GIVING MYSELF AWAY

CHARLES UPTON

GIVING MYSELF AWAY

FROM
BEAT GENERATION PROTÉGÉ
TO
METAPHYSICAL SOCIAL CRITIC

○ ○ ○ ○ ○ ○ ○ ○ ○ ○ ○

*A Cultural History of America
through
Fifty Years of Spiritual Seeking*

Angelico Press

First published in the USA
by Angelico Press 2025

© Charles Upton 2025

Thanks to Counterpoint Press for permission to reprint
Gary Snyder, "For/From Lew" from Poetry Now 2, no 5
(May 1996). Copyright © 1996 by Gary Snyder. Reprinted
with the permission of The Permissions Company, LLC
on behalf of Counterpoint Press, counterpointpress.com.

Thanks also to City Lights/Grey Fox Press for
permission to reprint poems from *Ring of Bone:
Collected Poems of Lew Welch*. Copyright © 2012 by
The Estate of Lew Welch; and from *I Remain: The
Letters of Lew Welch & The Correspondence of His
Friends, Volume Two*. Copyright © 1980 by Donald
Allen, Literary Executor of the Estate of Lew Welch.

All rights reserved:
No part of this book may be reproduced or transmitted,
in any form or by any means, without permission.

For information, address:
Angelico Press, Ltd.
169 Monitor St.
Brooklyn, NY 11222
www.angelicopress.com

ppr 979-8-89280-126-3
cloth 979-8-89280-127-0

Book and cover design
by Michael Schrauzer

If the fool would persist in his folly
He would become wise.
       o   o   o
I pounded on the wall
Till words obeyed my call.
— William Blake

CONTENTS

EXPLANATORY NOTE................. xi

OPENING
The Story of Someone's Life 1

CHAPTER ONE
The Planet of Home and Childhood............ 9

CHAPTER TWO
The Planet of Church, School and Town 59

CHAPTER THREE
The Planet of Lew Welch and the Beat Generation 87

CHAPTER FOUR
The Hippie Planet 140

CHAPTER FIVE
Kerouac-ing It: The Planet of the Road........... 205

CHAPTER SIX
The Planet of British Columbia: Death in Life 228

CHAPTER SEVEN
The Planet of the Underworld: Life in Death......... 252

CHAPTER EIGHT
The Planet of Revolutionary Solidarity 310

CHAPTER NINE
The Planet of the New Age 354

CHAPTER TEN
The Planet of Project MOVE 378

CHAPTER ELEVEN
The Planet of the Traditionalists 394

CHAPTER TWELVE
The Planet of Kentucky................ 476

CLOSING
The Planet of Remembrance 570

INDEX OF NAMES.................. 581

EXPLANATORY NOTE

The timeline of this book, as when I make references to my age, counts back mostly from 2023, though a few references to certain events of 2024 appear here and there.

When an asterisk (*) appears after the first instance of the name of an individual or an organization, this indicates that its name has been changed to protect both the innocent and the guilty. The names involved are "Donne," "Plunkett," "Plunkitt," "Planquet," "Stock," "Pilson," "Mark Fitzgerald," "Leanna Graham," "Randy, Rachel, Olive and Ruby Carson," "Nathan Boone," "Bob Ladroni," "Maggie Carlin," "Mick Mead" and "Custodian Properties."

OPENING

The Story of Someone's Life

IN MY LIFE I'VE CAMPED ON THE EDGES OF MANY worlds, I've haunted the borderlands. This book is a map of the itinerary that took me past quite a few of them, though not so close that the gravitational field of any one of those worlds caught me, preventing me from moving on: The late *real* Catholic Church, the 2000-year-old one, that died in the 1960s. The Twilight of the Beat generation, featuring Allen Ginsberg and Lawrence Ferlinghetti and Gary Snyder and Lew Welch. The Hippie Extravaganza. The Guru Parade. The Great "No" of the Vietnam antiwar protests. The Radical Left, fighting for peace in the era of Central America. The Neo-Shamanic Experiment, courtesy of Carlos Castaneda. The Neo-Pagan Revival. The San Francisco Poetry Scene, revisited. Social Justice Christianity and Liberation Theology. The New Age Paradigm that got old so quickly, an era that included New Age dream work and citizen diplomacy with the Soviet Union. The Twilight of Persian Sufism. The Invisible Byzantium of Eastern Orthodox Christianity. The world of service to the homeless on the soft mean streets of Marin County, California. The Traditionalist/Perennialist School of religious philosophers, of René Guénon and Seyyed Hossein Nasr and Frithjof Schuon and Huston Smith. The Last Days of Hillbilly Appalachia. The Hidden Kingdom of the Covenants of the Prophet Muhammad, of antiwar Islam in the Age of ISIS. True Muslim Sufism with the followers of Shaykh Ahmed al-'Alawi. Worlds I skirted, or loitered on the outskirts of, or else drank deeply from the waters of, but *only once*, since the price of every drink was an irreplaceable chunk of my life-energy.

Only Catholicism, into which I was born and out of which I died—and Sufism, into which I was born and in the arms of which I died—have been actual *lives*, not just a chain of temporary destinations, as experienced and remembered by tourists and/or soldiers through the medium of their snapshots or bloody trophies—that, and my marriage to Jenny Donne*, whom you will meet later on, when we come to the point where I myself met her, and therefore decided to embrace human life for real.

Three times my Sufi brothers told me: "You've got to write your memoirs." The third time I heard them (I am sometimes rather slow). So I had to ask the question: what in the story of my life could really be of value to others? If I had moved through the phases of it like a tourist taking snapshots, if I had viewed it as a process of "making memories" (a seriously weird idea), it would have had no value at all. But I didn't travel through those phases, those climes and countries, as a tourist; I traveled as a pilgrim. I moved not primarily from job to job or marriage to marriage, but from paradigm to paradigm, from belief-system to belief-system, from set to set. Nor did I travel randomly; my eyes were always on the prize. What exactly that prize was became progressively clearer as I checked out of each passing hotel and into the next one, but my direction of travel was always the same: toward True North, the direction of the Pole, toward what T.S. Eliot called "the still point of the turning world."

But every memory — if we come to it through *nostalgia* that is — is the memory of a loss: a return to the exact point where a past lifetime ended so you can finally *feel it end*, maybe for the first time. This is the ambiguity of all love for the past — and all fear of it. *Recall*, on the other hand, is something different: recall is the resurrection of the dead. In memory, the past pulls you back into its darkness, into the husks of everything you once thought you were; in recall, the light of Recollection draws your whole past forward into the clear circle of the Present Moment, into what the Sufis call the *waqt*, and St Thomas Aquinas the *nunc stans*, the "standing Now." As you remember the true shapes of the faces they rise up, out of the formless mass of your distractions and denials, the darkened hallways where you abandoned and ultimately forgot them; instead of being left behind as dead memories they are welcomed as living realities, allowing them to take the exact seats assigned to them in the great General Assembly of all places and times. But nothing can return as a reality until you release it as a memory. How can something rise from its grave if you're still holding on to it? How can souls come back from the dead if you never let them die?

From one point of view this is a book about a young Catholic boy of the Baby Boom generation who was born at an early age in the San Francisco Bay Area, grew up in "marvelous" Marin County, became a poet and a metaphysical writer and a social activist, led a life of serial monotheism as a spiritual seeker, got married, converted to Islam, became a Sufi, then moved to Kentucky after California and its counterculture — at least as far as what he could take from it, and it from him — had been pretty well used up. But what it really is, is an inquiry into the nature of *identity*, both real and imaginary. The truth to be drawn from the stock verbal exchange *Who do you think you are?* as answered by *Who do I have to be?*, is: you are never who you think you are; you are always who you have to be.

Every life is (supposedly) of interest to the one who lives it and has lived it; the question is, why should it be interesting to anybody else? "I fought in 5 wars" says the fictional autobiography-writer, "slept with 42 women, held down 27 jobs, traveled to 18 countries, received initiatory transmissions from 13 sages, knew 33 famous people" (etc. etc.) — but what *is* all that, exactly? It's only "stuff," only personal history. And, dear reader, it's not even your stuff. It belongs to the writer. You can't buy it, and he can't even give it away for free. "You've had an interesting life" someone might comment, and then possibly ask (perhaps only in his or her own mind), "If I read the story of that life, will *my* life become more interesting?" The answer, unfortunately, is "no." The whole matter is untransferable; there is no way you can invest in the non-fungible token known by the name of Charles Strother Upton, or any other token known by any other name. And of course there's also the question of "interesting to who?" To those in search of entertainment? To those looking for more idols to add to their collection?

And what about interesting to God? You'd think God would have to be interested in everything, since He has created everything, maintains everything in existence and sees everything as Himself. But beyond that, the notion, or hope, that God might take a special interest in those who take a special interest in Him is one of the pillars of religion—of *all* religion. And one of the things He is most interested in, in my estimation, is *objectivity*, both because objectivity makes no arrogant claims and because He is the Ultimate Object, who has no need for my limited understanding of Him to be Who He knows Himself to be. I believe this principle defines the specifically spiritual function of the personal memoir, seeing that true autobiography is the art that *objectifies a life*.

Nonetheless, a suspicion inevitably arises at this point: "Is autobiography all narcissism, or is it more on the order of the 'life review' that some people who remember Near Death Experiences have apparently gone through, given that this earthly life is itself a chain of births and deaths?" In answer to this question another question arises. Plenty of people—spiritual teachers and psychologists—say: "Whatever it is, detach from it, let it go." Other people—psychologists and spiritual teachers—say: "Take responsibility for it; own it." But what if it's true that to detach from your life and to own it are actually the same thing? No longer hidden inside you, no longer confused with you, there it is lying out on the horizon in plain view, clearly visible and fully recognizable as *your life*. If you are attached to it, identified with it, then it's invisible to you; if you detach from it, dis-identify with it, if you let it go, then you can see it. And if you can see it, then you can own it. Otherwise it owns you.

To do full justice both to my experience and to my habitual way of processing it, I have constructed this book not only as a personal history but as a cultural chronicle and a critique of mass psychology—because I *had to understand* what was going on in myself, in the world around me and in the attitudes of the people I met if I wanted to save my life. It is simultaneously a work of "magical realism" in which the paranormal events that mark virtually everyone's life (whether or not they admit it) are accepted as a matter-of-fact-presentation of the way things really are; a "Confessions of the Reformed Rake" like the one St Augustine wrote—except that, as a second-rate sinner, he had little to confess outside of women and Manichaeism; a record of spiritual seeking through many faiths, traditions and practices; an illustration of universal metaphysical principles not just intellectually but existentially, through a deep meditation on human experience; and an elegy for mass social and cultural breakdown over several generations, taking the reader as far as today's radical rejection of the human form. Lastly, it is a testament from the counterculture wing of the Baby Boom, demonstrating how our generation did its best to actualize the mass of potential we were born with in the three disciplines of Art, Religion and Politics, and punctuated by various meetings with remarkable and often famous men and women in each of these arenas. The planets of experience I traveled to and became a part of, the identities I took and abandoned, the suits of clothes I purchased and wore out and threw away, are listed above. Some are illustrated by poems, either mine or other people's, because I am a poet; some are announced by dreams or visions because these too are part of the universal human experience. But in any case I did not travel as a simple compact kernel of generic selfhood, gazing indifferently at Eiffel Tower or Roman Colosseum or Algerian Kasbah, noting all, transformed by none. To paraphrase William Blake from his "prophetic book" *Jerusalem*, "*I became what I beheld.*" (Is this celebration, or lament?) I adopted identities, lived out the consequences of them, then repented of them and died to them. I didn't just soar like an eagle, I also shed skins like a snake. Not only that, but I did all of this more-or-less consciously; a part of me stayed awake through the whole process. In some of my other writings I've criticized "identity politics" and the quest for identity in general, since Sufism teaches its adherents not to collect identities but to discard them, till the spiritual traveler recognizes him- or herself as the nobody he or she really is, and always has been. On the other hand, if you never identify with this or that thing, person or situation from the inner or outer worlds, nothing will *happen* to you; you will have no "experiences"—and we are apparently placed, for some reason, on this superlatively shaky and impermanent earth to have "experiences." But the habit of adopting identities is inseparable (unfortunately) from having them painfully torn from your grasp, even if you sincerely intended (imperfectly, as always) to let them go. To say *I am this*, on any level whatever, is to be *born*—and, inevitably (as we all know), to be born is to die.

Nonetheless the value of the identities I adopted is more than a simple case-study in the abnormality of normal psychology, because those identities had everything to do with various collective mind-sets and historical eras. All along I was asking: what do these people (and I am certainly one of them) believe in now? What do they aspire to? What useful values have they forged? What delusions beset them? What are the likely consequences of their nightmares and their dreams? — which is to say that I was both an observer of and a participant in 75 years (maybe 55 of them relatively conscious) of unparalleled cultural and spiritual change and transformation in the United States of America, and this earthly world.

EDGINESS

So I've always lived on the outer edges of different worlds — quite a list of them. This would naturally make a person feel like an outsider, as if he were on the outside looking in. From God's point of view, however, to live on the edge of *this* world is to live at the Center of Reality. The earth itself sits (or spins) at the edge of an average-sized galaxy, which lies on the edge of something bigger, which sits and turns at the edge of another something, bigger still — all of which, moving and spinning, is perched *at the edge of time*: not at the great conjectural center of Day One that the Big Bang is supposed to be, but at the edge of an ever-expanding bubble of spacetime, whose Center is both everywhere and nowhere. And the Earth (as opposed to the system of This World) is definitely *not* on the outside looking in — though our terrified fascination with the hugenesses of space and the vastnesses of time, coupled with our inexplicable fear of being just who and where and what we are, makes us feel (idiotically, but also sadly) alone in the universe.

So the edge is where I live — I always have. At the edge of grammar school and high school worlds, the edge of the Beats, the edge of the Hippies, the edge of Leftist politics, the edge of the New Age; at the edge of the poetry scene, the edge of the Perennialists; at the edge of Marin County California, at the edge of Kentucky: always on the outer rim, Janus-faced, looking both ways, simultaneously toward figure and ground, thesis and antithesis, inner and outer worlds, the established "thing" and whatever subversive termite or grub-eating woodpecker or foolishly struck match was destined to undermine and bring down that thing — intricate specific text and shapeless, enveloping Context — the word that presumes to say who I am, spoken by me alone, and the vast Silence, into and out of which every spoken word is born and dies.

And in reality (if we only knew it) that's where all of us live: square in the house of the First Speaker, thundering so loud you can't even hear Him, who lets each word He releases into the world speak itself out to its heart's content — until, easy or hard, early or late, it assimilates its lesson, and learns to keep its mouth shut. Thus, as William Butler Yeats said, in his description of my own particular phase in the great psycho/historical/eschatological system that appears in his book *A Vision* — Phase Eleven, the one he called "The Consumer, the Pyre-builder" — I am someone "who defends a solitude he cannot or will not inhabit," but also one "to whom becomes possible, for the first time, the solitary conception of God," as well as a person who habitually finds himself involved with "a quarrel with the thought of his fathers and his kin, forced upon him perhaps almost to the breaking of his heart: no nature without the stroke of fate divides itself in two." And so, from birth or even from before it, I have had one foot in this world and one in the next: that's the two into which I am divided. My wife Jenny seems to have both feet planted firmly in that other world and barely the tip of one little finger extended into this one — though, paradoxically, she seems much more firmly *incarnate* than I am — which means that her life-burden has been to be oppressed by *worldliness*, by what St Paul called "The Rulers of the Darkness of This World" — oppressed by rejection and denial, but simultaneously protected by her own invisibility. I, on the other hand, have been both oppressed and blessed, both cursed and flattered by This World; at the same time I have been profoundly drawn to that Other World and also deathly afraid of it. Consequently I have been able to find rest neither in the stability of full integration into the visible world (though what had seemed to be so stable to so many is now revealing itself to be profoundly vulnerable, volatile and threatened) nor in the inviolability of the Unseen. I'm partly in the monastery and partly on the battlefield; being half-cloistered, I'm like the warrior who is periodically healed (or half-healed) with prayers and medicinal liqueurs by holy monks between battles, or else by the maidens of the Grail Castle as he comes closer to his Quarry. And since I have found stable refuge in neither the inner nor the outer worlds, I am periodically brought into direct face-to-face contact with the militant Powers of Darkness.

For somebody like me to get anything said or done can only happen at the lip of Apocalypse, the thin edge of time — at the point of the Great Reversal, where the province becomes the cosmopolis and the marginalized tent-camp the capital city, where the flimsy membrane of the world-illusion finally wears so thin that it can no longer hold back the face of God, and the Center breaks through.

Apparently I was supposed to be here to see it. Now I do.

SEEKER'S CHOICE

When people who report Near Death Experiences tell us, "I saw that I had chosen and agreed to my present earthly life before I was born," what they are really talking about is the mysterious relationship between choice and destiny — about the fact that, when it comes to the most fundamental elements and issues and alternatives, you are entirely free to choose *one* out of all of them, and yet you never really could have (or *would* have) chosen anything else. As the Holy Qur'an tells us when recounting the day when the unborn potentials of all things were brought into Allah's presence before coming into this world, and He asked them: *Am I not your Lord?*, all of us, without exception, answered *Yea!* — because, more than earning Paradise, more than avoiding Hell, what we want most of all is to be our true selves — to know and speak our own true names. Your will is perfectly free at only one point: the point of either freely choosing your destiny, choosing to be yourself, or else rejecting that destiny and spending the rest of your life vainly trying to be somebody else.

Some people, the ones who are unable to face the pain of their lives because they can see no meaning in them, choose to deny their reality and their destiny — and almost all of us, in fact, go into this denial at one point or another; we choose the mask over the face and try to mold it so firmly to that face that the two become indistinguishable. I know I did this myself during the hidden years of my later childhood and early adolescence. But the thing is, *the face always wins*, though it may only win at the point of death — seeing that the mask, like your money in the bank, is one of those things that "you can't take with you." The mask is the self we invent, either as a kind of bandage (I almost wrote "bondage") in response to the blows of life, like the one worn by the famous Invisible Man in the movie of the same name, or else the barrier we put up to block the inner assaults of the true life we have denied, beating against the bars of her cage, demanding to be heard. William Blake called that mask the Spectre, and the true inner life the Emanation, perfectly encapsulating their relationship in four lines:

> My Spectre before me night and day
> Like a wild beast guards my way;
> My Emanation far within
> Weeps incessantly for my sin.

The Spectre is the life we try to invent for ourselves without God, the one Christ was talking about when he said, "if you try to hold on to your life you will lose it, but if you are willing to lose your life for My sake, then you will find it." He was telling us that our lives and our souls — the two meanings of the Latin word *anima* — are not our own; they came from Another and belong to Another. If we try to claim ownership over them, if we declare that "I am the master of my fate, I am the captain of my soul" (from the poem "Invictus" by William Ernest Henley), then we are on the road to destruction — whereas if we become slaves to Allah and reach the firm conviction that we have always been His slaves and could have never been anything else, then He is our total Life, in both time and eternity. When the Prophet Muhammad, peace and blessings be upon him, spoke about the Greater Jihad as "the war against the soul," he meant the war against the *pretensions* of the soul (our own pretensions that is) to independence and autonomy, its false claims to self-ownership and self-mastery. When I was immersed for two years in the paradigm of the New Age, half believer and half skeptic, acting the part of an "impartial observer," a kind of spy or anthropologist—the New Age that holds as one of its central dogmas the belief that "you create your own reality"—I sometimes felt like a kind of defective God, as if for some unknown reason I had been able to create a universe, but now, inexplicably and disastrously, found myself unable to manage it, helpless to prevent it from spinning out of control. These are the wages of the magical worldview—to find, to our infinite shame, that the final outcome of the desire for total power is total helplessness, coupled with a shameful inability to ask for help. This is the lesson learned by Hitler in the *Führerbunker*, by Napoleon on St Helena—in both cases, too late. So the Seeker's Choice is always to choose GOD's choice, and then let Him lead you where He will, through whatever taverns or caravanserais on the Silk Road between what never could have been and what never will be, through whatever heavens or hells or purgatories may lie, strung like pearls, along the paths of the Unseen. In the words of Hafiz, the Drunkard of Shiraz:

> The day this heart placed its reins
> In the hand of Your love,
> I gave up the desire for an easy life.

CHAPTER ONE

The Planet of Home and Childhood

SO MY LIFE HAS BEEN A JOURNEY THROUGH A chain of separate worlds, each one self-enclosed, like an independent planet. My childhood home—apart from the different childhood planets of school, church, vacation—was one of those worlds.

What's the first thing I remember of that world, the planet of childhood? *Sounds?*

What were the first sounds I knew, in my childhood home north of San Rafael, California, with the two big picture windows facing east toward the water, on the shores of San Francisco Bay?

To the east, trains, the engines reverberating distantly across the water when the wind was still. To the west more trains, the Northwestern Pacific before it stopped running (now returned, I hear, as a commuter line). The long bass drone of the diesel engine whistles. And the Catholic church bells, the noon angelus rung from St Raphael's. Closer in, the dawn rooster, from the chickens Ma Wagner kept in cages along with her pigeons and rabbits, a middle-aged woman who dressed in overalls like a man, like Tugboat Annie from the movies, back in the days when women generally didn't do that, and when those that did were recognized as a definite "type." Then eastward again, the fog horn—deep, solemn, mournful, another sign of early morning before the fog burned off—till the GPS put them all out of work. And the echoing traffic on San Pedro Road, up against the hills. These, along with the voices of my mother and father, my grandmother and grandfather, the noise of the wind, the waves and the yelping seagulls, and the joyful chorus of frogs from the nearby marsh when the rains came, were the first sounds I ever heard in this world.

But the East was the true vista, the gates of Sunrise, sun coming up red over the East Bay hills, or else breaking pure through the cloud-shelf, throwing incandescent snakes of quicksilver like caged lightning on the water—easy to see it exactly like that, once you forgot that the water was "water" and the sunlight only "sunlight"—all sent to make a radiant path for the King to my door!

Beyond our windows about a mile out lay the Marin Islands, the larger one with piers, two houses, tall eucalyptus trees; the smaller one (a rookery), covered with buckeye trees and dotted with white egrets. I used to row out to them in my rowboat. Once I buried a pirate treasure on the smaller one, made of rocks painted with gold paint, plus a plank contraption hanging from a tree to point the secret way to it, all straight out of "The Gold Bug" by Edgar Allen Poe. Beyond the low ridgeline across the Bay lay Mount Diablo, the tallest peak in the Bay Area, blue in the farther distance. And then Mount Tamalpais to the west—the home mountain, known to us as The Sleeping Lady. All-in-all it was a legendary, romantic world.

Our house, complete with a pier and sometimes a boat, was set on a bank just above a rocky beach, a few yards north of Chicken Point. The "chickens" the Point was named after were the quail, *las gallinas*, that used to fill the place; a few were still left, to accompany the black shelves of ducks out beyond them on the water. Canvasback. Sprig. Bluebills. Mudhens. The house had originally been a fisherman's shack before the advent of Bayside Acres, the oldest subdivision on San Pedro Road. Grey stone fireplace and chimney, still bearing the crack from the shock-wave when the ammunition ship blew up, far across the water to the northeast at Port Chicago, during WWII. Elegant redwood rafters and paneling. More rooms were added later to both ends to make a line of diminutive houselets, perfectly connected, with flagstone patio, outside kitchen, big garden of trees and paths on the other side toward the road, and another, higher patio up near the grape vines. A fish pond with goldfish, mosquito fish. And the fruit trees! Peaches, apricots, persimmons, grapes, apples, pears, figs, loquats, avocados, oranges, grapefruit, lemons, two varieties of lime, plums—and almonds too, the first to bloom in Spring. White blossoms. There was even a small rustic *Biergarten* overgrown with trees, in a nook in our hillside just above the Bay, with a walk-in refrigerator in a little concrete blockhouse coated with tar, containing a big keg of draft beer, complete with a spigot on the outside wall to draw from it. Clearly my father had been determined to make a paradise, a walled garden of the mysteries, just for me, little Charles Upton, his only child, to be the secret Prince of. How many times have I wondered whether, without the memory of that paradise, in rich rustic laid-back postwar Marin County in prosperous postwar America, I could have ever endured to stay down on this grim, tormented planet as long as I have. That garden, frail and impermanent, like everything else I knew in my earliest years, was nothing but a thin shell of beauty concealing Giant Forms of Terror—a white, abject terror that hid an even deeper Beauty, shining down into the midst of it from the Unseen Worlds. It was all part of the bait that lured and hooked me here: chained me to my post.

And the ships across the Bay that passed, north and south, through the deep channel near the eastern shore, seeing that our shore to the west was all tidelands, vast mudflats at low tide. Tankers, freighters (this was before those huge square high-piled container ships came in), sailboats, speedboats, cabin cruisers, sinister gray warships bound for Alameda or Mare Island—and, once in a while, a nuclear submarine.

I dreamt of those warships. In my dreams there were many more of them, bigger, more threatening. Real battleships. Finally I determined that some of those dreams were likely prenatal in origin, vistas of the San Francisco Bay of the wartime 40s. (I was postwar Baby Boom, born in '48.) Before taking the plunge into the womb of the woman who was to become my mother — still house-hunting as it were — I had undoubtedly been testing those waters, taking readings of the grim and shocking psychic atmosphere of planet Earth, and probably pretending that I could still opt out if I got cold feet, in the face of what I had most certainly been shown, all too clearly, of the heavy darkness of the earthly future — the massive catastrophes, the moments of exaltation nonetheless, defiant in the face of them, the various long slow dyings of so many things that I was required to love just so I could feel the loss of them — as also their eternity. The flesh that would all but choke my breath before it was done with me... and this after I had already formally agreed to forget the contract I'd signed, the one with the famous *why* clause, the full explanatory dossier, never to be opened till death or near-death.

But beyond the warships, beyond the jets from Hamilton Field to the north (long since decommissioned), old T-33 trainers with their big detachable fuel-tanks on the wingtips, screaming low over the water — tanks that the Chinese shrimp fishermen from China Camp collected after they'd been dropped to use as water-tanks before the city plumbing came in — beyond all that, and closer in, just up the hill, was Angela Pierce, the Girl herself, the first love of my life. Tawny olive skin, raven hair, the classic Virgin/Whore Catholic schoolgirl, half-Italian. She actually asked me to marry her once when we were about eight years old. I told her, with shameful, dishonorable rationality, that it was too soon for me to make a commitment like that because I couldn't know how our circumstances would change in the coming years. Yet she was the first woman (for woman she certainly was) who had the power to awaken my *anima*, the feminine soul of me. Angel indeed! Without her how could I have ever recognized Dante and his Beatrice, Layla and her Majnun? Or my own Jenny Donne?

And China Camp itself north along the coast, beyond Bayside Acres, beyond San Pedro point, also known as McNear's Point. It was a real Chinese fishing village subsisting on bay shrimp, settled by the Quan family and other immigrants of the Chinese Diaspora and further populated by Chinese laborers working at the McNear brickyard. It was once so important a settlement that, at least according to local legend, it was visited by Sun Yat Sen himself when he toured California in 1904. We know that he at least passed the Camp when he took ship from San Francisco to visit other outposts of the Diaspora in the Sacramento Delta, recruiting for the Kuomintang. When I was a child, the traditional Chinese junk the Quans fished from was still moored just off shore. Most of the area their colony occupied, along with the bulk of the McNear lands, was later turned into a state park or else papered over with subdivisions, a common fate of many of those ephemeral New World colonies basically started by single families, like the fictional town of Macondo founded by the Buendía clan in Gabriel García Márquez' *One Hundred Years of Solitude*. The story of a similar familial domain in Mississippi, founded by the grandson of a hunted, fugitive Scotsman and finally broken up for a golf course and housing tracts — just as the McNear principality was parceled-out for Glenwood and the golf club and housing of Peacock Gap — is told by William Faulkner in the final pages of *The Sound and the Fury*.

But Bayside Acres was my true village and domain; it was a perfect place for me to live out the childhood rituals that heralded everything that was to come in my later adult life — rituals that were based, at least according to today's hindsight, on the three archetypes of the Magician, the Acolyte and the Romantic. For Halloween I had the neighborhood kids over to our house to see spooky exhibits featuring a ghost that fluoresced under ultraviolet light and a boiling pot of dry ice whose mephitic vapors flowed down the sides of the container and spread out over the floor. For trick-or-treat, which all the local kids *and* adults participated in, I "went" first as a spaceman, but then as a magician and finally as the Devil, dressed for the last two roles in a black opera cape with a scarlet inner lining, sewn by my grandmother. I cast her in the role of a witch with her own dry ice cauldron at the door of her home a block away; she wore a rubber witch mask until I informed her, as delicately as I could, that she would probably look more like a real witch with the mask off... Yet holy rituals were just as attractive to me as evil ones. For Christmas (with a neighbor's help) I suspended a Star of Bethlehem over the street next to our house, made of silverized cardboard with a lightbulb in it, while in the little "well" at the foot of Beach Drive — a wooden roof on posts, part of a real well that had been taken out of service and filled in many years earlier — I placed a life-sized plastic doll representing the Baby Jesus in a wicker laundry basket filled with straw, with a flashlight under his head so he would glow in the dark. For the Fourth of July I staged public pyrotechnic displays with a mixture of store-bought fireworks and others I made myself from large masses of match-heads and pads of steel wool tied to rocks, which trailed long paths of sparks when you lit and threw them. (In such folkways, minus the Baby Jesus, you can clearly see the early seeds of today's Burning Man.) And for a different occasion, probably one of my own invention, I had my mother sew a mantle of purple cloth and help me make a tiara of gold-papered cardboard with glass jewels glued to it, with which I crowned and vested Angela Pierce, my almost-betrothed, as queen of my heart, just because she was my chosen Hagia Sophia, the innate and primal anima-image of my incurably romantic soul. And though she seemed a bit confused by the gesture, probably since she had been confronted for the first time with the formidable and mysterious burdens that come with physical beauty, she nonetheless submitted to the ritual.

But think of it: Who today could imagine a Marin County subdivision as harboring such apparitions as *Ma Wagner*? As actually being that normal? Along with figures like Pete Autsen, the neighborhood drunk, and Ray Rue, a retired San Quentin prison guard with a baseball cap and a schnozzola like Jimmy Durante... Ray had the greatest respect for my father, whom he'd known as a prison dentist; he always called him "Doc," back when that name was a term of respect offered to the professional class by the less educated who nonetheless still venerated the idea of education, still aspired to some modicum of elevation and refinement, if not for themselves then at least for their children; Mr Rue calling my father "Doc" was like an English peasant farmer addressing the local petty lord as "yer honour." We even had a village idiot, Chuck Tobener, who patrolled the neighborhood on crutches and knew all the little minute particulars of the place that nobody else, the people with driver's-licenses, had time to see or focus on. He was a child of the Tobener clan, our one "Oakie" family, a tribe of not-quite-rural blond-headed thieves and mischief-makers. If a *dramatis personae* such as I knew then in the neighborhood I grew up in, all of whom were necessary to the exact quality of the place and perfectly accepted as such, somehow made it within the borders of the Marin County of today, they'd immediately be deported, driven by the Sheriff to the county line.

Widening the radius a bit to Greater San Rafael, I remember an old "Chinaman"—the standard term of the time, back when all the laundries were run by the Chinese—dressed in his pre-Maoist native costume, who sold vegetables in town out of the back of a model-A Ford flatbed truck—imagine that! And Erskine McNear, scion of the McNear clan, the most prominent family on that coast, a tall, lanky, shambling, spastic hermit with a stutter, the only bearded man in town, who lived in a self-constructed shack on the considerable McNear lands, originally 2500 acres before they were broken up for subdivisions; if my father was the Squire of Chicken Point, Lawrence McNear was the Lord of McNear's Point with its public beach, dance venue and brickyard. His younger relative, Jeannie Powers—about my age—was our first up-front Lesbian (though she later married someone of the opposite sex), back in the days when you could be that without the slightest hint of Lesbian-feminist ideology, simply on the basis of personal quirkiness, as well as membership, by blood or marriage, in a crazy-rich clan of Scottish settlers in the process of transforming themselves from ranchers and rural-industrial brick-burners into mid-20th-Century California suburbanites.

This was 1950s suburbia in *California*? Once we knew, and were, real human *characters*; now all we will be, if the powers that be have their way with us, is caricatures, simulacra, ideologically-defined "identity-units," each complete with its electronic avatar haunting cyberspace — more real on the high-definition, pixilated screen than in the dubious flesh: post-modern ghosts, drained of all ancestry, all human substance.

And let me not forget to mention the other citizens of my neighborhood: the animals, the birds and the fish: For the Earth element, the fallow deer who visited all the gardens (though they were not always welcome); the racoons who found bounty in what we humans consider beneath us; the cottontail rabbits, the moles and the gophers. (I stroked a mole once who had left his hole in the earth, likely to die; I saw his seeking nose, his wide digging hands — and his mole-grey coat, the softest and smoothest I ever felt, fitting him to swim through the earth with the greatest of ease like a fish through the waters.) For the Water element, the game fish, mostly bass and smelt, though I believe we had flounders too, those weird, flat, squashed-looking fish with their offset, uneven eyes — squashed because they somehow contrived to turn themselves sideways so one of their sides became their belly and the other one their back, fitting them to flounder along the bottom to feed — and once I found half a sturgeon washed up on shore. Then the little leopard sharks, the stingrays, the small scurrying beach crabs and the leaping sand fleas — the mussels on the rocks — and, buried in the sandy and rocky shingle (a Brit term I never heard used in California, but the only one I can think of for that kind of shore), the clams: throw a rock and, within a radius of maybe three feet, a dozen of them would squirt in reply. My father even planted some oysters there once that he brought from the shores of the Pacific Ocean. And once in a while a seal would show her head above the surface not far from shore, curious to see what these land-dwellers were up to. Then for the Air element, the land-birds — many species including the robins, the sparrows, the blackbirds, the crows; the towhees, the bluejays, the cedar waxwings, the mourning doves — and then the sea birds: the crowds of sea gulls, the white egrets (two species, the larger American and the smaller Snowy), the ducks I've already mentioned, the solitary great blue herons — and afterwards the night-flying herons, smaller, whose "quock-quock" you'd hear every evening at dusk as they passed in formation back to their nests for the night. And as for the Fire element — who lived there? Only the insects are left to be named, the ones that for some reason the idea of Fire reminds me of: innumerable flies and beetles, the earth-born ants, the sow bugs and the pill bugs, the honey bees, bumble bees, those mean, challenging yellow-jackets, the mosquitoes, the dragonflies... and then the magnificent monarch butterflies with their brilliant orange wings who made a kind of deciduous autumn for the California trees, most of which are evergreens, not only the conifers but those beautiful naturalized Australian eucalyptus, the more abundant madrones and live oaks, and the bay laurels, their leaves narrower than those of the Mediterranean laurels but stronger as a spice, and a lot better (to my taste) in a good beef stew...

May all these little lives—each one vaster in the Unseen than we can possibly imagine—be reunited with their Original Names in the higher gardens, after their short assignments on this narrow earth are complete.

How do you know but that ever'y bird that cuts the airy way
Is an immense world of Delight, closed by your senses five?
   —William Blake, from *The Marriage of Heaven and Hell*

I BEGIN BY INVOKING THE ANCESTORS

My parents had me in their early 40s which was pretty late for those times, and since my grandfather on my mother's side lived with us, and my grandmother on my father's side in a charming little cottage a block away, I was exposed to worldviews and emotional auras that reached far back into the past. Walter Strother, my grandfather, was a true 19th-Century man; branches of his family, notably the Baskervilles, went back to the Tidewater Aristocracy of Virginia, those slaveholding planters who were proud not only of their own noble or royal bloodlines from Britain but equally so of their descent from New World royalty in the person of Pocahontas, daughter of Powhatan, High King of the eastern seaboard—though the Grand Dame I like to brag on, mine through the Strothers, is Eleanor of Aquitaine, patroness of troubadours and founder of the famous Courts of Love in Langue d'Oc. Some of those country gentlemen of the Tidewater later immigrated to Kentucky, leaving a few stragglers firmly settled here in the old Lexington graveyard in my adopted home town. From there they migrated to Missouri where my grandfather was born, and from Missouri to California's Central Valley so my mother could be born in Fresno. My grandfather had worked as a journalist in San Francisco, in a time when a man could be a journalist, a gentleman and an amateur scholar all at the same time, when not every reporter had to be an aspiring Walter Winchell; my own grandfather was actually, in demeanor, more like Woodrow Wilson, sober and studious. He was in lifetime mourning for his dead wife, the grandmother I never knew, a roguish, displaced Southern Belle he obviously doted on (according to the photographs)—he the earnest introvert, she the outrageous extravert. He read religiously, marking each book with a diminutive "alpha" followed by the exact date he started it, and an "omega" with the date he finished; some of those same books are in on my shelves to this day. His methodical nature drove my father crazy. He never smiled. And, on my father's side, my grandmother, Lillian Upton, as I knew her was a belle of another sort, an agéd belle of Belle Epoch San Francisco. She herself was a Hudson, descended from old salt-of-the-earth stock who hailed from the marshlands of the Thames, like Joe Gargery in Charles Dickins' *Great Expectations*. She lived in the tiny one-bedroom (or one-and-a-half bedroom) cottage Jenny and I later moved into, along with her brother Walter Hudson. He was the *slowest* man I ever met, having raised "puttering" to new heights. After inheriting $5000, she was able to build *three* houses in California, one on Catalina Island. In old photographs that I still have of her, she appears as a classic, raffish beauty in more-or-less Gibson Girl, Gay 90s style, a Great Lady of the Barbary Coast. She married a prominent Frisco citizen, Charles Hemenway Upton, another journalist, one-time night city editor of the Hearst newspaper the *Examiner*. My father's father's bloodlines were Norman, as witness the hatchet-face of the Northmen I inherited from him, though my own father got his fuller face from his mother's side. In her sweet old age, after a lifetime that had obviously featured plenty of high times—including, according to the photographs, a *ménage à trois* that encompassed her husband Charles and a female companion I was introduced to in childhood as "Aunty Frankie"—she radiated an atmosphere of what William Blake called "the lineaments of gratified desire."

But it was my maternal grandfather who might actually have made me a writer. He was the furthest thing from a raconteur, in no way glib or voluble; he never cracked a joke. Yet he actually READ to me, mostly from Mark Twain and Rudyard Kipling and the Oz Books, almost every morning at breakfast. (He tried to move on to James Fenimore Cooper at one point but I wouldn't have it; I must've felt about Cooper about the same way Twain did—who hated his guts—though I didn't realize that at the time.) So literature as *the score for the human voice* got into my ear early; it was likely this that prepared me for the teaching of my first and only poetic mentor, Beat Generation poet Lew Welch, who endlessly taught and insisted that *"language is speech."*

History. Scope. Visceral sympathy for older systems-of-sentiment. And, starting from that basis, a lifetime pilgrimage through different emotional climates, different histories, different worlds. Remembering them all. Seeing exactly how each one fit into the larger pattern, how it contributed to the heroism and the terror of the next phase, and the phase after that, ultimately to form the roots of our world of today, profoundly menaced from every direction, yet inspired by flashes of angelic lightning. The farmer—that craftsman who plants in one season and reaps in another—that man *has* to remember. Yet if I were to tell the story of my life and then *identify* with it, shoulder it like a backpack and walk around under the weight of it, that would be to embrace the true curse of personal history. Like San Francisco Beat-era poet Jack Spicer said:

> Dare he
> Write poetry
> Who has no taste of acid on his tongue
> Who carrys his dreams on his back like a packet?
> Ghosts of other poets send him shame
> He will be alive (as they are dead)
> At the final picking.

There is another way, however: the way of the snake, what Dylan Thomas called "adventures in the skin trade." As you dream of yourself, and tell the stories of those dreams on waking, you say good-bye to every one of them—forever. Like Salome doing the dance of the seven veils—which are the Vedic *koshas*, skins of the *Atman*—you strip away and discard into the karmic scrap-heap all the ephemeral personality-sheaths of the Absolute Self. Magda Cregg, Lew Welch's common-law wife (you'll hear more about her later) once produced a short film on that theme entitled *Take it All Off*, starring, as the sole actor and character, the famous stripper Blaze Starr, girlfriend of the Louisiana politician Earl Long as recounted in the motion picture *Blaze*, starring Paul Newman. As she danced she seductively removed her arms, like long black gloves, and threw them to the audience. Next her legs, one by one. Next her head. After that there was nothing left of her but a headless, limbless torso tumbling through black starry space. My wife Jenny had a dream like that once, a dream of Marilyn Monroe. Marilyn was giving all her clothes away—but as she did she was becoming afraid that, as soon as she had gotten rid of the last garment, she would no longer exist.

Non-existence? Not a bad fate—certainly better than the one she actually inherited.

MY FATHER AND MOTHER, THE PILLARS OF THE TEMPLE

My father, William Freeman Upton, had a rich and sunny soul, like the Sun itself in its golden afternoon: expansion personified. He was born under the astrological sign of Leo ruled by the Sun, the sign of nature and the human character in their ripeness and fullest outward expression, of boughs heavy with fruit—peaches, pears and apples—fruit fully ripe and ready to fall. In the words of Louis XIV the Sun King, "*apre moi le Deluge*." (Lew Welch too was a Leo, the name he took for his poetic persona; strangely but appropriately, they fell from the bough at roughly the same time, dying within a year of each other. My father was born on the 15th of August, the Feast of the Assumption, and Lew on the 16th.)

My father apparently grew up like a sturdy, happy, curly-haired, free-roving little weed on the streets of San Francisco, doted on by his stunningly beautiful mother, protected but not imposed upon by his prominent father, the man-about-town, needing little more than earth and sun and breathing-air to thrive. In any case, and based on his parenting style, that's how he looked to me. But like any light that's too apparent in this "world below the Moon," a shadow was hidden in him somewhere—and it's always the hidden shadows that bite. For one thing his parents were divorced in a time when that was much rarer than it is today, a sort of scandal, and it was obvious from his photographs that my grandfather (I have a vague memory of meeting him once in the driveway of our home) was a deeply depressed soul. He dealt with that depression through alcohol. I have a picture of him with a cracked smile on his face next to a gang of his cronies, not his professional associates but his lowlife boon companions—a Chinaman in traditional dress, a round-bellied jester in a sweater and snap-brim hat—sprawled on the deck of a boat moored at the dock, stoned out of his gourd and holding what looked like an uncorked *half-gallon* of gin. That's the only smile he flashed in all of his photos, the short-lived grin only to be found several inches from the bottom of a bottle of booze. My father must have been affected by the moral fall and undoubted social obloquy of his own father, but if it did he certainly knew how to hide it.

My father too, like many responsible solid citizens of his time, was what today we would class, legitimately or not, as an alcoholic. He would drive the three miles home from his dental office for a leisurely lunch, during which he would consume a large mug of beer. In the evenings he would down a couple of gin-and-tonics, and then—depending on what we were having for dinner—he would share a bottle wine with us, if appropriate from a culinary perspective, carbernet sauvignon or pinot noir by Louis Martini or Charles Krug if we were having red meat, Wente Brothers grey riesling if we were having the classic Bay Area meal of Bordenave's sourdough French bread and cracked bay crab. Then another mug of beer in bed before lights out. So drinker though he was, he was in no sense a drunk. He never became sloppily sentimental or abusively angry, and he never lost behavioral control. Nowadays we can't drink like that any more. The collective human soul is so filled with grief and loss and fear, and the anger that is the most common human response to this kind of suffering, that after one or two drinks we are in danger of becoming violent maniacs—and well-armed maniacs at that. We can't hold our liquor in these times because we can't hold the chaos of our souls. Nonetheless my father told the story of the time when, as a young man under the influence of drink, he had pulled a knife on someone, an act by which he had apparently scared himself straight as far as violence was concerned. After this he became a lifelong "moderate, social" drinker according to the standards of the time, though according to today's norms he would probably still be considered an alcoholic.

And my father definitely taught me to drink. As a child I would take a sip of his gin-and-tonic or have a glass of wine at dinner, and I would share the beer that was the beverage-of-choice when, beginning in early adolescence, I went duck-hunting with him and his friends.

The world of the duck-hunt was a true rite-of-passage, an initiation into the Masculine Mysteries. No girls allowed. As the poet Robert Bly expressed it somewhere (either in *Iron John* or *The Sibling Society*, I forget which), it was through activities like hunting that a boy would learn the wordless lesson of what it was like to be a man, of how the male body vibrated in tune with other similar bodies. Nobody sat me down to formally lecture me on the duties and comportment of my sex. As with any traditional craft initiation, most of the teaching simply happened through paying attention, then imitating. Nor was the act of attention in any way deliberate or regimented; it just happened. Nowadays we can't imagine *teaching* as anything other than one brand or another of ideological indoctrination, as if the human apprenticeship might be accomplished through *texting* alone, with once in a while a Zoom meeting thrown in. It's as if life has no *smells* any more—in this case the smells of mud and beer and ducks'-blood and smokeless powder and wet retriever-dogs and human sweat.

As for the mud, the name of our duck club, situated in the Yolo Bypass in the Sacramento Valley was "Gumbo Farms"—a name given to it by my father—after the supremely sticky mire we had to trudge through, in our waders (rubber overalls) or hip boots, to get to the duck blinds, which were like fox-holes made of yard-wide sections of concrete pipe sunk in the gumbo and surrounded by branches of grease-wood (also known as coyote bush) for cover. The Bypass existed to take the overflow when the Sacramento River rose too high due to the Spring snow-melt, during which time much of the land was turned into rice paddies.

The quarries were: mallard, sprig, wigeon, teal, spoon-bill for the ducks (rarely ruddy ducks or mergansers), then Canada geese and snow geese. We were also treated to the vision of the stately trumpeter swans, whose chorus can be perfectly reproduced on the common recorder (the wind instrument, not the electronic device). But the swans were sacrosanct; no duck hunter would ever be impious enough to take down one of these aristocrats. Nonetheless one of our club members, Jerry Kerr (a Scotsman from New Zealand) was careless enough on one occasion to shoot a swan, undoubtedly mistaking it for a snow goose, who are mostly white with black wing-tips. As soon as the transgression was committed, cries arose from the other duck-clubs around us: "Swans! Swans!" The result was a shame that took a long time to live down—though not one imposed by any kind of social pressure, but solely by the hunter's own conscience. (Jerry was the sweetest and most deeply sentimental of my father's friends, with a soul like the poems of Robert Burns; his constant back pain, due to a botched operation, undoubtedly led him to drink a bit more than the rest of us, not to mention the likelihood of codeine pills, the only oral "opioid" easily and legally available at the time.)

Sprig or pintail was the most choice duck of the bag, capable of being transformed by a competent cook into a truly memorable dish. My father would paint them with paprika and orange marmalade and broil them at the highest possible heat for the shortest possible time, since the interval between raw redness and gray dried-out failure was perishingly brief.

When the skin was crackling crisp but not burnt, the savory near-liquid fat around the tail was bliss beyond telling. Mallard was good and reliable—they were the largest breed—but rather bland. As the only wild duck that would sometimes abandon long-distance migration to breed and hybridize with the domesticated white Peking ducks, they were half-civilized already—and you could taste it. Wigeon were a fine duck, almost as good as sprig. And though the teal, a sweet-fleshed bird, were the smallest of all, they were considered second only to the sprig or pintail in quality; their wings sported inch-long rectangular patches of brilliant iridescent teal green. Spoon-bills or "spoonies" were second-rate, though still edible. Once the hunting-day was over the individual bags were pooled and the ducks distributed according to the precedence of each hunter in the order of the day—first chooser, second chooser, etc.—an order that might have been determined by lot but was more likely decided according to some pre-determined system I was not privy to.

Two memories from those duck hunts stand out. One was when a pair of ducks approached our position. "I'd take the front one, you take the rear" said my father. We both shot and both hit our targets. My father told that story for years afterwards. The second memory had to do with a mallard someone had brought down with a broken wing. I pursued it across the shallow water where it was swimming frantically for its life, looking back over its shoulder as I steadily gained on it; when I came up to it I reached down, grabbed it, and wrung its neck. "This is killing" I said to myself; more than simply killing a bird with a shotgun, this way was "personal." In earlier years virtually all Americans experienced killing almost daily, and sometimes—from time to time, in war or in defense of the home—the quarry would be a human being. William James remarked that only recently, in his time, had the cruel infliction of pain on other human beings ceased to be a common, necessary, and therefore acceptable practice; "civilization" had arrived. In our own time, of course, civilization is fast disappearing. Violence in the streets and the homes and the churches and the schools is common again, not just in war or to carry on or defend against some criminal enterprise, but more and more often in the form of some sad case of psychopathic "acting out," if not of calculated Satanic invocation. I am profoundly grateful that my experience of killing has been so mild (at least up till now) that I have never yet been forced to take human life—I was exempt from the draft for the Vietnam War due to asthma and chronic uveitis in my right eye. That privilege has been one of God's greatest generosities to me; apparently He was saving me for a deeper war.

My father's fellow duck-clubmen called him "Der Führer" because of his natural leadership abilities, which they accepted with feigned reluctance and in no way subserviently. How little such human relations are understood nowadays, in these dark and depleted times when the only "natural leader" is the Alpha Male, otherwise known as the bully. My father's leadership was expressed through his position as Chairman of the Marin County Planning Commission, and later his function as appointee to the Bay Conservation and Development Commission and the Regional Water Quality Control Board. (On one occasion, in the course of his performance of those duties, he had an interview with Ronald Reagan when he was Governor of California; it was during this time that Ron became notorious for his motto "If you've seen one redwood tree you've seen them all." I asked him about his impression of the Governor; "He's definitely a good actor" was his answer.) It was partly through these positions of responsibility that my father expressed his love of nature and his commitment to environmental stewardship. His other way of showing this love was through the art of painting that he took up at around 60 years of age, an art through which he became — at least on the basis of ten or so of his last paintings — a highly talented, self-taught impressionist of California landscapes. He never became known for this achievement, however, since he didn't travel in "arty" circles. His main technique was *impasto*, which uses the palette knife, applying the paint in thick streaks or dabs. And his major technical invention was to lay down a coat of red paint on the canvass, after which — in order to lend an impression of depth to his rendering of forest scenes — he would dig down, through the dabs of black and dark green and white and yellow that rendered his vision of evergreen foliage in bright California sunlight, till the red layer was reached, which clearly suggested patches or dapples of sunlight appearing deeper in the forest. Tragically, most of his paintings burned when my childhood home went up in smoke around 1972; my indelible impression is that he had decided to take those paintings with him to the next world. But three of the survivors still appear on the walls of my present home — and, to keep them company, a still life of duck, wine bottle and onion by fellow painter Jerry Kerr hangs above our dinner table. (My grandmother painted too. Like many women of her class and generation, she decorated porcelain plates and vases with grapes and flowers as one of the "accomplishments of a lady." She did watercolors of sunsets, oil paintings of birds. One of these, a portrait of a redwing blackbird painted on the lid of a tub of cottage-cheese, still hangs on our kitchen wall.)

So my father, seamlessly and with naturalness and ease, could have a family life, a professional life, a sporting life, a civic life and an artistic life, with no inner contradictions, no excessive tax on his time, none of the stress and strain that comes from the obsessive attempt to become a "well-rounded character" or a "Renaissance man." How poor we all are now in comparison! And perhaps our greatest poverty is poverty of time. We seem never to have enough time to *finish* things, to put a finish on them, burnish them to a high gloss. It's not just that there aren't enough hours in a day — there don't seem to be enough seconds in a minute. Time is simultaneously shrinking and speeding up, leaving us constricted, driven and exhausted. Either we can't find enough time to finish our projects, or else we are burdened with *too much* time, time that doesn't have enough space in it, time filled with numbness, fidgeting and self-flight, time that we have to "kill." Our work does not satisfy, our leisure (if we have any) does not restore. As René Guénon predicted, and saw, in his great prophetic work *The Reign of Quantity and the Signs of the Times*, as the cycle of manifestation, the present *manvantara*, winds down, time speeds up and progressively devours space, destroys the tranquil simultaneity that allows all things to effortlessly relate to one another in a common matrix; the contemplative faculty, the recollection-of-heart that would make it possible to see and feel the inner self and the outer world around it as a seamless unity — as a single, perfectly realized, jewel-like Form set in a boundless expanse — becomes impossible to us, this being one of the symptoms of the near approach of the Hour of Judgment. We are in headlong flight from, and simultaneously in mad pursuit of, each successive instant; even worse, we somehow think that this state of affairs can be cured by *moving faster*. We have lost what the Sufis call the *waqt*, the Eternal Present that underlies the flow of passing time, like a bed of smooth yellow stones visible beneath the surface of a clear running stream on a sunny day. As the Sufi teacher Ibn Abbad of Ronda put it, "The fool is the one who struggles to procure, at each instant, some result that Allah has not willed."

As a dentist as well as a painter, my father was a craftsman. He loved making things. Writing is also a craft in every sense of the word, but a craft of the nerves not of the hands; consequently it can't really be used to calm and center the mind like smithing or sculpture or woodcarving can — though it can certainly reduce a mass of unformed thought and chaotic feeling to an articulate mental form, and this too can serve the act of recollection, though in a relatively indirect manner, not so immediately as the crafting of a corporeal object. And though the great Sufi Jalaluddin Rumi, the greatest poet of the Persian language, called poetry "tripe" — it's difficult to imagine a viable Sufi order organized around a poetry collective! — in Sufism and related "estates" in the Muslim world, the traditional crafts (rug weaving, silversmithing, sword-making etc.) have often been fully integrated into the contemplative life. The same was true in the medieval West. The craft guild system was entirely initiatory in form, with its three grades of Apprentice, Journeyman and Master. Each guild would have its patron saint, just as the guilds of the Islamic world had their patron prophets, and in both worlds the craft in question was often given a symbolic philosophical or theological interpretation — which, in *Dar al-Islam* at least, would sometimes be subtilized and essentialized to the point where it could work as a support for the teaching and transmission of this or that Sufi doctrine or mystical secret. The same was true in the West in certain places and times, as witness the mysteries of the Freemasons, who may in fact have begun as a Sufi order active in the Holy Land, and who later lost their proper matrix when, under the patronage of the Templars, they migrated to Christendom.

My wife and I once attended a performance, at Pikeville College in Eastern Kentucky, of some of the medieval mystery plays from the Wakefield Cycle, one of which was performed exclusively by the Coopers' Guild, the barrel-makers. The theme of that play was God's creation of the world. Apparently the Coopers took the Seven Days of Creation as a template for the creation of a sound and shapely barrel, and the creation of the barrel as an eloquent and dynamic symbol for the creation of the Universe, which was envisioned as a kind of supremely well-constructed barrel designed to contain everything that exists. In so doing they consciously invoked angelic and Godly norms and archetypal energies to empower their barrel-making and bring it to perfection. As Dante said in his *Divine Comedy*, man creates his craftsmanlike and technological objects by imitating the *method* (not the products) of God's creative action — *natura naturans* ("nature in the process of naturing"), not *natura naturata* ("nature already natured"). In any case, the corporeal crafts (ideally at least) produce a recollection of the mind, the perceptions, the feelings and the vital energies that can't be had elsewhere at any price. No wonder William Blake symbolized the poetic faculty or Divine Imagination by his figure of Los the Eternal Prophet — a blacksmith. Here's the poem I wrote about that when I came under the guidance of my first real Sufi shaykh, Dr Javad Nurbakhsh of the Nimatullahi Sufi Order:

Under the Hammer

When you were at work in the quarry, breaking rocks,
A willing slave, a king hid in a ruin
I went and lay down
Under the hammers of your remembrance.
What I had made of myself, you unmade
With the craft of the quarryman and the mason.

When you were at work in the smithy,
A coal black smith, face gone dark
From staring into the fire,
I crept into the forge and lay down
Under the bellows of your remembrance.
Your face gave light
Till I reached white heat.

What refuge from the hammer, except on the anvil?
What refuge from the fire
But in the forge itself?
What does it matter if I become a cup or a blade, a stirrup or an axe-head
If I bear the stamp of the Master?

My father, as a craftsman, transmitted some of that spirit of craftsmanship to me, and he did so in two ways: first, simply by letting me watch him do it; secondly, by making available to me his supremely jumbled workbench built down one side of our garage so I could "play at making" just as he did. It was likely this, along with the books my grandfather read to me every morning at breakfast, that helped make me a poet, a *poietes*, a "maker."

As a maker my father made an arrow with a sharp steel head that he cut and filed himself. He made an "automatic fish-hook" composed of two sharp spring-loaded prongs held together by a ring to which the line was attached, such that when the fish struck the ring would slide down the hook, releasing the prongs to spring apart and impale the fish's jaws. He repaired a crack in the metal insert to the wooden stock of his 12-guage automatic shotgun using (somehow) pure gold as the solder. And he built (to my imagined design) a "sail-raft" that floated on inner-tubes fastened beneath the deck, complete with mast, red baleen sail, an actual motive screw operated by a hand-crank, and a wheel connected by lines to a working rudder. I imagined it *and he built it!* How many other things in later years was I able to meticulously imagine because I was somehow confident that they would actually take shape in the real world? (This book, perhaps?) He also made a pendant for my first hippie girlfriend, Megan Roberts, out of a beautiful multicolored stone I'd found at Limontur Spit on the Pacific coast of Marin; it had what looked like a moonlit landscape on it, painted purely by natural forces. He used one of his dental drills to drill a hole in it, then inserted a loop made from stainless-steel wire, fixing it with epoxy.

Megan (to jump ahead a bit in time) is quite a story in herself, a tale of young love and young sex, which I won't go into detail about here. I was 19, she was 15, thus making her "jail-bait" — except that her mother fully approved, aided and abetted. Though our affair was fairly short, it was eternal nonetheless. "Was eternal" may sound like a strange paradox, a mystery that I expressed in the 3-word proverb I once coined about the brevity of the *apparently passing* present moment: "Eternity doesn't last."

Her mother Adelaide was a divorced Irishwoman of a romantic literary disposition who had once known W. B. Yeats as a fellow-passenger on the bus she took to work every day in Dublin. She remembered him as perpetually talking to himself under his breath — always working, composing. Megan's father, whom I met only once, was a short, narrowly-built Welshman with a pencil mustache; in his mournful jauntiness he looked like an aging RAF ace from World War II. Megan was an accomplished jazz violinist, subject to high fevers of purely emotional origin; as a Pisces she had a deathly fear of sharks and was affected by a lifelong, unconsummated attraction to suicide. She once re-wrote the lyrics to the old rock song by

Leslie Gore "It's My Party and I'll Cry if I Want To" to read "I'll Die if I Want To," and had a dream that the reason LSD had appeared was that whoever dropped it would be immune to nuclear radiation.

During one of Megan's psychogenic fevers (she sleeping at her own house, I at mine) I had the following dream:

> I was a vain and arrogant samurai whose motto was "Seek the Clear Light." Suddenly a great challenge presented itself: a vast fleet of UFOs appeared, all hovering at the same altitude over the coastal waters of Japan. They covered the entire sky from north to south, equally spaced, stretching all the way to the eastern horizon. Each one was shaped like a huge transparent tear-drop with a glowing red eye in the center! In my arrogance I appointed myself a one-man diplomatic mission to make contact with our celestial visitors in the name of the Emperor, so I embarked in a small boat across the waters, rowed by a servant, and approached the nearest craft. Then my servant cried out: "See! The eye glows red!" At that point I became so terrified that I *turned into my servant*, as if to hide out as someone of too lowly a caste to be worth killing. At the same instant a heat-ray from the eye of the spaceship hit and vaporized both of us. I died, was reincarnated as Charles Upton, and woke up.

She and I also apparently had some level of dream-connection before we ever met, since both of us had powerful dreams in our childhoods of a huge red Moon — exactly as in Joel 2:31 and Acts 2:20, both of which predict that "the Sun shall be darkened and the Moon turned to blood" before the coming of the Great and Terrible Day of the Lord:

> In my dream I was sitting with my parents before the large picture window of our dining room that overlooked San Francisco Bay. An oversized Moon, red or pink, appeared over the waters of the Bay, which suddenly became filled with rockets exploding like fireworks; then two huge glowing spheres rose above the East Bay hills, red on the top half and yellow on the bottom. I was sitting with my mother to the right of our dining room table, with my father as a shadowy figure to the left. "What do you think it is, Billy?" she fearfully asked him. He said nothing, so I answered instead: "I think it's the end of the world!" (When I recounted this dream to my first Sufi shaykh, Dr Javad Nurbakhsh, he reacted with shock, and responded by saying: "Give up the desire for children.")

Megan was a prominent and desirable member of the common "girl pool" of my over-extended adolescent peer group, the Trumbly-Clan-plus-John Doyle (you'll learn about them later), passing on after me to the great Doyle, and then to various nameless outside figures. (The Marin County girls of that time were often quite cultured and literary while still being highly attractive and available; in their Shakespearean demeanor they were perfectly designed to populate the Renaissance Faire — which began in Southern California and then branched out into Marin — the Faire in turn being designed to show those girls off to the greatest effect. The change of the major public cosplay event from the Renaissance Faire, which took place in beautiful coastal woodlands, to Burning Man, set in a barren desert, is a perfect barometer of the demonic blight that has cast its shadow on American culture since the counterculture died.) Later, after she'd gotten married, had a son and was in the process of getting divorced, Megan became for a short time a good friend to my wife Jenny and myself. The last time we saw her was at a party spontaneously convened by a mutual friend, Kathy Kane (also known as Candy Kane — Kika Kane after she moved to Hawaii), who had the sudden intuition that soon none of us, in the extended group of generally hip Marinites of the Baby Boom who had known each other in the same neighborhoods or else in high school, would ever see each other again. She was right. Soon after the party Jenny and I moved, rather unexpectedly, to Kentucky, and bid Marin (and California) an eternal good-bye. Megan looked happy on that occasion, firmly at peace and snugly tucked in with her new boyfriend. (But I digress — just as life does, which appears — sometimes — as one long series of unclosed parentheses.)

Returning now to my-father-as-craftsman, and his possible effect in that role on my psychic development, I was also exposed at an early age to the primary materials necessary for the craft of Alchemy, the art dedicated to the *magnum opus*, the Great Work. Gold and Mercury I knew from my father's dentistry practice. On one occasion (add this to the list of "crazy-dangerous things that parents of Baby Boomers used to allow, if not encourage, their children to mess with," in the days before we all became puritanically timid) he gave me a vial of liquid Quicksilver to experiment with, bright and silvery, surprisingly heavy, like lead, and amazingly *quick* to escape across a flat surface. I was also familiar with dental gold, as on the day when I accompanied him to the old San Francisco Mint to turn in a bag of gold dental fillings for the standard $36 per ounce gold went for in those days and for quite a few years before and after, until it ceased to be the standard for our currency and became a commodity like anything else, subject to rise and fall in value based on market pressures. When that happened, its intrinsic value as a traditional symbol of the incarnate Intellect, the gold of the Sun hidden as a solid nugget in the body of the Earth, was lost to human memory. I also knew the qualities of lead and tin, which were available in various forms on my father's work bench. Add to these the copper of pennies and copper pots (back when pennies used to be made of solid copper), the silver of silverware, and the powdered sulfur used in gardening, plus the ubiquitous iron, and I had first-hand experience of the classical Seven Metals recognized by alchemy, by astrology, even by medieval herbology, according to the famous "doctrine of signatures" where each herbal remedy or poison was considered to be under the rule of a particular metal and the influence of the specific planet which ruled that metal. I had all that in my childhood and table salt too, which I inspected with my father's beautiful antique microscope, made partly of brass, through which I saw the microscopic paramecia from our fish pond dart and wriggle, and the amoebas ponderously extend their pseudopods — thereby determining that Salt (like diamonds) is composed of tiny cubes, the cube being the "Platonic solid" representing the Earth element. And so, with Sulfur and Salt added to the metals, I had direct knowledge in childhood of the Three Primary Agents of the "royal art" — Sulfur, Salt, and Mercury — as well as of Gold, the goal of the whole work. But *tin* among the metals was especially interesting to me since it's the metal of Jupiter, the ruler of my own astrological sign of Sagittarius. Most of us probably think, following the idea of the "tin can," that "tin" is just another name for sheet metal, probably sheet steel or aluminum, as in "tin rooves." Wrong. Tin cans got their name from the practice of plating steel cans with tin to prevent rust. Tin as I knew it appeared as several leaves of actual *tin foil* (*not* aluminum foil) sandwiched between the pages of a paper booklet designed to hold them. Tin is as white as silver (though more malleable) but heavy, like lead; in another way it resembles Quicksilver with the quickness removed — Mercury fixed and stabilized. As many of these things as possible I burned or melted (though thank God I didn't try to vaporize Mercury, poisonous as it is!), since I loved to play with Fire, the supremely transformative element. Through this I discovered that sulfur burns with a low, lurid, deep blue flame and emits a nearly-invisible fume (sulfur dioxide) that stabs deep into the nostrils, the sinuses, the lungs, the eustachian tubes. Mercury is cool, lambent and motile, Sulfur hot, dry and acrid; they are — as the alchemists of old undoubtedly realized — like eloquent physical symbols of untamed chaotic emotion and untempered willful thought. So the influence of my father's craftsmanlike character, coupled with his imaginative playfulness, was already storing my latent memory with concrete symbols of the hidden correspondences between matter and Spirit — symbols that neither of us were conscious of at the time, nor prepared to understand even if we somehow had become conscious. Symbols like that can't really be called spiritual, and are capable of leading in some very dark directions if they fall under the power of subversive influences. But under a truly celestial influence they can greatly broaden and deepen our understanding of the actions of the Grace of God upon the "base metal" of the human soul. (God, however, rarely showed His face in those days. He was still hiding Himself in the pregnant future — leading me on.)

And as my father loved to sport creatively with materials, so he also loved to play with words. He was in no way an intellectual or a literary type, nonetheless he had a great appreciation for certain authors, especially O. Henry and the naturalized California writer of boyish adventures and adventuresque poems, Robert Lewis Stevenson. He also relished classics like *Seventy-Five Years in California* by William Heath Davis and *The Discovery and Conquest of Mexico* by Bernal Diaz del Castillo. But his verbal playfulness seemed entirely congenital and intrinsic to the quality of his soul. He would re-write the lyrics of popular songs for comic effect, a habit that I picked up from him and still indulge in. And he invented zany meaningless phrases like "Outboard motor BOATS roBOTS," obviously listening in for the auditory textures of language itself apart from its meanings.

So he too was undoubtedly an influence on my life as a writer, someone who prepared me to hear what Lew Welch would later tell me. Gertrude Stein had the same kind of linguistic playfulness that my father had, a sport and skill that passed from her to Lew, who wrote his Ph.D. thesis on Stein at Reed College; it's clearly visible in some of his poems — "DIN POEM" for example. Lew worked with language like my father worked with wood and metal, going beyond American poet William Carlos Williams's "no ideas but in things" to the principle that "words are things, not ideas," and onward to the final conclusion that "only poets know that words don't mean anything." But the notion that "words don't mean anything," that all meaning comes from the person articulating it — an attitude Lew expressed in his maxim (adapted from Cocteau) "the poet does not ask to be understood, he *demands* to be *believed*" — is a two-edged sword. If you play with language in such a way that words lose their associated meanings and become pure autonomous shapes of sound — like (in Lew's image from "DIN POEM") a date palm tree full of garrulous sparrows making an unbearable racket — then language has become a passive material that lets you say what you mean to say *intentionally*; no longer will you fall into the trap of letting your words do your talking for you. On the other hand, if you begin to believe that there are no such things as objective meanings that transcend you and to which you owe allegiance, then you are on your way to becoming a nihilist and/or a chaos magician. Be that as it may, it was Lew Welch's struggle as a writer to make language as *concrete* as possible, to bring his writing as close as he could to the kind of craft that works on Matter rather than ideas — thus making it the sovereign medium for the transmission of *real* ideas, without all the unnecessary intellectual and aesthetic baggage. As Lew put it, "You can't build a poem out of anything but words, just like you can't build a brick wall out of anything but bricks." And it was undoubtedly my father's playful relationship to language, along with his nuts-and-bolts craft orientation, that prepared me to understand that teaching. (Who conspired, through these many converging influences, to make a poet and a metaphysician out of me? Who else but the Great Conspirator Himself?)

But am I really that *poietes*, that "maker" my early influences prepared me to be? Am I really Lew Welch's prize student, my father's only son? Always remember (*O nameless one*) that whatever "me" sees as firmly established is already on its way to oblivion. And never forget there is only one Creator, one Maker. Once there is an ego there is a history and a destiny — but, after the lynch pin is pulled, the Wheel of Birth and Death rolls elsewhere, out of the picture; it's no longer included in the frame.

And none of these potential influences from my father would have meant anything at all without his greatest gift to me: the fact that he accepted me. If a person has known that kind of acceptance early on, then (God willing) he won't be tempted later in life to sacrifice his eternal essence to defend his passing identity. When the Call arrives, he will gladly release that essence back into the hands of his Heavenly Father.

But I am also my mother's child — the fertilized cell, the embryo, the perpetually unborn fetus. That's part of the story too.

My mother, like her father, was a grieving soul. This may have had something to do with the death of her own mother, but the real center of it was my younger almost-sister Janet, who had died stillborn. My mother hid the grief of that loss throughout most of her life; it was only much later in our relationship that I even learned about it. It's likely that she somehow thought the loss of the child was her fault, judging from her attacks of profound guilt which she theatrically dramatized so as not to feel the depth of them; in any case she kept the tragedy a closely-guarded secret, something that called her (in the words of Corinthians) to "come out from them and be separate" — to come out from the easy relationship with the world that my father knew, and seek a kingdom not of this world. If I got part of my jovial and expansive disposition from my father, from her I received my strand of painful introversion, my nervous over-sensitivity, my lurking fears — but equally my sense of a Transcendent God. Not that she was reclusive or profoundly depressed; she had a good relationship with the other couples in her and my father's social group, and the kind of productive life of church service and charity work that was common among established upper middle class wives of that era. And, like many mothers, she sincerely loved the child in me, though she was increasingly threatened by the adult. But there was a raw wound buried somewhere in her that was not to be touched, a wound that she protected with an outer layer of drama-queen persona that fled from any expression of genuine feeling, though she was by no means the worst example of that condition. And the other side of this outer persona was that profound guilt she could never squarely face, neither own nor let go of. And as part of the same defense-system she had a not-fully-conscious air of haughtiness and class pride, one that gave her the common California prejudice against "Oakies." I once heard her describe the *declassé* Tobener family who lived in our neighborhood as "Jodie," or "Joadie." "Jodie" just means "Jewish" in Hebrew, so I assume that the word, which I'd never heard before and have never run across since, was a reference to the Joad family, the Oakie refugees from the Dust Bowl become California farm laborers in John Steinbeck's great novel *The Grapes of Wrath*.

She also had an unaccountable prejudice against the Irish — strangely so, because she was a devout Roman Catholic convert who knew and venerated many Irish Catholic priests. Her devotion to the Blessed Sacrament was so deep that whenever it appeared she would burst into tears; she had this reaction, she told me, even before she entered the Church. It was as if this scorn of the Irish were the unconscious revenge of her Virginia and Missouri WASP ancestors against her betrayal of her roots, her apostasy to Papism. (For all I know she might have thought of my friends the Trumblys, my over-extended high school peer group who you'll meet later, as a perfect example of those supposedly well-known "Joadie Irishmen." We should not expect prejudice, which is always unconscious to some degree, to be rational or consistent — any more than we should expect it to be *entirely* void of justification, just wrong enough to lack sufficient justification for its existence.)

As for her love for me, which was entirely genuine though rather stifling, one of her friends among the Dominican nuns of San Rafael, Sister Joan, once described it by saying that she loved me "desperately." Joan gave every impression of being a Lesbian, as a number of the Dominicans apparently were; her paramour, whether or not an open sexual partner, was Sister Pat — Joan the butch, Pat the fem. Pat used to carry around a teddy bear — reminding one of the character of Sebastian, the young, gay Anglo-Catholic aristocrat (innocent, childlike, and always drunk) in Evelyn Waugh's *Brideshead Revisited*.

My mother's desperation regarding me likely had much to do with how difficult it had been for her to deposit me on earth alive, especially in view of the earlier stillbirth — just about as difficult as it was for me to agree to being born and commit to staying down here in this darkened world. I was born by Caesarian section when that was much less common than it is today, due to the fact that the environment of her womb had begun to become toxic to me so they had to get me out quick. Luckily I had a good birth weight and wasn't really premature. But in any case, since I was the only child and likely to remain so, she was determined to hold on to me as tight as she could and not let me wriggle from her grasp like my stillborn sister Janet had done. Luckily I could remember, due to my religious education in Catholic school, that Jesus had once told his own mother, "Woman, what have I to do with thee?" At one point, after my father passed away, she turned her apartment into a speakeasy for the nuns so they could have drinking parties there when they needed a break from the convent. They named the apartment "Sarah's Tent" after the wife of the Prophet Abraham. They even kept a journal of their drinking events hidden under a cushion on the living room floor. When my mother died, the nuns arranged for that journal to be buried with her in her coffin.

(I must confess that I drank plenty of booze myself from that same cabinet when I lived at my mother's apartment, but I never got as far as the teddy bear stage, nor was I able to "achieve" homosexuality, though that's where the imagined suggestions to it surfaced most clearly in my life. As you will learn below in *Chapter Six*, my father had recently died of cancer, my childhood home had burned, and I—the only child—was living at one point in a small apartment with my bereaved mother and drinking like a fish, all this soon after getting dumped by my first live-in girlfriend and being injured in an automobile accident in a foreign land, British Columbia. Is anyone surprised that my sexual identity was on shaky ground? All traditional morality aside, I believe that some people are virtually born to be homosexual, but it's equally obvious to me from my own experience that other cases of homosexuality have to do with serious wounds to one's inherent *heterosexual* identity—an insight that "woke" psychology has now officially outlawed as "politically incorrect." God help the young man or woman who naively turns to the contemporary discipline of psychology for help in healing such wounds as that, even if they are not offered the transgender option so as to set those wounds in stone! That everyone who is gay has freely chosen to live that lifestyle just because they want to be bad, and that everyone who feels homosexual desires ought to be encouraged to come out of the closet, "accept themselves" and "guiltlessly" live them out, are two total lies—lies that seem diametrically opposed to one another but are actually in bed together, somewhere in the collective unconscious of this profoundly toxic society.)

As for her anti-Oakie bigotry, as soon as my Kentucky-born wife-to-be Jenny Donne came on the scene my mother saw red, immediately converting her prejudice against Oakies to one against Hillbillies. After Jenny had phoned me a couple of times at my mother's apartment, she asked me if Jenny was mentally retarded; I suppose she could tell that by the Appalachian accent. That earlier generations of her own Strother family had once been prominent citizens in Lexington, Kentucky didn't seem to matter in this context, any more than the fact that Kentucky was the traditional heartland, along with Louisiana, of Roman Catholicism west of the Alleghanies; Thomas Merton's Abbey of Gethsemani is in Bardstown, Kentucky. Undoubtedly Jenny had activated the ancestral prejudice of the aristocratic planter class in my mother's racial memory, those knightly blackguards who generally became Confederates during the Civil War, who collectively looked down upon the small freeholder class they dubbed "white trash," most of whom lived in the hill country, many joining the Union cause. Jenny actually ran into a similar prejudice from the premier living Kentucky poet, Wendell Berry, who had been one of her professors at the University of Kentucky. (I remember a dream I once had that's relevant in this context, in which a disembodied voice expressed the hope that "some day the dead would stop bickering with each other"—a hope that I fervently share.)

Strangely enough, Lew Welch, an Irishman from a well-to-do Arizona family who knew the Goldwaters, also adopted the common anti-Hillbilly prejudice of his adopted California—strange because the Hillbillies were and are mostly Scotch-Irish. He composed a rather foul parody of a traditional Hillbilly ballad, probably "The Banks of the Ohio":

> She baréd her bosom,
> I whupped out m'knife,
> Carved my initials on her
> Thin breast bone...

Maybe, since he was Irish, he had to think of himself as a lord, which was a hard thing to do in the populist, quasi-Leftist counterculture of the 1960s—as the old saying goes, "every Irishman is a Chieftain"—though he was still always in danger of being seen, by the likes of my mother, as a no-account bog-dwelling Mick, forever oscillating between the lace curtain and the mud hut, a Hillbilly in all but name. Here we can see once again—hopefully for the last time—how *class* has truly got no class at all, seeing that all the Eleanor of Aquitaines in the world couldn't begin to clean up one tiny corner of my disordered soul. How could they? They never learned how to do the necessary housework.

Due to her theatricality, her inner avoidance of grief, my mother was in perpetual flight from genuine feeling—a condition which led her to deny the validity of my own feelings on most occasions. When I would express a negative or inconvenient emotion, she tried to convince me that it was all an act; she would call me "president of the Actor's Guild." In so doing she taught me to distrust my feelings, as well as to dramatize them; was this another influence on my later life as a poet? And her flights would sometimes take physical form. On certain occasions she and my father would have silent fights that they were very careful to keep hidden from me. At the climax of these episodes my mother would flee the house, slam the door, jump in her car and drive into town to take the temporary veil with her girlfriends the Dominican nuns, her refuge from the World of Men. (Priests, like gays, didn't really count as men; in any case the Fathers usually appeared as isolated individuals, in relation to whom the nuns could always find strength in numbers.)

Nonetheless, at the end of the day, my mother gave me the greatest gift of all—greater even than the treasure of earthly life: the gift of the

Presence of God, along with a visceral understanding of what a *religion* is, a Way revealed by God and standing as a road and a ladder back to the fullness of His Presence. She told me once that, while pregnant with me, she had had a vision of the Uncreated Light. And somewhere, underneath all the grief and all the illusions we spew out, like an octopus spewing ink, to obscure and blunt the sharpness of that grief, lay my mother's primary love for me, and mine for her, on a level deeper than temporal memory can reach — the level where early childhood still swims, as Wordsworth knew in his "Intimations of Immortality," in the Shining Ocean of Beginning.

FAMILY JOURNEYS

From our home-base in San Rafael (to widen the circle once again), the three of us — my father, my mother, and myself — left our home-planet and hit the holiday road to wider California destinations in the satellite-planet of Vacation: Bucks' Lake and Snowshoe Flat in Plumas County; the Lair of the Bear, a campground for University of California alumni (like my father) in the Stanislaus National Forest; my Aunt Barbara's (my mother's sister) house in Beverly Hills; Somes Bar in Siskiyou County, on the Salmon River, a tributary to the Klamath, up near the Oregon border, the very country where Lew Welch became a Forest Sage for a year or so to write his *Hermit Poems*; and (without my father) to Mexico, along with my parents' friends the Pringles, to visit the Mesoamerican ruins in the Yucatan and the Aztec sites near Mexico City. Never had there been a time in this country — and certainly there never will be again — when the sense of adventure and the feeling (and reality) of *safety* were so perfectly united. Even death-enamored Mexico, land of the dancing skeletons, was relatively cool in those years. The world was our oyster.

CITY OF THE (VIRTUAL) ANGELS

Some of our earlier excursions were south to L.A., either by plane — the United Airlines DC-7, the last major piston engine airliner in service — or by train, the Coast Starlight, to visit aunt Barbara and her husband Charles in Beverly Hills. Barbara was the dominant sister of the two Strother girls; her parents (and my mother's) apparently took the position that "one should never contradict Barbara," which in practice, as my mother often reminded us, included allowing her to force my mother (Bonnie) to "eat rocks." When visiting our home in the North she would appear as the Great Lady, in full mink coat and dripping with diamonds — in broad daylight — making my mother seem mousey and nun-like by comparison. Barbara's husband, Charles Widmann, was from a part-German family who ran a coffee finca in Guatemala. Charles' brother Rudi was the more German of the two, loud, effusive and commanding. He was bald and had a bright red complexion that might or might not have been the origin of his name. Charles, on the other hand, was shy and retiring, more Latino-looking than Rudi; he rarely said much, limiting himself to whistling thinly between his teeth. Looking at this pair you could see how, in upper class semi-feudal Guatemalan society, the dominant brother would become the Patrón while the subdominant brother might join the priesthood. And Barbara, for all her show of dominance, was deeply jealous of my mother since she herself was childless, and she was probably equally jealous that my comparatively less-interesting, subdominant mother had landed a husband who, to all appearances, was more likely to produce children than Charles Widmann ever was. After Charles passed away from brain cancer, Barbara would phone my mother from time to time, and unload a stream of abuse as part of the grieving process. Her life came to a hard end when she suffered a stroke alone in her apartment, then had to sit paralyzed in a chair for days until she was finally found, taken to a hospital, and allowed to pass on from this life.

(*Memories.* Why are they significant? What makes them so? Why should the memories of one person be significant to anyone else? If they are used to build an individual identity they hold no significance beyond that identity; they are non-transferrable. But to the degree that they are released from the gnawing need to *be somebody*, they take flight. They are like a cloud of monarch butterflies or a flock of startled blackbirds rising from an open field—each one a finished Form, ready to die, ready to become immortal. They are the flora and fauna of the human experience in time now set free from time, purified of attachment and made ready to pass, either to future generations—if Providence grants us such—or back to the Night of the Unseen, to become the cells and molecules and firing nerve synapses of the Eternal Human Form, safe in the heart of God. The release of all the memories stored in histories and bloodlines, in places and objects, and in the age-old human mind, is what the Book of Revelations calls "the resurrection of the dead.")

Aunt Barbara's house was on a hillside, in the strange L.A. environment of milky smog and thin sunlight. From there we would take excursions to Marineland, where you could gaze through a window of thick, clear glass into an undersea world filled with groupers, sharks, huge sunfish and many other species, not to mention the Garibaldi perch, of a brilliant vermillion color like big goldfish; they were named after the followers of the Italian revolutionary leader Giuseppe Garibaldi, the Redshirts. Infinitely greater than Marineland was Disneyland, the Magic Kingdom, which provided a powerful (though artificial) visionary experience for a young child like myself living in the first television generation, before color TV, before the internet, and certainly before the virtual Disneyland known as the Metaverse. The only time I've flown in a helicopter was when we were taking one as a shuttle to Disneyland. With artificial natural environments and artificial three-dimensional apparitions, Los Angeles and its environs clearly demonstrated, for those with eyes to see, how Hollywood was beginning to invade and transform the real world, to de-nature nature. As for the Wizard of Oz himself, Walt Disney, it's as if he had been hired by invisible controllers from the Jinn-world to provide the young with advance advertising for the psychedelic revolution of the 60s — an "agenda" that is clearly visible, for example, in his cartoon tour-de-force *Fantasia* with its dancing mushrooms and its mountain that turns into Lucifer, which came out in 1940, a quarter-century before the widespread use of LSD.

SNOWSHOE FLAT

A later destination was Snowshoe Flat in the forests of Plumas County, up in the Feather River country. Snowshoe Flat was the second home of Bill and Augusta Dawson, professional friends of my father's. In those days people in the upper middle classes would sometimes share such vacation homes with friends, more as a kind of informal housesitting arrangement than as an actual time-share. The Flat, built on a flat or shelf of land overlooking a valley that held the little towns of Graeagle, with its saw mill, and Blairsden, with its delicious peach ice cream, was set in a forest of sugar pines, the ones with those huge, foot-long pinecones. It was a sturdy red cabin or chalet with a steep metal roof. The cabin had an old radio in a wooden cabinet that actually did seem capable, as in the *Twilight Zone* episode, of tuning in to old programs from the Golden Age of Radio, shows like "Fibber McGee and Molly." Memories from that era include the time my father, using a willow branch, experimented with water-witching (otherwise known as dowsing) to expand the capacity of the spring that fed the house; the Halloween when I and a friend from Bayside Acres, James Ringrose (my father was in the habit of inviting neighbor children near my own age to share our vacations with us) constructed a graveyard farther into the forest with rocks and bricks as headstones, each with a cardboard tag with the name of the occupant, complete with a white ghost-doll made from a bedsheet dancing above it that could be raised and lowered on a rope, as well as a long pipe that we buried under the pine needles so we could produce ghostly voices issuing from the ground. Two other things I'll never forget: the sweet smell of honeycomb from part of an abandoned hive that had fallen in the pine needles, mixed with the equally fragrant aroma of the pines themselves, and the night the sawmill at Graeagle burned, the fire clearly visible, from our higher vantage point, far down in the valley. How *at home on the earth* we all felt in those days.

SOMES BAR

Our major destination on the Vacation Planet was the town of Somes Bar on the Salmon River in the Siskiyou Mountains, steep forested country, rarely craggy, that reminded one of the highest of the Appalachians, except that the forests were tall evergreen conifers, pines and firs, rather than mostly second-growth deciduous trees (maple, beech, poplar, oak, birch, buckeye, etc.) like the eastern forests. The town consisted of one general store owned and operated by the Long family (Floyd, his wife Joe, and their children Butch, Judy and Lori) plus one or two houses, placed on a graded flat opposite the point where a bridge crossed the river. I remember standing on that bridge and watching the majestic runs of the salmon and steelhead through the crystalline waters, laboring upstream to spawn and die. From Google Earth I now learn that the bridge I remember was later torn down after the road it serviced went out of commission due to the construction of a new and wider road farther up the slope; the bridge was moved downstream, while the town itself—unless Google is entirely mistaken—came to rest upstream and on the opposite bank. (That Google Maps can be wrong has been abundantly proven to me over the years; for example, the Web now presents to us, as an old black-and-white picture of *Sawyer's* Bar, what is actually a photo of the old Somes Bar, just as I knew it. Who knows if we learn more or lose more as human history passes by? It may be impossible to definitively answer that question, given that we only remember what we remember, and always forget what we forget.) The new road was definitely a good idea, since the narrow old road south and west between Somes Bar and Orleans, a thousand feet up a sheer cliff from the Klamath River, was the most dangerous drive I've ever been on, with hardly any riverside barrier and plenty of blind curves around which might come barreling, at any moment, a huge logging truck driven by some daredevil who must've lived in the constant knowledge that it is *always* a good day to die. Butch Long himself died on that road, mercifully fast, when his pickup truck went over the edge.

The cabin we stayed in was on the left bank of the Salmon, directly across from the store and/or town which was (then) on the right bank. It was the property of Walter Anderson, another dentist and friend of our family. Walter Anderson was a "confirmed bachelor," middle aged and fussy, who in later life lived with his Scandinavian housekeeper who had been his dental receptionist before he retired, along with a Boston bull terrier called Rab, named after the Arabic word for "Lord." "Bachelors" are a kind of thing I don't think we have any more. The academic associations of the word imply that the bachelor was a kind of lower or apprentice degree in life, a preparation for the higher degree, that of the married state, but that's not how bachelors were necessarily looked at in those days. A bachelor was usually either a pleasure-seeking playboy or a kind of voluntary hermit as far as women were concerned, perhaps slightly misogynistic but still fully accepted as a recognized social type and condition. He might have been gay of course, but that was rarely considered or imagined. He was simply a bachelor, a life chosen for his own purposes, which was considered to be entirely his own business and nobody else's. "Singles" — not to mention "Incels" (what a horrible notion) — came a lot later.

Dr Anderson held his cabin at Somes Bar on a 99-year lease from the Forest Service. It had a corrugated tin roof and consisted of a large open porch that we used as a sleeping area during the summers — we usually vacationed there for maybe 3 weeks in August — and two main rooms, a bedroom with bathroom-and-shower in the back and a "living room" with miscellaneous, mis-matched, cast-off or second-hand chairs, a bookshelf, and an ancient wooden crank telephone that almost worked, from which the Somes Bar store (nowhere else) could theoretically be contacted, though we never used it. Separated by a divider of shelves and cabinets from that room was the kitchen area with a sink and an ice-box (cooled with store-bought block ice) and a wood stove, the stove fed from a woodpile in a cleared area to the side of the cabin, which required some chopping before the sticks would fit in; it was from that pile I learned what carpenter ants were, after one of the soldiers of that species bit my finger and drew blood. The rest of the insect life there was equally powerful, and included crowds of grasshoppers with red, yellow or blue gliding-wings stretched between their big jumping-legs and their bodies (wonderful for trout-bait), magnificent metallic emerald green beetles an inch long, and the biggest hornets I've ever seen, one of which — marked like a yellowjacket except bigger and colored black and white instead of black and yellow — sounded, when knocking on the picture-window, like somebody was tossing pebbles against the pane. (The yellowjackets were a perpetual scourge, so we set up traditional yellowjacket traps made of chunks of bacon-rind hanging by strings far down into deep cans or jars, just above a few inches of soapy water. The yellowjackets would gorge themselves on the bacon fat and then, too heavy to fly up out of those containers, fall back into the water and drown.) I also remember the snakes, especially a fine-looking brown-and-white-banded California king snake I saw one time, and the plentiful, playful chipmunks. I took a "playful" pot shot at a chipmunk once with an air gun, and killed it, not really meaning to. (Since then I have had a little pain in my heart, about the size of a chipmunk. Hunting for food is honorable; hunting for sport, or (worse) for distraction, is degrading.) And the Salmon River really was salmon country. One day a local fisherman brought us some salmon fillets which we smoked in the little smokehouse near the cabin over a slow fire of alder wood. Salmon smoked like that doesn't turn out like lox, moist and tender, but emerges dry, almost crystalline — but delicious nonetheless.

The cabin had no electricity, so we lit the place with those wonderful kerosene lamps with "mantles" — not the kind with flat wicks and an open flame, but the ones with ring-shaped wicks surmounted by tube-shaped mantles, hollow at the top, made of the finest imaginable open network of fired white clay, a network that would incandesce like tungsten filaments over the heat of the flame and give off a glorious light that was more like broad daylight than any lightbulb I've ever seen, whether incandescent or LED. And though we had piped water, a working faucet for the sink and a flush toilet, that water came from a spring farther up the hill behind the house. The cabin was also home to bats, who slept through the days in the little tunnels between the corrugations of the sheet-metal roof and the underlying planks. You could get up close to them and watch them stretching and yawning in their sleep like tiny gargoyles, their little white canine teeth as small and sharp as needles. One time one of them came out during the day and clung to the wall of the porch; since this was an abnormal occurrence and indicative of possible rabies, my father shot it dead with my BB gun and disposed of it. But did we worry that the other bats we slept under every night might have rabies? It never crossed our minds. This was before "safety culture" came in, the widespread emotional illness that caused the congenitally terrified people of England a few years ago to cut down a venerable stand of ancient chestnut trees just because a nut once fell on a child's head, conked him and raised a bump. We didn't worry about things like that back then; we slept sound in our sleeping-bags on the porch of our cabin every night with no fear of mosquito-borne illnesses or attacks by man-hating animals or any human criminal—listening, in our primal innocence, to the endless chant and moan of the river below us in the dark. One night, in the complex chorus of that speech, I heard the Battle Hymn of the Republic sung in actual human voices, as clear as if it had been performed by the Mormon Tabernacle Choir a block away. Nature was human to us in those days; we accepted the earth, didn't fear it, and lived at home in it.

(Parenthetically, one of the most interesting aspects of human perception is its ability to form intelligible patterns out of random masses of information, to engage in both visual and auditory *pareidolia*. Gazing at an old black-and-white cathode-ray TV screen—the kind that would produce, after broadcast hours, a random "snow" of dancing white dots—it was possible, and still is possible, to say to it "let a triangle appear," or a square or a circle or a figure-eight, and see the very same shape, clear as a snapshot, rise into view a moment later. And the same thing is apparently also possible with a complex collection of random sounds like the noise of a river flowing through a stretch of rapids. The night I heard the Battle Hymn I must have imagined that song for some reason, and then heard it outside me a moment later, clear as a bell, in the many voices of the river. Or was it really the voices of the Ancestors, gathering up their ancient passions and exploits and tragedies and recounting them for the benefit of us, the younger generations living downstream, both to release those memories as burdens and to make a gift of them as wisdoms? *We will show them Our signs,* says the Holy Qur'an, *in the world around them and also in their own souls, until they are convinced that this is the truth. Isn't it enough for you* [you human beings] *that I am Witness over all things?*)

Siskiyou County was Indian country, territory of the Karok (Karuk) Tribe, the "Upstreamers" — as opposed to the Yuroks, the "Downstreamers," who lived farther down the Klamath in Humboldt and Del Norte counties, and the Hoopa (Hupa) Tribe, newcomers from the north coast who moved in around AD 1000. The matriarch of Somes Bar was Mrs Langford, a half-Indian lady, highly respected and always consulted on important matters. She was the mother of storekeeper Joe Long, Floyd's wife, making their children presumably one-eighth Karok. Butch, who plunged to his death into the Klamath from the Orleans road, was fair, blond and blue-eyed, but with an Indian facial configuration, high cheekbones and "Roman" nose. Judy was a sulky, nubile, dark-skinned "maiden" (an honorific if not a strictly accurate title), while Lori, who looked more like Butch, was the sexiest 8-year old girl I have ever encountered, obviously headed for an explosive puberty. Once, after spending a day swimming the river (whose current was just gentle enough to make this relatively safe while strong enough to make it interesting; anybody with any free time, and young enough to do so, spent their summers in the river), on the shore I encountered a husky, dark-skinned Indian kid. "Want to fight?" he asked. "No thanks" I replied. I got the sense that, to him, a good fist-fight or wrestling match would've just been his way of saying "hello."

But the member of our party that really made an impression on the local Indians was our dog Tam, an Irish water spaniel, whose full name was Seventh Heavens Shillelagh Tam. Irish water spaniels are like big husky poodles with liver-brown tightly-curled coats, but with throats and tails nearly hairless, giving them their nickname "rat-tails"; their throats, covered with the finest fur, are smooth as mole-skin. When Tam first appeared on the river-bank, the Indians immediately took notice. "Is that a bear?" they asked. "He walks proud" one of them said, which was exactly true: he carried himself with chest out and head held high; he was not a dog to suffer fools lightly.

Tam was an aristocrat — never a cur or a bully, yet always ready to defend his honor. The "Seventh Heavens" in his name came from the kennel in the Sacramento Valley where he was born and raised, run by an old Irish woman, Mrs Murgatroyd. When we first took him home to our house on the shores of San Francisco Bay, he had a revelation; the scales fell from his eyes; it was his road-to-Damascus moment: *Water! And lots of it!!* He headed for the Bay like a shot and never left it until the feebleness of old age overtook him. Water spaniels were bred as retrievers and (being great swimmers) duck and goose retrievers in particular. But it turned out he was too wild to be trained for that purpose — not dangerous or violent, just ridden by his own obsessions and imperatives; he didn't have time for the lesser purposes to which human beings tried to yoke him. Every morning when we let him out of the house he would first stop and howl to the four directions — north, east, south and west — in order to announce his presence. Then he would begin his daily labors, which consisted of *diving for rocks*, then carrying them one by one up from the shore and depositing them in our garden. In his lifetime he must've moved literally tons of them. Ultimately we used them to keep the weeds in check between the trees, first putting down a layer of black plastic sheeting, then holding it in place with a layer of Tam's rocks. He was too lordly to be easily affectionate, though he was never mean or hateful. As he patrolled his domain, pacing back and forth along the water-line with a gait like the *tölt* of the Icelandic horses, the other dogs of the neighborhood took umbrage. "Who in hell does he think *he* is?" was their attitude. They would run after him and worry him, nipping at his heels. He was far too proud and aloof to pay them any mind — until they went too far and he felt that his honor had been impugned. His response on one occasion was to seize one of the dogs, roll him into the Bay waters — Tam's natural element — and *dunk* him, holding him under just long enough for that clown to learn his lesson. Another time we heard a commotion outside, and when we went out to our driveway we saw Tam with the neighbor dog Spike, a springer spaniel. He had Spike down on his back, pinned to the ground with his front paws on his opponent's outstretched floppy ears, steadily growling at him to make sure that, in the future, he would never again forget his *place*. It seems that people nowadays can't conceive any longer that that an animal could have a character and a destiny — "because," as Jenny comments, "they can't even imagine any more that a *human being* could have a character and a destiny!" Seventh Heavens Shillelagh Tam was definitely not a politically correct canine — probably (in part) due to the fact that we never had him castrated.

But to return to Siskiyou County: on one occasion when a school friend of mine, Michael Mooney, who was on vacation with us, dove from a rock in the river and hit his head on another rock under water, nearly killing himself, after which he had to be transported many miles to a local clinic from which he soon emerged with several stitches and a shaved patch on the front of his skull just above the brow, my father made a hairpiece for him out of Tam's fur and some adhesive tape to hide the bald spot in Michael's Irish red hair. (How *bad* we all were in those days! I wonder how many laws — probably most of them unwritten — my father would have broken if he were alive to do such a thing today, seeing that this country is presently affected by a horrible, humorless Puritanism, a Puritanism that is no longer Christian but entirely atheistic, and therefore truly sub-human, the worst of both worlds.)

Those northern California mountains were also Bigfoot country. Everybody believed in Bigfoot as a "cryptid," a not-yet-officially-discovered and classified species of animal; many had seen him. And the best film record ever taken of Bigfoot—the one with the female Sasquatch striding over the dry rocks of a river bed, looking sideways at the camera—was captured at Olive Creek on the Trinity River, a tributary to the Klamath, a little ways south of the Hoopa Indian Reservation. Yet now Bigfoot is beginning to appear all over the country, and is revealing himself more clearly every day to be not a cryptid but some kind of paranormal being, whose tracks will sometimes stop short in a field or an open stretch of sand and, without any backtracking, entirely disappear, as if the thing that made them had suddenly gone up in smoke. A friend of mine, Steven Speray, was recently contacted by a hunter of his acquaintance who encountered something resembling a Sasquatch in the wild forested country of eastern Pike County, Kentucky, near the Virginia border. It was man-shaped, abnormally tall and muscular, and able to travel at an impossible speed through the thick underbrush. At one point it turned to look at the hunter, then emitted a piercing howl or shriek that unnaturally vibrated *inside the man's chest*, leading both him and my friend to conclude that it must have been a preternatural entity, not any kind of unknown animal or primitive human being. Now that *cracks* are beginning to appear in what René Guénon called the Great Wall, the barrier separating the corporeal world from the quasi-material "etheric" world of subtle energies that closely borders it, various Sasquatches, Space Aliens, Werewolves and spooks of all descriptions are beginning to appear more and more frequently to more and more people. Once the church bells have been silenced and the crosses cut down, the door is open for the dark forces to dance. Somehow I have never been happy with entities like these. One gets the impression that virtually all children nowadays are attracted to things like Dinosaurs, Sasquatches and Robots, whereas I was always afraid of them and had nightmares about them. Sometimes I've imagined myself consulting a psychiatrist about these difficulties; I see myself telling him (or her): "I don't know what it is, Doc. I hate to admit this, it's a pretty embarrassing thing to own up to, but the thing is, *I just don't like demons!* I've been like this for as long as I can remember. Do you think you can you do anything for me? Is there any cure for me, or am I totally beyond help?"

Soon after our last vacation at Somes Bar—though I came back to the Anderson cabin once more with my friend Ken Bullock in later years, after my father's death, to try and help him through a dark period in his life—the Forest Service committed the unpardonable sin of cutting down the (presumably) Karok sacred tree on the flat-topped Mt. Offield, a lone pine visible from many miles around. That winter the Siskiyous were hit with what was then described as a thousand-year flood, the Christmas Flood of 1964, which devastated northwestern California and parts of

Oregon. Many bridges were washed out, many towns seriously flooded. Some were never rebuilt. In the dimension of horizontal, temporal causality, the cutting down of the tree and the flooding of the rivers have no discernable relationship—but in the dimension of vertical causality, where what is eternally commanded-to-be descends into, and becomes, what is transpiring at this very moment, they are like two beads on the one string.

PRE-COLUMBIAN (AND PRE-GANG) MEXICO

High School was largely the end of family excursions, but we did take one more trip in the early 60s in (probably) my freshman year—at least I and my mother did, along with our family friends the Pringles—to Mexico to tour the Mayan, Zapotec and Aztec ruins. The Pringles on that occasion were Brooks and Catherine, both dermatologists (Brooks was a member of my father's duck club), their daughter Alison and their son Bob, who was just out of the Peace Corps. A two-physician income was pretty hefty in those days; most middleclass families could subsist on only one salary, and still have a house and two cars and send their kids to college. Nonetheless the Pringles didn't live apart in the compulsory McMansion as people in the higher middle-income brackets do today; they had a nice house on a Marin County hillside in San Anselmo. Nonetheless that house, like that of my parents, was no larger than that of Betty and Howard Trumbly in San Rafael—the parents of my adolescent peer group the Trumbly Clan—which was easily affordable for them on the single salary of Howard, a master electrician who worked for Bell Telephone.

Our first stop was Oaxaca, from which we fanned out to visit the ancient Zapotec ruins of Mitla, Yagul and Monte Albán—Mitla with its intricate, decorative stone-work, Monte Albán a neat, almost miniature ceremonial city of honey-colored stone with perfectly preserved temples and plaza. My memories of Mexico are pretty broken up—first by railroad journeys on archaic Mexican trains with caged chickens and urine running down the aisles; by a flight on a single engine "air taxi," maybe a Piper Cub, up the long mountain valley from Oaxaca to San Cristóbal de las Casas in the state of Chiapas; and a second flight on an old DC-3, banging and slamming through the air-pockets, possibly the longest-serving passenger plane in world history (do some still fly?), held together with bailing-wire, the prayers of saintly mothers and the expertise of the kind of ingenious mechanics who kept the streets of Havana, Cuba alive with brilliantly-painted 1950s-vintage U.S. autos far into later years. And those memories were secondarily fragmented by a totally unfamiliar psychic environment. Where was it that I walked through that open-air meat-market with whole sides of beef hung up in the hot blazing sunlight, buzzing and black with flies? And where did I taste, for the first and last time in my life, a tiny dab of *wasp honey* from a paper comb I found on the ground?

A fascinating flavor, sweet like bee honey but with a tart sourness to it that intriguingly stung the palate...

Besides the ruins I have only two memories of Oaxaca. Since what is cutely called "Montezuma's Revenge" was affecting me, Brooks Pringle invited me to his hotel room for some of the cure. Brooks was quite a drug-user for a totally straight upper middleclass California dermatologist; he lived in a time when it was apparently understood and accepted that a physician would self-prescribe (unless his wife Catherine wrote the prescriptions for him), consequently he was a walking cornucopia of pep pills, tranquilizers, sleeping pills, and—paregoric, camphorated tincture of opium, which was certainly very effective for diarrhea, as well as for anything else that might have affected one at the time, whether physical or psychological. Since he was already half-shot on margaritas, Brooks proceeded to pour me an extremely liberal dose of paregoric, which I gulped down and then made my way back to the outdoor tables attached to the hotel. As I sat at our table I began to feel a tingling at the back of my neck—and when I turned around I saw an ancient Indian with dark glasses (though it was nighttime) staring directly at me from about three feet away.

The other memory of Oaxaca was of a museum we visited, the Museum of Oaxaca Cultures, where I saw, among various other exhibits I don't recall, a pre-Columbian crystal goblet—not glass crystal, but a vessel carved, or rather laboriously abraded, out of a single large crystal of quartz. That goblet *imprinted* itself on me, went directly into my brain, like a spike driven through the third eye. As I gazed at it, I almost fainted.

Later, during a train journey to Mérida in the Yucatán, I had a dream: *A ghost was putting on my body like a coat,* moving its arms up through my arms like sleeves; in each hand I held a crystal goblet like the one I'd seen in Oaxaca. This was before I'd read accounts of the type of Mesoamerican human sacrifice where the priest dresses in the flayed skin of his victim. So I must conclude that the goblet I'd seen in that museum, which Google tells me was found at Monte Albán (I actually saw that very same goblet again in Google Images!), had been made to contain human blood. René Guénon was right: the sites sacred to earlier religions whose spirits have departed do indeed contain toxic psychic residues of the kind that black magicians will sometimes "harvest" for use in their own inverted rites. Had I been inoculated against future temptations to dark magic on that occasion? Or was the vaccine as bad as the disease?

It was in Oaxaca that I learned the correct pronunciation of the Mexican "x," which I heard from the mouths of either the Zapotecs or the Mixtecs (both live in the area) speaking their native tongue. It's like a cross between the "ks" and the "sh" sounds, like a sharper "sh" made with the tongue placed farther to the front of the palate than our "sh," just behind the front teeth—a phoneme that reminds you of the hiss of a snake.

The other town we spent some time in was San Cristóbal de las Casas, south of Oaxaca, from which we visited the beautiful little Mayan city of Palenque with its 3-storey tower, built up against some low forested hills with a stream running out of them, right through the conduits and viaducts of the city. I walked alone for a ways up that crystal-clear stream, flowing without a trace of scum or moss over a bed of bare yellow stone, then knelt to drink a draught of the pure jungle water. And I was able as well to walk down the steep steps into the crypt of the great king Pacal Votan to view his sarcophagus—no guards, no guides, just a handful of befuddled tourists. That's the way the Mayan ruins were in those days; those necropolises were *just there*, largely unattended, the pre-Columbian dead still living relatively free of government control.

Various occult fantasts such as Ignatius Donnelly and Lewis Spence, as well as José Argüelles of Harmonic Convergence fame, have associated Pacal Votan with Quetzalcoatl, the Plumed Serpent, the Mayan Kukulcán; and it is true that various Mexican and Mesoamerican kings, such as the Ce Acatl Quetzalcoatl ("One Reed Plumed Serpent") of the Toltecs, took the god's name as a title. Even more interesting is the association of Pacal Votan with the Mesoamerican version of the legend of the Tower of Babel, in which René Guénon discerned the outlines of an ancient rebellion of the warrior caste against the priestly caste; Babel (which means "Gate of God"), like the pyramids of Mesoamerica, was likely a ziggurat—in Nahuatl, a *teocalli*, a "god-house." (How strange the resemblance between the Nahuatl *teotl* and the Greek *theos*, both of which mean "god.") Francisco Javier Clavijero quotes Francisco Núñez de la Vega, bishop of Chiapas, to the effect that "a certain person named *Votan* was present at that great building, which was made by order of his uncle, in order to mount up to heaven; that then every people was given its language, and that Votan himself was charged by God to make the division of the lands of Anahuac." Was that little tower I saw in Palenque actually the Mayan Tower of Babel?

San Cristóbal itself was a beautiful town with colonial architecture, set in a circular mountain valley ringed with peaks—an old caldera? We lodged in a clean, spacious, efficiently-managed hotel run by a well-organized Swiss matriarch, from which Bob Pringle and I explored the town, taking nips on our bottle of mescal, a kind of raw tequila (*con gusano* of course, which indicates that it contained a maguey worm, the caterpillar who makes its home in the maguey species of agave plant from which both mescal and tequila are made, and which functions as a label for the illiterate and proof of the authenticity of the contents). I'm convinced that if someone were to boil all the alcohol out of a bottle of mescal they could still get high on the residue—which just might explain the resemblance between the words "mescal" and "mescaline."

You got the definite impression that the main industry of the town was the manufacture of fireworks, which were of a single variety: black powder rockets on long stabilizing sticks surmounted by a simple black power explosive charge tightly wrapped in twine (possibly jute fiber). People set them off every night and often during the day. Could there really have been *that* many fiestas? But since Bob and I were modern, progressive Gringos we decided to improve on the tradition-bound local rockets by constructing an advanced, two-stage one. We bound the "motors" of three rockets together, and into the space between them we inserted the stabilizing-stick of the second stage, arranging the stages so that the weaker forward counter-thrust from the engines that was supposed to ignite the explosive charge would ignite the engine of the second stage instead. On the night we set it off, on a small hill in the middle of town, it worked perfectly—except that the rocket turned over before the second stage ignited, and consequently fired the second stage *downward* instead of up, right into the yard of someone's house, where it exploded with a muffled thud. I think I must have derived my general impression of the effectiveness of Peace Corps from that night's experiment, along with some of my sense of the meaning of the term "ugly American."

Four other memories of San Cristóbal stand out. One day we hired some horses to trek to a nearby town, and when the guy who rented them out laid eyes on me, his eyes narrowed. As his little joke he selected the worst horse of the whole string especially for me, the one with the terrible uneven gait that was stuck somewhere between a trot and a gallop—a nag guaranteed to bust my ass, which he certainly did. Finally I couldn't take it anymore, so I dismounted and began leading the horse by the reins back to town. I must've looked as angry and disgusted as I felt, because when I passed some Indian kids one of them cried out, "¡*El Diablo!*"

And though I might have passed for a White Devil on that occasion, the *real* Devil was undoubtedly the man I saw later in town: red complexion, hook nose, black hair, black goatee, glaring, leering grin, striding boldly down the middle of the street, walking a *coyote* on a rope. As he strode along another man, armed with a machete, emerged from a doorway on the left and began marching shoulder-to-shoulder with him. Then a third man appeared from a doorway on the right and joined the march. He was carrying a rifle. If the Estados Unidos Mexicanos ever decides to get rid of its present coat-of-arms, the Aztec symbol of the eagle with the rattlesnake in its talons, I vote for the symbol of Rifleman, Machete-man and Coyote-walking Devil as a perfectly appropriate replacement.

And then there was the open-air *mercado*, nothing but a roof on pillars—a roof with a concave curve like a Chinese pagoda, on top of which were large, bulbous ornaments, painted red, that looked for all the world like Buddhist *stupas*; as soon as that impression sank in, all the Indians shopping there suddenly looked like Tibetans. (William Burroughs too remarked on the Tibetan flavor of certain high-altitude Indian sites in Central and South America.)

I also remember, with fondness, the sundown ceremony of the local Indians, the Tzotzil and/or the Tzeltal. All the men wore shallow-crowned, circular, flat straw hats, each with a bunch of colored ribbons hanging from it—unless the man were married, in which case the ribbons would be tied up in a knot. On one of the dirt roads into town, at the top of the ridge that circled San Cristóbal, when their day's work was done they would sit by the roadside, under the three great, rough wooden crosses, and play a haunting, repetitive pattern on their huge home-made guitars with the big cigar-sized pegs: their evening *rāga*.

For the last leg of our southward journey we took the train from San Cristobal to the substantial city of Mérida near the Caribbean coast of the Yucatán. It was in Mérida that I saw the *paseo*, a Sunday evening courtship ritual where all the young people wishing to advertise themselves as seeking a mate will walk in procession around the plaza, the boys in one direction and the girls in the other. (Who walks clockwise—the boys? With the girls walking counter-clockwise? The girls walking on the inside and the boys on the outside? It stands to mythopoetic reason that the boys would walk clockwise on the outside and the girls counterclockwise on the inside, in line with traditional symbolism; I hope that whoever knows the actual form of the *paseo* will care enough to confirm this or deny it.)

From Mérida we took excursions to the major Mayan cities of Uxmal and Chichén Itzá—Chichén Itzá with the two Plumed Serpents flowing down from the apex of the classic pyramid on either side of one of the four steep flights of steps up the four sides, their dragon-heads at the bottom, and the city's ball court with the thick, horizontal stone "hoop" set high on the flanking wall, where either the losing team (some say the winning team) or else the player who made the most goals with their hard, solid rubber ball would be rewarded (according to some) with the sacred privilege of being sacrificed to the gods. With this kind of cultural background it's no surprise that a soccer game between El Salvador and Honduras morphed on one occasion into an actual war between the two nations, known as the Soccer War.

Chichén Itzá is where I first remember noticing the classic Mayan racial type: more-or-less triangular face, prominent "Roman" nose curving down from the forehead with almost no bridge to it, full lips, downturned "jaguar" mouth, and backward-curving skull like you will see in depictions of the ancient Egyptians, and sometimes in modern Africans with obvious Egyptian blood (this anatomical similarity puts one in mind of the "cocaine mummies" who recently turned up in Egypt—mummies that, on chemical analysis, were found to have cocaine in their tissues.

Some of the ancient intertribal or Metís societies of North America claim that there was commerce across the Atlantic between the New World and the Old in archaic times; it now looks like they were right). The Mayans also seem to have a tendency to be cross-eyed, which may be why they would hang a bead on their infants' foreheads so the child would stare at it, thus accentuating this quality which they considered beautiful, as they also accentuated the backwards-ness of their skulls by binding a board on their infants' heads, like the Flathead Indians of North America, or at least some of the tribes who go by that name. I have rarely seen a purer racial type than the Mayans of the Yucatán in the 1960s; they reminded one, in their highly standardized physiognomy, of the Watusi or the Han Chinese. (I'm using the past tense here because, judging from Mel Gibson's film *Apocalypto*, the Mayans of today — or maybe just the ones Mel was able to pick up on the docks as extras — are more mongrelized than they were when I met them, over half a century ago; the pure Mayan type may, slowly but surely, be disappearing.) I remember the vulgar comments of a couple of American tourists, a mother and her daughter, about this particular race of humans. "They *were* relatively advanced — *for their time*," the mother said. "What nobody seems to know is what ever *happened* to them." She had apparently failed to notice that the people all around her, the local inhabitants, were the very image of the reliefs depicting the ancient Maya that were carved on the pyramids they had come to stare at — nor did she seem to know that they were still speaking substantially the same language as when those temples were built. (Tourists, read your guide-books.)

It was in the Temple of the Columns at Chichén Itzá that I encountered my second Mesoamerican ghost, this time with my eyes wide open. I had separated myself from my group and gone aside, alone, to view the Temple, in the wall of which I saw what looked like an excavated tunnel, off the beaten tourist track. There were no "keep out" signs so I decided to go in. It was pitch black. As I stared into the darkness, the dancing dots of light and color that the brain fills any darkness with began to form themselves into a distinct figure with arms, legs and a head. Having no idea of what might be an appropriate way of addressing such an apparition, I made my way out of that tunnel as quickly as I could.

My other powerful memory of Chichén Itzá was of the *cenote* or circular natural pond or well, those cliff-sided sink-holes filled with black water that made human and agricultural life possible in the Yucatán. Those were the holes into which offerings to the gods were thrown; sometimes young virginal girls were cast into the *cenotes* to drown, in hopes that this action would bring rain. My wife Jenny, who has the "Mongolian Spot" on her sacrum just like the Mayans do, once had a dream or vision about how, supposedly in another life, she had been the one to bring this practice to an end — or maybe, as she now tells me, she actually read this story somewhere; in any case she immediately identified, on the basis of her past role as a family scapegoat, with the heroine of it. The idea was that the sacrificed girl would come before the rain-gods in the next world, the Chaacs, and implore them to send rain. Chaac was big in the Yucatán; some of the kings of Chichén Itzá were named after him. The heroine of the story, however, shocked and astounded the rain-priests by threatening, if she were sacrificed, to go to the rain-gods and tell them never to send rain again! So they let her go, being of course afraid to kill her, and that was the end of the cult of Chaac at that place and time. (A true myth? Certainly a story great enough to become one.)

After the temple-cities we took a vacation from our vacation on Isla Mujeres, the Island of Women, off the coast of the Yucatán near Cozumel—a slip of land so narrow that you'd think, for all its big modern hotels, that Huracán, the storm-god whose name means "Heart of Sky"—as if the Mayan shamans, flying through the stars in their astral bodies, had remarked on how closely the spiral Milky Way galaxy resembles a huge celestial hurricane—could wipe the whole thing out with a single wave. That night we slept in hammocks at a *pensión*. Bob Pringle had done his best to prank me on that occasion by suggesting that I ask the proprietor for a *chamaca*, which, in Mexican slang, means not "hammock" but "young girl"—but I didn't bite.

It was on the boat to and from Isla Mujeres that I encountered the true loveliness of the Caribbean Sea, a liquid atmosphere of pellucid turquoise blue, completely transparent for a hundred feet down, where vast sea turtles, sharks and manta-rays went gliding in majestic tranquility on their own chosen errands, oblivious to the ways of men.

Our last stop was Mexico City to view the Aztec ruins of Tenochtitlán, and the even more ancient and larger pyramids of the pre-Aztec, possibly Mayan city of Teotihuacán—but by then I was shot. The thin air at that altitude was sapping my energy with no time for me to acclimatize to it, not to mention the fact that I had had enough by that time of black magic, blood, and ghosts—especially of blood, in the arts of which the Aztecs had been the pre-eminent and unchallenged masters. So I just crashed in my hotel room. Except for the National Palace with its murals by Diego Rivera, I missed Mexico City entirely.

THE CONTINUATION OF MEXICO IN THE INNER WORLD

In the process of writing down this and other stories from my life, I begin to see that I was destined to encounter, investigate and understand the reality of psychic darkness, not on a gross level as in war or prison or *successful* criminal attack, but on a subtle one, in what might be called the world of the spirits. It's almost as if I had agreed to do this beforehand. Did anything good come of it? For one thing it undoubtedly taught me a level of "discernment of spirits" that has turned out to be highly useful in navigating our 21st-Century world where dark psychic forces appear to have infiltrated every aspect of human life. And it has certainly sharpened my longing for the Spiritual Light, even the faintest glimmer of it, and strengthened my gratitude to Allah for every time He has lifted the corner of the veil, allowing me to glimpse that Light.

It is also becoming clear to me that the brief trip I took through the remnants of Ancient Mexico in the 1960s set part of my soul on a course, or tangent, that only concluded in 1988, when I first stepped on the Sufi path. The first echo of it was my encounter, courtesy of Lew Welch, with Peruvian-born quasi-anthropologist Carlos Castaneda, who claimed to have been taught some form of archaic Toltec sorcery. The second echo was my and Jenny's pass through Central American revolutionary politics in the 1980s as part of the church-based Sanctuary Movement for Central American refugees. And my decision to go that route, strangely enough, also had something to do with Castaneda, who—though he quoted a poem by Peruvian revolutionary poet Cesar Vallejo in one of his books—was in no way a politico. That story is worth telling.

One of the "plant powers" described, and ingested, by Castaneda (or the *character* of Castaneda) in his first book, *The Teachings of Don Juan: A Yaqui Way of Knowledge*, was *Datura Stramonium*, Jimson Weed, also known as Devil's Weed. After my brief encounter with Castaneda courtesy of Lew Welch, as will be recounted in *Chapter Three*, I decided to sample it so as to catch (and be caught by) its particular quality. Rather than brewing up a broth of the highly-poisonous root, on a couple of occasions I simply smoked a bit of the dried leaf. As soon as the smoke of the Devil's Weed entered my lungs, I was *immediately* in the presence of a supremely dark force, clearly a *feminine* force, that demanded absolute respect. When in Her presence, any motion of arrogance or egotism or self-will on my part would be instantly punished; consequently the only way I could deal with Her was to simply sit still, in quiet self-effacement—as if in the presence of a poisonous snake I had to be careful not to antagonize—until Her influence passed. (Some of the qualities I have attributed in my books to Kali, the Hindu Goddess of Death, were undoubtedly derived, at least in part, from my experience with Jimson Weed.)

The second and last time I smoked the Devil's Weed I was at the apartment of Csaba Polony, a gracious and honorable proponent of what has by now become the Old Left—as different from today's unnatural, twisted, Cultural Marxist Left as can be imagined—during the time when Jenny and I were (briefly) part of a group we helped found called the Marin Committee for Central America (see *Chapter Eight*). I was debating within myself about how deeply I wanted to get into this Latin American revolution thing, when I glanced over to the window—and in a glass vase on the sill, making up part of a dry arrangement, I saw a sprig of Jimson Weed. I recognized it because I'd learned to spot it in the wild, in Marin County's San Geronimo Valley. I asked Csaba if I could smoke a pinch (in a pipe that was handy, if I remember right); he had no objections so I went ahead. As soon as I had drawn the smoke, I had a vision of Augusto C. Sandino, the Father of the Nicaraguan Revolution. (I remember how he smilingly passed his hand over his forehead, lifting the front of his cowboy hat.) "I am not a pure influence," he told me; "I have blood on my hands. But if you decide to go some distance with me, you'll definitely learn something of value." I believe it was at that moment that the next part of my life, the phase of Liberation Theology and solidarity with the revolutions of Central America, announced itself. As Lao Tzu said, "when occupations come to you they can't be avoided; when occupations leave you they can't be retained."

The final phase of the course that Devil's Weed had set me on was my involvement with the first (and probably the last) international folk event, Harmonic Convergence, and my meeting with the main inventor and organizer of the event, José Argüelles (see *Chapter Nine*). Harmonic Convergence, based on Argüelles' theories about the meaning of the Mayan Calendar, besides representing the peak of the New Age Movement, was a kind of sublimation of Latin American liberation politics mixed with various occult notions drawn from Mayan mythology—influences that might remind one of the ideas of Carlos Castaneda. All of those associations, for me, were under a kind of dark wing—a shadow that lifted as soon as I entered the world of (more or less) Traditional Islamic Sufism. *But did it lift entirely?* Nietzsche tells us that if you stare for long enough into the Abyss, the Abyss also stares into you. God can bring good out of evil, but anybody who reads this and then thinks "so then let's have more evil so we can have more good" will get just what he or she deserves. Those who are wounded in war—or at least some of them—will be better able to help other people with the same wounds; a person without PTSD will not be very helpful in a PTSD support group. Even so, doing things that could result in lifelong damage to the psyche can't really be recommended.

Nonetheless, whatever the conscious choices we make, life has currents, eddies, inside the larger flow of events. They are marked by intimations, omens, synchronicities; sometimes they are announced by dreams. If you seek their causes in visible conditions, or even in psychological tendencies and motivations, you won't find what you're looking for, because those causes do not lie in the river of linear time but in the Unseen Ocean which that river continuously arises from as invisible vapor, and endlessly returns to as visible and audible rain. The origins of those currents are relatively eternal in relation to their sequential appearance, which is why the real cause of a given fully-enacted life-scenario can appear at the beginning of it, or at the end of it, or at any number of points along the course of it. The true source of any journey does not lie in the first step we take on the road between perceived point of departure and projected destination, but in the road itself and the land it travels through — the actual ground under our feet. Like Plato said, "time is the moving image of Eternity."

THE DREAM OF MY LIFE

When I was five or six years old I had a dream that seemed to predict the whole course of my life; every time I go through a major life-change, I see something new in it:

> I am in a large, luxurious cubical room, paneled in dark brown wood. On each wall is a rectangle of red wallpaper, like cloth, as if it were made of red satin. Each rectangle leaves only a foot or two of the wood paneling of each wall visible, surrounding it on all four sides.
>
> This room is entered through glass doors on the right-hand wall, beyond which I have a vague sense of a traffic-filled street. I have apparently come into the room through these doors.
>
> In this room are all the people of my life. All my family, my friends, my acquaintances, and the suggestion also of all the people I am destined to meet in my future. A party is going on, with entertainment. Above us is a large, brilliant chandelier. In the far corner, to the left, is a big grand piano.
>
> The entertainment is provided by two figures near the piano. They appear to be North African shaykhs or marabouts; they are dressed in white djellabahs; each has a white turban or burnoose which covers the head and is wrapped around the neck beneath the chin. Their faces are black.
>
> The entertainment has to do with an animal which, in the dream, I think of as a "horse," though clearly it is a one-humped camel, a dromedary. The marabouts, who are armed with rifles, kill the camel, who then comes back to life. That's the entertainment. Anyone among the guests can request that the camel die in a certain way, after which it will again come back to life. I make the request, the next time they kill the camel, that it die with its legs buckling under it so that it twists to the left as it falls. I demonstrate this kind of death myself so that the marabouts will understand what I want, twisting to the left as I fall and making a "blaaaugh!" sound, like a camel, then standing up again. They proceed to shoot the camel so that it dies exactly as I have demonstrated. Then it comes back to life, and stands up.
>
> To the left of the large, red-papered cubical room is a doorway, which is reached by ascending perhaps two short steps. Beyond the doorway is a small, narrow room with plush, green-upholstered chairs, and a table upon which is a lamp with a yellow-green shade with yellow polkadots. Beyond this room is a darkened area of shabby, abandoned-looking halls

with cracked and flaking plaster. The other two rooms are in vivid color, but this rear area is all in black-and-white. I enter the narrow room and pass into the rear area, then I return to the cubical room. I leave the cubical room and then re-enter it for a second time, in exactly the same way. Then I leave it for a third time—but when I return to the cubical room for the third time, it is now pitch black, silent. Everyone is gone. I am alone.

At this point the dream becomes "lucid"; within the dream, I realize that I am dreaming. In my fear of abandonment I cry out to my mother and father, who I now realize are sleeping in the next room—in terms of this world. I want them to awaken me from this dream which has ended in such a frightening way. They hear my cries, and do in fact awaken me.

The shabby, darkened halls in the dream with their aging tile floors and cracked plaster now remind me of Angelico Hall on the campus of Dominican College (now Dominican University) in San Rafael, where the Garden School where I went to nursery school and kindergarten was located, and the steps up to the small room that led to those halls of the similar steps up from the entrance foyer of the School to the classrooms. The North African marabouts foreshadowed my entry into the 'Alawiyya tariqah, whose founder, Shaykh Ahmed al-'Alawi, hailed from Algeria. Did their appearance represent the rise of Islamic Sufism, at least in my life, as a compensation for the decadence of the Catholic Church? As for the darkness at the end of the dream, that still remains to be deciphered—not primarily through a meditation on its symbolism, though such investigations will always be useful, but by the greatest *mufassir* (Qur'anic exegete) of all, the ultimate Joseph of dream-interpretation, which is life itself. Nonetheless, some consideration of the symbols may be of help. The shabby, darkened rooms were to the left, which in the next world is the road to Hell and in both worlds can represent the side of the ego, what Sufis call the *nafs*. The right, on the other hand, is the direction of the Spirit, the road to Paradise. But why was the right-hand direction pitch black at the end? A foreshadowing of spiritual despair? Or did it, by any chance, indicate the station of ultimate annihilation in God? And in addition, just to further complicate things, the symbolism of right and left, when applied to the soul rather than the soul's imaginal environment, can have a reverse interpretation, according to which the right represents the Outer world—the side of the liver, the seat of self-will—and the left the Inner one, the side of the Heart, which is said to be bigger than sky and earth put together, big enough to contain God Himself. Was that blackness the picture of my perpetual difficulty in dealing with This World, the world of traffic-filled streets beyond those glass doors to the right of the great hall? An impenetrable difficulty that only annihilation-in-God might overcome?

As always, life will tell, though only if we possess the key to the interpretation of that life. But given that the blackness at the end of the dream was foreshadowed by the black faces of the two spiritual guides, who themselves stood to the left, I can hope that the second interpretation, annihilation in God, will be the right one—and will allow me to do the necessary work to make it the right one.

CHILDHOOD'S END

In his poem "THE ENTIRE SERMON BY THE RED MONK," Lew Welch writes: "We invent ourselves. We invent ourselves out of materials we didn't choose, by a process we can't control." The "self" we invent is the ego, which is both a necessary crutch that makes it possible for us to function in this world, and a Frankenstein monster that will eventually kill us unless we kill it first, or at least subdue it and train it to be a good guard dog who knows not to bite us or our friends, nor even to attack our enemies unless that's absolutely necessary, but simply to warn us of them, and warn them to watch their step when entering areas where they will have to deal with the vigilance of others. That ego is born in early childhood. I actually remember the day when it happened; it was in Catholic kindergarten. The moment unexpectedly arrived when I had the sudden insight that "Only *I* am *me!*" I expressed it to myself in exactly those words. And, later on, that ego will reach its "adulthood" when it takes its proper place in what the Muslims call the *dunya* and the Catholics "This World." The above dream, God willing, is about the annihilation of that ego, whereas the following dream, dreamt some years later, is about the "puberty" of it, its crystallization as the "me" I would now have to face the world with:

> I am with my grandmother in one of those storefronts on C St San Rafael, between 4th and 3rd streets. The room is mostly darkened and largely empty. My grandmother is sitting on something like a couch to the left. To the right there is a door in the wall near the back. Shining through that door, as if it were transparent, a spooky green face appears, shaped like the features of a Jack-o'-lantern. Then the door opens and a huge robot steps into the room. "A robot!" my grandmother cries. The robot walks slowly toward me with a lumbering gait. I am frightened, but as he approaches he becomes smaller and smaller—until, standing directly in front of me, he is just my size; he now appears to be a child like me. "Hello!" I tell him, feeling it's time to make friends.

Later I realized that the robot in the dream was like my own face in the mirror that hung on a pillar in front of each chair in Andy Pedroli's barber shop, which was in a storefront at just the same place on C Street where my dream was set. (Andy Pedroli had a certain local celebrity in San Rafael as a popular barber. He also looked just like Nikita Khrushchev, a resemblance people recognized when Khrushchev visited the U.S. in 1959.)

But *what was that robot?* It was a terrifying, artificial, mechanical, threatening thing—it was, in fact, *my ego*—the face in the mirror that William Blake called the Spectre. Yet I had to make friends with it, identify with it, overcome my fear of it. Childhood, since it contains the seeds of all that is to follow, good or bad, is certainly not all innocence—as Blake pointed out when he wrote:

> My mother groan'd, my father wept
> Into the dangerous world I leapt—
> Helpless, naked, piping loud
> Like a fiend hid in a cloud.

Yet that dream pinpointed the moment when the truly innocent part of childhood ended for me. From then on I had to halfway live a lie, and *be* a lie. God, including the God within us, is veiled by His manifestation—but, mercifully, He is also manifested by His veil. If this were not the case, we would be totally without hope. That's the inner-world interpretation. As for the outer-world one, I see this dream as a prediction of the mass dehumanization, in the form of transhumanism and artificial intelligence, that threatens us in the 21st Century.

MY MOTHER'S SOUL: A MEDITATION ON POETRY AND ALCOHOLISM

I'll end this chapter with a "meditation" that I composed at my mother-in-law's house on the creek at Long Fork, immediately outside of the little town of Virgie in Pike County, Kentucky, just after my wife and I left California. It was written five years after my mother's death, when our last ties with California, the San Francisco Bay Area and Marin County had been broken for good. In it I review another area or history of psychic damage, and another set of circumstances in which God threw me a lifeline—because who else could it have been? We may spend years fighting and struggling to rise out of darkness, and finally feel we have emerged into the light. That struggle is absolutely necessary. But did we really save ourselves, such that we now have the right to congratulate ourselves? Or did we make the supreme effort simply to catch hold of that lifeline, one we could never have thrown to ourselves—a help that could only have been freely offered by Another? The Qur'an tells us that God not only created us, he also created our actions. Yet if we had not *agreed to be created*, where would we be now? So here it is:

Preface

Beside the gift of my earthly existence, which I can never repay, I received from my mother—a Catholic convert to the pre-Vatican II Church—the greatest spiritual gift imaginable: initiation into, and an understanding of the intrinsic nature of, Tradition in René Guénon's sense, via one of God's great revelations to humanity: the person of Jesus Christ. I also received from her the greatest curse, transmitted when she declared to me, in a tone of haughty self-assurance and certainty as to her rectitude: "I did what was necessary to make sure that you would never love me." The only way I could sink to the depth of that curse, and see it for what it was, was through my later initiation—of my own free will and on my own responsibility—into the art of poetry, accompanied by fifteen years of alcoholism. And the only power that could have raised me from that watery grave was the power of Tradition itself, realized as a channel of the Grace of God. But even though she paid her debt to me even before she incurred it—nonetheless, she paid it.

The Meditation Itself

In the month of the sea-god Poseidon, ruled by the Moon, the month of the sub-incarnate waters, reservoir of shapeless biological energies, I invoke the soul of my mother.

My mother's soul was lost to her. Not lost in the theological sense; it's just that she never had met it. She didn't know where it lived, its likes and dislikes, what it ate for breakfast. She didn't know its name. In the gray dusk, on the rain-slick street, under the glaring lights of evening, when she might have encountered it, hurrying by, or maybe loitering, uncertain of which street to take, what name or what number—a stranger of strangely familiar aspect—she simply wasn't there. She broke the date—failed to make it. Didn't know it was to be made.

The soul that felt hatred or love or pain but didn't know it, the mind that knew what it felt because it had access to the pre-recorded script, but didn't know the soul that did the feeling, simply failed to recognize it—this was my inheritance. The ghostly unfamiliar mother who with silent, mournful defiance played the piano, frightening her little son because she did not answer, did not respond when he called her name, locked in her shell of music, played *smoke gets in your eyes, when deep purple falls*, sealed in a macabre and towering self-pity—the decayed southern belle, over sleepy garden walls, playing piano for the dead. The dead who were too uppity to answer when their names were called, the snob-ridden dead, aristocratic ghosts who were her only living family, to which her son was not admitted, only the stillborn daughter that preceded him—though his mother was well prepared to accept him at the last: one of her final acts, in the last weeks of her life, was to assure him of a niche in the crypt beside her: sealed and paid for. To put his mind at rest.

(When my mother gave birth to me, she brought forth her secret sorrow, and nursed it. Poor little stillborn daughter. Poor little boy-child, too weak to live, too good for this world. Poor little me.)

American gothic, you'd have to call it—not the stiff Yankee gothic of the famous painting but the pure Southern strain we call "Southern grotesque," the morbidity of it ripened like a fine cheese, the stench of clotted, fermented milk saying all there was to be said: that the soul is dead. That memory, proud and imperious, lives on, poring over the splintered bones of it, appraising the relics, fixing their value according to the accepted canons, in triumph over every ambiguous and shifting current of life. The pulse of that life — nailed in mid-stroke.

Bourbon whiskey opened the door to that crypt. That was my key. Sitting there in suspended animation, in her apartment with the creek out back, unborn and undead, I walked back through the decades, two centuries of them, through the soul of America. I was looking for the primal love that was pleased to receive back, into a shimmering, maternal paradise, the failed goldseekers, the circuit-riding preachers whose voice betrayed them at last, the settlers dead on the plains, bleached skulls of the buffalo their only headstones, all of them family, all welcome, all next-of-kin. It's as if you never left — brother, husband, son. I have remembered you back to the grove of your beginning. You should never have strayed from this changeless twilight. But now you're home again. I'll lift new butter from the churn, and light the fire. I'll make your bed. I'll even forget your names for you. This is memory's blessing; we'll make of every one of you the bright ghost of the hearth. Shining pennants, whipping in the wind, on the eve of painted battle. Thus we will honor you. *Lares* without separate character, no more different than one kernel of corn from another. Ghosts who swim like half-heard voices in the mother-of-the-corn, the brown bourbon whiskey — ironically called "the water of life" — through the waning half of the Moon's cycle. Fathers without name, without country. Faceless progenitors, whose sculpted heads now gleam, row upon row, in the blood of the setting sun.

It's always the soul, always the daughter, who is lost — stillborn on the eve of first love. The Kore! *Fathers,* she cries, *remember me. Return me to my mother in the sunlight above. Mount your horses, draw your gleaming sabres to defend my honor.* Deaf to her cries, the stone pillars stand, paralyzed in their eternal honor. Earless voices dinning through the caverns of that loss, reciting the unalterable code. Through the souls of Hart Crane, Twain, Hawthorne, Poe. Never the daughter to show her face above ground in my time, never any more. Never life to be carried on, never the generations to rise and taste the wind, and hew the wood, and plow and plant. Never the grave to be betrayed — not in my time. O Mother! This was your worship. This was your idol and your cult.

The false, dramatic emotion. Dramatized so as not to be felt. Duplicitous. Doubled against itself, soul against soul, that the soul never *be,* never see the light. Declaim it, or laugh it off, but never simply meet it. Never dare the human simplicity that puts us all, whether poets or men of action, to shame. Twain, whose moment of highest realization was as the twelve-year-old trickster, charlatan wiser in his boyhood than the adult hucksters and charlatans of his day, man-boy who couldn't be tricked because he didn't believe in God, so unlike the shorn and foolish sheep at the country tent-meeting, the credulous old ladies. That impish laughter was the seal on the coffin of his soul, delivering him at last to a horrible and killing nostalgia, to return to the scene where the crime was accomplished, the murder of humanity, the end of boyhood, the entry into the dead statue of manhood. Whose mature competence was simply to laugh it off, over the advancing years, sharpening the thorn that defends the heart—but too late. Murdered young—and then dancing. On all their heads. On all their graves. Wise and canny, over the solemn and hoodwinked dead.

All back to Poe, the great archetype. To sorrow for the lost Lenore, to Annabelle Lee in her kingdom by the sea, to the sister of Roderick Usher in her rattling coffin, cracking the great walls of the edified, the upright character. Till she brought down the house. Not one stone left upon another. And no lament can mourn it, no curse can requite it; it's like beating a dead horse; it simply isn't real. The world-acclaimed Shakespearean actor may declaim, may stuff his mouth with Lear and Hamlet, but drama begets melodrama, and then heads for the desert; the soul goes brittle and thin; the sodden soul turns to dried cracked plaster—*Achh!*

These are the pleasures of Hell. (Of course Hell has pleasures—who'd want to live there otherwise? The Devil too is merciful.) And what are they like? In a word, they are "Beardsleyesque." A sly incestuous eroticism, wrapped in plumes of mephitic vapor, black and olive green. The gas that rises off the surface of long-fermented emotions. To take pleasure in this, or to resist that pleasure, is to invoke an exquisite agony. The skill is just to watch it, like a snake about to strike, a jaguar about to leap—till it passes.

But can it be redeemed? asks the martyr. Rising, can it rise up to God? I know you don't like to hear this, says the wise man, but some things are none of your business. Suffice it to say that it cannot be redeemed in this vessel. The incandescent Name of God, descending into your soul, like a red-hot blade quenched in a barrel of cold water, boils it off. That's all you need to know. Remember the practice of the Prophet when he reached *the Lote Tree of the farthest limit* during his ascent through the worlds, his *miraj*: [*His*] *gaze did not waver, nor yet was it overbold.* And one more thing: when infernal pleasure turns to disgust, that's a good sign. That's the repentance of the unconscious psyche, the purification of the lower waters. So speak the name of *love* now; mouth it once, at least. Feel the hole that no curse nor lamentation can fill—only love itself, that shrunken, weak-fisted word, that drab pebble of God, waiting in the long-buried heart for something genuine—a kind word or simple act of courtesy—to give it the time of day.

Who was this Jesus my mother courted? The soul that could never be, could never live a real life, was still attracted like a moth to that candle. She told me once that before she converted to Catholicism, whenever she attended a Catholic mass and the Eucharist appeared, she would burst into tears. Tears of love, or self-pity? Pity, certainly, but maybe with a genuine core to it somewhere? *The world is cold; my sister abuses me; my parents let her do it—but Jesus understands.* Not tears of repentance, surely. But who knows? What is attracted to God must somewhere have God within it. Curse and lamentation won't do it, won't save me from falling into the pit she dug for me in life. Ghost of memory, go back to hell! Soul, weep out the last drop of your suffering. *Cry me a river*—but no, forget it, it's all a bit much—and like the wife of my teacher who killed himself once wrote: "Too much is not enough."

Where is the modest beginning of real human love? That genuineness, that simplicity? The great, drunken emotions, or the dry lack of them—neither can answer. But love knows the answer—love, the salt of the earth. Love the living. If you love them, then the dead—whatever is living in them—will have the love they need. Start with small helps and cares. Forgive, but briefly. Remember the quality of the moment, and don't violate it. Everything starts here, and it doesn't matter how near or how far away the end is; near or far, time is composed of nothing but these same simple moments. To be cared for, or thrown away. It's never too early, or too late. So begin. You have already begun. Start with the taste of salt, and the grand passions will subside. The water that rose in an immense tidal wave will go back to the well it came from, to be drawn when needed, in a vessel of moderate size, big enough for daily needs but not too heavy to carry.

Why break your back? Why flood the whole town? It's only water.

CHAPTER TWO

The Planet of Church, School and Town

CATHOLIC CHURCH AND CATHOLIC SCHOOL

In my childhood I didn't live in a town, though San Rafael was what was called, nominally, my "home town." I lived in a parish. There is a history to every place we live in that is no more *past* than the rock strata under our feet, though this is something that Americans in particular have a hard time understanding. Every day we walk on the earth of other lives; they hold us up, like the ground beneath us.

San Rafael was one of the California Missions, Misión San Rafael Arcángel, founded by Padre Junipero Serra and his compadres. There is a concerted attempt today to "cancel" Fr Serra, supposedly because of the Native Americans who led the life of peons—some of them virtual slaves—on many of the 21 California missions, but in reality because the global elites have decreed the co-optation, and eventually the liquidation, of all the traditional religions. What is forgotten is that there was a concerted attempt, after the Anglos took over California—culminating in the Bear Flag Revolt in 1846—to exterminate the original Native American population to the last man, woman and child. This took place between the 1840s and the 1870s. (The Revolt was headed by Captain John C. Frémont, and led to the secession of California from Mexico and its brief independent status as the Republic of California before it joined the United States of America.) Bounties were given for Indian scalps; the Indians were rounded up by local Anglo militias and systematically slaughtered. So the rule of the Catholic Missions, though harsh in many ways (the Mission system mostly came to an end around 1833) was much more benign for the Native Californians than the was rule of the Anglo Protestants. Sometimes the Indians were impressed by the mission militias and set to work in the fields, sometimes they came to the missions voluntarily, though they clearly wouldn't have done this if life hadn't become pretty hard for them already. They were taught farming and various crafts, and the Catholic faith; their ancestral religious practices, as was the policy with virtually all Indian religious residential schools in the U.S. and Canada, were prohibited. Nonetheless the Missions made some attempt, however imperfect, to "improve the lot" of the Native Americans; it was the Protestant Anglos, not the Spanish Catholics, who did their best to wipe them from the face of the earth. That's why I maintain that those with the impulse to tear down statues—a practice I do not support—should begin with John C. Frémont, not Junipero Serra.

So many of the California Indians had been massacred, and so many of the other Indian populations to the east permanently cut off from their traditional ways, that when the man called Ishi, believed to be the last of the California Yahi tribe, emerged from "hiding"—from what had once been home that is—in the Sierra foothills near Oroville in 1911, he was billed as "the last wild Indian in America." And even though many of the Florida Seminoles, and undoubtedly some remnants from other tribes, had never been rounded up and placed in the rural concentration camps known as "reservations," while many of the Pueblo tribes of the Southwest lived and still live in their ancestral cities—the oldest of which is Acoma Pueblo, Sky City, which (according to local tradition) was founded in 1144 AD—Ishi was rare in that he was from a tribe that had been believed for quite a while to have been totally wiped out. (This notion was disproved, however, when an attempt was made, in the year 2000, to return Ishi's preserved brain to his people for proper mourning and burial—the rest of his body had been cremated—after it was discovered that some of the members of the Yana subgroup of his Yahi tribe were still living.) He was taken in by the well-known anthropologist Alfred Kroeber of the University of California at Berkeley and housed at the San Francisco campus of the University on Parnassus Heights, until his death 5 years later—the same UCSF that in future years became the site of the well-patronized hippie looney bin, the Langley Porter Psychiatric Hospital, a kind of home away from home for many who'd temporarily driven themselves over one edge or another through the use of psychedelic drugs. My father, as a child, met Ishi at his home at the Museum of the University of California Affiliated Colleges, the older name for UCSF; he died when my father was 11 years old. I recount these facts based on an understanding that has slowly dawned upon me while writing this book: that contact with the world of the Native Americans has been a kind of sub-text to the story of my life, as it perhaps is to many of the lives of White Americans without our quite realizing it. And it may in fact be true that the hippies, with their beadwork headbands and their clothes decorated with pseudo-buckskin fringe, had somehow psychically picked up on this fact, possibly because their own White race was beginning to show the first signs of its future descent into "the scrapheap of history," like so many races before it. My wife Jenny, who obviously has a lot of Indian blood in her veins, always emphasizes that our White European values and ancestral traits need to be preserved—if only because those who accede to their own genocide, whether it is abrupt or by slow attrition, will have neither the right nor the power to complain about, or do anything to prevent, the genocide of anybody else. And she always points out that European culture, in the area conquered and brought under Roman order by Julius Caesar—not the Semitic culture of the Near East, even though it gave us Jesus Christ—was the seed-bed for the later development of

Christendom, and thus for the founding of the United States of America.

My childhood home on Chicken Point in San Rafael was built on what must've been at one time a midden heap of the Miwok tribe, since shellfish were one of their staples and the soil of our garden was saturated with shell fragments. Near the house we owned at one time and rented out, on a hillside on the higher tract of Bayside Acres, entire clam shells were visible in the soil. And at an angle of San Pedro Road just north of Paganini Point (named after the family who lived there, not the famous violinist), near where San Pedro School was later built, there was what we called an Indian Burial Mound—either a burial site or a huge midden heap—which was also home to an extensive burrow of ground squirrels with a big buckeye tree growing out of it, the first of our wild trees to flower in the Spring. The mound was later destroyed, probably to make room for the school yard—something that couldn't be legally done today. So we had obviously settled in Miwok country, over the homes and the gravesites of the earlier inhabitants. One of our prize possessions when I was growing up was a Miwok *metate* stone, used to grind their other traditional staple foods, acorns and buckeye balls. The acorns needed to be soaked for a while in a stream to leach out the bitter, astringent tannin, something that also had to be done with the buckeye balls to remove the poisonous ingredient, which was nonetheless useful to stun the fish from the stream in which the balls were being soaked, so they could be easily gathered. The Miwoks were at one time among the most populous tribes in North America. I once met the tiny remnant of them while they were picnicking at Olúmpali State Park, formerly Rancho Olúmpali, under Mt. Burdell near Novato. Olúmpali had originally been a Miwok village—a site that had been continuously inhabited, the anthropologists now believe, for as long as *eight thousand years*. When Christ was born, the forefathers of the little group I met sitting around that picnic table might well have been living in that exact same spot for six thousand years. If so, they'd been there for over three-thousand years longer (by some contemporary estimates) than the Mayans inhabited Mexico—yet all Marin County appeared to be to most people was a semi-suburban bedroom community for San Francisco whose *relevant* history probably went back no farther than the Hippie Era and the Grateful Dead. When I encountered them, the Miwoks were attempting to racially reconstitute themselves by the practice, genetically risky in so small a population, of marrying only among those few people of their acquaintance who were known or believed to have Miwok blood.

Living in a Catholic parish, founded by the Spanish who had supplanted the Indians and had in turn been trampled under foot by the Anglo-Americans—even though nothing was left of the original mission but two bronze bells hanging from a wooden frame outside what was called the "Mission Church," built next to the larger and more imposing St Raphael's Church—was like occupying one integrated cell in the "mystical body" of an intact Roman Catholicism, representing two thousand years of unbroken spiritual, cultural and civilizational tradition, spread throughout the world—a tradition that was not ethnically identified in any essential way, though it was represented in the San Rafael I knew mostly by the Irish and the Italians. The great bell of St Raphael's rang the hours and gave form and resonance to the day, for Catholics and non-Catholics alike. It could clearly be heard even three miles out, from where we lived farther north along the coast, separated from San Rafael proper by two ridges that came down from Black Mountain, the one closer to town called Axel Hill after the San Pedro Road grade that passed over it, ending in Paganini's Point, the other ending in Chicken Point. That bell gave notice, not only to the Catholic faithful but to all the spooks and goblins and UFO Aliens who hadn't quite yet shown their heads above ground by the time I was growing up, of the Presence of Grace. And on the summit of San Rafael Hill above the town stood the tall plain wooden white-painted Catholic cross, visible from a good distance away. Some years before my wife and I left California that cross was torn down, undoubtedly because it "offended" somebody—though obviously it's entirely acceptable, according to contemporary mores, to offend *some* people... All Christians, however, were not bothered by this change. In the 1980s, when Jenny and I, as elders of a small local Presbyterian church, were involved in the peace movement in solidarity with the revolutions of Central America and the Sanctuary Movement for Central American refugees—though "peace" and "revolution," to the more discerning sensibility, may seem rather strange bedfellows—I had the idea of re-baptizing the cross on San Rafael Hill "the Peace Cross" (not an entirely viable concept from my present perspective). But when I shared this proposal with another figure in the Marin County peace movement, the Rev. Doug Huneke of Westminster Presbyterian Church in Tiburon (a ghetto for the super-rich, appropriately named "Shark"), he reacted violently, ranting that the cross was "divisive" and should be torn down. Well, he got his wish. Perhaps it would have been better, however—in view of the precipitous decline of both Catholicism and "mainstream Protestantism" since those days—if he had remembered the words of Jesus Christ: "Blessèd is he who is not scandalized in me."

For a large chunk of my childhood, church was not a *part* of my life: beyond the borders of my house and my neighborhood, it *was* my life. Catholic School from nursery school and kindergarten through high school. Mass every Sunday. Weekly or monthly confession. The rites-of-passage of First Communion and Confirmation. Since Catholics practiced infant Baptism which nobody could remember, First Communion became for us like a rite of full initiation into the life of the Church—which, in theological terms, is exactly what it was. And the sacrament of Confirmation was the rite-of-passage having to do with puberty, conceived of as the stage of life in which spiritual warfare would become necessary—necessary because unavoidable. The first rite, the Holy Eucharist, took place at the age of 7 or shortly after, which was considered to be "the age of reason," after which the child was responsible before God for his or her actions, and therefore able for the first time to sin—consequently the child's first participation in the sacrament of Penance, his or her first confession, happened around the same time. The ceremonies surrounding First Communion included the characteristic Catholic processions, especially processions of young girls with white dresses and flowers in their hair—the first "flower children" of my experience. Those girls, like girls entering the convent in Mexico, wore veils like brides; they were preparing for their betrothal to Jesus the Bridegroom. (I remember meeting a girl once at an airport who was connected with the Hare Krishna movement. She told me she had been a Catholic nun who had fallen in love with Jesus, but she left her order at one point because, being modern and progressive, they would not let her love and marry Him in that simple way. So she chose Krishna instead, who had no such scruples.)

The Dominican nuns, whose huge old 4-storey Victorian Mother House was the oldest building on the San Rafael Dominican campus, underwent an initiation of three grades: Postulant, Novice and Nun. The Postulants dressed in black, representing death to the world. The Novices were clad all in white, symbolizing purity and receptivity; they were *candidates* for the cloister, preparing for the day they would take their solemn vows. (The Latin word *Candidatus*, from which we get our word "candidate," means "dressed in white"; in ancient Rome, candidates for office dressed in white togas, representing themselves to be *candid*, full of *candor*, and thus worthy to be *elected* or chosen.) Full Dominican nuns dressed in black *and* white. After my studies of metaphysics in later years, I saw that all this was in line with traditional alchemical symbolism, where the first stage of the Great Work—the *melanosis* or the *nigredo*, the "blackening"—is the death of the old self, the mortification of the worldly ego, of what the Sufis call the *nafs*. The second stage is the *leucosis* or the *albedo*, the "whitening," which is the work of becoming receptive, like the Full Moon, to the Sun of the Spirit. The third and last stage is the *iosis* or the *rubedo*, the "reddening," where the purified soul is imprinted, transformed from top to bottom, by the Divine Power of that Spirit. This is the Sacred Marriage, the *coniunctio oppositorum* or Union of Opposites, which produces the Philosopher's Stone, the alchemical Gold. But since we obviously can't have Catholic nuns parading around in scarlet habits (though that may come soon enough), the black-and-white habit of the fully professed Dominican nun represents the opposites that are to be joined, but draws the veil of esoteric and erotic modesty and secrecy over the Sacrament of the *thalamos*, the Bedchamber, which certain heretical Gnostic sects openly included in their list of sacred rites.

Up till the age of thirteen, the end of grammar school, those nuns *enclosed* me. In nursery school and kindergarten they represented almost the entire world beyond the family. Those were the days before color TV, when we had only 3 available black-and-white channels. There was not even a television in our house, so if I wanted to watch TV I had to go to my grandmother's house, a block away. That's where I saw those old cartoons with the swing soundtrack where, when a character would look at something, a dotted line would extend from his eyes to the object he was viewing; where crowds composed of a hippo a lion and a giraffe a hippo a lion and a giraffe over and over again (dressed like human beings), would flow past; and where the buildings and landscapes would all dance in time to the music. That's about as visionary as television got in those days (though some movies had a lot more to offer — *The Wizard of Oz* for example), which was obviously next to nothing when compared to the visual environment provided by the Catholic Church, with its magnificent sacred architecture and stained-glass windows. The nuns extended that impression for us by showing us striking religious artworks, including a set of beautiful color prints on biblical themes, the Nativity, the Crucifixion, Noah's Ark, the Garden of Eden etc. Before theology comes catechism, and before catechism, direct visual impression. No child, in this age of color TV, computers and smart-phones, can be educated like that anymore — but I did get that kind of education, and it went a long way toward setting for me the primary *mythopoetic* parameters of my worldview.

In Nursery School and Kindergarten I committed two major crimes or transgressions, for which I received the ultimate punishment: I was forced to sit in the *baby chair!* The first transgression had to do with a mimeographed outline of an apple that we were supposed to color in solidly with red crayons. "*Look* at all those white spots! Disgraceful!" said Sister Mary Ellen, pacing judgmentally between us, inspecting our work. I, however, produced something even worse than white spots, in the form of a network of red *lines* extending *beyond* the outline of the apple into the properly white space beyond! "What is this!" exclaimed Sister Mary Ellen in shocked disapproval. "That's how the juice gets into the apple" I explained — fairly rationally, I thought at the time. But it was neither rational nor orthodox according to the good sister, and so — into the baby chair with me. From my present vantage point I can clearly see that what I was doing was painting a portrait or diagram of the spiritual Heart, the point or organ within the subtle nervous-system of the human makeup that, when closed to the world, produces either spiritual petrification or *apophatic* mysticism — mystical consciousness transcending form — and when opened, either *cataphatic* mysticism — the vision of God's manifestation in all things — or else a lethal dissipation of soul. And my second transgression was like unto it. Once, at chapel in the Garden School building, instead of praying in English like the rest of the children, I prayed the Our Father and the Hail Mary in frog language — "croak *croak-croak croak-croak, croak-croak croak-croak* croak." Why not? Do not all creatures praise the God who created them? Perhaps they do, I learned, *but not in chapel* — so it was back to the baby chair for the second time. "I think I am becoming fond of the baby chair" I told the nuns. *Only now* do I see how those two baby crimes were essentially the same, and how they had everything to do with my basic configuration-of-soul. If the frogs, along with all things in creation, declare the Glory of God, that is cataphatic mysticism precisely. But if that openness-of-soul, the source of my tendency to "pray outside the box," fell short of the vision of God in all things, it might dissipate my essential spiritual attention, causing it to fall into a fragmented, "neo-Pagan" identification with elemental, subhuman worlds — the very temptation that the LSD-dropping hippies would be faced with around fifteen years later. (The lesson that religion needs to learn, over and over again, is: how to protect what's precious without stifling what lives and breathes. Parents need to learn the same thing.)

But it was also in the Garden School that I committed not merely a social transgression but a true sin of the heart. One of the kids was a bully who would continually get me in a head-lock — so when I had a chance to stick it to a weaker child, I took it. There was one little boy who dearly wanted to be my friend, but I didn't care to be bothered; my ability to reject him restored to me some of the feeling of power that I felt that the bully had taken away. On one occasion I told the child who wanted to be my friend that I would meet him on the other side of the school yard, a grassy area under some wide-spreading trees. He ran off to our rendezvous point, while I, proud of my cunning, ran the other way.

Every year Dominican would host a performance at Angelico Hall called Living Pictures. Children from the Garden School would appear on stage as *tableaux*, standing motionless in period costumes. I myself made my theatrical debut and swan-song as The Shell Gatherer, a child carrying a basket of shells, which in this case were mussel and clam shells gathered from the bay shore in front of my house. A 19th-Century painter, Charles Octavius Cole, painted a picture with that title, in stiff American Primitive style, in which the Shell Gatherer was a girl. Since I (*a secret sinner!*) had been officially branded a "good boy" by the nuns — all baby chairs aside — and seeing that even the angels had already been transformed into women in bad Catholic art by that time, some among the nuns (and my mother as well?) might have thought that to be a girl was the highest destiny to which I could aspire. Maybe, if I was very very good, God would allow me to be a girl in the next life. (Will we ever see a Ph.D. thesis entitled "The Roots of Transgenderism in the 1950s North American Catholic Ethos"? Probably not.) That was back in the days when boys were bad and girls were good. Irish boys drank and fought, Italian boys strutted and fought, while good Irish and Italian girls went to church with the old ladies, the ones dressed in black with black lace veils and black square-toed sensible Catholic shoes; at least that's more or less the way it was in the "old countries" and in the heavily ethnic Catholic neighborhoods of the eastern U.S. You could still see those old ladies even at St Raphael's when I was growing up, when religion equaled mourning and the earth was officially recognized as a vale of tears. There are plenty more tears in that vale nowadays than there were back then, but true mourning, *orgiastic mourning*—now that we need it more than ever—is apparently a lost art.

After the Garden School I moved to St Raphael's School in downtown San Rafael—"parochial school"—for grades one through eight. St Raphael's was part of a large compound that also included St Raphael's Church, the largest church in Marin County; the Mission Chapel with its gift shop and small museum of Spanish and Indian artifacts; and the priests' residence. It was a single integrated space, a unified world. The priests were Father McAlister the pastor, a man of sober sacerdotal dignity though generally free from pomposity and pretense, reminding one of Bishop Fulton J. Sheen without the flamboyance. Father O'Meara was white-haired, prematurely aged and bowed with some undeclared burden of suffering; he said daily mass alone at one of the side altars, with one altar boy and no congregants. He never heard confessions and never distributed Holy Communion. Father Dullea was the "fun" priest whose sermons kept all the kids entertained; he later became principal of Marin Catholic High School, in which incarnation (as you will see below) he was no longer fun. There were others who stayed for longer or shorter periods, but the only one I remember by name was Father Cain (a rather unfortunate name for a priest), a dark, intense young man with curly black hair and the beginnings of the kind of "charisma"—in the Hollywood sense of that word, not the theological one—that would have to do its best a few years later to fill in the yawning gap left by the withdrawal, radical yet finally not total, of God's Grace from a Church that had suddenly and savagely turned against its own traditions.

Confession was an experience of growing shame followed by the sudden release from shame, in which it was hard to tell the difference between the descent of God's forgiving mercy and the pure relief that that whole ordeal was over. It began with the "examination of conscience," a simple but very effective method for mass training in introversion, psychological insight and self-understanding. In the act of confession itself you could sometimes *hear God listening* through the deep contemplative listening of the well-formed confessor, acting not as himself but as an *alter Christus,* "another Christ"—a listening that was merciful but not indulgent, strict but not "judgmental" according to today's sense of that word—the perfect balance, on the sacramental level if not yet entirely on the personal one, between compassion and detachment. This quality, or virtue, constitutes the exact meaning of the Greek word *apatheia;* that this resonant term has now degenerated into the English word *apathy* is an exact barometer of the loss of faith in the Roman Catholic world and the various Protestant worlds that grew out of it. It was as if, by the power the Sacrament of Penance, in which the eternal listening of God was made effectively present, my sins were forgiven by being *dissolved in total acceptance*—not indulged, not excused, certainly not made light of, yet *accepted* nonetheless, in some mysterious way that is totally beyond description. It was as if God's absolute *listening* had sucked my sins away into the Void, into the Divine Emptiness, the apophatic intuition of the Great Mystery that is realized by the *via negativa*.

Confirmation, the rite-of-passage for puberty, remains for me nothing but a one-time memory of a more intensive catechization followed by a rite in which Archbishop McGucken slapped each of us on the cheek, gently but firmly, apparently so as to "beat the Devil out of us" in a humanly mild yet sacramentally powerful manner: one more "indelible mark" upon my immortal Catholic soul.

But Mass was the center, as it still is today—though in terms of "sensible consolations," what we Sufis call *ahwal* or "spiritual states," the more powerful rite was Benediction, with its clouds of frankincense, the golden "cope" of the priest, an elaborately-embroidered full-length cloak, and the gleaming gold and jewel-encrusted "monstrance" he held, like a blazing sunburst radiating from a pure white Center, in which was set a consecrated Host under glass—the Body and Blood of Christ. Staring hard at that monstrance with its Divine content, the pivot of the universe, my *ajña-chakra* or Third Eye was opened, and became one with the transcendent Point before me, resulting in wave after wave of flashing light.

In contrast, the Mass itself was more sober, because more sacred. I myself served at that rite as an altar boy or *acolyte*—the fourth of the seven Holy Orders, not imprinted upon me sacramentally but rather delegated by the authority of the priest under whom I served. Serving at Mass the sensible consolations were few because I was always afraid of making mistakes, and consequently I kept making them. Nor did receiving Holy Communion as an ordinary congregant result in any major "mystical" experiences. It was as if the transaction involved was between God in His nakedness and some level of my soul I could not yet fathom.

I remember one occasion when I was serving at Mass under Father Tierney at St Sylvester's Church, a small church near our home on San

Pedro Road. Kneeling at the altar, I thanked God that I had been born both into the True Church and also into America, the greatest country on earth; the coincidence of these two blessings seemed like a sign from Heaven directed to me personally. How amazing that I could have actually felt that way at one time, given the grim march of disillusionment and decline that was to follow! St Sylvester's had been a one-room schoolhouse at one time, with thick plastered walls of brick or adobe. The building survived the 1906 earthquake and in 1957 was purchased from the McNear family to become the a church of a new parish — or the chapel of a new subsidiary parish — since St Raphael's parish had grown so rapidly. An entirely new church, much larger, was even built nearby, but it had to be abandoned a few years later because it had been constructed on filled tidelands that ultimately wouldn't support its weight. It was as if this misfortune were an omen of the precipitous decline in the Catholic faith, and Catholic church membership, that was soon to follow.

PAROCHIAL SCHOOL

In St Raphael's School most of the teachers were nuns, with the exception of young, trim, curvaceous and attractive Miss Slavin, my third grade teacher, the niece of the lady who ran the mimeograph room, and old Mrs McDougal, who taught fourth grade and who, by her accent, was from somewhere in the Deep South. It was she who taught us how the Yankees in the War Between the States were all white trash, rude and uncouth, while all the Confederates were brave, gentlemanly, honorable and refined.

In grammar school we really learned *grammar*, the kind of grammar that even journalists for Reuters and the AP don't know nowadays (not to mention their dreadful spelling!). Our textbook series was *English Grammar and Composition*, which taught us not only grammar, spelling and writing style, but how to use libraries, dictionaries and reference books; narrative writing, letter writing, writing research papers; rudimentary logic and "clear thinking"; the art of public speaking; the art of listening; even how to recognize and critique propaganda — and this, remember, was the curriculum in Catholic *grammar schools*. Who learns all that in high school or even college nowadays? Anyone who wants to get a shockingly clear idea of just how dumbed-down America has become should get ahold of a copy of the *McGuffey's Reader* for grades 1–6, which first appeared in the mid-19th century and is still in use today in private schools and among homeschoolers. And we are not just denied knowledge, we are *taught to resist it* — as if resisting knowledge were an expression of our freedom and independence! But the truth is the exact opposite: to reject knowledge is to embrace degradation and slavery.

We were also taught geography, arithmetic, and European and American history — and given that the Catholic Church was the center of western civilization and culture for at least 1500 years, we received a pretty deep and comprehensive view of that civilization by viewing it from a Catholic perspective, just before it started to unravel. It's uncertain if such a perspective can be attained anywhere in this society today, except by an intensive course of self-directed study over a period of many years. Lastly, we were taught the fundamentals of the Catholic faith from the *Baltimore Catechism*, which established the foundation for my later study of metaphysics and comparative religion. But are even geography and arithmetic being seriously taught anymore? My friend Bill Trumbly, who worked for the Bell Telephone company (like his father had) in the 1970s, had co-workers who thought you could take a bus from California to England! And I'm confident that geographical knowledge, like almost every other kind of knowledge, has only gone downhill since then. (How many people today, for example, can even answer the question "where does the sun rise, in the east or in the west?" Somebody should ask that question on a national level and see what happens.) As for knowledge of arithmetic, electronic calculators have effectively destroyed it, which means that contradictory and impossible "statistics" can be quoted every day in the news and nobody even notices it. Because people no longer know how to do arithmetic in their heads, numbers are essentially meaningless to them. And is it any wonder that people who possess no knowledge of their own but rely upon whatever they happen to see on their computer or smartphone screens, from Wikipedia, Google, AI or wherever, might slowly become vulnerable to the paranoid notion that *everybody is lying to them*? Because they possess little knowledge of their own, anybody *could* be lying to them, man or machine, and they'd never know it. This is one of the roads by which ignorance destroys both mental health and social solidarity. As the Ghost of Christmas Present said to Ebenezer Scrooge in Dickens' *A Christmas Carol*, when he opened his cloak to reveal two ragged waifs, a boy and a girl: "This boy is Ignorance. This girl is Want. Beware them both, and all of their degree, but most of all, *beware this boy*."

In the schoolyard pecking-order, I was near to being bottom bird. The alpha male who delighted in bullying me was Ed Lencioni; I was his chosen victim. But why me in particular? Many years later, when I shared this question with a psychotherapist, he said: "Maybe that bully saw something in you that challenged him." That was certainly not my view at the time, however. I was much closer to adopting the attitude that German Romantic poet Rainer Maria Rilke took to his own schoolyard bullies when he told them: "I suffer as Christ suffered, quietly and without complaint, and as you hit me I pray to our dear Lord that He will forgive you" — though I'm very glad that I did not pour gasoline on the fire by expressing my feelings in similar terms! When you've been too *good* for too long you can build up a towering load of anger that might boil over at any moment into reckless violence; luckily, and with God's help, I was able to bring most of that anger out, step by step, in sublimated form, and apply it to some real work in the world, mostly intellectual work but some socio-political work as well; not for nothing is the Air element, the mental dimension, represented in Tarot cards by the Suit of Swords, the sword being a symbol of discriminating wisdom.

One of the most common and potentially useful ways of sublimating anger is through language, through verbal expression. It is my theory (subject to revision) that if you're good enough at cussing — or even better, if you're skilled in the traditional poetic art of satire, particularly if it's subtle enough so that your target only realizes he's been skewered after you're safely out of range — you won't be driven to resort to fists, knives or guns. The collective erosion of our verbal skills may in fact be one of the causes behind the present epidemic of violence in our streets, churches and schools; if you can't even explain something to yourself, much less get anyone else to take seriously the explanation you've arrived at, what response is left but frustrated violence, either against other people or against yourself? As we work on developing established spiritual detachment, sublimating aggression through wit and satire may at least have a moderating effect on our inner fury; even Jesus, while preaching "love your enemies," used merciless satire against those same enemies.

Nor was Ed Lencioni only a temporary oppressor; as you will see, he might have brought some serious damage into my life that I will carry to my grave.

One of my classmates in St Raphael's was my first love from Bayside Acres, Angela Pierce. She was in the process of growing up to be a Bad Girl, defined as a girl the nuns would immediately recognize as problematic. On one occasion she came to class with a "rat" in her hair, one of those inserts that helped "that kind of girl" build up her tall bouffant hair-do so as to become a "motorcycle Black Madonna two-wheel gypsy queen" (in the words of Bob Dylan from his song "The Gates of Eden"). Instead of talking to her privately and explaining to her that such a coiffeur was not appropriate for a good Catholic schoolgirl, the nun on duty shamed her in front of the whole class. (All the nuns were not like that, however. One of my teachers, after correcting me in class, saw how much she'd embarrassed me, so she phoned our home after school to apologize for hurting my feelings. It's not easy to make a solid marriage between moral rectitude and compassion, so the that the latter doesn't degenerate into laxity and the former into authoritarianism, but the ability to do so is a sure sign of success in the spiritual life.)

When I was in eighth grade, Angela Pierce and Ed Lencioni came together to set the stage for the first major intrusion of material and spiritual darkness into my life. Once I was sitting at my desk with Angela sitting directly across from me, in the next row to my right. I turned toward her and, for several minutes, gazed silently into her eyes. Lencioni must have seen this, because soon after (either on the same day or a few days later, I forget which), when we were together in what must've been a study session after school hours, he assaulted me — sneakily. He, after all, was the Italian Alpha Male, and Angela the lovely, olive-skinned, half-Italian Bad Girl; obviously she belonged to him, not to me. On the fateful day I was sitting at my desk, "minding my own business," when Ed started punching me, lightly and rapidly, on the right side of my jaw. This went on for quite a while, during which time I practiced "turning the other cheek" — or, rather, the same cheek. Pretty soon, however, I started to get dizzy, "punchy," and nearly fainted. I thought I could simply endure the ordeal, but that didn't turn out to be the case.

After this assault my neck began to get stiff, a symptom that I now recognize as the sign of a "subluxation," a displacement of one or more vertebrae. The stiffness didn't go away. Also, a nymph node on my right side, between neck and shoulder, became swollen. Not long after this, while I was with my father at our duck club in Yolo County, my right eye suddenly became inflamed, and whited out. The condition turned out to be chronic uveitis, which could be temporarily relieved with steroid eyedrops but which nonetheless resulted in thick masses of "floaters" invading the vitreous humor in the interior of my eye. This condition, over the years, slowly resulted in total blindness in that eye due to a cataract, which was partly cured by an operation, though later I developed glaucoma which required a second operation. I've never fully regained the use of that eye, though I can see well enough through it to retain some depth vision. I can't prove that Ed Lencioni's assault blinded me in one eye, but that's certainly what it looks like in retrospect.

That was the first major stroke of Fate I endured in this life. In the symbolism of dreams, the inner world is to the Left, the outer world to the Right — and the Right is the direction from which the major attacks I've endured throughout my life have come; in both of my major automobile accidents I was struck from the right, and both of them, like the attack at school, involved women. The first accident, in Canada, happened after I broke up with my first serious live-in girlfriend, Paula Wasserman. The second, in Kentucky, involved my wife Jenny — who, since she was sitting to my right, was injured more seriously than I was, though we were both pretty well beaten up; we had wounds in exactly the same parts of our bodies: right leg, right wrist and left ankle. Clearly the first two women were not to be mine — possibly, at least according to the symbolism of these injuries, because they represented This World, or were too intimately involved with it. But Jenny had never been granted membership in This World; this is undoubtedly why I was allowed to keep her as the Muse of my spiritual Path, symbol of the purity and simplicity my complex self-contradictory self longed for—and that is exactly what she has been to me for the past 47 years.

And the symbolism of blindness-in-one-eye was not lost on me either. Before entering Islam I was struck by the fact that the chief god of the Norse pantheon—Odin, the All-Father—was said to have sacrificed one of his eyes to gain knowledge of the Runes, the esoteric metaphysical principles that lie behind all manifestation; he did so by tearing it from its socket and casting it into Mimir's Well, the Well of Memory. According the genealogy of the Baskerville family, a tributary to my mother's family, the Strothers, I can actually claim descent from Odin, or Woden—or so say the *Saxon Chronicles* compiled by another ancestor of mine, King Alfred the Great. But that whole universe of Pagan symbolism was placed on the back burner when I took *shahadah* and became a Muslim, since in Islam the One-Eyed One can only be *al-Dajjal* the Deceiver—the Antichrist. It is usually said that he will be blind in his right eye, which is sometimes taken to mean that he will be able to see this world well enough but will be blind to the next—in other words, that he will be a total materialist. Here, however, the symbolism of Right and Left appears reversed, just as it does in the human nervous system where the left cerebral hemisphere controls the right side of the body and vice-versa. In any case, I now see my blindness in one eye as the symbol of an attack by the spirit of Antichrist that's abroad in the world in these latter days. He tried to draw me into his camp—as when I put myself in the way of the Devil's Weed, and took certain other destined missteps that you will hear about when I tell the story of my passage through the dark side of the hippie counterculture in Chapters *Three* and *Four*—and when the *Dajjal* ultimately failed in this, when he was driven back from the Fortress of the Heart, he took his vengeance on me. But precisely because he was able to wound me, I know him intimately; as William Blake says in *The Marriage of Heaven and Hell*, "He who has suffer'd you to impose on him, knows you." That's how I was able to write what some have called my *magnum opus, The System of Antichrist: Truth and Falsehood in Postmodernism and the New Age*.

It may seem strange to some that I've dealt with this lifelong wound in so symbolic a way, with so much poetry and mythology and self-referential melodrama—but the fact is that *trauma invokes the archetypes*; whatever has the power to shatter an earlier image of self-and-world that you accepted without question pitches you into the world of the Transcendental Powers. Every shaman knows this, which is why he or she risks not only sanity but life itself to find the Ordeal that will accomplish the break with consensus reality. But though the shaman seeks that break, the greater truth is that it just comes to him, or her. The spirits send it. God sends it. At one point we must conceive of a power of evil, a power named Satan or Antichrist, so we can avoid the blasphemy of attributing evil to God, Who is Absolute Goodness beyond all knowing or telling. But the real truth is, God has a bullet with your name on it: the jacket of it is Justice but the core of it is Love. Your greatest doom is also your greatest good fortune—but who can face or live with a truth like that, this side of the grave? As William Blake put it, "The roaring of Lions, the howling of Wolves, the raging of the stormy sea and the destructive sword are portions of Eternity too great for the eye of man."

One more universe of symbolism still has to be dealt with in terms of the lifetime-wound I received in grammar school—the universe of Courtly Love. In this constellation of meanings the beloved woman is the Soul; the Dark Knight who abducts her is the World—otherwise known as the power-motive; and the White Knight who must rescue the Soul—since it must at least be his intent and ideal to realize the purity that this Whiteness represents—is the conscious personality. It is always the addiction to Power that destroys or imprisons Love, consequently the one who vows to rescue Love from Power must use Power *against* Power—even against his own Power. This is why the hobbit Frodo's quest in J. R. R. Tolkien's *The Lord of the Rings* was not to wield the power of the One Ring against the evil forces of Mordor, but to sacrifice that Ring by casting it into the fires of Mount Doom. (The destruction of love by power, specifically magical power, is the central theme of the great Ukrainian/Soviet motion picture *Shadows of our Forgotten Ancestors* by Sergei Parajanov.) But the one who is wounded can't turn to Love directly because his wound, his deathly weakness, makes him crave Power—so he must struggle with Power to overcome Power, even as he is using Power to protect and rescue Love *from* Power; that's enough of an inner contradiction and an outer battle to last a lifetime. As the poet of Muslim Andalusia, Ibn al-Qabturnuh, says (in Lysander Kemp's translation):

> I remembered Sulayma when the passion of battle was as fierce
>   as the passion of my body when we parted.
>
> I thought I saw, among the lances, the tall perfection of her body,
>   and when they bent toward me, I embraced them.

That's Romance! That's the whole universe of Love and Death in four lines. You can't fake it; you can't simply "decide to adopt it"; either it comes to you or it doesn't—as a stroke of Fate. Heraclitus said: "Character is Fate"; I say: "Fate sculpts Character." And there is no disagreement between us; we are saying exactly the same thing. Fate is the outward projection of Character, just as Character is the inner coagulation of Fate. In the higher world, the world beyond time, they are simultaneous and inseparable.

And the strangest thing about my loss of sight in my right eye is that nobody believed it. My parents, who were the furthest thing from neglectful, treated it as if it wasn't happening. The same was true of my high school friends. Did I just not complain enough? Was I hiding it from myself? I rarely felt deep contentment or anything like peace, though I was not completely unfamiliar with these states, but I was certainly enthusiastic and euphoric more often than not—between the anxiety attacks. Did the face I put on fool everybody? For some reason these "explanations," while plausible, are not satisfying to me. It's as if what had struck me had come from so deep a place in the "collective unconscious" and/or the Unseen World that it was invisible to other people, half-invisible even to me. But it was not, and is not, invisible to God—that's why the constant remembrance of God has precedence over all investigations of material causes or psychological motives. He shows us His signs in the world and in ourselves, but He is the eternal Witness over both of them. We only imagine what *might* be; He knows what *is*.

So that's the end of that particular "grammar school memory." Because life is essentially holographic, the entire pattern of it can sometimes be seen reflected in a single event, no matter if it comes early or late. The real causes of things are not behind them in the past, but above them in the Book of Life.

And if your real life is made up of the events that mold you, I can truly say that nothing else really happened to me in grammar school. All the other little happenings dwindle to nothing by comparison—except the instruction I received in religious knowledge. Nothing happened but that stroke of darkness and the power to face that darkness—the power to know that Something greater than the darkness exists, and that it is possible to turn to It.

MARIN CATHOLIC HIGH SCHOOL

In high school I gradually became part of a group of male misfits who had little in common besides alienation from the official high school student establishment of sports and sexual conquest. Not that any of us (as far as I know) were gay or seriously afraid of girls; we were just oddballs—myself, Bob Trumbly, John McBride and the rest—and enjoyed each other's oddball company. One of our number, jazz afficionado Carlo Gardín, named our group "The Birdseed Community" after Arthur Birdseed, a character played by Steve Allen on his 1950s TV show. This is how Bohemias are born: not through any real community of belief or sentiment (at least to begin with) but as based on little more than a shared alienation from the dominant society, which requires that the Bohemians appreciate each person's uniqueness and encourage one another to express their individual quirks—as opposed to "straight" society where conformity to collective identity is stressed and individual quirkiness is frowned upon: the Carnies vs. the Rubes. (Those stock characters who appear in circuses, side-shows and the *commedia del arte* are not only quasi-archetypes but collective reductions-to-stereotype of different individual eccentricities.) The people who strictly identify individuality with egotism are misguided, because "straight" collective identity is also a form of ego; the people who identify conformism with ego-transcendence are equally misguided, since to hide our individual ego in some collective herd-ego is not the way to transcend it. Only the ego that stands forth in its nakedness can be struck down by God's ego-annihilating thunderbolt — though this is a hard station to reach, in view of the fact that Prometheanism — rebellious individual self-expression — is one of the most common, and therefore the most boringly collective, of all human attitudes or ego-postures.

As for the curriculum we were taught, it's my impression that we received a better liberal arts education in Catholic high school in the 1960s than many people get today in a 4-year college — and without the mountain of student debt that usually goes with it. On top of literature, history, writing, geography, mathematics and chemistry (with full recreational access to the powerful acids, the potent reducing-agents and the other toxic substances of the chemistry lab, and all the near-disasters that went with them), we learned religion, apologetics, Latin, and even a little Greek. As for myself, I was at the top of my class in the verbal (as opposed to the mathematical) section of the SAT.

Nonetheless both my studies in chemistry and my childhood attraction to playing with fire bore fruit during those years when a fellow student unexpectedly gave me a large jar of potassium chlorate, an oxidizing agent so powerful that you could probably mix it with sawdust and make a workable explosive. Instead of sawdust I elected to use powdered gardening sulfur and powdered sugar as my reducing agents. I constructed a set of scales with jar lids as pans so I could weigh the ingredients, then did the molar equations I'd learned at Marin Catholic so I could mix them in the correct proportions — after which I drilled a hole in a short length of steel pipe, packed it with the potent mixture, secured the charge with pipe-ends, and thereby produced a worthy, "professional"-level pipe-bomb or IED. I should have invited my friends over to witness the demonstration, but I couldn't wait. So that evening I took my creature down to the bay shore, placed it at the foot of a cliff where it couldn't damage any buildings, and set it off. The deafening roar, after two or three seconds, echoed to produce two clear "sonar" images of the two Marin Islands, just under a mile distant — and several seconds after that, a lower and longer echo came back from Mt. Tamalpais, 6 or 7 miles away. Sadly, after such a promising debut, I never did become any kind of a terrorist; I never even applied for a job in that field. As for the whole playing-with-fire thing, that came to an abrupt end as soon as marijuana entered the scene. Exactly the same sense of excitement we'd felt as kids when scoring illegal firecrackers or cherry bombs from some Chinaman in the City was now transferred to the world of drugs, whose inner "explosions" suddenly became much more interesting than the outer ones.

Our teachers were about two-thirds priests and one-third laymen; we had no women teachers since the students were separated by gender for the first two or three years, the boys taught by men, the girls by women. The boys wore "street clothes" while the girls still wore uniforms—just like new immigrants from India or the Islamic nations, where the women (until they learn better) will sometimes still wear traditional dress in public (those beautiful saris!) while the men more often appear in standard western proletarian attire of blue jeans and baseball cap, as they in fact most often did in their home countries.

Insofar as my teachers were "role models," two of them—both priests—stand out. The first was Father Pettengill, who half-initiated me into the world of mythopoesis, the other half of that initiation being provided by that pivotal book of Blake criticism, Northrup Frye's *Fearful Symmetry*, that was given to me by my first publisher, John McBride. Fr Pettengill brought before the eye of my heart such concepts from Biblical mythopoesis as Holy Wisdom, the Shekhina and the Kabod Yahweh, the Glory of God—which, when personified, bears similarities to the Archangel Michael ("he who is like God") and to the greatest of the Kabbalistic angels, the Seraph Metatron, as well as to Blake's Angel of the Divine Presence. It was from Fr Pettengill that I picked up the skill and habit of the "word study"—the practice of amplifying the meanings of a word based on its etymological associations in one or more languages, similar to the Jungian method of amplifying dream symbolism according to how a particular figure or image appears in world mythology. Without the Catholic use of the word-study technique there would probably never have been a *Finnegan's Wake*.

The second memorable priest from my high school days was Father Lacey, who showed me (without making much of it or turning it into a "teaching") how living the spiritual life takes real character—"backbone." Fr Lacey was a *mensch*. He never blustered or threw his weight around, yet he commanded immediate respect from a mass of tricksterish and potentially rebellious male students, as a man who had taken his medicine and paid his dues, and was consequently not to be trifled with. (On the other hand, our principal Father Dullea was the exact opposite: he loved to bluster and throw his weight around, but a backbone he had not.) And Father Lacey told us one thing that I've never forgotten: "True pride and true humility are the same thing"—a principle that was echoed, or commented on, many years later by Ron Harris, the Black shaykh of the San Francisco *khaniqa* (lodge) of the Nimatullahi Sufi Order, in two lines of a poem he quoted to us one evening:

> Everyone is proud of someone—
> And we are proud of God!

MCBRIDE

My impresario and press agent at Marin Catholic was John McBride, who apparently wanted to "stage" me as the performer that he himself couldn't be or didn't want to be. McBride gave me two of the books—outside of *Fearful Symmetry*—that most affected my intellectual development, though I finally had to reject the viewpoint of one of them: *The Phenomenon of Man* by Teilhard de Chardin and *Understanding Media* by Marshall McLuhan. Though Chardin, the Jesuit paleontologist, was a powerful influence on my worldview for some years—I even wrote a poem called "The Garden" based on his ideas which was turned into a broadside illustrated by Lew Welch's wife Magda Cregg, though I no longer consider it part of my "canon"—I ultimately understood that Chardin was an evolutionary pseudo-scientist and pseudo-metaphysician, a phony mystifier and spiritualizer of Darwin who, along with Hegel and Rudolf Steiner, believed in the error and heresy known as "the spiritual evolution of the macrocosm," which denies the entire Judeo-Christian-Islamic eschatological tradition, and the Hindu doctrine of cycles to boot, and is also one of the foundations of the New Age movement. But it wasn't until I read *The Reign of Quantity and the Signs of the Times* by René Guénon that I could finally see all the way through Chardin.

John McBride was an odd fish in a Catholic high school, or any high school. He was an intellectual and littérateur of the first order. He identified with T. S. Eliot. He once read a review he'd written of Eliot's "The Love-Song of J. Alfred Prufrock" to our English class; when he got to the part where he characterized the poem as exhibiting "semi-hypnotic verbal motifs" we just about fell out of our desks. On the other side of the aisle, though he was the furthest thing from an activist in later life, he had the makings of a Marxist-influenced Neo-Catholic even in high school (class of '66), which may be why he ultimately married Mariana, daughter of the famous Leftist poet Kenneth Rexroth. Once when our class was visiting the Catherine Branson School for a day, a girl's school and sister institution to Marin Catholic in the town of Ross, I recited Allen Ginsberg's *Howl* on the lawn to a circle of listeners which included McBride. After the declamation was done, as McBride and I were walking home, he kept shaking his head and saying "I'm just J. Alfred Prufrock, that's all I am, J. Alfred Prufrock"—the man in the poem who asked himself if he dared to eat a peach and who believed the mermaids would never sing to him. (Wasn't "freak out the Straights" half the hippie idea, all that universal love and brotherhood we preached notwithstanding?) Nonetheless McBride edited a literary magazine for Marin Catholic called *Forum* in which my poetry first saw print; after that he published a first edition of my long poem *Panic Grass*, before Lawrence Ferlinghetti brought it out, in another literary magazine he started at the University of San Francisco, and later in life he went on to become a respected poetry publisher through his

Red Hill Press. A poem of his own in *Forum* contained some lines that I'll always remember, which succinctly cover an essential point:

> I could kill myself
> but need the thought of dying
> more.

McBride would also organize campaigns with me as the candidate. It was through his string-pulling that I was elected King of the Mardi Gras, at which dance I appeared as Hamlet, dressed all in black and with a Marine officer's dress sword at my belt that had belonged to an ancestor of mine, Captain P. H. McCaull, who had fought in China in the Boxer Rebellion, plus a human skull we had laying around the house that my father had named "Yorick." He also somehow got me elected Rally Commissioner — me, the least athletic, most anti-jock of all students. (*How did he do that?* Stuff the ballot-box?) So I staged a mock sacrifice-of-a-virgin at a rally in the gym, suggested by the Beatles movie *Help!* and exploiting for the purpose a girl who had a crush on me and would do anything I said. I also recited a long, schmaltzy, lugubrious religious fable, translated from the Yiddish, entitled "Bontzye Zweig," until Father Dullea sent two big burly football players to haul me off stage (good for him!); a photograph of this incident appeared in our yearbook. All this must've been my idea of "pep" — though I'm confident none of it would be considered politically correct today, and would probably result in several lawsuits, plus (perhaps) a shooting or two. But it was a kinder and gentler era then, the era of horsefeathers, the first opening shots of the Hippie Revolution that would produce such figures as Wavy Gravy, the psychedelic clown, and — on the more political side — the leftist trickster and some-time Democratic Party operative, Paul Krassner. (Once, at the opening of the University of Creation Spirituality in Oakland, California, brainchild of the dissipated Catholic and later Episcopal priest, Matthew Fox, I met Jerry Brown, the once-and-future Governor of California, then mayor of Oakland, who told me that I looked like Krassner — which I do not and never have; possibly he was just picking up on my trickster sub-personality.) And though all these antics may have seemed lighthearted and harmless enough back in the mid-60s, in reality they were the beginning of some serious black humor designed to confront the very dark times that were coming.

WHITEWATER RAFTING IN IDAHO

One summer during high school, with some other Catholic students, I went white water rafting on the Salmon River in Idaho (not to be confused with the other Salmon River in California, tributary to the Klamath), a trip sponsored by the CYO, the Catholic Youth Organization. Our school bus plowed tediously through the Nevada deserts at 45 miles an hour, though we did finally reach our destination. From that trip — besides the rafting itself (which was exhilarating, though not enough to be frightening), I remember two incidents. In the first, we stopped at a landing occupied and run by a colorful, bearded hermit of the "grizzled prospector" type who had developed a side-show routine for the rafters. He showed us two things: a "Viking helmet" with horns, made of copper, (though real Viking helmets had no horns), that he had constructed himself with his metalworking skills, and a large glass jar full of mountain lion fetuses preserved in formaldehyde. (If only we could have taken selfies in those days so as to preserve all our various grotesque, anomalous and meaningless memories...) The second incident was something that I overheard one of the adults in the party—a red-haired man with gleaming eyes—telling to somebody else about the future development of test-tube babies, surrogate motherhood and human cloning, which he apparently looked forward to as fascinatingly sinister; when I remembered him later, it seemed to me as if I had encountered the Devil on that river. Those were the very things that had most horrified me, ever since I read an article on test-tube babies in the *San Francisco Chronicle* while I was still in grammar school. My parents or Catholic school teachers never mentioned these subjects, so my horror wasn't transmitted by them; it was apparently intrinsic to my soul, and therefore effectively absolute. I always hoped that I would die before these demonic things came to pass—but apparently God had other plans for me. (Parenthetically, I remember how shocked the woman reading the news was, on the premier leftist radio station of the Bay Area, Berkeley's KPFA, while reporting the first cases of surrogate motherhood, describing the process as "of *doubtful* ethical legitimacy!" That was in the days when the Left was still vaguely humanistic, instead of increasingly inhuman as it is today.)

THE HIPPIE THING

The Hippie Thing, like all major cultural changes, invaded from all points at once. Suddenly, in Catholic high school, I was no longer the *wimp*, the non-athletic *doofus*, the low bird on the pecking-order run by football stars and cheerleaders—or even by the apple-polishing prize students who kissed up to the priests. I'd never tried to climb that social ladder, and now, suddenly, I was near the top of a different ladder entirely: I was *hip*. There were seriously attractive girls who were no longer automatically gravitating to the alpha males, the quarterbacks; they were getting attracted to nervous, poetic, ironic, over-sensitive artist types—like me! I didn't struggle to get ahead; the world just changed as if to accommodate me. (According to the Jungian therapist Marie-Louise von Franz, it's often the women who sense the new cultural or spiritual potentials, and then proceed to weave the subtle emotional networks that will allow them to take shape.) Of course there were still those girls who were looking for the traditional masculine hero type—the type who, not too far in the future, would enlist to serve in Vietnam. But that *other* kind of girl was also appearing in increasing numbers, the type represented by the well-known anti-draft poster of the Vietnam era that showed the three beautiful Baez sisters, Joan, Mimi and Pauline, sitting seductively in a row under the bold caption that read: "GIRLS SAY YES TO BOYS WHO SAY NO"—an ancient anti-war strategy straight out of the comic farce *Lysistrata* by the Greek playwright Aristophanes. And it was three of those girls—Mary McGuinness (the leader), Janice Turini (the one who looked like Joan Baez) and the third slightly-overweight blonde one whose name I don't remember, the one Mary had re-named "Football," just as she had dubbed Janice Turini "Peter" (since Mary was trying her best to become a Lesbian as her sure ticket into Hipness, though later on she married and had a child)—it was those girls who officially stamped me hip. Those three, whom John McBride called "the Three Weird Sisters" after the witches from *Macbeth*, nearly turned me into a little Bobby Dylan with their powerful hip projections. But when did hipness really begin for me? It began when I was wounded by that bully in grammar school. That's the moment I started to become nervous and ironic and artistic—because *trauma is the root of the ego*. Hipness, like every other identity, is only a bandage wrapped to hide a wound. But trauma is also the greatest opportunity to sacrifice the ego that it itself creates—if you know how to give yourself away, and into Whose hands that gift must pass. Hipness is the *persona* game, according to the rules of which you must throw the dice for fame or shame. The real shame, however, comes not from losing the game, but from being foolish enough to play it in the first place.

The Hippie Thing also appeared simultaneously, outside the high school context, in the world of my adolescent peer group, the Trumblys. It was Jim Meisner—hipster rather than hippie, a friend of Bill who was the oldest Trumbly brother, a year or two older than me—who first turned me on to marijuana, the weak "Mexican Green" that came in palm-sized matchboxes at $5.00 a piece, before I had quite "learned" how to be stoned—by which I mean, learned how to recognize and cooperate with effects that were outside my range of psychic experience at the time. (Today's thermonuclear weed, unlike the dope of the mid-60s, requires no learning curve.) After turning on I wrote a poem about the dinosaurs I saw dancing and wrestling before my mind's eye, projected outward onto the dry, sunny California hills.

It was the Pied Piper flutes or Krishna flutes of the hippies, already audible in the distance, that spelled the end of my allotted time in the Catholic Church of my childhood—just as that Church, without my fully realizing it, was starting to die. To begin with, I was taught in apologetics class (*apologetics* being the art of defending one's faith to unbelievers, *not* apologizing for it, though Pope Francis seems not to have understood this distinction) that Pope Innocent III, in his Papal Bull entitled *Unam Sanctam*, issued *ex cathedra* ("from the Chair")—that is, as backed up by the full power of Papal Infallibility—had declared that "to be subject to the

Pope is, for all human creatures, a necessity of salvation." Yet I was being taught at the same time that people practicing other faiths than Catholicism or Christianity could be saved! This was the first *inconsistency* I had run into in my 10-plus years of Catholic education. Those who have never truly lived inside a traditional Catholic worldview — aesthetic, emotional, historical and theological — will have a very hard time grasping what a shock this was to me, especially in times like these when consistency has become a relatively meaningless concept, no longer prized, no longer struggled for. Since we are now in the postmodern age of quantum indeterminacy, of "social Heisenbergianism," an age defined by Ralph Waldo Emerson when he said that "a foolish consistency is the hobgoblin of little minds," the sense of uncenteredness and disorientation this obvious contradiction threw me into will be hard for many to believe, much less identify with. The astronomer-priests of the Bronze Age, who gave us our signs of the zodiac, must've felt a similar sense of cosmological disorientation when they began to realize that, due to the precession of the equinoxes which they had failed to allow for in their calculations, the eternal celestial order just didn't *work* anymore. However, this theological quandary would probably have remained a mere nagging worry at the back of my mind if it weren't for the fact that a number of the priests, my teachers, had obviously begun to lose their faith.

Father Surubi, a chubby Italian that my father liked to call "Father Cherubi," obviously had "issues." He was highly frustrated about something or other, and had a short temper. On one occasion he kicked a hole in the classroom waste basket. Later I heard that he had renounced the priesthood and married an (ex) nun. That's when I began to suspect that, in the far far future, ex-priests and ex-nuns would be the only people still interested in getting married. (Around 2005 Rama Coomaraswamy, who was ordained a Traditional *sedevacantist* Catholic priest while still married, had confided in Jenny and me that he believed that at one point marriage would actually be outlawed.)

Then there was the time when Father Kohles, who saw that I was struggling with my faith, deeply scandalized me by offering me "Pascal's Wager," which goes more or less like this:

> If God exists and I believe in God, I'll go to heaven, which is infinitely good. If God exists and I don't believe in God, I may go to hell, which is infinitely bad. If God does not exist, then whether I believe in God or not, whatever I'd gain or lose would be finite. Therefore I should believe in God.

What could be more *faithless* than an idea like that? Is believing in God something that you simply decide to do on a bet, like buying a lottery ticket? What would St Paul have thought of Blaise Pascal's version of "faith" after being knocked off his horse and struck blind by the Uncreated Light in the form of Jesus Christ on the road to Damascus?

Father Kohles undoubtedly thought he was showing a budding young secularist (one of the popular books of the time was *The Secular City* by "mainstream Protestant" Harvey Cox) how a Catholic priest could be just as hip and secular as any brooding, existentialist teen-age rebel, by the act of reducing the most momentous issue in human existence to a mere roll of the dice — but it didn't work. And the reason it didn't work is because I was in no way struggling with my faith in God, but rather with the absolutist claims of the Roman Catholic Church, which that Church itself had begun to become uncomfortable with.

And one of the last straws in terms of my Catholic identity had to do with the weird things that were happening to the most sacred rite of all, the Catholic Mass. It was still being said in Latin, but *a running commentary in English* was now provided, by some sort of anthropologist or tour guide inexplicably occupying the pulpit, so as to explain to the supposedly totally ignorant Marin Catholic students (after 13 years of Catholic education!) what the priest was doing and what it meant: "Now the priest is reciting the Introit; now the priest is performing the Consecration," etc. etc. This was undoubtedly done in order to erode, slowly but surely, the traditional sense of the sacred in the faithful so as to prepare them — by the gradualist or Fabian Socialist method — to accept the suppression of the Tridentine Latin Mass, the deconstruction of the sacramental order and the abrogation of much of traditional Catholic morality. So after being nourished for most of my life with faith, I was now suddenly being plied with sacrilege, in the belief that it would somehow appeal to me! Thinking back on the deeply-buried sense of shock and loss that characterized those times, I am reminded of Psalm 137:

> By the rivers of Babylon, there we sat down,
> And there we wept, when we remembered Zion...
> Those who carried us into captivity
> Required from us a song...
> But how shall I sing my Lord's song in a strange land?
> If I forget thee, O Zion
> (*O Catholic Church that they eviscerated before my eyes*)
> Let my right hand forget her cunning...

So it was the obvious cracks that had begun to appear in the edifice of the One, Holy, Catholic and Apostolic Church, against which even the Gates of Hell were not supposed to have the power to prevail, coupled with the ever-advancing flutes, drums and guitars of the hippie Spiritual Revolution, now much closer in the distance than they had been a year or so earlier — not to mention the rumors that "there's now this pill you can take called LSD that will let you *see God*" — that sealed my fate (my *freely-chosen* fate I hasten to add) as a Catholic apostate and hippie believer. And one of the strangest and most ominous "coincidences" of this terminal convulsion of Western Civilization was the fact that the widespread use of LSD and the Second Vatican Council happened at *exactly the same time*. Whether due to the machinations of the Freemasons, the Illuminati or Lucifer's social engineers (the fallen Cherubim), in those years the last pillar of Western Christendom was dynamited, and the House began to come down. (If anybody wants to hear an unexpected but entirely appropriate and poignant lament for this tragedy, let him or her listen to the song "I Dreamed I Saw Saint Augustine" by Bob Dylan.)

But since I was in the latter half of my teens when this slow disaster was taking place, I didn't yet have the discernment-of-spirits to tell the difference between my rebellion against the Catholic Church and my rebellion against the destruction of the Catholic Church; the two became confused in my mind. This confusion came to a head when, in my senior year, we held a seminar in a small amphitheater-like classroom built down the side of a hill. Its purpose was to prepare us for confronting "the World" outside high school; its two main subjects were sex and drugs. We were warned against Aldous Huxley's book *The Doors of Perception* and against birth control; a couple of us (that "couple," interesting enough, were me and Ed Lencioni, the guy who had sucker-punched me in grammar school) responded with smart-ass retorts. I bet the lecturer $50 that the Church would allow birth control within 10 years — though if he'd taken me up on it I would have lost because my timing was way off...

Not long after that, I had a dream:

> I was in a room like the one in which the seminar had taken place; at a podium at the bottom of the room stood a large professorial Serpent with spectacles, lecturing. As for me, *I was William Blake!* Challenging the Serpent Professor I jumped to my feet and declaimed: "All Hells are Hells of the Imagination, because the state of mind that creates the sin also creates the retribution!" In response to my outburst the Serpent reared up in anger, breathing fire — and in so doing, freed many souls from Hell.

The *coup-de-gras* came in my senior year as the Class of 1966 was preparing for graduation. Paul Schwab, a boy who had been in our class the year before and who had gotten a girl pregnant, had been killed over the summer in an auto accident. In an assembly at the gym, when Father Dullea was taking prayer intentions from the students — things that people wanted the priest to pray for at the graduation Mass — a girl asked Father Dullea to pray for the soul of the Paul Schwab. In front of the whole student body, *he refused to do so!* All my life I had been taught that Jesus was the Friend of Sinners, and that we were expected to pray for "the good souls in Purgatory" — and *now this*. And when someone else asked him to pray for the soldiers and civilians suffering and dying in the Vietnam War, he answered: "Hah! Do you want *more* or *less* war?" So when the assembly was over, and Dullea was marching around bellowing at the students as he liked to do, I bellowed back, from the top of the outside stairs leading to the classroom quadrangle, loud enough to raise an echo. He came up the stairs and confronted me, weakly. "*More or less war!*" I repeated to him. He couldn't even raise his eyes to mine; he kept staring at my chest. "Don't you need a haircut?" he queried irrelevantly. "My parents think I look real pretty just like this" I replied. It was my rebel apotheosis, my fifteen minutes of smartass fame.

The Russians have a proverb: "Befriend a priest, lose your faith." Why haven't we heard "Befriend a hippie lose your faith" from the Americans? Both are equally true. But just as not all hippies were faithless, not all priests are hypocrites. My wife Jenny's present priest in her little Traditionalist/ *sedevacantist* house church, Father Oswalt, is the model of salt-of-the-earth sanctity and simplicity — *intelligent* simplicity, not the naïve kind. More power to him, in this world and the next.

I often wonder if I was fully aware of what was happening to the Church, and to Western Christian civilization, in the 1960s, even though I experienced it in very intimate terms. I must have had some sense of it however, conscious and yet unconscious, since I wrote the following poem (in quasi-medieval English like Thomas Chatterton) while still in high school. It's not a great poem, I never published it, I don't even have a written copy of it... yet I remember it word for word:

> An eldern knicht
> By workéd way
> Ensconced the glory
> Of his day:
> With quest-fair dreams
> His road he trod
> The grail-poor world
> Unsprung from sod.
> Beggar-coining
> Sword in hand,
> Dragon-mapped
> He scoured the land,
> Braved pagan horde
> And martyr-kill—
> Saw not the dusk
> That ate his will.

o   o   o   o   o

After graduation from high school I attended the University of California at Davis for a total of 3 days, during which I quickly determined that the college professional track was not for me. In the process of signing the forms and talking to the right people so as to extricate myself from that institution, one professor said to me: "Don't let them grind you down." I've done my best, ever since, to follow that advice.

TOWN AND COUNTY

By comparison to church and school, my home town of San Rafael, California was nothing much. Though I lived there for 56 years, minus one year in British Columbia, one in Olema in West Marin and two in Petaluma in Sonoma County to the north, I was never really a citizen of it. With my friends I cruised Fourth Street in a '57 Chevy, the street made famous by the film *American Graffiti*, and I often visited my father's dental offices in the old Albert Building next to the Rafael Theater, but the town itself clearly belonged to others. My high school friends the Trumblys were citizens in good standing, being real live nephews of their uncle George who ran George's Pool Hall on Fourth Street, the site that later became the well-known nightclub and music venue New George's. But as for me, I was Out. Some people are born to be citizens of the world; they gladly fall into its clutches because they know of nothing else. Others are born into exile and never emerge from it until they leave this world behind. But whatever the names of those exiles are — and I will never know most of those names until I stand up from my grave at the coming of the Hour — they are my people.

To give a true feeling of San Rafael in those days there is no better source to turn to than the poem "San Rafael" by Caryn, the little schizophrenic Jewish girl who was attached to our circle, a poem which appears in a typed-xeroxed-and-stapled collection entitled *A Little Poetry* (subtitle WHEREFORE ART POETRY) that she probably composed and published in some halfway house somewhere, as "art therapy":

> For more than a decade
> My home has abide
>   To the sounds of your shoppers,
> Motorized bread winners,
>   School marms,
> Extra curricular chums,
>   Delinquency farms,
> An escape in the hills
>   Above the torn-down city hall,
> Home is a get-away
>   From nothing's call.
>
> O San Rafael,
>   The once industrial center
> Of San Rafael,
>   Your citizens light a rage
> Yet unmatched
>   By politicians of responsibility.
> Your draft board blew up,
>   You met many hippies
> The famed, the infamous came to
>   Graze in your political squalor...

The delinquency farm was the County "Honor Farm" run by the Sheriff's Department who managed the jails, as minimum-security a place as you could imagine; the "escape in the hills" might have been that old tunnel in San Rafael Hill above the town, probably dug for water, that the hippies had named (for some reason) "Hokey Pokey" and turned into a fairly secure dope hangout till the cops got wind of it; and the "once industrial center of San Rafael" was a piece of perceptive wit on Caryn's part that compared the feeling of San Rafael in the 1960s, with its run-down outskirts—a town which had never been any kind of industrial center to speak of—to a decaying mid-sized rustbelt city of the eastern U.S. . . .

But Marin County was a different matter; I actually did live there when I lived there. It was the land, the forests and hills, the dairy ranches, Mt. Tamalpais, the Pacific Ocean, and the people I knew and loved who knew and loved them like I did. I was an exile in terms of the human collective of San Rafael which, though it was as much working class as middle class, was still like an exclusive club I did not qualify for—but I was at home in Marin County, because that's where I could live as a human citizen of the Earth. I knew all the wild plants, how after the second rain of the season (usually in October) the *agaricus* mushrooms would come up— especially in the sheep ranches before they were bought out for the Point Reyes National Seashore—after which it was easy to gather a bushel an hour. I used to make a delicious tea from Marsh Mint (a kind of "Bog Pennyroyal"), Labrador Tea (camphoraceous and aromatic), and—the finest of all—Yerba Buena, also camphoraceous but minty as well, a creeping perennial shrub with ovate, opposite leaves, whose infusion refined and elevated the spirit. And as with James Joyce's Dublin after he permanently exiled himself from Ireland to the Continent—"to forge in the smithy of [his] soul the uncreated conscience of [his] race," as he says in *Portrait of the Artist as a Young Man*—when I left Marin County for good, and after enough years had passed, my exile (and homecoming!) to the Commonwealth of Kentucky ultimately transformed Marin County for me into a mythic landscape, eternalized by the power of Memory—who is, after all, the Mother of the Nine Daughters, those Ladies who at their best are nine different methods of recollection. It was a land I was deathly afraid of ever returning to in this life, lest the charm be broken and ravenous Past destroy me. Memory begins under the spell of Nostalgia (the internment, the eulogies etc.), passes through the purgatory of Disgust (the dismemberment of the corpse in the underworld), and finally comes to rest under the sign of Recollection—the true *re-membering*. Here's where you can glimpse the real difference between the nostalgia for past time, which is nothing but an endless dying, and the nostalgia for Eternity, which is the restoration of all things in the life of the world to come.

CHAPTER THREE

The Planet of Lew Welch and the Beat Generation

MY TRANSLATION FROM THE ROMAN CATHolic City of God into the Kingdom of the Counterculture, the hippie life, was fixed and confirmed by my meeting, when I was a Catholic high school student in the 1960s in Marin County, California, with my one poetic mentor and first spiritual teacher, Beat Generation poet Lew Welch. Less famous than Allen Ginsberg or Gregory Corso or Lawrence Ferlinghetti, but pre-eminent in his own rendition of the poetic craft and character and well-respected by the poets themselves—I always say that Welch and Jack Spicer are the two members of the Generation who, in the uniqueness of their achievements, deserve greater recognition—Lew had attended Reed College in Oregon with fellow poets Philip Whalen and Gary Snyder, and the three remained lifelong friends. He had been an advertising hack (famous as author of the phrase "Raid Kills Bugs Dead"), a fisherman on a commercial salmon boat, and a some-time cabbie. It was this job that gave him the inspiration for his poem "AFTER ANACREON," which begins with "When I drive cab"—just as each line of the ancient Greek poet Anacreon's "Wine Song" begins with "When I drink wine"—as well as providing him with several of his "Passenger Poems" based on various examples of unfiltered overheard American Speech from the back of his cab. Lew had also been the paramour of poetess Lenore Kandel, whose famous *Love Book* of erotic poems was declared obscene at one point, greatly boosting her sales.

When I knew him he was working at the docks in San Francisco as a longshoremen's clerk, and living with his "common-law wife" Magda Cregg (the mother of rock musician Huey Lewis) in a house at 52 Buckelew Street in the nearly 100% Black town, or rather housing development, of Marin City, our own version of "the projects." My high school friend Bill Trumbly rang me up one day to say that he was too hung-over to attend Lew's poetry class at the College of Marin in Greenbrae, so he suggested that I take his place. And so, in a landscaped garden on the College grounds, complete with a sunken patio and a grove of redwood trees, I met Lew; the only other student present was poet Mary Norbert Körte, a Dominican nun in the early stages of leaving the Order, and probably the Catholic Church as well. Unexpectedly, this strange...lean...intense...rawboned...plainly emphatic...deliberately concrete...painstakingly simple man seemed more interested in teaching us perception exercises than in talking about poetry.

"Take a look at those redwood trees over there" he said. "Now imagine the spaces between the trees as solid objects, and the trees themselves as empty spaces." And we did it; we saw as he saw. In so doing, we perceptually actualized (I realized later) the famous line "form is emptiness, emptiness is form" from the *Heart Sutra* of the Mahayana Buddhists, and learned how to see the world not as a set of literal objects—as our unconscious identification of things with our *names* for them had taught us to do—nor yet as nothing but fantasy-images inside our own heads, but as a third thing, placed exactly between them: a thing called an *apparition*.

The perceptual seed that Lew Welch planted in my psyche that day sprouted years later, on the occasion when, meditating with my eyes open in a redwood grove in Gerstle Park in San Rafael, California, the redwood grove was suddenly transformed into a birch grove: the redwood trees, empty; the spaces between them, birch trees. All those who have read *Shamanism: Archaic Techniques of Ecstasy* by Mircea Eliade will remember that the birch is the pre-eminent World Tree of the Siberians, the one that the Siberian shaman climbs in his death-defying and death-embracing trance, from world to world, from *loka* to *loka*, from nest to nest... Given that the Zenith, projected horizontally on the earth's surface, becomes the North, and in view of the fact that Lew Welch, as a Leo, identified with the Sun, it should come as no surprise that Hyperborea, the True North, "the land behind the North Wind," was known as the original homeland of the Greek god Apollo—Poet, Physician and implacable Archer—one of whose epithets (in Latin) is *Sol Invictus*, "the Sun Unconquered."

Strangely enough, *I Remain*, Lew's collected correspondence, contains his own evaluation of the kind of initiation he believed that he and I and Sister Mary had been granted, on that day I first met them in the late 1960s at the College of Marin, though I never came across his account of it until a few years ago, many years after his death. He said that the three of us had taken Orders of a higher degree than anything the Church could bestow. As of now I can't entirely agree with him on that score—especially since these "Orders" did not save him from his fate as an alcoholic suicide—but it is certainly true that we were imprinted, in those pivotal years, at that particular locale, in that specific moment, with some very strange and intense lore, which I now feel it my duty to pass on. It may be the case—possibly because I've never had children—that the Ancestors require this kind of transmission from me from time to time. Apparently they insist that I pass on some of the teachings they gave me before they will agree to release me (speaking in Hindu terms) from *pitriyana*, the Way of the Fathers that leads to rebirth, and allow me to pursue my call to *devayana*, the Way of the Gods that leads to Enlightenment, in the form of *tasawwuf*, the Sufi Path.

After the class I handed Lew a sheaf of my poems for his perusal—after which, a short time later, he wrote me to say, "you can be a poet if you want to," and then took me under his wide, sometimes shaky, and always superlatively alcoholic wing. That was my initiation. He mentored me as a budding poet during the last years of his life and the first years of my *conscious* life, reciting to me the classics (Yeats, Burroughs and others) and passing on some of the spiritual insights he'd arrived at, and paid for, over the years. But it was only in 2011 that I was told by a correspondent that Lew, in *I Remain* (a book I hadn't yet read at that point), had named me his "only heir"; I'm passing on that inheritance now. Like William Blake said in his "Proverbs of Hell" from *The Marriage of Heaven and Hell*: "In seed time learn, in harvest teach, in winter enjoy."

The movie *Big Sur*, written and directed by Michael Polish, about Kerouac's "black satori" at Ferlinghetti's cabin, south along the Pacific coast from San Francisco (where Lew apparently had a similar epiphany at one point), in which the character of Lew Welch appears as "David Wain," gets him all wrong. The film shows him as nervous, fast-talking and frenetic, whereas in reality he placed each word so slowly and precisely that it was as if (to use his own metaphor) he were laying a course of bricks. If there is any voice familiar to many that could be in any way compared to Lew's, it's the voice of Jack Nicholson. You might say that Lew was like a young Dennis Quaid with Nicholson's voice — but if you did you'd be wrong. His voice and face were his own, since he'd already been cast in his one lifetime role. He was so slow and sure and certain in his speech, and in the weight of what he said (even when discoursing on less-than-weighty subjects), that he actually taught several fully verbal adult males of my acquaintance, including Jack Boyce and Frank Dietrich, *how to talk*. After he died you would sometimes hear his exact voice coming out of somebody else's mouth. More often than not if you struck up a conversation with the speaker you'd find that he'd known Lew, most likely having sat next to him at the No Name Bar in Sausalito, along with actor Sterling Hayden and the other regulars, letting himself get stamped and sealed and imprinted with the exact shapes and cadences of that relentless, never-ending Voice. (Frank Dietrich, along with my friend Ken Bullock, was the one who introduced me to my future wife Jenny Donne, whom I first met at a poetry class taught by the highly accomplished and under-appreciated poet Jack Gilbert, whose *forte* was not passion sublimated by asceticism but the asceticism of passion itself — especially in the face of death. Frank was a solid suburban citizen and *amateur* poet living in Marin County, who divorced his wife Barbara for a younger woman, moved to the Sacramento Delta to manage a boat dock, and then dropped out of sight, never to be heard from again. Jack Boyce, who had become attached to Magda after Lew's disappearance, died, after tempting Fate by dancing, undoubtedly stoned, on the rafters of Magda's cabin, known as Purple Gate, in the strange, reclusive little coastal town of Bolinas, when he fell and broke his neck.)

Lew ended up introducing me to a number of the poets and writers of the Beat Generation. This probably prevented me from thoughtlessly immersing myself in the Hippie Collective, since thanks to him I now had the kind of literary identity, and acquaintance with important literary figures, that was supposed to make someone in my position a "detached observer" — so where the hippies wore colorful tie-dyed outfits, I tended more toward depressive existentialist beatnik black, with some Mod influence thrown in courtesy of the Beatles.

Probably my first experience of classical "beatness" was when I and Mary McGuinness (whom I've already mentioned, a budding Lesbian, proto-hippie and fellow student at Marin Catholic High School), made the scene at the Trieste Café in North Beach, which is on the (non-existent) National Registry of Beat Locations and Institutions. I had the flu. She gave me one of her codeine pills. We drank espresso, hunched over our table in depressive introversion, just like everybody else. We felt extremely *beat* — "tired and wily" as Allen Ginsberg described that same feeling in his early poem "Sunflower Sutra," the one about him sitting with Jack Kerouac on the railroad tracks in the Berkeley salt flats across the Bay, surrounded by trash and flotsam. From the present standpoint of the early 21st Century, I would now define "Beatness" as: "The humility enforced on extravagant souls by the necessary consequences of that very extravagance, accompanied by at least the vague notion that such humility might be pressed into the service of salvation and enlightenment." Lew, however, was not really beat in this depressive sense — though he certainly had his periods of fierce depression — since he was addicted to Solar Glory. His ideal, however, was not to enact a majestic royal sundown, but rather to sacrifice himself at High Noon: to die at the height of his powers.

Lew was probably the most philosophical and metaphysical of the Beats, though he hid that part of himself in a rather matter-of-fact and simple-minded style of writing — at least to certain ears. I remember when Lawrence Ferlinghetti said to me once, "Welch? He's just dumb." He loved truth but hated abstraction — like the Zen people when they warn against "the philosopher disease" — so he labored to render his fundamental perceptions of the nature of reality as concretely as possible, without fanfare, without drama, something like what William Carlos Williams or Gertrude Stein might have done if they had been informed by Dōgen or Lao Tzu. Ginsberg, on the other hand, presented his truths with trumpets and fireworks and lead-guitar riffs, more in the style of Walt Whitman raised to a higher pitch of energy by William Blake and the King James Isaiah. From the standpoint of the hippie era we usually think of Allen Ginsberg as the spiritual leader of the Beat Generation with Kerouac as a close second (though Kerouac was the true First Founder, with Burroughs as a kind of Merlin to Kerouac's Arthur). In many ways this is accurate, though Kerouac only led, by the time the hippie wave crested, mostly as a memory, having retired from the scene and moved to Florida to live with his mother as a bitter alcoholic right-winger before the hippie counterculture was in full swing—unlike Ginsberg who relished his position as cheerleader, or Welch and Snyder who composed serious manifestos to serve and instruct the young. But the fact is that Ginsberg, for all his pre-eminence as a metaphysical gossip, did not *intellectually penetrate* his influences as deeply as Kerouac did (especially in *Some of the Dharma*) or Gary Snyder or Philip Whalen or Lew Welch. (The uniquely spooky Jack Spicer had a different area of study, that being the world of "ghosts," particularly the ghosts of language—though his *magnum opus The Holy Grail* went way beyond his earlier linguistic and paranormal obsessions.) But it was Lew who (in my opinion) most clearly, and tragically, expressed the *existential dilemma* that only Perfect Total Enlightenment can cure. Reading *I Remain*, his collected correspondence, you can see with painful clarity how he was more desperately, deadly serious about questions that are central to the spiritual Path than any of the other Beats. Snyder took it for granted that he already knew. Ginsberg asked no real questions except "what lies beyond death?" and spent his life exploring the worlds generated by his consciousness instead of trying to dig down to the root of that consciousness. One gets the impression that it was *only* Lew who was continually asking: "What is the proper comportment for a human being? What is Truth with a capital T? How can I become the kind of person who has something to say worth listening to?" He was also one of the first to die, whereas Allen Ginsberg and Gary Snyder and Lawrence Ferlinghetti had enough solid bourgeois character (especially Snyder) to avoid alcoholism and drug addiction and live on into old age. As of this writing Snyder is still alive at 93, most likely as the very last of his Beat (literary) Generation.

Lew was not my "guru" or "spiritual master" in the usual sense. What he was was the man who provided me with my *life task*, a task he himself had not been able to complete. He did not give me this task by transferring it to me. Instead, we were drawn together by a common need and thread and destiny: exactly where he was at the end of his life "just happened," in some ways, to be exactly where I was at the age of 22. And our lives were strangely linked even before that. When I was vacationing with my family at that cabin at Somes Bar on the Salmon River in the early 60s, Lew was at his abandoned CCC (Civilian Conservation Corps) cabin, upstream at Forks of Salmon, years before I met him. That river was the terrestrial origin of "the clear stream of all of it" he writes about in his poem "[I SAW MYSELF]," the stream in which he imagined himself as "a ring of bone"—the phrase that became the title of his collected poems. I swam like a fish for many hours in that pure, clear, emerald-green water, appropriately *downstream* from where he was doing his forest hermit thing at about the same time, just so I could get the essential *drift* of his teaching before it was translated (later) into words. I even bought and sold a piece of land in the John Day country of eastern Oregon and camped on it with my new wife Jenny in the late 1970s (see *Chapter Seven*) only later finding out that Lew mentions that exact area in one of his letters. (Ginsberg also refers to that country in a poem, where he imagines the great Tibetan yogi Milarepa meditating as an anchorite in the mountains above John Day, right where my brief 80 acres were, though I'm sure he never knew about my foredoomed attempt to become a Mountain Man.) So it seems as if all the main events of our lives are pre-recorded somehow, written down in the Akashic Records, or on the Guarded Tablet, or in the Book of Life. While we are reading that Book, living that Life, we have to proceed consecutively, line by line, but this doesn't mean that the whole thing isn't already there, safe and complete in that other world, bound in a single comprehensive volume. As it says in the ancient Welsh poem "The Book of Taliesin," which is quoted by Lew in his own poem "WOBBLY ROCK":

> *I was a word in a book*
> *I was a book originally.*

LEW'S LEO

Lew invented a poetic persona for himself called "Leo" after his astrological sign. This allowed him to "be" the Sun, to "be" a Lion, etc. A friend of his, Kirby Doyle, a lesser-known member of the Generation — in one of those cheap pornographic paperbacks the Beats sometimes turned out when they needed cash, like the ones published under the Black Cat imprint by Grove Press — called him "Leo the Magic Lion," making him part of his own gallery of archetypal "heroes" that included Allen Ginsberg as "Aladdin Ginstrap" etc. etc. Once Jenny and I drove Kirby from Ferlinghetti's editorial offices/apartment back to his "home" in Marin County, a tent in the woods on the ridge above Woodacre in the San Geronimo Valley. The one thing I remember from our conversation was his great veneration for the U.S. Constitution — "*If* it's still in effect" I cynically added — and saw him jump.

Archetypal identities are a two-edged sword. Every human soul has a true destiny, but you have to have gone a long ways toward transcending your ego, with all its identifications and self-identifications, before you can see it. Otherwise it only appears piece by piece, step by step, in the course of your walk through life. Sometimes you can't even recognize these pieces when they're staring you in the face, consequently you come to the conclusion — as many have done in these times — that "life is random." *Adopting* an archetypal identity, however — which Jung seriously discouraged because it results in *hubris* — radically edits and simplifies the process. If all you are is that one archetype (instead of being a unique synthesis of all the archetypes, which is what each individual rendition of the Human Form actually is), it provides you with a ready-made character, and a ready-made fate to go with it. "Character is Fate" said Heraclitus, which is why "a man's gotta do what a man's gotta do." In exchange for the gift of a clear and certain identity, which comes with a specific costume provided by the Wardrobe Department and a particular stock character sent down from Central Casting, you have agreed to surrender your ability to *change course* in life. Consequently you have become *fey*, a highly useful word which is related to *fay*, the French word for "fairy," both *fey* and *fay* being derived from the Latin *fatum*, "fate." To be dedicated to a single archetype is to become *fey*, and—seeing that a given pre-recorded life necessarily comes complete with a given pre-recorded death—to become *fey* is always *fatal*, unless the spell is broken by the intervention of a higher Reality. The Regime of Fate is ruled by the Great Goddess, who appears as the Muse to all true lyric poets, and one of whose Irish avatars is as the Morrigan, the Goddess of War: thus Morgan la Fay from the Arthurian legends—the *Fata Morgana*—was both "Morrigan the Fairy" and "Morrigan the Fate." The great Irish warrior-hero Cuchulainn met Her at a ford once in the form of a feeble old woman, whereupon she challenged him. "You can do nothing to harm me!" he confidently boasted. "Certainly I can," she matter-of-factly replied. Cuchulainn knew he was a Hero, but he was ignorant of the One from whom his heroism came, and who was capable of taking it all back at a moment's notice with a single flick of her apron-string. I remember a poem that Beat poet Stuart Perkoff once recited to us at a UFO soirée at Helen Luster's house, a very dear and interesting lady you'll hear about later on. In it he announced to the poets of the Beat Generation and the Hippie Counterculture together (the lines reproduced here are an imperfect rendition, taken from memory): "She's coming for you now, poets—She's coming to *take it all back!*" Truer words were never spoken: She *did* take it all back, resulting in the rapid descent of the poetic art in North America, as the counterculture faded, from the sublime to the picayune.

We mustn't forget, however, that there are such things as *true* archetypal identities, based on the particular Name of God that is dominant in the makeup of a given soul. These true identities are not generated through identification, however: they just are. Sometimes we find them during the course of our lives; sometimes they remain hidden until we wake up in the next world. But whether we are conscious or unconscious of them, they determine to a large extent the course and quality and destiny of our lives, because they are nothing less than God's Will for us—the Will we all accepted in the timeless time before birth into this world when God asked us, *Am I not your Lord?*, to which we all answered *Yea!* [Q. 7:172]

Human identities in the Christian Middle Ages were more archetypal than the generic individualities of today. You were either a Peasant, a Lord (or Lady), a Cleric, a Craftsman, a Warrior, a Merchant, a Wandering Minstrel, a Perfidious Jew or one of the other pre-determined roles from a small handful of stock identities, each complete with its own proper duties and morality and comportment and ideal destiny—in Hindu terms, its own *dharma*. People then were more like Tarot cards. The unique individualities were all still there under the archetypal costumes that indicated membership in a particular caste or estate, but they weren't emphasized, encouraged and given free rein like individualities are today. Almost the only ways to opt out of this system were to become either a Monk or a Criminal. The Criminal would generally be a vagrant or vagabond, an *extravagant* person (one who "wandered outside," beyond boundaries), a *renegade* ("run-a-gate," someone who would sneak outside the city walls during the night). But both Monk and Renegade were still recognized types; Friar Tuck (from fiction) was a recognizable Monk; Francois Villon (from history), was a recognizable Renegade; his criminal brotherhood, the Coquillards, were more like a guild than a gang. Is today's *cosplay movement*—along with its sinister *Kumbh Mela*, the Burning Man—like the Renaissance Faire before it, our half-conscious attempt to resurrect the medieval Tarot deck of archetypal identities? On the other hand, nobody hates archetypal identities more than the Cultural Marxists; the main reason they reject even *gender* is because it's too *archetypal* for them. Even Burning Man, the exteriorization of the postmodern Collective Unconscious, is too chaotic and nihilistic to be properly archetypal. And this is entirely consistent: you can't be a thorough atheist without hating the archetypes, because the archetypes always lead back to God. In Islamic terms those archetypes, or Platonic Ideas, are, precisely, the Names of Allah.

You can still see traces of these old archetypal masks in English or Scottish ballads like "Mary Hamilton," which is a perfect illustration of how Character is Fate (Heraclitus), or "Lord Randall," in which the Great Goddess appears in the guise of the young lord's wife or beloved, who has rendered Randall "sick at heart" by feeding him poison. When Joan Baez, in the ballad "Henry Martin," sings of the brothers who cast lots to decide which of them was to "turn Robber all on the salt sea," we can see, first, how only Fate (in the guise of Chance) can decide who will be allowed and commanded to change one archetypal identity for another, and (secondly) how this change is as abrupt and total as the turning of a page in a book or drawing a card from a deck. "Leave me, I am not that man any more, I have *turned Robber*; depart from me, I am not that man any more, I have *turned Monk*." Lew Welch went through a Turn exactly like that near the end of his life, the turn from Leo to Turkey Buzzard—but we will speak of that later.

Lew Welch was in many ways a materialist—*matter* being cognate with *mater*, the Latin for "mother." He usually scorned Christianity: "Who could ever worship a *Holy Ghost?*"—though he once said to me (I was basically in my Blakean Christian period at that point), "Maybe Jesus really is your Master." But he had definite problems with God, which is undoubtedly why he chose Buddhism as a path, thinking to avoid the ultimate confrontation—even though the Tibetans in their *Book of the Dead* speak of that very confrontation as the first phase of true death, the encounter with the Clear Light of the Void, "thrilling, blissful, radiant." Kerouac names that very same light "The Golden Eternity" in his one true Buddhist sutra, *The Scripture of the Golden Eternity*. He had a vision of that Light when he stood up too fast from lying on his back on his mother's lawn in Florida, probably drunk—after which he fainted, fell, and saw it.

Lew's inability to accept the idea of God left him no approach to Deity but the Regime of Nature, which is necessarily the regime of Fate. And, ironically, it was this materialistic nature-worship—essentially the "paganism" of Sir James Frazer and Robert Graves (the two books he told me every poet should read were Frazer's *The Golden Bough* and Graves' *The White Goddess*)—that replaced for him any kind of effective, serious Buddhism, which would have started him out with certain basic behavioral requirements, such as "no booze." And so he fell back, at least partly, on a simple, literal worship of the earth and sun:

> Here comes the sun. It's the only god we've got. It's shining on the earth. It [*the earth*] is our mother. It is a big round ball [from *How I Work as a Poet*].

Consequently, instead of discarding identities until the last one was stripped off, he opted to take on *archetypal* identities—first Leo, then Turkey Buzzard; and choosing an archetypal identity for yourself is just another name for narcissism. The narcissist sacrifices his living flesh and spirit to the vampire of his self-image, and consequently lives a false life, a life of flight from Self. "We invent ourselves," wrote Lew in "THE ENTIRE SERMON BY THE RED MONK," "out of ingredients we didn't choose, by a process we can't control... All you really say [*supreme irony!*] is 'Love me for myself alone'... It is also possible to *uninvent* yourself. By a process you can't control. But you invented Leo. Forget it." Lew, in this poem, defines his poetic persona, "Leo," as the product of a *successful* act of narcissism—as if there could be such a thing—and explicitly rejects the spiritual Path, *the path of self-uninvention*. But no act of narcissism can really be "successful," simply because narcissism is a living hell. Gleaming in the reflected light of your own radiant image in the pool, you trap and lock the attention of everyone around you. But none of that attention really *gets* to you. All the love and admiration and compassion and help you so desperately (and silently) crave is attracted to and eaten up by that endlessly talking image, leaving the real you starving: this is the *oral hell* the Buddhists reserve for those they call the *pretas*, the "hungry ghosts." Lew was capable of making many people love him, but he could receive love from no-one. He let himself starve all his life for the love that might have saved him, because it would have destroyed his glorious self-image, his "Leo." Lew had so deeply despaired of the love he needed that he was finally willing to sacrifice himself to the self-image he mistakenly *thought* was actually getting it. But an image on a TV screen cannot receive love, and all who give their love to such a subhuman image, no matter how much poetic glory, how big a share of the King-Light it floods them with, are signing up for an extended stay in the bat-ruled Mayan underworld known as *Xbalbá*, the Cave of the Vampires.

IDENTITIES: SOCIAL, SEXUAL AND UNDETERMINED

I remember the one time Lew met my father, at our home in San Rafael. In Lew's presence he suddenly became the substantial burgomaster, Lew the furtive bohemian artiste. The glare of social shame briefly filled the room. I perceived this as coming much more from Lew than from my father, who was never one to "pull rank" in any way; he accepted virtually everyone he met because he was *interested* in them. Their good qualities delighted him; their bad or irritating qualities were reduced to fascinating foibles that only gave him more material for his wine-inspired tales illustrative of the human condition, told at our glorious dinners over the dinner table made from one thick, immense slab of polished redwood, at which he nobly presided as the one who carved the meat. Lew was apparently afraid that my father would think he was feeding drugs to his innocent young son (which he was, of course, but only marijuana, and that was to be had everywhere, from any or all of my friends); he made a rather lame joke about not being partial to LSD because it gave him "acid indigestion." Perhaps this incident was the origin of the myth Lew made up about me, a story in the genre known as "Irish facts," that I was not the natural son of my putative parents but a mysterious foundling, like a king's son secretly raised by shepherds until such time as, attaining his majority, he became ready to challenge his evil uncle, the bastard pretender, for the throne of the kingdom. It's a bewildering thing to be "princed" at so young an age; it saddles you with a mythic identity that you have to simultaneously live down and try to live up to, one that is destined to prove worthless in the markets of the world, seeing that the true and vulgar nobility in the American caste system is money and nothing else. And of course stories like this, in the Neo-Liberal society of today, are tantamount to admitting that your parents were Nazis, a situation that has forced me to consider just what "white privilege" might amount to in real terms. After pondering this question I've come to the conclusion that *one* of the most valuable aspects of this privilege is that you didn't have to think of yourself in terms of race at all (at least in California, as opposed to the Deep South), just as a heterosexual in those times didn't have to think of him- or herself in terms of gender identity. The work of defining gender was for homosexuals, the struggle to define racial identity was for Black people and Mexicans. White heterosexuals, not having to worry about such things, were free to develop other aspects of their character and their relation to the world—some of which were so impractical, at least for the more artistic wing of my generation, that they led to real disasters later in life. Nonetheless the socially-imposed need to define ourselves in terms other than those "automatically" provided by society was a form of oppression that the more psychologically privileged among us in the 1960s didn't have to contend with—and that group, strangely enough to contemporary ears, included plenty of people from both the middle and working classes; those who were not economically privileged could still be socially privileged in other ways. "Free, White and 21, plus Male, Straight and Marin County-raised" was all "straight" society gave me, seeing that I occupied a low rung in the pecking-order of my extended adolescent peer group, was too dependent on my parents and had very shaky economic prospects for the future—but seen from the perspective of 21st-Century America, that was quite a lot. An intact society, no matter what its limitations might be, can actually give you a *life*, an unquestioned identity—something that no-one in today's world is automatically assured of. "Society," in these times, is seen as nothing but a set of oppressive myths that every social group must create counter-myths to protect themselves from—and it was in fact the Beats, who mostly either rose into prominence from the working class or the underground of the *lumpen proletariat* or else descended from the established middle class into the Bohemian *demimonde*, no matter what level of privilege might have been available to them through their families if they had opted to pick up on it, who began to see things that way; that's what made them "beat." Jordan Peterson says that, though we don't have nobility in North America, we do have celebrity. To be a poet in the 1960s (and even later) except for maybe no more than two of the Beats (Jack Kerouac and Allen Ginsberg), plus Robert Frost, Robert Bly (a semi-Beat outlier) and Carl Sandburg, was to be at the very bottom of the totem pole of American Celebrity, something like what it must've been to be a Vaudeville entertainer in earlier years: fringe notoriety, Show Biz in the sticks—though I did, on one occasion (thanks to Lew's "management" of me) open at a rock concert in San Francisco for Country Joe and the Fish! (The Fish, man!) Sadly, however, it's becoming very hard for people to look at social realities like this anymore, whether past or present. Ideology, though it may have a sort of pedantic truth of its own, has trumped any truly humane social consciousness. At this point we can't see or respond to real people or situations, only to ideological dogmas—which, in effect, means: only to *words* (cf. Lenny Bruce's "racial epithets" routine, which everybody ought to listen to). And this realization, for me, throws light on one of Lew's most basic teachings, one that I don't yet fully understand, but still hope to: "Only poets know," he said, "that words don't mean anything."

In a way, Lew protected me from falling into the heavily homosexual Beat and post-Beat poetry scene in San Francisco, not through any moralizing influence but simply by being firmly heterosexual himself. Among the poets themselves, as I knew them, there was not a hint of homophobia. Allen Ginsberg and other gay poets (Jack Spicer, Robert Duncan, James Broughton, Peter Orlovsky, etc.) were entirely accepted in terms of their sexual orientation; this was not really an issue on any level, since the Brotherhood of Poets was dedicated to the art itself, not to the use of the art to serve any overt political or cultural or ideological agenda, not even a hip one. But it was most certainly a Brotherhood; a few girls, like Diane DiPrima and Denise Levertov (one of my favorite poets, Beat by age-group more than social identification, and not as universally known as she should be) were allowed in the club during the 60s and before; nonetheless poetry in those days, like rock music in the "classic rock" era, was mostly a man's game. Likewise political poetry, "the Poetry of Resistance," grew up largely under the influence of the leftist poets of Latin America like Pablo Neruda and Caesar Vallejo; it was pretty much a creature of the 1980s, though it partly developed out of the earlier world of anti-Vietnam War poetry—and, at least until recently, Latino poets have had a disproportionate influence in the world of Federal art grants, access to the position of U.S. Poet Laureate etc. On many levels the art of poetry has been co-opted to serve this or that political, usually quasi-Leftist agenda, and this is one of the things that seems to have effectively drawn the cloak of historical amnesia over the traditional religious identity of some of the Beat writers, especially their *Christian* identity. Who remembers what a pious Catholic Jack Kerouac was before he became a Buddhist, and to a degree even concurrently with his Buddhist identity, filled with the simple French Catholic quasi-Marian devotion of a St Thérèse of Lisieux, the Little Flower, or a Francois Villon? Who remembers that Denise Levertov and William Everson (Brother Antoninus) and Philip Lamantia formed a solid phalanx of Catholic Beats? Who remembers that even Gregory Corso and Jack Spicer dared to let the name "Christ" pass their lips once in a while? Who even remembers the pre-Buddhist para-Hasidic Allen Ginsberg of *Kaddish*, or that *Howl* itself contains the lines "where you will split the heavens of Long Island and resurrect your living human Jesus from the superhuman tomb"? I once had an interview with Brother Antoninus at the old Dominican Priory, since torn down, in the town of Ross in Marin County, and showed him some of my poems. Antoninus, as far as I can see, was the sole poetic successor to the supremely aloof and reclusive poet of the wild California coast, Robinson Jeffers. The meeting was set up by one of my teachers at Marin Catholic High School, Brother Christopher—a Dominican friar and repentant actor—since he knew I was a poet and thought I should talk with an older Catholic man of the same calling. Brother Antoninus later left the Dominican Order, and eventually the Catholic Church itself, to become a self-initiated shaman, which many poets of that time and place, if they happened to be at all attracted in that direction, somehow thought would be the easiest thing in the world.

As for the Catholic Gregory Corso, there's a great story about him in that role. When the top-tier Catholic movie *The Song of Bernadette*, about St Bernadette Soubirous of Lourdes (starring Jennifer Jones) came out in 1943, the young 13-year-old Gregory stole a white dress shirt (some versions say a suit) from a haberdashery so he could appear properly attired at the opening, as if for his first communion—for which theft he was arrested, convicted and sent to prison (not reform school as you'd expect). That way he could maintain his standing both as a Good Catholic Boy and as a Bad Boy and future Beat poet. The French criminal-and-choir-boy poet, Francois Villon, would have understood that action perfectly.

So official atheism descends. "Religious people" are all fanatics, potential terrorists, stupid simple-minded sentimentalists, deniers of science, deniers of the self-evident truth that human beings are nothing but biochemical mechanisms, holders to the fallacy that men and women are different from each other, non-celebrators of diversity, haters of nature, superstitious believers in imaginary spooks and outdated myths. And so, into the same dumpster with Oral Roberts and Billy Graham and Jerry Falwell, with Osama Bin Laden and Charlie Manson and Jim Jones, we dump Dante and Milton and Blake and Shakespeare, and much of Walt Whitman and Emily Dickinson—and pretty soon Jalaluddin Rumi too, after the covert official support for Islam has finished its work of destroying Christianity with Islam's help, and the day arrives (soon, very soon) when Islam must be destroyed in its turn, even in the West—not just with bombs but with the same official progressive-globalist cultural pogroms that effectively castrated Christ and thereby made it mostly unnecessary to bomb the pitiful remnants of Christendom (except in its ancient Mid-East heartlands, through our puppet-pals ISIS and their friends), since the Church had already been destroyed from within by a Second Vatican Council that effectively cut the heart out of it—not to forget the campaign to add Martin Luther King and Muhammad Ali and Thomas Merton and Malcolm X to the same landfill, all of them to be officially relegated to "the scrap-heap of history"—even *Buddhism itself*, now that the Dalai Lama has broken ranks with the globalists by comparing the EU-sponsored immigration of de-culturated quasi-Muslims now flooding Europe with the Chinese conquest of Tibet! Pope Francis is still cool of course, since he opined in an interview with Vatican Radio that "God does not exist"—but after him, my faithful believing friends, *le deluge*.

Withering under the incessant blows of this massive globalist attack on our collective cultural memory, its brutal re-writing of any history has not already been cleanly wiped from all human memory, we OF COURSE forget that the Beat Generation, and the hippies who followed them, were full of believers in God, or at least included plenty of artists to whom mention of God was no scandal, as it most certainly is today. Well before Dylan's Jesus-freak period, Native American-identified folksinger Buffy St Marie could sing Leonard Cohen's "God is Alive and Magic is Afoot," and the Quicksilver Messenger Service perform their powerful song "Pride of Man," inspired by the Apocalypse and the Book of Isaiah.

And we are also commanded to forget that it was entirely possible, in the San Francisco poetry scene of the 60s and 70s, to appreciate both a fascist fellow-traveler like Ezra Pound and a Soviet Ministry of Culture poet like Vladimir Mayakovsky — or Andrei Voznesensky, number two Russian poet in those days after Evgeny Yevtushenko, on the occasion of whose visit to San Francisco in the 70s I partied over a long weekend with other poets at the North Beach topless joints and Lawrence Ferlinghetti's City Lights editorial offices, showcasing for the Soviet cultural icon all the wonders of Western decadence, of which we ourselves were sterling examples. (I remember the car perpetually parked at the foot of the steep street below the offices, where a lone figure sat reading a newspaper for hours and hours — undoubtedly Voznesensky's KGB handler, or else his opposite number from the FBI.) We could unthinkingly accept both a poetry-writing Catholic monk like Thomas Merton and a Buddhist bard like Gary Snyder or Allen Ginsberg, both an all-but-straight Minnesota Midwesterner like Robert Bly and a strictly gay poet like Spicer whose only viable "range," outside of Stinson Beach for the summer season (though he did spend some time at Simon Frazer University in British Columbia), seemed limited to U. C. Berkeley and the cafes of Telegraph Avenue plus the officially gay boulevards of Polk and Castro streets in San Francisco — true cultural worlds-unto-themselves like the old Black Harlem used to be — with no feeling of dishonesty or sense of inner contradiction. But not anymore. Uniqueness of perception, depth of feeling and clarity of expression now mean little unless they are pressed into the service of some social agenda or other. Nature (beyond sounding the alarm about environmental destruction), spirituality and humanity are mostly passé today in the world of American poetry; the poets are not singers of the eternal themes but workers and activists, or else simple banal nihilists and/ or narcissistic self-advertisers who have rejected the struggle to render the sublime for the ease and convenience of reproducing the picayune. To simply see and feel and know has much less cash value than it did in the world of the 60s and 70s. (God willing, however, this may be starting to change. In 2016 my wife and I were asked to submit some of our poetry to an anthology called *Diamond Cutters: Visionary Poets in America, Britain and Oceania*, edited by Andrew Harvey and Jay Ramsay. A few of the poets included are now officially dead so as to establish a proper "tradition," but many of us are still walking around. The medieval monk or nun, along with their brothers and sisters up till the 1950s, had a system of collective support for renouncing the world, the monastery system; how were we poets of the latter days able to do something similar without benefit of such amenities? Only, I would claim, by the secret patronage of an unknown Friend—secret even to us, though we draw our every breath, and follow every beat of our heart, only by His largesse.)

The Beat world and the later San Francisco poetry scene that succeeded it certainly had their social ideals and stereotypes—we knew, for example, that we were not McCarthyites or warmongers or rednecks—but inside the borders of that world the dogma "Do your own thing, and don't bum anyone else's trip" was effectively absolute. The hippies inherited that dogma from the Beats, which meant that a refreshingly accepting and supportive atmosphere—one that probably saved my wife Jenny's life when she fled to California in the 70s from an abusive family situation in Kentucky—became slowly polluted with a taboo against any struggle to find and articulate real meanings, against any dogma other than the dogma of no-dogma. As Magda put it in two words: "WHATEVER, FOREVER!" On one occasion I remember talking with a long-time employee of City Lights Bookstore, Shig Murao, about my correspondence with William Burroughs in the late 1960s on the subject of the Church of Scientology as a dangerous cult. (I like to think that Burroughs' break from Scientology soon afterward had something to do with that exchange, though it's more likely that he had mostly made up his mind to jump ship from the Sea Org before we dialogued.) Shig was shocked. To him, the idea that I or anyone in the "hip" world would have a problem with somebody else's choice of a path in life was inconceivable—at least for anyone but a "Christian Evangelical bigot" or some equally unfortunate example of benighted humanity. (Notice the contradiction?) And it was out of this very attitude of admirable hipness and liberality (*not* to be confused with today's Liberalism, which has no liberality at all), by a number of large but nonetheless consecutive and clearly devolutionary steps, that today's world of Woke bigotry and Cancel Culture emerged. So maybe Hegel was right after all, in an ironic and inverted way, when he said that history moves by a course of thesis, antithesis and synthesis—or rather, as I would say, *anti*-synthesis. Society really does seem to *degenerate* by a dialectical process, one that's only made possible by firmly repressing, as we all dearly love to do, each phase of that history as soon as it's past. Maybe that's why Jack Kerouac saw himself as the "Great Rememberer, redeeming life from darkness"—like the Kabbalist Isaac Luria, who defined the spiritual life as the meticulous gathering up of the scattered sparks of the Godhead that had become lost in the wilderness of space and time when the Vessels of Creation were shattered. How many of our past lives, our lives in this world and this body, had to be shattered to set us here at the Center at last, at the point of Remembering?

But before we reached that point (if we ever did), *why couldn't we remember?* Maybe it's because we couldn't see where we were even when we were right there, and this because we basically had no *respect*, a word that literally means "to look again." It is the habit of the human race to gawk at our experience like somnolent television viewers; we don't respect our own lives enough to stand apart from them and grant them their own space so we can savor them and come to terms with them. This is because we *identify* with our experience, identify with ourselves. As opposed to this "natural" way of moving through life, the Sufi Path teaches its travelers to *dis-identify* with their past, with their present circumstances, with themselves, with everything—to dis-identify by a process of *remembering*—of remembering that God is the Only Being, and that we, along with the trees and the animals and the fish and the rocks and the stars, are nothing but the million mirrors He has created to reflect His Face. What God most wants from us is this very Remembering; all His moral and ritual demands exist only to support a great act of recollection—though if we turn them into idols through identification, which we so often do (seeing that the greatest enemy of religion is *religiosity*) they will only make us forget. Like Jack Kerouac said in his prayer of thanksgiving on the publication of his first book, *The Town and the City*: "God is the only critic who cares little for style."

MAGDA

Lew's common-law wife Magda (Maria Magdalena Cregg, née Barcinsky)—I could never think of her as a girlfriend or fiancée—was in every way an equal partner to him, and an integral part of my few years with him. She was a sturdy, blonde, big-boned, middle-aged Polish woman, a sculptor and filmmaker, who took to the Bay Area hippie counterculture like a spaniel to water. She had been the daughter of the owner of a textile factory in Poland when World War Two broke out, and tells the story of her escape with her family from the Nazis in their Fiat, with the family furs and jewels in the trunk. After they ran out of petrol they hired peasants to haul them from village to village with teams of horses, picking up a new team at each stop. She told of how she fell in love with the American English language as soon as she heard it on the radio, before she understood a word of it. After immigrating to the U.S. and marrying Hugh Anthony Cregg Jr., an Irish-American physician from Boston—a marriage that produced Hugh Anthony Cregg III, otherwise known as the rock musician Huey Lewis—she ended up, after a divorce, with Lew (Lewis Barrett) Welch, one of the top virtuosos of the American English she loved; Lew became

Huey Lewis's stepfather and was likely the inspiration for his stage name. I met Huey on a couple of occasions but didn't really know him; I was better acquainted with his younger brother Jeff who was more part of Lew and Magda's family during the time I knew them.

Magda, like Lew, loved to play with language. He writes of the time he was in bed with her when she woke up suddenly with a revelation: "The Far East is *west* of us, nearer by far than the Near East, and *mysteriouser*. Is the Middle East really the Middle West? And there aren't seven continents, there are six; Europe and Asia are stuck together in the middle." This became the poem "GEOGRAPHY" in his book *Courses*, a tiny pamphlet only slightly larger than a checkbook, the numbered edition bound in reindeer hide, which was conceived of as a concentrated epitome, in around 400 words, of all you can *really* learn in college.

After Lew's suicide, Magda became a kind of white witch (or maybe a little off-white actually) for the hippies of Bolinas, California, where she lived on the Bolinas Mesa in a green school bus that no longer drove, before Huey made it big with his band, Huey Lewis and the News, and bought her a house. Earlier she had spent a couple of years traveling the world in search of exotic psychedelics, plus pot seeds for new and more powerful strains of marijuana. She brought back Ibogaine from Africa and apparently contacted the same Amazon rainforest shaman that Allen Ginsberg and William Burroughs had discovered earlier, as recounted in their book *The Yage Letters*, making her one of the first people to introduce Ayahuasca (a DMT-based brew similar to Yage) into the U.S. counterculture, a drug that was nowhere near as common in the hippie pharmacopeia of the 60s and early 70s as it is today. And her horticultural experiments with weed resulted in the strain known as Purple Gate Purple, which (unless I'm mistaken) became an important contribution, a few years later, to a number of large-scale marijuana-growing operations in the coastal mountains of northern California. When Huey's song "I Need a New Drug" came out, we said to ourselves: "If what Magda brought back from her travels didn't do it for him, he's out of luck."

Of the writing Magda did after Lew's death, mostly unpublished, I always remember and quote one line: "Too much is not enough," which can be seen as a criticism of the hippie/Kerouacian "wow to everything" attitude, as well as of William Blake's proverb "The road of Excess leads to the palace of Wisdom." Maybe when the hippies said "too much!" they really meant it, though on an unconscious level; total openness to everything usually leads later on to a shutdown due to excess sensitivity and paranoia, resulting in a condition where an entirely different proverb applies — the "hell is other people" of Jean-Paul Sartre.

And I'll always remember one story she told from her childhood in Poland. Her family and the other folk in her area used to collect wild mushrooms, just as I and my family did in California, and when they had finished for the day they would take what they'd found, for inspection, to an old woman who knew mushrooms, so she could weed out any poisonous ones; after she had given a pass to the day's take, they felt confident they could eat them with no ill effects. Magda, however, suspected that the old woman had her own uses for the poisonous mushrooms she took possession of, uses that might explain the sudden deaths of this or that local thug or oppressive landlord from some mysterious disease. And she also explained the origin of the *witch's cauldron* by the fact that food can be preserved by two agents, heat and cold—so in a place and time without refrigeration, a big portion of the village food supply was often preserved in a gigantic, perpetually-simmering pot hung over a fire—a fire that was tended, and the pot stirred (understandably) by one or more old women. Since the fire had to be kept going without interruption, perhaps for months or years (or even centuries?)—this being the origin of the idea of an "eternal flame"—the pot might contain tiny remnants of the various foods eaten by the village stretching back for generations: meats, roots, grains, pot-herbs, mushrooms—thereby making it a real support for village unity and cultural continuity. I intuitively expanded on this motif by imagining that these old women would also take in young village girls as apprentices for a stated period, teaching them cooking skills and other elements of domestic economy, and once in a while one of these girls would stay on, renouncing marriage for the life of the "maiden aunt," to learn the deeper elements of the craft: the role played by Vesta, Hestia and similar goddesses. I saw in my mind's eye that this element of peasant culture and economy was the ultimate origin of various later colleges of priestesses or proto-nuns, like the Vestal Virgins of Italy or the convent of St Bridget in Ireland, both of which tended eternal flames just as the village crones had always done, those old women being the first and original "Mother Superiors." (Magda had plenty of lore like that stored away in the marrow of her bones, but hardly anyone to teach it to.)

THE ROGUES' GALLERY

On one occasion Lew had his horoscope drawn by Gavin Arthur—an elder statesman of the hippie movement, one of the organizers of the famous Human Be-In in Golden Gate Park, grandson of American president Chester A. Arthur, sexologist, gay "pioneer" who had apparently once slept with Neal Cassady, occultist who had known Maud Gonne and W. B. Yeats back in the old country, and astrologer to the Beat Generation. Lew related to me that Arthur had told him that the reason he drank was that he had so much fire in his chart—Sun in Leo with (I think) Aries rising—that he was trying to use booze, known to the Irish as *usquebaugh* (whiskey), "the water of life," to put out the fire. And alcohol does indeed present itself as pure spring water to those who are dried out with abstract thought and the ashes of self-will (in alchemical terms, the ones burned to the bone by the power of Volatilizing Sulfur—the fire—that has now switched over to Fixing Sulfur—the ash). We forget, however, that *usquebaugh* is actually *fire*-water, which is why it appears in the opposite mode to cold, shrunken and constricted souls (those oppressed by Coagulating Quicksilver) as the *flame* of life, this two-faced quality being one of the many ways in which "wine is a mocker" [Proverbs 20:1–3].

"Once slept with Neal Cassady." What a claim to fame. Was this Beat/Hippie thing really a salutary influence for a young not-quite-ex-Catholic boy such as myself? Everybody wants to be somebody by getting next to somebody. "I saw Robert Cummings once, sitting right there at the next table in the restaurant when my parents and I were visiting my Aunt Barbara in Beverly Hills." "Really? Robert Cummings? You mean that actor guy who used to play in all those old movies? The one with the sort of breezy attitude?" "The very same." "Robert Cummings! Wow." But after collecting all this baggage, all those things you can't take with you, how are you going to get through the needle's eye? That eye certainly can't be avoided. Like Lao Tzu said, "Knowledge is gained by daily addition; the Way is gained by daily loss, loss upon loss until at last comes rest." The universal and almost-universally-ignored advice is: *Slim down while you still can. Learn to travel light.*

But *everybody* was famous in those days in the hippie world, at least for three or four years. A culture-hero on every block. The Beat writers, especially Kerouac and Ginsberg, turned all their friends into celebrities and "heroes." Was this done in response to media attention, or were they fishing for that attention all along? And now the majority of American teenagers, when asked what they want to be when they grow up, say: "A celebrity." Famous for being famous. No longer do white kids even want to be Neil Armstrong, and Black kids, Michael Jordan, people famous for doing something. Under the regime of social media, the attention of thousands of strangers to a tiny, miniscule slice of who you are, or even a total lie about who you are, is the only thing that *makes you exist*. You are not a creature of God any more, only a momentary construction of the Strangers, the Aliens. And when you crave absolution you no longer confess your sins to God, but to the faceless masses, who are now (thanks to Facebook) no longer faceless. They are your Friends! People with whom you can "open up"! Did the Beats really start this massive slide toward narcissistic illusion? Which was then massively expanded by the Hippies? It certainly looks like it. As for myself, I'd rather be famous for being unknown—except for a number of rather obvious difficulties inherent in that approach. (NOTE: Anybody who wants to investigate the phenomenon of Celebrity as a replacement for Religion, and Religion as the thing that can redeem us from Celebrity, should view the film *Tender Mercies* starring Robert Duvall.)

Be that as it may, it was through Lew that I met a number of the celebrities of the Beat/Hippie world, poets and otherwise, most of them only briefly, as a kind of tourist on the streets of North Beach or on the mesa at the Pacific coastal town of Bolinas, the elephant graveyard of the Beat Generation. In North Beach, the poet Robert Duncan (for a moment) in his Sherlock Holmes cape, whose "Poem Beginning with a Line from Pindar" is a true masterpiece, and should convince anyone that "Beatnik Poetry" has been seriously misrepresented. Whimsical counterculture novelist and poet Richard Brautigan, just as briefly, in his quasi-ten gallon hat; he looked just like — Richard Brautigan. (His story is tragic. Having been unable to sell his latest novel to any publisher, he committed suicide at his house in Bolinas. His week's-old decaying corpse was finally discovered by a publisher's agent who had been searching for him everywhere, contract in hand.) Also in Bolinas, the sharp, scrawny, one-eyed Robert Creeley, a highly interesting "minimalist" poet who spawned a horde of much less interesting minimalists, whose "spare, sparse" verse, composed of short, chopped-up lines, unsuccessfully hid their common lack of anything really worth saying. His ability to survive a marriage to the beautiful, buxom, big-boned Bobbie Louise Hawkins, "also a poet," showed him to possess a hidden tenacity of spirit not apparent on the surface.

(*Famous, famous — or: forgotten, forgotten*)

Back in North Beach, a nine-second encounter with film director Francis Ford Coppola, as I was walking Columbus Avenue with his ex-brother-in-law, the poet Tony Dingman, part of the Coppola entourage and another student of Lew's. Tony had played the role of a corpse — actually a severed head — in Coppola's film *Apocalypse Now*; he did a great job, but of course the danger of a role like that is that you might become typecast. (See if you can find a copy of his poem "The Nine Muses of Brazil.") Earlier Jenny and I had met Tony in Bolinas when he was house-sitting for none other than Richard Brautigan. And, in his apartment on one of the Seven Hills of San Francisco, courtesy of Lew Welch, I had an evening with the prominent editor Don Allen, a gracious homosexual gentleman of the old school, who had edited Lorca and was known for producing the hugely influential anthology *The New American Poetry* for Evergreen Books, which features most of the poets of that era I've mentioned in this present book, though I was too young to get in myself. (Later I was rejected by its interesting but uncentered successor *The Young American Poets*, an anthology that amply demonstrated how America was pretty much incapable by that time of producing a new literary generation to succeed the Beats, partly because the best writing of my Baby Boom generation went into song lyrics, not books, as witness the oeuvre of the well-known

Nobel Laureate in Literature, Bob Dylan. That rejection was probably one of the best things that ever happened to me, since acceptance would have nailed me to a literary scene where I would've had to "be somebody," without having the power to determine who that "somebody" might be.)

(*Famous and/or slightly famous*)
Who else did Lew introduce me to? The folk singer Terry Cuddy, unknown but "famous" nonetheless, who was sent to San Quentin for the possession of something like one pot seed. When Johnny Cash played there he liked and performed one of Terry's songs ("The Green Hills of Marin" perhaps, with the line "San Quentin Prison/ In the green hills of Marin"?). Again in Bolinas, Lew took me to see Philip Whalen, a wonderful poet whose easy yet luminous wit in no way distracts from the weightiness of his subjects. Lew made the mistake of introducing me to Phil as "the hot young poet who'll put all us old guys to shame," to which Whalen replied: "He looks like Harpo Marx." And, last but not least, Grover Sales (jazz critic, publicist and historian), who said that I sounded like the premier hip/intellectual comedian of the time, Mort Sahl.

Lew also introduced me to Gary Snyder, the third of the Reed College trio of poets (Welch, Whalen and Snyder)—and on one occasion, in the basement of City Lights Bookstore, I met Gregory Corso. "Do you know who I am?" he asked, sheepishly. "Mr Corso!" I said with a bow. He offered me a pull on his half pint of vodka mixed with lime juice—and I took it. (*Initiation!*) I wonder if anyone realizes that Corso's major influence on American culture might have been his line from the poem "Clown," from *The Happy Birthday of Death* [1960]: "Time to return from star trek/ And scrub the earth." Never once did he think of suing Gene Roddenberry or his estate or the *Star Trek* franchise to put a permanent roof over his head...

Later on I had the chance to listen to Ed Dorn read from his well-respected poem-cycle *Gunslinger*, and had the privilege of hearing British poet Basil Bunting recite the entirety of his admirable epic poem *Briggflats*. I met the unique Black poet Bob Kaufman with Ferlinghetti and some of the guys in a North Beach café, smiling but saying nothing—Kaufman who, as a speed freak, had changed his name to Radio (cf. Jack Spicer's poem "Sporting Life") and who took a vow of silence after the JFK assassination. Jenny and I once had Thanksgiving-dinner-for-those-without-a-family with Kaufman's son Parker (named after Charlie Parker) at a house owned by some of the extended Grateful Dead "Family," on the invitation of Miriam Borkowsky, whose own story is worth telling:

Miriam was a perpetually near-homeless poetess with three children in tow; they often lived in their car. The university that housed her archive (University of Pennsylvania? I don't remember) once let her sleep the night, homeless, somewhere on campus, because it was the least (*absolutely* the least) they could do. Once when we were driving her and her children through the dairy ranches of the Marin County countryside, Miriam launched into a panegyric on the glories of agriculture, to which her 13-year-old daughter Eugenia responded, "Stupid *cows!*" Miriam then moved on to the elevating influence of the intellectual life. "Intelligence is *stupid!*" Eugenia retorted — then chuckled to herself when she got the joke... instead of ideals and values, apparently all she wanted was a real life. Years earlier Miriam had been diagnosed with cancer, which she kept at bay through severe fasts — though she spent a night on the floor of our home in San Rafael when that strategy had apparently stopped working for her...

On one occasion I also met the truly great poet Kenneth Rexroth, author of some of the finest and purest heterosexual love poems in the English language, in an Eastern Orthodox Church (Holy Trinity Cathedral on Van Ness Avenue) at the wedding of my high school friend and publisher John McBride (of Red Hill Press) to Rexroth's daughter Mariana, an ex-porn queen who had gotten religion, and who had arrived at Orthodoxy partly due to her studies under the great universal scholar of world religion and mythology, Mircea Eliade.

Rexroth, a committed Communist at one point, had left the Party (as so many did) due to the tyranny of Stalin that few knew about or would admit was real at the time, either that or the Nazi/Soviet non-aggression pact that nobody could ignore; along with Ezra Pound and Arthur Whaley he pioneered the introduction of the great traditions of classical Chinese and Japanese poetry to Western audiences with his wonderful translations. On the other side of the street, I met George Oppen at Frank Dietrich's house in Marin's Lucas Valley, another Communist and fine modernist poet, a member of the influential Objectivist School along with Louis Zukovsky, Charles Reznikov, Carl Rakosi, Basil Bunting and William Carlos Williams. Oppen renounced poetry for many years to work as a labor organizer, but he never renounced Stalin, at least while the dictator was alive. Of my poem *Panic Grass* he said, with a faint yet distinct irony: "We all thought it was very *poetic.*"

And then there was Jack Hirschman — poet, Kabbalist and "stage Communist" — whom I first met with John McBride at his friend Paul Vangelisti's house in L.A. before Hirschman moved to Frisco to become (at one point) the city's poet laureate. (Later I met him again at McBride's house in Berkeley, where John treated him, for some reason, as a kind of side-show exhibit, like a trained seal.)

McBride's poetry soirées were fascinating. At one of these gatherings we were treated to a performance by the Italian poet and "wag," Adriano Spatola. At another I watched as the participants first retired to various corners and doorways to practice their lines before coming out and launching into the opening gambits of Fascinating Intellectual Conversation, apropos of nothing in particular and based on such offerings as (after a couple of deep breaths): "Did you know that Paracelsus' real name was Theophrastus Bombastus von Hohenheim and that that's where our adjective 'bombastic' comes from??"

And on another occasion, also at Vangelisti's house, I was introduced to Charles Bukowski before he became the recognized Doyen of American Lowlife—a well-deserved title. At one point he handed his car keys to Vangelisti so he could pick up some booze, saying to him: "Be careful with my car, Paul—it's my soul." Later I saw him again at a poetry reading in San Francisco. At somebody's apartment after the reading, at a "meet and lionize the Poet" party, there stood Bukowski in the middle of the floor, silent, hunched over, beer in hand, stoically enduring his allotted notoriety, surrounded by several concentric circles of lionizers, all of them watching him like wolves, hardly speaking—waiting (I suppose) for the Divine Spark, or else the Concentrated Spirit of Lowlife, to leap from the Poet to his hungry, circling devotees. Sadly, no Spark leapt. Consequently, as soon as Bukowski left the room, the gathering launched into a rambling discourse to the effect that "Bukowski's washed up, man. Of course he was always overrated. What's he written in the past 6 months?" Soon after that I left the party myself and went down to the street, and there I saw him leaning wearily over the hood of his car, beer still in hand. "They're all up there putting you down, Mr Bukowski" I told him. "They say you've shot your wad, that you're finished as a poet." "Thank you," he replied. (Charles Bukowski was not an official member of the Beat Generation, but man was he *beat*.)

If people are attracted to you because you're "famous," sometimes they will try either to prostrate themselves to you, to beat you down so they can rise to prominence by stepping on your prostrate body, or else to just accidentally brush up against you, hoping some of the fame will rub off. It never does, however, and this is very disappointing to them, if not actually insulting. I wonder if this is where the practice of "sacrificing the god" in Pagan antiquity actually comes from, so exhaustively researched by Sir James Frazer? If so, maybe that's why I characterized poetry at one point, paraphrasing William James, as "the moral equivalent of human sacrifice"....

(But think of it, man—I could've been Mort Sahl! Harpo Marx! This young mechanic could've been a panic! *I could've been a contender!* Can anybody see where I went wrong? Was it only shyness and lack of ambition? Is shyness really what is now called "social anxiety disorder," a recognizable pathological condition, treatable or otherwise? Or is it actually the still, small voice of the Monk Within?)

Then (actually a lot earlier) came Lawrence Ferlinghetti, famous for real.

Through contacts provided by Lew I was able to publish two books of poetry at the age of 19: *Time Raid* (my juvenilia) through Don Allen's

Four Seasons Foundation, and the short epic *Panic Grass* in the City Lights Pocket Poets Series, my poem about the End of America. I purposely chose White on Black for the colors of the cover to reverse the Black on White of Allen Ginsberg's books—*Howl*, *Kaddish*, etc.—because Ginsberg was a Gemini and I was a Sagittarius, placed directly opposite him on the wheel of the zodiac. Like William Blake once engraved on the plates of *The Marriage of Heaven and Hell*, "Opposition is true friendship"—except that, later on, he erased it... I read the whole poem out loud—and I do mean loud—at a poetry reading at Glide Memorial Church on Ellis St, a gig Lew set up for me. That event is described as follows on the back cover of the book:

> Charles Upton read this poem at the San Francisco Rolling Renaissance poetry readings in the Sanctuary of Glide Memorial Church, Summer 1968. The Sanctuary shook.

After the reading, Lawrence Ferlinghetti came up to the podium and said, "Kid, I want to publish that poem." (Interestingly enough, a great grandfather of mine had been the pastor of the Methodist congregation that later moved to Glide Memorial. There were a lot of ministers in earlier generations of my mother's side of the family, the Strothers—plus journalists on both sides—so maybe that pulpit was in my blood.) In any case the upshot was, in the words of Lew Welch:

> More people know you
> Than you know.
>
> Fame.

So at 19 I was, or could have been, "the youngest member of the Beat Generation"—a completely inaccurate title—with absolutely nothing more to say. Consequently I withdrew. I hid out. I never did a public reading of *Panic Grass* again after it was published. My poetry fell apart, became corny or sentimental or eerily thin. I had no idea of who I was or what I was supposed to do with my life. For quite a few years, all I got out of *Panic Grass* was the knowledge that *at least I had done that*, even if the rest of my life was that of a socially and economically retarded nobody, virtually an unborn child.

I believe that the desire for fame almost always has something to do with the denial of shame—which is why those who seek fame and find it so often come to a shameful end. As the hippie/devotee girls used to chant (as if skipping rope) in the ashrams of their gurus:

> *One* to *me* are *fame* and *shame*
> *One* to *me* are *loss* and *gain*...

I hope they really meant it—because if fame and shame are not one to us in *apatheia*, through spiritual detachment, they will end up as one to us through being inseparable from one another, like two dead bodies buried in the same grave. Today that chant might be updated as "One to me are Likes and Unfriendings on Facebook"—especially since it is apparently now possible to *buy thousands of fake Facebook "likes"* from the online self-image brokers! Not only does fame continue to be a kind of phony friendship, but the contemporary world has finally conceived of such a thing as *fake fame*—something not worth a whore's compliment or a tinker's damn. Like the hookah-smoking caterpillar on the mushroom said to the proto-hippie seeker-girl, Alice, in *Alice in Wonderland*:

"WHO are *you*?"

(Sri Ramana Maharshi asked the same question, but definitely not with the same import or intent.)

GINSBERG

The main rogue in that Rogues' Gallery was, of course, Allen Ginsberg, who was the boss chicken of many pecking-orders, at the top of many heaps. He was the recognized leader of the Beat Generation poets. He was an early experimenter with psychedelics who wrote poems under the influence of peyote (an important catalyst for his *Howl*), mescaline, lysergic acid, nitrous oxide, ether (his poem "Aether" is an amazing tour-de-force), LSD (resulting in his beautiful poem "Wales Visitation"), etc. etc. He was a recognized guru—or at least a PR guru—for the Hare Krishna movement; for Shaivite Hinduism (largely through his *Indian Journals*); and for Tibetan Buddhism by his connection with the Tibetan Vajrayana teacher Chögyam Trungpa. He was a peace activist and a major leader, along with Jerry Rubin and others, of what might be termed the "anti-war riots" (which I attended) at or around the Democratic Convention in Chicago in 1968, and of the later Anti-Nuclear Movement. He was a serious investigator of the subversive activities of the CIA; his research in this area is now housed in his archive at Stanford University. And he was also a pioneer of the darker side of the Gay Liberation movement through his role as founding member of NAMBLA, the North American Man-Boy Love Association, an advocacy group for the legalization of pedophilia—a development that would be, beyond a shadow of a doubt, a major step in the direction of the worst evil the human race is capable of. Once lust is confused with love, once the belief becomes entrenched that all sex is good no matter what, virtually any delusion seems justifiable, no matter how terrible and obvious the consequences may be. Nonetheless he personally supported several Beat poets who had been less successful than he was in handling the alcoholic and druggy lifestyle that he had celebrated, or at least reported on with relish, as part of the developing hip ethos that he was one of the main spokesmen for. Last and possibly least, along with Neal Cassady, he was part of a diplomatic delegation representing the counterculture who met with the Hell's Angels in 1965 at Ken Kesey's house in the woods at LaHonda, California, at a "summit," fueled by LSD and rock music, that was designed to make peace between the Angels and the Hippies—an event conceived of by none other than the Kentucky-born originator of "gonzo journalism," Hunter S. Thompson. Quite a resumé! I seriously wonder how many of my later life-developments and projects, both healthy and unhealthy (and excluding the gay thing), were actually due to the influence of Allen Ginsberg. Like Dante Alighieri, Lord Byron, Percy Bysshe Shelley, W. B. Yeats, Ezra Pound, many of the revolutionary poets of Latin America, Walt Whitman, and to a degree William Blake, he definitely conceived of the poet as having an important leadership role in society—and Ginsberg was in fact widely acknowledged (in Shelley's phrase) as one of "the unacknowledged legislators of the world."

I first saw Allen Ginsberg at the famous Human Be-In in 1967, at the polo fields in Golden Gate Park. He was there on the stage along with Timothy Leary, Lew Welch, Gary Snyder, Lenore Kandel, Jazz musician Dizzy Gillespie with his famous up-angled trumpet, and the extraordinary poet Michael McClure. McClure was known among other things for his televised video of himself reciting poetry to the lions at San Francisco's Fleishhaker Zoo, as well as for his parody of T. S. Eliot's *The Wasteland*. Where Eliot's poem begins "April is the cruelest month," McClure's more leonine version reads, "GRAHHR, April!" The poem he recited on that occasion consisted of the simple, bare repetition of one line: *"And it is all perfect, this is really it."* And it *was* perfect for that occasion, striking the precisely appropriate keynote for the Now Generation, both quintessentially eternal and totally ephemeral ... but I guess you had to have been there to appreciate it. Ginsberg, playing his finger-cymbals, led the crowd in the Hare Krishna chant, while Leary gave his famous "Turn On, Tune In and Drop Out" speech: "Turn on! Embrace the psychedelic experience! Drop out of your jobs! Drop out of your high schools! Drop out of your universities!"—to which the San Francisco hippie crowd, already stoned out of their gourds with no help from Leary, responded with fair-minded and humorous condescension: "good for you, Tim!" That choir had already been preached to a long time ago. (A little bit later, in the light of subsequent developments, Lew amended Leary's rabble-rousing motto to read: "Turn Out, Cop Out, and Drive On.") Writing this, I begin to realize just how true it is to say that the leaders of the 60s counterculture, or at least a good number of them, were the poets—a hard thing to wrap your head around now that the poetic art (outside of music) has been whittled down to a precious few precious aesthetes, or word-bound "textualists," or self-advertising hip-hop rappers and poetry slammers, living in their own incestuous art ghettoes, talking only to themselves and listening to hardly a word.

The one other memory I have of that day was of the grim Hell's Angel standing spread-eagled, arms folded, on top of the trailer housing the electric generator, "guarding" it. He was cool for that day because it was a cool day, early in the psychedelic explosion, when the hurtling fragments of it were still unfolding in relatively slow motion. Later on, at Altamont, things would get a little more serious.

As for the Angels, who were nothing less than a criminal gang and who, according to Mike Bettis, a homeless Angel I worked with later when I was one-half of a tiny homeless service agency in San Rafael, were sometimes into Satanism. Like the Italian Cosa Nostra, they achieved a certain degree of social acceptance through style alone, which literally allowed them to get away with murder. The 60s counterculture, too, was in many ways an apotheosis of style. It was as if the Hollywood glamour-pot had finally cracked and boiled over (partly due to the influence of LSD), redistributing the available glamour from the elites to the masses, after which "traditional" glamour itself began to go out of style, like an inflated currency that no longer retains its old buying-power. Compare an actor like Clark Gable from the golden age of Hollywood to a typical actor of today—Johnny Depp for example. Gable, with his wide, glamourous Hollywood smile, glowed expansively for the cameras—while Depp, with his vulnerable, haunted expression, looks like he's not facing a camera so much as a loaded gun.

After that I saw Ginsberg—or at least he saw me—at the Rolling Renaissance event at Glide where I read *Panic Grass*. And later at the Big Sur Folk Festival at Esalen I had the privilege of being briefly groped by him. I didn't slug him, nor run away in shame and fear, nor was I at all attracted to him; I just took the whole thing in good part, as part of the enveloping Thing I was now a part of. It had nothing to do with sex—at least for me—only with Celebrity. That it represented galloping corruption for both Ginsberg and myself, though possibly we were being affected by different brands of that corruption, was completely hidden from me by the glamour of the collective drama we were immersed in.

Because Allen Ginsberg was *our guy*. He was the symbol—at least to anybody in the counterculture with any literary pretensions or interests at all—of the New Thing that was happening all around us, and inside us, whether we thought of that Thing as spiritual, literary or political. My friends from my adolescent peer group, the Trumbly-Clan-Plus-Doyle (heterosexual suburbanites to a man), called him by the affectionate nickname "Ginzy." On one occasion I secured an interview with him for me and my friends at Ferlinghetti's place. Sitting on the floor yet clearly sitting "in state," he literally looked bigger than life, expanded, inflated; he had the divine *afflatus*. I wanted to talk with him about some hare-brained idea I had related to the possibility of totally controlling one's own consciousness through self-hypnosis. "Have you actually tried any of this?"

he asked. "Did any of it work?"—legitimate questions that showed he had a greater practical grasp of reality at that point than I did. And I read him the poem I'd written about my powerful experiences after ingesting morning glory seeds (more about that later); to the line, "I saw their aspect, and I marveled at it," he replied "Marvelous aspect!"—which was pretty good poetic advice ("always seek concision"), only for a different poem and a different intent.

In later years he and I developed a kind of low intensity rivalry or general irritation with one another. In a letter that made up part of part of our epistolary debate around Chögyam Trungpa—you'll hear about that later when we come to The Great Naropa Poetry Wars—he accused me of writing "manic gibberish." "It would be more accurate to call it *intellectual* manic gibberish" I replied, "admittedly a difficult genre." (I'll never forget the story that Neeli Cherkovski, North Beach poet and biographer of several of the poets of the Beat Generation, told me about Ginsberg as the Buddhist Contemplative, his meditation session beginning with "Please don't disturb me, I'll be in deep meditation for the next hour" and ending with him leaving his cell every 5 minutes to bum a cigarette, ask "was that phone call for me?," make himself a cup of coffee, etc. etc.) And on another occasion, when he and Bhagavan Das, the Hindufied American spiritual musician that Ram Dass (Richard Alpert) had discovered in India—and who was one of the most conceited individuals it has ever been my misfortune to encounter—were performing at the College of Marin, Ginsberg told me that "we're doing this whole thing just to bring you down." Maybe the problem was that, as Sister Mary Norbert Körte had observed on one occasion, I was simply not a Beat Poet—a Neo-Blakean Visionary maybe or a Romantic Symbolist like Rilke, but not a Beat. In any case I had not shown any interest in doing what it took to become fully initiated into the Beat world, which would probably have included sleeping with Ginsberg. And in subsequent years Ferlinghetti and his colleagues began to lose interest in me as a poet and a potential Baby Beat, such as the poet "Antler," Brad Burdick, apparently later became; clearly I did not have "the scent of the pack."

Once, while the famous Naropa Poetry Wars were still raging, based on the pro vs. con reactions to the Tibetan Buddhist teacher Chögyam Trungpa (see *Chapter Seven*), I met Allen on Columbus Avenue; he was wearing a white suit. "So what's your problem with Trungpa?" he quickly asked, not really waiting for an answer—nor did I have one ready at that moment, in 25 words or less. The main thing he seemed to want to impress on me was that Trungpa had commanded all his male followers to wear white suits, which, he assured me, were easily and cheaply available from the Salvation Army. Maybe he thought that if I properly suited up, my objections would vanish...

The last time I saw Allen Ginsberg was at the Savoy Tivoli reading in 1979, when my wife and I were invited to read from our works alongside him, Lawrence Ferlinghetti and some other well-known poets—and when he died in 1997 I decided not to go to his memorial service in the City. I had no feeling of animus against him, I just didn't feel that I belonged there... and I was probably right.

It was different when Philip Whalen died in 2002, two years before Jenny and I left California for Kentucky. On that occasion I felt obligated to attend his memorial, conducted by Dick Baker Roshi at the Green Gulch Zen Center, due to Phil's relationship with Lew and the fact that Lew had introduced us. (In his later years Whalen had become an ordained Zen roshi at the San Francisco Zen Center, the sister-monastery to Green Gulch; I visited with him there on one occasion.) He was like a distant relative whose funeral was nonetheless worth wearing a suit and tie for because you felt you really should attend—though no suits and ties were in evidence on that occasion. We chanted some Buddhist sutras in Japanese and Dick Baker did an *ad hoc Tibetan Book of the Dead*-like thing where he tried to help Phil's consciousness-principle negotiate the after-death *bardo* by imagining him—since he had been an airplane mechanic in the Second World War—as walking through the spinning blades of a propeller and getting shredded to perfect annihilation in Nirvana. On that occasion I exchanged some words with Michael McClure and had a longer talk with Gary Snyder, who made a point of declaring to me: "Face it, Charles—Buddhism is *atheism*." Clearly, at that point, materialistic American Buddhism, coupled with environmentalist nature-worship—both of which Gary was heavily invested in—were becoming the new orthodoxy in the remnants of the counterculture world, an orthodoxy that obviously frowned upon the "straight" belief in God. That exchange resulted in "Is Buddhism Really Atheism? A Letter to Gary Snyder," which appears in my book *Knowings, in the Arts of Metaphysics, Cosmology and the Spiritual Path*.

In any case, as had become clear to me by that time, Sister Mary had been right all along: I was not really a Beat Poet, consequently I didn't have to totally identify with that world, or with the greater counterculture it was embedded in. At the end of the day, though it did temporarily open the door to higher consciousness and higher worlds, that counterculture was largely a realm of self-dramatization that ended in nothing but cheap fame, or oppressive obscurity, or degradation, or suicide! How bone-tired I had become of lowlife dressed-up with perpetually insufficient doses of glamour, magic and near-celebrity. Thank God that we are more than our biographies, more than our "lives"! What the world thinks you are plus who you think you are is nothing compared to what Reality *knows* you are. When you need self-knowledge, and to go beyond self-knowledge, why turn to any lesser Source?

THE ART OF POETIC RECITATION ACCORDING TO THE THEORY AND PRACTICE OF LEWIS BARRETT WELCH

I was tutored by Lew, briefly but intensively, in the art of reciting poetry, according to his doctrine that *Language is Speech*. In terms of recitation, this largely translates as "Straight Talk," thus (ideally) avoiding both emotive theatricality and "clinical" neutrality in the oral presentation of poetry. Lew's theory as to how poetry should be recited was based on his studied reproduction of prevailing American speech patterns, particularly when they arise from situations where the speech in question has some real work to do. That this was not simply a form of "method acting," a reliance upon one's uncultivated, pre-artistic emotional subjectivity, but rather a true art, or artifice, is indicated by the following lines from his poem "FOR JOSEPH KEPECS":

> The poem is not the heart's cry
> (Though it seems to be if you have craft enough)
> The poem is made to carry the heart's cry

As for the sound of speech with real work to do, Lew tells the story of the day he took a group tour through a California winery. As he strolled from point to point with the others, listening to the sleepy drone of the tour guide reciting a spiel he'd performed a thousand times before, suddenly the man's voice changed: "*Who's kid is that!?*" In this necessary, immediate and appropriate response to the situation at hand—an out-of-control child about to fall into a vat of wine—Lew heard the clear contrast between dead speech and living speech: heard it so clearly and permanently that it became, for him, a principle and a paradigm.

Lew's "tutorials" for Language-is-Speech are found mostly in his "Passenger Poems," as well as in "DIN POEM" and elsewhere. In "DIN POEM" an example of Straight Talk, also known as "everyday utilitarian speech in interpersonal situations," appears as follows:

> NEVER. NEVER PUT THE GOD-DAMN CAMERA IN THE GLOVE COMPARTMENT. I TOLD YOU AND TOLD YOU TO NEVER PUT THE GOD-DAMN CAMERA IN THE GLOVE COMPARTMENT. SO WHAT DO YOU DO? YOU PUT THE GOD-DAMN CAMERA IN THE GLOVE COMPARTMENT. AND ITS'S STOLEN! SEE?

If you can read this overheard or "found poem" out loud—presumably a husband's admonishment to a careless wife—and make it sound as it really would sound or actually did sound, then (as Lew would maintain), you can correctly recite poetry that is composed in American English.

One set of poems Lew tested me on to determine the level of my ability to recite were his "Passenger Poems," found poems from the period when he was a cab driver, based on samples of overheard American speech from some of the fares in the back of his cab. Here's one from a nurse, presumably a middle-aged woman disappointed with life, who now feels free to issue her complaint—half to herself, half before a cabbie-as-witness (someone she knows she will likely never meet again) in the anonymous intimacy of a taxi cab:

> I don't like cats kittens are alright I guess
> you can love 'em when they're little, like people,
> but then they grow up and take advantage of you
> and how can you love 'em any more?

The voice begins hurried and matter-of-fact, quickly lapsing into a self-pity that still falls shy of full disclosure, though its import is obvious enough—a self-pity likely fueled by alcohol, thus the cab. Once again, anyone who can recite these lines more-or-less as originally spoken, based on either an unconscious memory or a clear and conscious memory of how one or more Americans have expressed themselves in similar circumstances, can correctly recite American verse. (This, and the rest of Lew's tutorials, can and should be studied by all American poets who seriously want to learn their craft.)

And when it comes to Straight Talk in English-Language Poetry, the two consummate masters are John Donne and Frank Sinatra. Donne was not so much composing or reciting "poetry" as he was *talking*, the cragginess of his speech compensating for the tendency toward over-musicality of the (originally) Italian sonnet, and similar forms. Thus the correct way to recite him is to just go straight ahead, saying what he meant to say, and any concessions to the unreasonable demands of rhyme and meter be damned. Likewise Sinatra "talks" his songs rather than crooning them like Perry Como, which is one of the things that made him the greatest of the Italian-American pop singers. Plenty of great blues singers and jazz singers also know that art. When Lew first heard Jim Morrison sing, he compared him to Sinatra.

Just because Poetry is Speech, however, poetic recitation need not be didactic or conversational in tone. Speech that is both passionate and accurate can be, in fact must be, truly *sung*. I will never forget the night when Lew Welch "sang" me the Yeats poem "Byzantium." He truly rendered it as High Poetry, with consummate elocution, yet he never inadvertently wandered outside the walls of what is actually possible for standard American speech when functioning at white heat. Tight, slow, resonant, sonorous, incantory, deliberate—better than the interesting but nonetheless easily-bested magical sing-song of Dylan Thomas—he imprinted that poem indelibly on my memory: *stamped* me with it. One would "naturally" think, of course, that the high bardic declamation of Yeats in his "Byzantium," perhaps the most musically and symbolically dense and substantial of all his poems, could never be read in the same voice as "NEVER PUT THE

GODDAMN CAMERA IN THE GLOVE COMPARTMENT." One, however, would be wrong.

In his book *How I Work as a Poet*, Lew says: "My job [includes] learning how to become the kind of man who has something of worth to say." Only if you have something that you really think is worthwhile saying, not just some language-contraption you've strung together with bits of twine and paper-clips, will you have a chance to recite it *as if* you really meant it. This, however, will not absolve you of the need to learn the *art* of reciting it as if you really meant it. As with depth of character, so with poetic expression: you will need both the native capacity for it and the correct and appropriate cultivation of that capacity so it won't go to waste. Thus we can confidently assert, in Aristotelian terms, that the right recitation of poetry requires two things, the Matter and the Form: some thing that is really worth saying and the craft necessary to say it *as if* you really meant it, an art which still has to be learned and perfected — even if, in all sincerity, you already really do mean it.

Neither sincerity nor style, when taken alone, are enough. Without sincerity, style will fail; without style, sincerity will not "come across." A man chatting up a woman will fail if he has only the Form, meaning an accomplished style of approach ("That's a great line," says the Muse, "how many other women have you tried that one out on?"), or only the Matter, meaning real attraction and/or affection, since the woman knows that if the man does not have the courage to say what he really means with clarity and beauty, he will likely prove inadequate in other ways.

And so, yes, there is a third element necessary for the correct recitation of poetry: courage. The poet reciting either his or her own works or those of another will fail miserably if he or she is not really willing to put him- or herself emotionally on the line; this is part of what Ezra Pound meant when he said that "more poets fail through lack of character than through lack of talent." In the recitation of poetry, emotive theatricality and clinical neutrality, fake emotion vs. suppressed emotion, are two opposing ways of avoiding the moment of confrontation with *sincere* emotion, otherwise known as the Moment of Truth.

The full danger and rigor of this confrontation is classically expressed by Federico García Lorca in his superb essay "The *Duende*: Theory and Divertissement." Dietrich Bonhoeffer wrote a book about the Christian resistance to Hitler called *The Cost of Discipleship*; Lorca's essay on the *Duende* might well have been titled "The Cost of Poetry." Lew remarked on how many modern poets have died young of alcoholism, suicide, drug addiction; he himself ended his life at 44 as an alcoholic suicide. According to Lorca, the *Duende* is the dark, chthonic power behind all true poetry, true song, true flamenco or true bullfighting; he tells us that "the *Duende* will not approach at all if he does not see the possibility of violent death." When I read this definition to a Sufi of my acquaintance, Prof. Leonard Lewisohn, he said: "The *Duende* is the Majesty of God." (A perfect expression of the quality of the *Duende* can be found in the poem by Ibn al-Qabturnuh quoted in *Chapter Two* above.)

Dealing with the *Duende*, with emotional sincerity, requires the virtue of emotional asceticism, an ability to "hold one's feeling" that is akin to the capacity to hold one's liquor. This art is becoming increasingly rare in our time, which may be why so many contemporary violinists, for example, can scrape away at an astronomical rate (they call it "virtuosity") but seem unable to render emotional subtlety or sweetness; they likely fear that if they were to attempt this they would collapse, musically speaking, into slobbering emotional drunks—and they are probably right. It was this quality of emotional asceticism, this *continence* in the realm of feeling, that W. B. Yeats attempted to express in his notion (from *A Vision*) of the *antithetical tincture* (aristocratic and passionate), which is opposed to the *primary tincture* (democratic and sentimental):

> Cast a cold eye
> On life, on death:
> Horseman,
> Pass by.

Lew Welch's closest approach to this virtue was his technique, when reciting poetry, of inclining his head so that the tears that flooded his eyes would not blear his vision but drop on the page instead; in other words, he had trained himself to *weep* without *sobbing*, which is not an easy thing to do. I can usually only accomplish this if I am able to cause myself physical pain, as for example by driving a ball-point pen into my thigh while reciting. (Lew's next lesson, which he did not complete, would have been to train himself to *feel* without *drinking*.)

Emotional sincerity has nothing to do with song vs. speech, lyrical musicality vs. dry prosiness, Dylan Thomas' "Do not go gentle into that good night" vs. Robert Frost's "Good fences make good neighbors." It can be found or missed in opera; it can also be found or missed in a condemning judge's stark intonation of *"and may God have mercy on your soul."* The question is, can you stand the sincerity of the feeling—stand *next to* it as a clear detached observer, while simultaneously standing *in* it as the one fully bearing the weight of it? If you can't, then you'd better get off the stage.

In poetry, emotion is the Matter, which can only rise to articulation when the poet or the one reciting the poem has been touched by the Form of a profound truth, on whatever level that truth may manifest; it is also the Energy that fuels both composition and recitation. The Form is that which contains the Energy, allows it to *form itself*, prevents it from being wasted, and lets it be transmitted. As William Blake said in *The Marriage of Heaven and Hell*,

> Energy is the only life and is from the Body
> and Reason is the bound or outward circumference of Energy.

Those poets who can tap the depth and specific quality of the Energy both demanded and invoked by the Matter and the Form, and still keep this Energy within Reason, within the Form not imposed upon it but intrinsic to it — those who can be exquisitely careful, as in a Zen tea ceremony, not to spill a drop of it — can recite poetry as it should be recited. And, because Language is Speech, the poet who can recite well will probably be able to write well too, since his language is not a visual thing to him, as it is nowadays with those who text instead of talking, but fully inhabits his body, moves it, and therefore has the power either to save his life or to take it away, depending upon whether or not he *cheats*.

The timid (yet often violent), Neo-Puritanical, contemporary college-educated reader will, of course, have noted the plethora of gender-specific pronouns in this section, as well as the clear bias toward the masculine ones, toward the poet as "he." I believe this practice can be justified by considering this treatment partly as an historical exhibit, since I received my direct transmission of poetry-lore from Lew Welch in the late 60s and early 70s, and partly as a map of a particular psycho-physical formation. Poetry, to Lew Welch, was profoundly heterosexual, likely more so than to any other poet of his generation (Gary Snyder possibly excepted, with his lines "The Voice/ is a Wife/ to/ him still"), a generation in which few women of any stature rose to prominence — Denise Levertov being by far the finest exception — and which also included many gay male writers. The heterosexual male model of poetry is certainly not the only one, nor is it necessarily the greatest one, as witness Sappho, Emily Dickinson, Walt Whitman and Allen Ginsberg. But it *is* a model, a distinct design, a specific configuration of energy that must operate according to its own laws. Lew understood a man's speech as expressive of his essential masculinity — a masculinity that only exists, however, in a polar relationship with an essentially feminine energy, or force, or presence, without which no poetic expression (on the traditional heterosexual model) is possible: namely, the Muse. And while the power of the Muse essentially envelops, and profoundly moves, and in this sense dominates the male poet, this in no way undermines his expressive and intentional masculinity. On one occasion Lew expressed this truth to me with perfect clarity when he told me (forgive my bluntness), "the Muse doesn't suck you off." She *invokes* the male poet's expressive power, his active intent; she doesn't drain that power or usurp that intent. And it's entirely apt in this context to remember Lew Welch's cogent warning, from "LEO, IN ABSENCE OF FIRE," to the heterosexual Muse-inspired male poet about the occupational hazards of this approach to his art: "Anyone who confuses his mistress with his muse/ is asking for real trouble from both of them."

I believe that the poetic Muse, for Lew Welch, incarnated the power of *listening*, without which speech, no matter how passionate or how accurate, hurls itself ineffectually against a stone wall. As William Blake put it in *The Marriage of Heaven and Hell*, "the Prolific would cease to be Prolific unless the Devourer, as a sea, received the excess of his delights"; this is an expression of the *tantra* of poetic composition and recitation, precisely. On the other hand, according to contemporary gender mythology—which to my mind is profoundly sexist—*speaking* is active and represents authority, or *authorship*, while *listening* is passive and therefore represents a condition of relative oppression. This just goes to show how wrongheaded today's notions of both power and gender can be. A fundamental principle is missing in the idea that listening is a form of oppression—the principle that *listening is judgment*. The Ear of the Muse is rigorous, demanding, and not to be sidestepped, tricked or cheated: if she detects incompetence, insensitivity, vagueness, evasion, lying or any other form of cowardice in the male poet's offering to her, she will *immediately* deny him—by which I mean, deny his living human body—the energy he needs to take the next full breath. Simply stated, if a male poet, operating according to the heterosexual model of poetry, does not make the sacrifices necessary to perfect his art, to both become the kind of man who is worth listening to, and to learn how to say something *as if he really meant it*, then that art will shorten his life. His tryst with the Muse—as dramatized in "The Ballad of Thomas Rymer" (Child 37, C, B & A)—is a contract which must be fulfilled to the letter. And so:

> *A Paraphrase of Yeats' "Under Ben Bulben"*
>
> American poets, learn your job;
> Write whatever irks the mob;
> Stomp these wimps who fear to *mean*,
> Whose sole craft is to make the scene.
> Born yesterday, to the world they go;
> "Born again" they'll never know.
>
> *Cast a slim eye*
>
> *On dusk, on dawn:*
> *Driver, drive on.*

FREEDOM FROM THE WORLD OF WORDS

Beyond the strictly performance-oriented and "crafty" aspects of the poetic art, one of the central goals of Lew's curriculum was to create "freedom from the world of words"—a strange thing, one might think, for a poet to teach; yet that teaching was central to his own particular brand of "perceptual Buddhism," and was perfectly in line with the Buddhist aphorism, "to name something is to kill it." As Lew declared:

> Those who live in the world of words
> Kill us
> Who seek union with what goes on whether I look at it or not.

"Union with what goes on whether I look at it or not" was Lew's way of talking about what it might be like to reach absolute objectivity, remembering Frithjof Schuon's observation that "in order to attain objectivity it is necessary to die a little," and in the understanding that the world of words, our obsession with *naming* things, always veils objectivity by introducing the subjective element. He well understood that one of the main elements in *Sangsara*, the world of illusion-producing-suffering—if not the lynchpin of the whole thing—is the universal human tendency to mistake the names of things for the things themselves, after which we see the things themselves only through the lens of those names, thus his doctrine that "only poets know that words don't mean anything." When words cease—at least as the labels we stick on things, the frames-of-perception created by language—what does the world look like? The answer is: *Energy*. The world-beyond-words is what the Hindus call *Shakti*—another name for the Great Goddess, known to all inspired lyric poets as the Muse. As I've already (hopefully) made clear, but will now state again for emphasis, Energy is the Matter half of the Form-and-Matter pair from Aristotle's famous hylomorphic theory—which, when the two are married, helps beget what he called "substantial form," as when the *matter* of a poem, what the poet wants to say, is perfectly united with the *form* of the poem, the best and only appropriate way of saying it. All Matter, for the poem or for a life, is drawn from the reservoir of universal Energy, the universal potentiality for experience, otherwise known as the Cosmos. But the Form of that poem, of that life—the *soul* of it—comes purely from the Creator through the unseen world. There is no way to predict what form that form will take until it appears; it's all already there in the first moment of creation, but it only fully reveals itself as the poem is composed, or the life lived out.

For Lew—though he wouldn't have said it this way—the idea was to make the world of language part of the Matter, not the Form, to avoid the trap of expecting your words to do your talking for you by realizing that *words* don't mean anything, *you* do. (The question then becomes: do the words, your intent to speak them, and the form that intent takes, come from *you*, your ego, or simply *through* you from beyond you, from inspiration—which ultimately means, from the First Speaker Himself? It could be that Lew Welch's inability to answer this question is what ultimately ended his life.)

Lew worked to turn words into matter rather than form by comparing human language to the virtually-formless din made by a tree-full of sparrows, and gave us exercises designed to help us make this transformation, exercises made up (for example) of all the found poems and samples of American speech he exhibits in his "DIN POEM":

> Hi, man, what's happening? See you people later.
> Hi, man, what's happening? See you people later.
> Hi, man, what's happening? See you people later.

If William Carlos Williams (as I've already pointed out above), the mentor of many of the Beat poets (including Lew), could say "no ideas but in things"—a very Aristotelian poetic—Lew did him one better by maintaining that "words are things, not ideas," thereby leaving no way for Form and Meaning to arrive but from somewhere beyond language entirely.

TWO RIDDLES

As a further step toward producing freedom from the world of words, Lew composed three *riddles*—"THE RIDER RIDDLE," "THE RIDDLE OF BOWING," and "THE RIDDLE OF HANDS"—whose answers are entirely concrete. The solutions to these riddles are *not ideas*; they are nothing that the world of words could conceive of or understand, consequently nobody affected by "the philosopher disease" will be able to solve them. I'm leaving out "THE RIDER RIDDLE" here because it leads somewhere else, toward Shamanism; it's basically a way of finding your spirit helper or totem animal. (I'll get back to this riddle when the time comes to tell to the story of Lew's death and "continuance.") But the other two are more like *koans*. They can't be figured out by thinking about them; the only way to solve them is to let go of all philosophical and symbolic thinking, and make your mind as *concrete* as possible. Lew says about them: "They are Koans for beginners, making no claim for Perfect Enlightenment, but those who solve them will discover a deep spiritual insight." Unlike *koans*, however, they have explicit answers that can be told—but shouldn't; the answers offered should only be confirmed (or not). Both "THE RIDDLE OF BOWING" and "THE RIDDLE OF HANDS" have only one right answer.

As an introduction to these I'll give you the riddle from one of Lew's major poems, "WOBBLY ROCK," along with its correct solution, just to show you what I mean by "concrete"; and to introduce that riddle I need to say (in Lew's words) that Wobbly Rock is "a real rock/ (believe this first)/ resting on actual sand at the surf's edge:/ Muir Beach, California ... Hard common stone/ Size of the largest haystack/ It moves when hit by waves/ Actually shudders." Lew used to sit on that rock to meditate; it has a precisely square little step or cleft on it that makes a perfect meditation seat (half lotus). I've meditated there myself. Imagine how sitting in meditation on a huge boulder that rocks back and forth as the waves strike it—*k*-CHUNK, *k*-CHUNK — could teach, in a completely visceral, non-conceptual way, the Buddhist principles of universal *anitya* — Impermanence — and universal *shunyata* — Emptiness. And, paradoxically, you can only realize the *anitya* part of it, universal motion, if you become perfectly *still* — if, as Lew puts it, you "sit real still and keep your mouth shut."

Here's the riddle:

> *Dychymig Dychymig:* (riddle me a riddle)
>
> Waves and the sea. If you
> take away the sea
>
> Tell me what it is

This riddle brings together two (not unrelated) things that Lew liked to do: play with language, and point to the world beyond language, the *real* world. The solution is: If you take away "the sea" from "Waves and the sea," you get "Waves and," which, to the ear, is also "wave-sand." So the solution is something that anyone who has seen a sandy ocean beach has seen: the pattern of waves, or ripples, left by the ebbing tide in the drying sand. The whole conceptual universe of permanence vs. change, stationary vs. moving, Form vs. Matter is thus reduced to a single concrete visual image, available to anyone who's ever walked on a sandy beach. Subtract the word-play, and this is the precise mind that can solve the following two riddles. (I could add that "THE RIDDLE OF HANDS" and "THE RIDDLE OF BOWING" have to do with *jiriki* and *tariki* — two terms taken from Zen, denoting "self-power" and "other-power" — but this is just a later conceptual gloss; it's not really a hint but only a smoke-screen, a misdirection.) And so:

The Riddle of Bowing

In every culture, in every place and time, there has always been a religion, and in every one of these religions there has always been the gesture of bowing so fully that the forehead strikes the ground.

Why is this?

(There is only one right answer to this riddle)

COMMENTARY BY THE RED MONK

Sooner or later the gesture is necessary no matter which way you go. Suzuki bows with so much confidence we all feel bold.

The Riddle of Hands

In every culture, in every place and time, there has always been a religion, and in every one of these religions there has always been the gesture of hands clasped together, as Christians do to pray, in order to signify something important.

Why is this?

(There is only one right answer to this riddle)

COMMENTARY BY THE RED MONK

The gesture has but one source. Who would think to pick his nose, or cross his eyes at such a moment?

The man who claims to feel power between his hands is lost in forms and ideas. The man who clasps his hands and waits will never see the light.

Lew comments:

> It is no accident that people, everywhere, have always clasped their hands that way, for those purposes. Think about it. Why not any of the millions of other gestures and stances? Why, always, this one?
>
> The Riddle of Bowing is much the easier of the two. Try that first and use the same Mind to try to solve Hands.
>
> But please don't waste my time by telling me that Bowing shows respect for the earth or that you are vulnerable to a great power or you are submitting to something. I haven't got time for that baby-talk.

Lew told me the answer to "Bowing," and I solved "Hands" by myself, my answer later confirmed by Magda after Lew's death. Whoever wants to crack these riddles must conquer the Monkey Mind and get cured of the Philosopher Disease. (Anyone who thinks he or she has solved one or both of them is invited to apply to me, since I am empowered to say "pass" or "fail.")

LEW WELCH AND THE SPIRITUAL PATH

So Lew Welch was not just my only one-on-one poetic mentor but also my first real spiritual teacher and initiator — a strange thing, since he was also an alcoholic suicide, and what thing of value could an alcoholic suicide have to teach anyone? At the very least, I would say, the lesson of "Kid, don't end up like me." Yet there was more to what he had to transmit, much more, than simply the cautionary tale of his doom.

It is clear to me, looking back, that Lew knew he was drawing near to the end of his life — at 44 — and that the Hippie Spiritual Revolution was both the second wind and the last hurrah for him, as it was for many of the Beat Generation. He knew he had something to teach that was of true initiatory import, and that, having no children of his own, he had finally found the "vessel" into which he could pour it.

In a further attempt to "initiate" me beyond his teachings on the poetic art and freedom from the world of words, and while being very silent, yet (in retrospect) very clear, on the fact that he wouldn't be around much longer, Lew introduced me to two people who had everything to do with my future spiritual development: Samuel Lewis ("Sufi Sam"), and Carlos Castaneda. Sufi Sam, a kind of bridge figure between the hippies and the world of real Sufi initiation, foreshadowed my entrance into the path of traditional Muslim *tasawwuf*, while Carlos Castaneda was a lurid omen of my future magic-dabblings, my lifelong oversensitivity to dark psychic forces.

I always say that Sufi Sam was the real "Mr Natural," R. Crumb's guru character from his hippie-themed cartoons that appeared in *Zap Comix* and elsewhere. He was a *faqir* of the Chishti Tariqah, among several others. His biographical note on the website of the Lama Foundation says:

> Murshid Samuel L. Lewis is the first American born Sufi Master. His life stands as proof that real spiritual realization transcends any sectarian barriers — besides being recognized by eight different Sufi Brotherhoods, he was confirmed as a Zen Master, as a Hassidic rabbi by Hassidic rabbis, as a master of Yoga and as a teacher of Christian Scriptures. Murshid Samuel Lewis' gravesite is located at Lama Foundation [near Taos, New Mexico] and is considered a sacred pilgrimage site.

He was founder of the Sufi Ruhaniya International and the Dances of Universal Peace, still known as "Sufi Dancing" among many who continue to believe that Sufism is mainly a school of ecstatic dance like that associated with the Mevlevis, the Whirling Dervishes.

I met him on two occasions, the first of which was set up by Lew when he invited me to his poetry class at U.C. Extension in the City, where Sam was a fellow student. Lew placed me at the podium on some pretext and got me talking, commenting that I had "an almost pathological belief in the reality of ideas." I was conscious that I was in some sense speaking for and to Sam, whatever foolishness I might have been spouting at the time; I was also conscious that Sam was listening.

The second and last time I met him was at the San Francisco Theological Seminary in San Anselmo, a grey stone castle-like building with round towers and conical roofs, prominent on a small hill in the middle of town, where I had done the first public reading of my 1967 epic poem *Panic Grass* in the outside courtyard in front of the library before Ferlinghetti published it. (My friend Doug Trumbly had transformed the square white tower of the library, illuminated after dark by floodlights and visible over a wide area, into one huge strobe light for the occasion with a revolving shade attached to an electric motor.)

Be that as it may, the second and last time I met Sam he was speaking to a small class at SFTS about various subjects, which included (if I remember right) the founding of a peace sanctuary or peace garden in Jerusalem. The one thing I recall him saying was, "You can't tell the United States government anything." A couple of momentary encounters with virtually no personal interaction — yet that was my first in-person introduction to Sufism, which has been my chosen spiritual Path for the past 34 years.

As for Carlos Castaneda, I met him only once, even more briefly. How long does it take for a spark to leap from pole to pole to complete a circuit?—though in this case, I fear, it was a pretty dark circuit.

For those who have never heard of Castaneda, he was a one-time student of anthropology who wrote a series of books about his interactions with the Yaqui Indian *brujo* or sorcerer Don Juan Matus in Mexico, books that were highly influential on the hippie and the later New Age countercultures, and had an important role in moving the magical worldview closer to the center of mainstream U.S. culture. The books began by emphasizing the role of several "plant powers" including peyote, psilocybin mushrooms and Jimson weed, which guaranteed their popularity among the hippies, but soon moved on to a presentation of various magical techniques that did not require the use of psychedelics or "entheogens." The first book in the series was *The Teachings of Don Juan: A Yaqui Way of Knowledge*, published by the University of California Press in 1968.

I somehow skirted the edge of the Castaneda world, as I had done with so many other "realms" I have passed by, or through, in the course of my life. On one occasion I met a girl at a party in Marin County's San Geronimo Valley who claimed to have been a girlfriend of Castaneda's—but of course that might have just been a social passport to make herself more interesting (even though she was already plenty interesting as-is, from my point of view). I also knew the supremely witch-eyed San Francisco poet Erica Horn, who was acquainted with Carlos and claimed that whenever he caught sight of her he would always run. When I was working with the homeless in Marin County as one-half of the tiny social service agency known as Project MOVE (see *Chapter Ten*), one of our clients was poet James Brodie, who claimed to have been Castaneda's drug dealer, though it was clear that Brodie (in line with Plato's view of poets from the *Republic*) was an accomplished bullshitter of the first water. And some years after Castaneda's death I attended a talk at Black Oak Books in Berkeley given by another one of his women, Amy Wallace, daughter of the well-known novelist Irving Wallace and author of the book *Sorcerer's Apprentice*. She regaled us with a string of highly entertaining, sometimes hilarious stories about her experiences with the great man—stories that, when viewed dispassionately, were seen to be truly horrendous (breakdowns, suicides, etc.). It was as if she were whistling past the graveyard, using her witty and humorous takes on the Castaneda world to shield herself from the full import of the horrors she was recounting. One of the things that most puzzled her was the question of why she had never witnessed any events of high strangeness suggestive of "non-ordinary reality" during her years with Castaneda. Her explanation, rather touchingly pathetic, was that, out of his special love for her, he had undoubtedly shielded her from the dangerous world of magic that he so freely indulged in when playing with his other women, his "witches."

Richard De Mille, nephew and adopted son of famous movie producer Cecil B. De Mille, wrote a book in 1976 entitled *Castaneda's Journey*, partly debunking the Don Juan books. He repeats the opinion of psychiatrist Dr Arnold Mandell that Castaneda's "informant" Don Juan represented a coyote trick played by Castaneda on Dr Harold Garfinkel, his Ph.D. supervisor at UCLA. Since Garfinkel, as a good postmodernist, held that all anthropological data is fabricated by anthropologists, Castaneda simply fabricated Don Juan to out-Garfinkel Garfinkel. De Mille traces many of the supposed teachings of the Yaqui sorcerer and his colleagues, and the dramatic magical events recorded in Castaneda's books, to specific occult and literary influences that have nothing to do with Native American culture. (I picked out one of these myself: The "guardian" that appears in *A Separate Reality*, the second book in the series — a drooling, airborne monster a hundred feet high, doorkeeper to another dimension, that turns out in reality to be a tiny gnat, is straight out of the story "The Sphinx" by Edgar Allan Poe.) But even though it can be pretty clearly shown that Castaneda's books are at least partly fictional — in his later ones he himself comes close to dropping the mask of "reportage" — this only invalidates Castaneda as an anthropologist; it does not invalidate him as a sorcerer.

Carlos Castaneda was, in my opinion, the practitioner of some form of sorcery, possibly though not necessarily Native American, perhaps eclectic, perhaps of Toltec origin as he claims at one point, perhaps non-Mexican: Richard Dobson, a "neo-shaman" I used to know, maintained that "Don Juan" and his brother sorcerer "Don Genaro" were actually Navajos; he even told us their names. In any case I know that Castaneda was not a perfect charlatan when it comes to sorcery because, following some of his techniques, and not always with the aid of psychedelic drugs, I came up to the door of the world he proposed via several experiences of "non-ordinary reality" — and learned, in the process, that magic is very sad. Once, for example, while I was hiking upstream high on a trail above the Salmon River of California while practicing one of those techniques, the whole world to my left dissolved into a field of shimmering blue, as if the river had risen from its bed below and was flowing through the air beside me, just beyond the trees. If I had turned toward it at that moment, what would have been the result? What would have happened if the river had taken me? Nonetheless I ultimately concluded that I had no compelling reason to pursue that path; it was only later that I began to realize how close I had come to the edge of the Abyss. It is my belief that the main attraction to magic for many people is a sense of powerlessness; this was certainly true in my case. Like the Tibetans say, "If you are strong, fight; if you are weak, curse."

For some years Lew Welch used to conduct a yearly event at Muir Beach on the Pacific coast of Marin County, California called "The Full Moon

Mussel Feast," which took place on the day of the full moon in August, when the Sun is most often in the sign of Leo. Anyone's ticket to the event was to pick six mussels off the rocks at the beach and drop them into a large pot provided by Lew and filled with yellow onions and cheap white wine (chablis), to be simmered over the fire; this is what constituted the "feast." Various events, rock music etc., were also scheduled at the simple rustic lodge. In those days Muir Beach was privately owned, which made it a much cooler and more public space than it later became under the supposedly "public" National Park Service. At the 1968 Feast the Grateful Dead were scheduled to play. Rain had threatened to dampen the proceedings, but Lew, high and wild-eyed on peyote (Castaneda's little green friend "Mescalito"), let me know that "all that's been taken care of," by which he undoubtedly meant that he or one of his "allies" had dispelled the clouds by their shaman-power. It was on that occasion that he introduced me to Carlos Castaneda in person, the *Nagual* himself, whose ground-breaking though not entirely kosher first book *The Teachings of Don Juan: A Yaqui Way of Knowledge* (already mentioned above) had just been published. There among the naked and freaking hippies, *perfectly* out of place, stood a short, well-groomed Latino gentleman in a dark suit, a white shirt, and a tie! "Here is someone I'd like you to meet" Lew said, "Carlos Castaneda. He's just published a book that has become my Bible." I politely shook the hand of this incongruous personage, then ran off to freak with my contemporaries — though if I'd known "who he was" at that early date I would probably have tried to possess myself of a lock of his hair or some of his fingernail clippings. Nonetheless Castaneda entered my reading list, as he did the lists of so many of my generation. Simon and Schuster published Castaneda's third book, *Journey to Ixtlán* in 1972 — after which (several decades later) I began to realize that the perception-altering exercises designed to "stop the world" that appear in *Journey to Ixtlán* bear a great resemblance to the one that Lew taught to me and Sister Mary Norbert on the grounds of the College of Marin, the one where you try to see the trees as empty and the spaces between the trees as solid. Therefore I am forced to speculate that Carlos Castaneda could have gotten some of his "sorcery" techniques from none other than Lew Welch. So was Lew the real Don Juan, or at least a fragment of him? And would that in turn make *me* a kind of fragment of the real Carlos Castaneda? As fragmented as I was at that time, courtesy of psychedelic drugs, and given the developing collective belief that "reality" (as many now think) may be nothing more than a story that each of us tells about the Great Mystery, with no need that the stories should line up or agree with each other in any way, even that might have been possible after the Counterculture's dive into mass subjectivism, which postmodernism has now picked up and officially written into the social contract...

LYRIC SORCERY

When it comes to magic, after my encounter with Carlos Castaneda I confess that I dabbled a bit — strictly for recreation, of course, or to seek purely disinterested knowledge, or to take hold of the power to do good! No heavy, humorless power-trips for me, no intent to hurt, no black magic. On the other hand, as a laughing Mephistophelian hippie once said to me in the mountains of British Columbia, "I'll clue you in, Charles — ALL magic is black magic!"

I completely accept the reality of magic as a "psychic technology" that can produce actual physical results. I myself experienced the paranormal powers of the Philippine Psychic Surgeons on a number of occasions, both in the Philippines and in California, as I will detail later in *Chapter Seven*. Every civilization throughout history, except for the most recent and the most materialistic, has known about such things.

So it seems reasonable to say, from one point of view, that magic is a power that can be used either for good, or for evil, or simply for entertainment — at least when we see things from the psycho-physical standpoint. But when we consider magic from the Spiritual standpoint, our evaluation changes; we discover that the practice of the occult arts not only seriously undermines our basic faith in God but also damages our capacity to reach mystical realization, at least in any ongoing and stable way. Martin Lings, in *A Sufi Saint of the Twentieth Century*, recounts the story of the great Shadhili-Darqawi shaykh Ahmed al-'Alawi who indulged in Sufi *karamat* or miracle-working in his earlier life, all of which he later gave up, except for the practice of snake-charming — until he met Shaykh al-Buzaidi, the man who was to become his Sufi guide, who told him: "It would be better for you to learn to control the snake [the *nafs*? The *kundalini*?] that lies between the two sides of your body."

It was common for the San Francisco Poets in the 1970s and '80s to think of themselves as magicians or shamans, a pose that Carlos Castaneda undoubtedly picked up on when he coined his term "lyric sorcery." For example, a poet friend of mine once showed me, as a more-or-less magical object, a stone taken from the barrow-tomb known as the Grave of Queen Maeve, in Ireland. That night I dreamt I was a sacred swineherd; a boar came and slashed the outside of my right thigh, two or three inches above the knee — a wound I later identified as the wound of Odysseus, by which his old nurse saw through his disguise when he returned to Ithaca. This dream took place on the night of the first full moon after the winter solstice — the one night of the year, according to Robert Graves in *The White Goddess*, when the ancient Egyptians ritually consumed swine-flesh.

But it was Lew Welch and his wife Magda who initiated me into an essentially magical worldview, something that could only have happened in the context of the general hippie ambience of the Spiritual Revolution in the San Francisco Bay Area of the late 60s and early 70s, and with the help of that one momentary encounter with Carlos Castaneda, as well as (then and later) the use of psychedelic drugs—not to mention the imbalanced and unguided practice of kundalini-yoga, which blasted all my chakras wide open and acted as a kind of depth-charge in the deep waters of the psyche. And this paranormal wonderland that I was so incautiously exploring also owed a lot to the late Celtic Revival that formed part of the counterculture smorgasbord, and whose setting was the Mythic Marin County that psychedelics first discovered, then transfigured, and then (at least for me) mostly used up. Lew's poem about that mythic land, the one that earned him the unacknowledged title of Marin County Poet Laureate before that became an official county honor, was "THE SONG MOUNT TAMALPAIS SINGS," whose refrain—triumphant, yet doomed at the same time—is: *"This is the last place./ There is nowhere else to go."* In the 70s and early 80s, following Lew's influence, as well as that of both the Castaneda books and another book entitled *The Magic of Findhorn*, I got into the habit of going "elf hunting" while hiking through the beautiful coastal woods of California, with or without the use of marijuana or stronger psychedelics, and with a certain degree of success. (J. R. R. Tolkien's *The Lord of the Rings* trilogy was on the hippie reading-list, leading some of us to believe that, with the help of LSD, it would be possible for us to befriend the elves for real—if we could only live like Hobbits, which resulted in the construction of a number of half-buried "Hobbit-houses" in Bolinas and Stinson Beach. I remember a "mini-Renaissance Faire" in Bolinas that my wife and I attended; for all their lyrical, mythopoetic dress, never have I felt and seen a sadder people. By nearly becoming elves themselves they had begun to lose their connection with the human form, resulting in a terrible sense of loss and desolation.) My motive during these excursions was primarily "recreational" or "poetic"; what I didn't realize at the time was that these experiences, for all their seemingly harmless lyricism, were beginning to thin out the substance of my essential humanity, and open doors through which much darker forces would later gain entry.

 A few years ago, after listening (for the first time in many years) to the Fairport Convention's rendition of "Tam Lin" as sung by Sandy Denny, I went to Google Images to see what Carterhaugh in Scotland looked like, which was the setting for the faerie events recounted in that song. It looked exactly like the woods of Marin County—woods into which some early West Marin landowner had introduced a herd of pure white fallow deer. One could actually glide through those woods, stoned on some sovereign remedy or other, and run full up against the immortal White Stag, right before one's eyes, in mortal space and time. Once, under the sway of some boss weed, I ran through those woods, following the invisible contours of Power, till I burst into a thicket where, in the exact middle of a circular bed of pine needles, the scarlet, white-flecked Amanita Muscaria psychedelic mushroom stood in its lordly solitude, spirit power of the great northern forests of Finland and Siberia. I didn't even pick and ingest it; I simply stared at it until the subtle energy it radiated sank deep into my third eye. For around two years after that, whenever I smelled the quality of that original moment, a clear red dot would appear in the center of my vision: one of the several doorways to the Land of the Ever-Young. I learned where the air-and-tree elementals were most likely to be found—the Elves or Hamadryads or whatever you want call them—the very nooks, the very natural cairns with their ragged little trees, the very openings between two tree-trunks where the forest opens to unveil the Forest Behind the Forest, in which they love to take their seats. With a breathing-exercise I invented, and a softening and doubling of my gaze, I could peer in on them any time I liked; I no longer needed the help of marijuana or other psychedelics. In other words, I was *fey*—dedicated to Death-by-Faerie-Glamour, just as Lew Welch had been—or at least to abduction by that world's Faerie Queen for a term of years, like the ordeal the poet Thomas Rhymer went through at her hands, according to the Scottish border-ballad of the same name. I was becoming what is called *pixilated*—"pixie-led." Only the protective power of my later Sufi initiations prevented me from being summoned at one point to pay that debt in full. The baneful after-effects of those supremely *poetic* excursions, that superhuman trance with subhuman consequences, are accurately expressed in the following verses:

> INVADED—my subtle energy-body
> Filled with boiling sub-personalities—
> Ephemeral frothing bubbles of
>   self-reflexive subjectivity, totally
>   ignorant of each other's existence—
> Destroying all feeling for or hold
>   upon the Center—
> Scattering the constellations of
>   eternal Meaning and breaking
>   every bridge to Transcendence:
> These are the wages of the magic art—
> The sniggering laughter of the Jinn
> Pounding against the crumbling walls
>   of the human Trust
> In black Kali-yuga.

(Parenthetically though unavoidably, I can't resist telling the story of Thomas Rhymer. Under a tree he meets the Queen of Elfland, who tells him that if he kisses her he must be her indentured servant for seven years. He kisses her anyway and they ride away together on her milk-white steed into her faerie kingdom—something he undoubtedly agreed to because he was willing to pay any price to gain the power of eloquence, a tongue that would always be *believed*. "True Thomas" (as the Queen calls him), even though he is now living with the Muse herself, the very source of poetic inspiration, is required to not speak a word in her presence for seven whole years; if he does he will never be able to return to the land of the living. When the seven years are up, the Queen hands Thomas an apple for his wages—which, if he eats it, will give him "a tongue that can never lie." "Some gift!" he complains. "How can I buy and sell, or chat up the ladies, or advance myself at court if I can never lie?" "Too bad," she says, "and too late." "The Ballad of Thomas Rhymer" is the truest story ever sung, outside of Dante's *Purgatorio* and the *surah* The Poets from the Holy Qur'an, about the purgatory the Muse-inspired lyric poet must travel through if he wants to save his soul.)

During this period of my life, my experiments with the paranormal, on three of four occasions at least, went beyond lyrical visionary experiences like elf-viewing to the actual production of visible and audible phenomena in the outer world. These exploits, however, were on a much lower level than the Sufi *karamat* of the young Ahmed al-'Alawi: rank sorcery, and unguided amateur sorcery at that, though always with what I believed to be those "good intentions" with which the road to Hell is proverbially paved. The stories of this magick-dabbling are embarrassing to recount, since they exhibit a mixture of dangerous childishness and sinister fascination that I am still paying for, 40 years later; their only saving feature is that they brought me to the finished certainty that magic is real—shameful, perilous, sad, but real nonetheless. I'll mention only two examples of my magical triumphs; on both occasions I had ingested a small amount of the peyote cactus.

The first manifestation took place in a beautiful mountain meadow in a park in Marin County (Laurel Dell on Mt. Tamalpais). As I was hiking through, I came upon two girls who were running a loud, smelly gasoline generator to power their various primitive recreational devices, ruining the ambience for everybody else. At that time of my life I considered myself a Green Warrior and sworn enemy of Technology, so I squatted down and stared at the generator, zapping it with a beam from my Third Eye, willing it to shut down. After a few minutes, the girls came over and turned the machine off. Then one of them, bewildered, turned to the other one and said: "Why did we do that?" I don't think they even saw me. I had no intent to control their actions, but that's apparently what I had done—or what *something* had done.

The second instance took place in Marin and Sonoma counties, during a seven-year drought. I decided that I was going to try and bring rain through magical means—which shows you just how low I had sunk; I was a pretty serious alcoholic at that time. So I hiked out to Lake Nicasio (in Marin), a reservoir, which was almost totally dry. I climbed down into the dry lake bed. Using a technique suggested by (but not identical to) those in Carlos

Castaneda's *Journey to Ixtlán*, I emitted a series of short, explosive yelps, like little bullets of sound, and imagined that the echoes that returned to me from the sides of the dry lake carried *undines* or water-elementals (from the system of Paracelsus). When I believed I had caught one, I returned to my apartment (in Petaluma, Sonoma County) and on a strip of canvass I painted a small picture of the being as I visualized it; it looked like a stocky little midget, wearing a helmet and dressed in Japanese-style wicker armor. Below the picture I painted in the symbol for the water-element used by the Hermetic Order of the Golden Dawn, the group that Aleister Crowley (as black as any magician could be) and the Irish poet W. B. Yeats belonged to—Yeats, whose magnificent poetry almost redeemed from the Devil's grip the magical operations he sometimes used to catch the images for them. So then I believed I had constructed a "rain-charm." Did it "work"? Yes it did—in a way. Shortly after I completed it the pipes burst and flooded my apartment. Later I made a gift of the charm to a Neo-Pagan musician I knew in Berkeley, Sharon Devlin, a harpist with the traditional Irish band Sheila na Gig (for some reason I was never able to hold on for very long to magical objects)—and *her* pipes also burst. All of this, of course, could be considered "mere coincidence"; nonetheless I drew some clear lessons from these events: 1) that magic is real, and 2) that it's definitely not worth pursuing. It's truly amazing what God has allowed me to get away with over the years, though not without consequences, since I could easily have lost my mind, my life, or my soul. I suppose that He considered that I needed to know both the reality and the drawbacks of the magical arts for His own future purposes. I emerged from that world psychophysically damaged, sadder but wiser. It was as if I had somehow been "cracked open" to allow access for both angelic forces and a vast spectrum of "infra-psychic" if not truly demonic influences, entities that have caused me immense psychic pain over the years but also driven me to pursue a much deeper connection with the High King of Heaven than I might otherwise have done, simply to save my sanity, if not my life. In this regard I remember some lines from a poem I wrote back in Catholic high school: "I always knew that someday the Devil/ Would scare me into the arms of God." In any case it was due to this sort of extremely dangerous magick-dabbling, coupled with my use of psychedelic drugs and my abuse of kundalini-yoga, which I practiced with no guidance whatsoever, that I came to the conclusion that once you pass, knowingly or unknowingly, through the region of the demonic, your name goes into the Devil's rolodex. On the slightly more positive side, I gained a certain understanding of the methods and agendas of the Powers of Darkness, and also of the efficacy of traditional methods of petitionary prayer and spiritual prophylaxis for protection against infernal forces. Nonetheless, I must seriously discourage anyone else from making the same mistakes I did. If you go to war and get a leg blown off by a land mine, that experience might eventually result in some real spiritual growth on your part—nonetheless, for obvious reasons, I can't really recommend it.

I suppose that the above two "proofs of personal power," things that I experienced at nearly the lowest point of my life, are just the kind of thing that every 13-year-old witch-girl on Tik-Tok now dreams of witnessing, but as I see it today—and I have seen it this way for many years—the whole effort was essentially based on the fact that nothing of any worth was going on in my life at that point; it was the sort of dream of power that only the powerless can dream. Working "real" magic is like using a credit card to spend money you don't have just so you can feel rich. And to the degree that demons were involved, which is always true to one degree or another in cases like mine, they were apparently using the time-honored technique of claiming that I had overpowered them by my superior wizardry and made them my slaves, whereas the actual state of affairs was precisely the reverse.

And I should also include here the story of a magical exploit that failed, since it apparently came up against a superior potency. In the 1980s, after I had begun to identify as a (far from orthodox) Christian, I did a profoundly wrongheaded magical "working" to prevent the Dalai Lama's archive from being housed at the San Francisco Theological Seminary, as had been proposed—as if that were any of my business! That was back in the days when, after my passage through the Chögyam Trungpa world, I saw Tibetan Buddhism as a spiritual/cultural invasion that threatened to weaken the fabric of the Christian faith. Little did I realize at that time that the main factor that would end the unchallenged primacy of Christianity in the United States would largely be one of self-betrayal—an inside job—though this treachery was certainly aided and abetted by well-meaning but ignorant hippies such as myself. (At the seminary I also thought I saw, on one occasion, the CIA agent who had been assigned to the Dalai Lama—I forget his name—whose photograph had appeared in Thomas Merton's *Asian Journals*.) My "working" involved a puff of Jimson Weed and the momentary use, as if it were a magical object, of a small brass figurine of the Great Goddess of Crete that I found on a counter at the seminary; I picked it up, said "back, archive, back, Dalai Lama" inside my mind, then put it back where I found it. Later, at home, I conceived of a second movement of the spell, where I would burn—for some unremembered reason—an empty package that had contained sticks of incense. I placed it in our fireplace, went into the kitchen to get the matches—but by the time I returned, less than a minute later, it was gone. I concluded by this that the Dalai Lama still had some loyal and efficient bodyguards. But why—all the dangers and illusions of magic aside—did I think I could defend American Christianity from Buddhist encroachment by smoking Devil's Weed and magically invoking a *Pagan goddess*? What was I thinking? Was I thinking anything at all? Undoubtedly someone or something else was doing my thinking for me.

So what of value, if anything, might I and my readers learn through this review of my travels through the world of magic? Two useful lessons come to mind: 1) If you intend to use self-will to control the world around you, magically or otherwise, you will eventually find yourself violating the integrity and the freedom of other people, and: 2) No matter how much personal power you feel you are applying—and to make two teenage girls do something they don't want to do obviously requires a formidable degree of personal power—the *very notion that you possess such power* is having a greater effect on *you* than any effect the power you think you possess could possibly have on anything else. The magician is hyper-conscious of the influence he believes he is exerting on the world, but largely unconscious of the greater influence that the invisible world—possibly the demonic world—is exerting on him at the same moment. Seriously, who wants to become a psychic bully whose swelling sense of his own personal power only hides the withering away of his spiritual virility and moral strength? What greater weakness can there be than the attachment to power? If you are dedicated to developing personal power you are a slave to it—whereas if you truly are a slave to God, if you can say with absolute sincerity "not my will but Thine be done," then you are free.

Nonetheless, if I was touched by evil early in life (cf. my Robot Dream), even before I had reached "the age of reason" that would allow me to commit my own sins on my own responsibility—whether by magical means or under the power of some other vice—there must have been a reason for it in the greater Divine economy, though this fact (if fact it is) in no way constitutes an *excuse*; there are no "get out of jail free" cards in the realm of karmic justice. Apparently it was God's will that I be confronted by a clear and absolute choice, just as Lew confronted me with both Carlos Castaneda and Sufi Sam. In reality we're all confronted with a choice like that, but it's usually obscured by a mass of ambiguities, vague impulses, addictions, distractions and general scatteredness, such that we may end up walking backwards into Hell without quite realizing it. And one of the things that can most effectively hide the necessity of that choice is the *entertaining* quality of various psychic and psychedelic experiences, and the "war stories," we tell about them, the legends we like to weave around the serious missteps we've made and the wounds we've suffered because of them, our tendency to put them all down to "the interesting experiences of a rich and varied life." As with my impression of Amy Wallace's tales of her life with Carlos Castaneda, the *raconteur* will often trump the penitent. Certainly we can learn a great deal and gain substance and breadth of character from the darker sides of our experience, once we have made some progress in what Carl Jung called "shadow integration"—but not if we turn it all into a sideshow, a polished repertoire of travelogues and tall tales. We can never make a definitive break with the world of the demons and the Jinn while their antics are still entertaining to us. Not for nothing is entertainment sometimes called "diversion" — diversion from the duties we agreed to when accepting the human mandate. Unfortunately, it is very hard to renounce the *captivating* aspects of psychic experience, demonic or otherwise, for the simple reason that we have learned to use this experience as a way of shielding ourselves from psychic pain. A real commitment to walk the spiritual Path to the end, to place ourselves under the Will and the Mercy of God, will radically interrupt our addiction to psychic experience. This is why — like a person's struggle against any form of addiction — it will sometimes produce intense psycho-physical discomfort, which is nothing less than the pain of purgation, the rigor of purification; that's what St John Chrysostom meant when he said "prayer is a torture chamber." And the demons know quite well how to take this pain as their grand opportunity to convince you that God hates you and has turned against you, that your soul is destined for Hell and has even now begun to experience a foretaste of that infernal destiny. To misrepresent the hot suffering of Purgatory, which is the painful struggle to become receptive to a freely-given divine Mercy, for the cold despair of Hell, which is experienced only by those who have definitively turned against God, is one of the demons' favorite deceptions. And one of the most dangerous things about this kind of indulgence in psychic or poetic *glamour*, though among the least understood and the hardest to see clearly, is the fact that the power of such glamour directs our attention to, and falsely exalts, whatever is most shallow and decadent in our lives, while simultaneously throwing into the shadow whatever is most genuine and most central to our spiritual and physical survival. And when that glamour is finally dispelled, the hoard of faerie gold we nearly sold our souls for turns out to have been nothing but a pile of dry autumn leaves. The magical, poetic realm of psychic glamour is what the French aptly call a *demimonde*, a "half-world" — a world inhabited by wraiths who used to be human beings. People often seek such glamour hoping to free themselves from a "straight" world that has become petrified and moribund and has consequently turned into a kind of *demimonde* itself. What we now have, however, is a situation in which occult and Bohemian influences have invaded society as a whole, such that it has become virtually impossible for people to go either entirely "hip" or entirely "straight" — and a society like that is perilously close to breaking up.

THE NO NAME BAR

My close observation of Lew's alcoholism, and its ultimate consequences, probably had a two-pronged, more-or-less ambidextrous influence. On the one hand, it might have had something to do with my roughly 15 years as an (unadmitted) alcoholic, which ended abruptly and permanently in 1988 when I entered the Sufi path. On the other, it might also have catalyzed an end to my drinking all by itself. Lew used his booze as a fuel for speech and the kind of knowledge that speech might catch, never as a doorway to oblivion. When I knew him he was down to chablis and vodka, the forms of alcohol least likely to produce the worst hangovers and most likely to support the common alcoholic delusion that dry white wine can't hurt you and that vodka is relatively harmless because it is clear, clean and pure. At our master-apprentice sessions at his house in Marin City, he would drink at a steady, measured rate, applying nearly 100% of his booze-generated energy to his often truly inspired speech, which in turn was dedicated to transmitting the lore and practice of the craft of poetry as well as the kind of truth, often spiritual truth, that poetry could catch and carry. When he felt the tail-end of a given session winding near he would rather abruptly call it a night, always while he was still at the height of his powers. His speech was never slurred. I never saw him sleepy, or staggering, or sloppy-sentimental. He always kept one eye on the fuel gauge, and when he saw that the tank was nine tenths empty, he would pull over at the nearest motel and turn in for the night. As for his hangovers, these I never witnessed. Most of our colloquia began either in the evenings, in the afternoons, or late enough in the mornings to give him enough time to have drunk himself past the horrors of waking up. With the help of the hair of the seeing-eye, or the thinking-brain, or the talking-tongue dog that had bitten him the night before, he was able to set himself up to get through another day — until, of course, the whole thing finally fell apart.

But he was prepared for that too. The various self-help fixes he had attempted in earlier years had apparently included not only psychoanalysis and Scientology and Zen meditation but also the Gurdjieff work — so when it came time to sign, seal and deliver his final teachings to me, after which he knew he would be in no shape to transmit anything more but could only end up tearing down everything he had so skillfully built up in a hopeless and ill-conceived attempt to "go on," he deftly applied a technique that I realized, many years later, he must have taken from G. I. Gurdjieff — what might be termed "intensive attention and abrupt withdrawal." For a year or more Lew gave me nearly his total remaining attention. He encouraged me, instructed me, built me up, introduced me to interesting and important people, spread my name — then, suddenly, he seemed to lose interest. He was no longer as available as he had been before. From being the star pupil, the prince, I was now well on my way to being the forgotten pauper, almost overnight. Obscure. Diminished. Irrelevant. *Uninteresting*. But even though I was disoriented by this change, I wasn't really disheartened; maybe I was actually relieved. In any case, it slowly dawned on me that for him to cut me off, or loose, was a conscious decision made by Lew for some purpose of his own—an impression that was later confirmed by his wife Magda after his death. I now realize that Lew had first given me his teaching, then done what was necessary to force me to make it my own, without him. Since the pre-determined date of his suicide was fast approaching he didn't want me tethered to him any longer, both so I could live and so he could move on. It finally became clear to me that he was deliberately enacting the well-known piece of Zen advice: "If you see the Buddha, kill him."

THE MORAL OF THE STORY

So that's the core curriculum, the Lew Welch/Beat Generation course in a nutshell. But after all that, did Lew actually give me any viable "advice to the young," any "words to live by"? He did. They appear in his little book *Courses*—now a section in *Ring of Bone*, his collected poems—as "THE COURSE COLLEGE GRADUATION ADDRESS":

(1) Freak out.
(2) Come back.
(3) Bandage the wounded and feed however many you can.
(4) Never cheat.

As if to drive these four points home, Lew once said to me: "The time will come—when or how I can't tell you—when you will give your all." (His version of the giving of that *all*, which was first given to us before we ever knew how to ask for it, is told in his poem "HOW TO GIVE YOURSELF AWAY: THE SERMON OF GLADNESS," delivered at Glide Memorial Church, San Francisco, February 25, 1967.) It now looks as if my time of all-giving has finally come—after having already "finally come" plenty of times before—and it keeps on coming, stronger and more demanding every day. One of the things it apparently demanded of me is the book you now hold in your hand or face on some electronic screen. There is no way, however, that the *all* it asks for can be delivered to its destined Recipient—either face-to-Face or through any number of His proxies or surrogates—exclusively through the world of words. Beyond all words, beyond all thoughts, no matter what we do or do not do, that all-giving keeps on giving of itself. If we are asleep to the flow of that generosity it will simply pour over us and *erode* us, but if we are awake to it, it will give of itself not against our sullen resistance but with our joyous participation—through our *living* body, that is, not over our dead one.

CHAPTER FOUR
The Hippie Planet

HOW TO BE A HIPPIE

Besides the proverbial "sex, drugs and rock 'n' roll," plus the clothing and the hairstyles, the incense and the patchouli oil, what else did it take to make a hippie? What were the basic beliefs, the fundamental myths? Obviously peace and love, mysticism, pacifism and social justice were important, but was there a deeper layer of unquestioned attitudes underlying these manifestations? I believe there was—a layer I've divided into eight dominant themes:

(1) NATURALNESS

To the degree that 1950s "straight" culture emphasized the artificiality of the "outer man," and identified it with strength of character according to the Protestant work ethic—since it's undeniable that maintaining an artificial exterior requires a lot of energy and sacrifice—the hippies tried at all costs to be *natural*, while at the same time inevitably developing an artificial exterior of their own. Nonetheless, the turning-point between one collective social persona and the next did provide a moment of openness and freedom, short-lived as it was.

But exactly what did the hippies mean by "natural"? Emotional openness and sincerity; lack of social and class pretensions; tenderness and compassion; rejection of socio-political oppression; hatred for hypocrisy and injustice. Admirable virtues! But were they really "natural," or were they actually a holdover from western Christian civilization, or at least from the better angels of that civilization, minus their opposite, negative qualities—hypocrisy, compulsive morality, inquisitorial judgmentalism and the rest? Rousseau might have seen the first list as the virtues of the "natural man," but the Christian monks—and the Sufis—would be more likely to consider them to be the fruits of the "greater jihad," the struggle against the passions, against the many forms of egotism and selfishness that are intrinsic to the "natural man" when unredeemed by the Grace of God.

So there is "natural" and "natural." There is the naturalness of the primordial human nature possessed by Adam and Eve before the fall, what we Muslims call the *fitrah*; there is also the "naturalness" of the subhuman instincts—anger, greed, lust, etc.—before their redemption and *humanization* by the mercy of Allah; this unredeemed naturalness is what the Sufis call the *nafs al-ammara bi'l su*, "the soul commanding to evil." And—unfortunately but not surprisingly—the hippies never distinguished between these two forms of naturalness, which is why so many of their experiments in "living life in accord with nature"—in their communes, for example—came to such a sad end.

One of the hippies' favorite books was the *I Ching*, particularly in Richard Wilhelm's translation, whose commentaries on the 64 hexagrams represent a spiritual classic in themselves. Unfortunately, they never took to heart his commentary on Hexagram 25, *Innocence*, in which the following passage appears:

> Man has received from heaven a nature innately good, to guide him in all his movements. By devotion to this divine spirit within himself he attains to an unsullied innocence that leads him to do right with instinctive sureness and without any ulterior thought of reward or personal advantage... However, not everything instinctive is nature in this higher sense of the word, but only that which is right and in accord with the will of heaven. Without this quality of rightness, an unreflecting, instinctive way of acting brings only misfortune.

(2) DO YOUR OWN THING

One of the items that naturally comes up when you emphasize being natural is the collection of things you naturally want to do. The question is, is "your own thing" just the set of basic desires that you hold in common with the rest of humanity, made to seem like a special call from the Lord just because *you* are the one desiring them (this is how the *nafs* looks at it); or is it a *real* call from the Lord, the one thing that you would inevitably seek out, or that would unerringly seek you out, throughout your whole life, because it is intrinsic to you—your goal, your delight, your doom, your destiny, your lode star? Once, when I was working at the Marin County Library in the Civic Center building, the library hosted a Harry Potter event for the local kids. (Libraries saw Harry Potter as a blow struck for literacy, because the kids were actually *reading* the books.) One or two of the young people were dressed (more or less) as Harry, but the whole thing was stressful and disjointed somehow; a couple of the children were crying. The event was led by a middle-aged hippie clown who at one point told everybody: "You can be *anything* you want to be!" When I was helping him pack up his props after the gathering, I said to him: "In traditional fairy tales, like the Grimm's stories, the idea is not that you can be anything you want to be, but that you must find the *one* thing that is right for you—the Magic Bird, the Abducted Princess, the Water of Life—the thing that will show you who you really are and save the whole situation. What good is it to be confronted with an infinite number of choices when you have no way of knowing which one is the *right* choice, or even any idea that there *is* such a thing as a right choice?" In other words, if you're going to do your own thing, you'd better be very sure what that thing is, or at least be seriously looking for it—otherwise you might end up in the condition my friend Bill Trumbly described when I asked him, before I first took LSD, what he'd learned from it: "I learned that everything is possible, but nothing is likely."

So "do your own thing" was a very ambiguous imperative—like the self-contradictory idea that "*you got to be free*" (from the Beatles song "Come Together")—continuously oscillating between respectful tolerance and psychopathic self-will, between Ram Dass and Charlie Manson, between "respect others' choices because it's not your business to tell them what to do" and "*I* get to do anything *I* want, even if it hurts other people, because *my thing* is absolute." (When Frithjof Schuon, borrowing from Sartre, said that "we are condemned to freedom," he could only have been talking about freedom as conceived of by the ego, the *nafs*.)

(3) LOVE EQUALS "LIGHTEN UP"

While the hippie worldview included the idea of Romantic Love, as in "Children of Darkness" by Richard and Mimi Fariña or some of Bob Dylan's early songs like "Girl from the North Country," and later ones like "Love Minus Zero/No Limit" or "Spanish is the Loving Tongue," the more dominant ethic was best expressed by the one-time Marin County band, Crosby, Stills and Nash, in their song "Love the One You're With":

> If you can't be with the one you love, honey,
>   Love the one you're with.

Here the whole idea of Christian *agape*, of universal love, of the Brotherhood of Man and the Sisterhood of the Ladies, was translated into a command to universal promiscuity: if you can *be* anything you want to be, then why can't you *fuck* anyone you want to fuck? The concepts are strictly analogous. This was one more early sign of the end of marriage as a central institution in American society. Since love was supposed to be universal, it had to be collective; since it was collective, it had to be impersonal; since it was impersonal, it had to be shallow—"easy" precisely, as in the Beatles song "All You Need is Love" where the line "it's easy" is repeated over and over again. That was the Woodstock ethos. Anyone who has any idea of what Carl Jung meant by his concept of "individuation" will immediately see that such an attitude was designed to make the actualization of the Self Archetype impossible, to nip spiritual development in the bud. And it is even possible that the attitude in question was actually *designed with scientific rigor to accomplish this* by the social engineers, as is indicated by the fact that the first musical phrase of "All You Need is Love" is taken from the Marseillaise, the theme song of the French Revolution, and that in the cartoon version of the Beatles from the cover of the album where the song appears (*Yellow Submarine*), John Lennon is making not the V-shaped "peace sign" of the hippies but the heavy metal-identified "sign-of-the-horns" with the index and little fingers, which was not in general use at that point. In the name of love—a curse on love. As against that curse, I offer these passages from *Love and Other Difficulties* by the German Romantic poet Rainer Maria Rilke:

> For one human being to love another human being: that is perhaps the most difficult task that has been given to us, the ultimate, the final problem and proof, the work for which all other work is merely preparation... love... consists in this, that two solitudes protect and border and salute each other.

(4) SPIRITUALITY AND SELF-INDULGENCE ARE ONE

Throughout history, spirituality has most often been associated with asceticism and self-denial, if not self-torture. This goes back as far as the ancient shamans, for whom the rigorous and life-threatening shamanic ordeal was the key to spiritual insight and power — as it still is today. But there has always been a Dionysian stream as well, reaching far back into the pagan past. Both intense suffering and intense exaltation have the power to initiate an ecstatic break with consensus reality — and the hippies (not surprisingly) generally chose the path of Joy, Pleasure and Bliss, the path Eric Clapton and Cream were singing about in their song "I'm So Glad." The fact is, there was no other way to introduce an interest in mystical spirituality to the masses at large — at least in times like these — except by associating it with unparalleled self-indulgence. This doesn't mean, however, that plenty of suffering and rigor didn't come along with all that pleasure; it's just that this aspect wasn't emphasized in the initial ad campaign. Hard experience taught plenty of us, later on, that popping a pill of LSD was sometimes like going "over the top" into a hail of psychic machinegun bullets. Those of us who knew the score prepared ourselves as best we could for all eventualities; we were ready to except whatever consequences we might invoke, whether glorious or agonizing, by audaciously daring the Powers.

(5) THE PRIMACY OF EXPERIENCE

The hippies believed in the basically Romantic principle — the premise of Goethe's *Faust* — that "experience is the highest good." As Jimi Hendrix sang, "Are you really experienced? Have you ever *been* — experienced...?" Material possessions might get lost or stolen or misappropriated, and in any case you can't take them with you to the next world, but your *experiences*, according to this system of belief, will always be yours; they are inalienable: "The way you wear your hat; the way you sip your tea; the memory of all that — no, no, they can't take that away from me." (Did the hippies think that they could never get Alzheimer's? Even though they knew that weed could give you *instant* Alzheimer's?) Of course "experience" was (correctly) defined not as what we remember or anticipate, but as what happens *now*. But since even the most intense and insightful experiences can't overcome, all by themselves, our tendency to ego-identification, our habit of creating idols, experiences in the hippie world, as in all other worlds, tended to become possessions—elements of *karma*. ("It was the wildest acid trip I ever had, man; I became the Buddha! Let me tell you all about it.") And in terms of the quest for Liberation or Enlightenment, karma or attachment is, of course, the fundamental problem.

The idea of the primacy of experience had a powerful effect on how the hippies conceived of religion. The straight, pre-hippie religion of the 50s generally emphasized morality over experience—although, as was proven by William James' *The Varieties of the Religious Experience*, there were always those (the Pentecostals for example) to whom experience was paramount. But the notion that the essence of religion was limited to obedience to moral rules, plus the self-willed intent to believe traditional dogmatic formulations, was so strong in the early 60s that it inevitably generated its own antithesis: the idea that, when it comes to religion, *experience is everything*. And then LSD came along to apparently prove the truth of that proposition in terms that were, at least initially, very hard to deny. (Islamic Sufism, in common with every true spiritual Path, ideally keeps the correct balance between obedience and belief on the one hand and spiritual experience on the other—though to the degree that the "fundamentalist" Wahhabi/Salafis reject experience and idolize obedience, the more *antinomian* among the Sufis will be tempted to idolize experience and reject obedience.)

(6) THE BEST THINGS IN LIFE ARE FREE

Everything we have is a gift of God: our bodies, our minds, our world, all our human relationships, the water we drink and the air we breathe, as well as God's sustenance and guidance from the Unseen. Insofar as the hippies knew this, they knew the truth. No degree or quality of labor on our part can ever give us the power to provide these things for ourselves—though to preserve them, replenish them, and receive them with gratitude is the work of a lifetime. Luther and Calvin were entirely right when they declared that labor is insufficient for salvation, but entirely wrong when, or if, they intimated—or when those that read their writings came to believe—that labor is not necessary. Of course it is necessary, and the keynote of that necessity is, precisely, *gratitude*, gratitude for God's grace and guidance, gratitude for the breath of life. Some of the hippies, in following "the best things in life are free" ethos, overflowed with that gratitude; every time a new day dawned, they blessed the rising sun. Others, however, read "the best things in life are free" as a shoplifter or a selfish consumer of sexual partners might read it, believing that the labor of others, or the love of others, was theirs to take by right, that life owed them everything, while they themselves owed it nothing. Here we can see how the road to Heaven and the road to Hell, at least in their initial stages, look very much alike. (As for my own take on "faith and works," this poem pretty well covers it:

> God's mercy is like water:
> you can't create it
> the sky provides it —
> and if you don't drink it
> you will die.
> But prayer is like the fire
> hidden in flint:
> no heat nor light
> will come to you from it
> unless you strike!)

(7) A NEW AGE IS DAWNING

The official dogma of the Hippie New Age was enunciated by the band The Fifth Dimension in their song "Aquarius/Let the Sun Shine In" from the rock musical *Hair*:

> When the moon is in the Seventh House
> And Jupiter aligns with Mars
> Then peace will guide the planets
> And love will steer the stars
> [cf. *Canto Thirty-three* of Dante's *Paradiso*]
>
> This is the dawning of the age of Aquarius
> The age of Aquarius...
>
> Harmony and understanding
> Sympathy and trust abounding
> No more falsehoods and divisions
> Golden living dreams and visions
> Mystic crystal revelations
> And the mind's true liberation,
> Aquarius...

In *The Marriage of Heaven and Hell*, William Blake showed himself to be (as Allen Ginsberg well knew after the famous vision he had in which Blake spoke to him) the true prophet of the Spiritual Revolution of the 1960s:

> As a new heaven is begun, and it is now thirty-three years since its advent, the Eternal Hell revives. And lo! Swedenborg is the Angel sitting at the tomb; his writings are the linen clothes folded up. Now is the dominion of Edom, & the return of Adam into Paradise; see Isaiah XXXIV & XXXV Chap. 4...

This hopeful prognostication was contradicted, however, by the 8th major theme of hippie belief, which was:

(8) GET IT WHILE YOU CAN

While sincerely believing that the human race was entering a new age of peace and enlightenment, the hippies simultaneously felt — with good reason! — that at any time the world could go up in nuclear smoke. (And this was certainly not the only radical contradiction in hippie ideology; another big one was the notion that bloody revolution and universal peace were entirely compatible, as will be made painfully clear in *Chapter Eight*.) The perennial idea that life is short and that we should therefore eat drink and be merry for tomorrow we die was well expressed by Janice Joplin in her song "Get it While you Can":

> Don't you know when you're loving anybody, baby,
> You're taking a gamble on a little sorrow,
> But then who cares, baby,
> 'Cause we may not be here tomorrow.
> And if anybody should come along,
> He gonna give you any love and affection,
> I'd say get it while you can ...

Get It While You Can, like so many other hippie doctrines, can be taken in two opposite ways: either as an imperative to grab after all the pleasure and excitement you can while there's still time, or as a call to enter into the mystical silence of the present moment, the Eternal Now, the house where God lives, and which is also the Eye through which He eternally contemplates His creation. And how often was the first meaning mistaken for the second, and the second meaning taken as an excuse for the first! The essence of the first meaning is encapsulated in William Blake's saying "More! More! Is the cry of a mistaken soul: Less than All can never satisfy Man," while the second is perfectly expressed in one of his quatrains:

> He who binds to himself a joy
> Doth the wingèd life destroy,
> But he who kisses the joy as it flies
> Lives in Eternity's sun-rise.

And it was Blake again, also in *The Marriage of Heaven and Hell*, who perfectly synthesized the New Age and the apocalyptic aspects of hippie belief:

The ancient tradition that the world will be consumed in fire at the end of six thousand years is true, as I have heard from Hell. For the cherub with his flaming sword is hereby commanded to leave his guard at the tree of life; and when he does, the whole creation will be consumed, and appear infinite and holy, whereas it now appears finite & corrupt. This will come to pass by an improvement of sensual enjoyment.

God help the ones who were offered Guidance but rejected it. God awaken the ones who came into the field of that Guidance but failed to recognize it. God defend the ones who ignorantly listened to the teachings of demons, thinking they were angels. God shower His mercy on the ones who, though they failed to find Guidance, were ultimately found by It.

> Then to the rolling Heaven itself I cried
> What lamp had destiny to guide
> Her little children, stumbling in the dark?
> "A blind understanding" Heaven replied.
> *Omar Khayyam's* Rubáiyát; *Fitzgerald's translation*

THE PARADIGMATIC HIPPIE

The most hippie of the hippies we knew (and were) in those days was Mike Wilson, who lived in a house "organized" as an urban commune, with a downstairs apartment in which resided a bass-guitar player named Animal. In an earlier incarnation, around the age of fifteen, he had been "Michael St James," a pipe-smoking "author" in Irish fisherman's sweater and tweed jacket — not that he wrote anything much, since "author" was only his stage persona or trick-or-treat identity, the stage in question being his life. At Mike's house I met a pair of friendly traveling Mexican drug-dealers — no assault rifles or Aztec human sacrifices for them — and a young lady who commanded me in ringing tones to "Go to Nature, boy, just as Gautama did!" (Only later did I begin to suspect that the "Nature" she was referring to was most likely herself.) It was at Mike's house that I began to realize how, according to hippie folkways, it was the woman's role to run the household and bring in most of the money, while the man's job was simply to entertain, provide sexual favors and score for drugs. On one occasion, while working through a bad trip, Mike said to me: "Charles! I dropped acid, smoked weed, and shot cocaine in both arms — what do you do when *everything is everything??*" The answer, of course, was: "You wait till you come down and then stop taking so many drugs" — but I was not yet prepared at that time to offer so radical a solution... Because the dissolution of form into Infinite Possibility was the dogma of the age; order was a straitjacket, chaos was freedom. It was the rare hippie who would have understood the classical Greeks' fear of the Indefinite, their reverence for Limitation as a savior and redeemer.

Later on Mike and his cohorts moved to a hunting lodge in the woods, up the hill from Lagunitas in the San Geronimo Valley, that had once belonged to Teddy Roosevelt. They named it "Argentina" after the notion, or meme, that "Hitler is alive and well and living in Argentina." But why would hippies, the furthest thing from Nazis, name their living-space after the supposed last residence of *Adolf Hitler*? Undoubtedly because, in the words of Ralph Waldo Emerson (mentioned earlier), "consistency is the hobgoblin of little minds" — and because the shadow of total freedom is total authoritarianism.

THE THREE POTENTIALS

The counterculture wing of my Baby-Boom generation was offered three large masses of potential to actualize: Art, Religion and Politics.

(By Religion I mean spirituality in the widest sense of that word.) And because—thanks to intermittent support from my family—I was "independently poor" for most of my life, never free of economic anxiety but not always required to work full-time, I was given the space that allowed me to make some significant progress in actualizing all three. Of the poets of the Beat Generation I am aware of, only Allen Ginsberg and Gary Snyder were really able to touch all three of these bases, like Yeats and Dante did— though the same can be also said for some in the wider circle of poets in the Beat Generation age group—including the Nicaraguan poet, Catholic priest and one-time Sandinista Minister of Culture, Ernesto Cardenal. (Snyder once wrote that "whoever thinks sex, art and travel are enough is a skin-full of cow dung.") Lew Welch did Art and (up to a point) Religion, but not Politics; Jack Spicer did Art and, with his "ghosts," danced a bit around Religion; Ferlinghetti did Art and Politics (his Left Anarchism and general support of Leftist poets and writers) but not Religion, though he was willing to publish some who did. Timothy Leary and Ram Dass did Religion almost exclusively—though Leary's psychedelic evangelism had definite effects in the political dimension, and when he was a fugitive from the FBI he hid out in Africa for a while among the Black Panthers... Peter Coyote of the "Digger generation," older than most of the Hippies but younger than the Beats, did Art and Politics (in the form of acting and Digger-based social service), and then (much later) Religion when he was ordained as a Zen priest, while Bob Dylan (born in 1941, the same year as Peter) also did all three, though not concurrently: First Art, then Art and Politics; then just Art again; then Art and Religion (in his brief Jesus Freak period); then just Art. Joan Baez, like Phil Ochs, Pete Seeger and others in the folk world, did Art and Politics but neglected Religion. Of the Baby Boom, San Francisco Poet Roberto Vargas did Art and Politics, finally becoming the Nicaraguan ambassador to China under the Sandinistas; Jerry Rubin and Abbie Hoffman and Paul Krassner did Politics and little else; the classic rock bands did mostly Art, though they branched off from time to time into Politics and Religion. The Beatles, for example, did Religion mostly via Maharishi Mahesh Yogi and George Harrison, and Politics largely through John Lennon, but remained centered in Art. The Rolling Stones were even more Art-centered than the Beatles, though they made some half-hearted gestures toward revolutionary Politics in some of their songs, and toward Religion, or rather Anti-Religion, with their expeditions into "stage Satanism." And our dear friend Charles Manson made excursions into all three areas since he was a rock musician as well as a Satanic cult-leader, and also dreamed of sparking a wide-spread race war in the U.S., but he didn't really actualize any of the Three Possibilities (sorry, Charlie). So looking back over the whole field from my present vantage-point, Gary Snyder, Allen Ginsberg, Peter Coyote, Jack Hirschman and myself are the only five I can certainly place who did serious work in all three fields. There are undoubtedly many more — I know some possible names — but most remain largely unknown. As for myself, I was able to accomplish something in all three fields because I had the time: because I was *given* the time, just as I was given life, consequently I was largely though not entirely able to avoid the human destinies noted by the Sufi Ibn Abbad of Ronda when he wrote:

> Those who do not have to work for a living
> Are engrossed in every kind of nonsense,
> While those who must gain their livelihood
> Are so absorbed in this that they have time
>   for nothing else.

By God's grace, my life has been poised exactly between these two points. Plenty of nonsense is recounted and repeated in this book — but behind the nonsense, beyond the dissipation and the scatteredness and the self-indulgence and the distraction — like the drone of the *tambura* in Indian classical music, the base-line of the eternal Moment — lies the firm intent to make full use of the space and time that were given me in order to accomplish certain things that only space and time allow for — and then shape those accomplishments to be of real use to those with other gifts and other burdens. The ones who feel guilty for their good fortune, like those who foolishly waste it, will be numbered among the ungrateful.

THE HIPPIE INTELLECTUALS AND THEIR CURRICULUM

While there were plenty of know-nothing hippies who just wanted to get stoned, go to rock concerts and have more sex, the hippies definitely had a reading list (for those who were into that kind of thing) that showed them to be a lot more literary and more intellectually curious than people generally are nowadays. The reduction of the 60s counterculture (and the Beat Generation before it) to a handful of shallow stereotypes — even if some of the hippies participated in this reduction through unwitting self-caricature — is a convenient way of failing to come to terms with, if not actively suppressing, one of the most transformative periods in all of western history.

In our own time the literary and intellectual traditions of the western world, and the world at large, are being deconstructed in favor of this or that conspiracy theory (we never went to the Moon, the earth is flat, the human race is a genetic experiment of the Space Aliens, etc. etc.), or this or that special history or worldview of a particular subculture (Black, White, LGBTQ, Latino, Women's, Pagan, Christian, Environmentalist, Paranormal, etc.). In the 60s and 70s, on the other hand, subcultures had not yet radically diverged to become the mutually-exclusive planets-of-identification they are today, largely because the "western canon" — succinctly summarized by Richard Tarnas in his highly useful book *The Passion of the Western Mind*, which covers the intellectual, religious and artistic traditions of the western world from the pre-Socratics to Ginsberg — was still relatively intact. And because, thanks to Catholic school, I was able to understand what a *canon* was, I realized that other parts of the world — China, India, Dar al-Islam — had canons of their own, which were now equally available to me. The Indian canon had originally come to us largely through the Jesuits and the British Orientalists of the colonial period; the Chinese canon had been brought to the West mostly by the poets Arthur Whaley, Ezra Pound, Gary Snyder and Kenneth Rexroth, as well as by the various translators of the *Tao Te Ching* and the great translation and commentary of one of the hippies' favorite books, the *I Ching*, by Richard Wilhelm; and much of the poetry and some of other spiritual works of the Islamic canon, largely composed by Sufis or Sufi-influenced writers (Rumi, Hafiz and many many others) came to the world outside of academia courtesy of A. J. Arberry and R. A. Nicholson, as well as Goethe and Emerson before them. Soon after that moment of universal cosmopolitanism passed, however, the moment when I was privileged to come of age, this world intellectual synthesis of classical literature was either largely suppressed due to the rise of technological culture or else broken up (with a few exceptions) into the various trademarked fetishes of a collection of mutually-competing cults, subcultures and ideological gangs, while at the same time becoming marginalized in the academic world though the dominance of technocracy, Postmodernism, and Cultural Marxism.

Certainly the hippies themselves were a subculture, but their interests were much more catholic than those of most of the subcultures of today, embracing literary history; art history (including Surrealism, Dadaism and Art Nouveau as the genres out of which Pop Art and Psychedelic Art emerged, and not neglecting the acid-like volatilization of the visual world foreshadowed by Van Gogh and analyzed in the highly-influential prints of M. C. Escher, which looked back to Taoist philosophy as represented by the Yin/Yang symbol and forward to the mathematically-generated fractals); the history of political and comic cartoons culminating in such publications as *Zap Comix* featuring the quintessentially hip work of Robert Crumb; film history; labor history; Black history; Latino history; the history of slavery and slave revolts; the history and folkways of various North American and European subcultures such as those of the Cajuns, the Irish, the Appalachians, the Gypsies and the Jews; the history of Bohemian movements and enclaves; American Indian history and spirituality; the women's suffrage movement and the roots of feminism; gay liberation; the history of various peace movements; revolutionary history; Marxism; socialism; populism; anarchism; anarcho-syndicalism; the history of peasant revolts; environmentalism; Gandhian *satyagraha* and other traditions of civil disobedience, passive resistance, pacifism and conscientious objection to military service; the history of American communes and voluntary communities; subsistence agriculture; appropriate technology; organic farming; ethnobotany; the knowledge of wild edible plants; ethnomusicology; folk music and folklore; blues and jazz history; comparative religion; different schools of mysticism; psychology (Jungian, Reichian, Gestalt, etc.); various methods of alternative healing (herbal medicine, acupuncture, massage and bodywork, nutrition and nutritional supplements, reiki and other forms of energy-work); yoga and meditation; psychical research; shamanism; the history of Western occultism; world mythology; interest in primitive cultures, etc. etc.; the hippie wing of the Baby Boom generation was largely responsible for mainstreaming the majority of these areas-of-interest in Europe and North America in the 60s and 70s. As Allen Ginsberg expressed it in *Howl*, we were those "*Who studied Plotinus Poe St John of the Cross telepathy and bop kabbalah because the cosmos instinctively vibrated at their feet in Kansas.*" This was due in part to the fact that the liberal arts-based university system was still relatively intact, and—for all of its leftist civil rights and antiwar tendencies—much less ideologically-straitjacketed than colleges are today. Literary culture had not yet been deconstructed and replaced by technical culture. People still read books. (When something is truly destroyed in human culture, the memory of that obliteration is always destroyed along with it.)

But in the last analysis, all this intellectual ferment had no viable center to it in social terms; it did not carry forward or build upon the values of western civilization, which was the only civilization we had to work with. It was not a new phase of that civilization so much as the *bardo* of it—a word from *The Tibetan Book of the Dead* referring to the period between death and rebirth when all the primary ideas or archetypes that make up a particular human incarnation arise from the unconscious layers of that person's psyche in the process of dissolution and appear before him or her in visionary dreams. In my late teens or early twenties, after ingesting (on two occasions) small amounts of methamphetamine and then sitting down at my typewriter in an attempt to construct a cosmology that takes into account both matter and consciousness, I came up with a general law of manifestation—"growth hides, decay reveals"—and saw that Western Civilization, if not the world as a whole, was presently in the "decay reveals" stage—remembering that the Greek word for "revelation" is "apocalypse."

The curriculum that passed before our eyes in those years was made up of everything that had been excluded from the narrow, "straight" (or strait-jacketed) culture of the 1950s. It presented an *ad hoc* worldview stitched together from whatever had found no place in that weird and contradictory cultural synthesis produced by the emergence of the United

States as a global superpower and an almost unimaginably prosperous society so soon after the Great Depression and World War II, coupled with the equally unimaginable (and *unprecedented*) fear of total nuclear annihilation, and compounded by the profound collective trauma of the assassination of John Fitzgerald Kennedy. It was as if western society had received a sentence of death while still in relatively good health, and so became obsessed with finding a cure by investigating every "alternative therapy" under the sun, while at the same time reveling in its remaining youthful stamina in such a way as to burn it up that much faster. When Jimi Hendrix and Janice Joplin died from drug overdoses within a month of each other in the year 1970, I said to myself: "That was the peak; it's all down hill from here." *And it was.* Ever since that year, American society has been contracting. The economic expansion of the 80s and 90s was nowhere near as broad-based as that of the postwar era; it was, in fact, the reverse of that era. The keynote of U.S. prosperity in the 50s and 60s, the time when more people than ever before could own a house and a car, had been the redistribution of the national wealth to the masses, the inclusion of more and more Americans in "the American Dream." But the economic keynote of the 80s and 90s was the massive reversal of this trend, a disastrous about-face that laid the foundations for the society we live in today, when 1% of the population owns virtually everything. And the hippies felt this coming before anybody else — or did we actually help create it? In any case, the Baby Boom, for all the wealth we were able to amass, was the first generation in which a significant percentage of the upper middle class actually *sought* downward mobility, where the sons and daughters of doctors and lawyers chose the lives of petit bourgeois shopkeepers or working class carpenters — all because the *pressure of wealth* was too great to bear. (Whether that pressure was harder in the long run to bear than the *pressure of poverty* is an entirely different question.) My father could be relatively wealthy without being a hustler. He didn't feel he had to struggle for riches to prevent us from falling into the underclasses. In my adolescence he could work three days a week and still be comfortable and secure; he could use his money to buy leisure, and he knew how to savor it. Not so for many in my generation, and for most people in generations younger than mine. Time may still be money, but money is no longer time. In the Counterculture era there was still a large economic niche that made voluntary poverty possible, whereas virtually all poverty today is involuntary. Hippies who didn't hanker after big-ticket worldly goods as status symbols could live a true "shabby genteel" lifestyle, sometimes with considerable grace. The story of that world, only a few years earlier, is told in Lew Welch's unfinished novel *I, Leo* and Gary Snyder's poem "Hymn to the Goddess San Francisco in Paradise" from *Mountains and Rivers Without End.*

COLLEGE WITHOUT WALLS

My teachers and fellow-students in this Baby Boom college-without-walls were the Trumblys (or the Trumblys plus John Doyle), who provided much of the curriculum for a course of studies where, as the reader may have discerned in the form of the present book, film and music were as important as books.

I became associated with the Trumbly Clan, and their home in suburban San Rafael, only because their name began with "T" and mine with "U," consequently I was often seated next to Bob Trumbly in Catholic grammar school and high school. He had two younger brothers, Doug and Dan (Dan was the kid), and an older brother, Bill, who was the closest thing that I (as an only child) had to a big brother; Bill was the one I wanted to impress, the one I hoped would recognize and validate my achievements. He was more a hipster than a hippie, someone whose theme-song might have been "The Wanderer" by Dion (at least that was his persona-style) — though, like his father, he held down a long-term job with the phone company, made a stable marriage and had kids — until his wife Jennifer abruptly left him in middle age in an attempt to regain her virginity and become a high school cheer leader again. But he was also an aspiring intellectual who read widely in American and European literature, Marxism, etc. Whenever a new intellectual light bulb appeared above my head, I would run off to show it to Bill.

Bob was my age and in my class at school. If the other three brothers were fundamentally Irish (Bill and Dan being cynical and witty according to the traditional pattern), the French quality of the family emerged in Bob, who had slightly darker skin and tightly-curled black hair. Bob was the scientist of the clan who later did solid and well-recognized work in genetics, looking for a cure for cancer. But in the time and place when I knew them, four brothers living in a suburban house in Marin County with a basement all to themselves would naturally try to form a band, with Bob on keyboard, Doug on base, and Dan the drummer (though Bill, who was a year closer to the literary Beats and a year farther from the musical hippies, played no instrument). Doug recorded with Van Morrison at one point and did some gigs with him at Lake Tahoe, though that didn't last. But when it came to guitar players, especially lead guitar, the Trumblys had to look elsewhere — which is why, for short time, Doug also formed part of an ephemeral Marin County band called Trumbly, Ottenstein and Horiuchi, with Eddie Ottenstein on lead — a musician who, like many musicians of the time, didn't really talk but only "tweeted" monosyllabically — "Cool; boss; got it; no problem," etc. etc. The band was probably named (tongue-in-cheek) to suggest "Crosby, Stills and Nash."

But it was Bill, along with the Trumblys' next-door neighbor John Doyle, a towering Black Irishman from New Jersey with a lethal sense of humor, who aspired — half tongue-in-cheek — to turn the group into a literary generation following in the footsteps of the Beats. (Doyle was deadly serious on the subject of humor. He tried to kill me once by making me crack up during an asthma attack — bending me, gasping for air, over the hood of a car with the power of his mirth alone. With his one-two-punch of slapstick humor plus verbal humor, I'm convinced he could have taken Muhammad Ali himself, by first reducing him to a giggling tub of jelly and then beating him to a pulp.) And though I was low man on the totem pole in the Trumbly-Clan-Plus-Doyle (sometimes called The Birdseed Community after my oddball group of high school outsiders which had also included Bob Trumbly), I was the only one of us who actually became a writer. Bill, in a piece of choice wit, once addressed this situation when he inverted the Latin maxim *ars longa vita brevis* — "art is long but life is short," meaning that the human lifespan is usually too short to truly master a given art — to read *ars brevis vita longa*, indicating that an artistic interest too often ends up to be a sin of one's youth. Nonetheless John and Doug dabbled a bit. Since at one point they were both cab drivers, they followed Lew Welch and his Passenger Poems by producing taxi-related routines in a humorous vein, while perhaps the most interesting thing Doyle wrote during that time was a piece he published in the San Rafael High School literary magazine, portraying himself as one Professor McGroin and me as a naïve young visionary poet who ran around exclaiming, "O Rimbaud, its *real!*" and ending, when the my poet-caricature became disillusioned after encountering the rigors of real life, with the words

> The warm-blooded oviparous Ave is dead;
> Feathered mammals of the world glide in the shadow of death —
> O Professor, it's *real!*

I published some of their creations myself in a 1970s anthology (put out by the Other Voices Literary Society) of Bay Area writing I co-edited called *Because You Talk*, that title being a line taken from Doyle's piece "Because You Talk (Homage to Dewey Dell)," written in parody of William Faulkner's *As I Lay Dying*.

Doug's writing took the form of funny, witty little poems, jingles and verbal riffs, like these lines inspired by LSD:

> Then some joker walks up and hands me a brain pie
> Which I gobble down while examining the sky.
> Now I long to be in Napa, that's where I long to be
> Where the worms are very gentle and they do not stare at me.

"Napa" was the state mental hospital in Sonoma County. But his main achievement was his series of "basement tapes," brilliant comic productions he put together from snippets recorded off the radio and other sources, as well as routines of his own, rearranged in hilarious juxtapositions, plus various comic songs that he collaborated on with Doyle and his brothers. If there had been an internet in those days Doug Trumbly might have become a comic star on the web, but as it was, the whole thing remained on the amateur level, no more than a pastime. (His basement tapes also included guest appearances by Bob Trumbly and John Doyle doing routines of their own.) Imagine a cultural moment like that, where a middle-class-to-working-class group of friends, playfully cynical yet secretly serious on some inarticulate level, living in the suburbs with their parents, could collectively practice three different arts (music, writing and "virtual standup") and actually get pretty good at them, though not good enough to make viable artistic careers (which they didn't have the will for anyway). Does anyone have the room, or the time, or broad enough cultural interests to do anything like that nowadays? If they do, it will be all thanks to the internet. The Trumbly-Clan-plus-Doyle (plus me) might actually have achieved something significant, or at least notorious, if we had lived in this age of YouTube.

The Trumblys also had their own comic "metaphysical system" that they called "Levels." First Level was Straightness, saying something and really meaning it. Second Level was rudimentary satire or irony, saying something but meaning the opposite, as in "fat chance" or "big deal." Third Level was saying something as if you didn't really mean it while actually meaning it (see below). And the Levels went on from there. Those who understand how marijuana, all by itself, can produce a painful labyrinth of self-consciousness and missed social cues may be able to get some inkling of the mental/emotional mess we were capable of constructing through marijuana *plus* Levels. Once the Trumblys sprang a surprise birthday party on me. "Happy Second Level Birthday!" they told me, this being a good example of Third Level. First Level would have been just a sincere "happy birthday"; Second Level would have been "happy birthday, idiot (because you know we don't really mean it)"; so Third Level was "we know it sounds like we're pulling a cruel Second Level prank on you, but that's only because we want to joke you out of the idea that we would ever do such a thing!" So apparently the version of Perfect Total Enlightenment supposedly made available by the "Levels Metaphysic" of the Trumblys—the original prophet of which being none other than James Joyce—was, as we can clearly see in this example, the power to *laugh everything off*. Unfortunately, however, on that particular occasion I got half-stuck at Second Level, or rather at the dark suspicion that "is this really FOURTH Level, where they are only pretending to renounce Second Level a-la Third Level while actually slapping me down with it??"—consequently what might have been a happy event became an occasion for paranoia and hurt feelings. (Irishmen of the World! Admit that you can't laugh it all off. Renounce the false prophet James Joyce and declare your allegiance to the "divine ignorance" of Scotus Eriugena.)

The Trumblys didn't have a basically Beat or hipster character, or a hippie character either for that matter; they were far too secular for that. They had a Saturday Night Live character. They (we) resembled a Seinfeld ménage of quirky character-types with no group spiritual aspirations whatsoever, and hardly any cultural center outside a kind of satirical protest against human culture as a whole. SNL and Seinfeld are brilliant in many ways, but they have a serious dark side, one perilously close the surface: the tendency to use parody and satire to destroy any deeper meaning to life. Healthy humor works to pull down the idols of the ego; demonic humor builds up those idols. Healthy humor employs wit and rejects levity, while demonic humor—inspired by that class of demons known as the "imps"—immerses itself in levity. It turns its devotees into cartoons.

So it was all pretty childish after all. My Baby Boom generation were known to be the great pioneers of the over-extended adolescence, the rejection of maturity; we were affected by what later came to be called "the Peter Pan Complex." But the Trumbly Clan were in no way host to what Jung named the *Puer Aeternus* Archetype, the "eternal youth" shining with potential but afraid of actualizing it; that was more my own *forte*. The Trumblys, in their extended adolescent phase, were not lyrical yet impractical Peter Pans but the cynical debunkers of all such flower children and space cadets. Once I excitedly declared to Bob Trumbly, "*Everything is possible!*" "*Nothing* is possible" he glumly replied. According to their own terminology, the Trumblys' essential emotional tone, at least during that period, was "self-disgust." As for the psychedelic experience, which they certainly did not shy away from, they were virtually without any idealistic or quasi-spiritual take on it. Doug once said: "If only you could have all the incredible imagery that acid gives you without those *feelings*"; it was as if he were seeing into the future, calling for the fractal animation and virtual reality of the 21st Century. He wanted the phantasmagoria without the insight, the *maya* without the *moksha*. And he (or we), thanks to cyberspace, finally got his wish. I also wonder how much of my intellectual acumen and satirical wit I actually developed as a way of protecting myself from the quicker wit and more brilliant satire of the Trumblys, especially as directed against what they saw as my painfully unhip spiritual orientation. In the Trumbly world I was like Joyce's character of Leopold Bloom from his novel *Ulysses*, a rather slow and literal-minded secularized Jew, foil to the dancing, razor-sharp wit of "stately, plump Buck Mulligan" and his friends, the guy who could only think of the sharp and witty comeback he should have used at the party after the party was over. On one occasion Bill Trumbly even incredulously said to me, "You're a Jew!" Was I the archetypal social outsider, the man who—like a 20th-Century American Jew among WASPS—had to be smart because he wasn't "in"?

Be that as it may, these people, for all our divergences in taste and aspiration, which were soon to become apparent, were my true intellectual and artistic colleagues for the time we were together. Their audio curriculum, which was just as important as the books they read, included 60s rock (now "classic" rock), folk and folk-rock (Dylan, Joan Baez, Donovan and their ilk), Motown, rhythm-and-blues, a great collection of Delta blues, a touch of jazz... I remember the moment I first heard "The Gates of Eden" by Bob Dylan from his album *Bringing It All Back Home*, which caused me to collapse into the waste basket in amazement in the Trumbly basement. It was a true *paradigm shift alert*: the times they had a-changed beyond any shadow of a doubt. We were in a new era, enveloped in it and changing along with it.

And just as influential was the Trumbly collection of classic American stand-up comedy, which was heavy on social criticism and satire: Mort Sahl, Lenny Bruce, Bob Newhart, Nichols and May, Lilly Tomlin, Richard Pryor, the Smothers Brothers, George Carlin, plus a record called *The Wide Weird World of Shorty Petterstein* (1958), a brilliant parody of the Beat era which included the voice of Alan Watts as a pedantic professor interviewing a jazz musician named Jump Kalkenberger, as well as the National Lampoon record by some of the people who went on to found Saturday Night Live, the Firesign Theatre, and—William Burroughs, First Elder of the Beat Generation, who could legitimately be classed as a stand-up comedian in the serious black humor vein, as well as a master story-teller of science fiction, a leader in experimental surrealist prose, a forerunner to cyber-punk (his book *The Soft Machine* was likely the origin of our term "software"), and the closest thing we've had to an American Jonathan Swift for broad outrageous satire in the vein of Swift's *A Modest Proposal*, re-cast for the rising Luciferian technocracy of the late 20th century. These records, plus a solid reading-list of the major poets and novelists of the Western world, made up the multidimensional print and audio curriculum that constituted my actual college education—"college" defined as a *colloquy* of true *colleagues*—seeing that I had only attended a "real" college, the University of California at Davis, for a total of 3 days. This included a healthy bias toward the Irish (Joyce, Synge, Gogarty, Samuel Beckett, J. P. Donleavy, Brendan Behan) along with the list of required reading for the intellectual (though not spiritual) wing of the counterculture—*Walden* (Thoreau), *Growing Up Absurd* (Paul Goodman), *Education and Ecstasy* (George Leonard), *Walden II* (B.F. Skinner), *Understanding Media* (Marshall McLuhan), *Been Down So Long it Looks Like Up to Me* (Richard Fariña), *Tarantula* (Bob Dylan), *The Electric Kool-aid Acid Test* (Tom Wolfe), *1984* (George Orwell), *Brave New World* (Aldous Huxley), *The Power Elite* (C. Wright Mills), *The Rich and the Super-Rich* (Ferdinand Lundberg), *One-Dimensional Man* (Herbert Marcuse), *Love's Body* (Norman O. Brown), *The Wretched of the Earth* (Franz Fanon), the novels of

Herman Hesse, Nathaniel West, Jack Kerouac and Ken Kesey, the poetry of Allen Ginsberg, Gregory Corso and Gary Snyder, etc. etc., as well as Civil Rights Movement classics like *Soul on Ice* (Eldridge Cleaver), *Invisible Man* (Ralph Ellison), *Manchild in the Promised Land* (Claude Brown) and *The Autobiography of Malcolm X*, plus a smattering of the Existentialists (Sartre, Camus, etc.) inherited from a generation earlier; English, French and Spanish poetry (the English classics, Yeats, Dylan Thomas, Baudelaire, Rimbaud, Federico García Lorca); and French novelists like André Gide, André Malraux, Jean Genet and Louis-Ferdinand Céline.

Another important influence on the hippies, though of little interest to the Trumblys, were the *Whole Earth Catalogues* conceived and published by Stewart Brand, and the *CoEvolution Quarterly* magazine that grew out of them. The *Catalogues* were large-format pictorial anthologies of "appropriate technology," ecological theory, hippie literature (Ken Kesey, Gurney Norman, etc.), rural living tutorials and spiritual wisdom from the counterculture intelligentsia (many of them out of Esalen Institute), as well as from many folk and traditional sources. In them the uneasy partnership, or collision, between the imperatives of "back to Nature" and "on to Technocracy" that characterized the counterculture of the 60s and 70s first became clearly articulated.

To the basically secular literary and semi-hippie reading-list provided by the Trumbly Clan (primarily Bill Trumbly and John Doyle) I added the reading-list for the spiritual wing of the counterculture, known as the Spiritual Revolution, that the Trumblys generally frowned upon, since their worldview, though heavily influenced by the rock, blues and folk-rock music of the counterculture, also combined various literary identifications that were more neo-Beat than hippie, and thus more congenial to a brotherhood of cynical, anti-clerical, ex-Catholic Irish apostates than the hippie spiritual idealism of the time. The more spiritual curriculum that I was attracted to, in common with the literate wing of the 60s ethos, included all the scriptures of the major world religions and every imaginable school of comparative mysticism, with William James' *The Varieties of the Religious Experience*, *The Perennial Philosophy* by Aldous Huxley (whose approach is not to be identified with that of René Guénon, Ananda Coomaraswamy and Frithjof Schuon, the founders of today's Traditionalist Perennialism), *Mysticism* by Evelyn Underhill and R. M. Bucke's *Cosmic Consciousness* serving as ancestors to this eclectic survey of esoteric spirituality. And *The Varieties of the Religious Experience* with its accounts of experiences induced by ether and nitrous oxide, also showed itself to be an early ancestor to the psychedelic literature that was then being produced and discovered and re-discovered—books like *The Psychedelic Experience* by Timothy Leary, Ralph Metzner and Richard Alpert (Ram Dass), based loosely on the *Bardo Thödöl* (*The Tibetan Book of the Dead*), Leary's *The Politics of*

Ecstasy, as well as the two drug-related books Lew Welch suggested that I read: *Opium* by French poet and filmmaker Jean Cocteau—a successor to *Confessions of an English Opium Eater* by Thomas De Quincey—and *The Doors of Perception and Heaven and Hell* by Aldous Huxley, mostly dealing with his mescaline experiences: the very book I had been warned against in Catholic high school. Also part of the same genre were *The Teachings of Don Juan: A Yaqui Way of Knowledge* and *A Separate Reality* by Carlos Castaneda, the psychedelic stories of Ram Dass in his books and lectures, and, later on, the books and lectures of the ethnobotanist, "psychonaut" and DMT/Ayahuasca pioneer, Terrence McKenna. The interest in Castaneda also led those of us who hadn't already gotten there to the genre of Native American spirituality, as represented by such books as *Black Elk Speaks* by John G. Neihardt, *The Book of the Hopi* by Frank Waters, *Warriors of the Rainbow* by William Willoya and Vinson Brown, and *Seven Arrows* by Hyemeyohsts Storm.

When the 21st Century arrived, however, this psychedelic worldview was destined to undergo a major historical revision under the influence of the "conspiracy theory" mindset of the time, when the work of researchers like David McGowan, Peter Levenda and David Livingstone cast a whole new light on the Spiritual Revolution by revealing just how much of the counterculture phenomenon had been a social engineering job by the CIA, who provided the hippies with their precious acid courtesy of the notorious MK-Ultra mind-control program, first through figures of the counterculture intelligentsia like Ken Kesey and Allen Ginsberg. Even before the Beats and the Hippies became involved with psychedelics, various CIA types were fanning out through the world, consulting shamans and witch doctors from many primitive tribes, investigating their traditional psychedelic potions to see which of them might be useful for mind control, or else for enhancing the "remote viewing" capabilities of their agents for espionage purposes. The U.S. intelligence community apparently found yage or ayahuasca in the depths of the Amazon jungles even before Ginsberg and Burroughs did, and there is every indication that the CIA's interest in psychedelics expanded beyond the simple creation of mind-controlled zombies, as dramatized in the motion picture *The Manchurian Candidate*—Sirhan Sirhan, the assassin of Robert Kennedy (though probably not the *lone* assassin) might have been one of these—until it entered the field of mass social engineering. It's as if they sponsored the widespread dissemination of LSD throughout American culture so as to break down all the old paradigms of family, church, community and nation, in order to transform society into a shapeless plastic substance capable of being molded into new forms along Luciferian, technocratic and globalist lines.

The spiritual reading-list of the hippies prepared the way for, and was also partly provided by, the waves of gurus and spiritual teachers that washed over the counterculture in the 60s, 70s and 80s. The influence of the Hindus arrived first, largely initiated by the Vedanta Society (which harked back to Swami Vivekananda's inspiring appearance at the World's Parliament of Religions in Chicago in 1893), and building on a long-term interest in Indian spirituality in the English-speaking world, one of the less bitter fruits of colonialism, which is well represented by Christopher Isherwood's translation of the *Bhagavad-Gita* and Somerset Maugham's *The Razor's Edge*. This wave brought us the *Upanishads*, Sri Ramakrishna and Sri Ramana Maharshi, along with other important scriptures and teachers; the most popular account of the world of Hindu mysticism was Paramahansa Yogananda's *Autobiography of a Yogi*. In many ways it crested, expanding beyond the Hindu universe, in *Be Here Now* and the other books of Richard Alpert, otherwise known as Ram Dass, who was the closest thing to a Traditionalist/Perennialist that the hippie Spiritual Revolution produced. The Hindu wave was followed soon after by the Buddhist one, prepared for earlier by the Beat Generation's interest in the Zen tradition as surveyed by Alan Watts in *Beat Zen, Square Zen and Zen*, and which also included *Zen Mind, Beginner's Mind* and other significant works by Sunryu Suzuki, *Zen Flesh Zen Bones* by Paul Reps, and the books of Alan Watts himself. After this the Tibetan Buddhists appeared, most prominently represented by Chögyam Trungpa Tulku and several other prominent lamas who traveled to the West, the way prepared for them by the earlier books of W.Y. Evans-Wentz: *The Tibetan Book of the Dead, Tibetan Yoga and Secret Doctrines*, and *The Yoga of the Great Perfection*. The final wave of Buddhist influence came from Southeast Asia in the guise of the Vietnamese teacher Thich Nat Hahn and the American Buddhist pilgrim who intensively studied Theravadin Buddhism in the jungles of Myanmar, Jack Kornfield. And last to arrive in the hippie counterculture were the true Muslim Sufis, their trail to the West blazed by Hazrat Inayat Khan [1882–1927] and his student Samuel Lewis ["Sufi Sam," 1896–1971], the wheels of their wagon greased by the not-quite kosher non-Muslim "Sufi" Idries Shah [1924–1996], as well as by the fascinating and notorious G.I. Gurdjieff [d. 1949] and his followers, whose eclectic teachings embraced definite Sufi elements—the "enneagram" for example—mostly taken from the Naqshbandi Tariqah. The way for the Sufi journey to the West had been prepared a over a century and a half before Inayat Khan arrived by Johann Wolfgang von Goethe [1749–1832] in his collection of Sufi-influenced poetry *West-östlicher Divan*, by Ralph Waldo Emerson [1803–1882] in the U.S., and in England by Edward Fitzgerald's [1809–1883] classic translation of Omar Khayyam's *Rubáiyát* (quatrains). The widespread popular interest in Jungian psychology, and in world mythology courtesy of Joseph Campbell, his colleagues and predecessors—Sir James Frazer, Robert Graves, Mircea Eliade—arrived at roughly the same time as the Sufi influx.

Looking over this mass of influences from a short distance, and after a brief pause, it becomes possible to see how the various waves that carried Eastern religions and spiritualities to the western world have so often moved in sync with the political and military conflicts that have linked East and West: Hinduism from British Colonialism, Zen from World War II and (to a degree) the Korean War, the Tibetan Buddhists from the Cold War, the Buddhist teachings of Thich Nhat Hahn and Jack Kornfield partly in response to the Vietnam War, and the Sufis out of the twilight of the British Empire and the inheritance by the United States from that Empire of the "mandate" to influence, control and exploit the vast oil reserves of the Middle East, as well as in response to the fall of the U.S.-backed Shah of Iran, Mohammad Reza Pahlavi, during the Iranian Revolution. There is no deeper channel of cultural interchange than warfare, in the course of which the antagonists find themselves intimately *engaged* with one another on many different levels. (It may not be out of place here to mention the fact that my wife and I worked at one time as housecleaners for Jack Kornfield in Woodacre, California. We found him to be a fair and congenial employer, though the most convincing character-reference for Jack was the fact that his little daughter Caroline — sweet, sober, earnest and self-possessed — was the farthest thing from a Jewish American Princess or a Buddhist American Princess as can be imagined.)

And apart from the successive waves of eastern religion that broke against the coasts of the Americas, an interest in traditional Christian mysticism continued and grew through the hippie years, as exemplified by the Trappist monk Thomas Merton, who had many counterculture friends and connections, and by American Eastern Orthodox priest Father Seraphim Rose. Some of the hippies were reading St John of the Cross (*The Dark Night of the Soul*), St Theresa of Avila (*The Interior Castle*), and the works of Meister Eckhart; interest in the Greek Fathers of the Church, the *Philokalia*, etc., came a little later. This Christian influence was supplemented by the worlds of G.K. Chesterton, C.S. Lewis, as well as *The Hobbit* and *The Lord of the Rings* trilogy by the nominally Christian writer J.R.R. Tolkien, though these books actually had more influence on the growth of Neo-Paganism than on any truly Christian sensibility — on the earlier, softer, Celtic wave of Neo-Paganism that is, which culminated in attenuated popular entertainments like River Dance or Celtic Woman, not the later, heavier, "gothic" Paganism that morphed into the religion of Asatru and the Euro-Nordic influence on the Alt Right. And of course there were also plenty of much more sinister inputs pouring in from the history of Western occultism, via the Theosophical Society, Aleister Crowley's "Thelema" religion etc., plus the influences of Spiritualism, of psychical research in Britain and America (certainly a legitimate discipline on its own level), and of outright Satanism in the form of Anton LaVey's Church of Satan in San Francisco, which was a clear signpost pointing to the darker territory of the counterculture that gave rise to Charles Manson and also (up to a point) to Jim Jones. The highly significant book *The Morning of the Magicians* by Louis Pauwels and Jacques Bergier must not be forgotten, since it was an early popular manifesto of the incipient magical technocracy that has become dominant in our 21st-Century world. Equally significant in relation to the rise of that technocracy, as well as to the hippie belief in the Space Brothers and their UFO "mothership," were the "classic" science fiction books of the time: the *Foundation* trilogy by Isaac Asimov, *Stranger in a Strange Land* by Robert Heinlein, *Dune* by Frank Herbert, *The Martian Chronicles* by Ray Bradbury, *Childhood's End* by Arthur C. Clark, and the satirical, semi-science fiction books of Kurt Vonnegut—not to mention the unique, quasi-metaphysical, "neo-Gnostic" works of Philip K. Dick, a sometime resident of my home town of San Rafael, California, who had been a friend and confidante of poets Jack Spicer and Robert Duncan at U.C. Berkeley. Spicer himself, who declared "I write for the dead" and filled his fey and ruefully saturnine poetry with ghostly channeled voices, had a truly unique sensibility, partly informed by his studies in linguistics. He taught a workshop called "Poetry as Magic" in San Francisco and was the only gay writer I know of who saw his homosexuality (at least sometimes) as a sort of ironic and self-sabotaging twist of fate.

As for Anton LaVey, I can recount one strange memory that might relate to him. On one occasion, when I and my colleagues were driving the streets of San Francisco crammed into our hippie bus, we (or was it only I?) saw an odd miniature black "panel truck" (the ancestor of the mini-van, with no side windows behind the driver's seat) coming toward us on the opposite side of the street to our left. It was driven by a Mephistophelean figure with a shaved head and a black goatee. As soon as he had passed us I saw the *same* van driven by the same figure approaching us from the right on a cross-street. There was absolutely no way, no *normal* way, that this vehicle could have passed us on the left and then approached us, seconds later, from the right. I was not stoned in any way at the time. In those days, the golden age of long hair, pre-Skinhead and pre-Ken Wilber, nobody outside of Zen monks shaved their heads; a completely bald man would have had to have been either a monk or a cancer patient—unless, that is, he were Anton LaVey, who pioneered the shaved-head-and-black-goatee style for the Bay Area. So I had apparently witnessed LaVey *bilocating* on the streets of San Francisco in the late 1960s, which is why I remain convinced that he was much more than a mere "stage Satanist" whose devil-worship was nothing but a way of adding a new stylistic twist to the odd cosplay event or sexual orgy.

(In many ways the curriculum defined by the more spiritual elements of the above hippie book-list, after undergoing a radical editing and expurgation, reached a higher synthesis in the works of the Traditionalist or Perennialist School, which was unveiled to the western world at large maybe 15 years after the counterculture peaked. Perennialism was one of the later "planets" that my wife and I traveled to, and explored pretty thoroughly; it is a world I am still partly identified with. In *Chapter Eleven* you'll hear a lot more about this crucial development, which was one of God's last occasions for the mass transmission of spiritual wisdom to the human race before the Antichrist rings down the final curtain, and the Second Coming tears it in two from top to bottom.)

SCENES

Instead of relying on stable membership in family, church or political party — though these had by no means disappeared — the hippie lifestyle was lived mostly by "making scenes" — artistic, spiritual and political.

While poetry readings, film festivals and art exhibits were important, the major "art scenes" were the pop music concerts. This was an age when people waited for the next album from one of the major bands (the Beatles, the Who, the Rolling Stones, Bob Dylan, the Band et. al) to identify the next significant change in group consciousness, tell us what was going on in society, what to identify with, how to confront the future and remember the past, almost who to be. This was the same thing that earlier generations, at least the literary intelligentsia among them, had expected from the major novelists. And the most prominent poets, in the late 60s and early 70s, more-or-less rode on the coattails of the bands. During those years we had a true mass audience for the first and the last time in the postwar era (Dylan Thomas, Robert Frost and Carl Sandburg possibly excepted), and at least some of us did our best to provide that audience with the type and level of insights they were searching for to help deal with the upheavals of the times, as well as sharing with them the fruits of our unique, individual sensibilities and encouraging them to find their own idiosyncratic ways of viewing the world, and themselves. For a short time, it actually seemed to work.

I myself made enough scenes to feel I was part of the 60s counterculture, though I also kept some of my literary "unattached observer" stance so I wouldn't lose consciousness of what was going on through total identification with it. I visited the hippie Mecca of the Haight-Ashbury in San Francisco from time to time, but never really sank into it. Likewise I attended rock concerts at the Fillmore Auditorium and the Avalon Ballroom, immersing myself in a mass vibratory fusion of humanity and technology, viewing the first primitive, amateurish light-shows with their pulsating multicolored amoebas projected on the walls, losing all solid physical outlines, smoking electricity like grass and gulping it down like wine... but to what end? Some of these happenings were quasi-spiritual and/or political, like the famous Human Be-In mentioned above—but did any of this serve the arrival of the *shape beyond invention* that Lew Welch had wished for in his poem "INVENTION AGAINST INVENTION"? The whole thing was invention-*upon*-invention, becoming increasing shapeless and chaotic...

Outside the concerts, the other major cultural manifestations, the other big scene to make, were the "peace riots." Opposition to the war in Vietnam was an automatic part of the hippie manifestation, and in no way an unjustified one. For us adolescent peaceniks of Marin County it was mediated, at least in the year 1967, by an initiative called Vietnam Summer, which had an office on Lincoln Avenue in San Rafael, manned by a core of true activists (including Jared Rossman, younger brother of the more well-known Michael Rossman of Berkeley) and frequented by a motley crew of hangers-on. I was one of the hangers-on. I volunteered from time to time to staple posters to phone poles and to drive people to demonstrations and other events in my father's Chevrolet Suburban Carry-all, the primitive ancestor of the SUV and the mini-van.

The Vietnam War was the true beginning of the end of American innocence, exceptionalism and moral authority. We never recovered from it—and not just because we lost. It was the point of greatest expansion of the American Empire, the dark realization of Walt Whitman's "Passage to India," a poem that celebrated the doctrine of globalized manifest destiny carried as far as interplanetary space-travel. It was also the secret fulfillment of the American Doom announced by Herman Melville in *Moby Dick*, our irreversible day of reckoning, when the Ship of State dared the transpersonal powers, impaled itself on them, and started to go down—though it took another half-century for the full damage to manifest. After that grim stroke of fate, our judgment was set in stone. And the damage did not come only from the side of the imperialists and the warmongers, or from their enemies, the Viet Cong and the North Vietnamese, backed up by China and Russia. It also came from the pacifists and the peaceniks, from the conscientious objectors who burned their draft cards and the unsung and unpunished heroes who burned down the Marin County Draft Board—not to mention those hippie and yippie battalions, led by Allen Ginsberg, who chanted OM to levitate the Pentagon by pure magical thinking... (Ginsberg later repented of the Yippie antiwar demonstrations at the 1968 Chicago Democratic Convention because he saw that they were one of the things that got Richard Nixon elected.) Francis Ford Coppola's *Apocalypse Now*, for all its flaws, clearly demonstrated how the War-thing and the Hippie-thing were both parts of the same collective disaster, hopelessly entangled with each other in a single massive bleed-through. When something really ends, it ends at all points at once; the causes of its demise are not linear, but global; its executioner is Time itself. As Bob Dylan succinctly put it in his song "Desolation Row,"

> Praise be to Nero's Neptune
> The Titanic sails at dawn;
> Everybody's shouting
> "Which side are you on?"

The Titanic was the Pequod! Three years later, in 1968, I replied to him like this in *Panic Grass*:

> It's over with, it's all over, I need set no timetable
> Two years or fifty years, the course is mapped in bedrock,
>   the timetable is in the air, in the street outside, read it!
> Or I will read it to you, for a few minutes now, in the bond
>   my voice makes between us, an island against it . . .

THE PEACE RIOTS

Outside of the 1968 Chicago Democratic Convention, the main peace/war event I attended in the 1960s was the second anti-draft demonstration at the Oakland Induction Center:

> A By-Invitation Riot will be Held
> Tomorrow, October 17, 1967,
> At the Oakland Induction Center.
> Please Arrive Suitably Attired.
> First-come, First-clubbed;
> Non-Violent Resistance Trainees
> Will be Placed in the First Rank.
>
>   *R.S.V.P.*

We assembled. The cops assembled. We faced off. I was in the front row. I saw that the cop standing directly in front of me, about four feet away, was distraught, deeply ashamed. He couldn't meet my gaze.

The cops had set up their command center in a four-storey concrete parking garage just down the street. When the crowd of Our Guys saw them there, we spontaneously gave them the Fascist salute and all shouted *Sieg Heil!* in unison — a gesture that immediately struck me as disconcertingly ambiguous, if not outright creepy . . . so I immediately turned to the *left*, and faced *down* the avenue separating the cops and the demonstrators, instead of towards the cops like I was supposed to.

I am still facing in that direction.

Then the cops moved, clubbing the contingent who were sitting-in in front of the Induction Center entrance, clearing the doorway so the first busload of inductees could enter. One of our party, Caryn — that little schizophrenic Jewish girl who was part of the Trumbly "girl pool" — was clubbed, along with some other people we knew. Later Caryn told us that she's seen a cop openly weeping, an incident that made its way into *Panic Grass*.

As we drove back over the Richmond-San Rafael Bridge when the event was over, after coming out of the congested I-80 corridor and passing beyond the smoking, flaming Richmond refineries, things opened up till we could see, from the bridge, the wide expanse of San Francisco Bay, and Mt. Tamalpais beyond—at which point we could almost hear the scales falling from our eyes, an impression that was perfectly expressed and sealed for all of us when *what should come on the radio*, clear as a bell, at that very moment, but the song "I Can See for Miles" by the Who!

> I know you've deceived me, now here's a surprise
> I know that you have 'cause there's magic in my eyes:
> I can see for *miles* and *miles* and *miles* and *miles* and *miles*—
> (Oh Yeah)

After that day we could all definitely see a lot farther than we ever had before; a rendezvous with history will sometimes do that. (The next phase—for me at least—was the one announced by James Joyce when he said: "History is a nightmare from which I am trying to awake.")

THE GURU PARADE

A big part of that attempt to awaken from time was our quest for Eternity, which included, for my segment of the Hippie Revolution, an almost instinctive attraction to spiritual teachers and masters and gurus from the Mysterious East—a strange thing for a generation that prided itself on questioning authority!

In the 60s and 70s, we spiritual seekers of the San Francisco Bay Area didn't need to travel the world looking for mystical guides; such guides, from all around the world, were now making pilgrimages to us. These individuals might not in every instance have been spiritual teachers of the highest caliber—some were out-and-out charlatans—but a percentage of them were at least legitimate representatives of very ancient and powerful traditions. Yet there were so many of them, coming from so many different directions, that it became possible (as it were) to practice a different religion every week. This in itself tended to reduce religion to the job of collecting many different spiritual *experiences* rather than making a commitment to a particular set of beliefs and practices. Rather than doctrine, morality or the work of developing the character and purifying the soul, experience itself became paramount. The religious tripper developed into something like a restaurant or theater critic, "tasting" various spiritual influences, reviewing them and making a list of his or her "favorites"—yet something much deeper was going on as well.

The central *guru* ministering to the Spiritual Revolution, at least in the earlier years, was Swami Satchidananda Saraswati. After studying with followers of Sri Ramakrishna and spending time with Sri Ramana Maharshi, he became the *chela* of Swami Shivananda Saraswati, moving to the U.S. in 1966 and founding the movement known as Integral Yoga. He gave the opening address at Woodstock. On one occasion I sat directly in front of him in the first row of seats in an auditorium, giving him my totally (and rarely) undivided attention and becoming more profoundly still than I had ever been before in my life. It was on that occasion that I first understood, in my essence, the meaning of *darshan*.

But the Great Explainer of the spiritual Path to the hippies was (Baba) Ram Dass, Richard Alpert, one of the original "psychedelic triumvirate" of Harvard University, along with Ralph Metzner and Timothy Leary. His book *Be Here Now*, printed in a large woodcut-like font on rough unbleached paper for a "natural, organic" look, and with many illustrations, was and remains the hippie spiritual classic. As mentioned before, Ram Dass was the closest thing to a Traditionalist/Perennialist sage produced by the counterculture, and the most articulate by far of all the "gurus" of the time; his lectures, which I attended in both California and British Columbia, were important community events. His stories of his psychedelic experiences and his interactions with his yogi-guru in India, Neem Karoli Baba, were immensely entertaining, though his expositions of the ins and outs of the spiritual life went far beyond mere entertainment. If he had any central limitation, it was that he remained identified with his own eloquence and clarity of expression—an attachment that he seemed to recognize and accept as part of the "golden chain" or "veil of light" that many spiritual practitioners are bound to. When, in later life, he suffered a severe stroke that seriously limited his power of speech, I saw this as exactly the kind of mortification that his primary attachment called for—a mortification that, after an understandable period of struggle, he seemed to accept in good grace as the Lord's will. (As for Ralph Metzner, the least-known member of the psychedelic triumvirate, by the 1980s he was reduced to teaching on a second-string lecture circuit that included our little Santa Venetia Presbyterian Church in San Rafael, of which my wife Jenny and I were elders for a time, as you will see in *Chapter Eight*.)

But of all the gurus of my hippie days, the one who had the profoundest effect on me—both positive and negative—was the Sikh teacher of kundalini-yoga, Yogi Bhajan. As a missionary to the Counterculture his essential message was: "Attention hippies! Want to get high without drugs? Try kundalini-yoga—and then *watch what happens!*" I attended a couple of yoga classes in San Anselmo to learn his techniques, and then started performing such powerful methods as "breath-of-fire" while still smoking dope, taking psychedelics, and making no changes in my diet. And for all the revelations this yoga provided, part of the dark side of it, at least as I was practicing it, was that it turned me into a kind of floating head, all my life-energy concentrated at the Third Eye, everything below that like a blacked-out city, dark, frigid, abandoned by its citizens. "Down there" was where all the unfaced traumas and agonizing griefs were hidden, things that I apparently no longer had to worry about now because I had literally "risen above them"—though such "grandiose ascension" (as the poet Robert Bly named it) was not destined to last; the piper eventually had to be paid. The upshot was that my unguided and totally-undirected practice of kundalini-yoga completely unbalanced my psycho-physical nervous system and caused me to spend several years trying to fully return my astral body to my physical body—and, strangely enough, it was the *Castaneda* techniques that helped me accomplish this return, though after I had once again assumed physical form I mostly discontinued them. But at the same time, by blasting open my *chakras*, kundalini-yoga gave me direct experiential insight into all the major levels of consciousness, worldview and aspiration that make up the Human Form; whether I could ultimately stabilize or spiritually actualize any of these levels, and make them a balanced part of my life, was an entirely different matter. Nonetheless, since the level of being represented by each *chakra* concealed a specific bundle of *karma* that I was required to live out, purify and/or sacrifice, my spiritual development was accelerated in several different dimensions, though often in a painful and unbalanced manner. Suffice it to say that, in one way or another, I had begun to *pay*. *Experience* was expanded on many levels—but is experience in itself, even "spiritual" experience, true knowledge and love of God, and willingness to serve Him?

On one occasion I met Yogi Bhajan at the San Anselmo yoga class I was attending (I was living with my main hippie girlfriend, Paula Wasserman, at the time). I remember that he told us: "In the Piscean Age, ruled by Jupiter the planet of generosity, the contract was: 'Do your spiritual practices, purify your soul, and you will be rewarded.' Now, however, we are entering the Aquarian Age, ruled by Saturn, the hard taskmaster; the new contract is: 'Practice faithfully, purify your soul—*or else*'." He must've known that teaching such powerful techniques as breath-of-fire to a mass of scatter-brained drug-taking hippies was like teaching a child to swim by throwing him into the water—into shark-infested water at that, psychically speaking—to either sink to the bottom or swim for his life. Like so many approaches to the spiritual life during the Hippie Revolution of the 1960s, the promiscuous teaching of kundalini-yoga to all comers, like the widespread use of psychedelic drugs, was a sort of counsel of desperation. Experience was king! So when we students were talking with Yogi Bhajan after his class, I suddenly said to him (remembering the Jimi Hendrix song), "You are *really experienced*"—after which he peered at me suspiciously.

In hindsight, I see my difficulties with kundalini-yoga as a perfect cautionary tale about the dangers of an unguided and half-educated approach to the practice of *any* kind of yoga or spiritual technique. It will undoubtedly never be known just how many quasi-gurus the 1960s and 70s produced who, after dropping acid and practicing a little *pranayama*, suddenly "knew" a whole collection of mystical secrets that they immediately proceeded to "teach" to all and sundry: the blind leading the blind. It will never be known because most of these half-baked adepts later crashed in flames; only a few of them survived to become relatively sane and balanced practitioners of this or that contemplative spirituality.

The *kundalini* is a real and intrinsic part of the human makeup; it's not just some demon of occultism like some of the Evangelicals believe. But when you awaken it artificially by things like breathing exercises you are asking for trouble, especially when this is done *outside a context of Grace*. In terms of yoga, "Grace" is the protective and ordering influence of the Hindu or Buddhist tradition, plus the active guiding, redeeming and enlightening *baraka* transmitted by that tradition, usually through the person of one's guru — a *baraka* that only those who are duly initiated into a particular tradition have access to, or the power to assimilate, or any real right to approach. The Grace of any legitimate tradition, not to mention the direct Grace of God, has the power to awaken the *kundalini* on its own, in a balanced and harmonious manner, for God's own purposes and in His own time. Essentially, that's what the *kundalini* is: a response to Grace by the deeper levels of the human psycho-physical system. But when the *kundalini* is awakened in a self-willed attempt to *access* Grace rather than by a willingness to receive it as a gift, when it is used for a kind of raid on the mysteries, an armed expedition to take Heaven by storm, then the foolhardy and self-misguided yogi will be very lucky if the worst thing he or she encounters is the Angel with the Flaming Sword who guards the Tree of Life, blocking the Way and imperiously commanding the thief-of-fire to "go back!"

Other luminaries I encountered more or less as a hippie included Jiddu Krishnamurti, whose major claim to fame in my book was that he renounced the role of Messiah assigned to him by the Theosophical Society; Peter Caddy, of Findhorn fame; Rolling Thunder, the Shoshone (or Paiute or Cherokee or Hopi) medicine man, whom I met with Magda Cregg in Bolinas; professor Jacob Needleman, teacher at San Francisco State University, noted spiritual author and leader of the Gurdjieff movement in the Bay Area; various Tibetan lamas, including Chögyam Trungpa and the 16th Gyalwa Karmapa; Swami Muktananda, practitioner and teacher of Siddha-yoga and *chela* of the great Indian yogi of modern times, Nityananda; Jelaleddin Loras, son of Sulieman Dede, a deeply-venerated shaykh of the Mevlevi Tariqah (the Whirling Dervishes); Sant Darshan

Singh, the Sikh guru of the Shabda-yoga lineage brought to the West by Kirpal Singh; and Arvol Looking Horse, hereditary keeper of the sacred White Buffalo Calf Pipe of the Lakota, which was given to his ancestors, 19 generations back, by White Buffalo Cow Woman herself, divine emissary to the Plains Indians from the Great Spirit.

The basic theme of the one talk I heard by Krishnamurti was that East Indians have an insufferable sense of superiority.

Peter Caddy, whom my wife and I heard speak in Corte Madera, passed on to us the grave news that the magical Green Stone had been captured by agents of the Dark Side. He informed us that he had split with his wife Eileen so that he could find his feminine side and she her masculine one; his "feminine side" was apparently a much younger woman with whom he planned to found a Findhorn-away-from-home at Mt Shasta, though we later heard that this effort had not been a success. For those who haven't heard, Peter Caddy's claim to fame was that he was one of the founding leaders of the Findhorn spiritual community in Scotland, the premier demonstration-farm for the practice of horticultural magic, where cauliflowers the size of pumpkins were grown in poor, sandy soil through the agency of the Elves, the Plant Devas and other nature spirits, whom Peter and Eileen had contacted and made alliances with. These miracles-of-the-garden are apparently well attested; the story of this paranormal adventure is told in *The Magic of Findhorn* by Paul Hawken, a book that might be read as a companion volume to the more scientifically-oriented *The Secret Life of Plants* by Peter Thompkins and Christopher Bird. (I myself had a brief encounter with the aura of horticultural magic—that fey, liminal feeling—when I visited the house/shrine of Luther Burbank in Santa Rosa, California.)

Rolling Thunder was accepted as a "real" medicine man by the hippies, though he is considered to be a "plastic medicine man" by many of the Native Americans. For me he was simply another brief encounter on the edge of one of the innumerable worlds I passed through as a (supposedly) detached observer.

I visited Jacob Needleman one evening at his house in the St Francis Wood district of San Francisco. While we were sitting across the table from each other he apparently performed some sort of "magical passes" that I didn't notice at the time but must have picked up on a subliminal level (he was an accomplished stage magician and hypnotist), though I did note his mischievous smile. For three days afterwards I was in some sort of liminal state or light trance, until I realized my condition and shook it off. Undoubtedly—if I had turned out to be one of the "chosen"—I was expected to somnambulistically drive back to his house, under the subtle influence of the Master, and present myself for "initiation." Or maybe he would have told me: "You are here due to a post-hypnotic suggestion which you were susceptible to because you don't know yourself; since you are deficient in 'being' you are incapable of 'doing.' Travel with me for a while and I will help you learn how to free yourself from the other suggestions you are presently enslaved to." Even if that had been his intent, however, his way was not destined to be mine.

One of my more interesting experiences with Tibetan lamas of the Vajrayana tradition came during my meeting with a lama whose name escapes me. I was walking down the street in San Anselmo one evening when a local hippie-type I didn't know invited me to come and sit in a circle with his guru, who was about to hold an open-to-the-public meditation session. I followed him and sat down with the group. The lama led us in chanting *Om Mani Padme Hum*, the most common and universal of Vajrayana mantras, which we intoned so rapidly that I barely managed to keep up. (Apparently the Tibetan term for "chanting" is the same word that's used for the purring of a cat; after that session I understood why.) While chanting I entered a trance state in which I saw the lama on a subtler plane, with myself standing before him. "What is your name"? he asked me. "Charles" I replied. When the meditation was over and I opened my eyes, the lama said to me: "Hello, Charles!" I hadn't told him my name in *this* world, hadn't even spoken with him. He asked me if I had any questions, so I asked him—in line with my concerns at the time, and also with a question that has been more-or-less constant in my life: "How can spiritual energy be applied to political action?" He was (properly) shocked, replying (wisely) that the two had no intrinsic relationship with one another. But it's interesting that the one other Vajrayana empowerment I attended, outside of the Black Crown Ceremony (which you'll hear about in a moment), was a Green Tara Empowerment on the campus of the San Francisco Theological Seminary in Ross, in which the participants meditatively identify with, and assimilate the power of, one of the five goddesses known as the Taras, who are the field-manifestations of the Five Wisdoms represented by the Five Dhyani-Buddhas—in this case the green one, the goddess-consort or *shakti*-emanation of the Dhyani-Buddha Amoghasiddhi, who is the Buddha, or enlightened form, of *karma*, "action," which is related to the Air element; this was when Jenny and I, as members of the governing Session of Santa Venetia Presbyterian Church, were heavy into solidarity with the revolutions of Central America.

But of all my encounters with Tibetan lamas, the most powerful and permanently transformative was the following: In 1974 in San Francisco I attended a Black Crown Ceremony presided over by the Sixteenth Gyalwa Karmapa of the Tibetan Karmapa Lineage of the Kargyüpta Sect. Like the Green Tara rite, this was one of the many public "empowerments" provided by Vajrayana Buddhism, where the reflected grace of actual initiation is transmitted to the faithful at large as a kind of virtual initiation.

(Due to the strictures imposed by Chinese politics the Crown is now locked away somewhere, consequently the Black Crown Ceremony is no longer performed.) The Karmapa made his appearance flanked by several burly, severe-looking Tibetan guardian-monks, armed with quarterstaves. The ceremony began with the sounding of those huge, heavy, guttural Tibetan horns, shaped like alpenhorns. During the course of it the crowd meditated upon the figure of the Karmapa, who doffed his pointed red Tibetan "mitre" and donned the Black Crown; this symbolized, and concretely enacted, the dropping of his human identity and his assumption of the archetypal identity of Chenrezig or Avalokiteshvara, the Bodhisattva of Compassion. Those in attendance who were able to contemplatively "follow" this transformation were given a foretaste of the transcendence of their human limitations — something which could only have been actualized through full initiation into the Vajrayana Way, with all its attendant transmitted graces and directed practices — or, perhaps, through a future initiation into an equally valid Way.

After the ceremony a "receiving line" formed, made up of Buddhists, serious spiritual seekers, hippies, and flamboyantly costumed figures from San Francisco's Bohemia, along with such celebrities as Allen Ginsberg and Chögyam Trungpa, all waiting to receive the formal blessing of the Karmapa, which he administered by placing his fist firmly on the crown of the skull so as to open the Aperture of Brahma, the "eye at the top of the head" that the Hopis tell us should always be kept open. (The Gyalwa Karmapa himself had visited the Hopis during one of his tours of North America, on which occasion they recognized him as the "visitor from the East" predicted in one of their prophesies.) When I reached the Karmapa I presented him with the gift I'd prepared — a human bone that had been part of a cache of such bones stored in an old lard can in the basement/garage of my childhood home when I was growing up — the same bundle of human bones I'd swallowed some of the powder of in a little one-room apartment during my year in Canada, a highly dubious event you'll read about in *Chapter Six*. He took it, handed it to one of his guards, and laughed: "O *ha-ha-ha!*" (That "O *ha-ha-ha!*" has never stopped echoing, somewhere in the back of my consciousness, ever since that night.) Then he blessed me. (Those human bones had been a gift to our family from my great uncle by marriage, Reuben Vance "Doc" Vaughan — adventurer, world traveler, pharmacist, Federal narc, radio personality, and charter-boat captain to the Hollywood stars on Catalina Island, who claimed a fraction of Cherokee blood; those curious about his fascinating career should look up his autobiography *The Print of My Remembrance*. This leads me to believe that the bones could have been from one of the Channel Islands off the Pacific coast of California, where some of the oldest human settlements in North America have been uncovered. From today's perspective, I realize that this careless handling of human remains was deeply sacrilegious from the Native American point of view, though from the Tibetan and Christian perspectives there was little wrong with it. And, strangely enough, I later learned that the Karmapa's visit to the Hopis in Arizona had taken place only a few days before the Black Crown Ceremony where I met him.)

Sometime after attending the Ceremony, I had the following dream, and shortly after composed an exegesis of it:

> I am faced with a figure who is both the Gyalwa Karmapa and Merlin. He is wearing a conical hat like a "sorcerer's hat" or a Tibetan mitre. He directs my attention with a pointing-stick to a large diagram: the Sun in the Moon Cradle, which is a downward-curving crescent Moon upholding the Sun as in a boat, with long wavy rays radiating from its disc. The Karmapa figure points to six points on the lower crescent of the Moon and connects them, by means of lines, to six somewhat closer-together points on the upper arc of the Sun. I take this to mean that the Six Lokas or realms of illusion of the Buddhist Kalachakra or wheel of samsaric existence are a projection into the relative world of Six Forms of Enlightened Mind. Then the dream changes. I begin to dream about those ancient straight lines drawn on the earth's surface that John Michell, in his book *The View Over Atlantis*, calls "leys" — except that in my dream they are called "eber-lines." A voice says: "An eber-line can be drawn from any point to any other — but few remember that it is also possible to draw an eber-line straight up to God."

The following exegesis of that dream was composed in 1978:

> Re "leys": John Michell speaks of the discovery, made since the advent of aerial photography, of a series of perfectly straight lines of prehistoric vintage drawn all over the island of Britain. They are preserved in prehistoric earthworks, Roman roads, and short stretches of country roads and rustic paths. These lines take no account of geographic contours, but pass straight over all obstacles. Along a given ley (so named because the word "ley" or "lea" appears in many place-names along such routes) will appear a number of prehistoric sites, cathedrals — usually built on pre-Christian sacred points — or Celtic stone crosses, all in perfect alignment. On major sites, such as Stonehenge, Avebury, Woodhenge, and Glastonbury Tor, several leys are found to cross. Michell speaks of an identical system in China, where the lines are called "dragon-paths." Some believe these paths were channels established to conduct the flow of terrestrial magnetism, which was tapped on a seasonal basis by means of rites conducted at sacred "nodes" at various points along the track, points which were oriented to different heavenly bodies, as Stonehenge is to the Sun. He shows that similar ceremonies took place in Britain, one purpose of which was to stimulate the fertility of the earth. The British leys, like their Chinese counterparts, are also mythologically associated with dragons. (Since Ireland is known to harbor no native serpents, could the legend of St Patrick's driving of the snakes out of Ireland be a veiled reference to the suppression of such worship?)

William Blake, too, hit upon the idea of leys, which in his system comprise a Druidic "dragon temple" covering the whole of Britain.

So much for "ley"—but what about "eber"? Very well: while thumbing through S. Foster Damon's *A Blake Dictionary*, I ran into the name "Eber," under the entry "Peleg." These names were taken from the genealogy in the tenth chapter of Genesis, where Peleg and Joktan are given as sons of Eber (the eponymous ancestor of the Hebrews), Peleg being so named because "in his days was the earth divided." And later, while reading Charles Squire's *Celtic Myth and Legend*, I came across the name Eber again: According to ancient Irish chronicles, Eber Scot was one of the sons of King Milé—leader of the Milesians, the first Celtic invaders of Ireland—who, in a dispute with his brothers over the new land, suggested and saw to it that the land was divided. (This tale can be explained, of course, as a monkish attempt to reconcile Biblical history with Irish legend.) So, apparently, leys *are* eber-lines.

Curious; and it would have remained little more than a curiosity, had I not found, 28 years later, in the year 2004, the following passage from René Guénon's *Traditional Forms and Cosmic Cycles*, p. 24:

> Hyperborea obviously corresponds to the North, and Atlantis to the West; and it is remarkable that although the very designations of these two regions are distinct, they may give rise to confusions since names of the same root were applied to both. In fact, one finds the root under diverse forms such as *hiber*, *iber* or *eber*, and also *ereb* by transposition of letters, signifying both the region of Winter, that is, the North ["Hibernia," for example], and the region of evening or the setting sun, that is, the West, and the peoples who inhabit both ... The very position of the Atlantean center on the East-West axis indicates its subordination with respect to the Hyperborean center, located on the North-South polar axis. [Guénon's characterization of the two axes is right in line with the Lakota conception is recounted in *Black Elk Speaks*, where the North-South axis is "the Good Red Road" while the East-West axis is "the Black Road of Difficulty."] Indeed, although in the complete system of the six directions of space the conjunction of these two axes forms what one can call a horizontal cross [exactly as is represented in the Native American medicine wheel], the North-South axis must be regarded as relatively vertical with regard to the East-West axis, as we have explained elsewhere.

The eber-line which is "drawn straight up to God" in my dream is precisely the *axis mundi*, the vertical path; the six points on the arc of the Moon connected with six other points on the arc of the Sun are the cosmic realities represented by the six directions of space, North, South, East, West, Zenith and Nadir, placed in relation to the formless archetypes of these realities within the Transcendent Intellect; they are possibly related to the Six Grandfathers in Black Elk's great vision, and also to the vision recounted in the ninth chapter of Ezekiel of the "six men [who] came forth from the higher gate, which lieth toward the north." (See René Guénon, *The Symbolism of the Cross*; also Leo Schaya, *The Universal Meaning of the Kabbalah*, citations for "serafim.")

One further "event" connected with the Black Crown Ceremony remains to be recounted. When the Karmapa blessed me, I had a vision: I saw myself as a young Muslim woodcutter in Tibet, or somewhere else in the Himalayan region, bare-legged and wearing a shallow conical hat shaped like a Chinese peasant hat, except that it was made not out of woven rushes or bamboo but (appropriately) out of bark, probably birch bark. Nearby the Gyalwa Karmapa, or one of the earlier Karmapas of his lineage, was being carried in a palanquin across a clear shallow stream of ice-melt water flowing over a bed of pebbles. When I (as the Muslim woodcutter) yelled to him some smart-ass remark, he sent that remark *back* on me with great power, like a cry echoing, or a bullet ricocheting, off a rocky cliff. And only now, in writing this, do I fully understand that it was through that vision that the karmic task of spiritual practice and enlightenment passed to me from some deceased Tibetan yogi who had failed to complete it—whether or not he was actually the Gyalwa Karmapa in a "former lifetime"—till it came to rest, 14 years after the Black Crown Ceremony, with me in my Muslim Sufi "incarnation," one of the lives into which I was born in the course of this present life, in 1988, when I was initiated into the Nimatullahi Order.

I also had a powerful encounter with Swami Muktananda at a house in Berkeley, as part of another receiving line, each member of which received the Swami's *shaktipat*, a transmission of spiritual energy or *shakti* designed to activate the *chakras* of the subtle nervous system and awaken the inner *shakti* of the recipient, the *kundalini*. Muktananda's method of giving *shaktipat* was to hit me with a peacock feather (*wham!*). Afterwards, when I went outside into the garden, I started doing (half deliberately) an abbreviated Shiva-dance with one leg raised and arms outstretched: an example of the famous *kriyas* or spontaneous symbolic movements which the awakening of *shakti* will sometimes produce. After this experience I asked myself whether the *asanas* of *hatha-yoga* were not the separated and solidified snapshots of what had originally been an articulated and flowing Dance. (At the very least I can say that Muktananda's *shaktipat* was much deeper and more balanced than that of a certain Asha Ma, whom my wife and I met years later at an event at the San Rafael Public Library. The effect of her *shaktipat* was more like a hit of cocaine; I was so wired when I left the happening that I almost got us into an automobile accident.)

As for the Sufi tradition that was destined to become my spiritual Path, announced by Murshid Samuel Lewis and confirmed by the vision I had of myself as a Muslim at the Gyalwa Karmapa's Black Crown Ceremony, Jenny and I once attended a traditional Mevlevi *sema* (spiritual concert) at the Fairfax Pavilion in the Marin County town of Fairfax—a much more genuine and moving ritual than a later performance we saw of the supposedly-authentic Whirling Dervishes from Turkey after we moved to Lexington, Kentucky, who unconvincingly mimed being "slain in the Spirit" and showed themselves to be little more than a kind of Turkish *ballet folklorico*. On top of that we also attended—and unexpectedly became part of—another Whirling Dervish event at the College of Marin gym led by Jelaleddin Loras, who transformed a large crowd of totally untrained spectators into the very show they had come to witness by the power of his spiritual attention, turning us into a perfectly-choreographed wheeling mandala of scores of sacred dancers who ended our dance by all executing a creditable version of the famous Mevlevi "turning" exercise. I spun counter-clockwise on my own axis until I lost all sense that I was turning, but felt rather that I was standing still with the world turning clockwise around me—and all this with zero previous experience of the dance that was dancing me.

On another occasion I encountered the elderly Sant Darshan Singh, guru of the Shabda-Yoga lineage and successor to Kirpal Sing, at an event at Fort Cronkhite on the Marin Headlands. He appeared accompanied by a fierce old mustachioed traveling companion, a valet or bodyguard, like an antiquated family retainer, who glared at the assembled hippies, daring them to in any way speak out of turn or dishonor the Master. Darshan Singh's particular offering was the ability to awaken the *shabd* or Inner Sound in the brain center, which seems to be a sort of meditative extension of the "sound of silence" we often hear when we have blocked out the sounds of the world. His method of awakening this Sound was through the power of his "lyrical glance"—though, from my unenlightened point of view, that glance, severe and judgmental, was among the least lyrical I have ever encountered.

Later my wife and I met Arvol Looking Horse at the Pine Street Clinic in San Anselmo (offering acupuncture and Chinese herbs). The clinic had been made available as a site where he could meet with those interested in the Lakota Way after his tour with the Grateful Dead fell through—for which we should undoubtedly thank the protective wisdom of Wakan Tanka. He was there with his new American Indian Movement activist wife, a younger woman, whose "aura" was of an entirely different order. After his talk I had a brief exchange with him. I asked him if he was familiar with the books of Frithjof Schuon, a Swiss initiate into the Lakota tribe who wrote of White Buffalo Cow Woman and painted pictures of her. "I'm not interested in books" was his reply. Then something moved me to tell him: "Don't give the Sun Dance and the other sacred rites to the Whites. They have abandoned their own traditions—mostly Christianity—which means that they are now starving for the Spirit and in the habit of stealing whatever Spirit they can from the traditions of other peoples. If you become too involved with them they will eat you up." Quite a few years later I read that he had prohibited non-Native Americans from attending the Sun Dances he was connected with, though whether this prohibition is still in force I don't know. My colleague Dr John Andrew Morrow, a Muslim and a Metís (person of mixed European and Native American ancestry) from Quebec, recently complained that the "racial purity" rules of traditional leaders like Looking Horse meant that many of his own people could no longer participate in the Sun Dance. Everyone dedicated to maintaining a sacred tradition must now, it seems, wrestle with contradictions like this.

What a scattering of seeds! [cf. Matthew 13:1–23 and Luke 8:4–15] What a promiscuous hodge-podge of sometimes paltry, sometimes delusive, sometimes profound spiritual influences! It was as if all the esoteric traditions of the world, feeling that their end was drawing near — at least in their older cultural forms and contexts — were broadcasting their wisdom and *baraka* far and wide, flinging it to whoever was capable of picking it up on any level, whatever their capacity, whatever their intentionality, whatever their state. During those times and for quite a while after, things that had been done for aeons in secret were suddenly being cried from the rooftops — as if it were imperative to do this as fast as possible before it was too late. Realizing the Unity of God that lies behind all the heterogenous influences I picked up in those years has been the work of a lifetime.

And speaking of the scattering of seeds, at least three of the above list of spiritual teachers — Swami Satchidananda, Swami Muktananda and Yogi Bhajan — have been accused of sexually abusing their students, generally women, though their practice of lying about their liaisons was apparently more distasteful to their followers than the liaisons themselves. (Krishnamurti was guilty of an even more serious offense, which he took great pains to conceal — *he fell in love!*) Sarah Howard (I will introduce her later) tells of the time she was living in the San Geronimo Valley of Marin County when she suddenly stood up, took her car keys, went to her car, turned it on, and drove — as if under irresistible compulsion — to an unknown house, walked up to the front door, opened it, stepped inside — and there sat Yogi Bhajan! (Exactly what happened after that she never told me.) Clearly the Sikh guru had been fishing, with his big *Shakti*, for whatever other receptive little *shaktis* might have been in the vicinity.

As is recounted in the *Kalika Purana* (you can find a highly poetic précis of it in Heinrich Zimmer's wonderful book *The King and the Corpse*), even though Shiva is the adamantine *Shaktiman* or "power-holder," the pure Transcendent Witness, at one point His "power," His *Shakti* — who in one of Her forms is Kali — overwhelms even His supreme yogic detachment and draws Him into involvement with the dance of creation and destruction that His own absolute and perfect Attention and Detachment have projected. This reversal is portrayed in Hindu iconography as a sword-brandishing Kali dancing on the prostrate form of Shiva — Shiva with an erect phallus and a smile on his face: a perfect picture (though on a much higher level) of the fall of a dominant male guru at the hands of, and *into* the hands of, his female students, minus the *ego* that would ever attempt to resist such a fall. (And if Ram Dass ultimately avoided such scandals, it was only because he had no pretentions to celibacy—to say the least!) As we can see in the Last Supper and Crucifixion of Jesus, God can offer Himself to be broken up and scattered throughout His universe without fundamentally losing Himself, since this is how He redeems that universe: by an ultimately illusory dismemberment designed to save an ultimately illusory creation. Nonetheless the human nature of Jesus still resisted the ordeal in the Garden of Gethsemani, while ultimately agreeing to go through with it in submission to His Father's Will. Consequently what appears to be—and, on one level, what actually is—the corruption and dissipation of the Spirit through concupiscence and worldly attachment, may on another level be a dark act of Divine Mercy—a Mercy inseparable from Justice!—that is authored by Allah Himself, whom the Qur'an calls *the best of plotters*. That is His business, however, not ours; our business is to play the part He has assigned to us in submission to His Will. As Jesus succinctly put it: "There needs be evil—but woe to them through whom evil comes!"

TRIPS

> *Our companions warm themselves up with*
> *hashish. That's the devil's imagination.*
> *Even an angel's imagination is no great thing*
> *here—much less the devil's imagination.*
> *We would not be satisfied with the angel itself,*
> *much less the angel's imagination.*
> —Shams Tabrizi, "Sufi master" of Jalaluddin Rumi

Obviously you can't talk about the hippie era without describing people's highly revelatory experiences with psychedelic drugs, no matter how unnatural and fraught with illusion those "revelations" might sometimes have been. We received such intense epiphanies, learned such profound lessons in those years—except for the creeping suspicion that those lessons and epiphanies, while closely mimicking reality, might actually apply only within a fundamentally unreal world—only on the stage, on the screen or in the video-game—that they were the kind of "fairy gold" that, after sunrise, would turn out to have been nothing but a mass of dry autumn leaves. You might almost think that Shakespeare was foreseeing LSD when he had Prince Hamlet say: "I could be bounded in a nutshell and count myself a king of infinite space—were it not that I have bad dreams."

LSD

I dropped acid three times: The first time in the shape of a little blue pill; the second time in the form of half a "windowpane," a flake of a gelatin capsule impregnated with the drug; the third time as a square of blotter-paper carrying a dried drop of LSD solution.

Session One took place by a clear stream in the beautiful forested canyon below the Alpine Lake dam on Mt. Tamalpais. It was essentially a "Second Bardo" trip, "the Bardo of Experiencing Reality" (or rather, as I would now say, "Existence") according to the system developed by Timothy Leary and loosely based on *The Tibetan Book of the Dead*: Time slowed down immensely and became "spacialized"; the landscape was transfigured into a scene of *unearthly* earthly beauty like in the *Avatar* films; matter was transformed into, or clearly recognized as, a coagulation of energy — if I squeezed a stone it would vibrate and sizzle in my hand. The Celestial Light of Heaven almost came down, or started to; wings almost sprouted on my shoulders; large trees became sentient beings with faces like the "Ents" in J. R. R. Tolkien's *The Lord of the Rings*; I looked at an acorn cap and thought I was seeing a newly-hatched baby snake still coiled up as he had been in his shell. (Later at a café in Vancouver, British Columbia, after reading a poem based on that experience, I was told by another of the performers, a traditional London "busker" with his silver-studded leather jacket, that in my LSD vision of the acorn I had come upon a piece of Druid lore), etc. etc. At one point a short, gnarled little figure appeared whom I thought of as a "pirate." He was disgruntled, irritated, as if to say "Hey you kids! Get off my property! If you fall and hurt yourselves I could get sued!" (I was tripping with Caryn at the time). Later I realized that he was in fact a gnome, a spirit of the Earth element in the system of Paracelsus; I further realized that by dropping acid in that forested canyon by that clear stream of water we had done the equivalent of breaking into his house uninvited or even walking through his wall; no wonder he was angry! Here's the poem I wrote about that trip:

The Lightning's Kiss

I

the storm is directly above us:
   boiling fog,
surf crashing on the shoreline
   of the hills —
      mingling elements
flashing white, blue
   moil in a turbulence —
luminous webs
   vapours streaming
      and blotting the Sun
and revealing him again
      in his course —

    our external destinies
        rush to crazy oblivion
    in the sky above —

      here below,
          the Quiet:

    grey, green, dark & almost white,
the treetrunks boil up to Heaven!
      silver-muscled branches
    light up like bleeding arteries;
        slender arms and sinews of branches,
  sparkling hieroglyphs of leaves,
     architectural script of rock,
the face of the gnarled old vegetable Druid
     frowning thunderous from the roots,
       his countenance beating
          like a human heart —

and the creek is filled
  with men's voices
the single-minded, the inexorable
    in one motion through time —
  rare fluencies of speech,
sparkling emerald syntax
  in the masculine sunlight,
illuminating the brilliance
    of contention and declamation —

    sounds of crickets, secrets,
  goblets of Egyptian sound,
     moving downstream —

the linked syllables of Karma
    talking forever
 in the direction of the
      listening Sea —

and behind me, over my shoulder
    the Tyger growls —
chewing the bones of his prey to splinters
in a keening, crying Wind.

II

and the wind in the leaves
  is the voices of women
wailing in love
or lamentation —
coiling whispers around the treetrunks —

> drawing long shimmering cadences
> through the five-fingered strings of branches,
> and making an anguish of visible pleasure
> that moves through the forest
> like the cries of living violins
> as the bow draws over the nipples
> releasing a wind of singing
> that shivers in the branches
> and through the branches of my flesh
> like ripples through a
> shaft of smoke.

> (exotic poisons:
> vitalities coursing
> through rock & wood:
> the war outside
> by bomb, or dollar,
> is ground through
> wheels of Nature—
> or Nature herself,
> moaning
> like this,
> makes war outside
> this canyon:
> (the question
> should be: not
> Which is Origin, Man
> or what he sees,
> but:
> Where can I work—
> in these cool and
> harpstringed elements,
> or in the gut
> of the machine
> made of human hands
> these elements see
> in their Mirror?

If anyone thinks it is a "good" poem, this simply demonstrates the great gulf that exists between the aesthetic dimension and the spiritual dimension, though spiritual truth can certainly express itself by way of aesthetic beauty. The Qur'an calls the Jinn-inspired poets of pre-Islamic Arabia those who *say that which they do not*, and Rumi, the greatest poet of Islam, had the following to say about his art:

> My disposition is such that I don't want anyone to suffer on my account... I am loved by those who come to see me, and so I compose poetry to entertain them lest they grow weary. Otherwise, why on

earth would I be spouting poetry? I am vexed by poetry. I don't think there is anything worse. It is like having to put one's hands into tripe to wash it for one's guests because they have an appetite for it. That is why I must do it. [*Signs of the Unseen* (*Fihi ma-Fihi*), Threshold Books edition, p. 77]

Before my first acid trip I was apprehensive that LSD might peel away my outer layer of self-approval (thin as it was) and reveal all the rot inside; instead it peeled away the rotten layer of the outer man (thin as it also was) and showed me the inner man, pure in the sight of God. As Blake wrote in his poem "The Little Black Boy," "*I am black, but O! my soul is white.*" I pray every day that this unveiling won't turn out to have been a demonic deception.

Session Two was a First Bardo trip, the Bardo of "the Clear Light of the Void," the "set" for which I had posited by reading the *Diamond Sutra* and the *Heart Sutra* right before ingestion: No hallucinations, no visual or auditory distortions, simply the obvious fact that experience could go along quite happily with no *experiencer* there at all; as the Beatles put it, "Life goes on within you and without you." And since "I" was empty of self-nature, essentially snuffed out, the world I saw—the immense, beautiful, snow-capped mountains of British Columbia, viewed in pristine clarity—was equally empty. Nothing really there. This self-and-world annihilation only persisted, however, when I was alone; as soon as I approached another human being—a girl in this case—"I" began to come back into existence; from this I learned that relatedness, or polarity, is the principle of all manifestation—a truth that the Buddhists call "Indra's Net." As the *Heart Sutra* puts it: "Form is emptiness; emptiness is form." Precisely.

Session Three, which took place in the Anza-Borrego Desert State Park in Southern California, was probably a Third Bardo trip, "the Bardo of Seeking Rebirth," a condition in which ego-transcendence is blocked, and consequently the tripper (or the consciousness-principle after physical death) is experiencing the pain and suffering of chaos, leading it to attempt to escape from this chaos into some kind of stable form that isn't exploding in a million directions all the time. My "set" here may not have been as pure as that of Session Two, since I had already begun to read the books of "sorcerer" Carlos Castaneda. I had a brief experience of the higher reaches of the Second Bardo when the world appeared as a "tree" whose fruit was a constellation of Buddha or Bodhisattva images as in a Tibetan *thanka* (sacred painting or icon), but it didn't last; for the rest of the time I was just waiting to come down. When I closed my eyes, the cactuses and thorny chaparral bushes of the desert around me were reproduced as writhing, thorn-studded whips or cables, like the ocotillo plant. I stared at my Toyota Land Cruiser and just couldn't make out *what it was*: it looked like an ever-shifting 17-dimensional arrangement of wheels, pulleys and intersecting planes, like an M. C. Escher print. In this trip, like my two psilocybin trips, I was mostly just "doing time."

Mescaline and Peyote

The keynote of Mescaline, at least for me, was not the opening of any door to higher planes of reality, but the transfiguration of the material world, a vision of what Frithjof Schuon called "the metaphysical transparency of phenomena."

When I took my first mescaline trip with a friend, Randy Carson*, the main thing that was impressed upon us was how the world was made of *stuff*; the simple fact of the existence of matter gained a new and unexpected significance. And since we were an integral part of that world, we ended up sprinting from Laurel Dell (on Mt. Tamalpais), down Cataract Gulch, leaping from boulder to boulder so fast that one slip of the foot could have meant death, till we reached Alpine Lake below.

I took my second trip, with Paula Wasserman, on some sort of mescaline-based potion concocted by a local alchemist, at Limontur Spit on the Pacific coast of Marin County. We arrived before dawn and ingested the mixture; above us in the sky hung the constellation of Taurus, three precise stars — two above, one below — whose simple triangle *could* be nothing else than the head of a bull. It was a powerful trip, which included the moment when Paula was transformed into a smiling, shimmering, cut-glass figurine or ice sculpture, like an effigy of the Snow Queen — right in line with her pseudonym, "Paula Snow" — and another when, after a brief hyperventilation and holding of my breath, the world dissolved into a mass of scintillating electric-blue flashes. At one point Paula bent down, picked up something from the beach and handed it to me: it was a flat stone shaped exactly like a heart, as if perfectly sculpted to represent precisely that. The keynote of this trip was the excruciating sense of expansion and transfiguration that came over me as the drug began to take effect, which I expressed in the following poem, "The Teacher":

> He reached down, picked up a handful of sand, and said:
>
> "In each one of these grains of sand is all the pain of all the worlds.
> In this one grain is Famine, War, Pestilence and the Fear of Death.
>
> and this" —
>
> he poured out his handful of sand against the wind —
>
> "is Joy."

I dropped mescaline for the third time, on Inverness Ridge, with poets Gene Fowler and Helena Margarita Knox. Gene was an amateur astronomer, so we spent the trip star-gazing, figuring out where True North was, where the plane of the ecliptic crossed the sky, etc. Every time Gene shared a new item of astronomical lore, the sky changed; all the relationships and orientations clicked into a new pattern. Gazing at the constellation of Orion I saw it as a Babylonian archer, complete with kilt, conical helmet and heavy braided beard, holding a drawn bow and kneeling on one knee. Orion is usually identified with Nimrod, the "great hunter" who built the Tower of Babel in Genesis, but Orion/Nimrod is most often represented in a standing position. On mescaline, however, I saw him as the Babylonians themselves undoubtedly did, with one foot on the ground, and kneeling on the opposite knee to leave room for the bow.

Back at my house as we were coming down, Gene demonstrated a *petit magie*, one of his little magics. When a tiny winged insect landed on a sheet of white paper on the table between us, upon which Gene has been diagramming some of his mystical ideas, he drew a circle of power around her with a fine marking-pen, imprisoning her. She walked carefully around the whole circumference, testing it, but could find no way out. And so, invoking the third dimension, she simply raised her wings, and — to our delight — freed herself by flying straight up! All three of us (or rather, all four of us) were together, for that moment, in Haiku World.

My last major trip on mescaline — actually a mixture of mescaline and peyote tea — was a deliberate excursion, not into evil (*insha'Allah*), but into darkness. (The mere fact that I was not seeking evil did not mean, however, that evil was not seeking me.) Why I felt the need to take that trip at that point in my history I can't entirely remember, except that I had a nagging sensation that I hadn't done the necessary "shadow integration" to take my next step in life, hadn't seen deeply enough into the Dark Side. Or maybe it was because, after a long series of disasters within a period of under two years — my breakup with Paula, an automobile accident plus concussion in Canada, Lew Welch's suicide, my father's death from cancer, the destruction of my childhood home by fire — I feared that traumas were lurking in my unconscious that had to be faced now or else they would kill me in later years, so I opted for self-directed psychotherapy through the sorcery of psychedelics. If I am alive today it must be because God protects fools and lunatics. Which one was I? Both, undoubtedly.

I took this trip alone. The setting was once again Laurel Dell on Tamalpais, but this time I began at dusk rather than in full daylight. My plan was to hike down Cataract Gulch into the gathering darkness, so it would be night by the time I reached Alpine Lake. *I had no plans after that.*

This time both the set and the setting were magical — the kind of magic anyone might invent for him- or herself who had read Sir James Frazer's *The Golden Bough*, Robert Graves' *The White Goddess* and the works of Joseph Campbell and Carlos Castaneda, and had access to the correct plant powers to make all this mythology "real" — as long as he was willing to make himself unreal enough to meet it half-way. Both set and setting were specifically designed to evoke the archetype of The Hero's Journey through the Underworld.

Soon after ingesting the potion, I saw a man dressed in black coming down a distant hillside (to my *right*, thank God), wearing something like a black, straight-brimmed ten-gallon hat with no crease. He emitted a high-pitched whistle.

After I'd entered the Dell, I knelt and set a match to a dried sprig of Rosemary—to invoke the Goddess. Then I took a twig of Mistletoe—the Golden Bough itself, though the American species not the European one—and slowly twisted it, counter-clockwise, to open up the Underworld, to which it was the precise traditional Key. Aeneas used that same Bough to enter Hades, cross the River Acheron and meet with the spirit of his dead father. Then I hiked farther in and started descending the Gulch.

By the time I got down to the Lake it was almost full night. To proceed I had to crawl on all fours across a fallen tree trunk that bridged an inlet. Finally I reached the road and started the long trek back up the Mountain to where my car was parked. At one point I was challenged by beings who appeared in front of me as dancing vertical orange sticks of light. I kept them at bay by doing an exercise I'd found in one of the Castaneda books (plus some of my own additions), assuming a warrior-stance and slapping my thigh, while emitting sharp, percussive sounds that acted like an internal hammer against the point in the lower belly the Japanese call the *tanden*, the point from which the thick cable of energy that Castaneda calls "the Will" supposedly emerges.

Finally a car came by and stopped, carrying a visitor from the human world, the land of the living. He turned out to be a Park Ranger, arrived like an angel from heaven. He picked me up and drove me all the way back up to the Laurel Dell parking lot, which on foot would've taken hours. I tried to explain to him what had happened to me, without admitting to having ingested a psychedelic, though he must've suspected that this was the case. With no hassle and no interrogation, he let me off at my car, and drove on. *Thanks be to God, and His blessings upon His servants.*

Shrooms

All I can say about my experiences with psilocybin mushrooms is that they apparently did not like me. Peyote was congenial to me; its quality of *transcendental sobriety*, sobriety to the point of ecstasy, was in line with the better angels of my nature. But psilocybin was nothing but an ordeal. (When I would express this to my hippie compadres they were incredulous: "You don't like *shrooms*? Man, they're the best!") The first time I took them I spent the night alone in Randy Carson's steep basement room in his house on the ridge of Mt. Tamalpais above Mill Valley. I had no revelatory or mind-expanding experiences; the keynote of the whole long night was that *I would forget to breathe*. I'd be sitting there for several minutes and would suddenly realize that I hadn't taken a breath for quite a while. I had no sense of being starved for oxygen; as far as my physical sensations were concerned it's as if I could have sat there all night without ever needing to inhale. This, however, did not seem like a wise course of action to me, so I took a breath. Then, nothing again. So I took another one. I ended up spending eight hours doing nothing but *deliberately breathing*, one breath after another. The part of my brain that normally breathed for me, automatically and unconsciously as we do in sleep, had apparently shut down. That was the whole trip. (If I had actually gone to sleep, would I have died?)

My second and last trip on psilocybin mushrooms was taken with Randy Carson and his then-girlfriend, Carolyn Studer, the pastor of our little Presbyterian Church in Santa Venetia near the Marin County Civic Center, of which my wife Jenny and I had become venerable elders (you'll hear about that rather amazing life-planet in *Chapter Eight*). We began by smoking some weed at Randy's house in Inverness, then ingested the shrooms and drove up to the ridge above the town to go through whatever we had to. Randy was parrying and thrusting and strutting around as he often liked to do with his wooden practice samurai sword. When our time was finally up we drove back to his house. Later on Carolyn perfectly characterized the nature of our experience when she described it as "a Rolfing of the soul." (For those who don't know, Rolfing is a painful but highly therapeutic form of bodywork where muscles that have adhered to each other are excruciatingly pulled apart so they can move independently again.)

Morning Glory Seeds

My one Morning Glory trip was a uniquely powerful experience. I was living with Paula Wasserman in an apartment in San Anselmo at the time. During our approximately 9 months there, where our bedroom was decorated with a long horizontal scroll I created, inscribed with the several-foot-long synthetic word representing the last of the ten "thunders" from James Joyce's *Finnegan's Wake*, we smoked dope almost every day and experimented with strobe-induced trances courtesy of my father's 16-millimeter movie projector and an opaque film-loop with holes punched in it at the intervals corresponding to the alpha-frequency of the brain.

The active ingredient of Morning Glory Seeds is "organic acid," lysergic acid *amide*, without the diethyl radical that makes LSD. The Morning Glory high is transcendentally intense like that of LSD, capable of taking one far beyond the levels that peyote (for example) gives access to, yet it's much more organically grounded than acid is; it is still rooted in Earth. When the day came that we'd set aside for the trip, we ground up several packets of the seeds — Heavenly Blues, the other psychedelic variety being Pearly Gates (what names!) — ate them in dishes of ice cream, and then drove up to the top of nearby Bald Hill to trip. (Paula had costumed me for the occasion in a leather vest she made, the front of which was covered with feather-shaped or lanceolate-leaf-shaped patches of leather, all the same size and of many hues: lighter and darker shades of brown, dark red, yellow — all the colors of autumn leaves, arranged in an overlapping pattern like fish-scales.)

The central realization that came to me through that trip was the identity of the Real with the Good, which is certainly in line with the Christian concept of the Deity and which is also an important aspect of the doctrines of Frithjof Schuon, who emphasizes that the Sovereign Good is beyond the opposition of good-vs.-evil, given that God, since He is the Absolute, can have no opposite. As I expressed it in a poem I wrote about the trip, and which I later recited to Allen Ginsberg (it wasn't that good as a work of art so I didn't keep it): "You make it *better*, and *better*, and *better*, and *better*, until it's REAL."

At some point in the trip the impulse came to me that we needed to OPEN CHINA, so I decreed that this was to be so. (At the same time I saw that the roads that were cut into a hillside opposite us would grow and extend — until a point came, some time in the future, when that growth would simply stop. According to the mind-set I occupied at the time, this was very good news.) But did I ever ask where that imperative to "open China" came from? Of course not. The magician doesn't like to ask questions like that; he prefers to see all action as originating in his own sovereign intent; consequently the idea that the Principalities and Powers that lie behind the globalist agenda might have been manipulating me without my being aware of it never entered my head. It was much more congenial to me to think that I had, on that occasion, conceived the thought-form that would later result in Richard Nixon's ground-breaking diplomatic trip to China and his meeting with Chairman Mao, rather than that I had simply looked ahead into the future and seen this. To claim, like a *mere psychic*, that I had only foreseen this development rather than creating it myself was nowhere near impressive enough to match the intensity and exaltation of my experience.

Later on in the trip I encountered the seven Archangels — or (more properly) the seven Primordial Creative Demiurges — who originally unfolded the universe; it seemed as if I were one of them. (Later, in Leo Schaya's book *The Universal Meaning of the Kabbalah*, I learned that the beings I had met, or become one with, were the highest choir of the six-winged Seraphim, the ones who project the Six Directions — North, East, South, West, Zenith and Nadir — plus their common Center.) But once the vision ends and the trip is over, what does that amount to? You had been transfigured, you had assumed an exalted archetypal identity—but there was no way you could bring that identity back with you into your "ordinary" life, unless you did it through the very *hubris* of identification-with-the-archetype that Carl Jung warns us against as a kind of mental illness. Nonetheless plenty of people did that. After they came back—or half-way back—they held on to the memory of the identity they had temporarily assumed while tripping; they identified it with their egos, and consequently never fully regained the human form. So they named themselves "White Buffalo Cow Woman" or "Magic Snake-Power Man (or Snake-Oil Man)," etc. etc. and came out as fake spiritual teachers, self-professed magicians (either real or deluded), or simply as lunatics, like the woman we knew in Mill Valley who styled herself the Queen of the Nile and used to appear in ersatz Egyptian regalia at poetry readings and other events. But let's say you did succeed in coming all the way back into human form. Did you learn anything, did you gain anything of real value from the time you spent among the Eternal Seven? Maybe (just maybe) there might be some reason to know that such archetypal identities exist, but in terms of the spiritual Path, the whole excursion had been a waste not only of time but of precious spiritual potential—not to mention the danger that, if you revealed that you had been one of the Primal Creative Demiurges, somebody might lay at your doorstep the responsibility for the Black Mamba, the Smallpox Virus, the Monkey Pox or the Portuguese Man-o-War, and challenge you to justify such recklessness. The true spiritual Path begins with, and entirely addresses itself to, the *fitrah*, the Primordial Human Form—to what the Buddhists call "the human state hard-to-attain." As we Sufis explain it, the Human Form is not an archetype but the synthesis of *all* the archetypes, all the Names of God; that's why the angels, each of whom is formed on only one single Name of Allah, were commanded by Him in the Qur'an to bow down to Adam. As the universal synthesis of all the attributes of God we are His *khalifa*, His fully-empowered representative in this terrestrial world. But because we are also His *'abd*, His slave, we cannot *claim* any of these Names or Attributes as our own; in our own essence, apart from God's free and undeserved gifts to us, we are nothing—annihilated—snuffed out. It is from this point of absolute need that the spiritual Path begins—nor does this need ever leave us, no matter how much progress we make, since it is what we truly are. But if an angelic, archetypal identity somehow becomes grafted on to that nothingness, we can neither abase ourselves to the point of becoming a true servants nor allow God to exalt us to the point of becoming real *khalifas*. We are stuck in between—in the words of the *I Ching*, like a goat who butts against a hedge and gets his horns entangled, and so can move neither backwards nor forwards. Until this condition of false hybridization is healed, all progress on the spiritual Path is blocked.

The one other insight I remember from my Morning Glory Seed trip was my experience of *speech*—my own speech. I talked non-stop through the whole trip. I talked so effortlessly and endlessly and spontaneously that my speech became, at one point, just another one of the sounds of the world, like the hum of the traffic below us or the wind in the trees. *I was no longer talking because I was not.* And because *I* was not, a pocket gopher rose from the ground about a foot from my face, chewing a mouthful of grass; his long cheeks (his "pockets"), stretching about a third of the length of his body, were stuffed with it. And I kept on talking. If I had had an ego at that point, the gopher would've been alerted by my speech to the dangerous presence of *a human being with an agenda*, and would have immediately ducked back under ground to save himself. But as it was, he accepted my stream of human speech as no more threatening to him than the wind through the leaves of the bay laurels and the live oaks. We were both "children of the universe" (as the common hippie spiritual proverb went); we both "had a right to be here." And I maintain that this is the exact quality that the Judeo-Christian-Islamic tradition recognizes as the myth, and the visionary environment, of the Terrestrial Paradise, the Garden of Eden, where Adam and Eve—like the eternal Charles and Paula—still live at peace with the animals and they with each other, where the Lion lays down with the Lamb. In his "DIN POEM," Lew Welch notes and comments upon precisely this quality of human speech without a (recognized) human speaker.

And here we can also learn something about what *tantra* is, which is much more than just "the yoga of sex." If the mind can be quieted to the point where internal subvocal speech stops, the ego largely disappears, since that ego is 99% based on who we think we are and what we think the world is, which are based in turn on what we unconsciously *say* that we are, and what the world is. This is the "right-hand Path." But exactly the same effect can be achieved through complete "freedom of speech." I remember once when I was driving with a hitch-hiker up the slopes of Mt. Shasta in the Cascade Range, the most sacred mountain in California. I was talking, endlessly talking—until the point came where *I* was no longer talking because the "I" was no longer there. The speech went on; the speaker was annihilated. This is the *tantric* method, the "left-hand Path." (As I've already recounted, exactly the same thing happened to me on my second LSD trip in the Pacific Range of British Columbia: experience went on, but there was no experiencer. Life goes on within you and without you.)

The aftermath of my Morning Glory trip had only one obviously unfortunate consequence, based on the fact that we hadn't realized we should have soaked the seeds in water until the skins sloughed off before ingesting them, because the skins are where all the *strychnine* is; we only felt the effects of that ingredient after coming down. "Mild" strychnine poisoning is not a pleasant experience: slight diarrhea and the feeling of *shrinking inward* somehow at all points, coupled with the sense of having been transformed into a kind of boneless scarecrow from *The Wizard of Oz*. And look at the mixture of truth and illusion that trip delivered! Fantasies of magic and hubristic identification with the archetypes on the one hand, real (though temporary) ego-transcendence and insight into the nature of Divine Reality on the other. And furthermore, dear reader, please don't think that these experiences are "what you learn when you take Morning Glory Seeds"! As Timothy Leary and others have emphasized, the "set and setting" have everything to do with the quality and content of the experience — the "set" being the basic belief-system and intent you bring to it, and the "setting" the entire ambience, visual, auditory, olfactory etc., that sets the stage for it. Furthermore — though *I do not "advocate" the use of psychedelics or entheogens*, as should be painfully clear by now — if you do make the mistake of ingesting Morning Glory Seeds, be careful to get a relatively "organic" brand without such additives as mercury-based fungicides, etc. And be sure to soak them first!

Marijuana

Marijuana was usually smoked so continually, besides being comparatively mild, that specific psychedelic experiences generally didn't stand out as memories, though one did develop a connoisseur's palate for the differences between Acapulco Gold, the smoke of pure sunlight, those heavy opium-soaked Thai sticks, and the celestial Michoacan and Columbian *sensimilla*... however, I do remember four instances. In the first, after smoking some Panama Red, which provides a very jagged experience — possibly because its THC content far exceeds the percentage of CBD it contains — I closed my eyes and saw a repetitive wallpaper pattern made up of firing spark plugs. "Every interesting experience counts" is one theory...

In the second, after smoking some weed in the Trumblys' basement, I sat still until I had become just another piece of furniture or musical instrument in the room: the "me" was no longer in evidence. (I had a similar experience during a long bout of mononucleosis in high school, which kept me mostly bedridden for weeks. I got so little exercise that I developed serious insomnia, so my father brought me a single red capsule of seconal, the strongest of the barbiturates. After I swallowed it I lay staring at the plastered ceiling of my downstairs apartment in my childhood home, until, once again, the ego was snuffed out: there was the ceiling with its ridges and swirls and grooves of plaster, but there was no one looking at it.)

In the third, in a sea grotto at Limontur Spit, its walls encrusted with starfish, limpets, and chitons, I witnessed the birth of language, millions of years ago. Some event happened in the world, and simultaneously a *word* was born in the mind of the human witness to that event (in the mind of whoever I was or had been at that time), and was spoken out loud just as the event occurred—thereby resulting in the first dawn of the understanding of what a *name* is, the realization that: "That *sound* is the *name* of that *thing!*" In the words of the Qur'an: *We will show them Our signs on the horizons* (the outer world) *and in themselves, till it is clear to them that this is the truth.*

And then there was the silken experience of driving Highway 101 back from Mill Valley to San Rafael, stoned on champagne and black hashish, the fine thread of consciousness perfectly unbroken from nanosecond to nanosecond. Never once, after a thousand failed attempts, was I ever able to get busted for driving under the influence; all my automobile accidents were accomplished in complete sobriety, a sobriety that in itself sometimes disturbed my presence of mind due to the lack of any intoxicant to calm my thoughts... one of the spiritually seductive aspects of alcohol and drugs is that they can sometimes temporarily silence the "monkey mind," though over the long run they tend to make the jabbering of that monkey a lot louder and crazier...

(There is one herb, however, that I can confidently recommend for this purpose: the leaves of the uva-ursi or bear-berry shrub, called *kinnikinnick* in British Columbia—not to be confused with the eastern kinnikinnick of the Plains Indians, which is red cedar bark. One toke of bear-berry leaf, held and exhaled, and all sub-vocal speech abruptly stops, with no additional intoxicating effect: a useful "ally" for serious group consultations, where clarity and sobriety are required.)

Beyond these experiences, I should also report that one of the main effects marijuana had was to open the door for me to "clairvoyant archaeology" into the deep past—though there is no way I can prove the validity of my findings, or authenticate any of the mental artifacts I might have turned up during a particular "dig." In addition to grass, the best key to the past was good Spanish sherry—*oloroso* was my favorite—a vintage like Duff Gordon Old '97 or anything by Pedro Domecq. Sherry plus grass was even better. My mind would drift back through the traditional bodegas of Xeres de la Frontera—past the ritual bullfights and their possibly Cretan origin, where the first matador was Perseus and the first slain bull the Minotaur—past Barcelona, a colony of Carthage, founded according to legend by Hamilcar Barca, the father of Hannibal—Carthage itself being a colony of Phoenicia and its capital city Sidon, likely founded by distant ancestors of the mysterious Peoples of the Sea who, according to my own intuitional archaeological findings, were refugees from Atlantis forced to turn pirate after the ocean overwhelmed their homeland. Some say that Poseidon, the Greek sea-god, was originally Po Sidon, "Father (of) Sidon," possibly the chief god of the Atlantean pantheon—who, when he was overthrown by the Greek sky-god Zeus, wielder-of-the-thunderbolt, had his own thunderbolt snapped in two, leaving him with nothing but half-a-bolt: his royal trident. At the bottom of a bottle of good sherry—especially if the bucket you used to draw the water from that well was woven from the fiber of the hemp plant—you might well find the circular rings of Atlantis before the flood, of land alternating with water, lying out rich and opulent in the sun, and fearing nothing—the watery circles crowded with far-ranging ships, manned by the greatest merchants and sea-farers of the archaic world. And, as is proved by her many constructions of antediluvian polygonal masonry, Xeres de la Frontera herself was originally a part of Atlantis, whose greater portion went under the waves, in both Europe and America, when the seas rose at the end of the Pleistocene.

And then there were the excursions back to ancient Palestine where, after smoking, I dug and sifted the deep layers of human time at Jerusalem, Nazareth, Qumran, tracing the connections of John the Baptist and the Essenes to Zoroastrian Persia through the Mandaean Gnostics of the Mesopotamian marshlands, and of the Zoroastrian Magi to the Nazirite brotherhood into which Samson, the prophet Amos, John the Baptist and Jesus of Nazareth himself were all initiated—those "shepherds who watched their flocks by night" at the birth of Christ (i.e., those leaders of esoteric brotherhoods), the ones that Christian visionary Anne Catherine Emmerich saw meeting with the Magi who had come to witness the same birth, as well as the relationship of those same Nazirite Shepherds not only to the Good Shepherd but to the Sufis, whose name means "wool-clad" (as sheep are)—plus the resonance of the Zealot war-cry "Our Lord is Yahweh!" (never Caesar to be our Lord, but God Alone!), across six hundred years, to *La ilaha illa 'Allah*, "there is no god but God!" All the streets and alleys and by-ways of Pitriyana, the great Necropolis, dug and sifted by the fine picks and trowels of the herb *marijuana*—sister to the blond Lebanese hashish, subtlest of all the smokes and mirrors of the Old Man of the Mountain, Grand Shaykh of the Ismaili Assassins, that elixir being the chosen ally of all who begin everything but finish nothing, the ones *who say that which they do not*. Discerning the fascinating designs and patterns in a pile of psychic phantoms? Trying to fix up and organize and learn something of importance from a broken heap of dead karmic residues? What lessons on the *spiritual* level (not merely the psycho-historical one) can you derive from wandering for years and decades through the caverns of the ancestors? Only that *Memory is Eternal Death*.

Purple Gate: A Three-Day Inoculation against Deadly Yin Energy

> *My strength is perfected in weakness.*
> 2 Corinthians 12:9

This experience with psychedelic drugs makes up a sort of "medley" of substances and influences, consequently it doesn't appear in the above accounts of mescaline and psilocybin. After Lew Welch committed suicide, his "widow" Magda lived in a relationship with one of Lew's buddies, Jack Boyce, in a cabin he had built on the Bolinas Mesa, made out of timbers from an old railroad trestle. Jack, if you'll remember, was one of the people I met who had fully adopted Lew's voice, on a level that went far beyond mimicry and approached full identification. If that voice had been Lew's soul, it's as if Jack, by reproducing that voice, had become—at least half-way—his living reincarnation. Unfortunately, shortly before I renewed my acquaintance with Magda after Lew's death, Jack, who had been dancing on the thick, high rafters of his cabin, fell off, broke his neck and died. And so the cabin that came to be known as "Purple Gate" passed to Magda. Did Jack name it that, or did she give it that name after Jack's death? Whatever the answer, Purple Gate was generally recognized as signifying "the Gate of Death"—especially in view of the symbolic meaning of the color purple worn by Catholic priests during lent, for penance, and also for funerals. And to back up this funereal symbolism the story had been going around—was this before Jack's death or after it?—that Magda Cregg had in fact killed Lew Welch through something approaching witchcraft, or at least through her status as the sort of "Lady of Death" well-recognized in the hippie world, as in the song "Not So Sweet Martha Lorraine" by Country Joe and the Fish. (I met such a lady one time at Magda's residential bus on the Mesa. She actually tried to tempt me to suicide, since, as a student of Lew Welch, it would only be right for me to follow in his footsteps.) And while this belief in Magda's murderous intentions was really no more than a convenient projection on her by the men of that place and time, a reflection of their own fatal immaturities and tendencies to self-destruction, it's not as if she didn't *play into* those projections pretty thoroughly, and put them to use when necessary. When she brought the rare psychedelic ibogaine back from Africa, she boasted that "15% die." "The first time?" I asked her. "The first time" she confidently replied. She also wore a leather pouch around her neck containing a dried sliver of the pure white Amanita Verna, the Destroying Angel, one of the most poisonous mushrooms in the world, just in case the impulse seized her to follow Lew on his terminal trip into the Great Mystery. But I wouldn't call Magda a *femme fatal* so much as a "death-wife," the opposite of a midwife. Men with suicidal tendencies sought her out so she could ease their passage into the next world. Yet women like that would also sometimes *personify death* for the men in their lives in order to overcome their own fears. If you *are* Death, the theory goes, you can never die; if you are Fate you can decree the fates of others, but nothing fatal will ever happen to *you*. The counter-theory, which I myself subscribe to—though the activation of it requires a willingness to go through the valley of the *shadow* of death in the quest for Eternal

Life — was enunciated by the great English poet and Anglican priest, John Donne (an ancestor of my own wife, Jenny Donne), when he declared: "Death, thou shalt die!"

My own three-day sojourn at Purple Gate took place in the early 70s when the great Yin Wave that brought the brief Golden Age of the counterculture to a close was breaking over the hippie world — the wave that brought in the regime of feminism. Women were becoming tall and wide-hipped and powerful (like Bobby Louise Hawkins); men were becoming skinny and debilitated and effete (like Robert Creeley). The late 60s had been a time of what the *I Ching* calls "Old Yang," when the fullest outward expression of glorious masculinity, the era of shirtless blond-haired rock stars being worshipped like gods by hordes of subservient groupies, was just about to flip over into the "New Yin" phase of contraction and introversion. It was appropriate that this be the Age of Leo, the last days of golden California summer, before the vast Fall that was to come. It was the age of Shango, the great Yoruba stud and *orisha*, who became one of the main Voodoo *loas* — the thunder-and-lightning god who was so hypermasculine that he would suddenly go over the line, flip his sex and become a woman, this being why he was syncretized with the Catholic St Barbara, whose name means "bearded." (I remember the exact moment when, for me, this transformation took place. I'd driven down Highway 1 to Big Sur, and at one of those little cafes or art galleries that occupy many of the narrow, almost-vertical canyons set in the inner crooks of that road, I witnessed the following scene: A hippie swain, guitar in hand, was serenading his chosen maiden. When he finished his song, he opened his arms wide to her to receive his destined prize, as had worked for him so many times in the past — but this time his quarry reacted by crying "*yuccchh!*" and clearing out of the place as fast as she could. That's the precise point when I knew that the collective sexual weather had changed. After that I kept noticing how many very attractive women were doing all they could to hide that attractiveness, dressing in shapeless grunge or war surplus military gear. As global warming was just starting up in the outer world, the parallel global freezing in the inner world was already far advanced.)

My Psychedelic Retreat in the cabin of death began when Magda and I smoked some weed, then visited Don Allen, whom Lew had introduced me to some years earlier, the gracious, highly-cultured editor of Federico García Lorca and the Beats, at his house on the same Mesa. He served us bourbon (likely from the Old Literary Gentleman Distillery) to get us ready for the main events back at Purple Gate. These included Magda making me eat peyote and magic mushrooms *at the same time* "so they can get to know each other" (inside *me!*), and later on sharing with me a smoking mixture she had concocted of coca leaves from Peru mixed with dried flakes of the Amanita Muscaria mushroom, the scarlet one with the white flecks, which wasn't nearly as poisonous as the Amanita Verna, though definitely headed in the same direction...

Like my other psilocybin trips and my third and last acid trip, this session was largely characterized by endurance. Essentially, I became next to invisible — largely for self-protection, seeing that Magda, who was around 50, had offered herself to me sexually (though without much enthusiasm as I remember; I was in my late 20s at the time), to which I simply said "no thanks." I had withdrawn my masculinity from view and turned it over to the Heavenly Father for safekeeping. I was like Achilles disguised as a girl, hidden among women by his mother so he wouldn't have to — or be able to — fulfill his destiny to die as a hero in the Trojan War. (Let the reader note how the power of psychedelics to open the Collective Unconscious, especially when used outside the context of a living spiritual tradition and any effective channel of Divine Grace, tends to conduct the user through the psychic husks of innumerable ancient and exhausted Pagan deities and cults.)

And I was *so* invisible, my masculinity so effectively hidden, that I was actually able to sit in on the meeting of a witch's coven — a peyote-meeting conducted by Magda for the local women — who didn't even recognize me as a man, or hardly as a human being. I was nothing but a wraith, a ghost, a fly on the wall; consequently I might have been witness to things that no other man has ever seen and lived to tell the tale — unless he was lucky enough to get off with no worse a punishment than castration.

"Let's not invite any men to the next peyote meeting" one woman said; "let's just have *pictures* of men." "You don't want our bodies" I replied, "you just want our souls." *And yet I still live*, even at 74 — 30 years older than Lew Welch was when he blew his brains out.

Other ominous events occurred, symbolic of mitigated castration. I molded a perfect mushroom out of the local clay, placed it in the fire to fire it — but it broke. I started to shake Magda's ceremonial rattle — but it broke.

The last memory I have of those three days, however, was undoubtedly the most significant of all. Another young man visited us, sensitive and handsome and lyrical, wearing around his neck a scarf made out of tiny brass links, like fine chain mail — and this evanescent personage proceeded *to dance on the rafters for Magda just as Jack Boyce had done*, while reciting rhymed verse *ex tempore* — perfectly enacting the role of the poet tempting Fate and courting Death in service to the Goddess! (Shades of Thomas Rymer!) Even worse, and more dangerous, was the fact that his poetry was total crap — or was that actually what saved him? In any case, he was the very image of the famous *Puer Aeternus* of the Jungians, the Eternal Youth who is destined to die young at the Goddess' hands. It was as if that Youth had risen up out of my own unconscious and appeared in flesh and blood before me, as if he and his destiny had *split off* from me at that very moment and gone their separate way in life, leaving my path clear of his self-sabotaging and suicidal foolishness.

Looking back now on that final encounter, I can judge my three-day inoculation against Deadly Yin Energy, all those many years ago, to have been a therapeutic and immunological success.

Methamphetamine

I took the violent poison known as "meth" or "speed" only twice, in oral form, in very small amounts, because I wanted to sit down for once and "figure out the universe." What I figured out was that the universe — a word that means "one turn" — is what the physicists call a "standing wave," defined as "a wave that appears to be vibrating vertically without traveling horizontally, created from waves with identical frequency and amplitude interfering with one another while traveling in opposite directions." (These "opposite directions" may in fact be related to the bi-directional nature of time — *not* its theorized reversibility, which is absurd and self-contradictory, but the subtle temporal quality transmitted by the question: "Which way is time moving: from the past toward the future, or from the future toward the past?") But more to the point, since the universe includes both matter/energy and consciousness, it is better described as a "subject/object wave," something that is perpetually engaged in transforming *material energy* into *psychic experience*. Its perceptible material half (object) is continuously expanding and radiating energy while its psychic perceiving half (subject) is continuously concentrating and absorbing energy. When the available energy from the perceptible object is entirely transformed into subjective experience, when object is empty and subject is full, they exchange places. Completed perception (subject) now stops absorbing energy and begins to radiate it, thus becoming the object of the next cycle, while object, now exhausted, empty and no longer perceptible, begins to receive energy from what was once subject and, by transforming that energy into experience, becomes the subject of the next cycle. However, since we are not talking about a series of passing waves but a single standing wave, all the cycles, which are innumerable, are actually simultaneous. This is what Heraclitus meant when he said that "Immortals become mortal, mortals become immortal; they die each other's lives and live each other's deaths."

Is there any truth to this notion or is it nothing but a barren speculation, possibly influenced by my early reading of Teilhard de Chardin? And, if valid, could the notion of a universe that's defined as a cyclic-yet-simultaneous process of transforming objective energy into subjective experience help any further in the elucidation of the Anthropic Principle, which is precisely the contemporary rendition of the traditional doctrine of the Universe as the Macrocosm and Humanity as the (corresponding) Microcosm? However we answer this, the Matrix of the whole process, the Divine Reality that neither grows nor decays, in which subject and object are eternally united, did not appear in these cogitations. Because methamphetamine is entirely worldly—because it stimulates *ratio* but veils the *Intellectus*—it cannot see God.

A PSYCHEDELIC POST MORTEM

After completing the above account of my major psychedelic experiences, the thing that impresses itself on me is just how *uneven* they were. Mystical raptures and metaphysical insights were promiscuously jumbled together with magical fantasies (possibly of demonic origin), irrelevant static, and true death-traps. There was no overall guiding spirit. The whole thing was a crap-shoot.

René Guénon taught that rites and religions, as well as sacred sites like temples or pyramids, whose informing Spirit has deserted them, will often be polluted with the psychic residues that were once attracted to and sanctified by that Spirit, residues that have become toxic now that its influence has been withdrawn; this was his explanation of things like "the curse of King Tut." And I believe that the same thing can be said of the *memories* of psychedelic experience. Maybe God took a particular psychedelic session as an opportunity to send His Grace into the heart of someone who was so blocked from receiving spiritual influences that it took something as gross as a chemical to get through to him or her—but that doesn't mean that the person's memories of that experience still carry that Grace. After I first dropped acid and later tried to remember what had happened, my mind would travel back through the events of my life until it reached Acid Day—but instead of remembering that day, it would drop *through* it instead, as if through a hole in time, and end up *here and now* again. In other words, the true keynote of my experience with LSD was the unveiling of the *nunc stans*, the Eternal Present—and the Present is always Now. In comparison with that Present, the memories of any past unveilings of Now are the mere ghosts of eternity, regions of depleted reality that latch on to us like vampires, trying to keep themselves alive by stealing from us, and from our present quality of attention, the reality they lack. At one point in the hippie counterculture, stories of old acid trips were the stock in trade of every psychedelic raconteur (of whom Ram Dass—Richard Alpert—was undoubtedly the greatest, closely followed by "psychonaut" Terrence McKenna with his amazing experiences with DMT and Ayahuasca). But then, as if by collective agreement, a taboo was placed on stories of psychedelic experiences; nobody wanted to hear all that blather any more. Maybe people were just turning away from their mystical interests toward more "practical" concerns, considering that kind of Magical Mystery Tour to be a sin of their youth... but it is also possible that they instinctively sensed the toxicity of those memories and were acting to protect themselves.

Ram Dass was once told by his yoga teachers in India that he had a blockage in his *visshudha-chakra*, his throat center, due to his use of LSD. The *visshudha-chakra* is the center having to do with the speech and the thinking mind, while the next higher center, the *ajña-chakra* or Third Eye, relates to contemplative consciousness, to the direct perception of Truth. One of the long-term negative effects of psychedelics may be that they break down the natural barrier between thought and contemplation, thus removing the "guardian" that helps us to leave thought behind when entering into the contemplative Silence. What appears as inspiration when the higher contemplative mind speaks through the lower thinking mind may reveal itself to be nothing but mental pollution when the lower "monkey-mind" can't stop jabbering, even in the sacred temple precincts of the higher contemplative mind. Traditional spiritual paths have many safeguards against this unfortunate development—safeguards that the psychedelic "way" desperately needs, but which for the most part it has never even heard of.

THE DEVIL'S ROLODEX

If you've lacked any sense that higher worlds of perception exist than the material one, or if your attachment to your own subjectivity is so fixed that you've never conceived of the possibility of experience without an experiencer, then the use of psychedelics or "entheogens" may open your eyes. Nonetheless, when you "take a pill and see God," you've created several problems. First, you've limited God by turning Him into an experience of your own; certainly He is the ultimate Author and Experiencer of your experience of Him—and of all other experiences—but He is also immensely more than that, infinitely beyond all that. Secondly, if a simple material chemical can lift the veil from the Face of God, then God has been reduced to a mere physical reality, definable as one particular set of chemical- and/or energy-states of the human brain—and so when the brain dies and lies decomposing in the grave, God must be considered to be dead and decomposing along with it. On top of that, psychedelics sometimes have the power to breach the natural energy-barrier between the human psychophysical system and the surrounding subtle energy environment on a more or less permanent basis, thereby creating a condition in which the individual lacks healthy personal boundaries. You have opened up too far to all and everything, so you either retain that openness in all situations, including those where it is highly inappropriate, situations in which a degree of discretion and self-protection are required, or else you react against that excessive openness by closing down too far to everything, both intuitively and empathetically, thus going into what Jung called "the regressive restoration of the persona." In addition, many of the powerful impressions produced by psychedelics will sometimes remain with you for years on a subconscious level, long after you have detoxed from the physical drug itself. Under certain circumstances the heavy, negative or obscure impressions you might have received will form a kind of crust over the spiritual Heart on a deeply unconscious level, acting as a barrier to spiritual perception, while the more "positive" impressions will act to replace contemplative insight in the present moment with mere memories of such insights from the past, memories that can in no way be spiritually effective. Lastly, psychedelics may unconsciously open the user to demonic influences beyond his or her intent—influences that in some ways represent the inner-world analogue of the nefarious criminal and intelligence networks who've been involved in distributing psychedelics to the masses over the past 50-plus years—thus establishing (possibly but not necessarily) spiritually toxic connections that are likely to last until something intentional is done to remove them, or until God in the guise of Fate intervenes, causing you to finally act them out and so learn the "hard way"; I've described this condition as "going into the Devil's Rolodex." Can spiritually nourishing connections be established by the same process? Perhaps they can—yet such positive connections will need to be intentionally maintained and cultivated over the long term, and this is a work in which (to say the least!) drugs are of no help.

At this point in time, in the 2020s, psychedelics are undergoing a resurgence in academic and psychotherapeutic circles, often under much more "controlled" conditions than prevailed in the 1960s. I'm confident that these "entheogens" can be therapeutically helpful to some, especially those caught in various deep-seated addictions, conceptual/emotional traps and vicious cycles; they definitely do expand one's *psychic* horizons. What they cannot do, in and of themselves, is bring you closer to God in any fundamentally *spiritual* way. No pill can give you faith; no pill (not even MDMA!) can give you love. No pill can help you develop virtue or increase your willingness to make the sacrifices necessary to find love and realize wisdom—including the temporary sacrifice of psychological "balance" in the name of a higher good. Spirituality and well-being are certainly related to one another, but only obliquely. Sometimes a gain in psychological well-being brings you closer to the Spirit, sometimes a loss of such well-being does the same, since the rigor and suffering this loss produces may be the one thing that will force you to turn to God in faith as your only recourse. Seeking healthier psychic states is certainly a worthy pursuit; the only thing worthier is to accept all states, pleasant or unpleasant, expansive or contractive, as acts of God designed to remove the psychic veils that prevent you from following His Will and seeing His Face—which is to say, self-improvement must give way to self-transcendence at one point. As long these two are strictly identified, the true nature of the spiritual Path can never be grasped—though this certainly does *not* mean that the darker psychic qualities, especially those that may represent demonic interventions, should not be vigorously combatted and (God willing) healed. But beyond that, no artificially-induced psychic state, whether through chemicals or electronic or magnetic brain stimulation or anything else, can produce even true health on the psychic plane, since psychological well-being must be based on strength and clarity of character, not technological tricks. But do we even know what human character-development is anymore? If we define the human being as nothing but a complex bio-technological mechanism, then a tinkering-with and a tweaking-of the nerves and the genes is all we will be able to imagine as possible; the very concept of human character, and the *human dignity* that goes with it—in other words, an immortal human soul—will have been relegated (except for a "faithful remnant") to the dustbin of history.

HIPPIE REQUIEM

According to the famous proverb of William Blake, "If the Fool would persist in his folly he would become wise." I would only add: "If he survives." And if you end up becoming wise in any particular area, you will have to leave behind whatever foolishness might have made you wise.

When you're out of the game, you can reflect on the game. When, for example, you no longer identify with a particular mass movement or political agenda or collective worldly hope, you can contemplate in (relative) tranquility what you once enthusiastically supported or violently condemned. And since you are no longer a True Believer, you are willing to entertain the possibility that what you once identified with was not really worth your allegiance, that it had many negative elements and consequences, even that it was in some ways a swindle of massive proportions.

As my experiences with psychedelic drugs, including marijuana, receded into the past, I could afford to recall and meditate upon the fact that LSD was first distributed in the United States by the CIA, partly in the context of the infamous MK-Ultra mind-control program, which included experiments practiced upon unsuspecting American citizens that were worthy to stand beside those conducted in the Nazi death-camps (see the researches of David McGowan, Henry Makow and Peter Levenda). Timothy Leary was assigned to feed acid to the intelligentsia, Ken Kesey to everybody else; apparently the idea was to compare how it acted under "controlled conditions" with its effects in a totally free-wheeling, "party" atmosphere. And the hippies actually knew about this! They routinely said, "SURE we were a CIA experiment, man—an experiment that GOT OUT OF CONTROL!" Nor was the Agency simply interested in mind-control on the individual level, so as to produce Manchurian Candidate-like assassins for example. The CIA also likely sponsored the *mass* dissemination of LSD as part of MK-Ultra. According to Peter Levenda, in his trilogy *Sinister Forces: A Grimoire of American Political Witchcraft*, William Mellon Hitchcock (scion of the billionaire Mellon family), who was associated with CIA front organizations Castle Bank and Trust and Resorts International, as well as being Timothy Leary's landlord for his "psychedelic manor house" at Millbrook in upstate New York (see *Millbrook* by Art Kleps), paid a chemist by the name of Nicholas Sand to produce *millions* of doses of LSD. If this claim can be substantiated, then it was clearly their intent to drench the unsuspecting American populace with swimming-pools full of acid, in what might have been the largest mass social engineering project in human history.

Nor did the CIA only expose their victims and enemies — among whom we must include the American people — to the psychedelic drugs they had discovered and/or developed; they were also using them on themselves. The idea that the CIA wanted to employ psychedelics to "confuse and terrify" people is true as far as it goes, but they also apparently hoped that these substances could help their own agents gain magic powers: telepathy, remote viewing, etc. And they were also entirely willing to confuse and *delight* people if that would serve their ends. The hippie myth that the CIA were nothing but a bunch of uptight straight people who "couldn't hold their acid" and saw it only as a crazy-making pill needs to be permanently debunked. The Bohemian/Magician/Spy is a well-known type; both the Elizabethan occultist John Dee (the original Agent 007) and the Satanist Aleister Crowley worked for British Intelligence. The ultimate goal of the powers-that-be in terms of psychedelic research, which has made a vigorous comeback in the academic world in recent years, may be to create a type of "spirituality" where even mystical experiences that are valid on a certain level will serve to establish their control. They want to *own everything* — even mysticism, even spiritual aspiration, even God. And the fact is that LSD did initiate a sort of *bardo* or revelatory decay of American society; all the latent tendencies, good and bad, the dominant belief-systems, conscious or otherwise, were called up in a very short time, laid out for all to see — and much of the social, cultural and spiritual potential of America and the Western World rapidly exhausted in the process. The family was largely destroyed (not by LSD alone of course); Christian morality was undermined, including the concept of human dignity that is central to democracy; political responsibility was seriously eroded. And the social engineers simply sat back and took voluminous notes on the whole process. They noted the main trends, the major "cultural archetypes" operating in the "collective unconscious" of society, and devised various ways to appropriate, pervert, control and *counterfeit* every one of them. In so doing they helped initiate the sinister *Blade Runner* world we live in today. The hippies naively equated social control with a simplistic authoritarian repression; they rarely awoke to the fact that *real* control is based on co-optation, on the covert implantation of engineered beliefs and attitudes in the mass mind. The powers that be do not want heroes who courageously oppose them and die as martyrs; they would much rather find, or create, dupes who will obey their every command in the firm belief that they are following their own desires, their own creative expressions and "spiritual" intuitions, all in perfect freedom.

As the Hippie Counterculture waned, it separated into three strands: those who hurried to leave it behind, notably the "Yuppies" or Young Urban Professionals, whose name was coined partly to parody the "Yippies" of the Youth International Party founded by Jerry Rubin, Abbie Hoffman and Paul Krassner, and whose "coming out" was notably celebrated in the comic strip *Doonesbury* by Gary Trudeau; the Veterans of the Psychedelic Wars who, like those of The Greatest Generation who hit the Normandy beaches on D-Day, could never forget their own D-Day, which was Woodstock, or ever leave it behind, and so became paralyzed and nailed to the past; and the Hippie Rednecks, those downwardly-mobile Baby Boomers who might or might not have been part of the commune movement—and who pioneered the idea of home schooling before it became officially associated with the Right Wing—but who in any case gravitated toward the White conservative rural working class, and whose musical tastes, traveling from Bob Dylan and Janice Joplin, past the Creedence Clearwater Revival and The Band (particularly as represented by Levon Helm), through the Allman Brothers and Alabama, became generally Country/Western, thus explaining the long braided hair and pot-smoking ways of Willie Nelson.

As for the fading days of the counterculture in the San Francisco Bay Area, it was Magda Cregg who wrote the definitive epitaph for it:

> The poets took away poetry
> Musicians and cocaine took away music
> The people stopped dancing.

When Eternity falls, it splits in two; that's where the "ancient future" meme comes from—the sort of sensibility that leads us to imagine Flash Gordon storm troopers armed with ray-guns, but dressed as Roman centurions. It was Led Zepplin that aesthetically spearheaded the mad advance into the Future, in the direction of technocracy and transhumanism, our vast collective acceleration toward the liquid-nitrogen-cold, ozone-blue Dawn that lay ahead. And the Creedence Clearwater Revival began our great retreat into the Past, toward Sunset, through the fading embers of memory, riding the massive redshift that delivered us to a profound and killing nostalgia, the Sun on an Aztec altar off the Farallones, bleeding into the lap of Night... though, in reality, that retreat and that advance are simultaneous, being a single dual manifestation of "the sacred Red and Blue Days" spoken of by the Lakota, which stand as signs of the end of what the Hopis call "The Fourth World."

But what if we followed neither of them and just stayed where we are, letting the past return to the past by its own inertia and the future press on to the future through its own compulsion, leaving us simply standing here, free of both of them? What if we found out that Eternity never ended?

THE HIPPIES' SUFFERING

The hippies renounced privilege because privilege had cut them off from life—an exile that made them suffer. In flight from that suffering they rejected the burden of privilege, but also the security that went with it; in flight from both the suffering of privilege and the suffering of having rejected privilege, they sought pleasure wherever they could find it—particularly in sex, drugs and rock 'n' roll—and in so doing gave rise to a vast ocean of pain that their pursuit of pleasure both generated and blinded them to. And so, to escape the suffering created by "the pursuit of happiness" that was guaranteed them by their own interpretation of the Declaration of Independence, they doubled down on sex, drugs and rock 'n' roll. Some of the hippies, however, began to wake up—either because of LSD or else in spite of it (remembering that acid is not just a self-indulgence but also an ordeal, sometimes a deliberately chosen ordeal)—and therefore sought out the Spiritual Path that could both lead them out of suffering and give their suffering a meaning that would allow them to dedicate it: to God, certainly—whether they knew it or not—but also to the several surrogates of God, to the People's Liberation, to the Healing of the Earth, to the ending of their own suffering through spiritual detachment, to the willingness to suffer to end the suffering of others. They could do this because they were starting to learn how to suffer consciously and deliberately: "If you knew how to suffer you would know how not to suffer" says the Gospel of Thomas. They were beginning to understand the *mysteries* of suffering: what it would mean to suffer for "the good souls in Purgatory" like the Catholics say (which is what, from one point of view, we all are); and what it was to suffer for each other, as the Inkling Charles Williams taught in his theory of the mutual exchange and bearing of each other's burdens as our way of participating in the crucifixion of Christ; and what it meant to suffer in the knowledge that only God is the Doer, the Sole Performer of action, and the Only Sufferer of the consequences of action, and the One Who Alone is free from action and the suffering of action; and what it might be to suffer in the understanding that everything He sends, whether pleasurable or painful (as the Sufis say) is good; and what it would be to suffer in atonement for our sins, which are nothing other than our many and varied attempts to distract ourselves, by any means possible, including sex, drugs and rock 'n' roll, from the sufferings intrinsic to human life; and what it might be to undergo the suffering of the Bodhisattva who, having exhausted the suffering of his or her own karma, now inherits the karmic sufferings of all sentient beings, every one of whom the Bodhisattva vows to save, just as Christ on the Cross saved them—just as God saved them at the beginning of time in the very act of creating them, in the act of liberating them (as Ibn al-'Arabi teaches us) from the suffering of non-existence so they could play their destined roles in the suffering of existence, thereby opening them to the ocean of His Mercy: *There is no refuge from Allah but in Him* says the Noble Qur'an. Suffering, the taking on of suffering, the ending of suffering, the dedication of suffering—it's all the same story.

A few of the hippies ultimately woke up to this kind of knowledge. As for the rest of us who never did, along with those parts of my own soul that have willfully remained asleep, the resurrection that nonetheless must inevitably come of all the buried memories of the counterculture years, of those "years that the locust hath eaten" [Joel 2:25]—a resurrection that this book hopefully serves—must also re-awaken all the sufferings of those times, thereby giving us an opportunity, maybe for the first time, to embrace them, to be purified *of* them and *by* them, and to return them to the primordial creative Mercy that sent them down to us in the first place—thus allowing us, the hippie generation, to finish our chosen and delegated tasks before we finally quit this stage set, this ephemeral two-dimensional world, and meet our Maker.

CHAPTER FIVE

Kerouac-ing It: The Planet of the Road

IN THE LAST TWO CHAPTERS, SO AS TO TELL THE story of Lew Welch and the Beats and of the hippies who followed them, I had to get a little ahead of myself. Now, however, I need to go back and pick up my own personal timeline after high school, which will lead us across the same territory from a different direction, the direction of travel back and forth through what Allen Ginsberg punningly called "these States" (united or otherwise), then north to British Columbia.

In my circle of post-high school friends it went without saying that we would start criss-crossing the United States from coast-to-coast by car — like Kerouac did, but also following the directive of the famous ad-song "See the USA in your Chevrolet" as sung by Dinah Shore. Personally "discovering America" was much more attractive and less intimidating in those days than it is today. And hitchhiking and hopping freights, which we also engaged in, were even more interesting and more daring than the car trips, though they were a lot more dangerous than we were willing to admit at the time. Hitchhiking was accepted as a matter of course, though freight-hopping was pushing the edge a bit, even then. Still, in the four charmed years between 1966 and 1970, anything seemed possible, easy and relatively safe to us healthy young white men from the middle class in our early 20s, as yet free of serious trauma, who had enlisted under the banner of "Hip."

Seeking adventure — experience for its own sake that includes an element of risk — was something we were naturally attracted to. We lived in safe suburbs not ghettoes, and we were sure as hell not going to Vietnam, so how else (besides peacefully attending violent demonstrations) were we going to experience the harder edge of life? We all assumed that our role-model Bobbie Dylan had ridden freights, possibly from his "Song to Woody":

> Here's to the hearts and the hands of the men,
> Who come with the dust and are gone with the wind...
>
> And the very last thing that I'd want to do
> Is to say I've been hittin' some hard travelin' too...

So when we found out, in middle age, that he probably hadn't, we felt vaguely betrayed. That little wise-ass twerp suckered us into *what??*

When Woodie Guthrie rode freights during the Depression it was as an itinerant laborer, artistic or not as might be, with others who had been forced into that life: tramps, bindle-stiffs. (As the definition goes, "A tramp is an itinerant worker; a hobo is an itinerant non-worker; a bum is a non-itinerant non-worker.") But when I rode freights it was with $500 of travelers'-checks in my pocket. I lived in an era when voluntary poverty, voluntary danger and voluntary hardship (on a recreational basis) were still possible and desirable, and not just through rock-climbing, solitary long-distance hiking and x-treme sports — or else, if you opted to leave your amateur status behind and become a professional, by joining the mercenaries or becoming a front-line correspondent in a war zone or natural disaster. That is to say (if nuclear weapons and the draft are removed from the equation) that I lived in an era of safety.

Still, the world was getting more dangerous by the week. High-profile assassinations, violent demonstrations, race riots, exotic self-poisonings in the name of mystical enlightenment, with characters like the Hell's Angels and the Manson Family floating around somewhere in the mix, and with the great black rain of Vietnam always in the background... I've called those times "the dress rehearsal for the Apocalypse," with the Apocalypse itself being now. But all that was just icing on the cake to us, hot peppers to spice the stew. As the great Indian saint Ramakrishna answered when somebody asked him why there is evil in the universe: "It's there to thicken the plot!" That was our attitude exactly. It was at Altamont that the idea of evil as an exhilarating change-of-pace (Mick Jagger) and the knowledge of it as an all-encompassing and nearly-inescapable reality (the Angels) crashed head on against each other. And the Angels won.

Be that as it may, it was our plan and intent to seek a wide range of experience, experience *as if* for its own sake. Can you learn from experience? Working can teach you about work, relationships about relating to people, having kids about kids, but can *pure* experience without a conscious goal ripen into Wisdom? If the fool persists in his folly does he really become wise? The old Arthurian romancers had a concept they called *aventure*, which essentially means to cast your fate to the winds, like a questing knight, and then accept whatever comes, considering it to be a gift or a chastisement or a test from God — this being a way of enacting *not my will but Thine be done* in the most concrete of terms. But without God in the equation, the quest for experience in and of itself is a blind addiction that leads only to darkness and chaos. In Aristotelian terms (I always go back to Aristotle's "hylomorphic theory" for some reason), experience is the *matter*, but God — the Meaning, the Principle — is the *form*. The Tibetan Buddhist teacher Chögyam Trungpa compared experience to the manure that's used for fertilizer. In itself it's useless and has a bad smell, but when spread on the field of spiritual practice it can fertilize the crop of the Dharma. Experience can give *substance* to your character — though this is something that I only realized later in life — but your character also needs *form* (Lew Welch's "a shape beyond invention") if that substance is to be anything other than dead weight, just as that form needs substance if it is to be anything more than an abstract spinning of your mental and imaginative wheels. Experience is like the straw that the heroine must spin into gold in the Grimms' fairy tale "Rumplestiltskin." The idea is to collect as much straw as possible before spinning it — but not too much, since you don't want to be stuck with leftover straw when the period allotted for spinning is over. If that happens you will need to be "reborn" in one way or another to get the job done, and that is not a happy fate.

(The German novel or *Bildungsroman* that has to do with the relationship between form and matter, contemplation and experience, is *Narziss und Goldmund* by Herman Hesse, with Goldmund, the monk who leaves the monastery to seek experience representing the matter and Narziss his friend, the monk who remains cloistered, representing the form, both of whom discover by the end of the book that they learned essentially the same lesson. In some ways, during the years when I was an adventurer and a contemplative at the same time, I was both Narziss and Goldmund.)

1967

Besides a trip with Bob Trumbly in '66, south to Morrow Bay, Coalinga, the Monterey Jazz Festival, the first big one was the summer of '67, cross country to New York with Bob in my father's Chevy Suburban Carryall. How generous my father was! He himself had traveled cross-country by car at my age, for much the same reasons, so he must've seen us as following in his footsteps. The story of that trip, and of the times that framed it, is told in my epic poem *Panic Grass*, in which the journey begins like this:

On the eve of the storm we hurry
Preparing for the forced march
The re-enactment of legend, something we didn't invent
But must be sure of

Maybe even finish.

The car sits triggered, ready, in the cold half-light;
Premonition tries to draw a shelf of darkness over the entire sky.

Then we begin, moving out fresh & wild onto the morning highway, different beings,
Our lives turned up to the threshold of flame...

Before we left California we picked up a hitchhiker, Elliot — a classic long-haired hippie from New York — who was headed for the Big Apple. We took him all the way, and he returned the favor by piloting us into Manhattan through the vast, unfamiliar bridges and overpasses till the truck was safely stowed in a down-town parking garage, since we laid-back Californios didn't want to challenge the powerful Yellow Cabbies on their own turf, in a city known for raising road-rage to a ritual artform...

Mostly all I remember is momentary episodes, impressions, but one story is worth telling. The first day, after crossing the Sierras and getting half-way across the Nevada deserts, we made it to Battle Mountain and drove up on a hill above the town to sleep the night in the truck. (Was that on U.S. 40 or I-80? The interstate highway system had not yet been completed in '67; I know that farther east, in Kansas, it was still the old U.S Highway 40.) Just after sundown, as we were settling in, we saw a car coming up the dirt road in our direction — a car filled with young cowboys, obviously approaching with intent to hassle the hippies. They all wore black cowboy hats. When they reached the flat hilltop where we were parked they stopped, piled out of the car, and started ambling in our direction. At that moment I remembered that we also had a black cowboy hat in our truck, so I reached for it, put it on, and emerged to meet them.

As soon as they saw me with my black hat on, they stopped dead in their tracks, taken aback. After glancing back and forth at each other for a moment, they turned around (without a word), got in their car, and drove back down the hillside.

Such is the power — and the magic — of the illusion of *identity*.

As for our trip east of the western deserts, toward Wichita, Kansas, this is what *Panic Grass* has to say about it:

> I saw the Great Plains of Kansas at night, blood-eye moonrise to the left, to the right something else rising, we locked at 90 mph between;
> Bob gazing out wistful at the flying night, Elliot asleep in the back, radio probing the night for scraps of sound, becoming insane revival preacher screaming without boundary... then without warning someone else riding with us that night whose name I don't know...
> The preacher fading into urgent static, in and out
> War quickening in urgent message, in and out... "riot... Pentagon troops use teargas"... fading, rising, fading again... the broad flank of danger rising and falling like invisible waves of electricity, real fear claiming its nerve territory, swelling under the heart, then shrinking... the death breeze rising and falling, breathing out from the hurtling radio, exhaled from the eye of the Moon, squat orange satellite, poring over her mother tormentor in silent stone accusation — all mankind is bone and steel skeleton in long hugged explosion across Kansas...

When we got to Wichita in the evening we began asking around for where the hip-folk lived, and in no time we had met our compadres in the Movement. Motel? Forget it. In those days, for at least three or four years, all you had to do was cruise into any town in America (outside the Deep South), ask where Hippietown was, and you were assured of at least a warm floor for the night and some weed, if not a sympatico hip-girl to share it with you. After that charmed moment was over, a dark curtain of paranoia settled down — either prudently justified or certifiably neurotic — a curtain that has not essentially lifted for (by now) over half a century. Whitman's America, the Brotherhood of the Free, was finally realized in those few years, beyond any shadow of a doubt. It *was* all perfect, this *was* really it, but then—*après moi, le deluge.*

The hip crowd we fell in with that night in Wichita did not look to have been hip in any substantial way for more than three or four months—not long enough to grow the standard foot-and-a-half of hair—so Bob, Elliot and I could present ourselves as "missionaries" from California (and New York), there to bring the blessings of hippiedom to the slightly retarded but nonetheless highly receptive Midwest...

How do you become hip real fast when the situation demands it? One guy melted green crayons into his hair, and a bunch of people fanned out through the fields to harvest the gone-wild marijuana left over from the old commercial hemp-growing days—without a doubt the weakest weed I have ever smoked. And of course, to celebrate the arrival of the enlightened travelers from the West, some sort of blow-out or orgy was required, which in our case ended up to be something like a cross between one of Ken Kesey's Acid Tests (minus the acid) and an *Animal House* event for dissipated college students starring John Belushi (minus the togas). During the course of it I and my almost-girlfriend-for-the-night, whose name I don't recall, left the party to go find the local Gypsy fortune-teller, who read my palm. "You will live to be 97" she snapped in impatient irony, possibly after she saw that we were (or I was) unlikely to pay for her next-higher tier of available services...

Back at the house, as soon as we opened the door, long tall Gloria (buxom yet willowy) snaked up to me and planted a wet, skillfully-modulated kiss on my surprised yet grateful mouth, the party raging on behind... but nothing came of it. I was just not in the habit of jumping into bed with strange girls. For some weird reason I had to get to know them first—even to *like* them. I was an incurable and unlayable Romantic.

Not long after, after the beer and the dope had done their work, I crawled into my sleeping-bag on the living room floor and drifted off; the last image that came in through my eyes was the waiting-line that had formed for the Sex Room, which was modestly locked during each encounter, in line with the last tattered remnants of White Christian Civilization.

Then my sleep was interrupted by the *Alarm*: "Cops! Parked outside!"

The roaches! The ashtrays! The toilet! A new line immediately formed, this time to flush the evidence down the drain. So when the cops finally entered they must've been admitted by the occupants. There were no bull-horns, no door-pounding, no Swat Team—it was the Vice Squad instead. Half-shot, through the haze of the intoxicants, I sat up half-way from the floor to meet the gaze of an outraged but well-self-controlled Mom, sitting in a nearby chair, legs crossed, foot tapping rapidly. "So—where are you from??" she queried. "San Francisco Bay Area" I foggily replied. "Well—I suppose you people have your *beliefs.*" I allowed as how we did, though I couldn't remember any specific hippie beliefs worth repeating at that particular moment... so the conversation trailed off. (Saved, one more time, by the First Amendment.)

The final outcome of this encounter with the Law included no arrests, just (presumably) a rounding up of the underage girls to ship them home. It was no more serious in terms of legal consequences than a rousting of some high school kids for violating curfew. And Terry Cuddy, the folksinger Lew had introduced me to, had been sent to San Quentin Prison for possession of *one pot seed*. Talk about a charmed life. Even to this day, at age 74, I have no criminal record whatsoever. The pre-birth contract, enforced in this world by my guardian angel, must have had a clause that read: "Encounter, in a state of heightened psychic sensitivity, with seven brands of Darkness, no substantive material consequences outside of some physical injuries, agreed-upon spectrum of soul-traumas, each one a conundrum to be solved on the intellectual, emotional and spiritual levels..."

So the next day we were off, and onward, to Chicago, Pittsburg, New Jersey... then New York Itself: if I can make it there, I can make it anywhere! — as opposed to Marin County, which is better characterized by the contrary proverb, "If you can screw up there, you can screw up anywhere" (and plenty did).

After letting Elliot off to swim in his native waters, Bob and I checked in to the Albert Hotel in the Village, whose website now informs me:

> "Meet me in the bar at the Albert Hotel," Jimmy Stewart instructs Raymond Burr in Hitchcock's 1954 thriller, *Rear Window*. Then, as for decades, the hotel occupied a vibrant, iconic place in the cultural life of New York's Greenwich Village. From its opening in 1887, the Albert was home, hotel and hang-out for generations of artists, activists, writers, poets and musicians. Mark Twain lectured at the Albert. Hart Crane wrote [*part of*] his famous poem, *The Bridge*, in its rooms. Thomas Wolfe styled his fictional Hotel Leopold on the Albert. Anaïs Nin was a guest. Jackson Pollack visited, as did Andy Warhol. Rocky Graziano ate steak in its French restaurant. The Mamas & The Papas wrote "California Dreamin'" in the Albert. The list is endless.

But if the list is endless, put me on it too! Inscribe my name in the Book of Hip! All we knew was that the Hotel had something to do with musicians and was filled with sad rooms with hard beds, cracked plaster and no hot water. Bleak we knew it was, but we had no idea it was *that* bleak, that it was *artistically* bleak. And the amazing thing is, the poem I wrote about our '67 car trip, *Panic Grass*, was compared by Lew Welch to *The Bridge!* He did that in a half-darkened room at some get-together or other in Frisco after our return. I had composed the poem over the Winter of '67–'68, and on that occasion I read the whole thing to him. After I was done, he let me know — with deep sadness — that it was obviously a very important work, comparable to Hart Crane's classic epic of the great American Past updated into the Jazz Age and beyond. He was sad, I now realize, because *Panic Grass* had proved to him that the torch had been passed, his work was done, and so there was now nothing for it but for him to make his rendezvous with the Great Mystery, courtesy of a .22 caliber revolver.

Bob and I dined that night at the hotel restaurant, right where Graziano ate his steak. We ordered pork chops. The next night we returned. I was planning to flash a bit of my California wit to the waiter by telling him, "We'll have the usual"—but he beat me to it. "Good evening, sir—will you have the usual?" So New York wit trumped San Francisco wit that night, and it's way too late for a rematch.

Another night we made the scene at St Mark's-in-the-Bowery, the official Hip Church (Episcopal) of Manhattan, a sort of Glide Memorial East. I read a poem or two at the open reading, in a venue that had been host to Kahlil Gibran, Isadora Duncan, Martha Graham, William Carlos Williams, Amy Lowell, Edna St Vincent Millay, Carl Sandburg, and Houdini. One of the other performers was a strange Bohemian character, over six feet tall, lank, beardless and with long hair like Oscar Wilde, who sang in a falsetto voice while playing the ukulele: Tiny Tim himself, when virtually nobody outside of New York (including myself) had ever heard of him.

One thing that struck me about the crowded streets of New York was how so many people were talking to themselves—or else to an invisible presence, since the visible citizens totally ignored them. Today in the 21st Century, talking by unaccompanied pedestrians usually indicates cellphone use, and people talking to themselves on the street in 1967 California were either drunks or schizophrenics—but not even New York could have *that* many drunks and schizophrenics, so what was going on? It was as if people had surrounded themselves with clouds of language as a way of taking refuge inside their own brains from the raw, jagged edge of urban life—the sort of function that the Walkman fulfilled in later years. But some of them were actually screaming. I remember one wild disheveled old man who roared to the madding crowd, "GO BACK TO THE OLD COUNTRY!" Clearly nobody was tripping the light fantastic on the sidewalks of New York in 1967, and this was at the moment of the apex of America as a world power. It was obvious to me that the confidence and entitlement felt by the elites were not trickling down to the masses even then, any more than the imperial dominance of Great Britain brought any benefit to most of the citizens of Charles Dickens' London. Walt Whitman was taking a true look into our future when he wrote, in *Democratic Vistas*, of his fears that his beloved America would become "the fabled damned of nations."

Walking down a New York street one night, carrying a sheaf of poems, I heard a nearby pedestrian say to his companion, "there's one"; apparently it was Beat Up the Queers Night. They accosted me. "Whatcha got in that folder?" "Poetry." "Oh Yeah? Lemme see." He tried half-heartedly to wrench it from my calm, firm grasp, then simply gave up. I learned that night—though, as Socrates would have maintained, I must've known it all along—that it's very hard to slug somebody who is neither cringing nor fighting back.

And on another day, just before we left, I made an unannounced visit to Allen Ginsberg's apartment in Spanish Harlem, across the street from tenements like those, if not the very same tenements, that he had seen in his Blake vision—those "Motionless buildings of New York/ Rotting under the tides of Heaven." His door was covered with sheet metal in case the thieves and assassins attacked it with pick-axes and sledge-hammers. And in the stairwell, a big black-and-white poster of Ezra Pound.

After leaving the Big Apple, Bob and I took the southern route west, down the Eastern Seaboard to the Gulf Coast, then across, over Mobile Bay, to New Orleans—"mystic handbags in Bourbon Street's Arabian Bazaar, the Panderer's Box" as it was described in *Panic Grass*—the Big Easy. We spent our time in the French Quarter (where else?), and while there I took the time to grimly contemplate the building at 544 Camp/531 Lafayette Street, where New Orleans District Attorney Jim Garrison told us the John F. Kennedy assassination had been planned. As of today that building is a tourist trap on the JFK Assassination Conspiracy Tour, but I was there only four years after Dallas. And two years before that Dylan had written, in "Highway 61 Revisited," a verse (if not the whole song) that I always took to be about the Kennedy assassination:

> Well God said to Abraham, "Kill me a son"
> Abe say, "Man, you must be puttin' me on"
> God say, "No," Abe say, "What?"
> God say, "You can do what you want Abe, but the
> Next time you see me comin,' you better run"
>
> Abe said, "Where do you want this killin' done?"
> God said, "Out on Highway 61"

Mythic landscapes, landscapes of Hell! U.S. Highway 61 begins up near Duluth, Minnesota and ends down in New Orleans. *But how did Dylan know about the New Orleans connection to the* JFK *assassination* (if indeed he did know)? Garrison began his investigation of the assassination in '66, a year after the song was released, in '65; so Dylan couldn't have gotten any clues from him. This Zimmerman guy was ahead of his time for sure— or maybe his name was just inscribed somewhere in that same universal Rolodex, since if the abyss looks into you for long enough, you'll sure as hell end up looking into it. Hopefully that name, God willing (along with my own) has since been thoroughly expunged from the record.

After New Orleans, Texas and the Southwest, the highest deserts; the Colorado River and the Mojave Desert; then over the Tehachapis to Bakersfield to U.S. 101, north to the Bay Area, and across the Golden Gate Bridge to Marin County again.

It was like I'd never left.

1968

In '68 I did it again, this time with John Doyle, though when the truck broke down near Yellowstone National Park, Doyle bailed out and left me alone to wait till the repairs were done and I could continue on to Chicago to make the scene-of-all-political-scenes for the 1960s, the 1968 Democratic National Convention. While waiting I fell in with a Mormon girl from Utah by the name of Molly, who told me a story I promised myself I'd pass on if I ever got the chance:

Molly's grandfather had passed away, and at his Mormon funeral all the big Mormons, pillars of the Latter Day Saints and sons of the Prophet, started making fulsome eulogies for him, going on and on about all his good qualities, what a credit he had been to his community, etc. etc. When Molly couldn't take it anymore she jumped to her feet before the whole assembly and yelled "Hypocrites! When my grandfather was alive you all cheated him and swindled him any way you could — and now you have the nerve to sing his praises? Eat your words!" How proud of her I was — and even now, after 55 years, I still haven't forgotten her. The denouncing voice, raised in naked sincerity, and at great personal risk, has got to be one of the voices of God Himself.

The next destination, after the truck was fixed, was Chicago, the Democratic Convention. All I retain are isolated impressions, floating through a vast, all-encompassing energy-field of shock and chaos. The foot-soldier may say "I know what happened because I was there" (on D-day, or in the Tet Offensive), but he has no overview, he doesn't know what the generals know — the generals in this case being Abbie Hoffman, Jerry Rubin, Allen Ginsberg and their colleagues, who were nonetheless the farthest thing from armchair generals, putting themselves on the front lines, willing to share all the dangers and hardships of the troops. Because war it was — at least in a sense . . . theatrical war struggling to become real, to break through the TV screen to justify that great rap song by Gil Scott Heron of The Last Poets, "The Revolution Will Not Be Televised" — just as Vietnam was real war begging to become theatrical and unreal, to turn out to have been nothing but a dark, fiery dream, through the widespread use of marijuana and even LSD by the troops (those heavy, powerful, opium-soaked Thai Sticks that made their way to North America . . .). But the twain did not ultimately meet. The war in the name of peace that the counterculture convened was still a fantasy-revolution, no matter how serious we tried to make it in Chicago and elsewhere — even after the Symbionese Liberation Army (that fantasy-cadre undoubtedly concocted by the FBI) kidnapped newspaper heiress Patty Hearst and lost their lives in a burning house in L.A. under police siege, even after four protesters were shot dead by the National Guard at Kent State in 1970, as memorialized in the song "Ohio" ("Four Dead in Ohio") by Crosby, Stills, Nash and Young . . . and Vietnam still remained implacably real, even after Francis Ford Coppola's *Apocalypse Now* did everything possible to turn it into a cinematic reality... But we had to feel that our war at home was a real one, blood had to be shed, or else the deeply-denied survivor's guilt of having refused to share the agonies of the other half of our generation in the Southeast Asian killing fields would have been too great to bear.

Vietnam — the ultimate Altamont.

Driving into Chicago I picked up a Filipino dude of Melanesian or maybe Australian Aborigine extraction named Eliopanzo Peter Deal. Dark skin, flashing smile, he showed me his upper arm with deep criss-cross scars through the biceps, proudly announcing: "Machete!" Was the Convention drawing in not just hippies and yippies from all over North America but headhunters from the Pacific islands? One way or another it was a scene to make, a whirlpool that sucked in all the available flotsam within its range — a true *sangsara*.

Once down-town and with the truck safely stowed, I wandered from scene to scene — through Lincoln Park before the festivities, the staging-area, where an old Communist or labor organizer, nearly in tears, harangued the crowd: "It's the '30s again! 30 years I've waited for this..." But it wasn't the '30s again, not with Allen Ginsberg leading squads of hippie devotees against the police lines, chanting OM to quell the waves of rising violence with counter-waves of powerful vibratory peace... nor have the '60s themselves ever returned again in the half-century following. Events recall and anticipate other events, but they never repeat them — though there is some truth in Marx's ironic maxim, "In history everything happens twice — the first time as tragedy, the second time as farce." Nonetheless I was there, across from the ranks of the rifle-and-bayonet toting National Guardsmen, backed up by jeeps mounting .50 calibre machineguns, to watch the saintly hippie girl placing flowers in the gun barrels one by one — armed innocence, innocence armed with flowers, against the muzzles and butts of the rifles... maybe not since the Colosseum have we seen anything like that.

That night the whole thing happened. But where was I, sleeping in the back of my truck? Where was it parked? I don't remember... still, the next morning, through the bruised and wounded air, I returned to Lincoln Park, so soaked with residual eye-stinging tear gas that I couldn't even get in... And on the way out of Chicago I saw, as if straight out of Simon and Garfunkel's song "The Sounds of Silence," a big electric sign, high above the freeway — and the sign said "FINAL DAYS! EVERYTHING MUST GO! BUY CHRISTIAN CARPETS!"

Indeed.

Then on to New York for a day and a night in the East Village, and immediately back to California on Interstate 40, driving and musing alone.

RIDING FREIGHTS

One time John Doyle and I were hitchhiking on Highway 101 north of Petaluma. We had been at it for hours with no luck; the only attention we were attracting was from those drivers who "jokingly" tried to run us off the road. When — beat — we trudged back to town and shared our sorrows with a sympathetic Samaritan, he told us: "Screw hitchhiking. Why don't you just hop a freight?" The little Northwestern Pacific line paralleled 101 at that point, so we took his advice, and discovered that travel in an empty boxcar — as long as it was an "easy rider" with decent suspension — beat hitchhiking by a mile or more. That was our introduction to the art.

Later I returned to the Northwestern Pacific with a girlfriend, the cute and diminutive Judy Milani, with whom I rode from Novato to Arcata, just north of Eureka on the coast, the end of the line. At a stop we talked with the friendly old man who occupied the caboose — "featherbedding" as that used to be called, easy work for old-timers back when the unions were still strong — who had no problems with us riding in an empty boxcar, neither when acting as an official representative of the railroad, or of the law, or as an older adult worried that we inexperienced kids might be crippled or killed, since the 21st-Century moral panic of the "safety culture" had not yet appeared; life was too laid-back in those days to indulge in all that unnecessary worry. The Northwestern Pacific was like an easy training course for later big-time freight hopping, from California to Portland, Oregon, and later Seattle — and then the really big one, the Great Northern route from Spokane across two-thirds of the continent, to the outskirts of Minneapolis. (Some time later Judy and I hitchhiked to Oregon to visit that famous Family of the Mystic Arts commune — later Alpha Farm — that appeared on the cover of the July 1969 issue of *LIFE Magazine*, a temporary paradise of tall blond hippies, the women clad only in loin-cloths, inhabiting a log-built and dirt-floored Viking hall or Native American longhouse in an idyllic "natural" setting. When I passed through that commune again in 1971 with Bill and Jenny Trumbly on my way back to California from British Columbia, I saw just how temporary paradises like that can be, if "paradise" was ever the right word for such experiments... nonetheless Alpha Farm is still in operation, so maybe they made it after all.)

(Judy Milani, to give you a quick portrait, was a tiny, 4'10" "perfect hippie girl" of the time. Once when we were walking on the Pacific shore of Marin County at Limontur Spit we ran into a huge, bull sea lion. As soon as she saw him she sprinted toward him at top speed — though he weighed at least 15 times more than she did — with her arms held out to hug him! Flashing her a look of dismay and disbelief, he quickly floundered back into the sea and made his escape.)

Bill Trumbly and Doyle were the first to do some heavy-duty freight riding on the Union Pacific; I followed in their footsteps. Forget "riding the rods" in the literal sense of that phrase, which meant riding on the truss rods *under* the car, most of which had disappeared even by the 1930s. And when in the movies you see people running alongside a train and then jumping into a moving boxcar, that almost never happened. The idea was to find an empty boxcar in the yard, one with both doors open—because sometimes a strong jolt would cause a door to slide shut, which is why they were built with each of the two doors sliding in a different direction. (And it was also a good idea to find a plank or something to stick in the doorway so the door wouldn't slide all the way shut and lock.) Most likely it would present no problem if a hobo rode an empty boxcar, the bulls usually didn't care. If he fell off and got killed, the law would probably never become seriously involved except to note the death and collect the body—and obviously nobody was going to sue the railroad for "maintaining an attractive nuisance"! It was an era of "live at your own risk."

One of the best things about riding freights—outside of the contemplative solitude, if you were into things like that—was that the railroad tracks usually took a different route than the highway that ran between the same two points. No billboards. No worry about opposing traffic. Short wilderness vistas, mountains and rivers, that the eye of the pampered civilian motorist had never witnessed. And every once in a while a nostalgic snapshot of ancient, rusty, crumbling, rural-industrial America, old grain elevators, old quarries and gravel pits and the antiquated loading-elevators that served them. Industrial floodlights blazing late at night. Riding freights was like going back in time. And while I lament the death of the caboose, an imminently civilized amenity, there's no question that railroad graffiti has developed by leaps and bounds since the '60s and '70s, finally flowering into a unique genre of graphic art, influenced by gang graffiti and underground comix lettering but not to be identified with either, a style that rates its own lavish coffee-table book at least—though to show the originals in prestigious art galleries as they deserve would present considerable difficulties.

Doyle and I rode freights to Portland once, where we slept that night down on the hard gravel beach by the "thundering floodlit drydocks" as I described the scene in a poem I no longer have a copy of. The thunder came from the welding-torches that flashed and burned through the night. As suburban California kids with literary pretensions, industrial America was a vision to us, not a workplace. We were tourists through the fascinating exoticism of real life.

Later I took the same route alone. When I got to Portland I read poetry at the open reading at Alice's Restaurant—"Lament for Ignacio Sánchez Mejías" by Federico García Lorca if I remember correctly—in a location that I claim was the original establishment, though my Sufi brother Yusuf, with his Big Apple chauvinism, maintains that the original Alice's

Restaurant could only have been the one in Manhattan. Be that as it may, they both came from the song of the same name by Arlo Guthrie, another afficionado of railroad romanticism.

1969

Getting back to the main timeline, it was over the winter of 1968–1969 that I attended a hippie party somewhere in Marin. We were all sitting on the floor, leaning against the four walls (like the Persian Sufis do in their *khaniqas* as I was later to find out), passing the joints counter-clockwise. When one came to me I took a massive toke and nearly passed out, since it wasn't really a joint at all but a tobacco cigarette rolled like one, an herb I had never smoked. I got dizzy and fell sideways, and when I opened my eyes my head was in the lap of Paula Wasserman, the girl who was to precipitate a major revolution in my life. (Had she been watching for the first guy to keel over so she could pounce?)

Paula was a Jewish girl from New York whose parents had moved to Vancouver, British Columbia. She had that classy almost-English accent that a certain caste of New York Jews used to speak with (the poet Jack Hirschman, also originally from New York, talked just the same way) — an adopted upper class accent like the one used by George Plimpton and William F. Buckley, that you should not sound like that little underclass *schlemiel* with the glasses and the baseball cap in *The Man with the Golden Arm* starring Frank Sinatra. She took me home that night to her apartment in San Rafael's canal district, and we immediately "fell into place," like young hippies often did. When I got back to my parents' home I came down with a high fever. No flu symptoms, no head or lung congestion, just a fever so high that it left my bed totally soaked with sweat as if a bucket of warm water had been poured into it. Something in me knew, my soul knew, that Destiny had just knocked at the door.

So when the travel season came again — summer — we Paula and I set off to cross the country one more time, this time hitchhiking and riding freights; as Simon & Garfunkel expressed that particular fact and sentiment in their song "America," we simply "walked off to look for America." It was truly amazing and rare in those days, maybe uniquely rare in human history, how our music, for something like 5 years, perfectly expressed and encapsulated, month by month, the collective experience and trauma of the counterculture vanguard of our generation. The artists were seriously busting their asses trying to keep up with us, and they really did succeed for a while. Or were we really following them? Whichever way it was, for those few years at least, Art and Life were one.

We started by hitchhiking from Marin County to the town of Davis in the Sacramento Valley, where we caught the Union Pacific north, headed for Seattle. I remember riding an autorack (those freight cars made to carry automobiles), in the back of a Ford Ranchero, that long-discontinued coupe/pickup hybrid, which we picked for the easy ride that came from the extra suspension. Soon we were high up the headwaters of the Sacramento River, grinding through rocky granite mountains where the turns were so long that you could see the whole length of the train both before and behind, and so tight that the sound of the wheels against the rails, steel on steel, made a kind of shrieking, keening electronic music, eerily celestial, that vibrated high up in your skull, as if the metal itself were crying out in exultation and pain... When we pulled into the next yard a gentlemanly railroad worker motioned to us to "get down!"—since, as we found out later, the bulls generally didn't care if you rode an empty boxcar, but if you damaged the merchandise you were in serious trouble.

CANADA

So the freights took us as far as Portland, after which we hitchhiked through Washington and Oregon to the Canadian border, then crossed over into British Columbia, since Paula's parents lived in the Vancouver suburb of "West Van." Our exact itinerary is rather hazy to me after 50 years, but I do remember four episodes:

The first was our ferry trip across the Straits of Georgia to Vancouver Island, then across the island itself to the Pacific coast—specifically, to the big, crescent-shaped Wreck Bay, with wide beaches strewn with massive piles of driftwood, huge tree trunks and smaller branches from various logging operations, out of which we built a temporary shelter, as many other visitors had, and lived like beachcombers for a night and a day. The wild peas, eaten raw from their pods, were delicious. British Columbia, for some reason, has more cut, fallen and discarded timber than any place I've ever been. As Jack Spicer wrote about it—about Vancouver in particular—in an accurate portrait of its introverted, depressive mindset, based on a maddeningly constant light rain falling on a rather thin semi-pioneer culture dwarfed by a landscape of heroic mountains:

> Can
> A place in the wilderness become utterly buggered up with logs? A question
> Of love. They
> Came out of the mountains and they came in by ship
> And Victoria fights New Westminster. And
> They're all at the same game. Trapped
> By mountains and ocean. Only
> Awash on themselves.
> The seabirds
> Do not do their bidding or the mountain birds...

Then there was the beautiful evening we spent on the east coast of Vancouver Island at Nanaimo, the evening of Apollo 11, the first Moon landing, which produced a faint though quite distinct sense of disorientation and ungroundedness, one that I suspect has since become unconsciously permanent... I remember a poem I wrote about it—which I never kept, though it was published (if I remember right) in the journal *Sanskaras*; it had the lines: "[*something something*] shattering the archives/ To unpack the glistening meat of wonder/ A conflagration of daily bread..." At this point in my life, however, I resonate more deeply with Leonard Cohen's lines from "Sing Another Song, Boys":

> Ah, they'll never, they'll never ever reach the moon,
> At least not the one that we're after...

And though I'm no Moon Landing Denier, I would nonetheless like to direct the reader's attention to the motion picture *Diamonds Are Forever*—which came out only two years after Apollo 11—in which James Bond, played by Sean Connery, is shown fleeing from the bad guys through the Nevada desert in a dune buggy or lunar rover, which passes at one point in front of an outdoor movie set where a version of the moon landing is apparently being filmed...

And then, on the same trip to Vancouver Island, there was the night we spent in the donated apartment of one Terry Mirks while he was away, with the walls and ceiling papered solid with Playboy centerfolds of naked women. As we drifted off to sleep we experienced simultaneous astral projections, which we saw as being produced by some kind of subtle being that resembled a vampire... Later, back in Vancouver, when we told this story to Paula's best friend Frances—one of the most petite, cultured and ladylike females it has ever been my good fortune to meet, with a fine-boned loveliness reminiscent of Audrey Hepburn—she received our report with skepticism until we mentioned Terry Mirks by name. "*Terry Mirks?*" she exclaimed. "He is without a doubt one of the *weirdest* people I've ever known..." This, in my opinion, is just one more example of how we hippies opened every psychic door imaginable, then forgot to close them...

And where was it when Paula and I, hitchhiking, were picked up by some drunken Indians in an old clunker, three of them in the front seat and the driver arm-wrestling with the one on the far passenger-side as they drove? We ourselves were in the back seat along with an artificial leg, which one guy told us to "just throw that thing aside it's no good anyway"—(Indian black humor)—when our car side-swiped another vehicle. But since we failed to spin out or turn over, the Indians pulled over to the side of the road and let us out—because "the cops will be after us now, so good luck."

Then there was the classic moment when, on our way north through the interior to Prince George, we combined freight-hopping with hitchhiking by hitching a ride on a freight train that passed us in the yard—thanks to the engineer, who yelled out from his side window, "Hey HIPPIES! Got any grass?" We didn't have any, but were nonetheless invited to ride up front in the engine with the crew, watching the lamplit track flow back under the speeding train for hours into the night...

Yet on that stop we only briefly touched base in B.C.; soon we were down in the States again, on our way to Seattle.

OUT EAST

After we arrived in Seattle we hopped a freight that was headed east to Spokane. Somewhere on that leg of the journey we found an empty boxcar, only to discover that it wasn't empty at all, but occupied by five or six hoboes — real hoboes, that is, not impostors like us. "Christ!" one of them growled, "He's got a woman with him!" In response to this I quietly reached for my sheathed hunting-knife, strapped it on, then turned with a smile to our companions and gave them a friendly greeting. Paula was understandably intimidated, whereas I projected an aura of nonchalance, made possible by the fact that many of us hippies lived a kind of charmed life in those days — real or imagined — for maybe 4 consecutive years. My rule then, as with Teddy Roosevelt, was: "When in a dangerous situation, never show aggression and never show fear." Since I recently rediscovered Paula through Facebook, living on the shore of a remote lake in British Columbia — reconnecting with old friends being one of the few legitimate uses of that pernicious invention known as "the social media" — I can fill in some of my memory-blanks from her own account of that incident:

> In the early dawn light we were approached by two of the men. "Beans?" We were hungry, and gladly shared the cans of Boston baked beans and tiny jars of pickled cocktail sausages they offered. From the free store near the tracks, they said. In exchange we pulled out our block of cheese and loaf of crusty bread — bought at a tiny crowded delicatessen on a busy Seattle street. We ate quietly as our breakfast mates coached us on the best places for hoboes to camp and to find free food on this line, the Great Northern. Some towns offered food stamps, no questions asked. And then there were freight yards to avoid, yard bulls mean and menacing. These men, our new friends, were experts. We were rubes. We listened and nodded solemnly at information we would likely never need or use.

And here's another of her memories from later in the same trip, evidence of the way things used to be in the world of human relations, back in the days when the earth still had some salt in it, and we were still (North) Americans:

> We're high in the Rocky Mountains in Glacier National Park in the middle of nowhere, and suddenly we are approaching a tiny wayside railroad station. It's cold as can be for July. We're rolling oh-so-slowly through the station, no reason for this freight train to stop up here. We boldly sit just inside the open door, legs crossed close to the edge, to watch this event. On the platform, sitting on a wooden bench are two railroad men in classic striped overalls, eating their lunch. They look

relaxed and easy like, chatting with each other, more like farmhands than railroad men. When they spot us, the taller of the two had just enough time to toss his plastic bag full of the rest of his workingman's lunch in through our boxcar door. I panicked when I saw it come at me. I thought it was a bomb. Or maybe garbage. Trash thrown to trash. Turned out to be the best bologna sandwich I ever ate: white bread and mayonnaise and lots of butter and some soggy lettuce. He must've gone hungry that day; he'd probably worked much harder than we did. But man, we were grateful. So many simple kindnesses were shown to us two half-crazed hippies, that summer of 1969.

And Kerouac, in *Mexico City Blues*, 146th Chorus, perfectly caught the feel of the Rocky Mountain leg of that trip:

> The Big Engines
> In the night—
> The Diesel on the Pass...
> The Blazing Silence of the Night,
>   the Pan Canadian Night—
> The Eagle on the Pass,
>   the Wire on the Rail
> the High Hot Iron
>   of my heart...

With the Rockies behind us, we rode the Great Northern Railway, the one with the mountain goat logo, all the way across the Great Plains, through the whole of Montana and North Dakota, and part of Minnesota. On one long night of stopless motion, we felt the land's immensity, with solitude for our zazen, and the rhythm of our flight—the "CLACK-CLACK/ clack-clack" of the four front and the four back wheels of the boxcar across some shallow barrier—for our monkish silence. Then—in the long, wide eastward night of Montana, with Paula asleep in her bag at the head of the car—the moment came when I saw, from some far distant point, while peering from the open door of the boxcar at the flying darkness, vast inexplicable flashes of light, like God's flashbulb, a hundred times the candle-power of the biggest floodlight, illuminating the entire landscape. There's no way it could have been heat lightning, since the night was clear, and the flashes too regular for that anyway, in both intensity and duration. *What was it?* Some cousin to the UFOs I imagine, coming in through one of the widening cracks in this thoroughly crack-pated world.

The next day we pulled into a yard in Minot, North Dakota at dusk, where Paula stole a DO NOT HUMP sign off a boxcar to stick on her Martin guitar-case—because, "how *perfect!*" according to the standard hippie sensibility—even though that meant that some poor car full of delicate crystal glassware might have gotten humped, a crime we paid for shortly after, through instant karma, by getting humped ourselves by crashing into another string of cars, hard enough to couple our string to the one ahead of us and almost knocking us over. (For those who wonder exactly how a train can get humped, it gets run up over an artificial mound in the switching-yard so sections can be uncoupled and allowed to roll back to their proper tracks by force of gravity.)

Somewhere back along the line — Paula says Seattle — we had bought a salami, a hunk of dry jack cheese, and a loaf of bread — which, along with a canteen of water and some vitamin pills, is mostly what we lived on for 2000 miles; so by the time we pulled into Morris, Minnesota we were pretty beat. Somehow, though, we fell in with a merry Shakespearean acting troupe traveling by school bus, who, as evening descended, carried us in style to our next destination, which turned out to be a public park where they performed an act out of one of Shakespeare's comedies, possibly *The Taming of the Shrew* or *As You Like It*.

In Minneapolis — according to Paula's version of events — we somehow located a folk club with an open mike, where we successfully impersonated folk singers for a night, Paula playing her classic old Martin acoustic guitar and me the harmonica and the "sacred harp" — the name that the 17th century acapella shape-note singers of England gave to the human voice. (Why have so many Jews been attracted to Black blues and English/Scots/Irish folk music — especially New York Jews like Simon and Garfunkel, the New York adoptee Bob Dylan, and my own Sufi brother, Paul Yachnes? Even the traditional folk singer Jean Ritchie, from Perry County, Kentucky, married a New York Jew.) And, amazingly — at least according to my version of events — who should be on just before us but the Reverend Gary Davis, playing his famous guitar "Miss Gibson"! A hard act to follow — except that I remember this incident as having taken place in New York, not Minneapolis, and Paula, who certainly remembers our performance, doesn't remember the Reverend Gary Davis at all. Oh well; a half-century can do funny things to the memory. History is written by the victors, including those parts of yourself that finally emerged victorious over the other parts that didn't make it. History is all legend. Nonetheless I know that Gary Davis was for real; it was a real privilege to play on the same stage as he did, in that second-string music venue on that second-class circuit where so many of the masters ended up after the short wave of fame they rode during the '60s had petered out. And seeing how the United States of America has continued its long slide to Hell since the year of Our Lord 1969, there have been many times since when I've echoed the Reverend Davis' sentiment, from his song "Samson and Delilah": "If I *had my way/* I would tear this whole building down — *Good God.*"

From there we hitchhiked south along the Mississippi, down U.S. Highway 61. We enjoyed the hospitality of a farmer for one night, who let us sleep in his barn on the hay bales, and treated us to fresh milk the next morning. In Keokuk, Iowa, we ended up in the Negro part of town, across the tracks, where some Black folks "adopted" us and gave us the grand tour. Amazing! That was during the short short period when Black people were glad that young White hippies were "into" them, that we dug their way of talking, their music... they had no problem whatsoever with "cultural appropriation," it was all taken as flattery and admiration. We were in the age of Mose Allison, of Norman Mailer's "The White Negro." And how generous they were! They took us to a fast food joint selling soul food (because of course we needed that experience) and then to an all-Black club, and finally put us up for the night in a one-room shack with nothing but a bed, a battered TV and a few thin boards between us and a raging thunderstorm. As we were leaving Keokuk next morning in the rain, one cat pressed a wad of soggy bills into my hand and admonished, "What're you going to St Louis for, man? Kansas City's the place!" Then down river again, through the biggest thunderstorm I'd ever seen, bolts of the divine bombardment striking the earth by the fraction of the second in every conceivable direction.

NEW ORLEANS

In New Orleans we hooked up with some of the local hippies who likewise gave us shelter for the night. One of them, wearing a yard-tall top hat covered with black-and-white print fabric, had a prominent under-bite and a beard that grew up almost up to his eye-sockets, making him look just like a werewolf... a *nice* werewolf... and so with him at our side we walked the sidewalks of the Big Easy, immersed in our perpetual hippie Mardi Gras, till we ran into a man with a spider-monkey on his shoulder. When a child with tourist parents caught sight of it he cried out, in stunned, incandescent wonder: "*A monkey!!*" Seeing a monkey, for that child, in that moment, was like seeing God. And Paula and I also saw plenty of things that were equally astonishing to us.

And at one point, since we were in New Orleans, I asked around in my stupid innocence, or my stupid guilt, for where something like a Voodoo shop might be found. I was directed to a non-descript storefront without a sign and with totally unrelated products, like spark plugs and baby formula, in the shabby display window. When we entered it was like an old-fashioned pharmacy with high shelves filled with jars and canisters. Even though the bulbs were on, somehow there was no light in the room; it was a place that, as the internet now informs me, perfectly fit the description of the main Voodoo temple for North America, the central cathedral of that whole faith. I asked the Black proprietor if he sold anything like religious articles; the question seemed to terrify him. "Oh no, no, we don't, I don't believe we, we don't sell anything like that at this establishment..." What was he afraid of? Police spies? Or rival magic? Nonetheless that little shop might in fact have been the origin of the dream I had years later, in which two oily black hands emerged from beneath a wooden stage and started drumming on the boards, while a voice said: "By your leave, may I compose a few verses?

> Police cordon, please
> Police cordon, please
> Make way for an important visitor
>   from the underworld."

The "important visitor" was Eshu-Elegba, Legba Ati-Bon, the chief Voodoo deity represented by the central pillar of the Voodoo temple, which in turn stands for the *axis mundi*. The Voodoo *loas* are lower psychic reflections of the Platonic Ideas or Names of God in the world of the Jinn. Their archetypes occupy a high celestial plane, but they themselves, as reflections, are capable of sinking to the point where they become involved with infernal energies, which appears to be exactly what happened to them. As I said above, once you make certain connections, even with the best of intentions — or with no intentions at all to speak of — you go into the Devil's Rolodex.

And our next stop after that — perhaps directed there by the Baron Samedi, Mister Dead Man himself — was that famous graveyard with all the vaults above-ground, made necessary by the high water-table, where the doomed hippie heroes dropped acid in *Easy Rider*. We wandered around "picking up the vibes," crawling in and out of empty crypts, till I began to hear in my mind's ear the piping of ghostly voices, shrill and tremulous — voices that trilled far higher and then sank much much lower than the voices of the living ever could, as if they were seeking stable form only to lose it over and over again, now that the protective limits of the flesh no longer enclosed their wandering, shapeless motion. Through such little excursions, as I learned much later from René Guénon, I was picking up various "psychic residues" or "wandering influences" that would be a lot easier to initially attract than to ultimately get rid of.

HURRICANE

Near the end of our stay in the Big Easy we began to hear rumors of a big rock concert in upstate New York, at a place called Woodstock. Apparently people from all over the country were converging there. Our own "Woodstock," however, was Hurricane Camille, a Category 5, which made landfall in Louisiana on day two of that event, August 17, with winds of over 170 miles per hour. It was a small, tight storm, fantastically powerful, a bit like a big tornado.

At that point we were crashing in an the apartment of a sculptor that had been made available to us through the short-lived hippie mutual aid network of those times. It was on the ground floor of one of those old French Quarter houses, with super-thick (brick?) walls. Fearing that the street would flood, we enquired of the residents of the upper story whether we could ride out the storm on their level, but were informed that this higher plane was not available to "transients" like us. They were transients too, of course—as Siddhartha Gautama could have told them—along with the city of New Orleans itself, but this was way before Hurricane Katrina came to remind everyone of that obvious though universally-denied fact. So we made the best of it, and while the official occupant, the sculptor, was away, we did the responsible thing of closing and securing the windows and taping the panes with masking tape to protect from flying glass. But when he got back the sculptor would have none of it: he flung the windows wide to the wind and started sculpting madly, drawing energy from the storm, according to the Romantic doctrine that the true artist, at one with the Wild, has nothing to fear (except death) from Mother Nature. Continuing in Paula's words, "We stayed until the eye of the storm when we crept out into the streets, a 'no-go' zone patrolled by blue-lighted cop cars in the eerie quiet of the storm's center, and wound up in the corner bar where, as the storm re-surged, it was business as usual." Hitchhiking north the next day, we passed through forests where every other tree seemed to be broken off, and stretches of highway where the Gulf still covered half the road.

ONWARD

It may be that the Easy Rider Graveyard and Hurricane Camille, if not Voodoo Shoppe Number One, were the first distant announcements of an era of unprecedented trauma in my life, since directly after those encounters begins the period when, until Jenny Donne appeared, the timeline breaks up. I remember episodes, isolated events, but I can't always string them together on the same thread of linear time.

I remember that Paula and I hitchhiked along the gulf coast to the Florida panhandle; one of the rides who picked us up was a nattily-dressed red-haired scamp who proposed that I make Paula available to him for a fee, as if I were her pimp. Being at that time seriously deficient in the virtue of chivalry, all I could say was "You'll have to ask her; she's a free agent." At that time we were living under the hippie rubric of "If you can't be with the one you love, honey, love the one you're with"—from the song by Crosby, Stills and Nash—so how could I deny the same universal rights to a man who was generous enough to give us a ride, just because he was a "straight" (non-hip) guy? Did he not have equal claim on the liberating degeneracy we hippies were bringing to the world? Nonetheless we vacated that car as soon as possible...

But where was it in these United States that we were given hospitality on a hardwood floor by some barbiturate addicts? The time I woke up early in the morning only to find my hunting-knife laying unsheathed on a black hardcover bible between me & Paula? I freaked—until I remembered that, the night before, I'd placed it there myself in order to imitate an episode from the medieval romance *Tristan and Isolde*...in any case a trucker later picked us up and drove us up the eastern seaboard, all the way to New York, to spend our first night in Manhattan as the guests of another tribe of goofball bums who offered us their best available accommodations, through a warm city night, on the rooftop of a condemned brick tenement...For a very few years you could run into people who were at the bottom of both the wider social ladder and the hippie ladder who would still extend the obligatory hippie hospitality to other members of our larger movement...

And somehow the Clown Archetype followed us from city to city; we were always running into Clown references. At one stop somebody actually showed us a sheaf of his drawings of the Clown, pictured as if he were billowing upward like a helium balloon on a string, through a series of ever-changing scenes. In those days I got the impression that we had collectively decided, almost consciously, to enjoy the short farce that came between the tragedies, sensing in the pits of our stomachs that, Wavy Gravy (the psychedelic jester) notwithstanding, the Age of the Clown would not be around for very much longer...in any case our trip was rich enough in varied incidents so you could begin to see the synchronistic patterns between the discreet events, thus gleaning an intimation of the Big Trip that everything, whatever planet one turned one's attention to, was a part of...

So after a night or two at Paula's grandparents' apartment in Queens, eating borscht with sour cream and thin kosher beef, between which (if I remember right) I read my Moon Landing poem at an open reading at St Mark's-in-the-Bowery in Manhattan, we headed north into New England, planning to cross at least once through every state in the Union. (As it is, I've been through or to every one of them, except for Michigan and South Dakota.) We spent a night in Cambridge near Harvard University, in a sleeping loft with *mink* blankets!—because what use would a rich girl turned hippie have for a mink coat? Put it to good use, cut it up for blankets, so you and your friends can sleep, well-stoned, in sleek and creamy bliss...

And what would the hippies have been without such hedonism, the ad for the whole movement? "All you need is love" (by the Beatles), roughly translated into real English, most often meant "all you need is sex, or some other form of immediate pleasure." Doug Trumbly had a theory, based not on moral principles but on extensive personal research, that the more pleasure you experience the more pain you will have to experience, in direct proportion—and I can attest from my own researches that the more pain you undergo, the more pleasure you will be attracted to: not for nothing did William Burroughs talk about "the iron claws of pain and pleasure." Only sainthood knows how to transform pain into true love and sacrifice pleasure in the cause of real joy. That form of sainthood was offered to the hippies too — as it is, in fact, to everyone. Some of us accepted it and lived into it; most of us did not.

Then there was our side-excursion to Cape Cod, past the somber, seemingly half-deserted turn-off to Hyannisport and the Kennedy compound, and ending at Provincetown, where we somehow scored for another roof for the night. Outside the sky was streaked with semi-circular bands of cloud, the dwindling remnants of Hurricane Camille, and at one point we heard what must have been our landlord, talking, or trying to talk, with another unseen figure, possibly the person who'd offered us that temporary shelter — the owner's voice broken up with some sort of spastic speech-defect so that it sounded like "*Yeah-yeah-yeah-yeah*, OK-OK, *they, yeah-yeah, they can't stay, yeah-yeah-yeah*, OK, OK, *one night*, OK, *yeah-yeah-yeah*" etc., indicating that we might finally be wearing out our welcome on the road...

Because by that time we were just hitchhiking obsessively with little destination, and long-term exhaustion was beginning to set in. So we were lucky when Providence sent us a young couple in an old sedan who were headed all the way to San Francisco: working class/hip, silent and subdued, clearly fugitives or refugees from some unknown tragedy or the final phase of some expired life, the car stuffed full with all their few worldly possessions, chunking down on the shocks with every little bump. (When I remember them I always think of Dylan's song "Tangled Up in Blue.") They probably picked us up because they saw us as being as beat as they were... but the universal *charity* that covered the land in those days! The genuine Woodstock spirit, but for so short a time...

And so, from state to state, we drove in silence. Soon, however, I began to feel pretty sick; I figured it was probably that suspect hamburger that I'd eaten at the last stop. The thing turned into a serious case of dysentery — not the best condition for a cross-country hitchhiker. Our ride could certainly have dumped us at that point with full justification, fearing that I was contagious, but they just stoically accepted my condition, as they did their own. I also remember how their car needed repairs somewhere along the way so I stayed in the back seat as it went up on the rack, being too sick to walk... and all through that ordeal I never once feared death! Youth (until it dies) is truly immortal. As we neared California I phoned my father, informing him of my plight, and when we pulled into our driveway he met us at the door of my old house in San Rafael with the very paregoric I so sorely needed... a true home to come back to — though, as things turned out, its time still remaining was short.

CHAPTER SIX

The Planet of British Columbia: Death in Life

I N THE FALL OF '69, PAULA AND I "SET UP HOUSE-keeping" in an apartment in San Anselmo, one town west of San Rafael along Sir Francis Drake Boulevard, the main route west to the coast and the street where Clint Eastwood blew the punk away with his .44 magnum in *Dirty Harry*, though that was in the old quarry in Larkspur before it was dismantled to make way for the Larkspur Ferry and the shops at Larkspur Landing. That was the year I turned 21. *Panic Grass* had been glowingly reviewed in the San Francisco Chronicle, leading to a strange phone call where some sunny individual informed me that he was my press agent! I was so "detached from worldly ambition"—or rather so unbelieving that I could ever make my own way in a world like this—that I never even asked what his deal was and who if anyone had hired him; I treated the whole thing as a karmic joke. Kundalini-yoga had already begun to lift my consciousness far above mere material concerns, leading to the condition that Robert Bly, in *Iron John*, later called "grandiose ascent"—the flight of Icarus before the fall. Paula started making jewelry, and even rented a storefront in downtown Larkspur to sell it, drawing upon the shopkeeping instinct of her Jewish ancestors—but it didn't last. And soon enough it was Spring again, travel season, so we made ready to journey north to British Columbia once more. We'd bought a standard hippie van, a used VW bus, that my father helped us turn the back of into a neat sleeping compartment with a carpet-covered panel that could be removed to create seating-space. (This, of course, was before seat belts became mandatory.) And I now see that my travels in the 1960s had carried my father back to his own days as a young man making road trips across the U.S.—something quintessentially American that Jack Kerouac had in no way invented, just thoroughly chronicled for the first time: the pioneer spirit now become the vacation spirit; the "holiday road" ethos, inseparable from the work of John Muir and Teddy Roosevelt to set up the national park system; see the USA in your Chevrolet. Both Lew Welch and Jack Spicer had had to deal with what happened to the great American westward expansion when "manifest destiny" hit the Pacific Ocean and suddenly had nowhere to go any more—except onward to Vietnam. Lew wrote, about Marin County: "This is the last place/ There is nowhere else to go," whereas Jack—who died at 40 as Lew did at 44, and who had so much to say about San Francisco Bay Area dwellers as "coastal beings"—wrote in his masterpiece poem-cycle *The Holy Grail*: "Man/ Has finally no place to go but up: Galahad's testament"—Galahad being the grandiose ascender *par excellence*. "Up," for Spicer, first turned out to be the North, Vancouver, British Columbia, and specifically Simon Fraser University, where his colleague, editor and literary executor Robin Blaser taught. And then, of course, the final "up" of death.

And as for myself, I wasn't doing too well either. Maybe it was the aftereffects of psychedelics, or the radical psychophysical intervention of kundalini-yoga, setting off those depth-charges in the deep psyche; maybe it was the feeling that I was setting off into the unknown, into an inconceivable future—or maybe no future at all. And most certainly it was the shadow-cast-before of the life-changing disasters the next few years would bring, inaugurating an era of massive transformation, of "death-in-life and life-in-death" (Yeats). Nor was the "paranormal" shy of showing itself during that period, to complete the scheduled omens. I remember once during that period, when Paula and I were on the beach in front of my childhood home on San Francisco Bay, I saw, without benefit of drugs, a little orb of light traveling down her face from hairline to chin—after which, with an uncanny smile on her face, she briefly identified herself to me not as Paula but as a different woman entirely, a woman named "Marla"...

In the 1960s people moved west to San Francisco to become hippies; (the anthem of that migration was the song "San Francisco" by Scott McKenzie); in the '70s they moved there to become poets or to come out as gay. It's estimated that in that decade there were over 5000 poets in San Francisco. But the 1970s also saw a northward migration to Canada, spearheaded by Americans fleeing the war in Vietnam. But not everybody who became part of that flight was a draft-dodger, migrating out of necessity; for some it was just taken as the "next big thing." And so Paula and I, as it turned out—along with a few other people we knew—had opted, not quite consciously, to make ourselves part of that migration. Since she was a naturalized Canadian she had a reason to go there, a real destination, whereas I was just aimlessly seeking the next "scene." And so, in the 1970s, the two-century-old American westward population-flow, blocked in California by the Pacific coast, partly turned north, a 90-degree pivot that gave rise to the slogan "Don't Californicate Oregon," except for people like Magda who went south to Latin America or Indio-America instead—a move in some ways announced by Carlos Castaneda—while I was wandering around British Columbia. It took until the 21st Century for that flow to turn clockwise another 90 degrees to become today's eastward flight from California to various U.S. "red" states, where the social breakdown that my generation had initiated was not quite so far advanced.

So we crossed the Canadian border, drove to Vancouver, took lodgings at Paula's parents' home—and began to drift apart. Here's where the course of my life, largely thanks to the serious automobile accident that was soon to arrive, breaks apart into various "alternate timelines," yielding to my memory only isolated episodes. I remember throwing the *I Ching* and coming up with a hexagram that "proved" Paula and I would stay together, only to be met with a disapproving scowl. Then there was the time when I drove a party-girl to some hippie get-together or other, who almost sucked the lips off my face in the van; later, at the gathering, she sat on my lap, drawing another well-deserved scowl from Paula. *But why?* I hadn't come on to her; all I'd done was give off, in perfectly unconscious innocence, a more-or-less "unattached" vibe... On the other hand, I did nothing to ward her off—but that would have been terribly *discourteous*, wouldn't it?... suffice it to say that things were drifting in various cross-currents and contrary winds. And concurrently, on another timeline, Paula was getting together with one Howie Roman, a saturnine, self-possessed Jewish guy from New York with the same class-conscious accent that Paula and Jack Hirschman had, one that was successfully imitated—or inherited—from the likes of George Plimpton and William F. Buckley...

Was that before or after the accident? I don't remember. Be that as it may, the day came when I was driving our van on East Hastings in Vancouver. I began intoning a long Hindu OM, made a left turn, and was T-boned by an oncoming car. The van was totaled and I was knocked out; I was unconscious for about half an hour, coming to briefly as the ambulance crew was loading me onto the gurney, then passing out again till I woke up in the ER.

During my "unconsciousness" I had a vision: that I had come, or was conducted, before a panel of golden beings, probably seven in all, who were sitting at a semi-circular judge's-bench in front of me: my Board of Karma. Nothing was said that I remember, but I had the distinct impression that they were transmitting to me the marching-orders for the next phase of my life—or rather, for my next "life" in this particular body.

At the ER the physicians X-rayed me, found that I had no skull fracture or subdural hematoma, stitched up the wound on the right side of my head, gave me a shot of penicillin and a prescription for pain pills, and that was that. Paula soon appeared, looking shocked and frightened. Had this been an unconscious suicide attempt on my part, I wonder? Was she wondering the same thing?

Then they simply discharged me. "The hangman wasn't hanging" as the song goes, "so they put you on the street" (from "Do It Again" by Steely Dan). Thanks to Canadian socialized medicine, I owed nothing. And even though I was in the country illegally, no legal consequences followed. I never even thought of them, never found out who hit me or why he or she had never turned up; I was too shell-shocked to ask such questions. Maybe Paula took care of some of the necessary details, though I have no memory of that; I was totally knocked out of the game of practical, responsible human life—"occluded from space-time" in the words of William Seward Burroughs from *Naked Lunch*. Thinking back on it now, it must have been a hit-and-run.

In the coming weeks I seemed to make a fairly full recovery, with no serious after-effects. Little did I know that I had been traumatized, on both the physical and the spiritual levels, more deeply than I knew, probably more deeply than I have yet encompassed. A year or so later I started to get pains in my neck, and the right ride of my body became tight and weak. Had I received some kind of minimal brain-damage from the concussion? In reality it turned out to be a case of spinal subluxation which never entirely healed, which led me to patronize chiropractors for the next 50 years. But even deeper than that, my course of enlightenment-via-kundalini-yoga had been interrupted by the accident. In the "normal" course of things—if, that is, it had been possible to reach final spiritual Liberation by psychophysical means alone, without moral rectitude, without psychological insight and purification, without submission to God—the *kundalini*, which had already risen to the point where it had begun to activate the *sahasrara*, the "thousand-petalled lotus" in the brain center, would have fully united with that center, after which the *amrita*, the nectar of bliss and Enlightenment, would have flowed downward through the chakras until it opened the *hridayam* or Cave of the Heart: the seat of the *Atman*, the Absolute Witness, the Self. That, however, was not what my *karma* dictated; that was not God's Will for me. As with the bully in grammar school, the Darkness of This World had intervened—again from the *right*—to knock me off my imagined course and my hoped-for destiny, and replace them with God's knowledge of my *true* destiny and His silent pronunciation of my name—my *real* name: God in the mask of Darkness. This World is our enemy for sure, but on the deepest level—and this is not only a hard thing to see but a hard truth to accept—it is God and nothing else. As the Holy Qur'an puts it, in its characteristic, stunning concision: *There is no refuge from Allah but in Him.* And because my head had been struck and my neck wrenched, the Serpent Power was interrupted in its full ascent to the *ajña-chakra*, the Third Eye, and so came to rest—not entirely, but a large part of it—at *vishuddha-chakra*, the Lotus of the Human Voice, conferring upon me what has ultimately turned out to be an almost preternatural power of verbal expression. Out of His Darkness, God said: "Don't leave the world now, no matter how cruel it seems to you. *Stay there, and write.*"

And so I did.

After that, somehow (I don't remember how) I was given shelter, rent free, by one Jim Skerl, a sunny individual, black haired and blue eyed, that I'd met through Randy Carson. I lived with the hip Jim and his straight brother for some months as I "recovered." Thinking back now I am stunned by the amount of charity I received, in that foreign land, and took totally for granted, not because I was in any way ungrateful but because, on some fundamental level, I didn't grasp what was happening to me. By a combination of kundalini-yoga, the automobile accident, the trauma of losing Paula and the general hippie drug use I was engaged in, I had been knocked half out of my body without quite realizing it. I was stunned, punchy, sailing through life like a dream, consequently all I can provide as an account of this phase of things are isolated episodes or impressions, drifting totally unmoored from any recoverable sequence of memory. If nowadays we tend to define life as a collection of separate "moments," if we postulate the existence of parallel timelines, of the "Mandela Effect," of various experiential bleed-throughs into alternate versions of ourselves in the context of an enveloping "multiverse," I believe this simply indicates a state of profound collective trauma on a massive scale. If individual trauma can result in the mental illness known as Multiple Personality Disorder (now called Dissociative Identity Disorder), I believe that collective trauma can produce something very similar within society as a whole.

I remember hiking with friends into the big coastal mountains near Vancouver, into primeval forests, the ground covered with thick spongy moss, through thickets of brilliant magenta fireweed and thorny devil's club, up a switchback trail to a mountain lake framed with snowy peaks, one of which was an ancient extinct volcano so old that the slopes had eroded away to reveal the volcanic plug they had once concealed, a darker mass of less-eroded, harder rock forming a tremendous, vertical tower...

I remember the moment when, under the influence of grass plus a tin cup of the mouth-searing 151-proof naval rum, sipped straight—the correct use of which was undoubtedly to mix it half-and-half with water to produce the traditional 75½-proof "grog" of the British Navy—I solved Lew Welch's "RIDER RIDDLE," the one designed to answer the question "What beast do you ride?"—in other words, to discover one's spirit-guide or totem animal. The solution, unexpectedly, was Rattlesnake, the earthbound beast of the *muladhara-* or *root-chakra*, symbolizing (and possibly providing?) the basic ability to maintain physical, incarnate existence on earth, as well as to carry and process poison—something I desperately needed right then to keep my astral body from separating from my material body for good—unlike Lew's path, whose own solution to that riddle was Turkey Buzzard, which presumably allowed him the ability, or assigned him the fate, of soaring away into other worlds... Lew took the high road and I took the low road, which is why I'm still here in "Scotland"...

I remember my attendance at a free hippie banquet, at which we all sat on our heels at a long, low table where the latest big shipment of hashish was being divvied up—Vancouver being more of a hash- than a grass-town at that point—huge inch-thick cakes of it the size of tea-saucers if not dinner plates. Hashish was so integrated into Vancouver society at that time that we all knew of a *cordon bleu*-level French master chef who cooked with hashish and grass, a whole spectrum of different shades and qualities of it, allowing his many-course banquets—by invitation only of course—to provide the complete culinary experience, step by step; he insisted that his customers arrive at his establishment entirely straight, allowing him to act as the sole impresario of their total experience... But it was an appetizer of grass that was included in the banquet that night, and through it we reached such a perfect pitch of group consciousness that, when someone remarked "this is amazing grass," we all immediately launched into a perfect choral rendition of the old favorite "Amazing Grass," sung to the tune of "Amazing Grace," with words we all knew by heart, though they were composed, by group telepathy, only at that very moment: a classic "hippie miracle" of the kind that routinely punctuated our lives, making us believe that anything was possible...

I also remember the free dinner for spiritual seekers provided by the Hare Krishna people, which consisted of lush vegetarian *prasad*, food that has been blessed to serve as an offering to God. (Strangely enough, the Eastern Orthodox Christians have almost the same name for almost the same thing: *prosforo*, bread that's been blessed as an offering to God.) After the feast a little mystery-play was staged. A meditating *jñani*—a yogi whose *marga* or way-to-God was *jñana*, Knowledge—sat in tight-assed, self-willed meditation, intoning "Om" with gritted teeth and knitted brow. Then the beautiful spiritual troubadour Sri Chaitanya happened by, flourishing his Indian lute (or whatever it was), the very picture of a liberated soul whose *marga* was *bhakti*, the way of Love. Touched by the lyrical beauty of Chaitanya the *bhakta*, the yogi renounced *jñana*, the way of Knowledge, and embraced the way of Love and Devotion, whose patron and exemplar was the Lord Krishna, the cowherd of Brindavan. Sri Ramakrishna, of course, could practice both *bhakti* and *jñana* at the same time with no problem at all; nonetheless the Hare Krishnas, like many of the hippies, insisted that Love was radically opposed to Knowledge and intrinsically superior to it. (The Perennialist sage Frithjof Schuon, whom you'll meet later, had exactly the opposite prejudice.) And, on the other side of the spiritual smorgasbord, I visited on one occasion a 3-storey sub-par building of abandoned office spaces that had been taken over by the Jesus Freaks. While doing a few hatha-yoga *asanas* in one of the rooms to loosen up my neck and back, one of the Freaks caught me, and undertook to show me the error of my ways with great solicitude and concern: "No no brother, *that's* not the way..." To me it was like I was only doing pushups, but to him it was pure paganism or occultism, the straight path to Hell. Then there were the two young Freaks, one male and one female, who—bibles in hand—became engaged in a theological debate about whether or not they should sleep together, the man arguing in favor of that resolution on the basis of various "pro" citations from holy scripture, the woman backing up her opposition to it with equally authoritative "con" citations... what a fly-on-the-wall I was in those days, and on so many different walls...

And I also remember the two classic New Yorkers (from Brooklyn? The Bowery? The Bronx?), as if straight out of "The Bowery Boys" comic acting troupe starring Leo Gorcey and Huntz Hall, who identified Vancouver, if not Canada as a whole, as populated entirely by the "hicks" and "rubes" that New York mythology knew so well. So on one occasion they hired a cheap theatre where they put on a vaudeville act — actually more like a latter-day parody of a vaudeville act — with stock bad jokes and ineffective tap-dancing that nonetheless so wowed the locals that people in the audience started pelting them with money, both coins and bills, the whole thing being just about as "off Broadway" as you could get... not to mention the sad Jewish clown, also from New York, a classic young *schlemiel*, prematurely balding and with thick curly side-hair, who had no other identity than "clown" and no other prospects than whatever the destiny of "clown" might provide for him in the hippie world; taking pity on him I gave him my copy of Gershom Scholem's book on the Kabbalah, that he might begin his slow, laborious climb up the invisible Tree of Life... (how lost we really were in those days, all of us...)

Then there was the strawberry blonde English girl who had named herself "Orange Blossom" and who I attempted to become enamored of, though she herself was enamored of Jim Skerl. The day came when she was embracing the uninterested Skerl while I simultaneously embraced the uninterested her, creating between us an embryonic ouroboros that never succeeded in biting its own tail... she apparently saw me more as a brother, friend and spiritual adviser than a lover, which might have worked out on some level if only I had been gay... I remember an occasion when we were in the same apartment together, one of the donated temporary sleeping-spaces that kept me off the street during that time. Straight English girl though she was, she had dropped acid, so I placed my middle finger on her third eye and proceeded to "stir it open" with my superior hippie magic. "What are you *doing?*" she exclaimed in wonder — then gazed at me and said: "You're so *pure!*" Little did she know... however, I was still pure enough not to move down her chakras, one-by-one, giving her a subtle spiritual explanation of each one as I went, until at last I arrived at Number Two, the one described in the tantric literature as "her (the *kundalini*'s) favorite resort," thereby transforming the celestial, elevated LSD into an effective date-rape drug...

As I was cruising through these increasingly alienated and insecure experiences, I made the common mistake of many Americans in Canada, based on the idea that Canadians were just like Americans. They're not. For example, where Americans (at least of my age group) will often commonly communicate in terms of "routines," little skits or mini-dramas featuring satirical characters with different attitudes and accents — the cultural habit that gave rise to Robin Williams and Saturday Night Live, and which appeared in the original title of American-born poet T. S. Eliot's classic modernist poem "The Wasteland" as "He Do the Police in Different Voices" — even the most hip Canadians, at least in that era, would be entirely *straight* at that particular point. Just speak with the usual American illustrative humor and the normal Canadian would cock his eye at you and say to himself, "a looney, eh?" Consequently the percentage of missed and misinterpreted social cues, especially with the addition of cannabis, in mixed groups of Canadians and Americans could reach excruciating proportions, with neither group realizing quite what was happening, or why...

Still, I continued my earlier habit of patronizing the available gurus. These included the "Sufi" teacher Jack Schwartz, one of whose lectures I attended, as well as a representative of Human Individual Metamorphosis, a UFO cult headed by a couple known as The Two — the group who later morphed into a darker cult called Heaven's Gate, only to commit mass suicide in 1997 in Rancho Santa Fe, California, near San Diego. The huckster/lecturer, who in earlier years would have appeared in a striped jacket and straw hat and wielding a cane, showed us a series of complicated diagrams which, he said, indicated that it would be possible for us to activate *144,000 different senses* if we would simply sign on the dotted line! I expressed my reaction to this by dancing out of the room like a vaudeville entertainer exiting stage left to the *wah-wah* of disapproving trombones...

More interesting was the Theosophical white witch, a middle-aged lady with a hare-lip but a genuinely sweet and saintly disposition, physically deformed but spiritually beautiful, who liked to invite young hippies to her abode with an offer of good weed, to hold discussions of exalted spiritual subjects, and without a hint of proselytization. She had set up a Faraday cage, a wooden framework covered with copper screening that was electrified at an extremely high voltage, which was reputed to enhance the psychic sensitivity of those sitting inside it — though when I sat in that electric chair I felt that I was in the middle of a vast barren landscape, totally bereft of any vibrations of human emotion or organic life ... "they do not have 'emotion's oxygen' in that atmosphere," as William Burroughs once wrote of the environment of one of his imagined alien planets ... Then, walking home through the urban night, still stoned, I thought I heard, in the wind shaking the high-tension wires on the high steel towers, the voices of lost souls who had been magnetized by the current and couldn't escape, but were doomed to course along those pinging wires forever...

And since I was in the Great Canadian North where so many Native Americans and half-breed Indian/White *metis* lived (along with all the red-haired displaced Scotsmen of B.C., like Paula's and my friend, Graeme Foster), I decided to find a traditional medicine man with whom I could discuss my growing interest in shamanic rattles as spiritual tools. I finally found an old man, whose name I don't remember, and was granted an audience with him at his poor, run-down house on the north shore of Vancouver Harbor, in a patch of land still occupied by the Squamish Nation that went by the depressing name of "Capilano Indian Reserve No. 5." He let me hold his rattle, which had the words "Seremoniul Rattel" scratched on it with a ball-point pen. "All this" he said to me, passing his hand across the view outside his window, "all this once was trees, but now—no more." No Don Juan he, no Castaneda I, only someone willing to listen to his continuing list of the various things that, once upon a time, were, but now, sadly, are no more.

Nonetheless I was able, for the first but not the only time, to attend a lecture by Ram Dass, in many ways the spiritual highlight of my stay in Canada. "There's as much spiritual energy in this room right now," he told us, "as anywhere in India." I believed him then, and I still do. Group spiritual energy, however, is one thing, while dedication to the Spiritual Path, along with the laborious job of the discovery of sin and the purification of the soul from sin, by the guidance and power of God, is another thing entirely.

But perhaps my aimless spiritual seeking in Canada, and the general downward trajectory of the hippie counterculture in the 1970s, was best summed up by one young hip guy I encountered, who conclusively declared: "Unity is *boring!*" *Vidya-maya*, "wisdom-apparition," had attracted him to Liberation, which he had tasted for a moment but was unable to hold on to — and so *avidya-maya*, "ignorance-apparition," took him away again. So it goes — every single time. All the *truth* that danced before our eyes in those days! — even though, nine times out of ten, we took it as no more than a passing entertainment.

> You go back, Jack, do it again
> Wheel turning round and round
> You go back, Jack, do it again
> —"Do It Again" by Steely Dan

I was able, however, to make some "literary" connections in Vancouver. I did a poetry reading at Simon Fraser University that I was actually paid for, and had a brief affair with a congenial, 40-year old poetry-woman whom I encountered (and slept with again) later in San Francisco, during the orgies-of-welcome that attended the visit of Russian poet Andrei Voznesensky to Lawrence Ferlinghetti and City Lights — virtually my only "older woman" experience. We probably got together partly based on my publication of *Panic Grass*, which I myself had nearly forgotten. While in S.F. she was working at translating some of Voznesensky's poetry into English; on one occasion she asked me what word I thought was appropriate for a certain line and I replied "grip" — so if you ever read any of Voznesensky's poetry in English and come across the word "grip," you can be sure, swear to God, that that was my contribution. And speaking of encountering the same people in more than one place up and down the coast in those years, in Canada I actually ran into someone I'd met in Mexico years before, one Cornell Neumann, a scornful and insinuating young man, blond, rich, German, who was traveling the world with his mother. I felt that he was somehow my personal devil, sent to subtly torment and invalidate me. When I told him that, with the help of my parents, I'd bought a piece of land far up in the interior of B.C. (you'll hear about that later), he flashed me an ironic, mocking grin: "You're no *farmer!*" He was right of course — though it is definitely best practice not to get into a state, or into such company, where it is only the devils who are willing to tell you the truth . . .

And it may be that the expansive, acid-fueled hippie energy of the U.S. counterculture was simply incompatible on a basic level with the depressive, introverted quality of British Columbian society, a quality that was perfectly encapsulated for me when I stood on the street in a two-block long queue of silent petitioners in a cold drizzling rain, all of us waiting to be admitted to the federal government liquor store to be issued our ration of Victory Gin (cf. George Orwell in *1984*) . . .

Be that as it may, I finally graduated from crashing at friends' apartments to a room of my own in a building with a common bathroom and two other apartments, one occupied by a dusky, attractive young lady studying to be a cosmetologist, the other by a diminutive, elfin astrologer, with fine, longer-than-shoulder-length hair, plus a wispy beard and mustache; if he had been any smaller he would have been described as a "perfectly-formed midget." As for myself, at that time I was living substantially on air, in a room that contained nothing but a scrap of foam rubber for a mattress, my sleeping bag, a hot plate and an aluminum pot in which I cooked my meals of brown rice, vegetables, raw almonds, soy sauce and canned tuna, and a bare wooden floor. It was in that room that I composed several lines of verse, under the influence of some mescaline-soaked marijuana, that later found a place in my epic poem "The Wars of Love," and read with great interest *Tibetan Yoga and Secret Doctrines* and *The Tibetan Book of the Great Liberation*, as translated by W. Y. Evans-Wentz, who also brought us hippies (Timothy Leary included) the only English translation then available of the *Bardo Thödöl*, the *Tibetan Book of the Dead*. Three events stand out from my stay there. The first was a highly significant dream the next-door astrologer had about me, which I will share with you below, and the second, the attempted suicide by sleeping-pill overdose of the student cosmetologist, an ordeal which she seemed to survive with no ill effects — except, of course, in the invisible chambers of the heart:

because without doubt the store of darkness that lay hidden under the spiritual idealism and free-wheeling hedonism of the hippie generation will never be fully weighed and measured, except on the Scales of Akhira, in the next world — as witness the third event which, as I suppose I must now confess, was one of the darkest of all my excursions through the many subtle, psychic worlds I so "innocently" trespassed into during those years. If I remember correctly, it took place under the influence that same mescaline-soaked marijuana. After smoking, I ingested some powder from one of those Native American bones that my uncle Vance had given to my father — one of which I later presented to the 16th Gwalya Karmapa — in an attempt to awaken the former tenant of them from his sleep in the ancestral underworld. He duly appeared in my mind's eye, apparently very grateful that somebody had finally remembered him; nonetheless, without quite realizing it, I had committed two extremely serious sins — *cannibalism* and *necromancy*. And, idiot though I was, I was no more of an idiot than half of my hippie compatriots. *How did I survive?* How did I retain my sanity? How did I avoid becoming a Satanist? How did I retain my faith in God? It could only have been because faith in God is a gift of God, and because God saves whomever He will. But I wonder if that dark "experiment" was the source of a dream I had around the same time while living in that room, in which I left my body and astral-projected all the way to Sir Francis Drake Boulevard in Marin County, California, west of Fairfax, at the foot of White's Hill, where I entered an unfamiliar house — though in the dream it was supposedly the home, or the parents' home, of Desirée, one of my friend Ken Bullock's girlfriends — where I saw a large glass standing figurine of a cat with an elongated neck and gold-colored threads embedded in the glass. I especially noted it in case I ever wanted to search for that house in the physical dimension to prove the reality of my astral trip. During that flight also I became, for a split second, "The King of Corfu" (the Greek island), who — as I later learned from Google — could have been either King George I of Greece [1863], or Napoleon Bonaparte [1797], or Charles of Anjou [1267], or Philip the father of Alexander the Great [338 BC], or the sea-god Poseidon in the depths of the archaic past. My soul had been fragmented, refracted, into endless "reincarnational" worlds; it was a case of psychic devastation being compensated for, and hidden, by narcissism and the flattery of demons: "king" indeed! And finally, after my swift return-flight back to my sleeping body in Vancouver, I found it occupied by a "squatter" who appeared to be the soul of another human being who had recently died; when I "evicted" him so I could repossess my own legally-entitled body, I could hear him crying "Oh *shit* oh *shit* oh *shit!*" since he was now homeless again, at the mercy of the cruel astral winds... And virtually nobody in the counterculture world was capable of realizing how *sinister* such experiences were! They were just "far out" — no other evaluation was applied — and made great story-telling material for the hippie raconteurs...

INTO THE INTERIOR

Before returning to the U.S., California and Marin County in 1971, I took either two or three hitchhiking/freight train trips from Vancouver into the interior of B.C. in the year of 1970. My memory delivers them in 3 packets, but it's likely that the first two were connected, by which I mean, not interrupted by a return to the big city.

The first trip was my tour-of-inspection of the communes of British Columbia, which allows me now to report my impressions of that largely failed, because mostly unplanned, social experiment. The hippie communes that had any degree of staying-power, a few even surviving to the present day, were either based on some religious or spiritual belief, or else had collected around a strong charismatic leader — two stabilizing factors that were often found together. My first contact with that world was through a nicely designed establishment in the mountains that, like most of the communes of that place and time, functioned as a hostel for travelers. That one featured the common Demeter/Kore duo of Earth Mother and Nubile Maiden, the two main roles available to women in the hippie communes. The Persephone of the combo was a neat, bare-breasted, well-tanned young lass who helpfully informed me that "I really *like* sex," figuring that this piece of information would prove useful to me. And I might well have taken her up on her offer if it had not been for a guy who obviously considered himself to be her old man, watching us like a hawk from the next room and armed with a hatchet which he kept loudly chopping into a thick wooden plank. According to the free love ideology of the hippies, sexual jealously simply did not exist in the brave new world of the counterculture — except, apparently, for some of the men, who held on to that type of old age thinking which defined "free love" as the way to *get* girls, and strict monogamy — at least for the females — as the only reliable way of holding on to them.

After surviving the night I was informed of the name and direction of the next stop on the hippie nomad route, higher in the mountains along a dirt road, which turned out to be a frontier-style settlement. I joined the crowd at a rudimentary rodeo, where buckboards, each drawn by a pair of horses and pretty obviously manned by drunken drivers, were racing each other chaotically around a circular track — a driver falling off from time to time to either stand and run or fall and get trampled: good clean country fun. Nonetheless by the evening of that day I'd reached my next stopping-point, a remote hamlet with at least one well-tended dirt street to it, made up of a lovely collection of rural houses set in a grove of trees. It was there, on the following day, that I took my second acid trip, amid the stunning snowcapped peaks of the Pacific Range; I've already told the story of that trip in *Chapter Four*.

THE VALLEY OF THE THREE SISTERS

The next phase of Road Trip One — which might or might not have actually been Road Trip Two — took me to the Okanagan, that narrow strip of semi-desert east of the Pacific Ranges that widens when it enters into the U. S. until it ultimately becomes eastern Washington and Oregon, Nevada, Utah, the Mojave Desert, Arizona, New Mexico and West Texas. I traveled there because the hippie grapevine told me that the next point of interest was a commune in the mountains just west of the highway, in a place called The Valley of the Three Sisters, this being the name for a group of three mountains. After my ride dropped me at the right turnoff, I caught another ride up a six-mile dirt road which took me to a truly idyllic setting, with a good-sized plot of flat, tillable land, where the commune flourished — or maybe "withered" would be a better word, seeing that the human scene transpiring there, in contrast to the setting provided by Mother Nature, was far from idyllic.

One of the difficulties, perhaps the central one, was that there were too many men for the available women. The only stable female population seemed to be the standard Earth Mother and the equally standard young, nubile "maiden." And the other problem, of course, was the drug use — which, after the traveling hashish-vendor passed through, was largely responsible for the fact that these hippie "farmers" didn't plant on time and so brought in no crop that year; this undoubtedly explains why, over the winter, I met some of them again back in Vancouver. The general myth was that "Gaia is a bountiful Mother who provides freely and impartially for all" — even though it ought to be obvious to anyone that one of the main reasons human civilization was created in the first place was to protect us against many of the things that the Great Mother is so free and open with. (Civilization, of course, was one of the things the hippies were in flight from. Back in Vancouver I had published a poem in an alternative hippie newspaper that went on to win first prize in a contest sponsored by the "Anti-Civilization League," a band of grinning satirical tricksters who, like Frank Zappa, had targeted the hippie counterculture.)

As soon as I walked into the hippie homestead the hostess relieved me of most of the food I was carrying — specifically, a mixture of raisins, nuts and grains — an appropriation I didn't protest since, after all, they were offering me shelter. Like many communes of that time and place, the Three Sisters was on the hippie nomad route, and was therefore dedicated, according to the undoubtedly short-lived hippie dogma of the time, to taking in everyone who either traveled through or who wanted to "join." During my own short stay, these included, in addition to the Hashish

Candy Man, a wino bum who had decided to turn hippie since that appeared to offer him a better deal than the streets—all that was required, since he already had the beard, was to tie a rolled bandana around his forehead for a head-band—and some people from the eastern provinces, including several girls who were out west looking for adventure. One of them was an attractive young Jewish woman who, with a proud and challenging look, immediately stripped to the waist to reveal a pair of firm, shapely breasts: "A woman can be proud and stiff/ When on love intent," said Yeats in "Crazy Jane Talks with the Bishop." Since nudity and free love were part of hippie dogma, how could anything possibly go wrong?

HIPPIE SEXUAL POLITICS

Hippie nudity—female nudity in my case—always involved a kind of double message. Message One was: "Nudity is 'natural.' It has no necessary connection with sex at all. The human body simply is what it is; it is a part of Nature. Haven't you ever seen *breasts* before? I have them; your mother had them; they are nothing but a natural, organic way of feeding the young—so what's the big deal??" Message Two was: "This is *sex* and nothing else, pretty boy—sex, sex, sex!" So the male hippie was shamed for his desire—as if he were some sleazy *straight* guy watching a girly show, part of all that degenerate world that we had now left behind forever (all except for *you*, you pitiful loser)—while that desire was simultaneously being inflamed, under the theory that compulsory "free love" was also a part of "naturalness." And if he was in any way disoriented or demoralized by this double message, that simply meant that he wasn't *hip* enough. So the free love ethos had a power trip built into it from the beginning. Men had their own kind of power-trips of course, exemplified by the rock star stud with the hundred groupies, or the head honcho of the commune who—like many of the gurus of the time—had inherent sexual rights over all the women in the group, much like the king of the realm or the lord of the manor did under feudalism, who had the right to sleep with every new bride before her husband was allowed to, thus giving rise to surnames like "King" or "Lord" in the resulting offspring. When Prince Andrew took his pick of the young girls provided by Jeffrey Epstein, he was (in his Mother's estimation at least) simply exercising the traditional unwritten rights of aristocracy: "lords will be lords." But the power-trip laid down by the women was different, and was based on two different strategies. The first was the *Mutterrecht*, the primordial rights of the Earth Mother. In a culture where the women were so often the breadwinners, more capable than their men of holding down "shit jobs" in the straight world, and (at least in the U.S.) also often sources of additional income as single mothers through the Aid to Families with Dependent Children program—a culture in which the role of the men was to entertain, to provide sexual favors, to score for drugs, and sometimes (of course) to "save the world" as workers or leaders in various movements of spiritual or political idealism—the women, as in more traditional cultures, often ruled the household, took care of the children (of course), and laid down the law when it came to the antics of their less mature and responsible menfolk. And the second power-trip, as indicated above, was the sexual tease. Even if a woman had no intent to sexually manipulate men, if she was only a sweet, friendly girl who just wanted to have fun (and maybe even fall in love!), still, the tease that was *intrinsically built in* to the free love ethos gave her a certain power over men whether she wanted it or not, the power to shame and seduce, which many women found increasingly attractive, and were consequently seduced by themselves: the White Witch of Narnia had taken over the hippie universe (cf. C.S. Lewis' *The Lion, the Witch and the Wardrobe*). Consequently the unconscious power-motive worked to undermine and destroy the dedication to love that the hippies were consciously promoting. And this, precisely, was the root of the feminist development *within the hippie ethos itself*, independent of all ideology. In the more traditional societies of the western world, feminine sexual attraction and the necessary sexual denial that went with it of course also operated, but they did not contradict each other as they did under the regime of free love; they worked in tandem instead, since both were fundamentally oriented toward marriage. The various forms of marriage that developed in human culture over many thousands of years grew up in part to prevent the unbridled expression of sexual power and manipulation, of rape and seduction—which, if left unchecked, would destroy society. But as soon as these forms were jettisoned by the hippies, rape and seduction emerged from their cave, as vicious and primitive as they ever were—and they did their work. One of the results of this was the depersonalized hook-up culture of today, which ultimately allows only those who meet a set of increasingly twisted standards-of-sexual-attractiveness to have sex. This in turn has resulted in an obsession with plastic surgery, to the vast economic benefit of the medical profession; in the "incel" (involuntary celibate) subculture of woman-hating men; and ultimately in transgenderism, where for some men the only way of getting a woman is apparently to become one (or pretend to), and which has also taken the standard feminist dogma that sees traditionally masculine traits as positive and traditionally feminine ones as negative, the regime under which all a woman can really aspire to is to become a second-class man (because who, after all, wants to be a "girly girl"?), to its logical conclusion, leading many young girls to further enrich the "helpful and encouraging" medical profession by undergoing sex-change operations themselves with a view to becoming men. And so, taking the long view, we can see that the mores of free love in the hippie counterculture have ultimately led, in the 21st century, to the destruction of gender itself. The disintegration of human society has culminated in the deconstruction of the human form.

In the commune of the Valley of the Three Sisters, all these roles and dynamics were already in play. The group had its sexual tease, the young, nubile, bare-breasted maiden, concubine to the head honcho, whose only title to honchodom was his possession of her, since he certainly didn't exercise any responsible leadership as far as I could see. It had its Earth Mother, who managed the domestic economy and organized the gathering of the edible plants—wild strawberries, wild onions etc.—but who was less sexually desirable and obviously not available for that purpose. And, due to the sexual imbalance of only two (permanent) women to at least four men, not to mention the many temporary visitors, it had its "incels" too, who ultimately staged an "incel revolution"—in the form of a gang-rape—the night before I pulled up my shallowly-driven stakes and moved on. And undoubtedly the excess of psychic openness that these hippies exhibited was destined to result, later on, in the depressive introversion and the excessively "triggerable" sensitivity that are so in evidence everywhere today. So I had apparently gotten in, as a card-carrying member of the hippie counterculture, on the ground floor of the Worm that was destined to undermine, and ultimately destroy, Western Civilization.

Three further memories stand out from my Three Sisters experience. The first was something I heard from one young man of a depressive and saturnine temperament while sitting in a tree: "I'm going to sit here until I know what an old man knows" he said. Clearly he needed elders—but having rejected all the straight elders that would have naturally filled that role for him (father, grandfather, teacher, pastor, priest), and having found no *guru* he could unreservedly take as his adviser on how to be a human being, as well as (specifically) how to be a man, all he could do was try to mentor himself—*initiate* himself. He had to invent his own rites-of-passage out of nothing but his personal, dark and needful introversion, plus psychedelic drugs—and a passage to what, exactly? I believe that I understood his dilemma fairly well because, at the point in my life when I met him, I was doing something similar myself. The Catholic priests of my childhood were long gone, while my father, and my poetic mentor Lew Welch—though I didn't know it yet—would both soon be leaving this world. If I needed more "fathering," what other "Father" could I turn to, at that point, but God Himself? But did I really know how to do that? And was that my real intent?

The second experience was one of my own making, based on my reactions to the powerful hashish that had flooded the valley. Stoned, I sat before a pair of trees in the center of the field that the hippies—or maybe someone who'd owned the place before them—had named "the Marriage Trees," since it looked as if they were embracing each other. Listening, with my Inner Ear, to the wind blowing through those branches, I heard: "*Yyoouu wwiillll llivve...*" Then, looking down, I saw a shallow depression in the field, roughly the size and shape of a human body and sprinkled with wildflowers; I was convinced that a skeletonized corpse lay within it. At that point a "sorcerer's technique" came to me, like the ones in Carlos Castaneda's *Journey to Ixtlán*, which consisted of the explosive intoning of the syllables "ai-YIH-IH-IH," directed so that they rapped on my lower belly from the inside, on the point the Japanese call the *tanden*, the purpose of this being to prevent my fundamental life-force from being sucked out of me through that aperture by an encounter with Deadly Yin Energy. "He who tries to be his own guide has Satan for a guide," like the Sufis say... but since the Marriage Trees had told me that I would live, I most likely believed that I had to hold on to that worldview or else encounter the contrary fate...

The third experience was the deal-breaker. On the last night there, sitting around a campfire—but farther back in the shadows than the others—I heard several men, the "incels" of the group, planning a rape. We had been drinking that awful, toxic Canadian wine, the beverage that I claimed at one point was made by filling a railroad tank-car with Concord grapes somewhere in Quebec, adding yeast and sugar, tamping them down, then hauling that mixture across the continent to B.C., at which destination they opened the taps and bottled and sold whatever ran out as "wine." "And let's git that little Jewish girl too," I remember the bum-turned-hippie saying. But did I take it upon myself to warn the women? Not me. Nothing was required of me because I was only an "outside observer," a ghost, a fly on the wall. I was so out of it that I didn't even realize that I had been confronted in that moment with a serious moral challenge—so it might actually be true to say, at least at that point, that *I wasn't even a coward*.

Next morning, the air itself was wounded. Nobody talked about what had happened the night before, but the feeling that a disaster had occurred was palpable. The visitors were all packing up, preparing to move on. I was told by one guy that the next stop on the route was the commune run by "Frank the Sorcerer" on the shores of the Frazer River, but he cautioned me against going there because, according to him, "you two will only fight." Of course I didn't listen to him...

On the way to Frank's domain I stopped at a place where I encountered a Viking-identified proto-Pagan, unwitting ancestor to today's Alt Right. Having apparently done his best to become a blacksmith through pure untutored inspiration, he had forged for himself a kind of hatchet from a shapeless lump of iron, an object that he named "Gimli" after the dwarf in Tolkien's *The Lord of the Rings* (who was in turn named after the place where the worthy survivors of Ragnarök will live after the dissolution of the present world—*Gimli* in the Icelandic dialect—as recounted in the *Prose Edda* and the *Völuspá*). For all its cracks and fissures, at least that defective home-made battle-axe was something to hold on to...

To get to Frank the Sorcerer's place you had to cross the wide, deep Frazer River, where it passes through the desert strip of the Okanagan. It was crossed on a cable ferry, composed of a wooden raft big enough to carry at least one car—a conveyance that, since the cable it moved along was arranged diagonally to the width of the river, would be moved across by the force of the current; to return to the other shore you had to winch the cable farther up one of the banks until it was set diagonally in the other direction. But no car wished to cross at that time, so I and a couple of other travelers rode the ferry on foot. From the opposite shore we began a maybe six-mile trek by footpath. The sheer desert cliffs of bare orange rock on the opposite shore to our right were tall and impressive, pockmarked with many little natural caves of the kind that the Desert Fathers must've lived and prayed in along the Nile in the early days of Christianity. And when we finally reached the penultimate point of our trip, the edge of a steep canyon down to the river, cut by a tributary stream, we were confronted by a striking sight: a maybe 4-foot-tall, white-painted wooden *ankh*, the Egyptian symbol for "life," standing alone in the barren landscape at the lip of the ravine—as if to mark, with apotropaic, magical potency, the border of Frank's domain. And when we got to the edge, we looked down into a wide, steep, rocky stream-bed that held a lovely miniature "hacienda" of scrap-wood that Frank and his people had built.

Frank the Sorcerer himself was a tough little near-dwarf from Eastern Europe, always barking orders to his subordinates like a drill sergeant; he ran the place like a Gurdjieff boot camp, the orders that he gave interspersed with bits of spiritual wisdom. They lived on trout, insect grubs, goat's milk, Saskatoon berries, a few vegetables from the garden, and government flour. After we'd descended the steep bank into the canyon I was introduced to Frank; and also to the cottonwoods that we tried to cut for fuel, a clinging, rope-like wood that will bind any saw; and to the goats. (It was always goats with the B.C. hippies—goats, goats, goats. At those communes I drank the sweetest, and also the rankest, goat's milk of my experience. Goats were the ideal animal for the hippies of that place and time since they required little care and knew how to feed themselves.)

Being a subsistence economy, food-gathering consumed a good part of the day. Up the steep stream to fish for trout and collect grubs, then back along the trail by which we'd arrived to harvest the Saskatoon berries (also known as service berries or June berries) that grew on good-sized trees along the high cliffs above the river, which we later sugared and cooked, also adding a little lemon juice to acidify the mixture and keep down the bacteria.

Then the day came when Frank announced that he would be dropping acid, so he cloistered himself alone inside a tiny hut for eight long hours. When his time was up he emerged, making that swiping gesture to mime the dusting off of one's hands which indicates: "That's that." "Good session!" he informed us, before setting us to the next task.

Did Frank and I fight as the hippie at the Three Sister had predicted? Not quite... it's just that I was not *totally* impressed with him — and he knew it. He kept recounting his exploits, the many people who looked up to him and more-or-less followed him as a spiritual leader. "Look at this!" he exclaimed, showing me some craft object of other; "This was given to me by real Gypsies from the other side of the world!" "That's what *you* get" I said, with studied neutrality. It was probably my less-than-worshipful attitude that caused him to do his best to bust my ass by climbing the bank of his canyon at breakneck speed on our trip back to the river ferry; he almost succeeded, though I did barely manage to keep up. But though Frank ran his extended household like a miniature dictator, at least somebody was assuming responsibility! By this alone his scene was better than the scene at the Three Sisters, where leadership was almost totally lacking, resulting in toxic chaos, and ultimately violence.

That particular journey into the B.C. interior reached its apex somewhere in the far North, at another commune where the group was better organized than even Frank's outfit. They had a real house, not one thrown together by amateur hippie carpenters, situated on some good land with a fair-sized tillable field of loamy soil; I saw how deep and fertile it was when I helped my hosts dig a root-cellar. Since I was then probably at the apex of my physical strength in this life, I decided to walk down the railroad tracks to a town 15 miles away and then back, all in the same day, without stopping: 10 hours straight. (When I told my hosts where I'd been they didn't believe me; writing this story now I can hardly believe it myself.) That was the hike on which I saw my first and only wolf in the wild — not a re-stocked one but an original child of the earth I was walking on, long, lean and slate-grey. He emerged from the brush to my right, the side where the bank was, then faded back up the hill without a word as soon as he saw me...

When I say "better organized," however, I don't mean that these people were without the angst of their choices in life, and of the universal human condition. One woman was out from the East to try and kick her speed habit with the help of clean country living and her generous friends in B.C. — methamphetamine-lean and with the skull showing through the skin, not trim and healthy like the wolf was, though in some ways she was just as hungry... I ended up doing some foolishly "American" thing, like making an unguarded appeal to a stranger for a momentary sign of friendship, which made her absolutely livid: "You must *never ask!*" she announced—disciplining me, teaching me the hard discretion and self-denial that are necessary for survival on the human edge... and then there was the moment when I walked unguardedly through the door into the dining room and caught two girls at the table smooching like Sappho and Anactoria; they stared wildly away from each other when I appeared, looking this way and that... the B.C. hip scene, from Vancouver to the far interior, had lots of Lesbians in it, though the male homosexuals lived in some other scene that rarely crossed paths with hippiedom as I knew it.

Then, discovering that an adjacent lot was for sale at a reasonable price, I phoned my father down in California and put it to him that real estate would be a good investment for my future, even if I didn't make it as a farmer, consequently he sprang for the whole amount, thereby making me a Canadian landowner. So there is no question that, like quite a few other Baby Boomers out of the upper middle class, I was seriously over-protected and indulged; all my adventuring and danger-seeking were probably just my way of paying off the debt for that rare and dangerous gift, and of compensating for the darker side of it: if you're still economically dependent on your parents in adulthood, the least you should do is get busted up in a car crash...

The Vaishya caste (in Hinduism) makes money; the sacrosanct Brahmins beg from the Vaishyas for their daily bread; and the Kshatriyas, the warrior-caste that's situated between them, rules the Vaishyas and fights to protect the Brahmins... each has its own appointed suffering: the Vaishyas, work, economic worry and risk; the Kshatriyas, death and wounds; the Brahmins, the abysmal danger of spiritual pride, perhaps partly compensated for, and designed to be protected against, by an unacknowledged social shame in the face of Kshatriya courage and Vaishya practicality... only the Shudras, the lowest caste whose suffering is back-breaking physical labor, are allowed the kind of self-indulgences that the Brahmins, Kshatriyas and Vaishyas are ashamed of, and so willingly renounce... nonetheless the Brahmins, the highest caste, if they fail in their *dharma*, have nowhere to fall but into the ranks of the Shudras, and ultimately the Pariahs. The Bohemian—especially the poet!—is like a failed Brahmin, the degenerate scion of a fallen archaic priesthood now become a king in hiding among the lowlife, like the Jew Fagin in Charles Dickens' *Oliver Twist*. According to the Hindus, the Pariah or outcaste is the product of a mixing of castes, which gives him a heterogeneous and self-contradictory character—and that's the Bohemian to a T. (As for me, I have a more-or-less Kshatriya character, with a certain Bohemian, Brahmin/Shudra admixture. I live by campaigns rather than jobs, I move from war to war—bloodless war so far, by God's mercy—fighting not as a mercenary but as a warrior in the service of a King. Between wars I degenerate, I dissipate myself with the castle maidens, become fat and soft, a glutton and a drunkard; only the glory and the suffering of war have the power to bring me into focus again — until, God willing, the spiritual Path shows me the way of the Greater Jihad rather than the lesser, teaching me to leave the glory to Allah and the suffering to my ego, my *nafs*, that so richly deserves it but will, *insha'Allah*, finally learn how to use it.)

Nonetheless, even though being over-indulged sets you up for a life of shame and fear, my father truly *saved* me: not with money, not with permissiveness and largesse, but *because he believed in me*. And because I loved him with the greatest love of my adolescence and young manhood, I knew that I owed it both to him and to myself to live up to that trust. I will never forget the moment when, as a child of maybe five years old, he told me, with all the earnestness and blessing that were in him: "I want you to grow up to be a *good man*." (Have I fulfilled that great commission, my father? What will you say about that when we meet again?)

Because, without my knowing it, my father was nearing the end of his life. Some time during my year in British Columbia, he actually drove with my mother in his 4-wheel-drive Toyota Land Cruiser all the way from San Rafael in California Norte to the southern tip of Baja California; he wanted to be sure to make the trip before they put in the new modern road so he could travel by the old patchwork of partly-dirt roads through the most primitive "unimproved" back-country that was still available to him in North America... and it's amazing to me that my mother actually went with him! Later I realized that he must've known, or felt, that he had little time left in this world and wanted to spend it on one final adventure; I like to think that my own adventures in British Columbia had been part of what inspired him to take that step. And I get the idea that, wherever he went, the people of Mexico loved him. One old man actually offered him a house for free if he ever wanted to retire in Baja... imagine that for a place now infested with Satanic drug gangs who like to roll severed heads down the streets, like the Aztecs rolled them (in my imagination at least) down their bloody pyramids! Is it that the Earth is no longer worthy of us? Or is it actually we who are no longer worthy of the Earth?

LAST TRIP IN CANADA

Carried on by nothing (apparently) but the blind impetus of the Renaissance as it breached the protective wall of medieval Christendom in wave after wave of westward exploration, exploration that became the immediate ancestor of the directly-succeeding drive of American manifest destiny, ending at the Pacific coast yet still continuing, on another level, as the volatilization of that westward impetus created by psychedelic drugs and scored and choreographed by the rhythm of "classic" rock music — transmuting form into vibration and human intent into music, as if Shiva behind the veil of the Unseen had opened his Third Eye to inaugurate the *pralaya*, the dissolution of all things—I kept pressing on into the Interior, in both senses of that word. Until the inertia of that wave of travel was finally spent I just couldn't stop traveling, so I hitchhiked and hopped freights again, this time north from Vancouver to Prince George, ultimately bound for Prince Rupert on the Pacific Coast, just south of the Alaska Panhandle. Half-way to Prince George I stopped at 100-Mile House—not a house but a town—because my mother had asked me (of all things) to look up one Catherine Strother, an old relative of hers she had probably never even met in the flesh, who apparently lived there. It was this unlikely commission that led me, a nearly-penniless itinerant hippie, to make contact with a British Columbia rancher and his family, who in the "natural" course of things would've been more likely to slam the door in my face or drive me off with a shotgun. Asking around, I was given the location of the appropriate ranch, after which I trudged up to the corral, and yelled across the fence (politely, though as bluntly and arbitrarily as can be imagined) to the cowboy there who was wrangling a horse: "*Excuse me! I am Charles Upton, the son of the cousin of the aunt of* (etc. etc., I forget the exact terms of relatedness) *Catherine Strother; is this where she lives??*" It turned out that it was; I was apparently talking to her grandson, and this without benefit of any introductory letter or phone call. Nonetheless, *family is family*—so he stoically paused in his task and silently drove me up the hill in his pickup by the dirt road to the house where the old folks lived, at which threshold I was cordially received by Catherine Strother and her husband. (Come to think of it, maybe my mother had actually written her to expect me, though I either had no knowledge of that at the time or retain no memory of it now.)

And did I ever need that few days of hospitality! Teetering on the edge of burnout from too much hitchhiking and freight-hopping, coming down with a cold, and with the massive traumas I had recently experienced always threatening to bubble up to the surface, Catherine and her husband, by the grace and providence of God, gave me exactly what I needed at that moment: home-cooked meals of fried chicken, peas and mashed potatoes in a warm, snug house with no electricity or running water, yet with plenty of wood to burn in the stove and fireplace, a nearby well, the cozy light of the kerosene lamps, and the undefinable yet undeniable feeling of *family*, resulting in the miracle of total acceptance by total strangers. Catherine Strother, fishing for some cultural common ground with one of the hippies (myself) whom she knew expressed themselves mostly through music, shared with me her love for the songs of Elvis Presley. And since one of our few common experiences was 20th-century television, she told me how much she had loved the *Perry Mason* series, and allowed as how she wouldn't have minded if Raymond Burr had left his boots by her bedside on some cold night . . . for all I know, she might actually have saved my life.

My next stop after 100-Mile House, mostly recovered, was Prince George, where I slept for one night in a jolly hostel catering to hippies and another in a bleak, 50-cents-a-night shelter for the older, more traditional style of transients, otherwise known as tramps. Hard beds with thin mattresses, arranged dormitory-style on a bare concrete floor. From there I kept on and on, following my thumb, hitchhiking north through an increasingly trackless wilderness, headed for Prince Rupert. Alone, along the pure, cold, emerald-green Skeena River, singing and talking to myself, helping to hatch in the rookery of my imagination a globalist/New Age world where humanity would be united by a single electronic wavelength, tuned to the alpha frequency of the brain, reciting my mantra of *the Peace Frequency—One World—One World*. I was far out *way too far*, out on a shrinking limb, on a thread-thin tightrope across the astral Niagara, idiotically confident, inviting all the reckoning that was very soon to come.

When I finally reached Prince Rupert on the lip of the Pacific Ocean, just south of Alaska—a town with a Norwegian feel to it, set among the cold Canadian fjords—I fell in as usual with the local hippies. This time, however, while we were sitting at a cafe table, and just after I'd bought a hit of what purported to be MDA (an ancestor of today's Ecstasy, MDMA), which was then making its debut among the hippies as "the love drug," a new face and form appeared: those of an officer of the Royal Canadian Mounted Police—the Mounties. And, with a satisfied smile, he singled *me* out, asking me to accompany him to his car, then seating me next to him in the front seat. "It was a long chase," he told me, "but your case is now closed; the Mounties always get their man." Obviously he had mistaken me for somebody else—but how could I convince him of it? "Can I see a photograph of the man you've been after?" I asked, very politely. He obliged, showing me a picture of my near-identical twin, pretty much the same face, the same reddish beard—except that his eyes were listed (and appeared) as "blue." "Not me," I told him. "See? My eyes are green." Examining my face again, he confirmed this fact, and his own face fell. *Defeated.* He had been *so close* . . .

So he let me go. *He let me go even though I had no identification, was in the country illegally, and was holding a hit of an illegal drug!* (Let those who are open to such possibilities take this as proof of the existence of guardian angels.)

That night I bought a room in a cheap hotel, swallowed the tablet I'd bought, and discovered that, far from being the famous MDA that reputedly had the power to open even the hardest of hearts, it was probably something more like a speed-ball, a mix of amphetamines and barbiturates—a lowlife drug providing only a low-class high. Nonetheless the experience it provided me with ended up to be a significant turning-point in my life, because—while gazing at my image in the mirror—the image became the "real me," and the body gazing at it nothing but an empty frame, a human ghost. I was encountering what Jung called the "light shadow," all the responsibility, maturity and self-respect that had until then been split off from me, exiled and imprisoned in the Unconscious. *And it gave me a good talking-to*, impressing on me that it was time for me to get my act together, to grow up, to stop scattering myself to the four winds—in a phrase, to come back into the human form.

It was after this experience, and particularly after my razor-thin near-miss with the Canadian Mounty, that I saw that my "charmed life," my present available store of good karma, was about to run out—and that it was time to go back to California. So I booked passage south on a ferry that sailed the Inland Passage, past island after island, through narrow straits flanked on both sides by steep cliffs, thick with gigantic first-growth Douglas fir all the way to the waterlines, 465 miles as the crow swims, till we docked at Vancouver again. And after I'd found shelter there one last time, I got a letter through general delivery from my parents in San Rafael, complete with a newspaper clipping informing me that Lew Welch had disappeared from Gary Snyder's settlement of Kitkitdizze in the Sierra foothills, though rumor had it that he'd been seen again later. No one, however, had apparently been able to locate him with any degree of certainty. When something comes to an end (as I've already observed) it ends at all points at once; call this "synchronicity" or "destiny" or the work of Atropos with her scissors, no matter: that's just the way things are. And it's also the way things are when something really begins: its beginning can't be traced back to a single cause along the highway of linear time. It's a twinkle in the eye of every mother, though it remains mercurial and elusive until we learn how to "make it out," until the day when the Ceremony of Naming nails it down in mortal space and time.

o o o o o

These often sad and uncanny experiences, these states of dissipation and self-betrayal, did not simply foreshadow the disasters that were to come, which make up the subject of the next chapter—they actually required them. Be that as it may, I ask God now to bless everyone in this book whose names I have mentioned, or whose nameless faces or actions I have in any way recounted, whether He sent them to save me, or to chastise me, or simply to inform me, thereby allowing me to remember them in the pages of this book. "May all beings be well; may all beings be happy." I offer these memories to you, Lord, with no strings attached. You sent them to me originally, so now—if the time is right and if You are willing—please take them back.

CHAPTER SEVEN

The Planet of the Underworld: Life in Death

So when it came time for me to return to the States, Bill and Jennifer Trumbly came to collect me: more undeserved, and largely unappreciated, charity. (How did that ever happen? I don't remember ever contacting them to ask for the ride. Did my parents set it up?) The night before we left, when I was sitting with Bill in one of those big, bare Canadian beer-halls, our half-shot table-mate, possibly miffed that we hadn't introduced ourselves ("snooty Americans"), poured a mug of beer over my head. I accepted it stoically. No fight ensued. (Was it equally snooty of me not to accept his obvious offer of a friendly Donnybrook to liven up the evening?)

On the way south, Bill and Jenny came down with dysentery. Our first stop, since I was still half-way on the commune-route, was Tolstoy Farm near Davenport, Washington, just west of Spokane — a well-run organic farming collective of long standing, still operating as of this writing, inaugurated in 1963 and named after the Tolstoy Farm that Mahatma Gandhi founded in South Africa. All I remember from that stop is how I slept on a concrete floor in my sleeping-bag, listening to Bill and Jenny, on the same floor, retching all night.

In Oregon we stopped at the same Family of the Mystic Arts commune that Judy Milani and I had visited a few years before. During that visit the Family had given the impression (up to a point) of being tall, handsome, spiritually elevated dwellers in a primordial Eden. This time, however, they looked more to me like a pack of wrangling peasants with guttural voices and constricted brows, grabbing for whatever food they could get from the common trough — though maybe it was only my own state of mind that I was seeing. Nonetheless a definite downgrade seemed to have taken place, one that must've successfully been ironed out at some later point since the Alpha Farm that the Mystic Arts commune morphed into is apparently still in operation.

Our last stop before Marin County was Gary Snyder's Kitkitdizze settlement in the Sierra foothills near Nevada City. When I walked into the precincts and met Gary, he informed me that, yes, Lew Welch had disappeared one day, but the fact was that he never had been seen again; all the rumors of his re-appearance had proved false. I don't remember whether he told me on that occasion about Lew's suicide note; all I know is that I realized quite clearly at that moment that I would never see him again.

> Darkness, darkness
> Be my pillow...
>
> —*as sung by Janice Joplin*
>
> Down, down, down
> The dark lad-der...
> —*as sung by Buffy Sainte-Marie*

o   o   o   o   o

When I finally got back to my childhood home in San Rafael, I found that my father was dying of cancer—pancreatic cancer, essentially incurable in those days and still one of the worst forms. Did we know it at that time? Pretty much. He had lost a lot of weight, his complexion, death-gray. He came home from the hospital once with half his blood missing. We were working at a feverish rate to fix up the house and rebuild the pier, as if repairing our physical environment could somehow heal his body. I was also getting ready to call up my own entirely imaginary "shamanic healing power" to save him—until, after exploratory surgery, the worst was confirmed. At his bedside at Marin General Hospital, he told me, "I feel like quitting"—and then: "You've been a good son." No matter how great his own fear and anguish might have been at that moment, *he knew he had to bless me*—he didn't forget it.

(And then, one night, my mother—coming into my bedroom—the one that had been my grandfather's—and crying my name.)

That death, though clean and fairly quick, also had its sinister elements, as deaths often do—the occasion of a person's passing being well-known to bring out both the best and the worst in people. One of these mortal shadows was the intervention of Jeanette Pomeroy, a *femme fatale* of the kind immortalized in a song I've already mentioned above, "Not So Sweet Martha Lorraine" by Country Joe and the Fish. Ms. Pomeroy was one of those good-looking, menopausal, proto-New Age priestesses of Marin County, the Marin version of the "Mrs Robinson" character from *The Graduate* starring Dustin Hoffman. She had almost crowded my mother out of her rightful place by my father's deathbed, so hot was she to take possession of his soul by inhaling his final breath. She had returned not long before from Latin America where she had apparently picked up the Jaguar as her totem animal; had she also made contact with the descendants of those sinister Aztec Jaguar-priests who worshipped the god Tezcatlipoca, "Dark Smoking Mirror"? And upon her return she had changed her name to "Maya." When she told me this—we were sitting together at a café table—I raised my cup of coffee and toasted her with, "Here's to seeing through you." My mother remembers her sprinting at full speed down a long aisle at the Marin

Civic Center with a wide, athletic, straight-legged stride like the god Mercury in the FTD Florists' logo; an uncanny lady any way you look at her. Then later, after my father's death, when I was at her house to collect his beautiful old antique microscope and a bundle of human bones she had borrowed from us (the same ones whose powder I had consumed in that bare little room in Vancouver, one of which I had later presented to the 16th Gyalwa Karmapa), she had her two young daughters — one of them adopted I believe — strip to the waist at the table at the other end of the room, possibly in order to hook me into some kind of dark ritual, Ms. Pomeroy herself being maybe a little too old to perform that introductory function, except by proxy... I simply ignored them and got away with what I'd come for, still alive and breathing. This was definitely not the old, secure, civilized upper-middle-class Marin County that my mother thought she still lived in; clearly the hippie counterculture had done its work...

After my father died, I had a dream about him. I was in what looked like a waiting-room in a doctor's office, typical chairs, typical clientele — except for a woman who had a large Afghan hound on a leash, not a common sight for such a place. Then I was in another more non-descript space where I saw my father, lying on a pallet on the floor. "*Are you here already?*" he said. "Not really," I answered; "actually I'm just dreaming." Then I took him into my arms, tried to embrace him, but as I did he turned into a moldering corpse — so I let him go. "You're dead you know" I told him. "Oh yeah? Good-bye then" he quickly replied, and hurried off. Here is where I learned that the *deadness* of death has everything to do with holding on; trying to stop the fundamental flow of change is rebellion against life itself, because change *is* life — and death is the proof of it. This doesn't mean that we don't have to swim upstream against, and sometimes militantly oppose, the tide of spiritual degeneration of the End Times, just that the deeper, more basic flow we need to connect with is always moving in the opposite direction, back toward the Source it's always springing from and simultaneously returning to — though the flow of degeneration too is a lawful aspect of the Will of God, the aspect called *Justice*. We are placed in the way of that flow precisely so we *can* fight against it, thereby becoming the active ministers of Justice rather than the passive victims of it.

(I also remember the story my mother told of the death of her own mother, the grandmother I never knew. When she was dying and had lost consciousness, her family began calling to her: "*Are you still there? Can you hear us?*" In response she briefly came back to conscious awareness, only to fiercely inform them: "*You must never call someone back!*" Then she died.)

○ ○ ○ ○ ○

The next period of my life is nearly a blank. My father was dead, my mother and I occupied our house without him (for how long? Several months? As long as a year?), going about our lives in stunned silence.

Nonetheless I do have a few scattered memories from that time. Some time after my return from Canada, when my spiritual practice was entirely "experimental" and self-directed, I decided to do a spiritual retreat on Mt. Shasta in northern California, a mountain sacred to the original Native American inhabitants, and also considered to be a "power spot" by every occultist, Neo-pagan, and New Age group under the sun. I traveled there with two friends, drove up the mountain as far as the road went, and then hiked in, arriving at Horse Camp, set in a sea of fragrant "Shasta tea" (pennyroyal), and high enough on the mountain to give an unobstructed and stunning view. For three days I ate nothing but brown rice, and also observed a vow of silence.

On one of the nights I spent on the mountain, I had a significant dream — perhaps my first "lucid dream" (a dream in which the dreamer "wakes up" to the fact that he or she is dreaming) since early childhood. In the dream I was gleefully aware that, since I was "only" dreaming, I could now do anything I wanted — though the ironic look on the face of the woman I met seemed to say, "yes, but not without consequences." (Only after a certain amount of hard experience in later years did I begin to understand the meaning of that look.)

One evening, shortly after the sun disappeared behind a distant range of mountains, I sat meditating, facing west. In those days I used to meditate with my eyes open, and this evening, as I slipped into a light trance, I saw two points of light crossing the western sky, from right to left. The light they gave off was somehow more precise, more defined, more "real" than ordinary light — the first of my two UFO sightings. (Spectrographic analysis of the light emanating from certain UFOs has since revealed it to be richer in various blended wavelengths of visible radiation than light from any known natural or artificial source.) As soon as I noticed them, I became alert, attentive; I rose out of trance, came back to full waking consciousness — and the lights disappeared. Then I relaxed, centered my energy, sank back into a meditative state — and there they were again. I realized through this experience that UFOs habitually exist on a subtler plane of existence than the material — a plane that, however, is very close to the material and capable of impinging on it. The "craft" in question were not visible to my full waking consciousness, but neither were they mental images. They existed in a layer of reality that somehow came between psychic and the material — what some have called the "etheric plane." (In later years I used the "etheric sight" I had began to develop during my retreat on Mt. Shasta to investigate — in other words, to meddle with — the world of the Nature Spirits.)

It is interesting that my only UFO encounter up to that time coincided with the first lucid dream of my adult life. (I continued to experience lucid dreaming and/or astral projection for years, and finally became involved in attempts to deliberately produce it, basing them partly on *Lucid Dreaming* by Dr Stephen LeBerge of Stanford University, as well as the books of Carlos Castaneda and Jane Roberts. It was only after my initiation into a traditional Sufi order that my lucid dream experiences finally stopped.) Lucid dreaming involves a partial erasure of the border between waking consciousness and dream consciousness, between material and psychic reality; the self-reflexive awareness of the waking state—or something similar to it—now has as its object not the world reported by the five senses but the subtle psychic environment.

All this was very interesting to me at the time. It seemed like a harmless excursion into the wonders of the etheric and psychic worlds, magical worlds where the Imagination ruled, and where that Imagination, in all its subjectivity, could finally be "objectively" validated. And if these worlds, at least to begin with, were "magical" to me more in the Walt Disney than the Aleister Crowley sense of the word, I was to discover in later years that the heavy, humorless and sinister aspects of these subtle planes could not ultimately be avoided. It was on that mountain retreat that I took the first step on the "UFO research" track that was to result in all that I wrote on the subject in *The System of Antichrist: Truth and Falsehood in Postmodernism and the New Age* (2001), in *Cracks in the Great Wall: The UFO Phenomenon and Traditional Metaphysics* (2005), and in my second book on UFOs, *The Alien Disclosure Deception: The Metaphysics of Social Engineering* (2021).

Out of that obscure and hazy period between Canada and Jenny Donne, and the memories of it I've been able to stitch together, one other stands out—the memory of myself performing intensive yogic meditation, essentially based on kundalini-yoga, or rather on the inner psychophysical world that kundalini-yoga had opened up, plus certain Tibetan elements that I'd found in the books of W. Y. Evans-Wentz, while living at my childhood home in the apartment that had belonged to my grandfather, after my father's death. That practice was so intense that it actually raised a permanent "Buddha-bump" about half an inch high on the crown of my skull. When the Tibetans complete this practice, the Aperture of Brahma opens, which means that the fontanelles of your skull spread apart again like they were when you were an infant. After that the yogi walks around with a spear of grass stuck into the hole in his head as a badge of his proficiency. You might say that at this point I needed that kind of totally unguided *kundalini-* or *raja-yoga* (another general name for intensive psycho-physical practices) like I needed a hole in the head; nonetheless, it could be that this yoga made me more receptive to the "gift-waves" of the 16th Gwalya

Karmapa when I attended his Black Crown Ceremony a few years later at Fort Mason in San Francisco, as I have already recounted in *Chapter Four*, as well as opening me, in later years, to a more-or-less permanent intuition of the Angelic Hierarchy.

This development was accompanied by a dream:

> I find myself speeding down freeways of a thousand lanes, I am shooting all my friends with lasers. Then "the Guru" appears before me, shaved head, generally Buddhist appearance; all the chaos of the lasers and the freeways is now inside my mind. "You're not going to ask *all* those questions, are you?" he says. Then he simply looks *through* me, as if I were an open window—and when he does, all the chaos of my mind, which is also the chaos of "me," simply dissolves.

Then, after an indefinite period in the Limbo of shock and grief after the death of my father, the other shoe—of that time's predestined disasters—dropped. One night I dreamt of something like a demon, which I foolishly took to be one of Carlos Castaneda's "allies," a word generally synonymous with "familiar spirit." In the dream I grabbed hold of him, intending (in Don Juan/Castaneda fashion) to "tap him for personal power." "And then I jumped *into boiling oil!*" he blurted out, which I simply took as his way of trying to scare me so I would release him. The next morning, however, the house caught fire due a leak in our oil furnace, and was damaged badly enough to become uninhabitable. I had seen clots of black soot rising from the furnace chimney the night before but had failed to read the signs, and turned up the furnace higher than usual since the night was cold. My mother and I might have burned to death, if it were not for the fact that the house, being made of redwood, was much more fire-resistant than one built of pine or fir would have been. I tried to put the fire out myself, desperately looking for a hose that I could attach to the spigot of the sink in the garage, even running to a neighbor's house, demanding a plastic garbage container that I could fill with water to douse the flames; somebody else called the fire department—but it was all too late. I ran back into the burning house, against my mother's screams, to retrieve my sheaf of poetry, but that's all I could salvage. The house itself was a total loss. Some neighbor gave me a shot of brandy and a sweater to wear since I was only half-dressed. And somehow I made it, that evening, to the Trumblys' house, where I announced: "My house just burned down," to which shocking revelation they replied with stunned silence. Nonetheless, after the usual booze and grass (and they must've fed me too), they let me sleep on the basement floor. And while lying there a vortex opened up, just to the left of me on that same floor—the vortex of Death. I'm convinced that if I'd accepted its invitation and chosen to enter it, I would have died that night. My mother stayed the night, as we both did for a week or so afterwards, at the Pringle home in San Anselmo.

Friends — for all their limitations as perceived according to our fastidious narcissism — are sometimes life itself.

But what about that demon who had apparently burned my house down? Had my magick-dabbling connected me with forces much darker than I'd ever suspected? I certainly wouldn't deny it... and yet there's more to events like this than simply the triumph of evil powers: because, like the Catholics say, God grants these forces a certain amount of free rein for His own purposes, or like the Muslims say, nothing happens that is not Allah's Will. I remember what I once heard a Black radio preacher say while I was driving my car in San Rafael: "One thing the Devil hates to admit is that he is working for God and no one else." In hindsight I can see that if we had remained any longer in that hellish limbo of a house whose living spirit had departed, both I and my mother might have been destroyed. A few years later, after Jenny and I had moved into what had been my grandmother's house in the same neighborhood, the residual darkness of my childhood home, which we'd sold for a paltry sum to a new owner as a "fixer-upper" though it might have gone for two million if it was still intact, actually resulted in a murder: a husband had tried to stop an angry wife from fleeing their marriage in a car, and she ran him down.

> You may be high, you may be low
> You may be rich, and you may be poor
> But when the Lord
> Gets ready,
> You gotta move.
>
> *"You Gotta Move," as sung by*
> *Mississippi Fred McDowell*

And not only did our house burn; the vast majority of my father's beautiful paintings burned along with it — exactly as if he'd decided to take them with him, to hang on the walls of his new home in the other world. Here's the poem I wrote about that time and experience:

The Death of My Home

My father did not know
how to mourn:
and so an old sorrow rose
unexpectedly in him one day
and killed him
in the flower of his age...

So I went back with my mother
to my old burned house
where the trees were dying
and returning new in a human shape —

> The wall burned out and opened to air,
> the sky and the cry of the gulls and the sea-sounds
> threaded through what was once ribbed secure
> in the old days, like weeds through a fragrant carcass,
>   changing its purpose in death —
>
> Twenty years in a monastery, senses refined by light work,
>   mind occupied with a symmetrical dogma,
>   angelic inhuman quarter of the heart fed with cut glass
>   & organ chant
>   all that the soul might be left free to remember the
>   branch outside the window
> heavy with blossoms, and the patio of the trellised vines
> as they are forever at the first blessing,
>   reached for by a drowning hand.

And soon after our house burned, when I was staying in an apartment above a garage that had been donated for a short time by another of my mother's friends, I almost died a second time due to a gas leak. If I'd been a smoker I might have blown myself to smithereens; as it was, when my mother phoned me one morning, awakening me from my half-asphyxiated sleep, I answered her call with the words: "Hello... Death..."

This, however, was the end of the bonfire of my karmic vanities for that phase of things. Soon afterwards my mother found a good apartment right on the creek in the middle of San Anselmo, and I moved in with her to begin the next chapter of my life. And even though I can date my true alcoholism, not just my intermittent heavy drinking, from the time of the fire, nonetheless the deck had been swept clean of past attachments, making room for the arrival of Jenny Donne.

HEALERS

But before Jenny came, and since by that time I was traumatized and damaged on many levels, I began to patronize the vast spectrum of healers available to me in California at that time. To deal with the after-effects of my automobile accident in British Columbia I tried polarity massage, which was helpful, and began my lifetime relationship with chiropractic, which was even more helpful. I became involved with various kinds of "energy-work," including Reiki and something called Shen Therapy, each one of which (and I will include acupuncture at this point) seemed to put me in touch with a totally different layer of the highly-complex subtle energy-field of the human body. I even had an Edgar Cayce-like dream that suggested an herbal treatment, though I noticed no clear effect. In addition I began to patronize various psychic healers who practiced the ancient shamanic technique of "etheric surgery," the work of removing negative coagulations from one's subtle "etheric" energy-body so as to affect both the astral — the psychic level per se — and the physical. Their help was real, but limited.

One of these was the Rev. Plume, a hurried little Cockney who, as he was working on me, psychically plucked various items from my consciousness, such as my birth in the month of December, and recited them back to me, presumably to increase my faith in his powers. Even more interesting was the healing method of Betty Bethards of the Inner Light Foundation, a true Marin County spiritual luminary, renowned as a psychic before that word could be used to describe half the people you knew. (Yogi Bhajan had apparently told her, "You're not a psychic, you're a mystic.") She taught a form of meditation that incorporated the circulation of energy through the body to the rhythm of the breath, up the back while inhaling, down the front while exhaling, which was similar to the Greater Circulation in Taoist yoga as detailed in *The Secret of the Golden Flower*, as well as the Kriya-yoga of the followers of Paramhansa Yogananda; it also had some affinity with the technique of Rebirthing that I touched in with a few years later. I met her once for a psychic reading—I was around 30 at the time—at which time she told me that "you won't be known as a writer until you're 60 years old," which turned out to be exactly the truth. But the most interesting aspect of her ministry was her healing technique. The client (me) would lie on his back in a reclining chair while the healing team surrounding him would work to lift his etheric energy-body out of his physical body, clear it of various "hot-spots," and then press it back down into the physical. Lying in that chair I felt that it was vigorously rocking back and forth—but when I opened my eyes I saw that it wasn't moving at all. This treatment had a distinct lightening effect on my psycho-physical system—though I was never sure whether the etheric/physical reintegration had been entirely completed by the time the treatment was over; I often felt quite "spacey" for some time afterwards.

Another interesting experience in healing involved a Marin County psychic healer whose name I don't recall, a woman whose conceptual framework seemed limited to Freemasonry and Theosophy. She recounted a number of my supposed past lives, which included (predictably) an Egyptian prince who was barred from becoming Pharaoh because he was a hunchback. She also put me in (imaginative) touch with several of my spirit guides, one whose name was "Tili" and another female guide whose name began with "Theo," though the healer couldn't hear the rest of it. This "Theo" became, in my imaginative life, Theodosia, a Gnostic or Neo-Platonic philosopher of late antiquity, reminiscent of Hypatia of Alexandria, who functioned for me as the presiding Muse of the Blakean/Gnostic phase of my relationship to the Christian tradition—a generally individualistic and pre-Traditionalist period of my life—which was highly influential in the composition of my epic poem *The Wars of Love*. I saw her once in a vision of a "lifetime" in which I was the young son of a fisherman on one of the Greek Islands, waking up before dawn from my bed that consisted of a pile of fish-net laid out to dry on a stone floor, possibly a quay with some kind of shelter built on it, preparing myself for the coming day's labor. In the same vision I saw Theodosia, a beautiful woman with a regal bearing and a prominent aristocratic nose, apparently being accosted by a gang of uneducated Christians who were attacking her as a pagan, much like the Christian mob that ultimately murdered Hypatia for the same reason. (On the other hand, when I later saw a portrait of the famous Byzantine actress and courtesan Theodora, who later became the empress-wife of the Emperor Justinian, I beheld the very image of Theodosia as I had known her. If the Taj Mahal in Agra is the architectural image of Mumtaz Mahal, beloved wife of the Moghul Emperor Shah Jahan, the architectural image of the Empress Theodora is the Hagia Sophia in Constantinople.) The healer ended our session by reciting to me an *ex tempore* poem that I could use to summon spiritual guidance; it included the lines "O soul of wisdom and light/ Seek thou the Eye of the all-seeing world..." — an invocation that I never used, considering its dubious origin and its obvious connection to the All-Seeing Eye of the Freemasons. And were those past lifetimes actually "real"? Since I, following René Guénon, do not accept the literal reality of past lifetimes, but rather tend to explain the apparently quite striking evidence for them in terms of metempsychosis or psychic inheritance rather than reincarnation, I look at this sort of visionary data either as a symbolic dramatization of present psychic conditions or as a picture of the particular spiritual issues I was sent into this life to work out, or both. The hunchbacked Egyptian prince was most likely a reflection of my *vishuddha-chakra* blockage, exacerbated by the injuries I received due to the attack of the bully in high school and my automobile accident in British Columbia, and Theodosia an expression of my need to investigate the Gnostic "Shadow" of Christianity before being willing and able to understand it as an integral Tradition — a need that was undoubtedly in response to the destruction of the Traditional Catholic Church by Vatican II and the traumatic effect of that global tragedy on my spiritual life.

But undoubtedly the most radical and mind-blowing form of healing I availed myself of in those years was that of the Philippine Psychic Surgeons.

THE PSYCHIC SURGEONS

In the approximately two years between the time I first met Jenny at Jack Gilbert's poetry class and when we started a serious relationship, two shockingly transformative events happened in my life. The first was the destruction of my childhood home by fire, and the second — equally shocking but on an entirely different level — was my trip to the western Pacific to experience the powers of the famous Psychic Surgeons. The official evaluation of the Surgeons simply places them in the category of medical frauds, though a National Institutes of Health study did go so far as to admit that "It was found that psychic surgery did influence illness. Whether it affects the underlying disease remains uncertain" [https://pubmed.ncbi.nlm.nih.gov/1566128/]. I am confident that the psychic surgery world, like the world of mediumship to which it is closely related, is filled with fraud, but I am equally convinced that the Surgeons who worked on me were the real thing.

A short time before I learned of the Psychic Surgeons, I had a dream that seemingly predicted our meeting. I dreamt that I heard the beating of a shaman's drum—*poom-poom-poom-poom-poom-poom-poom-poom-poom*—after which a figure in the shape of my father appeared (though I knew it wasn't him), who said to me: "You're beginning to develop some shaman-power yourself now—*what are you going to do with it?*" Then I looked beyond him to the Marin Islands that were visible from my childhood home—though instead of being covered with buckeye and eucalyptus trees as they were in real life, they were thick with poison hemlock.

So, not long after, I flew to the Philippines as a psychic tourist looking for spiritual/physical healing. In Manila I became separated from my tour group, more-or-less deliberately, but finally found my way to the hotel where our first encounter with the Surgeons was to take place. A typhoon was making a pass just east of us over the ocean, with clouds of the most brilliant magenta I had ever seen.

Manila itself was under martial law courtesy of President Ferdinand Marcos, which explained the soldiers in the streets carrying ancient bayonetted rifles that looked to be of WWI vintage. Maybe every sixth person in the crowds appeared to be ill or malnourished, yet the feeling in the air—compared to affluent Marin County, California—was surprisingly laid back, even though large areas of the city were made up of nothing but rude shacks built of corrugated sheet metal, the streets between them little more than open sewers. As an example of the local wit—or, more likely, an expatriate wit—I saw a bar with a large colorful sign that read "The Ugly American."

Back at the hotel (which was overrun with young prostitutes), our party was being prepared for the upcoming healing sessions through a series of lectures on spiritualism, mostly from the standpoint of the prominent French philosophical spiritualist, Allan Kardec. Most of the Psychic Surgeons identified as Christians—Christian Spiritualists, that is, though they claimed to work by the power of the Holy Spirit Himself. But a few retained their original pre-Christian identity, seeing that psychic surgery is actually an ancient shamanic technique, prevalent in Southeast Asia but also reported from other parts of the world. For example, early explorers of Tierra del Fuego at the southern tip of South America talked about similar powers exhibited by the Native American shamans, though they saw these healers (as most contemporary investigators do) merely as masters of hypnotic suggestion and slight-of-hand. During the introductory lectures it was explained that the Surgeons worked with spirit helpers, yet no excessive claims were made for the efficacy of their methods, which was said to be about the same as that of conventional medicine: one-third cured, one-third improved, and one-third unchanged. Nothing was said about the frequency of "iatrogenic" outcomes—injuries or illnesses produced by the physicians themselves—though word-of-mouth suggested that these were largely unknown among the patients of the Surgeons.

When the Surgeons actually worked on me, I saw and felt them reach their hands directly into my body, the flesh parting around their fingers like clay or water, after which they removed some sort of foreign tissue from the incision, which spontaneously closed as soon as their hands were withdrawn. Sometimes there was a slight sensation of pain and a few drops of blood, but no residual pain whatsoever. They worked on various parts of my body, including my right eye which they actually popped from its socket, which they then scraped clean of some noxious substance before returning the eye to its proper place; I know this because, while coming out of the semi-trance the operations seem to place you in, I looked up and saw the line of American psychic tourists I'd just been part of standing there with their mouths open; it was one of them who later told me what had happened. I felt absolutely no pain, either during or after the operation, and suffered no ill effects. However, though the discomfort I'd felt in that part of my body noticeably improved after the treatment, my sight did not improve. And my roommate, who had a club foot, reported that they had broken his foot open right before his eyes, then put it back together again. Nonetheless I never felt that these events were actual *miracles*, since a true miracle is not simply a paranormal event but a Divine act of instruction and revelation that operates on many levels at once; its visible material effect is always the outward sign of an inner spiritual transformation. The Surgeons operated on a lower level than that, as the masters of a kind of ancient psychophysical technology that certain sectors of the human race apparently relied on in the days before mechanical technology took its place. Wonderworking saints, on the other hand, do not see themselves as the agents of the miracles they perform. Humanity works through skill—with or without God's help and guidance—but only God performs miracles.

After processing these highly "non-ordinary" experiences, I came to the tentative conclusion—with little supporting evidence—that the material the Surgeons remove from the human body is not always originally present within that body in the same form; it may sometimes represent a "materialization" of the subtle etheric pattern of the disease in question so as to "ground it out," something like releasing a charge of static electricity by walking barefoot on wet grassy earth, though in the case of psychic surgery the "charge" in question is released in fully materialized form — temporarily at least, since the foreign matter that is produced has sometimes been reported to spontaneously dematerialize later on, like the "angel-hair" sometimes thrown off by UFOs. And I've come to the further conclusion that one of the drawbacks of etheric energy-work, whether or not areas of the physical body are actually dematerialized, is the danger of a kind of "psychic post-operative infection," where the etheric energy-field that has been made permeable by the surgery doesn't immediately solidify again, thus allowing more negative influences to creep in without being detected; this may result, in the words of Matthew 12:45, in your latter state being worse than your former one.

But I did meet some interesting individuals on that trip. There was a group of people in our party who spoke English with a Russian accent; somehow the impulse came to me to ask them: "Are you Doukhobors by any chance?" They answered in the affirmative. I knew about the Doukhobors, whose name means "spirit-wrestlers," from my stay in British Columbia. They are a sect of dissenters from Russian Orthodox Christianity, known for their nudism and other eccentric practices, maybe a bit like the group Rasputin was apparently connected with before he became a monk — true Russian peasant visionaries, who had had to migrate to B.C. to escape persecution. My other memorable encounter was with a girl (amazingly) from Marin County, terribly injured, who invited me to her room. She made a point of exposing to me the lower part of her body, her pelvis, withered and mutilated from a near-fatal automobile accident she'd had when her car went over a cliff on Mt. Tamalpais; she was apparently daring me to accept her even in her terrible condition, and thankfully I accepted that dare. She offered me some grass to smoke, but I didn't feel safe making myself that vulnerable in such a psychically alien environment.

A day or so later our group left Manila by bus and traveled to the mountain city of Baguio, the Surgeons' main stronghold, where the more affluent citizens of the capital would migrate during the summer months to avoid the heat. The Philippine countryside was beautiful, the women dressed in simple brightly-colored dresses and the men in colorful short-sleeved shirts, many of the houses on raised posts to protect them from the floods, the rice paddies tended by farmers driving *carabao*, water buffalo, with their wide, graceful, swept-back horns like crescent moons — still my favorite members of the bovine race. In Baguio we were worked on by more Surgeons, who were reported to be even more powerful than the ones in the lowlands. These included Josephina, clearly the most venerated and respected of all, who worked on my neck, on the after-effects of my auto accident in Canada, which she improved quite a bit in terms of reduced pain and stress. She also apparently removed some calcium deposits, according to the description of some of the onlookers. And at one point on the trip, whether going or returning from Baguio I don't remember, we stopped at a beach where I bought some beautiful seashells from a local vendor, cowries and others, and had a chance to briefly swim in the warm waters of the South China Sea. Back at the hotel some other Surgeons worked on us, including the well-known Orbito brothers, after which we boarded our plane and flew home to North America.

The sensation of being operated on by the Psychic Surgeons was like nothing else in my experience, though its aftereffects in some ways resembled those of Betty Bethards' etheric surgery. At that extremely low point in my life my faith was weak, weak enough to require signs and wonders to build it up — and so signs and wonders were mercifully provided. It was more than I deserved though probably much less than I should have asked for, seeing that my present 'Alawiwya Sufis teach that you should never ask the All-Merciful for less than the *Ma'rifa*, the Knowledge of Allah. But if you are still partly possessed by a materialistic worldview, maybe you need to see, at least once, that what we think of as normal, relatively stable, matter-of-fact *matter* can actually be altered and de-materialized by subtle forces operating from an unseen dimension. My main gift from the Psychic Surgeons was simply a full acceptance of this basic fact, which was later of real use to me when I began writing on the UFO phenomenon, particularly in my book *The Alien Disclosure Deception*. In that book, as well as in two earlier ones, I attribute to UFOs and their alien occupants the power of temporary materialization, which is one of the common talents associated with the race of beings known to Muslims as the Jinn. The "spirit helpers" who have allied themselves with the Psychic Surgeons appear to be of the class known as "the faithful believing Jinn," as opposed to the unfaithful Jinn, the *shayatin* — the demons.

A few years later, in California, I encountered the Surgeons again on several occasions, who freely operated in the Golden State until the Feds came down hard on them as medical frauds and shut down their operations. Among other things, they worked (quite successfully) on the aftereffects of a painful prostate infection that seemed to me to be the result of an encounter with, and purification from, profound sexual evil, based on a shocking revelation by my (now ex) friend, Randy Carson; you'll hear more about that encounter in *Chapter Eleven*. During one of these sessions I talked with another client, who told me the story of the time the Surgeons had removed some rock fragments that were imbedded his leg due to an explosion. He described how the rock had emerged not as a number of splinters but as a single stony mass, as if the fragments had all melded into one for easier extraction by the power operating through the spirit doctors — this being more evidence of the malleability of matter when accessed from the immediately-pre-material dimension of the etheric world. The etheric plane is situated directly between the corporeal dimension which we perceive through our five senses, and the astral dimension that most often appears to us as mental imagery, including dreams; it is essentially identical to the Kingdom of the Jinn. Visual thoughts are astral; visual perceptions of the outer world are corporeal; well-defined, apparently-really-out-there-in-space hallucinations are most likely etheric: three different densities of substance or levels of vibration. But though this sort of knowledge is interesting, and possibly useful on certain levels, it is a serious error to identify it as Spiritual in any way; it's best left to the technologists, the psychic healers and the magicians.

In any case, my first pass through the world of the Psychic Surgeons concluded with another dream, after I had returned to my mother's apartment in San Rafael. A female spirit-being named "Eagleaxis" came to me, lifted me out of my body and carried me straight up to another world. ("Eagle" symbolizes spiritual elevation; "axis" is the *Axis Mundi*.) We came to a darkened amphitheater with circular tiers of seats filled with objects that looked like students' desks; they were shaped vaguely like crosses—and there sat my father, hunched over in the gloom, drinking from a pint of whiskey. "Father!" I said, "I am here! Don't you recognize me? I am your son!" "*Ahhch*, who is my son?" he replied, bitterly and with little interest in my presence. And even though I still pursued my shamanic experiments for a while after that, this dream, spiritually speaking, was the end of them. The amphitheater was darkened; nothing more was being enacted or revealed there. If I really wanted to be a student, I needed to sit in one of those desks shaped like a cross so I could learn my lesson: that not personal power but self-sacrifice was the true Way. Not my will but Thine be done.

THE TAIL OF THE TIGER

Some time after returning from the Philippines, through my connections with the alternative spiritual scene and the poetry scene in the Bay Area, I began to get wind of the new guru on the block, a Tibetan Buddhist I've already mentioned by the name of Chögyam Trungpa; he was a *tulku* (a recognized incarnation, like the Dalai Lama) of the Kargüpta Lineage. He seemed to be more conversant with western ways than most lamas, and his books were both insightful and accessible. Not only that, but he had already drawn Allen Ginsberg and William Burroughs into his circle. In those days of the waning of the counterculture, many people were looking for a more traditional and established spiritual Path as a way of "cleaning up their act," consequently a number of the San Francisco poets followed Ginsberg—who was beginning to present himself as a convinced Buddhist—in Trungpa's direction. I was one of them, but though I investigated Trungpa's world, I never officially entered it.

It, however, was already beginning to enter me, specifically through the medium of dreams. The first of these was the one recounted above where the Guru appeared and asked me, "You're not going to ask *all* those questions, are you?"; the next in the same series was the following:

> I abruptly confront Richie Bell, someone I knew from the San Francisco poetry scene, who happened to be quite short; he is dressed in traditional Japanese armor and wields a wooden practice samurai sword. "*What is the principle man doing right now?*" he says. I take this as a test of my present state, since if I were to think of him as "the principle man" I would flinch, and he would cut me, whereas if I considered myself to be the principle man I would become overconfident, and he would cut me. Then I am sitting next to Chögyam Trungpa, directly to his right. After making some encouraging remarks, he hands me a metallic disk with the number "18" stamped on it, which I place in my mouth; this indicates that I am to be 18th in his teaching-lineage.

Trungpa himself was the 11th Trungpa Tulku, but I suppose if one included the transmission of Vajrayana Buddhism from Tilopa of the Nalanda University in India to Naropa to Marpa the Translator to the great yogi Milarepa, plus the lineage of the Gyalwa Karmapas, and did some fancy juggling, one might calculate that Trungpa was 17th in some line or other, which would make me, apparently his potential star pupil, number 18. The only problem with this notion is that I was in no way qualified to be number 18 in any teaching-lineage whatsoever, so where did this piece of spiritual flattery come from, and what was its purpose?

Be that as it may, not long after these dreams arrived and soon after my house burned, I drove to Colorado to be part of a meditation retreat at Trungpa's rural quasi-monastery in the foothills of the Rockies, The Tail of the Tiger. While there I scanned the selection of Buddhist girls, seeing if any of them matched the "Anima-image" I carried in my heart, which I describe below. One of them did, but I was warned by one of the men that "she's really screwed up," so I didn't press my advances. I was introduced, however, to another woman from Mill Valley in Marin County who ended up becoming my one-and-only (though rather short-lived) Buddhist girlfriend, a liaison that led to a significant encounter with a Buddhist "dharmic" astrologer, the one and only person to cast my natal horoscope. His system was the common western one, but his purpose was relatively unique: not to plot his client's *fate* but to clarify his or her *dharma*, defined as the unique form of life or "right livelihood" that would most directly serve the cause of that person's Enlightenment. He told me that I had a "locomotive temperament" — a crisis-motivated or *kshatriya* character that was best expressed in strenuous "campaigns" rather than steady, plodding efforts — and a *socio-political dharma*, the destiny of the activist, something that proved itself true in later years in terms of two major efforts: the

Sanctuary Movement (as a Christian) and the Covenants Initiative (as a Muslim), both of which you'll hear about later on.

Two other memories from the retreat are significant. I was sitting on the grass with some other participants in the meadow surrounding the meditation-tent during a momentary thunderstorm, when I shared with one man my fantasy that I would die through being struck by lightning. "There was a tiny bolt of lightning right over there, just as you said that" he said. As the *mantra* of the Trungpa world goes, *Om Ah Hum Vajra Guru Padma Siddhi Hum. Vajra* = lightningbolt.

The second memory was even more interesting. I was sitting with the group in the tent waiting for Trungpa (who was always late). On a little table next to his empty chair sat an open bottle of saké, Trungpa's favorite drink. I made some remark to one of the men about the danger of leaving a bottle of expensive saké unguarded. "Why don't you take a hit?" he asked—so I did. At the moment I swallowed the wine, I remembered the dream I'd had about Trungpa handing me the number "18." Was this what Richard Thompson of the Fairport Convention, in his song "Farewell, Farewell," meant by "drink(ing) the light to be"? Be that as it may, such light that has come to me was not destined to arrive from that direction; I was simply skirting the edge of one more planet, one more world.

THE COMING OF JENNY DONNE

But it was in the very center of that darkness, at the deepest point of it—Lew Welch and my father dead, still traumatized by my car accident, my childhood home burned—that Jenny Donne came into my life, to become the keynote and the cause and the essential fragrance of that life for the next half-century (at least). But first I had to be pounded dawn far enough to be able to see her, and finally meet her, on the "dark and bloody ground" she sprang from (this being an epithet for her home state of Kentucky), and from which she was already rising, in a slow, solid and unbroken line, by dark grace and naked will alone, toward the light. I came from the potential light and the half-born light and the false light, the light that could only become true, only finally become itself, after being baptized in darkness. She came from the real darkness that alone can play host to the true light—if only the pilgrim in question can *see* it, and not lose faith in it. As it says in the first chapter of the Gospel of John, the King James Version:

In Him was life, and the life was the light of men.
And the light shineth in darkness; and the darkness comprehended it not.

I asked Jenny's present *sedevacantist* Catholic priest, Father Michael Oswalt, whether the word for "comprehended" in this passage—in the original Greek—means "understood" or "surrounded, as in a siege, so as to conquer." His answer was: "probably both." You can only truly reach a *comprehensive* understanding of a thing if you can view it globally, from all sides at once, leaving the secret of it no avenue of escape. So I would say that the darkness of evil found no way to penetrate Jenny, while the Darkness of God, of the Majesty of God, became the crucible in which that Light, the Light of men, could be born.

In Eastern Kentucky, under the regime of her abusive parents, Jenny had been — to use Kierkegaard's terminology from *Sickness unto Death*, which is useful in so many ways — in "despair of necessity." Things *had* to be a certain way — a hellish way. And not only was there no way out of those truly demonic conditions, but the acceptance of them — conditions of endemic violence and profound spiritual blindness — was considered by her immediate family to be an indication of moral strength and uprightness of character. She was beaten regularly by her father, Fred Donne, from when she was a babe in arms until the age of 16, when she went to school with an injured eye and her blouse dappled with blood. This precipitated a friendly visit from the High Sheriff of Pike County, who cautioned Fred, a respected member of the community who was both a high school principal and, even higher than that, a *basketball coach* — being of that old, tall, white Kentucky stock that Abraham Lincoln came from, the men who ran the game before the Black players took over — that such exhibitions did not reflect well on his character, might ultimately jeopardize his social standing, and so should probably be discontinued. That's as far as it went — though such an event in our time would have resulted in an intervention from Child Protective Services and possibly state prison for the perpetrator. And beyond the physical violence, the psychic violence she had to endure was, if anything, worse. Everything she *was* was officially denied, and — if recognized — immediately punished. As she expressed the consequences of that oppression in an early poem: "I can't see myself now, and I can't find any pictures of myself." She was the classic scapegoat in a narcissistic family dynamic ruled by her mother, Lola, for whom her father Fred, in his violence, might simply have been acting as a pawn, a surrogate, since she was adept at turning her habitual anger at the injustices of her life into a cold, silent rage that apparently induced certain people within the range of it, if they were at all vulnerable to anger in its outward expression, to act it out for her — in other words, to assume the scapegoat role that might well have included both her daughter and her husband. Here's one of the poems Jenny wrote about those years:

Silence

Silence, you are beside me and I have to fight you, I who
    never go to the wars.
And the wars happen all the time.

> Silence, you are lying to me. You tell me lies every day. Even
> when I don't speak, you lie to me.
> Silence, I have to talk to you in a weak language. I've had to
> make my language vulnerable. I wanted a strong language
> more than anything and I needed strength. It must be
> that all the strength I've built up so slowly and carefully within
> myself
> doesn't matter to you. You've put agony into my creative energies
> and I can't help but believe that you want to destroy me.
> Silence, do you want to destroy me? You keep bringing me material
> I can't control.
> When I was sick last week I vomited on the floor
> and for a whole day I was too weak to clean it up. I believe
> you caused that.
> If I don't confront you then everything I say
> will be worth nothing in the world.
> To whatever it is in me that wants to destroy and kill.
> The silence is hate.
> Hate kills.
> Silence, do you remember how jealous I used to be of my sister.
> I wrote a story once about a girl who hated her sister
> very much, and when the sister died, that girl
> started to become like her sister.
> Silence, when my great uncle died you made him ask again and again
> for my sister,
> and never once ask for me.

That's how it was. So when Jenny escaped from Kentucky and moved to the San Francisco Bay Area of California in the 1970s, with nearly zero resources both economically and psychologically, to immerse herself in a social milieu that was almost exactly the opposite of the one that held sway in Kentucky, that heroic flight was a true liberation for her. Those were the days when it was still possible to run away and join the circus, or run away and join the hippies. The '60s were a relatively collective and extroverted time for the artistic types of the San Francisco Bay Area, while the '70s, partly in reaction to the excesses of the hippie counterculture, were more individual and introverted. '70s "individualism" was not the self-assertive kind that began to grow up in the 1980s; it was more sensitive, more intimate, though maybe a bit more depressive (as opposed to the spiritual/political mania of the 1960s and the economic mania of the 1980s), yet there was still room in it for people to breathe, explore their psyches and their relationships, and generally find themselves. On top of that—at least in the San Francisco poetry scene of those years—people tended to support each other in that quest, in the work of discovering, cultivating and expressing their own characteristic personal qualities, whatever those might be. A poem that accurately rendered a unique or idiosyncratic quality of one's own personality or sensibility, or that of someone else, was considered to be a "good" poem. And, interestingly enough, the central conceptual expression of that ethos was Jungian psychology, with its introspective orientation, its investigation of the "archetypes," its willingness to look at the "Shadow," its quest for "individuation." Even sectors of the Catholic Church had begun to adopt a generally Jungian perspective during those years. So "pop Jungianism" became a kind of intellectual *lingua franca* for the San Francisco poetry scene of the 1970s. The poets were reading Jung, Erich Neumann, Esther Harding, Helen Luke, Marie-Louise von Franz, Irene Claremont de Castillejo and (later) Clarissa Pinkola Estes, Jean Shinoda Bolen and Marian Woodman. And since two of the major tools of the Jungians were dream interpretation and "active imagination," the art of that time reflected these practices, which were expressed poetically in the "deep image school" of poetics; the poets had begun to see themselves as something like psychic aquariums filled with sharks, turtles and multi-colored tropical fish. Maybe this actually was narcissism of a kind, but it was much less standardized and competitive and self-sabotaging than the vicious narcissism of today, infinitely more supportive and accepting of *individual* (not collective) differences. And this was exactly the world that Jenny needed for that phase of her life. It was only decades later that the openness-to-possibility of California culture clearly began to degenerate into the other brand of despair recognized by Kierkegaard, the "despair of possibility," though the seeds of this degeneration were already doing their work in the 1970s. "Open-mindedness" and "acceptance of differences" ultimately became oppressive collective attitudes that ruthlessly punished any attempt to develop a mature and stable character and an inner moral compass. The regime of Neo-Liberalism and political correctness had begun to rear its ugly head, an oppressive Liberalism with zero *liberality*, the immediate ancestor of today's "woke" ideology, according to which the tolerance and encouragement of "other voices" that had characterized California in the '70s ultimately flipped over into its exact opposite, this being an inverted, anti-traditional and *anti-human* orthodoxy enforced by a vicious cultural and even legal inquisition. So the day finally came when we had to get out of California.

I came together with Jenny through the mediation of two of my friends, Frank Dietrich and Ken Bullock, who had gotten to know her at Jack Gilbert's poetry class; they suggested that I attend that class, intimating that there was a girl there who I might like to meet. Frank was a middle-class Marin County suburbanite living in Lucas Valley (the head of which valley was later purchased by George Lucas—no relation to the original namesake—to be turned into Skywalker Ranch), where he lived with his wife Barbara. He ran a liquor store in the City. Somewhere along the line he had met Lew Welch and later decided to attend his poetry class at the

U.C. Extension. He told us that Lew had awakened him from a lifetime of somnolence and conventionality by giving him — as Lew himself phrased it (in my remembered version) about the influence of one his own teachers — "an irrevocable intimation of sweetness and size," and had done so through the medium of Human Speech. Consequently Frank became an *amateur* poet, which every true poet must be and should always remain, no matter how professional he or she may become in later life. "Amateur" means "lover."

Ken Bullock was another friend of mine from the hip/artistic milieu of Marin County, though he want to Drake High, not Marin Catholic; I met him at the antiwar office of the "Vietnam Summer" movement in San Rafael in 1967. He had a contradictory and ironic sensibility that made a permanent contribution to my own. He was obsessed with the maddening realization — just as I have been obsessed ever since I knew him — that people often have little idea either of what they are literally saying or of what they actually mean, particularly when spouting "conventional wisdom," no matter how "hip" or "progressive" such so-called wisdom might be. If psychobabble and spiritbabble and politicobabble ever had a sworn enemy, it was Ken Bullock. He wore his hair long like Oscar Wilde and spoke in wittily-inverted paradoxes just like Wilde did. He possessed a negative intelligence and a destructive wit in the best senses of those terms. He could tear down anything, and whatever he tore down most often richly deserved it. (In terms of Yeats' system of character-types from his great channeled text *A Vision*, he could only have been a Phase Nineteen, "The Assertive Man.") He eventually became (what else?) a theater critic, since theater at its best is a way of waking up to, and from, the unconscious theatricality of "real life," thereby freeing ourselves from our mechanical tendency to memorize and mouth our lines without actually realizing what we are saying.

Jenny and I met a few more times after Jack Gilbert's poetry class, but then she faded away for around a year, finally ditching me — after an attack of self-sabotaging shyness — at a proto-New Age exposition or trade-show inspired by the arrival of the Comet Kohoutek in 1973, an event that was ancestor to the Whole Life Expo that used to take place in the U.S. (headquarters in San Rafael at one point) and is now situated in Toronto. That year, the year of her disappearance, was when my childhood home burned, after which she began to "tentatively" call me at my mother's apartment in San Anselmo where I was then living; it was through those phone calls that we really met. Big things, things destined to last, often have to start small; as the traditional farmers say, "plant at the dark of the Moon."

Everything indicates that Jenny and I had been searching for each other in the subtle dimension for some time before we encountered each other in the flesh, lending credence to the theory that certain important earthly relationships are planned and plotted before birth, in the proto-terrestrial world. As a child she had told her mother: "When I grow up I'm going to move to California and marry a poet." Likewise, in the time leading up to our meeting, before I knew her name, I was doing my best to triangulate her location, through dreams and active imagination, by pursuing an "Anima-image" with dark hair and green eyes, like Dante's Beatrice. Jenny's hair, though it had auburn highlights, was dark enough, and her eyes—now more-or-less hazel, were greener when I first met her—something that indicated, to me at least, that she was more liminal, more *fey* at that time than she was later, since she had needed to make a direct connection with the Powers out of sheer desperation, simply to survive. When I first met her at Jack Gilbert's class I remarked, "obviously you're a witch," which was a stupid yet often-effective come-on to women in that place and time—though Jenny, as it later turned out, was properly afraid of my own magical liminality, this being one of the things that helped me to eventually moderate it. Still, the hopeless oppression she had faced earlier in life might actually have driven her to some extremity like witchcraft if she hadn't renounced it; she once told me once that she'd given up Tarot cards because she was afraid she might start doing magic with them. She even received a love-letter once from a warlock in Australia who had somehow seen some of her poems and thought he had found a kindred spirit. Carlos Castaneda, in his later books, maintained that, while your average everyday witch has an orange aura, the most powerful witches have green ones; likewise the poet Kathleen Fraser, in her poem "How I Understood You in Another Way" from her book *What I Want*, wrote of Jenny:

> There was a definite change of color in the room.
> Among us, green made itself a presence,
> a presence, as if it could have been the season,
> but I think it was Jenny as an instrument
> whose tenuous place in
> that space between the couch and the ceiling
>   spoke for how
> each of us breaks into pieces yet continues to flow.

The San Francisco Bay Area in the 1970s was a borderless sexual playground, from which Jenny, by her abrupt intervention, liberated me definitively. It was as if we who made up the remnant of the counterculture were collectively dedicated to burning up, in one huge bonfire of human potential, the accumulated erotic assets of the ages. Once sexuality is separated from reproduction and considered to be a purely "recreational" activity, its real nature has been lost sight of—and as one of the social critics of the time observed, as soon as the entire quest for human happiness and spiritual fulfillment has been loaded on to sex, sex has been given a burden too great for it to bear—an intuition that has proved itself all too true over the succeeding years. But while my fantasy-self, which consulted only the false infinity of its own fantastic desires, claimed it wanted to drown in the sea of women, something else in me always kept my head above water.

In '70s San Francisco the sex scene and the poetry scene partially overlapped. You would go to poetry readings where some of the poets would be strippers or public "sex workers" from the local clubs. It was important for a lot of those girls to be "artists" and "intellectuals" as well as erotic exhibitionists to prove that they were "well-rounded" (hoping you will forgive the pun). One of these, "Marlene," who in a poem by a colleague of hers was celebrated as "the one who does the Naked Dance of Love," did her best to seduce me, but I was a tough nut to crack. I didn't put up much conscious moral resistance in situations like that, nor did I shrink into shyness and social anxiety either; I just suddenly became too stupid or naïve, or too distracted by this or that intellectual train of associations, to (apparently) catch the enticing aroma of the dish that had just been set before me. My mind was elsewhere, not due to any lack of desire but in response to some silent inner phone call that interrupted what you'd think anybody would have seen as the main chance. After our one evening together petered out, Marlene produced some verses about our encounter, of which I remember only one line: "Later on, you weaken into feeling..." So she actually did get something out of me on that occasion: a poem. And she wasn't the only San Francisco girl in those days who tried the erotic/poetic method for bridging the gulf between art and life. Jenny had a good friend, Nellie, who produced a whole cycle of verses about her various brief affairs; Frank Dietrich told us that he had once resisted her advances because he didn't want to end up in (or as) one of her poems. Since it was the age of *experience*, we sometimes treated each other not as persons but simply as experiences we were having; as Jimi Hendrix put it: "Are you really experienced? Have you ever *been*... experienced?" How strange it was nonetheless that Jenny, who was so unlike most of the art-people and the sex-people of 1970s San Francisco, was still accepted in that world as she never had been in Kentucky — probably because people of that time and place were still really interested in each other, fascinated by each other's unique individualities, just as they were with their own. If it was the Age of Narcissism, at least it was a shared narcissism with a certain amount of generosity to it.

But where did those silent interrupting phone calls come from? My guardian angel? Or was it really that my solidest bedrock of desire was to exchange eternal vows with a soul mate, to fall in love rather than simply to fall in sex? (Lew Welch too complained that, instead of gorging himself at the table of sex like he thought he wanted to, he always fell in love.) Did I somehow understand that the more times you're willing to settle for second best, the less attainable that "best" becomes? In any case, at the moment when the road to the embodied perfection of unreality finally opened up, in the form of the official proposal of a menage-a-trois including another female from Judith, my Buddhist lady friend at the time—a woman I was hopelessly *pretending* (to myself) to be in love with—Jenny Donne appeared and broke the whole thing up, setting me on a different life-road entirely. Interestingly enough, my mother actually liked Judith, a practicing psychotherapist, in whom she undoubtedly saw a worthy successor who could fulfill her protecting and controlling function in my life after she was gone, but (as I mentioned above) as soon as Jenny made her first phone call to me at my mother's apartment, she was profoundly threatened. "Who *is* that girl? Is she *mentally retarded??*" she asked—as all people with an eastern Kentucky accent undoubtedly are, to California ears. My pious Catholic mother would undoubtedly have looked the other way if I had patronized prostitutes, but for me to turn my eyes to Jenny Donne was an unconscionable betrayal—understandably so, because after my father's death I was all she had, and because she must've sensed that I was suddenly becoming serious about life. I had already declined Judith's menage-a-trois offer based on an *I Ching* reading—having frivolously flipped a coin to determine my erotic destiny, like the almost total idiot I was at that time—but it was Jenny who cleared that whole situation out of my life for good. Following the traditional canons of the poetic art she wrote a scathing satire against her rival, but what actually chased those other women away, like shrieking frightened birds, was her implacable earnestness, the terrifying sincerity of her that made those women feel, in Yeats' words, how "Love is like the lion's tooth." And she made me feel it too. When Jenny came I realized, in the core of my being, that if I wimped-out now, at what was probably my last real chance for true love, if I failed to fix this lady's scarf to my lance and call on mounted Death to meet me on the field, I would have no real life. In this society we used to say "join the army, my boy, and go to war; it'll make a man out of you." I never went to Vietnam due to chronic health conditions that made me 4-F (the "unsuitable for service" category of the draft), but my true war began when I said "yes" to Jenny Donne. Why? Because she lived under interdict by the Rulers of the Darkness of This World; as soon as we married, I too was "the enemy" as far as This World was concerned. The Principalities and Powers immediately put a price on my head; from then on I was in the crosshairs of the Gnostic Archons. (If that sounds, at this point, a bit excessive, paranoid and melodramatic—just you wait.) Around that time I wrote some verses that later became part of my epic poem "The Wars of Love":

> I say all will be pressed into service.
> I say all will be required to fight.
> The passive, the coward, the innocent will be trampled down,
> Unless locked in single combat with Antichrist
> In mountain solitude and stillness.

Invoke, therefore, the war in your marrow;
Call on the fight you were born with, that enemy
Whose lie is cut and tooled, precisely,
To cover your single truth.
Pick targets. Each man is alone with all men
In this night of war. The conglomerate form of Death
Stands guard on each human door,
Solid to the bullet, and the chisel — like those cliffs in the Sinai
In which our skirmishers discovered, still living
The imprisoned forms of men!

And this is my poem to Jenny herself:

To My Wife

somnambulistic, I sweep the river —
— it carries the bones of the dead —
the Roman centurion — wounded by
magic — become a serpent — his plume
and armor roll pulled by the current
along the lucid bottom, the wave-striped
cobbles —

all that I was — broken. all that I
called myself — the shards of my name
taken by the river. and, nameless,
my bone and my pith — my will
is a great cable — it will not
let you fall. beneath my ribs the
day is breaking — while you mourn
the passing of my shadow, confused
in the traces of the night —

for a moment you will miss me
while the day is taking us — my wife.
my true one. the reason
I have not died. the foundation
of my work — for a little while you
will not know the strength of my love —
you will see me taken by reveries —
by battles whose field is hidden
from you — while I hide myself
in indifference, or foolishness —

— but know that I have come to you
out of a distance farther than I can
remember, and not die. because I am
skilled in lamentation. because I
did not recoil from the pain I

> owed to the wound I suffered to
> those whom once I loved.
> I have finished it. I have paid the price.
> I am free. Now bind me.

Jenny's life so far has been based on a simple dialectic. The *thesis* was Fate, Kentucky, the despair of necessity; the *antithesis* was Chaos, California, the despair of possibility; the *synthesis* was, and is, Destiny, Kentucky again but this time on her own terms, under the rule not of Fate but of Providence. Only a profoundly *simple* soul — not naïve, not lacking in intelligence or sensibility, just woven on the loom of a deep, contemplative sobriety — could achieve, in two radical, simple steps, a Destiny like that.

In any case, though for a relatively short time, Jenny was integrated into my wider circle of poetic friends. In partnership with John McBride and Ken Bullock, she and I helped co-create the notorious "Fake *Poetry Flash*," an audacious yet necessary act of purgatorial satire through which we skewered the Bay Area poetry scene, doing our best to drive the money-changers out of the Temple (though they snuck back in the next morning with their tails between their legs), nailing some of its biggest idols, puncturing a long row of its biggest balloons: Robert Bly, Michael McClure and plenty of others. Ken contributed the majority of the text, including all the best satire and the sharpest one-liners.

For the benefit of the uninitiated, I should say that the *Poetry Flash* proper was (and apparently still is) a calendar of Bay Area poetry readings and related events, plus reviews, which had become so nauseatingly precious and pretentious, both pseudo-intellectual and pseudo-artistic, by the time we declared war on it — 50 years ago — that a blow for freedom had to be struck. At that time the *Flash* took the form of a single once-folded 11-by-17 sheet. We simply took one of their monthly issues, complete with the official *Poetry Flash* logo and schedule in their recognizable typography, and inserted our own satirical reviews, thus guaranteeing that it would take some time before one of the brighter bulbs in the poetry scene (Jack Hirschman, as Jenny remembers) realized it was a spoof. We printed up our edition in an obscure print-shop in Santa Rosa, then mixed them in with the "real" *Flashes* in the newsstands and newspaper-dispensers in Berkeley and the City. The upshot was that the editor of the *Poetry Flash* called the District Attorney to report a major crime — though in later years the *Flash*, in a retrospective issue, acknowledged the FPF as "one of our more mysterious editions."

But for all of Ken Bullock's consorting with poets and thinking in poetic terms, he never became a serious writer while I knew him; like Doug Trumbly and John Doyle, he wrote for sport, not to find and express truth. When I was editing the poetry section of the *Because You Talk* anthology for the Other Voices Literary Society, he submitted a "manuscript" which consisted of a plastic garbage bag filled with scribbled bar napkins, which I laboriously sifted to separate out the nuggets. So why were my friends so literary and at the same time so averse to becoming writers? Though it may sound strange to contemporary ears, I suspect that one reason was that I alone of all my friends (John McBride possibly excepted) was actively seeking God—the ultimate Context, the final Point of Reference. Maybe if I'd grown up in New York it would've been different, but in California, for all its pseudo-spirituality, the quest for the Source was one of the few things that gave life sufficient form and meaning, above and beyond the enveloping chaos, to make possible the conception and writing of books.

But the saddest thing about my relationship with Ken was that not long after he had helped bring Jenny and me together, he rejected both of us. It was as if he'd discovered that he had lost his status as (in pop Jungian terms) her "intellectual animus," and didn't like that one bit. My initial perception was that he had turned on me for some dark reason known only to him; maybe he felt the same thing about me. I remember when, at the funeral of the father of one of our mutual friends, Mark Adler, who later became a successful classical composer working in the film industry, when we were each throwing a clod of earth into the grave after the coffin had been lowered, I said to Ken: "Let's bury the hatchet just like this"—but he would have none of it. So that was that.

The immediate surface excuse for Ken's attitude was that I had expressed no interest either in deifying Ezra Pound or in typing up manuscripts for McBride's Red Hill Press so as to achieve brief mention in the fore-matter of some of his books—which should not have been surprising since I was already a published City Lights Poet who didn't need to pick up the crumbs from somebody else's smaller table. Later on, however, I realized two things. The first was that Ken, and soon enough the Trumblys as well, had lost their "respect" for me because I had no desire or instinct to throw my weight around as a big literary honcho; they must've thought that, since I was apparently too foolish and naïve to take my rightful place in the poetic pecking-order, I deserved to be demoted to bottom chicken. And the second realization, which look a lot longer to come into focus, was that Jenny Donne represented a personal value-system so different from that of California's poetry scene, and its spiritual scene as well, that her union with me had unknowingly precipitated a silent revolution that could only express itself as a shocking rupture between me and almost everybody I knew—including my mother. Jenny was, simply, indigestible by hip California culture, just as she had been by Kentucky "middle class hillbilly" culture. Where what Saturday Night Live called "the Cyalifornians" were dedicated to the "sporting life" of singles-culture shallowness, plus an aesthetic orientation characterized by "deep surface" and little else—in Kierkegaard's phrase, to "the despair of possibility"—Jenny was silently and passionately serious, more serious than they could possibly imagine, serious enough to strike a deep, unconscious terror into the souls of the flakes and mountebanks of the Golden State. So they finally had to cast her out, and me along with her. Thanks to her I was ultimately rejected by just about everybody I knew: Ken Bullock, the Trumblys plus Doyle, even major elements of the San Francisco poetry scene. And as soon as my break with the Trumblys became apparent, Ken moved in to "take them away from me," to replace me in their affections and/or projections and help them elaborate and expand their negative image of me. And I remember a poetry reading I once did at the San Francisco Art Institute which included a poem about my upcoming marriage to Jenny. Afterwards a member of the audience came up to me with a concerned look on his face: "Hey man, don't do it man" he told me, "don't do it, your life will be over, it'll destroy you." I thanked him for his concern, but I already knew he was wrong, because—as it turned out—that's when my real life actually began. But it was Magda who gave me the most explicit lecture on the error of my ways: "Don't marry her, she is a *straight girl*, she will want *appliances*, she will demand a washing machine. Instead of getting married, just have kids; kids bring their own money with them" (i.e., via the Aid to Families with Dependent Children program). According to her I should aspire to become the no-account boyfriend of a Single Mom who was my "baby-mama." And my mother put it even more succinctly: "*You* can't get *married!*" So a straight Marin County widow of the professional class and the Bohemian widow of a Beat poet were of one mind when it came to Jenny Donne. Even Jack Gilbert's consort of the time, Michiko Nogami, told Jenny (though in a nice way), "We didn't think you would *ever* get married!" And last but not least, since according to the Trumbly mythology, I too was the last guy anyone would imagine getting married, when I actually did it, all the Trumbly girlfriends suddenly looked at their own guys in a different and highly unfavorable light, which certainly did not ingratiate me to the group at large. Even Caryn, the lowest chicken in the Order of the Trumblys, complained about "these Kentucky girls coming in here and marrying up all the men." And so—providentially—as soon as I married Jenny Donne, many ways parted for good. (When people ask me how I learned psychology I often say, "as a social survival skill"—seeing that the San Francisco Poetry Scene in the 1970s was a sort of advanced laboratory of social destruction. We were carrying on "pure research.")

So when Jenny came, I went to war. Looking back now I can see that I've always had formidable enemies arrayed against me in the Unseen World, enemies capable of reaching all the way into this visible world when they figured it was time to slap me down hard and then tempt me to despair. They were always there—*but I wasn't fighting them*: Then, when Jenny came, I had to fight them. I had to fight them because she kept *making them visible* to me. Over and over again these unexpected, weird attacks would get thrown at her from some arcane, unknown direction, materializing through people who had absolutely no idea what they were doing, or why. I would always try to counter them, but as soon as my blow landed (always verbal mind you, never physical), it would end up slapping the face of some poor clueless schnook who probably didn't deserve it, while the actual, invisible culprit had already skipped ahead to his next chosen host for his next two-second-long act of demonic possession, before moving on yet again to the victim after that, to prepare for the next attack—the next attack against *us*, not just against Jenny. We were next to each other in the same trench, sworn allies who were much more than doubly effective against our hidden enemies while working together—I the Sagittarian Archer providing the intent to fight (as inspired, however, only by Jenny), and she, the Libran, taking care of the intelligence wing of the operation, weighing and evaluating on her sensitive Scales the adversaries that stood against us. She was like the blindfolded statue of Justice whose blindness to This World was the unmistakable sign of her sight penetrating into the other one. And I was the blade in her hand, the active, militant response to what Justice brings to light: the Sword of execution. Excessive drama, you say, if not inflated melodrama? The very identification-with-the-archetypes that Jung warned us against? Possibly. Yet sometimes you have to see things that way, because that's how they inevitably present themselves, again and again. Drama is a serious imbalance that has to be paid for down the road, yet in extreme conditions it can be the very adrenalin of survival. The only way to avoid *hubris* in situations like that is not to try and de-potentiate the archetypal realities by reducing them to the mundane—no matter what you do or do not do they will manifest themselves, one way or another—but to submit to them as Names and Acts of God; to say (in the words of the *hadith*), "there is no might nor power but in Allah"; to vow (in the words of Job), "though He slay me I will trust in Him: but I will maintain mine own ways before Him." Instead of identifying with the archetypal powers, an identification that brings nothing but arrogance and harm, the only valid way of confronting them is to let them humble you. You will never have enough power to triumph in a contest against such forces; only God can provide the power necessary, and He always retains the exclusive right to use it for His own purposes. All that is required of you in relation to the Almighty is: first the petition, then the submission: "This, Lord, is my deepest wish—yet not my will but Thine be done."

But then, if all outcomes are in God's hands, *why the enemies?* There will always be things inimical to you in life, which are apparently there to teach you: 1) To stand up for yourself; 2) To renounce revenge; 3) To return good for evil, precisely in that order—because if you don't know how to stand up for yourself you will dream of revenge forever; if you don't renounce the revenge you have dreamed of, even when you are capable of enforcing it, you will never emerge from the hell of anger and hatred; and if you don't learn to return good for evil, then love will never come into your life. So at this point in my life's journey I would judge that those who are tempted to anger, hatred and revenge because they have been forced to endure injustice have inherited a specific portion of the spiritual darkness of the human race, either to purify and enlighten it or to be crushed under the weight of it. If I hadn't loved Jenny, though it seemed that the whole world hated her, I would have betrayed love and cast it out of my life, but to love only Jenny, Jenny as *against* the world, would be to make an idol out of her, after which all the love I had for her would have eventually turned bitter. Love is universal and relentless, it seeks to penetrate into every space that lacks it, and it will not renounce this quest until nothing is left *but* love—an outcome that, beyond the thin film of passing time, is not only entirely possible but necessary and inevitable: because love is not simply the ideal the Spirit strives for; it is the real nature of things. If it were not, how could the Bodhisattva ever dare to say: "Sentient beings are numberless, I vow to save them all"? So having enemies is apparently necessary to the work of overcoming hatred, anger and bitterness; it's the weight you need to lift to build enough strength to win the fight. How can you learn to love your enemies if you have no enemies?

And among those enemies was almost the entire evaluation of Jenny imposed on her by her parents, and the flaws in the evaluation that was imposed on me by mine. Jenny and I essentially grew up without real names—she because her given name was "Jenny," which was not really a contraction of anything and was therefore the name of nothing in particular (unless that of a female mule), and I because everybody called me by the nickname "Skipper" or "Skip," a name that even appears in my high school yearbook. A rural southern boy might tell you his name is "J.D." "Glad to meet you, J.D." you might reply; "what do those initials stand for?" "*Stand* for? They don't stand for nothin'. That's just my name—*Jay Dee*." And, less than auspiciously, I got my name Skipper from Pete Autsen, the neighborhood drunk. When my mother returned to Bayside Acres after giving birth to me in San Francisco General Hospital, Pete said (inquiring after my existence), "Is the Skipper on deck?" So neither of us had real names, names we could hope some day to be worthy of. Jenny first received her real name when she was baptized into the Russian Orthodox Church in the 1990s as "Genevieve," which allowed her to take as her spiritual guardian Saint Genevieve, the patron saint of Paris. As for me, Charles Upton, I was named after my grandfather, Charles Hemenway

Upton, the San Francisco patrician who later fell from social grace as a divorced alcoholic. Maybe that fall is why my given name of Charles was never emphasized—though my mother would sometimes call me "Bonnie Prince Charlie" after the Jacobite Young Pretender, and intimate that I had some mythic connection with Prince Charles Windsor, now King Charles III of England, who was born a month before me. (*Pretender* is right!) So I continued to be "Skip" until the publication of my first book, *Panic Grass*—the one who would skip promiscuously from thing to thing and had skipped many important stages in life. But when I expressed my uncertainty to Lew Welch about what name I should publish under, he said: "Let's do this the way the Zen *roshis* do it: *What is your name?*" "Charles Upton" I replied. After that, having become Charles Upton, I could look back to and claim Charlemagne as a distant ancestor on my mother's side—something that "Skip Upton" could never have done (though it is claimed that most people of European descent are related to Charlemagne in some way or another). You get no special privileges or virtues from your illustrious ancestors, nor any guilt either—all you get is a mark to meet, a mark that becomes a mark against you if you fail to meet it, plus a list of ancestral crimes to dis-identify with. Your real name does not ascend to you from the past through your bloodlines but descends from God in Eternity; the reason that God can *call* you at any moment is because He alone knows your real name.

Enemies aside, however—whether visible or invisible—the events that took place after my house burned have become hazy in my mind, since that was the lowest point of my life. I know I started seeing Jenny in her tiny room on Fillmore Street with no furniture and her bed a pad on the floor, just like that room of mine in Vancouver had been. But it was still during that damaged and darkened time that she and I took a "pre-honeymoon" to the Strawberry Mountains above John Day in eastern Oregon, where I'd bought 80 acres of steep, rocky, brushy land, hardly useful even for grazing, with the proceeds from my sale of that piece of much better land I'd bought earlier in northern British Columbia. I never occupied either of them, but I still sold both for a profit. We lived in a tent, and during our stay I swallowed a big lump of the peyote tar that Lew's wife Magda had given us as a pre-wedding present after we "announced our engagement," which didn't do much, but gave me the opportunity to place that bundle of human bones, undoubtedly of Native American origin—the same bones whose dust I swallowed in that poverty-stricken little room in Vancouver during my year in Canada, one of which I'd later handed to the Gyalwa Karmapa—inside a hollow tree to mark my territory. It didn't work, of course, because those bones weren't my bones to begin with, but at least they were on their way out of my life, since we never returned to John Day after our one and only visit.

The time then came when we visited the farm of Bill and Jenny Trumbly in Lodi in the Sacramento Valley (they were not farming it themselves, just renting a farmhouse next to a plot of tokay grapes that was being raised by a subcontracting farmer who lived off-site), and bought from them a camping trailer — exactly the same brand and style of trailer that had been at my father's duck club, strangely enough — which we later drove to Olema in Marin County, where we lived for a year in a trailer park. It was a tight fit, but Jenny's presence made the space capacious: wherever she was, was home.

(The night before we left Lodi, I had the following dream:

I dreamt of Jesus Christ, who told me that some day I would be famous. Answering him, I said: "I have been a priest of Ra, I have seen the Kaaba, and I have been conquered by you — what could fame possibly mean to me?" Then he presented me with two purple amethysts, placing one on my forehead and the other in my heart.)

Then finally, one year later, we returned to Bill's farm for our wedding. Though he's no longer in this world — he and his brother Doug died rather young, both around the same time, after we moved to Kentucky — I'll always be grateful to him for his generosity in providing the space for our inauguration. Having the wedding there was both a pledge of friendship and an act of defiance as far as my relationship to the Trumbly Clan plus Doyle was concerned; they had seriously balked at the very idea of the step I was taking, but they ultimately accepted it. The night before the ceremony, when I sat drinking beer with Bill at his dining room table, it occurred to me (as I remarked to him) that "this is my bachelor party." Bill's response was: "The only thing more inconceivable than you getting married is you ever getting divorced." That was his blessing on our union, and it was the right one — hard, but true.

The minister who witnessed our union was a spiritual healer, one Greg Schelkun, whom I'd met during my quest for the Philippine Psychic Surgeons; he had studied under them at one point. We invited the whole Trumbly family, John Doyle, Jenny's parents, my mother, Ken Bullock, and the poet Eugene Ruggles, who had just been nominated for the Pulitzer Prize. Gene, a dedicated alcoholic, was known for such drunken exploits as phoning up Idi Amin one night — the dictatorial and genocidal president of Uganda [1971–1979] — to ask him "Where do you get off, man, murdering 80,000–300,000 people??" (He actually got through to the palace, but apparently the President was otherwise engaged.) As for the refreshments, we provided *too much booze* of many different kinds, plus a beautiful smoked organic ham that the dog ended up getting. The ceremony took place on the bare dry ground of the farmyard, inside a circle of green ribbon (which we still have). Jenny wore a dress designed by myself and sewn by Jackie, the wife of a bookstore owner in Mill Valley — a delightful

British couple; her husband had been an acquaintance of Colin Wilson, the British "angry young man" and author of *The Outsider*, as well as various highly interesting books on occult and metaphysical subjects. It was of the darkest green velvet possible, almost black, with deep red piping on the hem and under the breast. Jenny wore a wreath or coronet that I'd made for her from silver wire entwined with holly (symbolizing peace and holiness), ivy (fidelity), and rosemary (remembrance, fidelity, and also the Virgin Mary). So I had crowned and vested Jenny just as I had Angela Pierce, the Girl of my childhood, so many years ago. Since both our birth-moons were in Taurus we were married on the Taurus Full Moon, on the ninth of the October, 1976 (Sun in Scorpio). The words of the ceremony were the traditional Anglican ones from *The Book of Common Prayer*.

When the ceremony was over my mother told us "be good"—to which Greg added, behind his hand: "*Be bad*"—then we jumped into our truck and headed for the hills for our honeymoon—the foothills of the Sierras that is, to the town of Volcano and a beautiful old stone hotel of gold rush vintage, a place Doyle had recommended. It was a lovely setting, but our reception turned out to be less than cordial. Our room had various hand-made objects decorating the walls, quilts and such, with notes attached that said things like "This quilt was sewn by our grandmother! *Do Not Touch.*" When we asked for our room key the woman manager told us, "There is no key; we're on the honor system here." Later she walked into our room unannounced, even though we had not been reveling, making lots of noise or breaking the bed. (So much for our first honeymoon—and some "honor" system!) We had reserved the room for two days but in the morning we checked out early and drove back in the direction of the Sacramento Delta, to the little river town of Rio Vista and the cheapest motel we could find. But it had a TV in it and we'd brought a bottle, so that's where we spent our real honeymoon.

Meanwhile back at the farm (as we heard later) the oversupply of liquor we had provided was having its effect. Gene Ruggles ended up falling and breaking his cheekbone on the corner of an outdoor ping-pong table, making it necessary for Doyle to drive him a fairly long distance to the nearest emergency room, which resulted in the legend of "the night the Pulitzer Prize nominee poet broke his cheek on a ping-pong table and I saved him." I've always wondered whether John Doyle, a mighty drinker in his own right, had himself been saved by this incident and his charitable nature from an even worse fate on his long drive back to Marin County.

TRAILER LIFE

So Jenny and I spent our first year together in a tiny camping-trailer at a trailer park in Olema, where Sir Francis Drake Boulevard, the main east/west artery from the settled part of Marin to the rural West Marin of the dairy ranches, meets the California coast highway, Highway One. That was our crucible. It was impossible to say "I need some space," so each of us had to become the space for the other, while at the same time occupying the mysterious third space that was defined and invoked by our relationship. During that year we read *Heaven and Hell* by Emmanuel Swedenborg, in which we found the doctrine "that a married couple make up a single Angel in Eternity" — and since every Angel is his (and her) own space, delimited without, Infinite within, we found that we had all the space we needed.

LEW WENT SOUTHWEST

Some time during that year in the trailer, I had a dream of Lew Welch. He was at a blackboard, doing something called "Chalk Speak," like a football coach will do "chalk talk," diagramming the plays for the players. After that dream I got a map of the Sierras, looked for some place name that sounded like Chalk Speak, and finally picked "Spanish Creek." (I was wrong.)

In the last words of his suicide- and/or self-occultation note, he had said: "I went Southwest" — Southwest, we must assume, from his point of departure, Gary Snyder's Kitkitdizze, near Nevada City in the Sierra foothills. And so, with that tiny clue, plus what the dream appeared to have told me, I decided to set off to find him — either dead, alive, or in some third state that was impossible to define. Nor was I alone in such a quest, since Lew, by writing his poem "SONG OF THE TURKEY BUZZARD," and doing what was necessary to insure that his body would never be found, had set up a powerful ambiguity in the minds of the stoned and liminal poets of the time: had Lew simply committed suicide (an uninteresting and depressing theory), or had he undergone some arcane shamanic transformation, actually in some sense shapeshifting into a Turkey Buzzard, just as Castaneda's Don Juan, instead of literally dying like some unimaginative Bourgeois nobody, had instead gone with his pal Genaro to "the land of the red bugs," those tiny insects, much smaller than the smallest ant, that you could actually see scurrying over the lichen-spangled rocks of rural Marin County — if you took the time, as Lew put it, to "peer into Tiny"? So I drove in my Toyota Land Cruiser (that had belonged to my father, the one he took to Baja California) to Samuel P. Taylor State Park in the San Geronimo Valley, east along Sir Francis Drake Boulevard, and picked some Red Larskpur Root — an herb the Miwoks used for divination and/or suicide — then headed for Spanish Creek in the Sierras. I hiked in, found a place down by the creek itself, and pitched my tent. That night I ingested just a *tiny* sliver of the Larkspur Root, and lay me down to dream.

I dreamt that Lew Welch was alive and well and living in Milwaukee, Wisconsin.

Back in Olema, I consulted Directory Assistance and found that there was *one* Lew Welch listed as living in Milwaukee, Wisconsin. I wrote him a letter to the effect of "if you're not the Lew Welch I knew this is going to be a *really* weird letter, so let me apologize in advance." I got no reply.

(Like all my other experiences with magic, this one taught me two things: 1) that magic is real—sort of—and, 2) that it's not worth the practice. Who would risk death, really, just to establish an astral connection with Milwaukee, Wisconsin?)

Then, much later, while looking again at a map of the Sierras, I realized (idiot) that Lew in my first dream, with his "Chalk Speak," had really been trying to say "Jack's Peak," the name of an actual mountain in El Dorado County. There it was on the map, south*east* of Kitkitdizze, above the southwest shore of Lake Tahoe.

But then, years later, Google Earth was born, and when I looked at the satellite photo of Jack's Peak in the Sierras, all I saw was a totally barren and inaccessible wilderness of snow and rock. No roads, no visible trails.

However, it turns out that there's another Jack's Peak in the Coast Range near Monterey, in a state park that's named for it, just off Highway One—the highway that forms part of Geary Street in San Francisco, hits the coast, turns south, becomes the Great Highway, then travels farther and farther south to Big Sur and beyond. From that Jack's Peak, you can see the Pacific Ocean. In Lew's words:

> I like playing that game
> Standing on a high rock looking way out over it all:
>
> *"I think I'll call it the Pacific"*

—from "WOBBLY ROCK"; and, from "THE SONG MT. TAMALPAIS SINGS":

> This is the last place.
> There is nowhere else to go.

You could make the case that Lew was not a man to die surrounded by high mountains, any more than Harte Crane was, though his relentless idealism might have told him different. *Man follows the Sun.* Like the Stamper brothers in Ken Kesey's *Sometimes a Great Notion*, it should have been the Ocean for Lew Welch—the place where the Sun decides to set. Yet he began from Kitkitdizze and sent a dream of Jack's Peak, which could have been the one near Tahoe; and he told Frank Dietrich, "Up in the Sierras there's these shear granite crevasses hundreds of feet deep. You could balance on the edge of one, blow your brains out, and topple right in; you'd never be found." He also noted that the totem bird of Milarepa, the great Tibetan yogi, was the Vulture—which is why, after Jenny and I had moved into the house that had belonged to my grandmother in Bayside Acres around three years later, I mailed a Turkey Buzzard feather that Lew Welch "sent" after his death to a Dzogchen Lama in Nepal, along with a picture of Lew and twenty American dollars, asking the Lama's prayers for his passage through the *bardo*...

But the Jack's Peak in Monterey County lies south-southwest-and-by-south of Kitkitdizze. If forensic dreams are ever to be relied upon in the run-off of resting-places, if "in dreams begin responsibilities," then I vote for there.

And whether that Jack's Peak, or that other one in the Sierras, holds his bones, too tough for even Buzzard-beak to crack, or whether that mountain was just one of his dream-time way-stations on the road between Here and There (which is the only road there is), there is still a reason to name it: because every *name* is a *step*.

No step from Here to There is ever final, of course; like Jack Kerouac said in *Mexico City Blues*, "You just numbly don't get there." So it's best, I think, to conclude all these attempts to end it all in the words of Lew Welch himself, from "HIKING POEM/HIGH SIERRA":

> Trails go nowhere.
> They end exactly
> where you stop.

THE JOHREI FELLOWSHIP

One of the providential influences that undoubtedly helped us survive our lean year as Marin County trailer-trash, and several of the hard years after that, was provided by a more-or-less New Age Japanese church known as the Johrei Fellowship, whose main function was to channel Johrei, the "Divine Light." Johrei was similar in some ways to the more familiar Reiki, except that it was more standardized — every church or center or practitioner connected with the Fellowship was clearly channeling the identical energy, which varied in intensity but never in quality. The recipient of the Light would sit across from the channeling minister, who then raised his or her hand, from which emanated — without physical contact — a subtle yet quite noticeable psychospiritual energy; it was as if a cool wind of light were blowing through one's atoms and molecules, flushing out dark clots and clouds of psychic impurity which, after being released from the subtle body, rose and disappeared into the sky. I became connected with the Johrei Fellowship — as a recipient but never a member — because I was then in a dark enough spiritual space to need what the Catholics call "sensible consolations," constant reminders that *Grace is real*, the kind of proofs and demonstrations that only those of little faith require. In many ways it was "cheap Grace" according to Dietrich Bonhoeffer's terminology, since it was offered without charge and required no commitment, no repentance, no struggle against the *nafs*, the lower self. It was as if, instead of forgiving my sins and giving me the power to continue to say "no" to them, it simply removed the *psychophysical consequences* of those sins — at least temporarily. I believe that Johrei did help to save me from ultimate despair during those years, but it did little to aid me in the real spiritual work that the true Path requires.

Our first experience of Johrei was provided by a member of the Fellowship who lived as a house sitter in a large house on a hill above Lake Nicasio, not far from Olema; I forget how we first heard of him. My initial response to the experience was suspicion, as if to say "what right has this foreign energy to break in on my own freely-chosen spiritual darkness?" Yet I always came back: to the San Francisco Johrei Center on Portola Avenue, on one occasion to the North American headquarters of the church in Los Angeles, and often to the house of Johrei practitioner Kathy Blackwell in San Anselmo, who was destined to be so helpful to us in the future. At the San Francisco church, while receiving the Divine Light, I would "channel" it in my imagination to other people and situations, visualizing various resolutions, purifications and healings. I have no way of knowing if this had any real effect—except for one piece of evidence. Some years later, while I was working with Sarah Howard in Project MOVE, our homeless service agency (as will be recounted in *Chapter Ten*), she underwent one of the frequent emotional crises that volatile artistic types like Sarah and I were subject to, though I forget exactly what precipitated it. Since this was in the era before cellphones (except for the rich), I had no way of contacting her, so I went to Kathy Blackwell's house instead and tried to "contact" her through Johrei. Later, when I let her know about my attempt to send her some "second-hand Johrei," Sarah let me know that, while she was sitting in her car in a state of turmoil, a sense of peace suddenly had descended upon her. "Was that you?" she asked. "It looks like it was" I answered.

PETALUMA

So after our year in the trailer was up, we left Olema and moved into a cheap, sub-standard mother-in-law apartment, the ground floor of two units, behind a house at (prophetically) 313 Kentucky St, Petaluma: bedroom, bathroom, small living room, kitchenette—that was it. No telephone and no TV, just a radio. We were each-other's go-to media sources, each other's only internet. We had to do a few indoor repairs on the apartment, but with a second-hand rug and furniture bought in San Rafael, and some of the few paintings by my father that had escaped the fire, we made a very attractive little love-nest, arts-nest and booze-nest, where we spent the next two years. They were years, for me, of heavy drinking, with lots of straight, hard liquor, whiskey and brandy. Yet it was in those years that I also began work on my own kind of metaphysical essay (on a typewriter of course; the personal computer had not yet appeared)—possibly aided by another chemical intoxicant, namely the loaf of greenish-black peyote tar that Magda had given us as a wedding present. We used to smoke little balls of it in a pipe, which put us in a more-or-less continuous liminal state (or more likely just me, since Jenny wasn't particularly fond of drugs)—no major psychedelic experiences, just a trace of second sight that finally made itself useful, for a relatively useless if not negative purpose, when I came to construct the "rain-charm" I've already told you about in Chapter Three.

The only person we (almost) knew in town was old Walter Anderson, a retired dentist and friend of my father's, the man who leased the cabin in Siskiyou County where my family used to vacation. It was into this world of isolation, alcohol and concentrated psychic energy that Bill and Jenny Trumbly and his brother Doug penetrated on one occasion, in an attempt to visit us. They had just been to something called the Frogonian Festival, somewhere in or near Petaluma, a periodic event sponsored by a well-known disk jockey of the time, Al "Jazzbo" Collins, whose motto (in the words of the *bandito* from *The Treasure of the Sierra Madre*, played by Alfonso Bedoya) was: "I don't have to show you any stinkin' badges!" They were, of course, drunk—drunk and slumming. Jenny Trumbly stayed outside, refusing to cross the threshold; she tried to stop Bill from entering our abode but failed, so we opened the door to welcome him and his brother. Doug Trumbly, after peering around suspiciously, said with scornful disapproval: "How didja make this place look so *nice??*" Apparently they were hoping to find us living in conditions sufficiently degraded to let them feel better about their own state—but no such luck.

HELEN LUSTER

One of the more interesting people we became acquainted with while we lived in Petaluma was the poet Helen Luster. The biographical note to her archive, held at the University "at" Buffalo, tells us the following:

> Helen Luster, 1913–1985, was born in Evanston, Illinois. She was a political activist for peace and a poet for three decades. Luster was a co-editor of *Trace* literary magazine in Los Angeles, founder and president of the Los Angeles Poetry Center in 1966, and co-led poetry workshops in her home with Paul Mariah. She was a student at [Chögyam Trungpa's] Naropa University, Boulder, Colorado for 10 years where she was also Allen Ginsberg's personal secretary. Helen Luster was also a student of parapsychology and active in that community. She was a member of seance and crystal groups and spoke at conferences on the subject of clairvoyance and synchronicity. A lot of her poetry is automatic writing.

Helen was a dear soul, dear in the "ding-y" sense; she lived in San Rafael (not a very long drive for us) with her more practical and introverted sister, Betty. She literally worshipped Allen Ginsberg, whom she took as a kind of prophet; in her poetry she styled him the Green Man, the late 20th-Century incarnation—for all his gayness—of a pagan fertility god. And, yes, her poetry showed every sign of having written itself, according to that more-or-less choppy style which was not so much an imitation of Robert Creeley's verse as the form he inadvertently gave the rest of us permission to try our hand at; Ginsberg himself characterized her poetry simply by saying, "She's learned her lesson." It was not really as a poet we knew her, however, but as a UFO enthusiast, who held highly entertaining monthly UFO soirées at her home off Lincoln Avenue. It seemed that she lived for the day, or night, when she might actually see a "real" UFO, though while I knew her she was still waiting. The closest she came to the revelation she sought was the day when a mysterious pink fuzz began to "manifest" through her air conditioner. It was undoubtedly some of that spun-glass insulation that was beginning to decompose, but she hoped against hoped that it might really be a message from the Space Brothers. My own later interest in UFOs and Aliens, which, as mentioned before, I first wrote of in *The System of Antichrist* (2001) and later updated in two further books, *Cracks in the Great Wall* (2005) and *The Alien Disclosure Deception* (2021), had much to do with my connection with her circle. It was Helen who first introduced us to the books of Jacques Vallee, the greatest of the UFOlogists, and played tapes of his lectures at her gatherings. Without this entré Jenny would never have spotted Vallee's book *Messengers of Deception* at a used bookstore, a book which became so central in opening our eyes to the whole world of social engineering.

Once upon a time the Trumblys, in an attempt to satirize me out of my spiritual-seeker, space-cadet identity, played me that brilliant LP by the Firesign Theatre, "Everything You Know is Wrong" (1974), which roasted almost the entire New Age/pop culture scene of those years, including the motorcycle daredevil Evel Knievel ("Rebus Kniebus"), the psychic spoon-bender Uri Geller ("Nino Savate"), and the whole world of the UFO crazies. They thought I would be properly chastened, but I was in fact delighted. So I borrowed the record to play for Helen's UFO group, and they too were delighted. (Like many of us had learned as poets, *insult is the sincerest form of flattery*, since it proves that the person offering said insult is "only jealous.") In any case, the Helen Luster Circle heralded our later graduation (or demotion?) from the poetry scene to the world of the New Age. In addition, for those who might be interested in certain little-researched aspects of the Great Naropa Poetry Wars (see below), I would suggest that they delve into the Helen Luster Archive, since it might contain the only copies of my epistolary debate with Allen Ginsberg on the subject of Chögyam Trungpa, which I sold to her at one point when Jenny and I were short of funds.

ALLEN GINSBERG AND THE GREAT NAROPA POETRY WARS

As I've pointed out above, Chögyam Trungpa appealed to many in both the hippie and the Beat generations who were looking for ways to reach a more stable spiritual and psychic standpoint after the excesses of the '60s. Once again it was Allen Ginsberg who led the migration of seekers from two generations of American Bohemia toward Tibetan Buddhism and the Vajrayana. I myself was more or less on the edge of this movement. I've already told the story of my trip to Trungpa's Tail of the Tiger outpost in the Colorado Rockies for a meditation retreat, though I never visited his main headquarters, the Naropa Institute (now University) in Boulder. I was attracted to Trungpa partly because his books exhibited a rare mix of intelligence, accessibility and relevance to the times. His teaching style blended the traditional Vajrayana with what I can only call a reckless degree of openness to the U.S. counterculture. I view Trungpa as a kind of "berserker" who exposed himself to many dangers as he plunged into the fading world of the hippie "Spiritual Revolution" so as to bring the Vajrayana to the west, whatever the cost might be to himself personally. And that cost was pretty steep, seeing that his alcoholism eventually got the better of him; he ended up dying of cirrhosis of the liver. (William Burroughs too was drawn into Trungpa's orbit; I briefly corresponded with him after the scandals mentioned below emerged in the Trungpa world, just as I had in 1968 when he was in the process of breaking with Scientology, but this time he held fast to Trungpa's Vajrayana. Undoubtedly he was old enough and near enough to death not to want to risk jumping ship after he had found a vehicle potentially capable of carrying him to the Farther Shore.)

The Great Naropa Poetry Wars—which is also the title of a book about these events by the poet Tom Clark—were sparked by the following incident: during a drunken party, Trungpa ordered his "vajra guards" to seize and strip the well-known poet and translator W. S. Merwin and his fiancée Dana Naone, whose desire to be alone together on the equivalent of their honeymoon was considered discourteous to the Master. Not surprisingly, this assault generated a great deal of controversy in the Trungpa world, and in the world of American poetry generally in the 1970s. Poet Ed Sanders, a member of the New York rock band the Fugs, mounted an investigation into the incident—which Trungpa immediately co-opted by offering to let him teach a course at the Naropa Institute on "Investigative Poetics." Sanders took him up on his offer. I myself played a brief and peripheral role in the Poetry Wars through an epistolary dialogue with Allen Ginsberg, who adopted the "pro-Trungpa" position vis-à-vis my "anti-Trungpa" stance. (When I briefly met with Merwin and Dana Naone, she expressed appreciation for my willingness to criticize Trungpa, an appreciation that Merwin clearly did not share.) At that point I was beginning to sense that my generation's attraction to the "feudal/hierarchical" system of Tibetan Buddhism represented the end of the spiritual freedom and self-determination of the counterculture and possibly of its generally liberal political stance as well, though I had not yet come to the realization that these "progressive" tendencies, having passed their peak, were eventually destined, all on their own, to reach an extreme point that negated much of their earlier free-wheeling character—a turn represented by the repressive "woke" culture of today—but also that that my generation's spiritual aspirations desperately needed a more traditional grounding if they were to survive and develop. At the same time, I felt the first foreboding of the deconstruction of Western Christian Civilization that is so widespread in these times, the injection of a degree of heartless Asian depersonalization—a depersonalization that was and is the *shadow* of Asia, not its substance—into the sense of human dignity and the eternal value of the individual soul (*not* the individualistic ego) that, for all the betrayals of this principle our history is littered with, had characterized the western world up until then. So it wouldn't be wrong to say that my unwillingness to place myself under Trungpa's yoke heralded my later connection with Santa Venetia Presbyterian Church, Liberation Theology and the Sanctuary Movement for Central American refugees, which you'll read about in the next chapter, while my initial attraction to Trungpa later bore fruit in my connection with the Traditionalist School of "comparative metaphysics" and my entry into the Sufi Path (see *Chapter Eleven*). And it was also during my psychic struggle against Trungpa's influence that I began to learn how a person can free him- or herself from deep psychological and spiritual identifications that were either wrongheaded to begin with or else had outlived their usefulness—the art of "self-deprogramming" that has saved my soul on more than one occasion. The basis of that art is a firm faith in God coupled with a keen sense of the *transcendence* of God, which together lead to an understanding that no form in this world of manifestation can or should be mistaken for the Absolute. As we Muslims say, *Allahu Akbar*, "God is Greater" (than whatever you can see or imagine), and *la ilaha illa 'Allah*, "there is no god but God." The true de-programming is not a re-integration into mainstream society after bondage to a cult—since mainstream society (assuming that it still exists) is in many ways a cult in itself—but rather a victory over idolatry.

My tryst with Trungpa ended up teaching me certain tactical lessons in the practice of psychic combat. Such combat, as I conceived of it then, is often carried on in the dream state, and is the furthest thing from aggressive magic designed to hurt; it has nothing to do with the casting of "spells" but is strictly limited to breaking them. One of the many things I learned while engaged in such combat is that it is sometimes necessary, while traveling the path from ego-consciousness (which is inseparable from an identification with some aspect of This World) to Spiritual or Heart-consciousness, to confront and overcome certain psychic powers that are apparently distinct from the individual psyche, powers that will rise up against you, blocking this transition. These powers, though they may actually be deeply-buried aspects of your own psyche that are difficult to recognize as such—or else, from another point of view, denizens of Jung's Collective Unconscious, since certain layers of your psyche are in fact deeply collective—will often appear, precisely, as demons; in any case they must be dealt with as such, whatever their true nature may ultimately turn out to be. Phenomenologically speaking, it is useful to separate these entities into two classes: those whose power lies in swiftness and quick attack, whom we could call "the Rangers," and those whose effectiveness is based upon maintaining a fixed standpoint from which their power can be exercised, the ones we might name "the Wardens." The Rangers include the more familiar demons of obsession and temptation, while the Wardens are those powers who infest locations and possess human beings. But there is also a higher class of these Wardens who manage various human collectives of belief and activity—as well as the *egregores*, the collective-thought forms of these collectives—including religious or "spiritual" traditions that have fallen away, to one degree or another, from the Truth that God originally designed them to protect and manifest. When criticizing Trungpa to Ginsberg and attempting to fight free from the Vajraguru's influence, I encountered various entities of this class, whose strength did not lie in tactical maneuver but in their well-established, "fortified" positions. They were the sort of beings who operate on the basis of context rather than exploit, as Trungpa did when he took the wind out of the sails of his critic Ed Sanders by inviting him to teach a class designed to investigate Trungpa's misdeeds on Trungpa's home turf, the Naropa Institute; at the time I compared them to psychic minefields. And my encounter with them undoubtedly influenced, up to a point, my conception of the Gnostic Archons—those Principalities and Powers, deeper even than the dark side of Trungpa's collective, who are entirely capable (at least with the help of plenty of alcohol) of making no less a figure than the Eleventh Trungpa Tulku dance to their tune. Of course I was drinking pretty heavily myself at the time... nor have I been able to forget a sentence I wrote while passing through Trungpa's world, one that clearly demonstrates my own complicity in the system that had entrapped me: "I consider Chögyam Trungpa to be a con-man subtler than I am, and thus a valuable teacher."

I certainly don't mean to imply that Vajrayana Buddhism, undeniably one of the highest pinnacles of human spirituality, is intrinsically demonic—even though the Tibetans are known for their practice of "converting" various demons to Buddhism, leading them to Liberation and then employing them as "Wrathful Guardians of the Dharma"—only that any unconscious human collective that exercises a manipulative influence over its members will include a demonic element, whose firmly-entrenched Wardens will strictly define the limits of both the activities and types of consciousness that are possible within that collective and the spectrum of the *authorized* methods of opposing it. My own advantage, on the other hand, lay in mobility, since my goal at that point was not to become a settled member of Trungpa's collective but to free myself from it so I could move on to my next assignment. My challenge was to criticize, and separate myself from, the degenerate aspects of Tradition without rejecting Tradition itself, and at the same time to stay faithful to my hard-won individual understandings without seeing myself as a freelance spiritual genius who might even have the right to found his own religion. If you wander one millimeter to the right or the left from the Straight Path between those two extremes, you will end up as dead meat on the highways of the Unseen.

(Some years later, when Jenny and I attended a workshop led by neo-shaman Richard Dobson in preparation for Harmonic Convergence [see *Chapter Nine*], I learned that my way of dealing with Chögyam Trungpa, and other individuals and situations I became involved with but ultimately had to break free from, actually had a name in the doctrines of the Twisted Hair Society, an inter-tribal *metis* medicine society publicly represented by one Harley Swift Deer (whose reputation in other respects I can in no way vouch for). It was called "tyrant-stalking." Swift Deer had something he called the Tyrant Wheel, which described the 8 major types of "tyrant-situation" and the methods of dealing with them — in 7 out of 8 cases, without open conflict; it had certain similarities to my own "Neo-Gnostic" system of the Four Archons (see *The System of Antichrist, Chapter Five*). Before encountering Swift Deer's system I had absolutely no evidence that anyone still alive in this world had arrived at my kind of insight into the *esoteric* dynamics of psychic oppression. According to the Tyrant Wheel, Trungpa functioned for me as an "East Tyrant" — the type who, like many false or fallen spiritual teachers, tyrannizes by inducing you to project on them the *Imago Dei*, the God-image we all carry inside us, so that you begin to fear that if you oppose them in any way you will earn the Wrath of God. The way to stalk a tyrant like that is through something like *sacrilege*, which is done simply by saying: "*You are not God*—you're a human being just as I am; we stand on the same ground, subject to His Judgment and open to His Mercy. *There is no god but God.*" But to do that you will need to have a conscious relationship with the *living* God, the only One who can shrink the East Tyrant down to size; if you try to fight that kind of tyrant ego-to-ego the game is already lost. And you will also need to realize, if you find yourself the victim of such a tyrant, that you yourself had a hand in creating him.)

As for that "next assignment," or maybe the one after that, it was not slow in announcing itself, since it was during my debate with Ginsberg and my participation in the Great Naropa Poetry Wars that I had a significant dream: I was standing on a high place looking down into a wide valley, a valley that was filled with a vague, shifting mass with flecks of color in it. Then a clear voice declared: "al-Ghazali is coming." When I woke up, I realized that the shifting mass was really a vast throng of people. Abū Ḥāmid Muḥammad ibn Muḥammad al-Ṭūsiyy al-Ghazali [1058–1111] was one of the best-known and most influential Sufis in the history of Islam—the sage who, more than any other, was able to reconcile inner mystical Islam or *tasawwuf* with outer *shari'ah*-based Islam in the mind of the *ummah*, the Muslim community.

This dream was certainly in line with the vision I had had at the Gyalwa Karmapa's Black Crown Ceremony, while we were living in our trailer in Olema, in which "myself" in another lifetime appeared as a Muslim woodcutter in Tibet—which means that, even before I had ever imagined becoming a Muslim, Islam and Tibetan Buddhism were already at war in my soul. But why? And why did I feel that my decision not to accept Trungpa's "invitation" in this life had placed me in such a life-and-death struggle, such that the simple decision to say "no thank you" to him had set me in conflict with apparently demonic powers? Thinking back over it, maybe something that I heard Trungpa say at the Tail of the Tiger might provide a clue: "If you break your tantric vows" he told us, "you go to a hell that is worse than Auschwitz"—which might have applied obliquely to me even though I had never formally made such a vow. And the fact is that Jesus said something very similar, about Judas, in Matthew 26:24–25:

> "Woe to that man by whom the Son of Man is betrayed! It would have been better for him if he had never been born." Then Judas, who was betraying Him, answered and said, "Rabbi, is it I?" He said to him, "You have said it."

Judas had certainly received "initiation" into Jesus's inner circle—but then he turned against his Master and betrayed him to his executioners, so it definitely seems as if a similar principle were being expressed by both Jesus Christ and Chögyam Trungpa. Two big differences, however, are that Jesus was not using terror to keep his disciples in line before the fact since had already been betrayed by Judas, and that Judas' betrayal was not only a self-betrayal but a direct attack on Jesus, whereas to break one's tantric vows would be a self-betrayal and nothing more—not to mention the fact that Chögyam Trungpa was no Jesus Christ! It's undeniably true that anyone who has come into intimacy with the Sacred and then gone on to reject it has prepared for him- or herself a terrible fate. On the other hand, what Trungpa said, the way he said it and the context in which he said it, could certainly be taken as a manipulative threat against his followers for purposes of control, a perversion of the Sacred in service to a cynical power motive, and thus as an example of the same kind of betrayal that it warned against. *Which version is true?* Because I did not formally enter Trungpa's circle but only skirted the edges of it, I have not had to answer that question, nor do I feel capable of answering it even now. Nonetheless I see it as entirely appropriate to quote the following couplet from William Blake's poem "Auguries of Innocence":

> The truth that's told with bad intent
> Beats all the lies you can invent.

My connection with the Poetry Wars ended when Allen Ginsberg, along with some of Trungpa's other students, led a meditative anti-nuclear sit-in on the railroad tracks near Rocky Flats, Colorado where a train carrying either fissionable material, nuclear waste or nuclear weapons (I forget which) was scheduled to pass. I sent him a telegram—a recognized way of emphasizing the importance of a message in those days—saluting him on his action, since I wanted to avoid bad blood and end our debate on a positive note of "no hard feelings."

BOTTOMING OUT

The lowest point of our stay in Petaluma came when I lost my wallet at a pay-phone, which was our only channel of communication with the outside world. At the same time my over-the-counter asthma-inhaler had run dry, so I was forced to phone my mother in San Rafael to ask if she could buy me one and drive it up to me, which she refused to do. She was still doing freeway driving at that point, but San Rafael-to-Petaluma was nonetheless quite a drive for an elderly woman. (Later someone found the wallet and returned it to me, though at this point I can't imagine how that happened, since people had no way to contact me.) In any case, before I was able to cash a check and buy a new inhaler, I was hit by a serious asthma attack, lasting for 48 hours. I had to struggle for each breath, and sleep (except for brief moments of oblivion) was out of the question. At that point I had no clear idea what a dangerous situation I was in; I could have easily died. If anything like that were to happen now I would immediately dial 911, but in those days I had resigned myself to living without the kind of safety-net I have today (shaky though it is). As I fought for air, I slowly came to realize that the emotion underlying the attack was anger—anger that I had no way of requiting or expressing. This situation was dramatized by a dream I had during one of the times I briefly nodded out, in which a German shepherd suddenly jumped from the trunk of a car and attacked a short Jewish man who resembled a familiar character-actor: the cruel master and the helpless victim, anger at the world and anger at myself, had come together in my psyche, and were close to choking the life out of me. Looking back over events like this, I am always amazed that I have absolutely no police record, have never been in a serious fist-fight, and have never owned a gun. Somehow I must have known how to sublimate all that anger and put it to work, or at least part of it—perhaps through a combination of social activism and the kind of literary self-expression that let me write this book. If you have enough cultural points-of-reference—the supply of which is shrinking with each new generation as "western civilization" becomes a thing of the past—you can understand your anger instead of just acting it out, and learn to express it through such vehicles as passionate invective or satirical wit, instead of with fists, knives and guns.

In any case, I survived—and it was not long after this that another dream clearly announced the arrival of a new phase of my life. In the dream I saw my father—and this time, unlike the dreams I had had of a figure in his likeness both before and after my trip to the Philippines—I knew it was really him. He was pointing to a bed of strawberries, like the strawberries my grandmother grew in the plot outside the picture window of her home in San Rafael. Strawberries, which were first associated with the goddess Venus and later with the Virgin Mary, traditionally symbolize love—since they are red and heart-shaped—as well as (in Christian terms) virtue, purity and perfection. I knew that my father was telling me, through that dream, that it was time for us to move into my grandmother's house in Bayside Acres, which we soon did, in the year of Our Lord 1979, and which we occupied for the next quarter-century.

This move precipitated a series of shocks—and not just for us. While the house was being prepared, we moved for maybe two months into an apartment in San Rafael's Canal District, the same area where Paula Wasserman was living when I first met her. For the typical San Rafael resident a move to the Canal signified a loss of status, since that area was the closest thing in Marin to a *barrio*, and only losers among the White race went to live with the Mexicans. On the other hand, the happy, beaming Vietnamese family who lived next door to us were definitely not stuck away in some ghetto like we were; they were living in an opulent paradise beyond their wildest dreams: a neat, clean apartment complex where all the utilities worked and no guards were needed—and it even had a swimming-pool! But it was during our time in the Canal that I had a second major asthma attack, which caught me again without an inhaler—one that was so intense that I immediately called an ambulance, which took me to an ER where I could receive a shot of adrenalin. And during that attack I had a clear vision of Ken Bullock, incandescent with hatred for me. I saw that he had hoped against hope that my exile from Marin County would be permanent so he could "take over my position"—however unenviable that position might have been—but now I had foiled his plans. Later on I felt some of the same hatred, though on a much smaller scale, from Doug Trumbly and John Doyle. But since I had never deliberately crossed or insulted either of them, though I did have a few brief squabbles with Ken and probably unconsciously said some inconsiderate things to Doug, I came to understand that their hatred had a big impersonal element to it. It was not so much a case of interpersonal conflict as one of *heresy*; somehow I had denied one of the central unwritten tenets of their faith, had failed to recant, and now deserved to be burned at the stake.

(Nonetheless, quite a few years later, John Doyle — after reading my book *The System of Antichrist* — contacted me out of the blue to say: "We were wrong about you; we were wrong to treat you so terribly" — a rare and admirable gesture!) Nonetheless, even as I write this, I begin to see more clearly than ever — and maybe for the first time — what infernal *evil* was uncovered when Jenny and I came together. Our love, which has lasted half a century and only gotten deeper, was born out of an ocean of hate, undoubtedly the same hate she herself had been born into in Kentucky, and that had almost killed her. Exiled from my home territory, rejected by my mother, by all my friends — even by many of the San Francisco poets! — just because I loved Jenny and took no pains to hide it. The demonic hatred now spreading like a dark stain over the Earth, though it must've been latent in the human collective since the first moment of the Fall, is not the old familiar kind of hatred we can easily identify with — hatred of the oppressors, hatred of the enemies, fear and hatred of the underlings, hatred of the personal rival, hatred of the strangers. It is, precisely, a hatred of love itself, the kind of hatred that makes us pray for some dense metallic asteroid to drop out of space and destroy us, that makes us entertain the insane possibility that we were not created by God out of His mercy and generosity but as a genetic experiment by horrific, ghoulish Aliens; the kind of hatred that makes us reject *even gender*, and in so doing curse the very continuance of human life. When Jenny and I were married, something in the Pit saw red — and whatever that Thing was, and is, it did not just feel anger: it also felt fear. Clearly we had struck an exposed nerve in Hell.

And a second shock was much more serious than the first: In order to move into my grandmother's house we needed to evict the present tenant, a Mrs Butler, whose family lived, or had lived, in their own home about a block away. When we went to inspect the house before she was scheduled to vacate, we saw that her dog had used a place in the hallway as his restroom, consequently the house stank of urine, and the floor, with the help of termites, had rotted away. On that occasion she told us what a shock it had been for her to be told she had to move — and a few months after she left and we moved in, she died. Yes, we had to save our lives — but did we have to kill someone else to do it? For a long time after that, possibly even till the present day, I've felt a huge sense of debt — and so, a decade later, when I was contacted by Sarah Howard and invited to work with her to serve Marin County's homeless [see *Chapter Ten*], I jumped at the chance. And we actually did save some lives — but is it really a life for a life? Does saving a life cancel the debt of taking one? I don't think so. Each action, good or bad, generates its own karma, and is punished or rewarded in its own terms. Karma is not quantitative, and is therefore non-transferable. Thank God that karmic retribution can be superseded by God's forgiveness, and that, in the words of the Prophet Muhammad, "acts are judged by their intent." All I can say in my defense is that I never intentionally meant Mrs Butler any harm — but my guilt for her death would still have destroyed our marriage if, somewhere, I had not felt and accepted God's forgiveness. Beyond this, I can only recount one striking incident that, even though it should really have no bearing on my case before the bar of eternal Justice, may still be relevant. Some years after we returned to Bayside Acres we were visited by a neighbor child, who was young enough to have been born after we moved in. After looking around the house, which he had never visited before, he turned to us and said: "I used to live here."

UNAVOIDABLE GNOSTICISM

When you suddenly find yourself in violation of certain unwritten rules that inhabit the collective unconscious of society, dark prohibitions and imperatives that in some ways act like conscious psychic entities — when you discover that "we wrestle not against flesh and blood but against Principalities, against Powers, against the rulers of the darkness of This World, against spiritual wickedness in high places" — then you have come to the point of the Gnostic Crisis, after which the world will necessarily appear to you as an engineered control-system, a cosmic prison created and maintained by deluded-and-deluding false gods — the Archons. *Those* heavens do not declare the glory of God, nor does *that* earth show forth His handiwork: He totally transcends them, being a virtually inaccessible Reality that has no part in either the material or the psychic universes of a fallen order-of-perception, which is why the Gnostics called Him "the Alien God." And if you want to free yourself from that prison (as Lew Welch phrased it), "The only way out, is OUT." It was to address the Gnostic Crisis that I began work on my epic poem "The Wars of Love," a poem that took me 33 years to complete. It is based on a system of Four Archons: established Law, mysterious Fate, rebellious Selfhood and dissolutionary Chaos — largely unconscious psychic influences that, as the most common and fundamental *misperceptions of the nature of God*, are the dominant principles of the system of global oppression and delusion that St Paul called "the Darkness of This World." (A more complete epitome of the "modern Gnostic system" the poem is based on appears as the chapter "The Shadows of God," Chapter Five of *The System of Antichrist*.) In my struggle against these Archons, I learned that to try and tap the power of one of them so as to use it against the others is a losing game, since — though they seem to be in perpetual conflict — they are secretly in league with one another behind the scenes. As I moved from planet to planet of experience in the course of my life, adopting, assimilating and then discarding the various worldviews provided by Art,

Religion and Politics, my insight into the nature of these Archons helped me learn how to free myself from them, by teaching me never to idolize as Absolute any limited form in the material, psychic or intelligible worlds, but always to say *Allahu akbar*, "God is greater" (than whatever you can perceive or imagine), and *la ilaha illa 'Allah*, "there is no god but God." Only a God who transcends all forms, who can never be limited to any of them, has the power to express Himself through all of them, to manifest through all intellectual, imaginative and sensible appearances, which are none other than His Acts, His Names and His Signs. This is why I was able to compose poetry without identifying as a "poet," to articulate theology without identifying as a "theologian," to carry on political action without identifying as an "activist." If I hadn't undergone this strenuous course of training, I could never have survived the mass ideological insanity of the 21st Century. In terms of orthodox Christian theology, as well as of the Primordial Tradition of which Christianity is one branch, the heresy of the Gnostics of late antiquity was that they accepted the Transcendence of God but denied His Immanence — and this is indeed a real heresy, by which I mean that it is simply not true. But it *is* certainly true, given the truncated cosmology to which it properly applies, that God transcends the fallen order of perception known as "the Darkness of This World," a counterfeit universe of deluded powers and power-based delusions.

THE REINCARNATION THING

So the whole period between my return from Canada and the advent of Jenny — or maybe between that return and our entry into Santa Venetia Presbyterian Church — was in some ways the pit of my life. I was excessively liminal. I had been given access to in a vast amount of *potential* but lacked the necessary *form* to actualize it — which is another way of saying that, partly due to alcoholism and drug use, I was too involved with the psyche and not sufficiently centered in the Spirit. When one's outlook is generally more psychic than Spiritual, the inherent multiplicity of the psychic world is often dramatized in terms of "memories" of former lifetimes. So it might be right to say that the *moksha* (Liberation) or *bodhi* (Enlightenment) that the dharmic religions of Hinduism and Buddhism envision partly as the *ending* of reincarnation, as liberation from the Wheel of Birth and Death, represents (or includes) an ascent from the psychic level to the Spiritual level. When your life is partially disintegrated, filled with cracks and fissures and with no clear direction — as so many people's lives are nowadays — it is "natural" to begin to think in terms alternative selves, past and future lifetimes. If the present self and the present life don't seem to be working out, maybe you should begin to surf the available channels until a more congenial self and/or life can be located. And the notion of "former lifetimes" also seems to answer the question of *why* a particular soul is destined to confront the specific evils and temptations and opportunities it must encounter in life: it's all in response to the wise or foolish choices, the good or bad intentions, that "you" enacted in a former lifetime. But since that lifetime is conceived of as the product of the karma generated in an even earlier lifetime, you are ultimately stuck with an infinite causal regression that really doesn't answer the central question—the question of "*why me?*" This is the question that Job was commanded to ask, only to be confronted by a tremendous parade of mysteries whose meanings were hidden from him (at least initially) under the terrible Majesty of God. In the last analysis, that question can only be answered by faith—the faith that God knows best, and that the unfathomable goodness of the Almighty moves in ways that are not our ways—though we must never forget that faith, as "virtual gnosis," is "the substance of things hoped for, the evidence of things not seen." The contemporary stories of Near Death Experiences we hear so often today generally give a simpler answer: that before we were born we all agreed to undergo these trials for the good of our souls—though I tend to see stories of such pre-birth memories as symbolic fables designed to dramatize the mysterious union between individual free will and God's eternal decree, in that primordial "time" before we came into the realm of existence. However—short of the kind of faith which accepts that all God does is good—the question as to why a particular soul needs a particular trial to realize that good inevitably takes us into areas where the *idea* of reincarnation, or at least something closely resembling it, presents itself as one possible answer: an answer that is clearly inadequate, but one that seems, at least at a certain point, to be inescapable.

According to René Guénon, the belief in reincarnation is nothing but a misunderstanding of a reality known as *metempsychosis*. I am not "really" somebody else inside, some deceased person from the past—any more than that deceased person was really me inside all along—nor am I destined to turn into some new, third, as-yet-unknown person after I die. Each of these three persons, even if we happen to discern some sort of connecting link between them, was, is and always will be a separate individual, unique and never-to-be-repeated.

Speaking for myself, I have been able to remember at least two apparent former lifetimes. One was as a second-rate, drug-addicted "beatnik" jazz musician, probably a saxophone player, who died young from an overdose; the other was an SS officer assigned to the personal staff of Adolf Hitler at the Berghoff near Berchtesgaden. Not a very distinguished lineage to say the least! When I told my one-time reiki practitioner, who also does past-life regressions or akashic records readings, about my Nazi lifetime, her response was, "But you're nothing like that!"

Precisely. And the reason why I am nothing like that is because what we are dealing with here is not reincarnation, but metempsychosis.

Metempsychosis is "psychic inheritance." Just as we inherit our physical traits from our ancestors via DNA, so we also inherit psychic "material" from various people who have passed on: tendencies, interests, skills, dilemmas, weaknesses, strengths, even memories. If a friend or relative passes away, he might will me some of his possessions, such as his library or various articles of his clothing—but even though I may wear the clothes of my deceased friend, or even re-configure my mind by reading his books, this will certainly not lead me to believe (unless I am mentally ill) that I actually *am* him. Likewise I may inherit memories, knowledge, and various other psychophysical configurations from deceased persons I've never met. This inheritance may be from people who died before I was born, but it can also come to me from people who happen to pass away during my lifetime on earth; I may inherit these psychic tendencies at birth, or at any time during my earthly life. And these psychic inheritances come to us not simply as blessings or curses, "good karma" or "bad karma," but as *tasks* given us to accomplish for the development and edification of our souls. Indications are, in other words, that the psychic tendencies represented by the SS officer and the junky jazz musician were passed to me so they could be transmuted and purified.

The first evidence of my "beatnik lifetime" was the interesting fact that, from as soon as I was able to talk (I was born in 1948), I started calling my entirely "straight" and middle class parents, for no discernible reason, "Mommy-o and "Daddy-o," this being the common beatnik slang for "Mother" and "Father." Later on, possibly around the age of 14 (I don't remember exactly), when I was visiting my Aunt Barbara in her house in Beverly Hills soon after the death of her husband Charles from brain cancer, and while listening to some piece of music on the radio that I can't now identify, I remembered my beatnik life.

The evidence of my "Nazi lifetime" was more striking. As a child I created a monogram or symbol for myself—I called it my "insignia"—which consisted of an angular "S," like one-half of the quasi-runic double-S symbol in the insignia of Hitler's Schutzstaffel—the SS. This S was intersected by a horizontal line and surrounded by a circle, which made it look like a cross between an SS standard and a swastika. Maybe this can be partly explained by the angular S that appeared on the uniform of the character "Sparky" in a children's radio program of the time, "Big John and Sparky." Sparky was a sprightly elf dressed in a semi-military uniform who had been Big John's ventriloquist dummy in an earlier, pre-radio incarnation. For some reason I called the S on his costume, which I must have seen on some piece of merchandise related to the radio show (I recently confirmed the existence of such items via Google Images) the "Space S," thereby doubling the S as if to echo "SchutzStaffel." More telling, however, is the fact that I named a particular large rock, visible from the dining room window of my childhood home on the shores of San Francisco Bay, "the Eagle's Nest." It was only in 2012 or 2013 that, after realizing that Hitler had named the retreat built on the rocky mountain above his Berghoff villa near Berchtesgaden "the Eagle's Nest," that I searched for images of it on Google—and discovered that one view of the knoll on which the retreat was perched was nearly identical in appearance to the rock of my childhood—the same general shape, the same gray color, the same bunched, uneven texture, though of course on a much larger scale.

The notion that I might somehow be the "reincarnation" of a Nazi SS officer gained further credence in my mind from a dream that the diminutive elfin astrologer I mentioned in the last chapter had about me while I was living in that single bare room in Canada. One night this evanescent personage dreamed that I was a Nazi hiding out in the Himalayas disguised as a guru, a holy man; at that time I had not yet come to the intuition of my "Nazi lifetime." (One is reminded here of the various Nazi excursions to Tibet to find the "Asian Aryans," and of SS officer Heinrich Harrer, author of *Seven Years in Tibet*—the book that was made into a movie of the same name starring Brad Pitt—who escaped from POW confinement in India when World War Two broke out, and ultimately traveled by foot with a companion all the way to Tibet to become a friend and confidante of the present Dalai Lama.)

Furthermore, the idea of the Himalayas suggests a third possible "past lifetime," a Tibetan one. As a child I had believed that my mother's dresser, which featured a decoration of deep maroon curtains below the table-top, was home to a dragon. This dresser was also associated in my mind with a particular, distinctive smell—an imagined or remembered smell, since the dresser itself had no scent. It was only after I attended one of my first Tibetan Buddhist rituals, conducted by lamas dressed in the exact color of the curtains of my mother's dresser, that I encountered that very same smell in "real life"; it was the smell of Tibetan incense. In addition, that Bay Area psychic healer I had patronized soon after my return to California from British Columbia had, as you'll remember, given the name of one of my spirit-guides as "Tili." This name meant nothing at all to me at the time—until the moment when, driving home from the meditation retreat at The Tail of the Tiger in Colorado, where I'd met Trungpa, to California with some of Trungpa's disciples, I told them the story of the healer and the spirit-guide, in response to which one of my companions informed me that "Tili is another name for the Indian tantric yogi Tilopa, the founder of the Kargyüpa Lineage [Trungpa's tradition], the guru of Naropa," Naropa being the Indian Buddhist Mahasiddha who flourished at the great Buddhist university of Nalanda and acted as guru to Marpa the

Translator, who was instrumental in bringing Indian tantric Buddhism to Tibet. Marpa himself was guru to the pre-eminent Tibetan yogi, Milarepa. So this whole Tibetan Buddhist development, with all its attendant signs and wonders, apparently represented a possible spiritual Path for me that never fully materialized — one that was ultimately replaced, in 1988, by the Sufi Path — a radical change-of-orientation that had been clearly announced in "the Dream of My Life" (as recounted above in *Chapter One*) which had come to me when I was about 5 years old, and was powerfully reinforced by the vision I had of myself as a Muslim woodcutter in some place like Tibet — which, if you will remember, had come to me during the Black Crown Ceremony conducted by the 16th Gyalwa Karmapa, Trungpa's spiritual superior, in 1974.

That's the totality of the "evidence" — but evidence of what? Had I actually been an SS officer, a junky jazz musician and a Tibetan yogi in "former lifetimes"? The first fact that argues against this explanation is that the jazz musician would've had to have been a younger contemporary of the SS officer; he could not have been one of that officer's "future lifetimes." And there remains, of course, the fact that my core values in this life have been as different from those of an SS officer as can be imagined — although, as a card-carrying hippie, I certainly could have been imagined, at least for a while, as the reincarnation of a beatnik junky. As for Tibetan Buddhism, it was as if my interrupted attraction to it represented an influence that *would have* manifested as an apparently "reincarnational" connection with Kargyüpta Lineage *if I had opted to avail myself of that particular "past life."* But since I chose not to become attached to Tibetan Buddhism in this life, the result was (paradoxically enough) that I never actually had been a Tibetan yogi in a former lifetime, whereas if I had chosen to go with Trungpa, then that former lifetime would legitimately have been "mine" via metempsychosis. The implication here is that all possible pasts and futures are projected from Now and return to Now. Once there is an ego, the antecedent causes and future potentials of that ego are projected in both directions throughout time, which is why the dissolution of that ego is also the end of reincarnation: freedom from the Wheel of Birth and Death.

What specific life-tasks or "karmic assignments" did I inherit from a junky jazz musician, from an SS officer, and (most likely) from a Tibetan yogi? As for the jazz musician, it has turned out that one of my major life-tasks has been to become involved with American Bohemia — with the Beat Generation, the '60s counterculture, alcohol, psychedelic drug-use, the world of poetry, the world of art — and then, over quite a few years, to struggle free of that world and the psycho-social mind-sets that defined it, so I could work to redeem certain real spiritual values from that realm of experience and transplant them to a higher plane.

So it's as if I inherited the condition, the subtle material design, which that junky jazz musician left behind when he died—not as a *fate* (though it might have been that if I had never awakened to it and put it to work), but as a *task*. In other words, one task I chose, or was given, as I entered this life was: to collect the insights available to the American Bohemian psyche and life-style, purify them of negative elements, and dedicate them to spiritual and metaphysical realization. And there is no question but that my mentor, Lew Welch, who died an alcoholic suicide, was desperately, fatally dedicated to the same task, possibly more so than any other member of his generation, because he knew that the completion of that task was, literally, the only way he could save his life. He—a great athletic runner in high school—got half the way there, passed the baton to me, then collapsed from exhaustion. It was the *tasks* of that junky musician and that Beat poet—the tasks, not the destinies—that came to me, one from before birth and one during this life, as aspects of my own chosen and destined portion of the common human work: to return the soul of humanity, both individual and collective, to its Divine Source. That return is ultimately inevitable, but one of the aspects or stages of that inevitability is that it happens *through us*, through our spiritual labor, which includes the work of purifying the soul-material we have inherited from those who have passed on before us.

As for what I inherited from a Nazi officer, it undoubtedly had to do with my *dharma* in this life to apply spiritual energy to socio-political work. And it may well be that that poor deluded idealist attached to Hitler's personal staff at the Berghoff also dreamed, at least in his younger years, of pulling down lightning from heaven and using it to raise the demoralized German people to new spiritual heights. Unfortunately, the form into which he finally poured the projection of this aspiration was that of the sleek, Luciferian SS. Therefore his task, though possibly well-conceived, was in no way brought to a successful conclusion, but was devoured before completion by the Powers of Darkness. And so that potential passed to me to finish, in a hopefully more positive way. I worked on the purification of that influence and the completion of that unfinished work through two major life-tasks that you'll hear about further on: the Sanctuary Movement for Central American refugees, and the work of disseminating the Covenants of the Prophet Muhammad with the Christians of the World during the rise of ISIS. And if it's true that I inherited a further karmic assignment from a Tibetan yogi, that unfinished task was certainly taken up in all seriousness when I entered the Sufi path.

Seen from a slightly different perspective, it's as if the SS officer/junky jazz musician polarity were a projection, into the dimension of reincarnation, of the often bipolar quality of the poetic temperament—unless we call it, in my case, the actual origin of that temperament—particularly since the Nazis pioneered the use of methamphetamine in warfare, engineering a character-configuration that was diametrically opposed to that of a heroin-addicted saxophone player. In any case, my challenge here has been not to use the quality of one "lifetime" to compensate for the other — despair to sedate mad aspiration and aspiration to hide from despair — but to place both qualities together on the scales and so strike a balance by which it's possible to realize, remembering the words of my Catholic high school teacher Father Lacey, that "true pride and true humility are the same thing."

When I was a child maybe four years old, I used to have recurring dreams of something like a seismograph reading with an oscillating pen and a moving sheet of paper; the pen would swing faster and faster as some kind of tension built up inside me, then slack off as the tension eased. I associate these dreams with the basic discomfort I have generally felt with incarnate life on earth, and also with a streak of unregulated self-will lodged somewhere in my psyche that might have tended to violence if I hadn't sedated the pain it caused with various dissipations and a general attraction to low-energy states and situations, as symbolized by the SS officer vs. the junky jazz musician in my "past life memories," or the decaying darkened hallways vs. the glaring red room with the rifle-toting Sufis in my Lifetime Dream — a temporary strategy that definitely needed to be transcended at one point. My task has apparently been to transform the passive aspect of this polarity into submission to God's will and the active aspect into zeal in enacting His commands, which ultimately come down to the same thing. Like Jung said, God comes to us through our weakest function, not our strong points, our talents and accomplishments: He is reached not through triumph, but through the kind of spiritual poverty that shows us how much we need Him. It has taken me a lifetime to fully address this task, since that whole complex has been nearly too hot for me to handle in many ways. Self-will is a mysterious rats'-nest in any case; it doesn't just manifest as rebellion but can also appear as obsessive and prideful obedience. How much of my life have I spent trying to obey God's commands without His help, without asking for His help, without accepting His help, without admitting I needed His help? Real obedience lives far beyond the level of heroically kicking your own ass to further the Good; it is most at home in the place the Taoists call *wu wei*, "doing without doing." As Yeats expressed it in his poem "Among School Children":

> Labour is blossoming or dancing where
> The body is not bruised to pleasure soul,
> Nor beauty born out of its own despair,
> Nor blear-eyed wisdom out of midnight oil.

When Milarepa's disciples asked him (not noticing the contradiction in their question), "What great Bodhisattva or Mahasiddha were you in a past life that you were able to reach Enlightenment in a single lifetime?" he answered: "I have no idea. All I know is, the day came when I realized that my former practice of black magic had created such a mass of bad karma that I'd *better* reach Enlightenment in a single lifetime or my goose would be cooked." So Tibet's greatest yogi — at least on one occasion — apparently rejected the relatively exoteric idea of reincarnation for the more direct approach of seeking salvation and Enlightenment as if this present human incarnation were the only one we have to work with. Thinking in terms of past and future lifetimes dissipates your spiritual intent; thinking in terms who you are now, and what is required of you, concentrates it.

LEW WELCH, REINCARNATIONALLY RECONSIDERED

So I believe that *something* like reincarnation is real — but it's not what we usually think it is, not what it seems. And Lew Welch, interestingly enough, also apparently had an experience of "reincarnation in this life." He told me once that, during a serious illness (probably a drug overdose) he had had a vision of an orb of light with an oriental-looking face inside it that traveled up his reclining body until it dropped into him at the level of his navel and disappeared. This apparition was the origin of his figure the Red Monk (remembering that Tibetan lamas dress in dark red) that appears as a "commentator" in some of his poems. He said that he felt that he had literally been reborn through that experience, that he had a different soul inside his body now than the one he'd been born with.

So my ultimate karmic task, the one I inherited from Lew Welch through *metempsychosis in this life*, was something other than the writing of poetry. It had to do with self-transcendence, with "dying before you die." He expressed the challenge of that task, which he left incomplete when he committed suicide, in two questions:

HOW CAN I LEARN TO GET OUT OF MY WAY?

and:

The question only a German could ask:

"*How can I try not to try?*"

Lew defined and expressed this central human task, this universal metaphysical and existential dilemma, *perfectly* — a dilemma that, in its own terms, on its own level, is *perfectly* insoluble. In Volume Two of *I Remain*, his collected correspondence, in a letter to Robert Duncan that he never sent, Lew gives us his deepest and most revealing picture of this struggle for what, in his poem "THE ENTIRE SERMON BY THE RED MONK," he calls "the path of self-uninvention":

After the radiant vision of openness, yesterday, I saw myself a ring of bone in the clear stream, and vowed never, ever, to close myself again.

○ ○ ○

... [*earlier*] at Ferlinghetti's Big Sur cabin ... I got the most radiant vision of openness. I saw how this was all meaning. That I was only a mess of gates. That having Human Being is to have many many gates, that it *all* all flow through.

That it was right, too, that we have a Self. That it *all* be transformed. Different on the way out.

Magnificent! But then he says:

And all of this was so powerful my penis came erect, with no sex to it, as the old saying goes "putting your prick through the window, and fucking the world" with helpless love!

What is this? Some black satori?

For I cannot stay open to it. It hurts too much. But what is it that hurts?

○ ○ ○

For whatever it is that hurts. Whatever it is that needs to rest from time to time. Whatever it is that can be opened to the flow of it, or closed from pain.

This must be killed again and again!

The really tragic thing about the drowning and gunshots and the irreclaimable madnesses [*i.e., the breakdowns and suicides of so many poets*] is this:

They, Poets all of them, missed the truth by a quarter of an inch.

You do not have to do it with a gun. You really do not do it with a gun.

Though, lately, I begin to wonder how many more times I can kill this thing. Is he always going to grow? Will he always be that same shape? Is there some error to the way I keep doing it. Perhaps I try to come *back* from it, instead of resting on it, when I'm *through* with it ...

Ultimately Lew did miss the truth, by even less than a quarter of an inch. He missed it by exactly twenty-two one-hundredths of an inch: the width of a .22 caliber bullet.

In my opinion, the essence of Lew Welch's fatal dilemma, and ours, is that *I*—the ego—cannot uninvent itself, transcend itself, kill itself, since it must assert itself and maintain itself in the very act of trying to do away with itself. "How can I learn to get out of my way?" You can't. "How can I try not to try?" You can't. You can't kill the thing that closes and denies itself, or opens so wide it hurts, no matter how many times you try, no matter how many lifetimes you end with a single gunshot to the temple.

So Lew's main error was the notion that he had to do it all by himself, all by his little struggling ego alone. And he fell into this impossible contradiction for only one reason: because he couldn't deal with the belief in, or face the reality of, God. The only way you can try not to try is to realize that only God is the Doer. And the only way you can get out of own your way is to embark on the Way of Another. Unless you can accept the fact that Reality or God or Enlightenment—whatever you want to call it—is not something that *you* must struggle to create, but Something that is already there, beyond the borders of suffering and illusion, then the Buddha's challenge to "work out your own salvation with diligence"—which in the right context is the key to the whole spiritual life—is only a curse. As William Blake put it in his *Jerusalem*, addressing himself to the Reality that lies beyond the illusory ego:

> O Saviour, pour upon me thy Spirit of meekness & love:
> Annihilate the Selfhood in me, be Thou all my life!
> Guide Thou my hand, which trembles exceedingly
>   upon the Rock of Ages.

CHAPTER EIGHT
The Planet of Revolutionary Solidarity

THE NEXT MAJOR PHASE OF OUR LIVES AFTER our return to Marin County, namely our connection with Santa Venetia Presbyterian Church from 1983 to 1985, and our participation in the Sanctuary Movement for Central American refugees, was one of the most powerful, the most definitive, and the most complete of all the "planets" I have visited in this life. It summed up, and also ended, a lot that had gone before, and acted as an omen and an announcement of much that was yet to come—and yet there was an awful lot of *maya* in it. *Maya* is the most supremely ambiguous of all the Primal Powers. It's not simply illusion since it is nothing less than the Principle that manifests the Real. Yet even as it reveals Reality it simultaneously hides It, and the main way it hides It is by convincing you that it has finally and definitively revealed It. Our lives had apparently reached their True Form at last in Santa Venetia—yet as soon as that apotheosis was achieved, those supposedly perfected and fully actualized lives were suddenly revealed (if we were willing to look) as a theatrical performance produced and directed by the Mistress of Illusion Herself. Santa Venetia represented the most complete union in my life so far of the three potentials that were given to the Baby Boom to work out: Art, Religion and Politics. Yet because we had no stable idea of how to hierarchicalize them, our synthesis of them ultimately fell apart. Only if Religion is put first can Art and Politics truly serve—otherwise Art will become empty dissipation and Politics a dark and violent obsession. The problem was, we had only a very shaky idea of the what Religion was in and of itself. We had the Gospels, Liberation Theology and the Protestant social gospel tradition, but when it came to what Religion really is when placed in the ultimate crucible, the vessel where there is nothing in all the realm of existence but God and the human soul, we were woefully ignorant. We had religion, we had art, we had politics, but we had no idea how to rank them in a true order. Kierkegaard rightly put morality above aesthetics and spirituality above morality, which for us would have meant politics above art and religion above politics... but we couldn't do that because it was all religion as far as we were concerned; we were a church, weren't we?

It was in Santa Venetia that I came closer than ever before to making—or maybe "receiving" would be a better word—directly through the medium of love, of *agape*, a true synthesis between spirituality and social action. But exactly what kind of "love" was it? It presented itself as deeper and more willing to face reality than the thin, sex-charged, drug-based, music-inspired "love" of so many of the hippies — though they too had their serious side — since we who espoused it were attracted to self-sacrifice and possibly even martyrdom, like Martin Luther King and others had suffered in the Civil Rights Movement, though with another part of ourselves we knew such outcomes weren't very likely. But did we really love each other, or were we just having the greatest fun of our lives? Because that was never really tested, I can never know for sure; like the French poet Pierre Reverdy said, "There is no such thing as love, only proofs of love." The Salvadoran peasants and refugees we were dedicated to defending certainly weren't having anywhere near as much fun as we were... and there is no doubt in my mind that I myself was attracted to at least the *idea* of political martyrdom in those years because I had not yet come to a true spiritual and mystical conception of Christ's declaration that "He who seeks to retain his life will lose it, but he who loses his life, for My sake, will find it" — something that I only began to see in its true light when I came to an understanding of the Sufi doctrine of *fana'* and *baqa'*: Annihilation of one's separateness and eternal Subsistence in Allah. If submission to the Will of God and dedication to the Straight Path result in corporeal martyrdom, then so be it — and yet the greatest willingness to suffer for a cause can never produce, or equal, the willingness to be annihilated in God, because the former is a choice of the ego while the latter is a gift of the All-Merciful.

But before I plunge too deeply into the Santa Venetia experience, and into our passage through the wider world of Leftist revolutionary politics, I need to review certain phases of the history, both individual and collective, that delivered us to its door.

OUR FIRST HOUSE

Our connection with Santa Venetia Presbyterian Church, as well as with the peace movement in Marin County and the greater Bay Area in the 1980s, was made possible because our lives had reached a greater level of stability in our new home. It was a small, one-bedroom place with no garage, but beautifully designed by my grandmother to make the most of the limited space. It had a little patio with a brick fireplace outside the kitchen window, a lemon tree in the front yard, a plum tree in the back whose fruit we could pick from a window in the bedroom, and from the living room a beautiful view of Mt. Tamalpais, plus a big acacia tree in the grassy vacant lot next to us that was part of our property — a tree where I used to play as a child. The acacias of California, leguminous trees like the eastern locust, blossomed in the Spring with masses of fuzzy little flower-heads, brilliant yellow. They were not native but grew wild by that time throughout coastal Marin. The house was warm and welcoming with the spirit of my grandmother, as if pouring in through some invisible door from a place that was clearly more than memory. The walls and the floors glowed with her presence.

It was during our stay in that house that we worked as housecleaners for the overworked homeowners of Marvelous Marin, through which role we saw into the some of darker and more repressed corners of the Marin County psyche, relieved from time to time by momentary flashes of light. Our clients ranged from the Buddhist teacher Jack Kornfield at the top of the scale, down to Betty Ellett around the middle, a retired radio personality from the South whose major mark of distinction was that she "knew Goober" from the old Andy Griffith TV show; and finally ending up in the dens of various well-to-do Marin County witches who were pure hell on earth. One of the unfortunate dynamics we encountered was that as soon as we would familiarize ourselves with a particular house enough to do a good job cleaning it, the part-time housewife we worked for would become jealous of our intimacy with the home she hadn't quite been able to fully occupy, translate that jealousy into suspicion, and ultimately fire us.

It turned out that the section of San Rafael where Betty Ellett lived was Santa Venetia, host to the church where the next major phase of our lives would be set. Santa Venetia was a semi-depressed area that also contained the Marin County Civic Center, that futuristic building designed by Frank Lloyd Wright that has appeared in at least one sci-fi film. The Center was laid out more-or-less like the Starship Enterprise with the Marin County Library, in which I worked for some years, occupying the "saucer section." But the area surrounding it, far from basking in its reflected glow, fell instead into the shadow of it. Why is it that the skid rows of so many American cities lie in such close proximity to City Hall? Is it just to make it easier for the cops to reach their monthly arrest quota, or for those on welfare to receive their monthly dole? If the United States of America were a true democracy, the centers of power would radiate empowerment and validation into their immediate environments instead of draining those qualities so as to establish their own power and validity by contrast with the surrounding lowlife—as witness the depressing fact that one of the worst skid rows of all is nearly the whole city of Washington D.C. Likewise so many colleges nowadays will radiate an energy of stupidity, so many churches an aura of sin. "Prisons are built with stones of law, brothels with bricks of religion" said William Blake.

RUNNING OUT THE SANDS OF LIMINALITY: THE GHOST OF LEW WELCH

The history of Santa Venetia Presbyterian Church and the Sanctuary Movement for Central American refugees will be coming soon, but first I need to tell the story of the tail end of the most liminal period of my life, where I was required to finish up my interaction with the ghost of Lew Welch. While we were living in that trailer in Olema I had tried to track down Lew in what was undoubtedly the other world; after we moved into my grandmother's house, he started trying to get through to me.

Lew Welch, like many poets of the Beat/Hippie era, sometimes thought of himself as a magician, an identification that usually grew up when the poet in question was failing in either his or her art or his or her life. And undoubtedly his most successful magic act was to conjure up a posthumous cult for himself, so as to mystify and glamourize what was, after all, just one more sordid alcoholic suicide. As we have seen above, he did this through a poem entitled "SONG OF THE TURKEY BUZZARD," which was his poetic suicide note; the poem, which came in answer to the third of his three spiritual riddles, "THE RIDER RIDDLE," is basically a way of finding your helping spirit in the form of a "totem" animal or plant; the riddle goes like this:

> If you spend as much time on the Mountain as you should,
> she will always give you a Sentient Being to ride: animal,
> plant, insect, reptile, or any of the Numberless Forms:
>
> What do *you* ride?
>
> (There is one right answer for every person, and only
> that person can really know what it is.)

"The Mountain" was Mt. Tamalpais. Lew asked this riddle of himself and, though he wanted "Cougar" more than anything, he got "Turkey Buzzard" instead. In "SONG OF THE TURKEY BUZZARD," he says:

> The rider riddle is easy to ask
> But the answer might surprise you.
>
> How desperately I wanted Cougar
> (I, Leo, etc.)
>   brilliant proofs: terrain,
> color, food, all
> nonsense. All made up.
>
> > *They were always there, the
> > laziest high-fliers, bronze-winged,
> > the silent ones.*
>
> o o o
>
> Hear my last Will & Testament:
>
> Among my friends there shall always be
> one with proper instructions
> for my continuance.
>
> > *Let no one grieve.
> > I shall have used it all up
> > used up every bit of it.
> > What an extravagance!
> > What a relief!*

> On a marked rock, following his orders,
> place my meat.
>
> > *All care must be taken not to*
> > *frighten the natives of this*
> > *barbarous land, who*
> > *will not let us die, even*
> > *as we wish.*
>
> With proper ceremony disembowel what I
> no longer need, that it might more quickly
> rot and tempt
>
> my new form

So the buzzards will eat Lew's guts and that's how he will be "reincarnated" as a Buzzard God. Lew's meat, in dying, will achieve new life as buzzard meat. That's all there was to it.

As an American Buddhist, and also as someone with an appreciation for *The White Goddess* of Robert Graves, Lew tended toward a simple materialistic nature-worship, intermittently relieved by the supernaturalism of the Tibetans and the preternaturalism of W. B. Yeats and Carlos Castaneda. So how does a materialist conceive of immortality—apart, that is, from the ministrations of transhumanism and cryogenics? Lew's way was to opt for what is called "poetic immortality," which is essentially *immortality in the memory of the living*. But he went a step further. I believe that Lew Welch also wanted to be *held in a stable form and a conscious state after death* by that same memory. That's why he founded his Buzzard Cult. He wanted to trap and hold the attention of the living after his death so as to maintain his identity—something he undoubtedly also did during life. When the Mexicans, on the Day of the Dead, put tortillas and tequila on the graves of the departed, they are doing the same thing. They are trying to keep the dead "alive" as ghosts—well-fed ghosts who will hopefully be satisfied enough not to vampirize the living. Lew, however, may ultimately have been unable to avoid the vampire trip, as witness at least two copycat suicides I certainly know of, those of Jack Boyce—an "accidental" death that was undoubtedly suicidal in intent—and "Burl," a sleepy, sodden youth who attached himself to Magda after Lew disappeared, and who ultimately jumped off the Golden Gate Bridge. But what is kept "alive" by the psychic energy of the living is not the actual spirit of the departed, but only the ghostly residue of the unredeemed psyche—in other words, the *ego*: the original vampire. In the words of W. B. Yeats, from "All Souls' Night," Lew ultimately wanted to be one who had

> ...a ghost's right
> His element is so fine
> Being sharpened by his death

> To drink from the wine-breath
> While our gross palates drink from the whole wine.

That *is* a pretty classy-sounding afterlife—until you actually get there and see what it's like. And the saddest thing is, so many of us (including myself) "bought" the Buzzard Cult. Whenever we'd see a turkey buzzard sail over, we'd say, "there goes Lew." The Buzzard Cult allowed us to deny *everything*: that Lew, by his suicide, had demonstrated at least some pretty serious flaws in his spiritual life; that all those glamourous bohemian death-trips were nothing but simple despair after all; that we too needed love, and to give love, but had despaired of ever finding it, had given up on it so long ago we couldn't even remember it, despite all the counterculture propaganda of the Beatles and so many others, their wan, pastel mewing about "love is all you need." (It wasn't love we were singing about, it was only sex... and ultimately it wasn't even sex we were singing about, it was only pornography, only *images*—"sexual" or "spiritual" as you will.) Lew trained us to seek inflated glamour instead of true love—love, of course, being "romantic," "unhip," something requiring a degree of basic un-self-flattering humility, some grain of genuine, sincere, unglamourous humanity—which Lew finally descended to (thank God) in his late poem "TO MAGDA." But how Philistine, how Bourgeois it must've seemed, at least to a part of him. How beneath the Pride of the Lion! And how bleak and terrible the foreboding, in the craw of the glamour-addict, of the Cold Turkey to come, the terminal deadness of reality without all that psychic glamour to keep it hopping. To endure that deadness without looking away—this being the essential skill and function of "the salt of the earth"—is the sole key to the renewal of life, that and a basic faith in God, an understanding that Reality, in Lew's words, "goes on whether I look at it or not." In Shakespeare's *The Merchant of Venice*, the portrait of Portia, Bassanio's beloved, is found in the leaden casket, not the gold or silver ones. Only the heavy lead of necessary limitation—found, accepted, lived with, and finally loved—can be transmuted into the Alchemical Gold.

Nonetheless Lew's informal but unaccountably powerful "initiation" of me had a profound effect on my spiritual life, both positive and negative—and even its negative aspects were not without their uses and insights. His death, tragic as it was and filled with spiritual darkness, nonetheless helped put me consciously in touch with the next world, and not only in a negative way.

In his book *Axe Handles*, Gary Snyder has a poem entitled "For/From Lew":

> Lew Welch just turned up one day,
> Live as you and me. "Damn, Lew" I said,
> "you didn't shoot yourself after all."
> "Yes I did" he said,

> and even then I felt the tingling down my back.
> "Yes you did, too — I can feel it now."
> "Yeah," he said,
> "There's a basic fear between your world and
> mine. I don't know why.
> What I came to say, was,
> Teach the children about the cycles.
> The life cycles. All the other cycles.
> That's what it's all about, and it's all forgot."

I'm virtually certain that this poem was based on a dream of Lew that Gary had. (Gary Snyder is one of the best, if not *the* best, dream-poets in the English language.) Around the time it was probably written, and certainly before I read it, I also had a dream about Lew, which resulted in the following poem; the last four lines of it were dictated, word for word, in the dream itself:

> I saw the Sun built up in the distance, like a temple on a plain
> Animals crashing through forests inside its face:
> And my dead teacher, seated, on the orbit of the Earth,
> Musing on his old love the Earth and Sun,
> And allowing himself, sadly,
> To forget it.
>
>> *This is the age when all stories have been told*
>> *The dead going on without poetry,*
>> *And poetry telling them the*
>> *Truth of gravity's art.*

I believe that these two poems are parts of the same "message" from Lew. For him to be sitting on the orbit of the earth in my dream is also a reference to "cycles," but with a different twist — more like the Buddhist "wheel of existence" that the Buddha is no longer whirled around by because he's now sitting at the center of it, with the universe turning around him — like the *Qutb* of the Sufis, the pre-eminent saint of the age, who is known as the Pole.

Many people had "visions of" or "meetings with" Lew after he disappeared. Stories of his reappearance abounded — but, in the long run, none of them panned out. Tony Dingman wrote a poem about the posthumous Lew Welch that took off from the line "I went Southwest" from the suicide note that Lew left at Gary Snyder's place (the prose one, not "SONG OF THE TURKEY BUZZARD," which is the poetic one), and plotted a line on the globe stretching Southwest from there, imagining Lew as turning up at many of the points along that line, in many lands.

Lew "appeared to" or "contacted" me as well. On one occasion, after Jenny and I had moved back to Marin County, I felt a maddening psychophysical vulnerability, like an ice pick to the base of my skull; I had to cover that area with my hands to prevent my consciousness from becoming totally scattered. Under the command of that sensation I drove with Jenny to the grounds of Indian Valley College in Novato, where the buildings were set in a wooded area, largely uncleared. Walking through those woods we heard a noise that sounded like the breathy hiss of a Cougar—a real possibility, though a rare one, in that country—after which I saw a large feather on the ground. I bent down and picked it up. It was a Buzzard feather. After returning home with it and smoking a joint, I decided (because I didn't want to retain a "talisman" that would connect me to wherever Lew was now, and because I have never been able, for some reason, to hold on to magical objects), to burn it in our fireplace so as to send it back where it came from; and when I did, I saw an image of him in the glowing coals and heard his voice saying: "Things don't change here as fast as I thought they would." (LORE NOTE: The base of the skull, known in acupuncture as the Jade Pillow, is the door to the psychic world, the kingdom of the Jinn, whereas the *brahmarandhra*, the Aperture of Brahma at the crown of the skull, is the door to the celestial world, the Angelic Hierarchy.)

This is the wages of the Buzzard Cult. Lew had thought that our attention to him after his death would keep him in quasi-human form and save him from "the second death," but all it really did (maybe, maybe) was imprison him in a kind of twilight zone, a darkened Limbo where spiritual progress is excruciatingly slow. If so, it would have been better if we'd done what we could to turn him loose—and holding on to a false, idealistic memory of the "great teacher" when we should have been praying for the Liberation of a despairing soul in torment was not the way to do it. Lew *was* a great teacher in many ways, but if his students are ever going to *matriculate* we will have to confront his last, and toughest, lesson: that who you think you are plus who other people think you are is nothing but pure illusion.

After I burned that first feather, Lew sent me a "replacement" during another hike in the woods, which I sent to that Dzogchen lama in Nepal I've already mentioned, asking for his prayers for the posthumous Liberation from the wilderness of the *bardo* of the consciousness-principle of Lewis Barrett Welch, my first true spiritual teacher.

THE LONG ROAD TO SACRED ACTIVISM: A RETROSPECTIVE

The Catholic writer Charles Péguy once wrote: "Everything begins in mysticism and ends in politics." Be that as it may, mysticism and politics were the poles between which the current of my post-WWII Baby Boom generation—or at least the "counterculture" sector of it—primarily flowed. And it was at Santa Venetia Presbyterian Church that the biggest spark to date leapt across the potential difference between those two poles, the only bigger spark being the one that sparked the Covenants Initiative that lasted from 2013 till 2019, based on the research of Dr John Andrew Morrow into the Covenants of the Prophet Muhammad with the Christians of his time; you'll hear about that particular exploit in *Chapter Twelve*.

As I've already made clear, my entire formal education consisted of 14 years in Catholic school, from nursery school and kindergarten through high school, mostly in the Roman Catholic Church as it was before Vatican II. Around 1966, however — as recounted in *Chapter Two* — my identification with Catholicism began to wane, just as the traditional Church and its sacred sacramental order were being deconstructed, though at the time I was not entirely conscious of these developments. Nonetheless I expressed my feelings about them in *Panic Grass* [1968]:

> Despair! Christ has burst your churches and
> cracked your tabernacles wide,
> and the Glory of God has fled into the mountains!

As already recounted in Chapters *Three* and *Four*, the pole of mysticism in the late 1960s was best represented by the *dharmic* religions of Asia, Hinduism and Buddhism — or at least those aspects of them that survived importation into the West — the practice of which involved yoga, meditation, and veneration of the *guru*, though we promiscuously mixed these influences with Shamanism (primarily Native American), Spiritualism, occultism, magic, the quest for psychic powers, and every non-traditional "spirituality" under the sun. Western Christian, Jewish and Sufi mysticism also played a part, though their influence was less central. And of course the whole mass was energized, and rendered increasingly chaotic, by the liberal use of LSD and other psychedelics.

The '60s were the decade when the post-WWII civil rights movement, the growing popular interest in mystical spirituality, and the protest movement against the Vietnam War met and cross-pollinated. From, say, 1967 through the early '70s, the dominant expression of the activist pole of Péguy's dyad was the anti-war movement. To the people of my age group, late teens to early twenties — at least those of the hippie persuasion — this movement was more or less taken for granted as part of the *zeitgeist*. We would show up at riots and anti-war demonstrations in much the same spirit as we attended spiritual gatherings or rock concerts; they were simply part of the "scene," and we were hell-bent on making that scene. Our older compatriots, particularly those with backgrounds in the civil rights movement, were often better-trained as serious activists, and tended to follow either various schools of Marxism, or else the non-violent resistance theories and tactics of Mohandas K. Gandhi and Martin Luther King. But I and my contemporaries in Marin County, California were little more than hangers-on. In most cases our "commitment" involved little study of political theory or training in the tactics of protest, nor did it (in most cases) grow out of any real personal insight based on serious thought or struggle. The military draft was enough to "radicalize" us, and the protest songs of the era were all the "theory" we felt we needed.

However, since we were attending anti-war demonstrations, patronizing the teachers to be found on the guru circuit, and dropping thermonuclear acid, it was natural that we would begin to ask ourselves how mysticism and politics might be brought together in a single practice. Allen Ginsberg and others had introduced such notions as intoning "OM" during demonstrations, in order to spread "waves of peace" and generally empower the movement whose operative word was — peace. So it was probably inevitable that the polarity between the radical encounter with Reality with a capital R provided by LSD (sometimes at least, and not without many subtle delusions and negative consequences), and the various forms of militant collective blindness we were sworn to work against (though also sometimes forced to participate in), would posit a "dialectic" of sorts. *Thesis*: "Everything is possible!" *Antithesis*: "Nothing is possible; history is an unstoppable juggernaut." *Synthesis*—?: (We'll have to get back to you on that one—in this life or the next.)

For me and my emerging peer-group, the San Francisco poets, the 1970s was a decade of introversion. The "consciousness" explosion of the '60s was subsiding, leaving depression in its wake. Alcohol increasingly became the drug of choice, though not to the degree (heaven forbid) that it crowded out all the other drugs. Feminism was turning a cold fire-hose on the hippie love-fest, generally pooping the party; at the same time that the identity of "poet," at least for our social sector, was partly replacing the identity of "hippie." When I first met Lew Welch in the late 1960s, poets were few and far between—a handful of the Beats and a few of their younger protégés, such as myself, John Oliver Simon, David Meltzer, etc. A few years later there were an estimated five thousand poets in the Bay Area, whose collective efforts in the name of self-advertisement—as well as the apparent belief that anyone who knew how to talk was therefore virtually a poet, so serious study of the art of poetry and artistry in the practice of it be damned—was one of the factors that has made poetry almost a hated art in this country. As the Marxist/leftist poets pursued their course with the help of Pablo Neruda, Cesar Vallejo and other "poets of resistance," we "deep image" poets were studying the Jungians, and devouring all the mythopoesis we could get our hands on of whatever historical era—Joseph Campbell was a big influence at this point—seeing it largely through Jungian eyes. In the terminology of the *Bardo Thödöl* (the *Tibetan Book of the Dead*), the 1970s were "the *bardo* of seeking rebirth," the collective attempt to return to something like a human form by sweeping up the dead leaves of the soul we'd shed along the road, after LSD and the cosmic melodrama of the 1960s had blown us to the four winds.

The fitting end to this era was the Iranian Revolution of 1979, which foreshadowed a return to politics with a vengeance, and heralded an era in which ideologized religion would become more central to political struggle, in the western world and the world as a whole, than it had been (perhaps) at any time since the Reformation and the Thirty Years' War. (Significantly enough, the Nicaraguan Revolution took place in the same year.) The churches had already become deeply involved in the anti-war movement of the 1960s, a development that was well represented in the Catholic world by various "radical priests" like the Berrigan brothers and by the tradition of Dorothy Day and the Catholic Workers movement; in the Evangelical Protestant world by Martin Luther King, the Sojourners community and others; and in Quakerism by the American Friends Service Committee, whose main focus in the '60s had been support for conscientious objectors to the military draft. In the 1980s, these various expressions of the North American "social gospel" tradition coalesced and gained a new impetus through the movement of solidarity with the revolutions of Nicaragua, El Salvador and Guatemala, and the struggle to block large-scale U.S. intervention against them.

The theoretical context for the peace movement of the 1980s was provided by Liberation Theology, which arose, mostly in Latin America, through a cross-pollination between radical leftist politics and the post-Vatican II Catholic Church. The central ideologues of this movement included Gustavo Gutierrez, Juan Luis Segundo, Dom Helder Camara, Leonardo Boff, and Ernesto Cardenal, Catholic priest and poet, whose three-volume book of dialogues, *The Gospel in Solentiname*, was an important influence. Father Cardenal, who later became the Minister of Culture of Nicaragua under the Sandinistas, had a parish on an island in an archipelago in Lake Nicaragua; his congregation was made up mostly of the local fishermen and women. But due to his international reputation as a poet and Marxist/Catholic intellectual, his parish became a place of pilgrimage for intellectuals, artists and revolutionaries from many parts of the world. Cardenal organized dialogues between the peasants, the local activists and the visiting intellectuals, who together began to develop a Theology of Liberation which was equally a creation of the intelligentsia and the uneducated poor—a very interesting development in both political and cultural terms.

In the mid-1980s, Liberation Theology appeared to my wife Jenny and myself as a viable way to unite religion (if not mysticism) and politics; we responded by joining Santa Venetia Presbyterian Church, a small missionary church under the authority of the Presbytery of the Redwoods, that was to become active in the Sanctuary Movement for Central American refugees, along with many of the local Catholic churches, as well as the Liberal "mainstream" Protestants. The pastor, Carolyn Studer, aspired to participate in the Sanctuary Movement, so she "packed" the Session (governing board) of her church with activist insurgents—us. This caused a few members of the congregation to leave, but most accepted this development in good faith. (This was a better outcome than was experienced by many churches that went through the same sort of "imposed radicalization" process in the 1980s, which often led to serious splits in the congregations involved.) Consequently Jenny and myself remain lifetime elders of the United Presbyterian Church. [NOTE: "Santa Venetia" is the name of no Christian saint, but rather of a housing development in San Rafael, built around some tideland sloughs, which a developer in earlier decades had tried to market as a kind of "Venice by the Bay," though I can't imagine any place on earth that looks less like Venice. Nonetheless a real Italian, Frank Sinatra, once owned 539 acres of land abutting Santa Venetia that later became part of China Camp State Park.]

The precipitating events for the Sanctuary Movement included the murder of three American Maryknoll nuns in El Salvador for the crime of working to improve the lot of the peasants, and the assassination of Archbishop Oscar Romero—who had begun to denounce the government-led Salvadoran death-squads—by death-squad killers while he was saying Mass in a hospital chapel. I wrote a poem about Romero's assassination that was published in the Catholic *Maryknoll Magazine*.

The moral rationale for the Sanctuary Movement was as follows: Since it was well-known that the United States, with the help of the National War College, had provided training to the death squads, and that the terror in El Salvador was driving many Salvadoran from their country, we had a duty, both as Americans and as Christians, to protect those refugees who made it to the United States. The Salvadoran refugees, as illegal aliens, were considered to be criminals under federal law, so we resurrected the old tradition which held that criminals fleeing the civil authorities could be granted sanctuary in Christian churches, where they would remain exempt from arrest as long as they stayed on the church grounds. Not all the refugees we were working with lived on church property of course; nonetheless we invoked the spirit if not the letter of the old sanctuary rule to serve them.

POETS—AGAIN? (A DIGRESSION)

During this period my wife and I re-connected with the San Francisco poetry scene. The "Caucasian" poets of the Left were partnering with the Latino poets of the Bay Area—like Roberto Vargas, who later became the Nicaraguan ambassador to China—to express solidarity with the revolutions of Central America; the main centers for this political/cultural ferment were the Mission Cultural Center in San Francisco and La Peña Cultural Center in Berkeley. But before I tell the story of that re-connection, I need to depart again from the central time-line in order to ask some questions about what the spiritual essence of poetry might be, poetry in itself, and recount some history of our connection with the poetry world between the time of the death of Lew Welch in 1971 and our intense but brief identity as "cultural workers" in solidarity with the revolutions of Central America in the mid-1980s, and ending with a highly revealing episode that took place at the beginning of the 21st Century.

Ezra Pound once said: "Poets are the antennae of the race." It's been more my experience, however, that we are actually more like "the mine-canaries of the race," the ones who first pick up all the toxic influences and cultural diseases that will later spread throughout society; if the poet sitting next to you keels over, you'd better put on your mask and go into quarantine as soon as possible. As poets, our psychic immune-systems are in a generally weakened condition, something that is both an occupational hazard and a necessary element in the particular kind of sensitivity proper to the art. Those of us who survive our various infections with minds and bodies relatively intact will have built rare immunities — not to mention the fact that we sometimes become world-class social diagnosticians.

The pure quest for experience always involves what the Christians call "sin," which can be partially defined as the sort of action that relies on self-will and an unreflecting emotional attraction to various objects of desire, and therefore compromises our primal connection to the Source of our existence. Sin ultimately leads either to conscious repentance or to the conscious or unconscious denial of God. But can we really recognize sin without experience? The *shari'ah*, the Sacred Law of Islam, or any moral system based on Revelation, says that we can. Yet is not every saint, except for the rarest class of them, a repentant sinner? The Law does not absolve you of experience, of the pure quest of the ego for its own self-expression, but it does show you how to recognize that misguided and *errant* quest, even in actions that had once seemed entirely pure and un-self-interested. First the Law discovers sin, then the Remembrance of God absolves it — which is why the genre known as "Confessions of the Reformed Rake," like the one produced by St Augustine, will always have its place, seeing that sin, at least for most of us, seems to be a necessary step toward an understanding of what virtue is and a commitment to developing it. William Blake said, in his "Proverbs of Hell" from *The Marriage of Heaven and Hell*, "If the Fool would persist in his folly he would become Wise" — wise enough to leave that folly behind. He also said, "The Road of Excess leads to the Palace of Wisdom," simply because "You never know what is enough unless you know what is more than enough." "Hell" to Blake, at least in that fairly early poem from which these quotes are taken, was not the Kingdom of Evil but the Kingdom of Energy and Experience, which is why he said of his master John Milton, author of the great *Paradise Lost*—both of them born under the sign of Sagittarius, just as I was—that Milton was "a true poet, and of the Devil's party without knowing it." Goethe, in his *Faust*, the fundamental theological treatise on the Romantic spirit, was wrong to say that pure experience alone, whose patron and guide is the Devil himself, will lead to salvation *without repentance*, without the painstaking discovery of sin and the painful purification from the bonds of it. Likewise the surah "The Poets" of the Holy Qur'an tells us: *Shall I inform you upon whom the devils descend? They descend on every sinful, false one. They* [the sinners] *listen eagerly, but most of them* [both the sinners and the devils, the Jinn] *are liars. As for the poets, the erring follow them. Hast thou not seen how they stray in every valley, and how they say that which they do not? Save those who believe and do good works, and remember Allah much, and vindicate themselves after they have been wronged?* To *say* something but not *do* it is to extend the name and image of Reality into imaginative forms that one has neither the power, the integrity, nor the *right* to fully realize. It is to create phantasms, to go into debt to Reality Itself, and thereby to wrong oneself, sometimes mortally. Poetry is boast, only action is proof; to *know* more than you can *be* or *do* is to be ravished, and then sorely punished, by the Reality on whose ground you have trespassed without invitation, purely on the basis of arrogance and self-will. The poet who *vindicates* him- or herself after having inflicted great self-wrong is the one who has paid, with spiritual warfare and suffering, the debt he or she incurred when arrogantly claiming the power of Divine creative speech—speech whose function is *to say what is*—and has thereby become an honest human being. This is what it means to be "as good as your word."

Jenny and I essentially quit being public poets in December of 1979, right after we had a chance to read our poems along with Allen Ginsberg, Lawrence Ferlinghetti, Jack Hirschman, Peter Orlovsky, Jack Micheline and other luminaries and/or dim bulbs at the Savoy Tivoli cafe, North Beach, San Francisco—our 15 minutes of fame. We spoke for Beauty and for Romantic Love in Marriage, and were heckled for it—but no problem and no blame: we needed to see the clear line between where we were headed and the counterculture we were in the process of leaving, and so that line dutifully revealed itself. I appeared later for a few seconds in a "retrospective on the '70s" segment on one of the local network TV stations, without sound, making some emphatic silent point to Ginsberg after the event. And in the following years the poetry scene itself, that had been the prophetic voice of two generations, dwindled to an abbreviated, self-referential art ghetto; the relevance of poetry to the society as a whole that gave the Beats and the '60s counterculture poets (who mostly wrote song lyrics) their significance and their context became a thing of the past—so Jenny and I slowly moved on into other worlds.

In the 1980s however, before we had entirely faded from the scene, we took another pass through the poetry world as "poets of resistance," though not in as high profile a way as we had done when we were under the brief patronage of the Beats. This was during the era when the Leftist writers of the Bay Area were working in solidarity with the revolutions of Central America—although, as we were soon to find out, even the seriousness of this commitment did not have the power to overcome the petty jealousies that poets are so often affected with, and which we participated in to a certain degree ourselves. As Blake accurately phrased it in his "Auguries of Innocence": "The poison of the honey bee/ Is the artist's jealousy." Jenny, during that time, was running into the common literary problem of me being considered "the Poet" and her simply "the wife (who also writes)," which came to a head at the poetry salon of one Doreen Post* in Marin County's Mill Valley, in the days when the traditional role of the Art Hostess was having possibly its final fling. (I believe that it was through Doreen that we first met the poet Gene Ruggles.) Doreen had organized a poetry reading at a local library to which "everyone" was invited except Jenny—so she decided to take action. She did this by showing Doreen the translations of some poems by one Susana Ibañez, an anti-Fascist revolutionary poet of Argentina who had supposedly been a cause célèbre in that nation's "Dirty Little War" of 1976–1983—poems that were actually written by Jenny herself. Doreen was extremely impressed and eager to get in touch with the author, until Jenny revealed to her the true identity of the mysterious Susana—obviously not because she hoped to secure a better position in the poetry scene, but simply as a well-crafted parting shot. A little later we told the story of this prank to the poet Gene Pilson*, who was living with poetess Erika Horn at the time. Gene had once suggested that I make Jenny wait for me at an appointed rendezvous to "put her in her place," since this was during a time when one of the ways a male poet would "show support" for another poet of the same sex was to dis his wife or girlfriend behind her back, under the theory that "we guys need to stick together against the bitches" (a theory that I never subscribed to); this was undoubtedly part of the mostly-unconscious response on the part of men to the feminism of the 1970s. So when Gene heard how Jenny had dealt with Doreen Post*, he totally freaked. "You couldn't have done that to somebody like [big] Doreen!" he shouted at her, trembling in disbelief—"you're frail, and weak!"—so I guess it was still OK to kiss up to the *big* bitches while demeaning the decent women who didn't want to be bitches at all, and so were relatively ineffectual in the poetry scene. "Lemme tell you how we settle things like this down at the union hall, *Jack*" Gene went on—"not with words, but with bullets!" By so doing he perfectly illustrated the ghetto-born principle that the pussy-whipped man will often resort to violence to prove his manhood; to make up for your single Mama beating on you, you turn around and beat on your girlfriend, or maybe join a gang. But however the male poets might have consciously reacted to the growing dominance of feminism, the whole idea of "the return of the Goddess" that was dominant at that time affected the men as well; according to the general mythology of the poetry world, the Goddess was identified with the Collective Unconscious, and the Collective Unconscious with the Muse. This was one of the things that gave the Divine Feminine ethos of the '70s its distinctly numinous quality, which could have been a powerfully liberating thing—if only there had been a real Divine Masculine component to go along with it, something that poet Robert Bly attempted to provide in his book *Iron John*. The era lacked the presence of a true Spiritual Father, like the Wakan Tanka of the Lakota or the Christian God the Father, and this inevitably put the men (speaking in more-or-less Jungian terms) at an archetypal disadvantage—because masculine spirituality was, of course, beginning to be ideologically frowned upon in those days as "patriarchal," in line with the irreversible collective impulse—based, as René Guénon observed, on the growing dominance of the Substantial Pole over the Essential Pole in these Last Days of the Kali-yuga—to deny the Divine Transcendence. This left the Hero (often degraded to the level of the paramilitary thug, like the character of Rambo as played by Sylvester Stallone) as the highest expression of the masculine spirit, while the more common expression, particularly among the poets, was the dying-and-resurrected (and often castrated) god, the *puer aeternus*, who goes through all his transformations within the enveloping magic circle of the Great Mother, and so never meets Her face-to-face as an equal—a cycle of fatality that Lew Welch for one never entirely broke out of, as we can see from his poem "A WARNING OF TAMALPAIS":

> Let all quick-eyed, prideful girls
> take note of this
>
> and every willing, head-strong boy
> beware:
>
> Nothing in all the Universe, is more
> sickening to see
> than a good man, trying, and he
>
> plagued by a bad woman!

We can discern in the radical gender-imbalance of the 1970s the roots of the androgynous destruction of gender that is so widespread in the world today. What a seedbed of social degeneracy the San Francisco poetry scene was in those years! It was a true wave of the future.

But even after we had formally broken with the poetry scene, at the beginning of the 2000s, my friend and fellow Lew protege Tony Dingman, ex-brother-in-law of Francis Ford Coppola and member of the Coppola entourage, invited me to read poetry at the director's new café/bodega in the American Zoetrope building on Kearney St in North Beach, more or less to help Tony's reading series get started; my payment was a bottle of red wine, produced by Coppola's winery and sold at the café, which I gave to Jenny who gave it to an Eastern Orthodox priest so he could transmute it into the Body and Blood of Christ. So when the evening arrived, there I was, laboring and sweating away at the podium, declaiming from my high-energy long-lined epic poem "The Wars of Love." The audience just kept chatting on; absolutely no one was listening. Finally one woman turned to Tony, the impresario, and asked: "Shouldn't we be paying attention to the poet?" "Don't worry about it, no problem, just hang loose" Tony replied. It was at that moment I realized that THIS WAS NOT A POETRY READING. It was nothing but a virtual, simulated poetry reading to keep up the image of an artistic North Beach for the tourists, with shaggy Beat poets perpetually ranting away in the cafés, just like in the olden days. I had not been invited to read my poetry as an artist and performer; I was not, in fact, a poet at all in that context—I was a Chamber of Commerce shill. And that was 20 years ago.

THE MARIN COMMITTEE FOR CENTRAL AMERICA

To pick up the main thread of this narrative, however, I must return to the time, almost 40 years ago (as of 2023), when I made my second major pass through anti-war activism. As with so many other major phases of our lives, it was Jenny who opened the new territory for us, in the 1980s, of solidarity with the revolutions of Central America. She believes that she probably identified with the oppressed of El Salvador and Nicaragua due to her own condition of oppression early in life; because the pain of that oppression was too great for her to face, she projected it on the outer world and attempted to overcome it there, instead of dealing with it in the inner world where it actually lived. In any case, Central America, solidarity with the revolutions of Central America, opposition to U.S. intervention in Central America, was in the air; along with the anti-Nuclear movement, it was the central rallying-cry for the American Left and the remnants of the counterculture in the 1980s, when the activist contingent of the Baby Boom was still young enough to automatically ask, "What's the next Cause?"

Jenny was probably first led toward an interest in Central America via the vogue in Spanish-language verse that was growing up in the Bay Area poetry scene, beginning in the Beat days with an interest in Federico García Lorca and the Spanish Civil War, as well as in Spanish poets like Antonio Machado and Juan Ramón Jiménez, then moving on to the politically active Leftist poets of Latin America like Cesar Vallejo (published by John McBride) and Pablo Neruda (translated by Robert Bly). This led to her decision to take a class in Spanish at Indian Valley College, where she got a clearer sense that Central America was going to be the keynote of the next wave of political commitment for our generation. It was at Indian Valley that she met one Frances Steadman, a local politico, who was the paramour of our one-time left-wing Democratic candidate for Congress, Phil Drath. On one occasion, at Frances' house in Mill Valley, Jenny and I met Peter Coyote, who introduced a folk singing group (Jenny doesn't remember their name). They sang a song by traditional Kentucky folk singer Jean Ritchie based on the Book of Genesis. Later on we also attended a lecture there given by a Tibetan Lama, whose name we have also forgotten.

Be that as it may, it wasn't long before we became acquainted with the greater circle of the Leftist politicos of Marin County, who seemed to be centered around the rich old Communists of Mill Valley like Irving Fromer and his clan, Milen Dempster and Helga Lohr-Bailey. But how did these classless-society types end up doing so well under the Capitalist system? My theory is that, because they accepted it as axiomatic that Capitalism would eventually self-destruct due to internal contradictions—though not without the help of a violent revolution at one point—when 1929 came along they (or their parents) did not share the prevailing illusion that the market would just go up and up forever, making everybody rich, but were able to read the signs of the impending crash and sell out in time. Nor did they have any scruples against playing the Capitalist system while it was still there to be played; Friederich Engels himself was, after all, a Capitalist.

Our first step toward "revolutionary solidarity" was to form an organization called the Marin Committee for Central America, which included us, Irving Fromer, Cheryl Zuur from the South Bay (who was to become our Fearless Leader), Danny Wakoff, a classic New York Jewish radical of the Baby Boom (I had the impression during those years that all the nicest and most laid-back New Yorkers had migrated to California), and a few of the other Marin politicos and peaceniks. Irving Fromer, a card-carrying Communist, was the bearded patriarch of Marin's far Left. Once, at his house in Mill Valley, I stood in the shadows as a young Communist zealot explained to us why the Soviet invasion of Afghanistan was "a fraternal gesture in support of a popularly-elected government" etc. etc. (I didn't buy that idea then and have not been moved to purchase it since.) Through Irving and his comrades we met Gianna Eason, a slim, witty and attractive Italian lady, whose central belief seemed to be that "revolution should be *fun*," and her "frenemy" Hannah Creighton, a one-time red-haired beauty who had just reached middle age and was beginning to realize that her days of trading on that beauty were coming to a close...

At a solidarity meeting at The First Congregational Church of San Rafael, when the Rev. Lou Riley was pastor there, we met Cristián and Christina Opaso. Cristián was a young Chilean immigrant, Christina a classic blonde Marin County hippie chick; for a short time we and they became close friends. During that time my favorite music group was the Chilean band Inti Illimani, while Cristián's favorites were Jimi Hendrix and Bob Dylan, the grass always being greener on the other side of the cultural divide.

Christina, who worked as a telephone operator, told us a great story about an encounter she'd once had, on the job, with Alan Watts. Watts, in a high state of English irritation and entitlement (possibly due to a serious hangover) had contacted the phone company over some issue or other, and reached Christina — who knew who he was, either because phone operators already had the Caller ID that hadn't yet been made available to the general public, or just because she recognized his voice. "Oh Alan" she replied. "I always thought of you as a highly evolved spiritual being, a perfect example of equanimity and detachment; I'm *so* disappointed in you." "Oh, ah, ah, I'm *terribly* sorry, please, forgive me for my most unseemly (etc. etc.)" was his response. At least he didn't claim to be a Crazy Wisdom Guru who had the *right* to be snappish and hung-over...

During our short time with the Marin Committee for Central America we met with a group of church people in San Francisco who were organized as a *comunidad de base* or "base community" — a voluntary association of the Catholic laity (and, later on, the laity of other Christian churches) as first defined by the Second Vatican Council, as well as through a meeting of the Latin American Council of Bishops in Medellín, Columbia in 1968. Such groups were convened for the purpose of Bible study, often within the context of the struggle for popular liberation and social justice. Fr Ernesto Cardenal's community of Solentiname, serving the population of the islands on Lake Nicaragua, was a *communidad de base*. Guiding the discussion for that evening was the well-known Brazilian social philosopher Paulo Freire, whose book *Pedagogy of the Oppressed* developed the important idea of "internalized oppression," a kind of collective version of the well-recognized psychological syndrome of codependency in abusive relationships. My own analysis of the Gnostic Archons as the Rulers of the Darkness of This World was undoubtedly influenced by some of his ideas.

Another "figure" we met during that time was the Mexican-American politico Tony Medrano, a resplendent image of the heroic revolutionary, with bushy moustache and head of luxuriant hair, who in his earlier years had been the mousey little Dominican friar Brother Diego, one of the teachers at Marin Catholic High School in the years I attended, who never spoke and whose face I can hardly remember. Certainly the movement for the People's Liberation had accomplished his own glorious emancipation, if no one else's. (I don't mean to imply, however, that he was all show and no substance; he was jailed in Guatemala at one point while on a fact-finding mission for a human rights organization.)

In any case, there was no question but that Liberation was in the air in those days. On one occasion Bianca Jagger herself spoke — at San Rafael

High School! — on the events unfolding in Central America. The Marin Committee for Central America even received a packet of information from Smith College in Massachusetts, asking if one of their students might intern with us — though we were definitely in no position to accede to such a request.

YET ANOTHER TAKE ON "RELIGION AND POLITICS": JOAN MCCARTHY

One of the most notable people we met during this time was Joan McCarthy. She had been a Catholic nun who was appointed mother superior of a convent in Mexico when she was hardly out of her teens; in that capacity she was treated as a kind of seeress by the Mexican peasants. Then at one point a choice was presented her: should she go to South America and become part of the Liberation Theology movement (under either Leonardo Boff or Dom Helder Camara, I forget which)? Or should she accept the invitation of a local "white" *bruja* (sorceress) to study traditional Mexican sorcery? She had partnered with the *bruja* to defend the peasants from oppression by the "black" *brujos* of the region, who at that point had a monopoly on medical care in the remote rural areas. Anyone who became ill had to resort to these people, who were most likely running a sort of protection racket, threatening to use their magic to make people sick instead of curing them if they didn't pay up. Joan and the *bruja* were training young local men as herbal doctors so as to undercut the power of the *brujos*. The *bruja* had told her: "I will show you the powers of the Garlic Flower, of the Silver Sword, and of the Cross — but the greatest power of all is love." Joan, however, chose the path of Liberation Theology, and left for South America.

This story highlights one of the questions that will always come up when any attempt is made to unite mysticism and politics: the question of magic. Spiritual power is infinite, social conditions are finite — so why not simply "tap" the power of Spirit to transform social conditions? What is routinely forgotten when this question is posed is: *whose agenda do we intend to follow?* Is it we — as individuals, or as members of a movement — who have the right to say what spiritual power shall be used for? Is such power just sitting there passively in the higher worlds, like oil in the ground, waiting for whoever has the ability and the *chutzpa* to drill for it? Or does God Himself have a plan for the use of that power — a power which, of course, is exclusively His in any case? I remember how on one occasion Jenny and I attended a lecture at the La Peña Cultural Center, by a rather unsavory young couple, on the subject of Mexican sorcery. After the lecture I asked a question: "If there is such a thing as Liberation Theology, could there also be such a thing as Liberation Sorcery?" "It's hard to use spells against bullets" the speaker answered. But what I should have said — I'm still kicking myself for not having thought of it — was: "Yes — but think of the possibilities for psy-ops and military intelligence." (I later discovered that these possibilities had already been thoroughly explored by the CIA in their "remote viewing" experiments and a number of similar efforts.)

One more story featuring Joan McCarthy remains to be told. On one occasion we attended a lecture and "testimony" by Joan at Westminster Presbyterian Church in Tiburon, hosted by the pastor Doug Huneke. She spoke on the plight of the Salvadoran refugees who were being driven from their homeland by death squads trained at the U.S. National War College. Rather disconcertingly, however, one of the members of the congregation turned out to be a military officer attached to that very college, who (unsurprisingly) took umbrage at Joan McCarthy's presentation. How Doug Huneke negotiated the ensuing turmoil I never discovered, but he clearly survived it, since he finally retired only just this year (2023).

BECOMING "POETS OF RESISTANCE"

One of the people we met at the Mission Cultural Center during our time with the Marin Committee for Central America was the poet Nina Serrano; Jenny and I read poetry with her once at the Center. Nina had a background in theater, radio, and film; she had worked on films about Fidel Castro's Cuba, Salvador Allende's Chile and the Nicaragua of the Sandinistas. In Cuba in 1968 she met exiled Salvadoran poet Roque Dalton, with whom she co-authored a TV drama about the legendary Dalton Gang that was aired on Cuban television. Dalton had tried to join the Farabundo Martí National Liberation Front but was told that his proper role was as a poet/propagandist. Like many revolutionary writers of the time he rejected the idea of being "merely a writer," feeling called to make a full military commitment and, if need be, die in the People's cause. Consequently he remained stuck between the roles of a rifle-toting footsoldier and a public spokesman for the revolution, with the final result that another insurgent faction he had joined, the People's Revolutionary Army, became suspicious of him and had him assassinated. For some reason, lyric poets — like John Keats and Lew Welch, like Dylan Thomas and Alden Van Buskirk, like Federico García Lorca and Cesar Vallejo — often die young; they are enamored of death and seem to attract it, as if death were their Muse — a quality that once led me, as I already mentioned above, to paraphrase William James' notion of "a moral equivalent to war" by defining poetry as "the moral equivalent of human sacrifice."

But where did this temptation to seek martyrdom for the People come from? I felt it myself, momentarily at least, when I was at Santa Venetia. So did Cristián Opaso, until I told him more or less what the FMLN had told Roque Dalton: that this was a media war, at least in terms of North America, so that's where our duty lay. Even the comic actor John Belushi, at least according to one story that Jenny remembers, was saying to himself during that time—just before his death from a cocaine overdose—"What am I doing here in the U.S. working as a mere comedian when I should be dying in El Salvador?" But why this attraction to heroic revolutionary death? The hippies of the anti-Vietnam War Movement never felt that attraction; even the freedom riders of the Civil Rights Movement, though they knew that death on the front lines was possible, weren't dominated by it. Were we really that committed to sacrificing ourselves for the People in the great global struggle against Imperialism, against the Darkness of This World? Were we just dramatizing the feeling of "survivors' guilt" that came from hearing so many heart-rending stories of death and torture? Were we by any chance being influenced by the collective ancestral psyche of pre-Columbian Latin America, where human sacrifice played such a big role? Or were we actually being unconsciously tempted by the Principalities and Powers to sacrifice ourselves *to* the Darkness of This World to save it the trouble of killing us, and so help it build its power?

During that time I began collecting poems for an anthology in solidarity with the Salvadoran revolution, working with a sweet Salvadoran lady, Maria-Rosa, who was also based at the Mission Cultural Center. Maria-Rosa believed, according to one of the short-lived cosmic myths of the time, that the world was getting cooler instead of warmer, which meant that Central America would be transformed, as one of the fruits of the Final Revolution, into an Earthly Paradise, where Man and Nature would come into a new partnership to bring ultimate liberation to the human race—a sentiment that was expressed in one of the common proverbs of the Salvadoran revolutionaries, "God and our mountains fight for us." James Laughlin of New Directions had agreed to publish my collection. Then one of the Bay Area Salvadoran politicos "appropriated" the project (I should have fought to keep it), because who was I, a mere Gringo, to presume to edit the works of dedicated Salvadoran revolutionaries!? The upshot was that the anthology was never published, leaving the market on Salvadoran revolutionary verse to be cornered later on by American poet Carolyn Forché, who had traveled to El Salvador under the auspices of Amnesty International. Another less-than-successful project was my attempt to bring Ernesto Cardenal, then Minister of Culture of Nicaragua under the Sandinistas, to the Bay Area. (Cardenal had studied under Father Thomas Merton at the Trappist Abbey of Gethsemani in Kentucky. Merton, also a poet, acted as a kind of spiritual adviser to the peace movement and the increasingly rudderless Catholic Church after the Second Vatican Council, reaching out to Buddhists, to Sufis, to poets and peace activists—despite the fact that, to my way of thinking, he was becoming increasingly rudderless himself.) Cardenal and I corresponded for a short time, but nothing came of it; later he was invited to San Francisco by the more established poetry commissars of the Mission District, working in concert with Lawrence Ferlinghetti's City Lights Books who had published my *Panic Grass*. Poetry in this context was considered to be a kind of motivational tool. It was not quite propaganda, but it was nonetheless expected to fulfill a utilitarian function under the rubric of "cultural resistance." During those days we became friends with people like poet Fernando Alegría, a colleague of Chilean national poet Pablo Neruda, who (as you may remember) had been part of the Leftist Allende government in Chile, serving as cultural attaché to the United States. Allende was assassinated in a military coup backed by the United States; his government was replaced by a *junta* headed by dictator Augusto Pinochet, known for his practice of "disappearing" his opponents. Part of that story is told in the movie *Missing* (1982) starring Jack Lemmon and Cissy Spacek, while the First World movement in solidarity with the revolutions of Central America appeared in 1980s pop culture, in all its poorly-grounded romanticism, through songs like "Indian Girl" by the Rolling Stones, and "Fernando" by — almost unbelievably — ABBA! Looking back now, I begin to get a clearer picture of just how much our solidarity with the revolutions of Central America was the fruit of a media effort, one in which Hollywood joined hands with the leftist/counterculture media establishment of the time, which included *The Rolling Stone*, Pacifica Radio, publishers like New Directions and City Lights, some of the major rock and pop bands, Leftist/Liberal journals like *The Nation* and *The New Republic*, underground newspapers such as the *Berkeley Barb* and the *Village Voice* — even *Playboy Magazine* up to a point — and which was still quite powerful in the 1980s. This consortium was ultimately responsible not only for various revolutionary-solidarity-themed pop songs, but was itself influenced by the revolutionary songs of the Chilean *Nueva Canción* movement (which originated in Portugal) as performed by artists like the celestial tenor Rafael Manriquez and the Andean folk ensemble Inti Illimani, who inspired the shrill, distant flutes in the introduction to "Fernando" and who also recorded the song "El Condor Pasa," written by Peruvian composer Daniel Alomía Robles and famously recorded and furnished with lyrics by Simon and Garfunkel. It also produced, in addition to the motion picture *Missing*, other films like *El Norte*, written and directed by Gregory Nava, which dealt with the plight of Latin American illegal immigrants to the United States, and *Salvador*, starring James Woods and Jim Belushi and directed by no less a luminary than Oliver Stone, the subject of which was the Salvadoran Revolution itself. The Mills of *Maya*, at least up to a point and with a disconcerting tendency to sell out to the opposition when the price was right, seemed to be grinding in our favor.

Fernando Alegría told us a striking story during that time about Pablo Neruda, a story that needs to be remembered. Neruda had always said, half-jokingly, that after he died he wanted to come back as one of those little eagles native to the Andes. Then, after he died in the hospital—twelve days after Allende was assassinated by Pinochet and his *junta* during their bombardment of the Moneda, the presidential palace in Santiago (Neruda believed that he himself might have been helped on his way to the next world by an order from Pinochet to his doctors that he be secretly poisoned), Neruda's wife contacted Alegría to report an amazing occurrence: one of those little Andean eagles had come through a window into Neruda's study, and refused to leave. "What is your explanation of this event?" Alegría asked. "Oh, it's just Pablo" answered the poet's wife.

ALL ROADS LEAD TO SANTA VENETIA

The Marin Committee for Central America never really became a viable organization, however. We had a few meetings to talk about how to address the Central America situation, but nothing substantive happened in that direction until, at a meeting of Marin church people who were investigating Central American revolutionary solidarity and the Sanctuary Movement for Central American refugees—at Rev. Lou Riley's First Congregationalist Church of San Rafael if I remember right—we met the Reverend Carolyn Studer, who invited us to become part of her Santa Venetia Presbyterian Church, since she needed sympathetic insurgents in the Session, the church's governing body, people who would vote for the church to join the Sanctuary Movement. We quickly agreed. This was not a difficult decision for me to make, since the background that many Baby Boomers had in both the "spiritual revolution" of the '60s and the peace movement against the Vietnam War, which had included religious activists like the Berrigan brothers as well as church-based peace organizations such as Sojourners, the American Friends Service Committee (the Quakers) and the Buddhist Peace Fellowship—all still quite active in the '80s—had perfectly prepared us to accept the Latin America-born hybrid of Religion and Politics represented by Liberation Theology. And once we became part of the church-based Central American solidarity movement of Marin, we discovered that networking, organizing and "evangelizing" within the churches was a very convenient way to mobilize support for a cause, since the people we wanted to reach were already organized and meeting at least once a week; we were preaching to a captive audience. So the Session voted, the resolution was passed, and Santa Venetia became a Sanctuary church.

THE DRAMATIS PERSONAE

In Santa Venetia we found a ready-made social group who, since we were united by a cause, were spared the tentative and uncertain process of approaching each other as individuals. Below are some of the people we met and knew during that time:

The Reverend Carolyn Studer

Blonde, blue-eyed, witty, highly attractive Carolyn Studer was a "preacher's kid" whose father was also a Presbyterian minister. She wanted to make him proud and follow in his footsteps, but she also wanted to be an artist and a musician—she was an accomplished jazz pianist—so it is possible to speculate that being the pastor of a small "mission" church in solidarity with the revolutions of Central America allowed her to play both parts simultaneously, both the "good girl" and the "bad girl." In any case, as the magnetic focus-of-attention for the Santa Venetia community, she was the visible agent of our group's unity—a role that, as I see it now, became increasingly burdensome to her as the months went by. (As an example of her highly entertaining wit, she once observed that "People think that 'God helps those who help themselves' is out of the Bible, but it really came off a redwood burl somewhere.")

Barbara York

Barbara, according to her own self-description, was a Christian rendition of the Southern California "Valley Girl," straight out of Bible Camp. Every bit as blonde and attractive as Carolyn, she was continuously surrounded by a cloud of boyfriends whom she referred to as "the herd." She too had trained for the ministry, but she never seemed able to find a position she could stick with. How such a quintessential "straight girl" could have fallen in with group of pot-smoking would-be Leftist radicals can perhaps be better understood if you watch the YouTube music video of ABBA's "Fernando"; the band member Agnetha Fältskog, allowing for the inevitable distortions of caricature, might be taken as a kind of alter-ego of Barbara York. Yet Barbara, for all her professional limitations, had a streak of real faith and piety that I don't believe Carolyn Studer could match.

Charles Hernon

Charles Hernon was a short, florid, raw-boned Scotsman who had once been employed by the BBC in Britain; his main credit was that he had worked with Patrick McGoohan on the TV spy series *Danger Man*. He had attached himself to Santa Venetia Presbyterian like a barnacle to a rock; as the self-designated sexton of the church, he in some sense "went with the building." Charles became our Chief Media Officer, which mostly translated into "camera man"; he saw definite cinematic potential in the Sanctuary Movement, as well as in Carolyn, the blonde, good-looking Presbyterian pastor, as its poster-girl. He was always floating big ideas about how this potential could be exploited—most of which came to nothing—but he was nonetheless largely responsible for the aforementioned video our church produced, called *Through the Needle's Eye*, which I'll have more to say about below. Charles had named me "Producer" of the film largely to give me a sense of entitlement but still keep me separate from the nuts-and-bolts production work, even though I had named the film, come up with the idea of inviting a Vietnam Vet to apologize to the refugees who appeared in it for the actions of the U.S. government, and appeared in it myself to recite Jenny's poem "The Mountains"; still, it would clearly never have happened without Charles Hernon. I remember one time during the editing process, when I had been told to stay home and not interfere, that I was so psychically in tune with what was going on that I phoned the church to tell them "don't make that cut!" *"How did you know we were about to make that exact cut??"* they incredulously asked. In any case, Charles Hernon added a dour, astringent element to our congregation that nonetheless worked perfectly as a necessary seasoning for the heterogeneous mulligan stew that we were. He kept calling Carolyn "Carlin," an old Scottish word for a witch, a harridan, an unsavory old woman; I might have been the only one who knew what the word meant since I'd encountered it in the old border-ballad "The Wife of Usher's Well." But he made up for it, and for his shabby treatment of me as a "serious artist," by giving me a single-shot bottle of his favorite scotch, Famous Grouse, which was so smooth on the palate that I've characterized it as "the Old Bushmill's of scotch whiskeys"; so I suppose we must call it even.

Dave Pittle

Dave Pittle was another ordained Presbyterian minister without a church of his own, who had some kind of background as a missionary in Latin America. He was heavy-set, jovial, bearded, the very image of the epicurean gourmet; he drove us on a tour of the Napa Valley wine country once. He liked to call Carolyn Studer "Sister Carolyn," jokingly comparing her to Aimee Semple McPherson. His theological position might be described as "Orthodox Liberalism" in that he believed that God was good, generally well-meaning, but too weak to do much about it. Dave's God was the Celestial Liberal (the pre-Woke "guilty" Liberal that is), presiding ineffectually over a world whose evil He was helpless to control. Nonetheless he introduced a more or less adult influence into our church that helped balance out some of the more extravagant "creative" flakiness we were oversupplied with.

*Leanna Graham**

Leanna was Santa Venetia's "sex girl." (Doesn't every church need at least one of those?) She was short, full-figured, attractive and likeable, and friendly to everybody, especially the married men of the congregation (including me, though in my case she had no success). She had an affair with one of these, Steve, who was more-or-less in an open marriage, allowing her to temporarily become part of his family's ménage. Experience has taught me that it is very hard for Christian churches in the U.S.—and not only the Liberal churches—to preach against sexual sins. (Jenny's next stable church after Santa Venetia, St Nicholas Orthodox Church in San Anselmo, also had its sex girl while Jenny was worshipping there, who largely escaped censure because the only sins that the Orthodox seemed to take seriously were sins of eating; Jenny remembers one occasion, during the time she was attending St Seraphim's Orthodox Church in Santa Rosa, when the priest refused to baptize one of the catechumens because he had caught him at a restaurant eating chicken during Lent.) As for Santa Venetia, the major if not the only sins were various violations of Liberal social mores, human rights and standards of social justice. When it came to sex, however, that was sacrosanct: openly preaching against sexual misdemeanors would have been considered "going too far" in a Puritanical direction—though Carolyn did once announce in a sermon to the women of the congregation that she had no intention whatsoever of sleeping with their husbands... In any case, Leanna was not alone in her collectively-sanctioned promiscuity. When the power of the Holy Spirit descends on a group, everything depends on whether or not that group has, or is, a vessel strong enough to contain it. The Spirit is Infinite Life, but life on the human level needs to be limited, properly ordered and correctly channeled: you can't water your backyard garden with Niagara Falls and expect to harvest a crop. The Pentecostal Fire may begin as cloven tongues of flame above the crown of the head, but later it descends from there, chakra by chakra, until it reaches Chakra Number Two, the sexual center, where it too often gets stuck—especially if the spiritual keynote of the group is fellowship alone, with little commitment to self-mastery and purification of soul. When sexual energy becomes formless and overcharged and is directed toward unconscious group cohesion rather than attentive and caring personal love, it can falsely masquerade as the virtue of universal charity, thereby justifying its excesses, while at the same time sowing the seeds of bitterness and spiritual darkness for the future.

However, Leanna's* obvious sexual availability had one touching but silently tragic consequence, directly related to our work in the Sanctuary Movement: a young Salvadoran refugee, most likely of the peon class, fell in love with her. Why would he not? She was young and attractive; she was unmarried; she was with a church working to help refugees from Central America; marriage to an American woman would help him gain legal status in the U.S.—and so of course she represented Life to him, on so many levels. Therefore, even though she had no balcony to be wooed on, he began wooing her in the traditional manner—with a guitar. It all came to nothing, yet it was a poignant moment I've never forgotten.

The same kind of loose behavior we were involved with in Santa Venetia apparently sometimes took place at the antinomian *agape* feasts of the early Christians, behavior that was likely based in part on a misinterpretation of Galatians 10:13, "Christ has redeemed us from the curse of the law" and similar passages. This is why the Epistle of Jude warns against false teachers who "turn the grace of our God into lasciviousness." And we certainly had our own love-feasts, our famous pot luck dinners, and (for the "inner circle") our pot-smoking sessions, where *fellowship*, whether or not it was always strictly Christian, assumed the status of a quasi-sacrament; the ultimate result of this formlessness and lack of vigilance was a creeping depersonalization that finally closed the Spirit's door. I've always said that my two years at Santa Venetia Presbyterian Church were like the hippie commune experience I'd never had during the '60s, especially since Carolyn, myself and a few others smoked grass nearly every day for a solid year—a practice that energized the group psyche and made everything more interesting and clairvoyant and liminal, but did little to maintain healthy personal boundaries, not to mention any stable contemplative center. We were doing serious work and taking real personal risks, and when you are involved in things like that, one of the most dangerous things you can do is use sex and drugs to suppress *fear*. We needed that fear to inform us and protect us.

As for Leanna, I once heard her say, half to herself: "I think I'm becoming corrupted." Later she invited some male church members (including myself) over to the house in my neighborhood where she was working as an *au pair*, on which occasion she entertained us clad only in a towel; her guests were at least ten years older than she was. "Why don't you go after guys your own age?" I admonished—and later on, she did. After the church folded when Carolyn left and then later re-opened, she did marry a guy her own age; we attended their wedding at a park on Paradise Drive on the Bay shore between Larkspur and Tiburon, the ceremony performed by Carolyn, in what was probably her last appearance before the church community. Finally Leanna and her husband moved to Las Vegas, Nevada and had kids. Revolutionary solidarity, and play time, were over.

Mike Lyons

Mike Lyons was certified to operate the largest cranes in the world, those huge steel arms you see rising above skyscrapers being built; he was Leanna's paramour for a while. He lived in a Chinese junk at one of the San Rafael yacht clubs, a boat that briefly became the Santa Venetia church boat. We didn't have a bus like some churches did but we did have a junk with a dragon painted on the sail; we could've gone from yacht club to yacht club around the shore, evangelizing the party-boys, the lonely divorced and/or ejected husbands and the weird introverted hermits of the Bay Area—though to exactly what doctrine I'm not entirely sure—except that Mike had other plans; he needed the junk to live in.

As our church began to retreat into history, Mike Lyons became a Zen Buddhist. I remember something I said to him once while drunk: "I don't need to become Enlightened because God is already Enlightened." "You're wrong, Charles; Enlightenment only means anything if *you* become Enlightened; you need to be serious about it and work at it." He was right of course—but, in another way, I was also right: because to say that God is already Enlightened is the same thing as saying that all things have the Buddha-nature—including me. If I wasn't already Enlightened somehow, somewhere, my quest for Enlightenment would be a hopeless struggle. Like the Zen people say, "If you want to become Enlightened, you first have to be Enlightened."

Charles and Eileen Dubbs

Probably the best representatives of those elements of the pre-Sanctuary Movement congregation who had responded amicably to the transformation of Santa Venetia Presbyterian from a neighborhood community church into a hotbed of Marxist sympathizers—as most but not all of the original group had—were an elderly couple, Charles and Eileen Dubbs. Charles and Eileen were the *real* Fred and Ethyl Mertz from the *I Love Lucy* show; the resemblance was unmistakable. And, just like Fred and Ethyl, they had been vaudeville performers in their earlier years. They were good examples of the totally heterogeneous makeup of our group in terms of age, background, and point-of-origin—suggesting in some ways the motley crew that collected around the "Fisher King" Elwin Ransom to fight the system of Antichrist in C. S. Lewis' *That Hideous Strength*—clearly demonstrating that the Holy Spirit makes His selections based not on any worldly-recognizable criteria but on the secrets of the Heart. In our case, however, the Spirit was not so much mustering the latter-day saints for the battle of Armageddon as providing us with an amazingly intense but nonetheless short-lived set of experiences, either as a test, a purification, or an exposure to certain powerful impressions, that would prove useful to us somehow, somewhere, in this world or the next.

These were not the only "principals" of our church family, but the above portraits should be enough to give you an idea of its interesting, multifarious, mongrel quality.

THE CHURCH ROUTINE

Santa Venetia Presbyterian Church was an incredibly tight-knit group; it was like nothing else I've ever experienced, either before or since. The "ministerial team," a loose collection of members of the Session and others who were close to Carolyn and sometimes smoked dope with her at her apartment, often met for breakfast in the church kitchen. This was undoubtedly a form of the well-known Protestant "prayer breakfast," except that these get-togethers went far beyond prayer. We talked and talked, and shared everything; our mutual trust, untested and unchallenged, knew no bounds. And our evening pot-lucks, often scheduled to coincide with various presentations by community groups or members of the congregation, were even more extravagant, and better attended.

Our Sunday services, beyond a few prayers and the singing of the "doxology," featured entertaining and thought-provoking sermons by Carolyn, and on rare occasions by other preachers (including myself). The congregational singing was delightful, based on our songbook, which was a mixture of standard traditional Protestant hymns like "Rock of Ages" and a good selection of contemporary folk, light rock and folk-rock numbers. During those two years I sang as I had never sung before, and learned in the process that—at least for me—there are certain emotional layers of the soul that only music and song can touch. As I discovered both there and with my first Sufi *tariqah*, music has the power to awaken and dissolve deep-rooted emotional knots and crystallizations, so that the Word of God can take root in the Heart—but if those coagulations are released while nothing from a higher spiritual plane immediately takes their place, the soul is sometimes made vulnerable to occupation by less salutary influences, as Mozart and Mick Jagger clearly attest.

The evening presentations, which were often political in nature, were interspersed with amateur theatricals, many of which seemed to be based on people's past experiences with high school plays or Christian Bible Camp, as well as various group exercises derived from the pop psychology of the time. Jenny did one in which, dressed in a white Mexican wedding dress, she performed "The White Parrot," a Spanish fairy tale she'd found a version of in a book by Jungian psychoanalyst Marie-Louise von Franz; Jenny cast herself as the parrot. And I led a small group in a contemplative visualization based on an exercise I'd developed called Strategic Insight Meditation, which was supposed to allow one to submit pre-conceived questions to one's "higher self"—whatever that might be—and receive practical and workable answers.

(Then the day came when Carolyn hurried in, obviously distressed about something, and presented us with a "jazz sermon" on the piano instead of her ordinary Christian one in the English language. It seemed on that occasion that she was going through some emotional crisis that couldn't be put into words, one that only music could express.)

VISITATIONS

And then our church began to attract people; people began to hear, somehow, through some channel or other, how "something was going on" at Santa Venetia Presbyterian. For example, a new worshipper appeared, a woman, who prayed with her hands held palms-up before her, like the Muslims do. When we asked her who she was, she told us that she was (of all races) an Assyrian—a people I knew nothing about except for their appearance in the Old Testament as imperialists and oppressors of the Jews — and in a short story by William Saroyan entitled "Seventy Thousand Assyrians," where the narrator, an Armenian immigrant to the United States (like Saroyan's parents), gets his hair cut by an Assyrian barber who tells him that, of all that great and ancient race, only seventy thousand remained. What, or who, had called her to worship with us? There can't be many Presbyterians among the Assyrian Christians, most of whom live in Iraq, speaking Aramaic and largely belonging to one of four churches: the Chaldean (Catholic Uniate, whose Bishop-in-exile, Francis Kalabat, would play an important part, thirty years later, in the "Covenants Initiative" you'll hear about below), the Nestorian, the Jacobite or Syrian Orthodox, and the Syrian Catholic. Jenny remembers that she was a resident of Santa Venetia, someone who had probably had a hard time finding a branch of her home church in North America, but didn't seem to care overmuch about where she worshipped because she knew that "the letter killeth but the Spirit giveth life."

Another unexpected visitor who became an integral part of our congregation was one Hunter George from the state of Mississippi, a large, bear-like man who identified with that animal and who had a background as a redneck spiritual guru; he told us that he had maintained his guru-like demeanor of high energy and spiritual peace by the liberal use of methamphetamine (the energy) combined with barbiturates (the peace) — though his drug-use was now a thing of the past. Then there was the frantically attractive lady in her late thirties, clad in panty hose and short shorts — "she needs a good stuffing" was Charles Hernon comment — who showed up at the church because she was feuding with her husband, a wealthy Latin American honcho of the dictator caste; this was in the days when Marin County was becoming the home away from home for the expatriate ruling class of half the world. She had apparently decided to go over to the revolutionaries and *salvatruchas* just to spite him, specifically by writing a check to help us fund our film featuring the torture-testimonies of Latin American refugees. "I *bought you*" she told me once after issuing some order or other. "You did not buy me" I replied; "you just bought some of my time." Lastly, a more prominent figure arrived to make a presentation at our church one evening, this time by invitation: none other than Ralph Metzner, the third and least well-known of the Harvard psychedelic triumvirate that included Timothy Leary and Richard Alpert. (Art Kleps, in *Millbrook*, his book about Leary's "psychedelic manor house," had characterized Metzner as someone who, like so many of us nowadays, was "still looking for a technical answer to a philosophical question.") Metzner led us in a Wild Man Dance, during which he transformed us all into trees — though happily the spell wore off before the time came for us to get into our cars and drive home.

OTHER EPISODES

In the course of our work with Central American refugees we had some interesting encounters beyond the local Peace Movement church people and the Salvadoran cadres. On one occasion Carolyn and Jenny had an interview with the prominent feminist theologian Rosemary Radford Reuther; Jenny only remembers that she had some mild disagreement of opinion with her. Then there was the time when Carolyn and I met with the Methodist Bishop of (I believe) Ecuador. Carolyn was going on, in hippie-fantasy style, about how aid flights to El Salvador should be organized through which shipments of electric guitars would be parachuted to the insurgents, etc. etc. The Bishop's response was: "You are a very attractive woman and I'm sure you mean well, but — to speak quite frankly — the last thing we need in the Central American situation is any more *cowboy diplomacy*."

As another example of the "loose cannon" syndrome, a local church person involved with the Sanctuary Movement whose name I don't recall told us the story of the time when, before a trip to El Salvador, one of the local Marin politicos had given him a shipment of *watches* to be delivered to someone in that nation. The church person saw no problem with this, until he realized (or was told) that the only possible use of such a shipment would be to provide the insurgents, many of whom were penniless peasants who had never owned a personal timepiece in their lives, with watches they could synchronize before mounting an attack. If the Salvadoran authorities had come to the same conclusion, that naïve American idealist might never have been heard from again.

Then the day came when some little girls from the neighborhood burst into the church, which also functioned as a kind of community center, and announced: "We found Huey Lewis!" And it was true; apparently Huey was then renting a house in Santa Venetia. Later I met him at his door to make some pitch or other for our church and our movement; I believe that the vague possibility of a benefit concert was briefly discussed — but (not surprisingly) nothing came of it.

The most intense interaction between our church and the Santa Venetia community, however, came when we were looking into the possibility of sponsoring a homeless shelter on the church grounds. We had already become part of a project where various churches would shelter the homeless for a night on a revolving basis, but this proposal involved a more ongoing commitment. In response, the mothers of Santa Venetia — whom we named "the Mama Bears" — were up in arms. Their leader in this entirely understandable crusade for moral decency and the safety of Santa Venetia's children was one Marsha Blackman, who was certainly a natural leader and a tough mama to deal with, though her credentials as an ethical standard-bearer might have been called into question by the fact that she was also one of the editors of *Hustler Magazine*, the raunchiest adult publication in the U.S. during the 1980s. We Christian Marxists certainly had no monopoly on moral ambiguity! Such contradictions as these are one of the occupational hazards faced by of anyone who, in either a small or a big way, decides to try and change the world. In any case, the "community input" meeting at the church on the question of the proposed shelter did not go exactly as we might have wished—to say the least.

THE CARSON INTERVENTION

One of my own most ambiguous decisions while I was at Santa Venetia was to "fix up" Carolyn with my friend Randy Carson. My idea (as if it was any of my business!) was that if Carolyn had a man in her life she would be less likely to inadvertently destabilize the congregation through the unbounded broadcast of unassigned sexual energy—so I talked her up to Randy as both desirable and available. One of the effects of their liaison was that Randy Carson offered to make his conflict resolution skills available to Santa Venetia in the context of the clash between the church and the Mama Bears. This led to a rather incongruous community event where techniques that had been highly successful in a corporate setting were being applied in an entirely different context. The encounter seemed to go off pretty well, yet in the long run nothing fundamentally changed. And the spirit that Randy brought in—something I had undoubtedly been blind to due to my friendship with him—was in many ways incompatible with the Christian ethos and system-of-sentiments our church was founded on. Randy was more of a Viking, a "son of Thor" who identified with the warrior caste and spirit, Germanic and Scandinavian, as well as with its Japanese equivalent, the Samurai. His spiritual Path was the Japanese martial art *aikido*, in which he held an advanced black belt. The quality of medieval Christian knighthood, however, the ethos of chivalry, was not one of the arrows in his quiver. He tended to see Power as the central principle of reality, as expressed in the dynamics of conflict and conflict resolution. It is true that every human situation includes a power dynamic, and that the more you know about how power operates, the more deeply you will see into the situation you are presently considering. Nonetheless, Power isn't everything. The Divine qualities of Love, Wisdom, Knowledge, Detachment, Self-sacrifice are just as primal, and every bit as universal, as is the quality of Power. If all you can see is Power, then the proverb "if your only tool is a hammer, everything you see will look like a nail" perfectly applies to you. Nonetheless the bottom line for that phase of my life was that the Spirit that had animated Santa Venetia was beginning to withdraw, so the intrusion of foreign and incompatible elements was, at the end of the day, inevitable. Consequently I can and must forgive Randy for the clash of his spirit with ours, just as I must forgive myself for bringing him in. I forgot to ask what God wanted, nor did I hear anybody else taking pains to remind us that this is always the first question that must be asked, no matter what situation we confront.

SACRED ACTIVISM AND "SPIRITUAL" POWER

At Santa Venetia, having moved one or two steps away from magic and closer to prayer, I started experimenting—as I've already mentioned—with a type of visualization called Strategic Insight Meditation, "trying it out" on members of the congregation. The idea was to form a question as an image, submit it to the angelic plane or "higher self," and receive an answer in return, also as an image. The problem with practices like this, as I later slowly realized, is that they give the illusion that intuiting the Will of God and acting on it can be carried on simply as a "technique," a way of manipulating information, without reference to one's total moral and spiritual state. You can't distance large portions of yourself from piety, devotion and submission to God by defining spiritual intuition as no more than a kind of psychic "search engine" and expect not to run into serious problems. If you attempt this—and most especially if you are "successful"—you will have opened yourself to spiritual delusion.

Also during my time in Santa Venetia I began experimenting with prayer networking for the purpose of empowering the Sanctuary Movement, an approach that would expand immensely during Jenny's and my later pass through the New Age. On one occasion an "informant" from El Salvador, under the sponsorship of the Reagan administration, was scheduled to testify before Congress about Russian involvement in the Salvadoran revolution; we in the movement were worried that this would be the prelude to large-scale U.S. intervention, not simply the kind of small-scale proxy war that was already going on. I responded by reaching out to the dozen or so branches of the Johrei Fellowship in the U.S., who channeled long-distance Johrei as well as providing one-on-one "treatments" (free of charge), and who also forwarded prayer-intentions submitted by its members and fellow-travelers to the spiritual powers under whom they worked. I wrote a letter to all the Johrei churches in the United States, asking them to pray not for any preconceived outcome to the upcoming Congressional hearings, but simply that the truth be revealed. The upshot was that the informant in question, contrary to all expectations, denied any Russian involvement in El Salvador. But the most interesting aspect of this exercise in "white magic" was the fact that the testimony took place *before* any of the prayer-requests I had sent could have been received and acted upon. Someone less "liminal" than I was at the time would simply have concluded that the prayers I had requested had had no real effect—and I certainly don't blame anyone who accepts this as the most obvious and rational explanation. The lesson I drew from it, however, was an insight into the principle expressed in the Book of Isaiah, where God says: "Before they ask I will answer" [Isaiah 65:24]. Spiritual causality is not limited by time; the influence of the First Cause does not arrive horizontally from the past, or even from the future, as in the case of Aristotle's "final cause"—the notion that the ultimate goal of a particular action may be considered to be the actual cause of it—but rather descends vertically from Eternity. But if God answers prayers before they are formulated, what becomes of the "prayer of petition"? Doesn't petitionary prayer lose all its function and meaning if the visible effect precedes the visible cause? Yes and no. If God knows "beforehand" what we will ask Him for, nothing prevents Him from answering prayers that we haven't prayed yet, though of course we will never be able to prove the relationship between such prayer and its answer; in this case prayer of petition is transformed into prayer of thanksgiving. Furthermore, according to Sufi doctrine, we can only effectively petition God if He has already commanded us to submit that petition—if He has said (in effect) "ask Me for something." And if a particular outcome "was always going to happen anyway," then the fact that someone prayed for that outcome was also always going to happen anyway—the prayer and its answer making up a single synthetic destiny. This principle is encapsulated in the prayer of the Sufi Bayazid Bistami, "O God, You know what I want"—the import of this being that if our petitions to God are actually reflections of His desire to grant those petitions, then the highest form of piety and submission to His Will is not to grasp after the desired outcome by importuning Him, but rather to allow it to rest, undisturbed, within Him, while becoming profoundly receptive to its influence. In retrospect, I can now see that this attempt to apply spiritual force to political action was an important turning-point in my pilgrimage from the illusions of white magic to the realities of submission to God, from "I will the good (or my idea of it) and call upon all spiritual powers to empower that will" to "not my will but Thine be done."

But was Truth really served by that testimony before that Congressional committee, on which occasion I had prayed that the truth be told though the heavens fall? A large-scale U.S. invasion of Central America would have been an unmitigated disaster for all concerned, on both sides; I'm still glad that it was avoided. Yet there is also no doubt in my mind that the Russians *were* involved in El Salvador, and possibly the Chinese as well; it stands to geopolitical reason that all players who had any stake whatsoever in what was to happen in Central America during those years had to have had some involvement, whether large or small, in the events transpiring there. Perhaps the larger truth would not have been *served* by a revelation of Russian involvement, but neither was the entire truth in any way *told*. What *hubris* we were affected by in those years to be so certain that we knew God's true will for that historical moment, and so confident that our own actions served it!

Nonetheless, for around two years in the mid-1980s, a deep spiritual influence was moving through Santa Venetia Presbyterian Church, which was certainly felt beyond the boundaries of our little congregation. The Holy Spirit—at least as we saw Him—was being poured out upon us, bringing together a powerful union of social action (rightly considered in Christian terms as a commitment to corporal works of mercy) and God's Grace as expressed through love and fellowship. Add to this the high drama of opposition to the U.S. government, which would have earned many of us five years in Federal prison for conspiracy if the Feds had decided to act, and the result was a very potent mix indeed. And even though the ideology we held to was in many ways based on a falsehood, the sincerity of our faith-commitment was still a powerful force that, at least to some degree, served the Good: thank God that, in the words of the Prophet Muhammad, peace and blessings be upon him, "acts are judged by their intent"! (It was only later that some of us began to realize how dearly we would have to pay for the *mere falsehood* of our ideological position.)

THROUGH THE NEEDLE'S EYE

As I've already mentioned above, our church's major project during the time I was there was a film called *Through the Needle's Eye*. It was based on testimonies of Argentine woman refugees who had been tortured during Argentina's Dirty Little War, which we presented in the context of similar events now taking place in Central America. I recited one of Jenny's poems, "The Mountains," in the video, which was written in sympathy and solidarity with the sufferings of the oppressed in El Salvador and elsewhere—though in retrospect it could just as easily be read as a critique of that struggle and that solidarity. We also invited an American veteran of the Vietnam War, a member of the veterans' peace group Swords to Ploughshares, to formally apologize to the Argentine women for the actions of the U.S. government. We were told later that this video had helped other victims of torture find the courage to give their own testimonies.

DUSK

But for all the strength and truth of the Spirit that moved us, we remained without a vessel strong enough to contain that Spirit and apply it to the real heart of our spiritual lives. Many U.S. "progressive" Christians were being drawn to social action during those years. In one sense this was an overflow of the Christian charisma expressed through corporal works of mercy; in another, it was simply a way to stir up the dying embers of faith into a strong but temporary new blaze by seeking social "relevancy." In our own case, too much of the essence of the spiritual life was being lost in conflict with worldly conditions to allow for the deepening of our devotional and contemplative center. We were willing to struggle with the world in the name of God and make real sacrifices in the pursuit of our *image* of God's justice, but we had little idea of the way, or even the need, to struggle with ourselves; in Muslim terms, we had volunteered for the lesser *jihad* as a way of shirking our duty to fight in the greater *jihad*. And if we dreamt of dying as martyrs for the People's liberation so that our worldly identities would survive in the People's memory, this simply transformed those identities into idols and blocked us from renouncing them and remembering God Alone, as the contemplative Path called us to do. And so the manifestation of the Spirit in and through us had a set limit to it; after that limit was passed, nothing was left for us but the outer darkness, filled with the weeping and the gnashing of teeth.

Various signs of the coming dusk began to appear. For one thing, it became clear to us that some of the various Salvadoran politicos we were working with had been lying to us. On one occasion, during an event at the church, one young trickster, with narrow eyes and a sly smile, told us: "O no! There are no *Communists* fighting with the Salvadoran rebels! Rest assured (you stupid, gullible Norteamericano church people) that we are entirely pure of that stain." Satanist graffiti, on one occasion, appeared above the church door. And the building next door was purchased by the Da Free John (later Adi Da) organization and turned into his Marin County headquarters; busloads of hippie peons were shipped down from his stronghold at Clear Lake to work on the site. One of them was a 40-year-old woman with the dress and demeanor of a 15-year-old hippie girl. She peered around with a spooked look on her face at the "outside world" she'd heard cautionary tales about; she looked as if she hadn't been outside of the Da ashram in twenty years. [NOTE: Da Free John or Adi Da, 1939–2008, was one of the ever-changing names of Franklin Jones, an American teacher in the Hindu yoga tradition with a background in the Psychedelic Revolution, a *chela* of (among others) Swami Muktananda — whose *shaktipat* I had once received — author of many highly intelligent and perceptive books, and a self-styled Avatar of God whose degree of realization apparently surpassed that of all the avatars, prophets, saints and gurus of the past; he has been characterized by some as a cult-leader.] And as I've already recounted, the mothers of the greater Santa Venetia community, whose "latchkey kids" attended a day care center on the church grounds, went to war with us when we voted to become a homeless shelter. Then one of our congregants, Rich Cavangnolo, died by electrocution during an accident at work. Finally we realized that a couple of visitors to the church obviously thought they had walked in on some kind of cult meeting, and beat a hasty retreat. We had definitely lost many of our personal boundaries due to the intensity of the group experience; *had* we become a cult? And as our light faded, the Presbytery of the Redwoods, the church's parent body, was suddenly no longer willing to indulge the antics of a "mission" church that was not pulling its own weight in financial terms. So things changed, we slowly drifted apart, and Carolyn Studer was ultimately replaced as pastor. She moved to L.A. to play jazz piano with Al Jarreau, and later went to work for the Disney studios, whom she claimed stole her idea for the TV program that was later to become *Touched by an Angel*. (The female Irish angel in the series was, in my opinion, a kind of idealized Carolyn Studer.) Ultimately the original congregation of Santa Venetia dispersed, after which the church became host to a congregation of Korean Presbyterians.

With the end of Santa Venetia Presbyterian Church as we had known it, our identification with the Liberation Theology movement also ended. There is no doubt in my mind that without the large-scale involvement of North American churches in the opposition to U.S. intervention in Central America we would have seen a much greater bloodbath in that region, accompanied by a destabilization of much of the western hemisphere, most likely including the large-scale incursion of the Central American death-squads into the United States itself. But even though Liberation Theology, with its "option for the poor," did base itself partly on the Gospel call for Christians to perform corporal works of mercy, nonetheless a true marriage of Christianity and Marxism—that is, of theistic spirituality and atheistic Communism—is not a viable possibility in either theological or socio-historical terms. (In view of this it may be no coincidence that Thomas Merton's last speech in Bangkok, immediately before he died by accidental electrocution, was on the subject of "Marxism and Monastic Perspectives"; if anyone wishes to take this tragic event as a sign of God's displeasure I would certainly not object.) No matter how idealistically we might have pursued it, no matter how heroically we might have fought and sacrificed for it, no matter how sincerely we believed we were serving the cause of God's Mercy as expressed in the struggle for human liberation, such a two-headed beast as Liberation Theology is contradictory, ill-conceived, and dishonest at the root. Simply stated, it was based on the lie that "a man can serve two masters," a lie that we are still paying for, and paying dearly, in the 21st Century. And the fact is, much of the moral authority and spiritual capital of Christianity, and especially of the Roman Catholic Church, was squandered in those years through the more or less successful attempt to block U.S. intervention in Central America. Real material good was done in the dimension of time; much spiritual good was lost in the dimension of eternity. And the fact is that the Catholic Church, after the rejection of its traditional dogma, the deconstruction of the sacramental order, the pedophilia scandal which resulted in the bankruptcy of whole archdioceses, the closure of so many churches and the departure of millions of the faithful, no longer possesses the kind of social influence and moral authority that it spent so recklessly on helping "the World" in the 1980s.

Elements of the U.S. Catholic Church—notably Catholic Charities—have retained even to this day their commitment to helping Latin American immigrants illegally cross the border from Mexico into the United States that they embraced during the days of the Sanctuary Movement; this represents the grassroots aspect of the infiltration of Marxism into the post-conciliar Church. However, while some refugees from the south are still fleeing political oppression, they are now accompanied by plenty of members of Mexican drug cartels and other criminal and/or terrorist organizations. And where, exactly, is the line to be drawn between helping refugees and enabling human traffickers? In this year of 2023, it is estimated (subject to corroboration) that something like 30,000 *unaccompanied children* crossed illegally from Mexico into the United States; it is very difficult for me to believe that a large percentage of them were not scooped up by the kind of child sex-trafficking networks that were exposed in the 2023 motion picture *The Sound of Freedom*. According to National Public Radio—not a news outlet where you'd expect to run into the kind of anti-immigrant sentiment usually identified with conservative Republicans—the immigration from El Salvador to the United States that began in the 1980s has led to a vast increase in the power of the Salvadoran drug gangs, which is what the revolutionary cadres tended to morph into, especially after the revolution, as soon as they embraced drug trafficking as a source of funding—just like Colonel Oliver North did on the other side of the fence, the side of the Nicaraguan Contras who also dealt drugs, and who were backed up in their activities by President Ronald Reagan. Salvadorans operating in the relative freedom of the U.S. have been able to build narcotics-trafficking networks much more easily than they could have done in their native country, after which these networks are simply exported back to El Salvador. MS-13 for example, one of the most violent of these drug gangs, actually devolved from a paramilitary organization set up to defend Salvadoran refugees in Los Angeles. The "MS" in its name stands for *Mara Salvatrucha*, "*mara*" meaning "gang" and "*Salvatrucha(s)*" being a reference the Salvadoran insurgents of the 1980s who were connected with the Farabundo Martí National Liberation Front, named after the leftist national poet of El Salvador, Farabundo Martí. So times change. What is mercy and justice in one era can unexpectedly become cruelty and injustice in another. Politics is the art of the ephemeral.

At one point during our years with the Sanctuary Movement, an interesting and quite moving document was circulated, a statement by a woman guerrilla fighter somewhere in Latin America. She called upon the monastics of the Catholic Church not to abandon their contemplative vocation in order to become activists and revolutionaries (and, I would add, social workers), but rather to continue to man the post where God had stationed them, since *they* (in a certain sense) were part of what *she* was fighting for. Unfortunately, from the standpoint of 2023, I can only conclude that, at least in terms of its "official" ideology, the Catholic Church—except for a tiny remnant of the Traditional faithful—has remained largely deaf to her plea.

But God still heard my prayer during those years—no matter how ill-conceived it might have been at the time—that I would be given the chance to bring together, in a legitimate way, spirituality and social action. Sincerity neither can nor should ever triumph over Truth—and yet, in some mysterious way that we can never fully predict and often can't even begin to understand, it will always somehow serve that Truth. The real answer to my prayer finally came, thirty years later, when the re-discovery of the Covenants of the Prophet Muhammad with the Christians of his time allowed me to act as one of the founders of an international interfaith peace movement, the Covenants Initiative, that was based explicitly on the socio-political Will of God as expressed directly through one of His chosen prophets; it was through the effect of that Initiative in my life that the lesser *jihad* finally began serving the greater. And who should my partner and leader in that movement, Dr John Andrew Morrow, turn out to be but a veteran, just as I was, of the non-intervention movement in solidarity with the revolutions of Central America in the 1980s, though his theatre of operations was centered more in Guatemala than in El Salvador. The story of our partnership is told below in *Chapter Twelve*. After those thirty years of disillusionment and instruction, God was finally giving us a second chance to get it right!

ANOTHER "TURNING"

So I had now reached a point in my activist career where I was subject to the common disease of disappointed idealism, or (in my case) "Leftist burnout." We had discovered that the Salvadoran revolutionaries were not saints, that there was plenty of infighting among the various factions, and that even just and successful revolutions were often not able to maintain their earlier idealism—to say the least. I had seen several of my contemporaries, who had come to the same point, flip precipitously to the Right, becoming followers of William Buckley, etc. I vowed not to take that route—and so, rather than moving to the Right, I consciously decided to go *up* instead, to opt for subtler and supposedly more "spiritual" forms of activism. I was just on the cusp of transcending that binary circuit of the human brain which sees everything in either/or, for-or-against terms, that believes there are only two sides to every question—a circuit that the Devil can use to great advantage. When the *Princeps Huius Mundi* is allowed to draw the sides—Right against

Left, Man against Woman, Black against White, Red State against Blue State, Muslim against Christian—he has virtually guaranteed that whichever side you take, damage will be done and darkness spread; as Rama Coomaraswamy liked to say, "the Devil doesn't care which side of the horse you fall off of." The spiritual Path requires that you transcend the *dvandvas*, the pairs-of-opposites—which means that learning not to get stuck in the contradictions of social ideology is one step toward, and also one of the effects of, the transcendence of the *dvandvas* in the inner world. Sometimes, of course, a faithfulness to eternal Principles will require you to take sides, but it will also teach you never to *absolutize* the side you take, since you've realized that *partisanship* is always necessarily a *partial* viewpoint. When the Pharisees asked Jesus whether or not it was lawful to pay the Roman tax, they thought they'd caught him in the net of the opposites. If he answered "no" he would be arrested by the Romans and tried for sedition; if he answered "yes" he would lose his base among the Zealots and the other militant anti-Roman Jews, and simply become irrelevant. But when he answered "render unto Caesar the things that are Caesar's and to God the things that are God's," he slipped their trap. Transcending the socio-political *dvandvas*, however, is something that most people with a radical political commitment find it almost impossible to do, or even to want to do, since they see anyone who claims to have achieved this as some kind of wishy-washy "moderate." The truth, apparently, is that it sometimes takes the blessing and guidance of a Prophet like Muhammad, who had a socio-political as well as a spiritual mandate from God, to fully make this transition.

Roughly contemporaneous with the Sanctuary Movement was the Anti-Nuclear Movement in which, once again, poet Allen Ginsberg played an important role; several "progressive" churches in Marin who hadn't been attracted to Central America had become involved with the best-organized and most successful thrust of that movement, the Nuclear Freeze campaign. In 1967 Ginsberg had been involved in a mass peace demonstration, along with 70,000 peace activists and acid-heads, which included an effort to *levitate* the Pentagon by the application of group psychic energy. (Was anybody really serious about this possibility? And did it really matter?) Next year in '68 he was leading troops of *Om*-ing demonstrators at the Democratic National Convention in Chicago, whose surrounding peace riots I had attended. And in the late '70s and into the '80s he was a leader in the Anti-Nuclear Movement, in which capacity he composed a powerful poem entitled "Plutonean Ode" where he *cursed* the highly radioactive, artificial element plutonium, much as prohibitionist Carrie Nation in earlier years had cursed the Demon Rum. All these efforts well exemplified the "magical populism" for which the hippies were known.

By the late '80s, much of the impetus of the hippie magical populism was being carried on, in altered form, by the New Age Movement, whose style was less confrontational and who tended to act more through "psychic networks" of stay-at-homes than mass demonstrations, though they certainly had plenty of public events, largely in "workshop" form. The New Agers were adept at national and even global networking, and this at a time when the internet was still in its infancy. And it was the New Age that Jenny and I initially turned to, after Santa Venetia descended into darkness, to take our attention off of the pain of that demise and give us a new Cause to believe in, a new form of Sacred Activism to pursue, a new way to make a working union between Religion (or rather Spirituality) and Politics. The story of this turn (or was it really just a temporary vacation?) is told in the next chapter.

AFTERSHOCK

I put off finishing the present *Chapter Eight* of this book until the last—especially the episodes on Santa Venetia Presbyterian Church—because I suspected for some reason that they would present the greatest challenges. And I was right: In the process of writing this chapter, a great terror came over me. The memories I called up shockingly impressed upon me the fact that during our years of solidarity with the revolutions of Central America we had been in the presence of the greatest evil and the greatest *illusion* we had ever encountered, either before or since. A rattlesnake you have seen is still dangerous if he lies ahead of you on your path, but the rattlesnake that you don't see can be fatal. We all knew that something terribly dark had happened when Santa Venetia folded, but we never suspected the real truth: that this darkness had been there from the beginning.

The evil of the Nazis, though they had no qualms about using the Big Lie when it suited them, was in some ways fundamentally honest: "Our goal is to eliminate the Jews, subjugate the Slavs, crush the weak, and secure greater *Lebensraum* for the German people." It's all there in *Mein Kampf*. But when Karl Marx and Friederich Engels, in *The Communist Manifesto*, said: "Workers of the world unite! You have nothing to lose but your chains," they told a bigger lie than Adolf Hitler ever dreamed of. Hitler openly invoked the powers of evil; the Communists co-opted the powers of Good—the virtue of Charity, the love of Justice—and then lied about it. Hitler killed possibly 16 million people; Stalin and Mao together murdered as many 120 million.

That's the first layer of illusion. The second layer was the lie that Liberation Theology, a Communist ideology that called religion "the opium of the people," could honestly and legitimately be wedded to the Christian imperative to perform corporal works of mercy, to invite the poor to the banquet. It is certainly true that the Communists have defended the poor and provided for their needs many times since the *Manifesto* was published — though the Christians have always outdone them in this — but once they triumph in a given nation, the churches are usually shut down, the priests murdered, the people taught that there is no God. Even the Sandinistas of Nicaragua, for all the help provided to them by the Catholics after Vatican II, are now running afoul of the Catholic Church, and being branded oppressors by many who once supported them. When my colleague in the Covenants Initiative, Dr John Andrew Morrow (see *Chapter Twelve*), met with Ernesto Cardenal when he was ex-Minister of Culture of Sandinista Nicaragua, the confused and aging poet-priest rambled on, in Deist mode, about how God had created the universe and then gone away, leaving us all in the lurch, which meant that the mandate for managing and improving that universe had now passed to the human race, and to humanity's vanguard, the heroic warriors fighting for the People's liberation. Such a hopeless, contradictory conception is certainly one of those allowed for by the formless and chaotic theological speculations of the Novus Ordo Catholic Church after Vatican II, which also included the vaguely Hegelian, process-theology-influenced, Chardinian notion that God is some obscure, struggling Consciousness, always seeking greater power and integration but never quite getting there, much like *El Pueblo* in their struggle for freedom. It was as if the church-and-party line had finally become: "Some day, my friends, we will reach the great classless Omega Point that Father Teilhard promised us — but until then, our slogan and lament must be, in the words of Berthold Brecht: 'Ah we, who desired to prepare the soil for kindness, could not ourselves be kind.'"

The third layer of illusion was our willingness — I might say, our compulsion — to use our feeling of fellowship, and the sincere yet untested emotions generated by taking up "the option for the poor," to quite successfully divert our attention away from the above contradictions. We had forgotten Christ's words that "the poor you have always with you," meaning that we will always be confronted with the imperative to exercise charity for those in need, "but you will not always have Me." Well did Frithjof Schuon preach against the error of "sincerism," the notion that sincerity of subjective belief can obviate the deficiencies of objective error! If you call upon the Holy Spirit in sincerity and faith, and then use the power of that Spirit for a purpose or in a manner that God has not sanctioned — especially if you do so *without even asking Him what He wants* — you will invoke immense darkness. The Prophet Muhammad, peace and blessings be upon him, taught that "acts are judged according to the intentions behind them" (a teaching that Frithjof Schuon, for one, apparently ignored). Yet the good intentions that can lead the soul to Paradise in the next world can do nothing whatsoever to negate or ward off or mitigate the evil consequences, in this world, of such intentions misapplied in ignorance — especially *willful* ignorance. Knowledge does not free us from the duty to love, but neither does love absolve us of the duty to know — to know, and then to act accordingly.

And the fourth and final layer of illusion, perhaps the most destructive of all, was the one that affected our personal feelings and relationships. A lot of people were hurt when Santa Venetia Presbyterian Church fell; some may never have fully recovered. It wasn't just the various squabbles that grew up when the energy that had given the group its cohesion began to fade (including some of the trips that Carolyn ran when she began to fear she was losing her authority) — it was also the fact that so many of the people who had given the appearance of being lifelong friends suddenly turned into rather distant acquaintances when the matrix that had made those friendships possible was no longer in force. Without *real* friendship, without true constancy and loyalty between individuals, the impersonal shadow of a counterfeit *agape* was cast upon our scene, a shadow that was not the universal love it had pretended to be but hardly more than an ephemeral collective co-dependency or group identification. And the effect of this profound disillusionment was that both our ability to relate to groups in a sound and conscious way, and the similar yet opposite ability to make and maintain authentic one-on-one relationships, were wounded. Our high-energy co-dependency had damaged our ability to discern and maintain healthy boundaries, without which no true love, either individual or collective, is possible. True love requires *respect*, a word which literally means "to look again" — to look beyond our initial identification with or aversion to a person so we can begin to see who they really are, *apart* from us, thus making possible that higher way of being-together which only appears, in Rilke's words, when "two solitudes protect and border and salute each other."

CHAPTER NINE
The Planet of the New Age

WELCOME TO THE NEW AGE

One day, after the era of Santa Venetia Presbyterian Church and the Sanctuary Movement had passed, Jenny woke up and said: "Now I want to be a spiritual tripper!"

"Spiritual tripping" in the second half of the 1980s essentially meant involvement with the New Age movement, so we ended up on a 2-year tour-of-duty through that world, partly as believers, partly as skeptical observers. As for myself, I wanted to get a picture of what remained of counterculture spirituality and see what it had morphed into now that the "classical" hippies had begun to fade back into the annals of history. And since we entered more-or-less as activists, or with an activist background, it was natural for us to become involved with the "psychic peace movement," as part of the collective oscillation of the "alternative" sector of the Baby Boom generation between the poles of mysticism and politics. My perpetual question about this period is: were we really exploring the potential of organized mass "consciousness" to change material conditions, or were we just taking a kind of Caribbean fantasy-cruise as a well-earned vacation from hardball *realpolitik*?

FROM "SPIRITUAL REVOLUTION" TO "PARADIGM SHIFT": RETROSPECTIVE NUMBER TWO

At this point it wouldn't hurt to take another look at the origins of the hippie Spiritual Revolution and how it was similar to, and different from, the later New Age development. (For a useful perspective on the "cusp" of this transition I refer the interested researcher to *The Greening of America* by Charles A. Reich.) So many influences came together to make the New Age, so many books influenced the development of it, that I can't do more than give a quick overview of them here. Spiritualism, Theosophy, Rosicrucianism, Freemasonry, and the Hermetic Order of the Golden Dawn must of course be included, along with a number of other strands derived from the history of western occultism, not to mention British and American psychical research and the books about and example of the "sleeping prophet" of Kentucky, Edgar Cayce. In terms of the printed page, the three authors most influential (in my opinion) on the New Age ethos were Jane Roberts, channel for the teachings of the entity known as "Seth" who appeared in such books as *The Seth Material, Seth Speaks* and *The Nature of Personal Reality*; the set of books comprising *A Course in Miracles*, channeled by Helen Schucman; and the writings of Carlos Castaneda that I've already dealt with above. And *The Aquarian Conspiracy* by Marilyn Ferguson provided a comprehensive overview of the whole movement. Outside of the works of these central figures, a number of other important books were published that epitomized, or even initiated, several practices and disciplines that are still alive and well today. For the practice of "channeling"—which began in earnest under the name of "mediumship" with the Spiritualist movement of the 19th century—an influential book was *Opening to Channel* by Sanaya Roman and Duane Packer; for out-of-body experiences and the study of them, *Journeys Out of Body* by Robert Monroe; for thanatology and near-death experiences, *On Death and Dying* by Elizabeth Kubler-Ross and *Life after Life* by Raymond Moody; for advanced psychical research, *Psychic Discoveries Behind the Iron Curtain* by Shiela Ostrander and Lynn Schroeder; for the contribution of New Age ideas to the rise of globalism, *The Call*, *Everyday Miracles* and *Re-Imagining the World* by David Spangler and *The Global Brain* by Peter Russell; for the rise of technocracy, *Future Shock* by Alvin Toffler; and for the growth of the religion of UFO-worship, *The Pleiadian Agenda* by Barbara Hand Clow. As for a critique of New Age beliefs from a more traditional standpoint, important books were *The Hidden Dangers of the Rainbow* by Constance Cumby, *The Soul After Death* by Fr Seraphim Rose, and my own *The System of Antichrist: Truth and Falsehood in Postmodernism and the New Age* [2001].

The roots of the New Age were latent in the hippie movement from the beginning. Just as the Communist Party was not dominant in the 1960s peace movement—which was largely populist and spontaneous in nature rather than the product of any organized Leftist vanguard—but was nonetheless always there, better organized and with a clearer agenda than the peace movement as a whole, so such occultist organizations as the Theosophical Society and the Freemasons, though not dominant in the hippie Spiritual Revolution, nonetheless exerted their influence, an influence which came to the fore in the New Age movement of the 1970s. Hippie spirituality, as we have already seen, was mostly a hodge-podge of traditional religions and spiritual practices, largely of eastern origin—with the mystical aspects predominating—promiscuously mixed with Shamanism (primarily Native American), Spiritualism, occultism, magic, the quest for psychic powers, and every non-traditional "spirituality" under the sun. Western Christian, Jewish and Sufi mysticism also played a part, though their influence was less central than that of the dharmic religions of Asia. Sixties spirituality grew in part out of the earlier importation of Hinduism into the West, mostly through the Vedanta Society, and of Buddhism in the form of Zen, which was the dominant spirituality of the Beat Generation (though by no means universal among them) who preceded the hippies and provided them with much of their worldview. And the whole amalgam was energized and rendered increasingly chaotic by the use of LSD and other psychedelics.

The hippies of North America were drawn mostly, though not exclusively, from the middle classes. Many, however, became downwardly mobile, since the hippie movement was in part a rebellion against middle class values. Consequently many young people whose parents were of the middle class and who had groomed them for careers in the professions ultimately became carpenters, house painters, auto mechanics, etc. This trend among the hippies of embracing the crafts and the trades rather than the professions was related to — though certainly not to be strictly identified with — a tendency among some hippies or ex-hippies to adopt aspects of the more conservative values of the rural Christian working-class they were coming into contact with through the back-to-the-land movement. The late hippie phenomenon of the "Jesus Freaks" foreshadowed this development. A hippie carpenter could still have long hair and smoke marijuana; nonetheless he and his family might also exhibit a tendency to seek economic and social independence somewhat in the "frontier" spirit of earlier generations of Americans, even gravitating toward the kind of rural "survivalism" now mostly identified with right-wing extremists and "patriotic" militias. Certain countrified hippies, with their bearded men and their women in "granny" dresses, even gave the impression of being a kind of strange, hybrid, latter-day Amish — Amish with the addition of sex, drugs and rock-and-roll.

Many of those among the hippies who resisted the pressure of downward social mobility and who hadn't destroyed themselves through drugs, ending up in mental hospitals, jails, or on skid row, were inspired instead to "clean up their act" and return to the professional career track in the Reagan years, driving themselves hard to make up for lost economic time; these were some of the ones who became the "yuppies" (Young Urban Professionals) of the 1980s. Nonetheless, many of the ex-hippies who were now part of the professional classes retained their interest in "alternative" spiritualities, which they sometimes re-packaged as motivational and organizational "paradigms" for use by corporate management, following in the footsteps of Andrew Carnegie and Norman Vincent Peal, though with the Christian paradigm now replaced with new ones drawn from non-Christian sources. (I learned about that world largely through Randy Carson, who once invited me to a lavish villa in Hillsboro, California, where the CEOs of Hewlett-Packard and other major Silicon Valley tech companies pow-wowed with their psychics, witches, neo-shamans and New Age gurus. I was immersed on that day in the world of "yuppie spirituality" — perhaps best represented by the highly-influential Erhard Seminar Training or EST, founded by Werner Erhard, which in turn grew out of the Human Potential Movement that formed an important part of the New Age and was one of the things that distinguished that manifestation from the hippie Spiritual Revolution that came before it.) Among the dominant influences of the time were the Sino-Japanese martial arts, as expressed in such works as *The Book of Five Rings* by Miyamoto Musashi and *The Art of War* by Sun Tzu, re-envisioned in terms of the economic combat carried on by corporate capitalism. It was this post-hippie resurrection of the entrepreneurial spirit, a spirit brilliantly analyzed in its original form by Max Weber in his seminal *The Protestant Ethic and the Spirit of Capitalism*, and specifically as expressed through one of the central spiritual currents of that ethic—namely, Norman Vincent Peal's *The Power of Positive Thinking*—that made elements of the New Age spirituality of the 1970s and '80s feel like a kind of non-Christian Pentecostalism. The founders of the personal computer revolution—Bill Gates, Steve Jobs, and Steve Wozniak—in some ways anticipated, or were even a part of, this gravitation of ex-hippies towards the professions, which also had affinities with a renewal of the American entrepreneurial spirit among elements of the counterculture in the '70s—though this trio of cyber-geniuses were also undoubtedly influenced by the hippie attraction to the crafts and trades. Rather than becoming businessmen working in large corporate offices under constant supervision, many early hippie techno-adepts opted to tinker with computers in their own shops or garages like smiths or potters, later marketing their creations. These "New Age yuppies" were followed by a younger generation of petty bourgeois entrepreneurs who identified with the same New Age values and thought of themselves as members of the same movement as the "progressive, New Age" yuppies, though they occupied a much lower economic class.

In order to serve the yuppies and small-scale business people of the '70s and '80s, who both emerged from and succeeded the hippie movement—at least those of them who retained their identification with "alternative" (non-Judeo-Christian) spiritualities, or grew up in an ambience dominated by these spiritualities—the New Age Movement appeared. The direct antecedents of this movement were western Spiritualism and Theosophy rather than the religions of India and China. Their central practice was (and is) the "channeling" of various "spirit entities," one of whose major functions was psychic healing, and their central hope was for the emergence of a "new paradigm" that would supplant both Capitalism and Christianity, both materialistic technocracy and the social influence of "old-style" macro-economic forces. Nonetheless the New Age practitioners were much more open to modern technology, including computer technology, than the hippies had been, who by-and-large flourished before the appearance of the personal computer. The hippies, however, especially via the back-to-the-land movement, and their expertise in the electronic technology necessary to produce rock music, had their own attraction to "appropriate" technology—one that is best represented by Stuart Brand, editor of the widely-influential *Whole Earth Catalogue* and its successor periodical the *CoEvolution Quarterly*.

The New Age attraction to modern technology, and to the assumed "spiritual" potentials of such technology, made it in some ways the ancestor of today's transhumanist development, as well an environment congenial to the growth of various brands of "UFO spirituality." And we should also mention at this point a more "literary" approach to alternative spiritualities, paralleling the growth of the New Age movement in the 1970s and 1980s, one that was best represented by *Gnosis* magazine, edited by Jay Kinney and Richard Smoley — who, interestingly enough, when they felt the need to "go straight" in their later years, joined the Theosophical Society and Scottish Rite Freemasonry respectively. This literary occultism, after hybridizing with certain surviving elements of hippiedom — primarily the mystical relationship to the natural world as mediated by various psychedelic "plant powers" which was well-illustrated in the opening scenes of the cinematic version of J. R. R. Tolkien's *The Fellowship of the Ring* — became one of the major tributaries to post-'60s Neo-Paganism.

But the less literary, less well-read, less historically conscious, and more technology-savvy New Age had greater influence than these "literary occultists" did, which allowed the New Agers to act as the vanguard of the movement toward globalization and one-world-government (not to mention transhumanism and artificial intelligence) — something that the more literary and historically-educated members of the post-hippie counterculture, including many Neo-Pagans, were less attracted to and more suspicious of.

As the 1990s drew to a close, the New Age as an influential popular movement was on the wane. At the same time some of the dominant teachers of the movement, such as "futurist" Barbara Marx Hubbard, were being inducted into the world of the ruling elites and their globalist think-tanks, which was in many ways the logical ultimate destination for the "New Age yuppie" in socio-political terms. Given that one of the major doctrines of the New Age was "create your own reality," those New Age practitioners who were able to "manifest their dreams" in the economic sphere had their belief in New Age principles triumphantly validated, while those (clearly the majority) who failed in their economic hopes ultimately concluded that the teachings of their New Age gurus — people like Starhawk (the New Age witch), Shakti Gawain (author of *Creative Visualization*) and the ever-present discarnate entity Seth as channeled by Jane Roberts — were all impractical fantasy, and either did their best to return to their Judeo-Christian roots, plenty of which had dried up and died in the meantime, or else became disillusioned with religion or spirituality of any kind. As of this writing, however, elements of the New Age, and of the psychedelic counterculture as well, seem to be making a comeback in certain quarters, especially in the area of UFO research and NDEs (Near Death Experiences), though in many cases (most NDEs excepted) they appear to be even more infiltrated and controlled by the elite agenda of the Powers That Be than they were the first time around.

And the New Age movement, from the beginning, might well have been an even more deliberate and well-engineered mass social engineering job than the hippie counterculture was, which was based to a large degree on the mass dissemination of lysergic acid diethylamide by the CIA—though it would be wrong to claim that either movement was simply created by the social engineers out of the whole cloth, since both of them embraced elements of a true creative populism, as well as appealing, however falsely, to the innate spiritual aspirations of the human race. In his last book, *Manifesto for the Noösphere: The Next Stage in the Evolution of Human Consciousness*, José Argüelles, who brought us perhaps the most influential event of the burgeoning New Age, the one known as "Harmonic Convergence," drew upon the theories of one Oliver L. Reiser [1885–1974] as laid out in his *Cosmic Humanism* [1966]. Reiser was a scientist who developed an early version of superstring theory, was praised by Albert Einstein, and proposed the actual creation of Teilhard de Chardin's "noösphere" by technological means, as well as a project for human eugenics through manipulating the radiation of the ionosphere; he apparently believed that mass radiation poisoning, such as was experienced at Hiroshima and Nagasaki, might ultimately have a eugenic effect upon the human race. According to researcher Drew Hemple,

> Reiser's book *Cosmic Humanism* was held in the highest esteem by a think tank called the Institute for Integrative Education. This think tank was set up by Forest Products magnate Julius Stulman and its office was then located at the UN Plaza. Its board of directors included the family that directed the nondualist Theosophist [*Theosophical?*] Society [*which branch we are not told*]; it also included scientists from Harvard and Yale. The goal of this Institute, as spelled out in their flagship academic journal *Main Currents in Modern Thought* [1940–1975], was to review all prominent academic journals and integrate all knowledge to the goals of nondualist theosophy. With this in mind, the journal had a very advanced interest in eastern philosophy, paranormal research, eugenics, higher dimensional physics and social engineering.

Apparently the term "nondualism" as used by Hemple does not refer to the Hindu Advaita Vedanta, but to the agenda of creating a One World society by technological means. Hemple also claims, without supporting evidence, that José Argüelles, who passed away in 2011, had CIA connections.

If my own experience is any indication, it would seem that the True Believer sometimes has to take a tour of duty as a Paranoid Conspiracy Theorist before he can moderate and balance out the effects of his earlier limitless idealism; when and if such balance is finally achieved, worldly idealism is transformed, *insha'Allah*, into trust in God, and bitter cynicism into sobriety and detachment from the world. This need to balance idealism with paranoia led me to speculate in later years that Harmonic Convergence and similar events might actually have been designed to function as a tender-minded advance guard for the tough-minded economic and political globalization process and the push for a One World Government. Certainly there was, and is, a lot of One World idealism in the New Age, as well as a wide cross-pollination between various large, established, well-funded New Age/Interfaith organizations, such as Esalen Institute, Share International and the World Parliament of Religions, and the think-tanks of the globalist elites. New Age teacher Barbara Marx Hubbard, for example—heir to the Yo-Yo fortune (yes, you heard me correctly) and past honors graduate in political science from the Sorbonne—went on to become one of the directors of the World Future Society along with Robert McNamara (formerly the U.S. Secretary of Defense and president of the World Bank), Maurice Strong (who had been secretary general of the UN Conference on Environment and Development), and scholars from Georgetown University, the George Washington University, and the University of Maryland. Most of us who had entered the New Age from the hippie counterculture simply took leaders like Hubbard as "our people"; we almost never asked ourselves, or anybody else, what powerful established interests might have *sent* leaders like her to lead us, and exactly what destination they might be leading us to.

THE PSYCHIC PEACE MOVEMENT

As for Jenny and myself, we definitely needed a spiritual vacation after the Sanctuary Movement and the cadres of the Far Left, so we "naturally" gravitated toward the more ethereal aspects of the social and spiritual potential of the Baby Boom generation. If the world couldn't be changed through heroic socio-political if not military action, maybe it could be helped through prayer and meditation; consequently the brand of activism we were attracted to during the second half of the '80s had to do with the mass application of "spiritual" energy to social change, as exemplified by Pathways to Peace headed by Avon Mattison, the International Day of Prayer for Peace that was "handed down" to the New Age masses by the UN and the World Council of Churches, and the ever-memorable Harmonic Convergence, which took place on August 6/7, 1987—the first and probably the last international "folk spirituality" event, conceived of by the visionary artist and student of Mesoamerican religion José Argüelles, on the occasion of which I made both my debut and sang my swansong as a New Age teacher. It's hard for me to write about this period of my life due to its inherent lack of substance, which produced a sensation best described as "the unbearable lightness of being" (the title of a book by the Czech novelist Milan Kundera, set in Prague before the Soviet invasion of 1968). You know how when you inhale a lungful of helium gas and then try to speak, your voice goes into treble register, making you sound like a child, an elf or a cartoon character? That's what those days felt like to me. The spirituality of the post-counterculture masses had lost its connection with the *objectivity* of spiritual Truth, and replaced it with the *mass subjectivity* of the "collective unconscious," or rather of collective consciousness, as its chosen replacement for God. *We* were God now, and so it was up to us to shift the paradigm, usher in the New Age and *prevent the apocalypse*. Imagine the *guilt* felt by someone who believed that he and his compadres had both the duty and the power to save the world from being destroyed, but who was then forced to confront the relentlessly-looming failure of that Great Work, on all levels. And the fact that it was a fake guilt based on a fake responsibility did not mitigate that feeling of guilt in the slightest. This was the point where I essentially parted company with Allen Ginsberg, who became a leader in the Anti-Nuclear Movement, which was an example of the more grounded and realistic peace activism of the time, one that resulted in his powerful "Plutonean Ode" already mentioned, which was written not only as a conscious and deliberate spell against plutonium, but as a curse directed against the Gnostic Archons, whom he mentions by name. This was his own temporary excursion (from the slightly more stable standpoint of the Tibetan Buddhism of Chögyam Trungpa) into the kind of "magical populism" that the New Age masses had totally immersed themselves in. Ginsberg might actually have been picking up on the fact that the New Age movement as a whole (as opposed to the more earthy Neo-Paganism) was actually a form of Gnosticism that, speaking in Christian terms, denies the Incarnation, and therefore denigrates the human form. (If you want to get a clear idea of the quality of New Age Gnosticism, there is no question but that the central text to be studied is *A Course in Miracles*.)

New Age spirituality sought *subtilization* rather than wholeness. The goal was to manifest social transformation and personal abundance in the material world; nonetheless the entire thrust of the "spirituality" of that time was to *separate* oneself from the body and the material world—primarily out of fear—so as to reach some imaginary Archimedean point from which that body and that world might be influenced; this was one of the central contradictions in the whole movement. And after such a massive collective misstep, what was left for us to believe in but "spirits," like the UFO Aliens, who were nothing in reality but the etherialized masks of materialism, atheism, and transhumanism—of Satanism, in other words, since those "aliens," according to every reliably traditional account of their nature and activities, are demons and nothing else? There is no surer path to a true darkness than the exhaustion that comes after seeking a false light. Is it any surprise that overt "organized Satanism" is now coming out of the closet? My generation thought of Altamont, the Manson Family, the Jonestown Massacre (whose cultural roots, despite Jim Jones' Evangelical background, were largely in counterculture San Francisco), the Zodiac Killer and the Son of Sam—all but one of these being California phenomena—as weird isolated anomalies unexpectedly popping up from time to time out of a general movement toward peace, love, spirituality and social justice. But hadn't we blazed a trail for them in every way imaginable? Hadn't we opened the door for the Devil with every conceivable key? The world of the 2020s is now so dark, our society so degenerate, our souls so wounded, the environment so damaged, the future so bleak, that it is almost understandable that some who are still trying to believe in a Supreme Power ruling the universe would see that Power as evil. In view of the world's condition, Satan as Supreme Overlord, the *Princeps Huius Mundi*, is simply becoming more *plausible* to some people than an all-powerful and all-loving God.

But in the 1980s the dialectic of degeneration hadn't progressed anywhere near that far. It was an idealistic era of kinder and gentler horseshit; we were still channeling "angels." I will now quickly innumerate the main bases I touched on my spiritually homeless wanderings during those years. I have already described above the New Age healers I consulted during that time—Betty Bethards, Rev. Plume, Rev. Greg Schelkun, various Reiki practitioners, the Johrei Fellowship, and others—so I will concentrate here on those groups and individuals who had some connection with, or pretension to, social action.

PATHWAYS TO PEACE

In terms of my shift of focus from peace activism in solidarity with the revolutions of Central America—a contradiction that should have been obvious to us at the time, but wasn't—to New Age peace activism based on channeling "peace" as an "energy," the first organization I made contact with was Pathways to Peace, founded by Avon Mattison, who passed away in 2021. Their website describes them as follows:

> Since its inception in 1981, Pathways to Peace has worked with the UN to expand awareness of and engage in the International Day of Peace, which is held annually on September 21st [and] has grown from a single event of a few hundred people into a global movement that reaches hundreds of millions... Established by a unanimous United Nations resolution in 1981, it provides a globally shared date for all humanity to commit to Peace above all differences and to contribute to building a Culture of Peace.

Based on my status as a Lifetime Elder of the Presbyterian Church (USA) that I had earned as a member of the governing Session of Santa Venetia Presbyterian, I introduced a proposal to the Presbytery of the Redwoods—a regional administrative body covering northwest California north of San Francisco—asking the Presbyterian General Assembly to adopt a resolution in support of the International Day of Peace. The resolution ultimately passed. (Why not? It cost them nothing, and me next to nothing. At least I was not trying to pave the road to Hell with good intentions—only the road to nothing much.)

"SUFI" DANCING

Around the same time, in an attempt to keep up at least a small remnant of the devotional life Jenny and I had known in Santa Venetia, we connected with the Dances of Universal Peace, which I will have more to say about below. The DUP had a headquarters and dance venue in San Rafael; though the Dances were not strictly speaking New Age, they were still part of the general New Age ethos of the time. They were a project of Sufi Ruhaniat International, founded by none other than Samuel Lewis—Sufi Sam—whom Lew Welch had introduced me to all those years ago. This was the well-known "Sufi Dancing," and dancing it certainly was, though I can't be quite as sure about the Sufi part. At least it helped us keep our spirits up after the loss of Santa Venetia—though when I phoned them one time to ask when Ramadan began that year, nobody seemed to know.

GLOBAL FAMILY

Then, somehow—I don't exactly remember our itinerary—we became involved with a New Age peace organization called Global Family, run by Jeff Daley and other Marin County New Age yuppie professional types, whose main thrust at that point was citizen diplomacy with the Soviet Union, such as was made possible by the *glasnost* of Mikail Gorbachev. (Other groups have since appropriated the name, but the Global Family that I knew no longer exists.) I remember walking into their office at one point and immediately becoming intrigued with a number of high-tech-looking monitors placed on several desks, all appearing fascinatingly advanced. In answer to my questions I was told: "These are computers; right now they are talking to *other* computers—all the way on the other side of the world, in Russia!" That was my first encounter with the personal computer, which at that point was still more or less a "business machine" that could mostly be found only in the offices of large corporations. It was through Global Family that I met such luminaries as Barbara Marx Hubbard and Stanley Krippner, people who were part of the unofficial but always-striving-to-become-official Steering Committee of the New Age, many of them associated in some way with Esalen Institute, the central think-tank for the hippie and New Age counterculture on the West Coast. (Barbara Marx's Hubbard's name was placed in nomination for the vice-presidency of the United States at the 1984 Democratic convention—making her the first woman to be so honored—after which she spoke to the assembled delegates.) It was at a Global Family gathering that I suddenly saw that we were being inspired and/or directed by a vast consortium of invisible "angelic" beings hovering above us—entities who, at this point in time, I identify as the Jinn. These were clearly the "good" demons as opposed to the "bad" demons—possibly those "angels of light" the New Testament warns us against. Maybe some of them had good intentions and believed they were helping humanity, but the higher beings of the Kingdom of Light, not to mention the lower ones in the Kingdom of Darkness, certainly knew better. (After Jenny and I moved from California to Kentucky in 2004, I decided to try and find out whatever became of Jeff Daley. I discovered that he had renounced the New Age, moved north to Clear Lake, and converted to Evangelical Christianity.)

HARMONIC CONVERGENCE

It was through Global Family that I was drawn into the vortex of the aforementioned event known as Harmonic Convergence, which represented the greatest point of popular expansion of the New Age ethos on a global level.

Harmonic Convergence was the first and probably the last international folk-event—though, as we shall see, it was not as spontaneous an expression of the global counterculture as we had been led to believe. Hippie/New Age missionaries fanned out across the globe, informing anyone who would listen that a big spiritual opportunity was on the horizon. If we all pooled our psychic energy and spiritual intent, according to whatever spiritual tradition or ritual form or magical technology we happened to be following at the time, together we could save the world and usher in a New Age for humanity. The Convergence was based on José Argüelles' book *The Mayan Factor: The Path Beyond Technology*. According to his calculations (which have been disputed), the Mayan calendar was destined to "end" on August 6 & 7, 1987, when all the cycles, epicycles, and cycles-within-cycles that the calendar was composed of concluded at the same point in time.

When a tribal people faces a collective dilemma, such as an epidemic, adverse weather, the disappearance of game or social disorder, the traditional response is to resort to the shaman, who consults the spirit powers to determine a way beyond the difficulty. On the theory that the human race is a kind of global tribe (as Marshall McLuhan had taught us), Harmonic Convergence might be described as "a mass shamanic event." We had decided to consult the spirit powers on a collective level, as if we were all shamans to one degree or another. This led to an unprecedented amount of outreach as the leaders of the Convergence brought the news of the coming paradigm-shift to religious and tribal leaders, witches, wizards, shamans, Druids, North American Indian tribes, Australian Aborigines, African witch doctors, Amazonian medicine men and even the Mayans themselves in Mexico and Guatemala, impressing on them that a Great Day was coming, a Day when we were called on to unite our collective psychic and spiritual energies on a global level to save the Earth. (Who had appointed these leaders? Or were we all the leaders in some way? Did José Argüelles simply think the whole thing up all by himself? From my present point of view these questions were never adequately answered; they were rarely even asked.) Be that as it may, Harmonic Convergence was the "ancient future" meme incarnate. But one of the most interesting aspects of this outreach, at least to me, was that the global networking necessary to organize the event in some sense provided a sort of human template for the widespread development of the internet that was shortly to follow. So much for "the path beyond technology"!

On one occasion, during the lead-up to the Convergence, I met José Argüelles, who took one look at me and told me that I was to be properly situated on the central pillar of one of his crypto-Kabbalistic quasi-Mayan diagrams — apparently a very flattering designation. It should always be remembered, however, that according to the Argüelles mythology, Harmonic Convergence was merely a preparatory event for the *real* paradigm shift that was to take place on December 21, 2012, which — according to some calculations, not all — was the day the Mayan calendar actually ended for good. This resulted in a highly publicized event, with relatively negligible effects, that came to be called The Mayan Apocalypse. It only remains to be pointed out that Harmonic Convergence and the Mayan Apocalypse represent one more case of the theft and bastardization of Native American religion by non-Native Americans — not in naïve and misinformed appreciation like the hippies did it, but apparently for much more cynical purposes. The *real* Mayan Apocalypse took place in Guatemala in 1981–1983 when the Guatemalan army massacred the Quiché Maya. They destroyed 626 villages. Over 200,000 people were killed or disappeared, 1.5 million were displaced by the violence, and more than 150,000 were driven to seek refuge in Mexico. Were these tragedies remembered and mourned on December 21, 2012? If they were, I never heard of it.

My own observance of the Convergence consisted of an overnight "ritual" I led on Mt. Tamalpais on the days in question; it was my first and last appearance as a "New Age teacher." Jenny was the "fire-keeper" for the event, a role she identified (courtesy of certain Neo-Jungians, like Jean Shinoda Bolen) with Hestia or Vesta, the Goddess of the Hearth, patroness of sacred domesticity; the Roman Vestal Virgins, as well as the primitive "convent" of St Bridget in Ireland, were keepers of a perpetual sacred fire. As for me, I wore a teal-green shirt for the occasion, the heraldic color of Quetzalcoatl/Kukulcan.

We were making it all up as we went along. We invented a "medicine wheel" according to various rumors about what such a thing might be, and all did our thing, applied our best energies to make things better on a collective level, for Humanity and the Earth.

When the sun rose the next day and I surveyed our "sacred space," I remarked that it looked like an abandoned Voodoo site. Later Jenny told me that she had felt totally out of place during the festivities, that she had hated the whole thing. How we were able to avoid spiritual or material disaster on that occasion is beyond me — except for the suspicion that maybe good intentions actually do count for something after all, no matter how misguided their expression might be. In any case, looking at that phase of my life from the perspective of 36 years, I see that Harmonic Convergence was the final exhaustion of the karma I had generated, or inherited, during that trip to Mexico, over 20 years earlier. Apparently it really is true that God protects fools and lunatics.

But I at least got a poem out of it:

Before the Convergence
Granted, we all have to pass again
Through whatever it was that killed us,
Transposed through the lookingglass right to left,
Enfolded in a wall of shimmering quicksilver,
To emerge where the Anti-Self lies in wait for us,
Extending a sly, left-handed handshake on the
Opposite shore of Death —

But, remember, José Argüelles,
There are two kinds of mirrors:
The dark smoking mirror of Tezcatlipoca
Where the soul is twisted till it becomes the mask,
And the crystal mask of Quetzalcoatl,
Holding not the face that is seen
But that other face — the one who watches.

The mirror masks and it unmasks,
It unveils and it disguises.
Wishing to hold himself something other
Than the face in the volcanic glass,
Quetzalcoatl on his raft of serpents
Was exiled to the Western Paradise —

While the fool who thought he *was* the mask
Curled up like a snail shell
Fossilized in limestone —
The *caracol* at Chichen Itzá —
To become the hell inside the mirror.

THE AFTERMATH OF THE CONVERGENCE

I remember a party I attended at Barbara Marx Hubbard's house in Mill Valley after the Convergence. Every face wore the same puzzled expression. *Had* we shifted the paradigm? *Had* we saved the earth? Had anything happened at all? And beyond that, what was next? Time had supposedly ended — and yet here we were, birds in the trees, the traffic outside, the sun still rising and setting. Should we maybe *keep* shifting that paradigm on a yearly basis, just to make sure? We had no choice but to keep pumping out that positive energy...

For some the answer was "yes," consequently a new international peace prayer day was celebrated the next year, 1988. Was that the same prayer day I had briefly been involved with earlier, the one sponsored by Avon Mattison and Pathways to Peace? Possibly, though I haven't been able to establish this for sure. I participated in that successor event as well, along with New Age pioneers Jon and Deki Fox who channeled an entity known as Hilarion, possibly named (somehow) after the Christian anchorite St Hilarion the Great [AD 291–371], a name that was later hijacked by the Theosophists C.W. Leadbeater and Alice A. Bailey and re-branded as an "ascended master." (Jon and Deki later got burned in a pyramid scheme called the Airplane Game, specifically designed for young entrepreneurial New Agers, which drew upon the New Age beliefs that "you create your own reality" and "everything is possible"—that is, upon Søren Kierkegaard's "despair of possibility." I tried to explain to them in simple terms how a pyramid scheme works, only to be told "No! We are drawing upon the Infinite Abundance of the Universe!") I remember setting up a peace prayer event with them at the Mission Chapel at St Raphael's Church. The pastor, Fr Kennedy, was hugely suspicious of it, but the directives from the Second Vatican Council had undoubtedly told him to be open to other "traditions" (even if the tradition in question had been invented only a few weeks earlier), so he sucked it up and let us proceed. All I remember is that we formed a circle and worshipped an inflatable globe of the Earth. (The same Vatican Two influence drove my mother out of the Santa Sabina retreat center at the Dominican Convent where she had volunteered for years, having ultimately been there longer than any of the nuns. The breaking point came for her when they hung a Whole Earth Flag outside the door and put a Buddha on the altar.)

PEACE PRAYER POST-MORTEM

So what was the ultimate effect of the various world peace prayer days that began in the 1980s—of Harmonic Convergence, of the International Day of Peace, of the Mayan Apocalypse? Is it possible that all this effort on the part of many thousands if not millions of people had no real effect whatsoever—except to divert their attention away from true analysis and labor and into barren magical thinking? Perhaps something of value was accomplished, who knows? Nonetheless these events were deeply infected by, if not actually based upon, two fundamental errors.

The first error was the New Age doctrine that "consciousness creates material reality"—a notion derived in part from the fact that all creative human constructions, such as a building or an organization, begin as conceptions before they become established as facts. What is routinely forgotten in this way of thinking is that buildings do not build themselves, nor do organizations organize themselves. The initial creative conception (the Form) must come into a fruitful relationship with the capital, the labor, the materials, and the pre-existing circumstances that allow for the organization to be developed or the building to be built (the Matter). The belief that the subjective pole—consciousness—has precedence and authority over the objective pole—material conditions—is the essence of false magical thinking, just as the belief that material conditions strictly determine consciousness is the principle of the worst, most hopeless and most fatalistic forms of materialism. Traditional metaphysics, on the other hand, makes clear that God is the First Cause of both consciousness and conditions, which together constitute the creative polarity by which He manifests the universe. In the words of the Qur'an, *I will show them My signs on the horizons and in their own souls until they are satisfied that this is the Truth. Is it not enough for you, that I am Witness over all things?* [Q. 41:53].

The second error—or heresy, or blasphemy—is to put a human collective in the place of God, as if the pooling of the consciousness, the attention, the psychic energy of millions of human beings could somehow *add up* to the Power of God. This is not only impious, but frankly absurd. Those who rely in their prayer upon the notion that millions of others are praying at the same moment are not relying exclusively upon God—and a prayer that does not rely exclusively upon God is no prayer at all. This goes double, of course, for prayer that is offered by those millions to a heterogeneous assortment of entities, "angels," spirit-guides and incompatible conceptions of the Divinity that, on certain levels at least, actually contradict each other. Each individual one of these faces of God may or may not be spiritually lawful and efficacious for the ones devoted to it: God is vast, His Mercy inexhaustible. But to worship them all at the same time can only produce a spiritual cacophony that might in some cases actually amount to a demonic invocation. Furthermore, no human collective—even if it follows a single unified revelation—can totally submit to God; only the individual can do that. This is the reason why all world-changing revelations sent by God have come only through individuals, not some sort of prophetic committee, and why no spiritual community, no matter how faithful, has ever became a saint. If God, within the context of a particular religion, allows or commands the community to pray *as* a community, this is only to support each individual within that community in his or her individual submission to Him; to the degree that this principle is lost sight of, the religious community in question—the *sangha*, the *ummah*, the mystical body—becomes not a real community of the faithful but an idol that destroys true faith at the root. If many individuals appeal to God, each in his or her own divine intimacy and solitude, great and miraculous things can happen—if God wills. Your brother's faith in God can support and strengthen your own faith, but your faith in him—if it has begun to *replace* your faith in God—is worse than useless. As for your *shaykh*, your *guru*, your *staretz*, faith in him is equivalent to faith in God to the degree that he is annihilated in God. But as soon as your attachment to him as something other than God begins to veil the Uncreated

Light, most likely because (consciously or otherwise) he is subtly provoking that attachment — or as soon as your attachment to the feeling of community support and validation begins to replace your reliance on God as your sole Sustainer — then that spiritual leader and that religious community will be very fortunate if the worst thing that happens to them is... nothing at all.

GROUP DREAMWORK

Concurrently with my interest in the New Age I had begun to become seriously involved in what came to be called "group dreamwork," under the influence of the Castaneda books, the "Seth" material channeled by spirit medium Jane Roberts, and the various studies of dream incubation and lucid dreaming that were being carried on in the scientific community by Stanford University's Stephen LeBerge and other serious investigators. (The Stanford Research Institute figures prominently in the development of New Age ideas; Michael Murphy, co-founder of Esalen Institute, came out of Stanford.)

To Sigmund Freud the term *dreamwork* denoted the process through which the psyche manufactures dreams. The New Age, however, to whom the term "light workers" was familiar (we of the spiritual *avant garde*, laboring to effect the great Paradigm Shift, were all "light workers"), used the term "dreamwork" to describe the activities of those involved not only in dream interpretation, but also in dream incubation, lucid dreaming, and the notion of applying insights and powers derived from dreams to the transformation of material conditions. Here we can see, in this radical re-definition of the word "work," how one element of the New Age ethos was a kind of sublimated, volatilized, psychologized Marxism; probably as good an example as any of this tendency was Theosophical Society spinoff Benjamin Crème, who included Marx in his heterogeneous list of sages, prophets and avatars.

If you mistake the psyche for the Spirit, if you accept that subjective experience can create and dominate material reality, as when human beings conceive of, design and build technological devices that affect the world — in other words, if you believe in "mind over matter" — then *dreams* will appear at one point as the royal key to both knowledge and power. The next step after that is to define the spiritual path partly in terms of *dream-control*, based on the ability to set up *lucid dreaming*. The Primordial Tradition however, of which all true and God-given religions are branches, does not accept the theory of mind over matter, but understands both consciousness and the universe perceived by consciousness as the polarized manifestation of a unitary Divine Reality that absolutely transcends them. Certain Hindu scriptures define both the belief that mind creates matter (the magical error) and the belief that matter creates mind (the Darwinian error) as heresies — whereas the truth is that God creates both, maintains both, and expresses Himself by means of both. God transcends subject and object, and is most fully realized when subject and object are united; He can only be identified with pure Subject—with the Atman as the Universal Witness—when the subjective ego that perceives a subjectively-conditioned "objective" world is dissolved; and the Atman, without dividing itself into witness and witnessed, witnesses nothing but Itself.

In addition to the books of Jane Roberts, Castaneda, and the dream-researchers identified with Stanford University, New Age dreamwork was heavily influenced by Jungian psychology, by John C. Neihardt's *Black Elk Speaks* which recounts the story of Black Elk's great vision that was later ritually enacted by his entire tribe, by *Journeys Out of Body* by Robert Monroe (since out-of-body experiences, also known as "astral projection," and lucid dreaming have a number of similarities), and by the tradition of shamanic dreaming as a whole. Dreams are also important in Islamic Sufism, which I was soon to become connected with; according to a *hadith* of the Prophet Muhammad, peace and blessings be upon him, "dreams are the 46th part of prophecy." Generally speaking, however, the Sufis do not try to incubate dreams or develop the power of lucid dreaming; they concentrate instead on following the *shari'ah* and staying constant in their spiritual practices, their litanies and invocations, during which efforts they will remain vigilant for signs of Allah's guidance that might appear through *any* channel, dreams included. If you try to control your own dreams you will place them under the power of the unconscious ego, the *nafs*, which will ultimately lead you astray. You can never become responsive to the guidance of Allah if you expend all your spiritual attention trying to guide yourself.

As for me, after Harmonic Convergence I took to New Age dreamwork like a spaniel to water, expressing it in terms of three main efforts:

The first was *The Harmonic Convergence Book of Dreams*. Before the Convergence I sent out a call through the New Age networks I was connected with, asking people all over the world (if my call was destined to reach that far) to send me accounts of any dreams they happened to have on the night of August 6/7 1987, and subsequent nights. After the event the dreams started coming in (sometimes accompanied by drawings)—mostly from the United States but a few from other countries—and I collected them. This was before email had become common, so the whole thing happened through the international post and the U.S. mails. I bound these accounts, along with a few of my commentaries, in a xerox edition I called *The Harmonic Convergence Book of Dreams*, which I made available to some of the New Age dreamworkers of the Bay Area.

What did I learn from this excursion into the "group mind"? First off, I confirmed that such a thing as a group mind actually exists. People in different parts of the world did in fact dream up similar or identical images on the nights in question, images that did not appear to have any direct connection to the imagery or ideology published by the organizers of the Convergence. Two of these were the *octahedron* and the *horse*. The octahedron (two pyramids base-to-base) is the Platonic solid representing the Air element, Aquarius being a Fixed Air sign, so in this context that shape would suggest something like Air in crystalline form, presumably related to the astrological fact that the Earth was soon to enter the Age of Aquarius. And the horse was the central symbol that appeared in the Dream of My Life, though in that dream it had looked more like a camel. So *there you have it*: that's the totality of the "evidence." Make of it what you will. As for myself, I no longer have a copy of *The Harmonic Convergence Book of Dreams*—though there might still be a few texts floating around somewhere—since I got rid of it as part of my great Bonfire of the New Age Vanities that was to happen around a year later, when most of that part of my life (gratefully) went up in smoke.

My second post-Convergence thrust was to found something I called Gate of Horn, a short-lived "group dreaming network" where people would agree to attempt to incubate dreams on the night of each New Moon, in an attempt to gain insight into how to solve specific challenges faced by the earth and the human race in these apocalyptic times. ("Avoiding" or "solving" the apocalypse was a dominant notion in those years; people had apparently forgotten that "apocalypse" means *revelation*.) The name was derived from the ancient Egyptian notion that false dreams come through something called the "gate of ivory" while true ones arrive through the "gate of horn." A few people had a few dreams and sent the accounts to me, but nothing much came of it.

My third and last excursion was the creation of something I called The U.S./Soviet Dream Bridge, as my contribution to the various attempts to carry on citizen diplomacy with the Soviet Union that different New Age and peace organizations, including Global Family, were sponsoring during the *glasnost* years. The New Age angle was in part inspired by the fact that certain "alternative spirituality" types—neo-shamans, theosophists and others—were then starting to surface in Russia; the Communist regime had been just as repressive to them as it had been to traditional Eastern Orthodox Christians, but now—thanks to Mikhail Gorbachev—they were able to practice openly. Consequently, in the 1980s the New Age peace movement in the U.S. was beginning to make contact with their Russian counterparts, a development that had undoubtedly been foreshadowed by G. I. Gurdjieff's decision to teach his brand of semi-traditional occultism in the West; one of his major disciples, A. R. Orage, had even started a journal called *The New Age*. My own contribution, via the Dream Bridge, was to ask Russian and American dreamers to incubate dreams on the same night to see if a psychic connection could be made between them; my invitation to participate in that attempt was delivered to the Russian dreamers by the prominent psychologist and parapsychologist Stanley Krippner of the Saybrook Institute—who, in 1993, had published the results of a number of dream telepathy experiments he conducted along with other researchers at the Maimonides Medical Center, though he had been involved with dream telepathy since 1969. The Dream Bridge turned up *one* dream that seemed to show a thin, feeble telepathic connection between East and West: a Russian and an American dreamer had both dreamed, on the same night, of something that looked like a log cabin.

FROM THE NEW AGE TO TASAWWUF

And that was it. After those efforts, my connection with New Age dreamwork, and to a large degree with the New Age itself, came to a close. But outside of Jenny's ongoing influence for the good, why did this happen at that particular point in my life? It happened because I stopped short—suddenly and providentially—and said to myself: "Charles, what the *hell* have you been up to?" I realized that I had gone too far in too many unknown directions, into a world without guides or signposts, but not without powerful psychic influences pushing their own agendas, most of which I was probably unconscious of. So at that point I turned 180 degrees, and made for the world of traditional esoteric spirituality with all deliberate speed—specifically, the province of Islamic Sufism, known in Arabic as *tasawwuf*. No more spiritual freelancing for me, no more devising my own meditations, no more inventing my own religions. It all had to end some time, so it was best that it should end right now.

The story of the New Age phase of my life would not be complete, however, without mention of the world-class group dreamworker Barbara Shor, whom I met on one occasion in the Bay Area, and who was at the cutting edge of self-directed research into the practice of group dreaming. Ms Shor had apparently created a thought-form or specific "location" in the astral or imaginal plane that she named The Octagonal Room; a door set in each of the eight facets of the Room opened onto a different probable future or imaginal reality. She and her cadre of group dreamers would agree to "meet" there on specific nights in the dream state, and they often succeeded; they would actually see each other, experience similar environments, exchange words, and clearly remember these experiences upon awakening. In other words, Barbara and her compatriots had gone a long way toward experimentally establishing the objective reality of the Psychic or Imaginal Plane, just as I had done—in a much less striking way—in the *Harmonic Convergence Book of Dreams* and the U.S./Soviet Dream Bridge. But exactly who Barbara Shor was, or who if anyone she represented, was not entirely clear to me; I was not yet in the habit of asking questions like that. She lived in one of those huge apartment buildings on Park Avenue in Manhattan; apparently she was descended from a long line of famous

Orthodox Rabbis (Kabbalists?). And it was through listening to her that I began to understand how the idea of being connected with the CIA was no longer an object of fear and loathing, as it had been for most of the hippies, but was beginning to be considered "hip." This was before I learned of the widespread connections between the psychic and intelligence communities that came to light through those well-known experiments conducted at the Stanford Research Institute and Lawrence Livermore Laboratory, some of them involving the famous paranormal spoon-bender, Uri Geller—a bleed-through of worlds that I was first alerted to by the book *Messengers of Deception* by premier UFO researcher Jacques Vallee, and which was later extensively researched by writers like Peter Levenda. Furthermore (strangely enough), Barbara Shor's name was once mentioned, apparently apropos of nothing, in an episode of one the versions of the *Stargate* Sci-Fi TV series, as if that ancient, futuristic Stargate apparatus, which could supposedly open a trans-dimensional portal to other locations in spacetime, were the TV version of her Octagonal Room. Interestingly enough, Stargate was also the name of a project to research and develop remote viewing, conducted by the Defense Intelligence Agency, the Stanford Research Institute and the U.S. Army from 1977 to 1991. (If you'd like to learn more about Barbara Shor and group dreaming, see if you can find a copy or internet file of Issue 22 of *Gnosis: A Journal of the Western Inner Traditions*, which came out in the winter of 1992, in which her article "The Promise of Shared Dreaming" appeared. It was through my connections as an often-published writer in *Gnosis* that I arranged for that article to be published.)

I'm very glad that I didn't participate in any of Ms. Shor's experiments, however, seeing that several members of her dream group became involved in serious accidents or developed unexpected physical ailments not long after I met them. And soon after that article appeared in *Gnosis*, Ms. Shor herself turned up with the rare blood disease that finally ended her life. Had their psychic excursions torn some subtle psychophysical barrier designed to protect the integrity of the human form? Speaking only for myself, I didn't wait around to find out. This is one of the virtues of living on the edge of various worlds—of just passing through rather than becoming totally identified with them—because to the degree that you are identified with them you will inherit their maladies along with their wisdoms, and pass when they pass. In any case, it was obvious to me that the New Age impetus had peaked, consequently the need for a stable spiritual path and some true and reliable guidance was impressed upon me in no uncertain terms.

But why Sufism? The true and sufficient answer is, "because God willed it." It is nonetheless possible, and not entirely irrelevant, to say something about the interlocking contexts in which that Will began to appear.

Before the Convergence and in preparation for it, I had attended a "Neo-Shamanic" workshop taught by one Richard Dobson, who had a background in Sufism, specifically the Nimatullahi Order based in Iran. When I met him he was apparently on the path from Sufism to Shamanism (though he might have been practicing both concurrently for some time), whereas I was traveling in the opposite direction, though I didn't know it at the time. In addition to that ambiguous influence, Jenny and I—as I've already mentioned—began attending the Dances of Universal Peace soon after we departed from Santa Venetia, a devotional form developed by Samuel Lewis—the "Sufi Sam" Lew Welch had introduced me to—who had grown up in Fairfax, near my home town of San Rafael. Sam, whose style was fairly loose and heterodox, was a kind of bridge figure between the hippies and the world of legitimate initiatory Sufism, in the days before the more orthodox Sufi groups began arriving in the States. Nonetheless he possessed a valid initiation himself from the Chishti Order, and reputedly also from at least one *tariqah* based in Central Asia. I experienced The Dances of Universal Peace as a harmless, benign and uplifting form of devotion to God, though these practices seemed to have little in common with Sufism and Islam as I later came to know them; nonetheless they helped Jenny and I heal, or at least survive, the emotional wounds we had suffered when Santa Venetia Presbyterian Church descended into darkness. So it was when the New Age faded from my life that my first tentative connections with Sufism began to surface.

As for the New Age, I have no doubt that some people have taken important steps on their spiritual Path through New Age ideas and practices. God appears to us through the forms we are willing to accept—though if these forms are incomplete or erroneous they will eventually submit their "bill," which can sometimes be pretty steep. My often cynical tone in recounting my two-year passage through that world is not meant as a judgment on any individual—except myself: the bitter taste in my mouth came from the realization that I was simply not where I was supposed to be. It's true that if you're on your way toward a real goal then every step through territory where you "don't belong" is a step in the right direction—but if you believe you've already reached that goal when you're actually a thousand miles away from it, if you never feel like a stranger in a strange land when you actually are in a strange and hostile territory, then your quest has most likely failed. But beyond all questions of my own spiritual progress or the lack of it, from the perspective of the present day I see myself as having participated, during those years, in the destruction of several truly sacred and God-given traditions, in order to replace them with—what exactly? Fake spirituality at best, and at worst, inverted spirituality. And though God certainly retains the right to free anyone from the prison of objective error in response to that person's sincerity, nonetheless—a prison is a prison.

How do you even begin to pay a debt like that? Read on.

THE BIG NO

While I was busying myself with organizing safaris into uncharted psychic territories and generally ushering in the new paradigm, Jenny was quietly doing what she liked to do best: frequenting libraries and bookstores to see what books might want to jump into her hands. In our Jungian period, largely as San Francisco Poets, she had discovered the works of Marie-Louise Von Franz in that way, as well as the books of Idries Shah, which formed a quick and temporary bridge for us between the mythopoesis of the Jungians, Robert Graves, Heinrich Zimmer and Joseph Campbell and the deeper and more spiritually practical world of the Traditionalist School, and Islamic Sufism. At the same time she decided to take a non-credit class on comparative religion at the College of Marin, in which the teacher made a point of advising the students *not* to read the books of one Frithjof Schuon—the result being that, when browsing at the Dawn Horse Bookstore in San Rafael, run by the Da Free John (Adi Da) people, her eye fell upon a book by the offending author, which she decided to purchase.

That book changed both our lives. It opened the door for us to the world of the Traditionalist School, otherwise known as the Perennialists—to the writings of René Guénon, Ananda Coomaraswamy, Titus Burckhardt, Martin Lings, Seyyed Hossein Nasr, Marco Pallis, Whitall Perry, Charles LeGai Eaton, Huston Smith, et al., who between them articulated a metaphysical view of the nature of Reality and an understanding of the spiritual Path that was higher, more comprehensive and more solidly integrated than anything the worlds of Jungianism, symbolic mythopoesis, New Age psychic spirituality or the spotty and drug-polluted "traditionalism" of the hippie counterculture could offer. The Traditionalist canon had the power to raise the whole discourse on the spiritual life to a higher level, one that clearly demonstrated how the "esoteric" centers of the major world religions—however difficult those centers may be to contact in these times of darkness—provide an infinitely deeper and more sophisticated understanding of metaphysics and the spiritual life than anything to be found in the heterodox esotericisms of the western world, or the magic, occultism and psychic spirituality of any world; as Ibn al-'Arabi declared, human knowledge (given that the human form is God's representative on earth) is higher than Jinnish knowledge. The Traditionalists threw the clear light of day on the distinction between psyche and Spirit and the primacy of Spirit over psyche; in so doing they signed the death-warrant for my connection with New Age spirituality or anything like it. For the first time since my membership in the pre-Vatican II Catholic Church, I felt I was in the presence of a comprehensive view of reality that, as far as I could see at the time, was totally unified and left nothing out.

But I was still lagging behind Jenny, who tends to feel that she can't move on in life, that she has never yet moved on even once, and then suddenly finds herself in a totally different world, light years beyond her past viewpoint and interests, with no visible intermediate steps whatsoever. I remember one time when we were sitting in our car at the San Francisco Theological Seminary in Ross. I was spouting off about the *novus ordo seclorum*, the New Revelation we were preparing the ground for with our little New Age doings, when she stopped me cold: "No! There will be no New Revelation for this cycle; Islam was the last. This whole cycle-of-manifestation is coming to a close."

And I really *heard* her; as William Blake said, "The truth can never be told so as to be understood, and not be believed." That was the beginning of what was to prove to be the greatest *enantiodromia* (change-into-opposite), the greatest *metanoia* (change or transformation of mind), of my life. I saw at that moment that the whole counterculture impetus had finally run its course and exhausted whatever spiritual potential it might have had, though it took me quite a few years to eliminate all its echoes from my life. If the true Catholic Church I had once helped to destroy had still been in evidence at that point I might have returned to it, but it was nowhere to be seen — until much, much later.

As of this writing, the New Age as a widespread popular movement, at least in its original 1980s incarnation, has been on the wane in North America for some time, likely because the practicality for real life of such techniques as "channeling" and "creative visualization" began to be questioned by the rank-and-file. But as the social power of New Age beliefs in their original form began to retreat from our collective consciousness in the 1990s and early 2000s — though such things as the "Mayan Apocalypse" of 2012 showed that it still had a degree of influence — some of the surviving leaders of the movement, as we have already seen in the case of Barbara Marx Hubbard [1929–2019], began to be inducted into the world of the ruling elites and their globalist think-tanks, if they hadn't actually arrived from that direction in the first place. And the New Age influence, or something like it, also appears to be growing in academia, backed by heavy patronage from various foundations and government agencies — as evidenced by the newly legitimized concentration on UFO research, the revived interest in psychedelics, the growing openness of "science" to the study of paranormal events and powers, and the increasing fascination with Near Death Experiences, both on the popular level and within the scientific community — developments that were influenced and legitimized to a degree by the public revelation of the CIA "remote viewing" project and similar efforts. Elements of the New Age ethos have also influenced Evangelical Christianity on a more-or-less unconscious basis, and have become generally diffused, though in diluted form, throughout many areas of society. The result of all this, exacerbated by the dominance of cyberspace and the internet, has been a general "volatilization" of our worldview, a retreat from interaction with solid material reality into a nebulous world of mental/technological images and psychic impressions, images that masquerade as, and tend to take the place of, the traditional sense of a transcendent spiritual order. One result of this technologically-mediated psychologization of both the spiritual and the corporeal worlds—a development whose "metaphysic" is in many ways derived from quantum physics—has been the gradual replacement of Judeo-Christian monotheism in western society with a *de facto* polytheism, resulting in the vision of a universe peopled with many "entities," and of both space and time as composed of multiple versions of themselves, leading to a general dissolution of our view of reality, and of our own humanity. It's as if the world were ending, not in a single cataclysm that terminates a real established order of things, but in the progressive disintegration of that order at every point. We don't have real "places" with unique qualities any more, only various regions of abstract quantitative space. And with the fragmentation of unified linear time into a mass of alternative timelines, we no longer have a common future, and find it increasingly difficult to envision our own individual futures. So it appears that the New Age movement was not the inauguration of a new universal paradigm as it had hoped to be, but simply one more herald of the end of time.

CHAPTER TEN

The Planet of Project MOVE

MY TWO YEARS WORKING WITH THE HOMEless on the soft mean streets of Marin County, California [1989–1991] made up a distinct episode in my life, the second attempt in a row (after my work in the Sanctuary Movement for Central American Refugees with Pastor Carolyn Studer) to Do Good as the faithful lieutenant to a charismatic female leader—in this case, Sarah Howard, Director of Project MOVE. (Doing Good certainly doesn't hurt, if you can avoid turning yourself into a demon by identifying with it; it is even commanded by God, within the limits and according to the norms He has established. But in no way is it the highest goal of human life.)

I have always recognized my excursions into social action as in some sense energy-overflows from whatever spiritual practice or commitment I was involved with at the time. The relatively formless political protests of the '60s were in certain ways the outer reflection of the equally formless hippie spirituality. My involvement with the Sanctuary Movement for Central American refugees via Santa Venetia Presbyterian Church in the 1980s was the temporary and ephemeral "incarnation" of whatever influence from the Holy Spirit might have been able to filter down through Protestant social gospel spirituality. And my involvement with the Covenants of the Prophet Muhammad with the Christians, mostly between 2013 and 2019—the only "excursion" that seemed to have a real and potentially permanent effect on the world (permanent, that is, while the world lasts)—came out of my connection with the Sufism of the 'Alawiyya Tariqah. But, beginning in 1989, my work with the homeless of Marin County, in partnership with Sarah Howard as the other half of a tiny homeless service agency, arrived as an expression of my recent entry into the Nimatullahi Sufi Order under Dr Javad Nurbakhsh. He had told me that this kind of work was "the best," though he in no way directed me to become involved with it—at least through the visible channels of the daylight world. Be that as it may, my first contact with homeless service work had actually been at Santa Venetia Presbyterian, when we became part of a revolving homeless shelter program that moved from church to church.

I first met Sarah Howard when I was just out of Marin Catholic high school. She was a trim, good-looking Jewish girl that some of my friends knew, with wavy light-brown hair tending to red—hair that I like to identify, rightly or wrongly, with an Edomite heritage. She had an aura of sensitive suffering that was quite attractive to me at the time.

Sarah had gone to Drake High in Fairfax, the high school of the intellectual elites that John McBride had briefly attended at one point. Some of the brainier and more artistic students from other schools would actually audit classes there—especially those of the famous Cappy Lavin, Jewish mentor to Marin County's best and the brightest. (Virtually all of my girlfriends, until I met Jenny who became my wife, were either Irish or Jewish, thus lending credence to the unprovable but suggestive theory that the Irish are one of the Lost Tribes of Israel, though Sarah herself never actually became "mine.")

Of the Marin County schools, San Rafael High was the standard all-American small town high school, the "American Graffiti" institution that my first hippie girlfriend, Megan Roberts (half Welsh, half Irish) attended. Football. Cheer leaders. ROTC. And Tamalpais High was the school of the bad guys; it actually had some *Black* people in it since it was close to Marin City, our official Black ghetto. I remember the days when there was only one known Black girl living in Marin County outside of Marin City—Pia, a beautiful full-figured Mulatta (back when such a type as that could still be recognized), while the only Black guy in our circle for quite a while was Calvin Scott, a poet of Shakespearean demeanor who, along with myself and my friend Randy Carson—an accomplished haiku poet—recited from his works as part of the Poetry in the Schools program.

Sarah was the daughter of Ken Howard, one-time head of the Communist party for Northern California, who still played an important behind-the-scenes part in the Liberal power-structure of Marin County. He was directly descended from the Adams family of the U. S. Revolutionary Elite, the Boston (area) Brahmin family that gave us two presidents, John and John Quincey Adams. Further back he came from the distinguished Howard family of England, the Anglo-Catholic Dukes of Norfolk, who were seated at Castle Howard in Yorkshire—the location where the great PBS series *Brideshead Revisited* starring Jeremy Irons was filmed. Sarah tells of the first time her father visited the Castle. He was sitting on a bench in the grounds when a Howard family retainer whom he'd never seen before stopped and greeted him: "Good day, Mr Howard," he said. "Good day," Ken replied, "but how do you know my name?" "Oh, the family features are unmistakable sir." (I remember the day I attended Ken Howard's memorial gathering in Mill Valley. Not only was Gary Giacomini there, the big West Marin rancher and chairman of our Board of Supervisors, but the music was provided by Mimi Fariña, sister to Joan Baez, who sang "Amazing Grace.")

Sarah's mother, on the other hand—who had died some years before I renewed my acquaintance with her—had been a Russian Jewish immigrant, descended from a long line of Orthodox rabbis and *tzaddiks*, who fled to the West to escape the pogroms, so Sarah found herself the product of the most Hebrew of the Hebrews and the most *goyishe* of the *goyim*, a mixed ancestry that in her case had not yet quite "jelled" (like the Anglo-Indian/ Jewish bloodlines of Rama Coomaraswamy, whom you'll meet later), leaving her, both racially and personally speaking, a kind of radically-eccentric hyper-individualist without the moderating influence of a definite racial type; such an anomaly usually takes several generations to establish itself after a radical mixture of bloods. Nonetheless she identified much more with her Jewishness than with her father's Anglo contribution.

Sarah as I knew her was brilliant, witty, volatile, artistic, a talented poet (I ended up editing her collected poems at one point), and someone truly heroic in her defense of the needy — including herself. She was moved to take up work with the homeless partly by seeing kids she'd gone to high school with living on the streets. Likewise one of our clients turned out to be a guy I'd known at St Raphael's parochial grammar school; he was sheltering inside a children's play-house in the playground at Gerstle Park. Sarah definitely lived on the edge, presenting a textbook example of overcompensation for a number of handicaps. She was epileptic and had been born with spina bifida, a dangerous and painful condition, yet she was an accomplished modern dancer. She also had some strange powers. She was hugely psychic, capable of charming wild animals (she could walk right up to a wild deer and pet it) and also had the ability to hear sounds on a lower register than virtually anyone else on earth. She could actually hear earthquakes well before the ground began to shake. In addition she knew how to "charm" the mentally ill, especially schizophrenics, a talent that helped her get a degree in psychiatric social work from Boston University, and fitted her to run a homeless service agency — at least temporarily — on the streets of Marin County. If anybody I ever knew "lived by her wits," it was Sarah Howard. In Boston she had set up a program to "mainstream" schizophrenics by providing them with college scholarships, since statistics show that schizophrenia often goes hand-in-hand with a high I.Q. What idea could be more brilliant, more audacious, more unstable? And she definitely knew how to "cultivate" the rich and famous. Once when Gary Snyder and some others were reading their poetry at the College of Marin, she and I were sitting (not together) in the front row. After the reading, when the poets were taking questions from the audience, I asked them, "Who or what, according to your conception, is the Muse?" As they were looking back and forth at each other, figuring out how to respond, Sarah piped up and said: "*I* am!" Later she told me that Snyder had taken her aside and given her a stern lecture on the possibly serious consequences of such an act of sacrilege. I wonder if, as a high officer in the College of Poets, he also offered her, on that occasion, an appropriate, convenient and pleasurable way of paying her karmic debt?

My acquaintance with Sarah was renewed when, in 1989, she tapped me to work with her as the other half of Project MOVE, which she named (for some reason) after MOVE, the Black revolutionary cadre in Philadelphia that was bombed from the air by a Philadelphia Police Department helicopter in 1985, resulting in the destruction by fire of an entire city block, 61 homes. Maybe she meant "move IN" to permanent housing, our goal for Marin's homeless, or maybe she was just referring to her own ability to MOVE so fast that the consequences of her actions could never catch up with her. In any case her debut on the national social service stage, a venue which none of us had heretofore realized existed, resulted in a true media circus, including an appearance on Good Morning America, where she revealed to the people of the U.S. the well-concealed secret that "The homeless are just like the rest of us!" In so doing she reversed the famous exchange between F. Scott Fitzgerald and Ernest Hemingway, where Fitzgerald declared "The rich are not like you and me," to which Hemingway replied, "Right — they have more money." Nonetheless, no financially secure American wants to entertain the inconvenient truth that he or she could lose it all at any time and end up on the street next to someone who might have been equally well-housed only a couple of months before; one of our clients in San Rafael, for example, had recently been a vice-president of Bank of America.

The *Marin Independent Journal* described the bursting upon the scene of Sarah Howard in the following terms:

> Anywhere else, an invasion of panhandlers on a street of pleasant shops would inspire shopkeepers to hire a security guard. But here in the heart of Marin County, where promoting psychic health is a civic duty as sacred as voting, the Downtown Merchants Association has hired a psychological counselor.
>
> She is Sarah Howard, and her instructions are to act as a roving dispenser of self-esteem to the approximately 150 homeless people who appear to be living here.
>
> On a recent afternoon Ms. Howard, who holds a master's degree in psychology from Sonoma State University, walked the main street smartly dressed in white silk and linen, poised to offer her services to anyone who looked homeless.
>
> "It's a new idea about how to treat homeless people," she explained. "You bring them into the community and the community responds... The real essence is rehabilitation," she said. "It takes extra time and extra people so they do not feel like rejects from society and can regain a sense of self-esteem. We don't want these people to feel worse; we want them to feel better."

Who can argue with that? However, the convenient media myth that psychiatric social workers dealing with homeless clients could only be found in Marvelous Marin, the heartland of the Me Generation, the land of "I Want It All Now," was far from the truth. Maybe our method of outreach and our relationship with the Downtown Merchants' Association departed from the norm to some degree, but there were undoubtedly plenty more clinically-trained social workers throughout the country involved in homeless service work who likely didn't appreciate being implicitly classed as anomalous, flaky dispensers of touchy-feely pop psychology. The media just saw the whole thing as a hoot, an outrageously humorous caricature, whereas in reality a lot of serious work was being done in many areas by dedicated people under far-from-ideal conditions, outside of the energizing, distorting and life-draining circle of *glamour* created by publicity.

This is not to say, however, that Sarah did not play into her media image up to a point, which (of course) worked to invoke the archetypal conflict and jealousy that exists between the Creative types and the Solid Citizens of the business and government establishments—between those who, in the typology of Søren Kierkegaard from his *Sickness unto Death*, are in "Despair of Possibility" (the people who limit themselves to what *might* be) and those who are in "Despair of Necessity" (the people who limit themselves to what they think *must* be)—an antagonism that can be roughly translated into late 20th Century American English as the Hippies vs. the Straights. We had Creative Ideas about how to deal with the problem of homelessness, while all our patrons-slash-opponents had was business savvy and money. Ideas were natural to us, while making money was a sort of esoteric mystery; the reverse was true of our opposite numbers, who treated our Ideas as a rare commodity that we had somehow cornered the market on but had no real right to since they were the "real" people and we were only pirates and poachers. Consequently they were not only dismissive of us but also hugely jealous, especially in view of our ability to command media attention. No matter how impractical our ideas might have been, our "practical" opponents treated them as solid gold, things they would gladly provide the funding for if only they could gain legal title to them first; they saw our creativity as an inexplicable magic power that we had somehow learned to exercise but had no real right to. We mystified and discounted each other's talents, but envied them at the same time. If these two abilities had been organically united, something miraculous might have happened—but such was not to be, seeing that the union of the Possible and the Actual requires both radical humility and a willingness to personally suffer, to endure a phase of total helplessness, and neither we nor our opposite numbers had the stomach for that.

In any case, Project MOVE opened a small office on Fourth Street in the building next to the Albert Building where my father's dental office had been. We had almost no furniture or office equipment, and the things we did have looked (appropriately enough) like they'd come from the Goodwill or the Salvation Army; maybe they actually had. But that small room nonetheless became one of the indoor bases that the homeless of San Rafael knew they could always touch, if they so desired, without being "surveilled" or "processed."

Being indoors, however, was difficult for many of them. In trying (against all odds) to make the homeless feel like accepted members of society, we had to work against something resembling the "imposter syndrome." Some homeless people felt wrong and out of place while indoors, as if that was not where they properly belonged; this often manifested as a kind of claustrophobia that made them long to return to the "freedom" of the streets. (I remember one occasion when Sarah had set up TV interviews for some homeless people we knew with PBS station KQED Channel 9 in the East Bay; our clients were extremely nervous in the studio and couldn't wait to get back outside where they "belonged.") And undoubtedly the experience of being temporarily sheltered in a series of situations they knew would soon end was often felt as a cruel tease that they wanted to avoid as much as take advantage of. So we began to understand that homelessness, on one level, is actually a kind of addiction. As the reality of being *forced* into homelessness comes ever closer, some people deal with this terrifying and traumatic reality by telling themselves (and eventually others) that homelessness was actually their own free choice, that they were liberated spirits who loved to feel the earth (or else the concrete) under their feet and the open sky above their heads. Certainly the end of the finally hopeless struggle to stay housed and employed was often felt as a relief, but it was a relief that could in no way compensate for their precipitous fall into the hell of homelessness. The truth is, however, that when someone is faced with two interpretations of a situation (or, parenthetically, two interpretations of another person's character), one pleasant and the other unpleasant, the temptation to concentrate on the pleasant interpretation and repress the unpleasant one will be very powerful. Be that as it may, there is an invisible threshold that the newly-homeless person eventually sinks past, after which what had been a floor supporting them becomes the roof of a dark cellar that prevents them from rising again to the surface of the earth where the majority of their fellow humans stand, walk and live their lives—and that sort of ascent, up from homelessness to reliable shelter, is a monumental undertaking both logistically and psychologically. Just as certain people will avoid trying to improve their health or overcome a handicap because they have *identified* with illness or incapacity, so homeless people will often identify with their status as homeless; they will sometimes even adopt "street names" to help solidify that identity, so they won't end up being *simply no-one*. (We Sufis may talk about transcending or renouncing identity, but you have to have an identity first before you can sacrifice it; to give your goods away and to have them stolen from you are two radically different things.)

A good example of this was "Bondo Bob" Conroy, the "mayor" of a homeless shanty-town (or box-town) occupying a vacant lot on San Rafael's Francisco Boulevard, a settlement that went by the name of "Bondonia."

Bondo Bob, in his "sheltered life," had been an auto-body repairman who named himself (or was named by others) after Bondo, a common body-filler used to fill in creases, punctures and dents in automobiles. As mayor of Bondonia he was respected for his ability to inject a degree of order into his domain, and also for his unpaid profession of repairing donated or abandoned bicycles to give a bit more mobility to the citizens in his charge. Bondonia met its end when the County ordered it bulldozed; that's when we came to understand an almost-universally applied "extra-legal" principle that appears in no constitution or written law or legal judgment: that those who have no address *lose the right to have possessions*. In other words, the "authorities" universally assert the de facto *right to trash or steal anything belonging to a homeless person*, even if they bought it with their own hard-earned or hard-begged money, and no matter how valuable it might be, with no legal consequences whatsoever. I tried to assert the American citizen's right to have possessions on that occasion in one of the County offices at the Marin Civic Center, but was dismissed with incredulous laughter. Of course this kind of radical, extra-legal expropriation or destruction of the few things necessary to maintain the life of homeless people will routinely result in deaths, but it's clear that the Declaration of Independence with its "right to life, liberty and the pursuit of happiness" does not apply to the homeless any more than it did to the slaves, and that if one becomes poor enough one will effectively lose one's American citizenship, not to mention one's recognized membership in the human race.

A perfect example of this sort of extra-legal expropriation is the case of Dean Hadhazy. Dean was a world-class portrait- and figure-painter in the neo-baroque style (though he worked mostly in pastels), who had studied in Europe, including Venice. He was of Hungarian descent, having grown up in the same neighborhood in the Bronx as Tony Curtis; they had exactly the same accent. Dean lived in a one-man camp in the San Rafael woods at the foot of Black Mountain near Dominican College (now University), a stone's-throw from where I went to kindergarten. (If California has become a Mecca for the homeless, this has everything to do with climate, since snow is virtually unknown outside of the High Sierras—though Mounts Tamalpais and Diablo in the Bay Area would get a dusting every few years—so it is possible, though barely, to live outside all year round in Sunny California. Nonetheless, recent statistics show that only 10% of California's homeless are from out-of-state.)

One of Dean's masterpieces was like a dark, existentialist version of the Sistine Chapel with a sky full of flowing figures in sombre colors; another was an "ideal" portrait of David Packard, co-founder of the Hewlett-Packard Corporation. He was dressed, with cape and medallion, as some kind of Renaissance Lord Mayor or Freemasonic Grand Master, posed in front of a *ruined façade of Notre Dame*, as if darkly predicting the tragic fire of

2019. The portrait was luminous, combining the regal character of a Roman Emperor with some arcane spiritual essence that I can't easily define; in comparison to it, the photograph of Packard that Dean had worked from merely presented the image of a mean, cranky old man.

Then the day came when I got a frantic call from Dean: "My camp has been raided and all my artworks stolen!" This was very puzzling to both of us, since a hater-of-the-homeless would be much more likely just to trash the camp and deface and destroy the paintings, not steal them. Finally, on investigation, we found that Dean's paintings had been stolen by Dominican College itself! Some employees of Dominican had found his camp, seen his paintings, and concluded that, based on their obviously high quality, they must have been stolen by some homeless person either from the College or else from the Dominican Convent next to it; the old Victorian Mother House was full of baroque-style Catholic art, and Dean's works would not have looked entirely out of place on its walls. So his paintings were ultimately recovered. Unfortunately, however, his expensive set of professional pastel crayons never turned up, "finders keepers, losers weepers" being the *de facto* Highest Law of the Land.

So who else did we know? One was Bob King, the quasi-official "leader" of, or "spokesman" for, San Rafael's homeless. He undoubtedly received payments from the City or the County, as indicated by the fact that he was indoors more often than most, and he likely repaid this generosity (at least according to rumor) by acting as a police spy. At one point he set his sights on Sarah as his ticket off the streets, resulting in a series of love letters in which he presented himself as "an old sailor looking for a home port" — though he was firmly denied entry by the port authorities. And San Anselmo had its "mascot" homeless person, undoubtedly a schizophrenic, who was sometimes known as the "Viking." The mascot-homeless role allowed the citizens of a town or neighborhood to discharge their charitable duties by choosing a designated individual as the official recipient of their concern, since it's easier to feel compassion for one unfortunate person than for hundreds; this also allowed the sheltered to deny the real extent of the problem. ("Mascotting" was undoubtedly mostly a suburban practice; in urban areas with large homeless encampments it became harder, and a lot less sentimentally attractive, to choose only a single mascot. Humanity, by number, becomes faceless.)

Last but not least, who should turn up among our clients but the Black poet Calvin Scott, older and more battered, whom I'd recited poetry side-by-side with in the Poetry in the Schools program, and who in the intervening years had been typed and profiled by the criminal justice system as a schizophrenic madman. Once a month the cops would waylay him and shoot him up with a long-lasting dose of the antipsychotic medication Haldol, to moderate his madness and return him to bourgeois consensus reality as far as was possible for a soul like his—Haldol that eventually gives you incurable Tardive's Diskinesia so you will be sure to walk and jerk like a madman as well as talking like one. But was he a madman all those years ago when he luminously declaimed from Rilke's *Duino Elegies*, and made them live? His sublime recitation of the last line of the Seventh Elegy—"*Inapprehensible, aloft!*"—still echoes in my memory.

Also, interestingly enough, our role as advocates for the homeless made us privy to a major historical event that the general public was not yet aware of. At one point an Iraqi ship owner appeared who offered to make his ship, moored in San Francisco Bay, available to us as a homeless shelter—an unexpected and initially puzzling event that only became intelligible to us after the U.S. invaded Iraq in Operation Desert Storm. Undoubtedly the merchant feared his ship would be impounded if not confiscated after the U.S. went to war, and was looking for a way to prevent this, and maybe generate a revenue stream at the same time. Little did he realize that we were not the source to turn to where money was concerned.

We discovered in our work that if homeless people could form stable couples it was easier for them to get off the street, so we sometimes found ourselves in the role of matchmakers—as what in Yiddish are called *shadchens*. Common-law marriages like this allowed the couple to pool their SSI checks, and also gave them the ability to *envision a future*, and the motivation to work toward it. That, however, was over 30 years ago. As marriage continues to dwindle as a social institution, this path from homelessness toward stable shelter is undoubtedly fading away along with it.

Then there was the homeless man, also a schizophrenic, who lived in a greenhouse on the grounds of the Falkirk Cultural Center in San Rafael, a Victorian mansion that served (and still does) as an art gallery and music venue. On one occasion he ran afoul of the police when he started breaking the glass walls of the greenhouse. After doing a quick translation and exegesis of his statement to them, originally delivered in Schizophrenese, we determined that this was his proactive response to climate change, since he had read that earth-warming was likely being caused by the "greenhouse effect." He took personal responsibility for the Earth, as we are all now being indoctrinated to do; it was just that he was rather hazy on exactly how to go about it. God willing the rest of us will be at least a little bit clearer on the right way to proceed.

We also learned about the fully-employed homeless, who worked 8-hour shifts 5 days a week, usually at minimum wage, and still couldn't afford to put a roof over their heads. These people were adept at appearing clean and well-groomed—sometimes more so than the general populace—but they could often be picked out due to their strong aroma of hand-soap from public restrooms, since the closest thing to a bathtub or shower they could usually access was a restroom sink. And the public libraries doubled, of course, as homeless day-shelters, which resulted in the homeless often being more literate and well-read than the sheltered population. In the days when cell phones were rare and expensive, a cheap paperback was often the only form of media a homeless person could afford; my own copy of *Hunger* by Norwegian novelist Knut Hamsun—a book about the author's experience of homelessness as a young man, which has sometimes been hailed as the 20th Century's literary debut—was a gift from a homeless person.

Other gifts were sometimes offered in gratitude for our services—a fine leather briefcase, a smart sports jacket—undoubtedly stolen property that had proved difficult to fence. The jacket came from a middle-aged, working-class homeless man from the Deep South who was in Sunny Marin County with his wife, undoubtedly seeking the same climate that had made Fairfax the site of the Arequipa Tuberculosis Sanatorium for women after the 1906 earthquake, which later became a Girl Scout camp. Sarah had arranged for a series of free acupuncture treatments for him at the Pine Street Clinic in San Anselmo, which cured him of some serious mobility problems, for which sleeping on the hard ground in the cold had undoubtedly not been very helpful. When I received the jacket I told him, "thanks, as long as you didn't get it off a dead man"—something I probably shouldn't have said; nonetheless I still thought I should briefly frown on illegal activities as my civic duty (though it was clear that I had no scruples against receiving stolen property), for which gesture I received an equally-deserved frown in response.

Since Project MOVE was a non-profit we could receive all sorts of heterogeneous in-kind donations for the tax write-off, as witness the acupuncture treatments. On one occasion some outfit gifted us a huge truckload of unsold cosmetics—organic shampoos and face-creams, things like that. We piled it all into a pickup and drove it to West Marin to be stored in Sarah's garage in Inverness, but on the way the top-heavy load fell off the truck—though we were able to salvage enough of it to provide the residents of a homeless encampment that the County had temporarily donated the land for, on a small hill near the Marin Civic Center, with fancy organic soaps and unguents. It was better than nothing—seeing that "better than nothing" was about all we could provide in any case.

The central project that Project MOVE became involved with was a convalescent program for the homeless, part of a larger voucher-for-shelter program which temporarily housed homeless people in local motels. The ER at Marin General Hospital served the homeless for free, usually when they were already at death's door, and then released them when it was considered safe for them to convalesce at home—the result being that one woman, after having had half a lung removed and still with a high fever, was discharged, shelterless, into the cold Marin County rain. These were the kind of people we did our best to pick up and house at the famous Bermuda Palms Motel (famous to those who've heard of it) on Francisco Boulevard, otherwise known as Litchfield's, palatial according to the canons of the 1950s—Richard Nixon himself had once stayed there—which by the 1990s had assumed the status of a City-and-County-designated whorehouse, undoubtedly paying rent to the City of San Rafael via kickbacks to the cops and allowed to operate to keep the whores off the city streets and to give the police a window into (and possibly a skim from off the top of) the local drug trade.

The Palms had a rich and storied past. Built by millionaire construction magnate Irving "Whitey" Litchfield in the late 1940s, it was advertised as "California's Las Vegas, a complete hotel resort: luxury swimming pool, color TV, nightly dancing and clean, sun-drenched rooms for less than $10 a night." Whitey later added the Flamingo Ballroom, the Camelia Dining Room, the Bali Hai Cocktail Lounge, the Mural Room for private dining and the Continental Room for conventions. Duke Ellington, Count Basie and Lionel Hampton played at the Palms. The famous stripper Lili St Cyr performed there. John Wayne and Lauren Bacall stayed at the Bermuda Palms while filming *Blood Alley* at China Camp in 1954. Humphrey Bogart and Robert Mitchum also made their appearance. And Whitey, an amateur boxer, set up a training camp there some time in the '50s, which was frequented by the likes of Sugar Ray Robinson, Bobo Olson, Rocky Marciano, Max Baer, Rocky Castellani, Paddy DeMarco and Joey Maxim. Don Cockell trained there for his World Heavyweight Championship bout against Marciano on May 16, 1955. And in the rock era of the '60s, the ballroom—known intermittently as the Euphoria and Pepperland—featured the Grateful Dead, Janis Joplin, Frank Zappa, Steve Miller, Boz Scaggs, the Sons of Champlin, Joy of Cooking, Captain Beefheart, Leon Russell, Elvin Bishop, Clover, Commander Cody, Linda Ronstadt, The Quicksilver Messenger Service, Hot Tuna, Pink Floyd, Tower of Power, Chuck Berry, Sly and the Family Stone, Country Joe MacDonald, the Youngbloods, and Van Morrison.

Sarah and I met Whitey once in the ancient shuttered nightclub complete with scattered abandoned tables, stage for the performers, floor that opened onto a swimming pool in Great Gatsby style, and the dusty and bedraggled *papier-mâché* palm trees of another era. It was in this environment, completely overrun by prostitutes and with a fine haze of cocaine sparkling in the air (that being mostly the era of snow rather than crack) that we were tasked by the County of Marin with saving human lives, with zero medical knowledge and zero resources beyond the motel vouchers. And we did save lives—at least a few of them and temporarily, as all life-saving must be.

Whitey himself passed away in 1995.

Glamour always ends in degradation because glamour *is* degradation. Nonetheless, based partly on the last fading spiritual impetus of the counterculture, we did save a few lives, some of which had clearly been brought to the brink of disaster by the counter-culture itself. When homeless Hell's Angel Mike Bettis reached out to us (apparently the Angels offer little or no retirement package), I found him in a motel room at death's door, his skin corpse-grey from internal bleeding, but I was able to get him to the ER in time. When he actually did die a few months later, it seemed like the entire San Rafael homeless community went into mourning for him; they even organized a memorial procession in his honor.

Then there was the young couple we couldn't save; all we could do was the Mother Theresa thing of witnessing and blessing the woman's death. She had obviously been ill for a long time and was consequently extremely unattractive, and possibly "mentally challenged" as well. Her boyfriend was the only one willing to stick by her, to protect her on the streets; nonetheless he still beat her from time to time. Sarah's response to this was to call him a "sociopath." "He's not a sociopath" I replied — "he's a sinner"; there's the difference between the secular and the religious worldviews in a nutshell. And what moral judgment could be considered appropriate in a situation like that? Maybe the subtlest and truest morality is simply to suffer with the people involved, and with the situation, and with your own reactions to the situation; that's where real reward and punishment are worked out in the most exacting of terms. When she was dying in the hospital I was there with her boyfriend to give what support I could. She was already in a coma, nonetheless he still tried to get through to her, telling her that he loved her; for a moment she seemed to notice and respond. "I think she heard me," he said. "I think you're right," I answered.

A second couple we worked with, Tim and Rebecca Huerta, did better. Tim was a "classic" Irishman who took his wife's last name; Rebecca was working with a phone answering service in town. They slept their nights in a homeless shelter. Tim got on the wrong side of the shelter managers because they wouldn't let him escort his wife through the streets on her walk to her job site, highlighting the fact that homeless shelters are actually more like minimum-security prisons. It was on the Huertas that I tried out that intuitive technique I'd developed while I was at Santa Venetia — Strategic Insight Meditation — which was designed to get specific answers to problems from a supposedly higher source. Asking how to help them, I was directed to a Catholic priest I didn't know, another Irishman, who was the pastor of St Sebastian's Church in Greenbrae. When he and Tim met they immediately warmed to each other, with the result that the priest provided him and Rebecca with the room in his residence reserved for the housekeeper, a position that was presently vacant. What happened to them after that I don't know, but at least they'd taken a step in the right direction. As for my "New Age" spiritual technique, it went the way of all similar experiments soon after I joined the Sufis, having come to the conclusion that such self-invented attempts at consciousness-extension are of limited value, and sometimes even dangerous — mostly because they tend to imperceptibly replace faith in God with worship of oneself. But this one "worked" on at least one occasion, though it was only a poor substitute for the certainty that God answers prayers, even if you haven't yet learned how to make sense of the language He speaks in.

As a social service agency we were expected, of course, to go for funding — but how could two people with no clerical staff, most of whose time was taken up with direct service to the homeless, ever write a grant, especially with little to no experience in doing so? The San Francisco Foundation, which managed the famous Buck Fund, set up by the Marin County philanthropist Beryl (not Pearl) Buck, was the perpetual tease as far as funding was concerned, but it never put out. I get the definite impression that most of the bucks from the Fund have gone to the Buck Center for Research in Aging, which, instead of helping 200 poor people live 5 or 10 years longer, seems to be designed (though I could certainly be wrong here) to allow a handful of transhumanist billionaires to achieve physical immortality — until, that is, the world ends, or a brick falling from a crumbling building takes them out. The peanuts-level funding that we did get came largely from the Board of Supervisors discretionary funds, which meant: from Gary Giacomini, whom I later found out that Sarah had been in bed with in more ways than one; she was willing to make that sacrifice to serve the poor and the destitute of Marin County (including herself), and also undoubtedly as a way to mourn and emotionally compensate for the death of her father. Our pitch essentially was: "We'll work for next to nothing and deal with populations nobody else will touch," which in our case meant homeless schizophrenics. We also had the supremely naïve and idealistic idea that the social service agencies of Marin should *work together* to solve the problem of homelessness! *Stupid hippies, what were we thinking?* It was a world of cutthroat competition. The standard routine, once funding was secured, was to set up a nice office, hire a competent staff, pay everybody's salaries, and then *maybe* provide some services to the community if any resources were left over. Lying about your degree of success to keep the grants coming was of course considered to be best practice; when a particular social service outfit claimed to have gotten (say) 5000 people off the street, all this indicated was that their *intake*, on some level or other and with innumerable repeat appearances, had amounted to maybe 5000 occasions; "off the street" often meant no more than one night in a cheap motel. It may be that the County motel voucher program for the homeless had evolved only so that the agencies administering it could report higher numbers of clients.

So Project MOVE was perpetually impoverished—until the day when every hippie do-gooder's dream came true: *The Grateful Dead wrote a letter promising to do a benefit for us!* The problem was, however, that once we had that letter in hand we suddenly thought we were big rock promoters, which was the furthest thing from the truth: we didn't even know how to *find or talk to* a big rock promoter, at least to begin with. It was at this point that Sarah began talking (half humorously but with entire seriousness) about setting up a Buddhist residential community for the homeless; she even started scouting possible sites. Never mind that she wasn't a Buddhist and had zero idea of what Buddhism was all about—she was a Jewish Hippie, wasn't she? Of course she was a Buddhist! (That was in the days when so many Buddhist teachers, like Jack Kornfield, were of Jewish extraction. It was clear, at least to me, that they needed to get out from under the thumb of the wrathful Yahweh who had treated the Jews so harshly as payment for their status as the Chosen People—but *religion* was the one thing they couldn't leave behind, which is why "non-theistic" Buddhism presented itself, at one point, as the ideal solution.) During that time we schmoozed with Peter Coyote, the Hollywood actor with the social service background (courtesy of the Diggers) who had also been close to Lew Welch and who ultimately became "the voice of PBS"; with Benjamin Harrison Lehmann Jr., the stepson of the famous actress Dame Judith Anderson; and with Robin Williams' mother, a delightfully dramatic and personable southern belle type. (Sarah had known Robin slightly at Redwood High School in Marin County's Larkspur; she described him as very quiet, but always listening.) So we had set our sights on the local celebs. Sarah once talked with Dame Judith by phone, who commended her for doing something "real and important" whereas she, the Dame, was only an actress—nonetheless, from my point of view, Sarah Howard deserved an Oscar for more than one of her performances. Another on that list was Prince Peter Andreievich Romanoff, first in line (at the present writing, at least according to one of the several competing theories) to be head of the Romanoff family, and therefore, potentially at least, the Czar of All the Russias. Handsome and with the tightly-curled hair of the standard prince, he was working as an auto mechanic at a garage in Inverness. At one point he married a local Sufi woman. Do the dreams of regime change in Russia presently being entertained by the U.S. government include the possibility of a Czarist restoration? Who knows? In any case—looking ahead and hedging my bets—I offered to be his speech writer if he ever found himself in the running. He told me he would think about it. And last but not least, Sarah got us invited to an event at Jerry Brown's place when he was running for President of the

United States in 1992. When we met him he was living in San Francisco in an old fire station, with the traditional brass pole for the firemen to slide down and a polished hardwood floor where the trucks used to be parked, an ideal space for large receptions. His father, Edmund G. "Pat" Brown, past Governor of California, also made an appearance that evening. Maybe Jerry already vaguely knew who Sarah was through her Democratic Party connections in Marin; nonetheless, instead of the traditional "It's an honor to meet you Mr Brown (etc. etc.)," Sarah opened with, "Hi — can I be Vice-president?" "We are not quite yet at that point in our recruiting process, but we will certainly take your proposal under advisement (etc. etc.)" he replied, woodenly. This kind of encounter was a perfect example of the *fun* of working with Sarah Howard — the sort of fun that *almost* paid us back for the pain.

In addition, while scoping out a site for the planned residential community for the homeless, Sarah made contact with a real estate agent, Katherine Blackwell, an acquaintance of mine who happened to be a member of the Johrei Fellowship that had been so helpful to me during the darkest period of my life; that's how the uplifting and healing channeled energy known as Johrei, the Divine Light, briefly became one of the services provided by Project MOVE to Marin's homeless. Once when Kathy was showing a potential site, Sarah told her: "There was a murder here" — which turned out to be correct. That's how psychic she was — psychic enough to have made her living at the pea-under-the-nutshells game, if that were ever required to keep body and soul together; as it was she tended to "pay herself back" from time to time by monetary slight-of-hand for her sometimes unpaid services to the homeless. At one point she even went so far as to cast the equivalent of a "spell" designed to cause a certain woman to lose her job so her sister Nina could get it instead; the act had suddenly suggested itself to her out of nowhere, and she felt it had also provided her with the power to complete it. Here we can see how simply doing good is not enough to protect you from evil, since both good and evil have to be harvested in their own terms; "good karma" does not automatically cancel out "bad karma." God can forgive any transgression, but this forgiveness operates on a much higher level than karma does; it cannot be calculated in terms of it. And you also need to be very clear on where the real Good is coming from, and refuse to accept "help" from any other direction.

But Sarah finally did land a big rock promoter, the biggest of all — Bill Graham himself! So it looked like we had all the pieces in place for the Dead benefit and the beginning of a track for future funding; however, that was not to be. One day Sarah and her until-recently-homeless boyfriend, John Burke, appeared at the door of my and Jenny's house. Her face was covered with blood. (John, a Vietnam vet who could fix anything from a helicopter to a computer and who was one of Sarah's once and future clients, had AIDS, which was right in line with her habit of going for love relationships with a built-in escape clause. Once at the Palms I had to tell a roomful of whores that "John has AIDS you know," a rather awkward revelation that was nonetheless required by the remnant of my "straight" bourgeois conscience. However, thanks mostly to cocaine, nobody seemed to care. That's what cocaine is for after all; it's the ideal anesthetic, both physically and emotionally. I remember one night when my friends and I were smoking weed, while two or three of us were snorting cocaine at a separate table. As I glanced over to them, they appeared as if they were photographed in black and white, while the rest of the room was in color. That's what cocaine does, and is: it washes all the color of feeling out of the air, and the human soul.)

The story she told was as follows: The night before Sarah had been with Bill Graham, talking up the Buddhist residential community. Ideas flew and expectations mounted. High from the bull-session—and a number of other things—Sarah ran her car into a tree on the banks of Paper Mill Creek while driving home to West Marin. The people who found her and drove her back to the more settled part of Marin County to look for medical care stole her purse, and she ultimately ended up in the drunk tank. She had just been released. So I drove her and John to my bank in San Rafael, Wells Fargo, so she could cash my check for $50 to get home. But while I was waiting in the parking lot for them to return, a news flash came on the car radio: *"Bill Graham was killed last night in a helicopter crash."* A storm had been raging, his pilot had counseled against flying—but Bill had said "what the hell, let's chance it," so they ended up colliding with some high-tension wires. Had Sarah in fact killed Bill Graham by drinking, smoking and talking him so high that night that he lost all caution? Or had Francis Ford Coppola actually killed him, years earlier, by placing him in the Playboy Helicopter (from which he later disappeared) in *Apocalypse Now*? No court or jury in the land would convict either of them, and the Higher Court of Appeals provides no public records. In any case, she had apparently crashed her car at the very moment Bill Graham died. So when Sarah and John returned from the bank, I had to break the news. Her reaction was a perfectly calm and matter-of-fact shock, as if she recognized this horrendous outcome as precisely in line with the true quality of the moment.

So, no Grateful Dead Benefit, no Buddhist Homeless Shelter, and soon enough no more homeless service agency. I could say more about Project MOVE in its fading months, but I feel that it's about time to bring this story to a close—because, seriously, how can you follow an act like that?

CHAPTER ELEVEN
The Planet of the Traditionalists

FOR MOST OF OUR MARRIED LIFE, JENNY HAS been the first to catch wind of major new developments; for example, she was the one who first "discovered" the movement in solidarity with the revolutions of Central America. Previously she had found the books of Marie-Louise Von Franz, probably the most interesting of the Jungians, whose most important work was in the area of the psychological exegesis of fairy tales, which she also related to dream interpretation. Next Jenny discovered the intriguing books of "Neo-Sufi" Idries Shah, collector (and also partly author?) of the corpus of the humorous yet perceptive Nasruddin stories, probably best described as Muslim folk tales. Most of Shah's output was in the form of Sufi "teaching stories," similar in style to the tales of the Hasidim. He also produced several very insightful books on the collective psychology of human self-deception, as well as *The Sufis*, an overview of the tradition of *tasawwuf*—valuable though not without a few worrisome errors and subterfuges; it had an Introduction by Robert Graves. Reading Shah's books was like eating peanuts or popcorn; you could go through a whole bag of them in no time. Unfortunately, he was also one of those so-called Sufis who claim that Sufism can be separated from Islam, which is like believing that the Franciscan Order of monks could become a religion of its own, outside of Catholicism (though I don't mean to suggest that something that crazy couldn't actually happen, given the craziness of our times and the ongoing dissolution of the Roman Catholic Church). All these foreshadowings, however, were destined to converge on the higher ground of an entirely new viewpoint: that of the Traditionalist or Perennialist School, founded by French metaphysician René Guénon and headed at that time by a Swiss philosopher named Frithjof Schuon.

Schuon was on an entirely different level than Shah, the Jungians, the Pseudo-initiatory and Counter-initiatory spiritualities (two of Guénon's categories) of the New Age, and the spotty and eclectic "traditionalism" of the hippie counterculture. His works on traditional metaphysics and comparative religion raised the entire discourse on mystical spirituality to a higher intellectual level. Nor was Schuon alone in his radically liberating perspective; he was recognized as the contemporary leader of a group of writers on traditional metaphysics and comparative religion that had included both René Guénon and Ananda Kentish Coomaraswamy, the Anglo-Indian writer on traditional art and metaphysics. Numbered in the present roster were Ananda's son Rama P. Coomaraswamy, Professor James Cutsinger of the University of South Carolina, the Iranian Sufi and religious scholar Seyyed Hossein Nasr who still teaches at the George Washington University in Washington D.C., and—despite his earlier counterculture connections—the well-known popular writer (though equally serious and scholarly) on the world's religions, Professor Huston Smith. Other members, both living and dead, included Titus Burckhardt, Martin Lings, Julius Evola, Marco Pallis, Charles le Gai Eaton, Alvin Moore Jr., Tage Lindbom, Lord Northbourne, Whitall Perry, Harry Oldmeadow, et al., all of them working on a strikingly elevated level. On top of that, Martin Lings, Dr Nasr, Prof. Cutsinger, Rama Coomaraswamy, Huston Smith and a few others—not to mention Schuon himself—were still actively writing and capable of being contacted.

Soon we immersed ourselves as deeply as possible in these writers and their books, which produced a true and complete *metanoia* in my spiritual outlook. From René Guénon I not only learned about his own version of the doctrine that Schuon called Transcendent Unity of Religions, perhaps the central teaching of his School, but about the Primordial Tradition from which all the Divine revelations ultimately branched, as well as the difference between true and false religion, between Tradition and Counter-Tradition. Guénon had been raised a Catholic as I had; largely between the World Wars he threw himself into every form of occultism and pseudo-religion he could find, just as I had done (though not so extensively) in the '60s, '70s and '80s—Theosophy, Spiritualism, Martinism, the occultism of Éliphas Lévi, Neo-Gnosticism etc.—from which he emerged with the unshakable conviction that these various "alternative" religions were nothing less than the many manifestations of the Powers of Darkness, which together constituted what he called the "Counter-Initiation." At the same time he was studying and seeking true initiation into, and writing books about, what he came to consider the valid and legitimate wisdom-traditions and spiritual Ways: the Hindu Vedanta, Taoism, Islamic Sufism, etc. He hoped to re-awaken the Catholic Church to its own metaphysical and esoteric traditions through a better understanding of the eastern religions where traditional metaphysics and esoterism were more intact than they were in the West—he dialogued for a time with the Catholic Neo-Thomist philosopher Jacques Maritain—but ultimately he despaired of this hope, converted to Islam, accepted initiation into a Sufi *tariqah*, and left Europe for Egypt, never to return.

Frithjof Schuon was a Muslim and a Sufi, but he is most often identified with his principle of the Transcendent Unity of Religions, which holds that God has sent more than one valid revelation to humanity, and that all these revelations or wisdom traditions—Judaism, Christianity, Islam, Hinduism, Buddhism, Zoroastrianism, Taoism, as well as such "First Nations" spiritualities as the Native American Sun Dance—are speaking, from their widely-differing points of departure, about the same Transcendent

Principle (God to the Christians, Allah to the Muslims, etc.). Furthermore, each one of these revelations—if it remains intact—provides a complete Path of Return to that Principle. Certain verses of the Qur'an say essentially the same thing. Nonetheless the differences between the religions are also necessary and providential, since they were designed by God to operate within different cultural frameworks and appeal to different human types. Consequently, to promiscuously mix the religions—for example, by attempting to practice more than one religion at the same time—is wrong-headed and destructive, and unnecessary as well, given that, in Schuon's words, "each religion contains all the religions, because the Truth is One."

All this gave me quite a bit to chew on. If anybody had ever *mixed religions*, it was certainly me. And without a doubt I had been deeply involved in spiritualities that were clearly Counter-Initiatory according to Guénon's criteria. Nonetheless I had always maintained my interest in the traditional revelations, side-by-side with the more suspect beliefs and influences of hippie and New Age spirituality. But somewhere, in my heart of hearts, I had given the traditional revelations precedence. My pre-Vatican II Catholic education had taught me that there is such a thing as a *science* of metaphysics, and given me an instinctive feel for what a *religion* is, a revelation sent by God to man; both these lessons were of great help when I began my investigation of the non-Christian religions while still in my teens. But it was not until I plunged into the writings of the Traditionalist School that I realized that the non-traditional spiritualities were not simply of lesser value than the traditional religions, but were in many cases actually opposed to them—sometimes naively and unconsciously, sometimes consciously, actively, and with a ruthless and openly-declared determination to sweep them off the face of the earth. This realization ultimately led me to write what some have called my magnum opus, *The System of Antichrist: Truth and Falsehood in Postmodernism and the New Age*, which came out in 2001. In that book, besides providing a comparative eschatology based on the end-time prophesies of eight religious traditions, which I compiled in a deliberate attempt to "update" René Guénon's prophetic masterpiece *The Reign of Quantity and the Signs of the Times*, I also provided a detailed refutation, according to the principles of traditional metaphysics, of a number of New Age belief-systems, most of which I myself had accepted at one time. These included the "sorcery" of Carlos Castaneda, the channeled "Seth" material of Jane Roberts, and *A Course in Miracles*. In the process of composing *The System of Antichrist*, I "wrote myself out" of both the hippie counterculture and the New Age.

If I had been "ripe" for a serious relationship to the spiritual Path in the '60s, I might have gone for some form of hippified Hindu yoga—for which one of the textbooks would certainly have been *Be Here Now* by Ram Dass (Richard Alpert), whose lectures I had attended in both the U.S.

and Canada—or possibly the kundalini-yoga of Sikh guru Yogi Bhajan, who (as you'll remember) I met on one occasion. If I had ripened in the '70s, my choice would likely have been Tibetan Buddhism, particularly the brand brought to the west by Chögyam Trungpa, a teacher that many of my fellow poets (largely under the influence of Allen Ginsberg) had been attracted to, as I've already made clear. The fact is, however, that I became ready for a serious commitment to the spiritual Path only in the 1980s — the decade when, mostly through the work of Robert Bly and Coleman Barks, the Sufi Jalaluddin Rumi had emerged as the most popular poet in the English-speaking world, just as more-or-less traditional Islamic Sufism was becoming established in the West. Seen from this point-of-view, my choice of Sufism as a spiritual path was little more than a function of its availability and my readiness.

But that's neither the whole story nor the real story, since when seen from the standpoint of the Dream of My Life I recounted in *Chapter One*—the one with the black-faced North African marabouts or Sufis in white *jellabas*—my rendezvous with Sufism was pre-planned and pre-accepted. That dream was so powerful that whenever my life has gone through a major change I've returned to it, each time seeing new aspects to its symbolism, which continues to be relevant and enlightening no matter what point-of-view I see it from. So the truth is, I was destined for Sufism from the beginning.

In any case, Jenny's discovery of the books of Frithjof Schuon drew us into a world and a worldview that determined the main current of our spiritual development for the next thirty years. Schuon's perspective on things of the Spirit was sober, comprehensive, profound, and relevant in many incisive and unexpected ways. He had the spiritual universalism that up until then we had only encountered, in a much less satisfying form, in the world of religious liberalism—in other words, he accepted that God had sent more than one valid Revelation to humanity, and that more than one of these Revelations might be effectively in force at the same time, thus avoiding the kind of militant religious exclusivism that is always in danger of placing opposition to religions other than one's own on a higher plane than the in-depth practice of the religion one actually professes. This, however, is where any resemblance to religious liberalism ended, seeing that his take on the world's great faiths was in no way modernizing or progressive. On the contrary, it was profoundly traditional—I might almost say, profoundly *adult*. Where the "traditionalism" of the hippie spiritual revolution was an entirely hit-and-miss affair, that of Frithjof Schuon was highly informed, integrated, culturally sophisticated, and all of a piece. For comparative religion and universal metaphysics, Schuon seemingly had no peer, at least in any of the contemporary spiritual literature that either myself or my wife were aware of at the time.

And we did in fact end up contacting, or at least communicating with, six names on the above list of Traditionalist authors. Undoubtedly the most gracious and helpful people we met in the Traditionalist world were Seyyed Hossein Nasr, who put us in touch with several congenial friends and teachers, and Prof. Huston Smith, world-renowned writer on comparative religion, whose book *The World's Religions* (formerly titled *The Religions of Man*), a highly-readable popularization of the subject that never sacrifices sound scholarship and subtle insight for accessibility to a wide readership, has become a classic. Huston was truly "a gentleman and a scholar," a congenitally sunny soul who radiated a genuine positivity that was free from the slightest taint of hypocrisy and narcissistic "charisma." We first met him at "CCC," the Community Congregationalist Church of Belvedere-Tiburon, a church we'd originally been introduced to through our work in solidarity with the revolutions of Central America and the Sanctuary Movement for Salvadoran refugees. CCC was the biggest Liberal church of Marin County, probably bigger and more influential than even the Unitarian Universalists; they were in the habit of hosting speakers from many religious and spiritual traditions, since the further a nominally Christian church departs from traditional Christianity, the more holes appear in the fabric of its ministry that tempt the ministers to plug them by fragments taken from other faiths.

Huston Smith was perfect for a role like that, not only because he was the recognized doyen of comparative religion studies in the English-speaking world but because he had also participated in the early research on psychedelics conducted by Harvard University. We ran into him again at one of the highly interesting symposia held by the Ibn 'Arabi Society on the campus of U.C. Berkeley, several of which we attended and through which we immersed ourselves in an abstruse yet surprisingly stimulating world of highly intellectual spirituality, one that bore definite similarities to Schuon's perspective and served as a perfect preliminary introduction to it. Later we became acquainted with Seyyed Hossein Nasr, with James Cutsinger, and with the most spiritually significant of our Traditionalist contacts, Rama Ponnambalam Coomaraswamy, son of the co-founder with René Guénon of the Traditionalist School, Ananda Coomaraswamy; cardiologist to Mother Theresa; one of Schuon's "Christian *muqaddams*" (representatives); in later life a licensed psychiatrist; and finally a traditional *sedevacantist* Catholic priest, as well as an exorcist who worked in the New York area with the fascinating and controversial Fr Malachi Martin—a mercurial figure who sometimes seemed to be a *sedevacantist* (someone who believes, like Mel Gibson, that "the Seat is vacant," that all the popes following Pius XII have been false), sometimes a conservative Novus Ordo priest ("Novus Ordo" being the *sedevacantist* term for the new version of the Catholic Church that grew out of the Second Vatican

Council), sometimes simply a jurisdictional and theological loose cannon who changed like a chameleon to match his surroundings and play into various people's assumptions about him. Nonetheless *everybody* should read his *Hostage to the Devil* (one of the best and most readable books on demonology) and *Windswept House* (a thinly-fictionalized exposé of the "resident evil" within the post-Vatican II Catholic Church).

The Traditionalists initially fulfilled two functions for us. First, they represented a clean break with the counterculture and the New Age spiritualities, while at the same time raising a few of the themes that these spiritualities had promiscuously played around with to a higher and more integrated level. In addition, they provided a new intellectual approach to mystical spirituality that protected us, at least for a while, from the traumatic heartbreak of the fall of Santa Venetia Presbyterian Church that had devastated other members of our once tight-knit group, sometimes permanently. We needed something a bit more cool and detached at that point, something with a degree of *sang froid* in it that manifested clarity, *apatheia* and spiritual objectivity. We were looking for a space where we could park our wounded feelings; only gradually did we come to the dual realization that the subtle, unofficial but nonetheless pervasive tendency in the world of the Traditionalist School to identify Love with a strictly devotional *bhakti*, placing it on a lower plane than *jñana* or Knowledge, would have to be paid for rather heavily down the road, and that not everything in Schuon's circle—to say the least—was really as cool and detached, or as truly Traditional, as our first impressions had led us to believe.

THE NIMATULLAHIS

In any case, our growing connection with the Traditionalist School opened up a number of fertile spiritual possibilities. Dr Nasr, in one of his books, had provided a list of the more-or-less traditional and orthodox Sufi *tariqahs* operating in the west, one of which was the Nimatullahi Sufi Order from Iran, headed at that time by Dr Javad Nurbakhsh. And since that *tariqah* had a *khaniqa* (Sufi lodge, the Persian equivalent of the Arabic *zawiya*) in San Francisco, Jenny and I decided to check it out.

There we met with one Ron Harris, a Black man who was later appointed the *shaykh* (in Nimatullahi terminology, the local leader) of that particular *khaniqa*. Nurbakhsh himself, whom we addressed as the Master, held the title of *Pir*. To Jenny he quoted from the Gospel of Thomas: "If you bring out what is within you, it will save you; if you fail to bring out what is within you, it will destroy you." And to me he told the story of the dervish who traveled to Paradise every night in his dreams, but nonetheless ended up dying on a dungheap. When I got home I gulped down my usual nightly quart of Rainier Ale—but somehow my heart wasn't in it. And the next day, when I opened what turned out to be my *last* quart of what was popularly known as the Green Death, I just couldn't drink it. If I joined the Nimatullahis I would have to become a Muslim for real, and I knew that alcohol is prohibited in Islam — consequently alcohol left my life at that very moment, and I haven't taken another drink in the past 35 years. It's not that I never craved alcohol; the craving, which was sometimes pretty fierce after 15 years as a confirmed alcoholic, came and went, first every week, then every month, then every three months, etc. etc. It's simply that I never once considered giving in to it. I sought no psychotherapy, no Alcoholics Anonymous, not even any nutritional support; I simply relied on the unbreakable certainty that I would never drink again. Will-power was not involved — unless the will in question was the Will of the Almighty. It was not a question of effort, it was an effect of Command. By that time I had been smoking marijuana no more than two or three times a year (psychedelics had disappeared some years earlier), but pretty soon that indulgence was gone for good as well. Such experiences as astral projection also came to an end around the same time, seeing that I had involved myself with them through an essentially magical paradigm where the ego, not Allah, is the "Doer." My excursions in the direction of God as a distant reality were coming to an end; I had begun working on the premise that, as Allah has informed us in a *hadith qudsi*, "Heaven and earth cannot contain Me but the Heart of my loving slave can contain Me." And as the Heart is the crucible of the Spirit, so the human body is the crucible of the Heart.

So *something* was definitely going on! And not long after that, Jenny and I joined the Nimatullahi Order, though she moved on a few years later. We were initiated according to the ancient Persian rite where the postulant presents to the initiating shaykh a coin, a ring, a piece of rock candy, a nutmeg, and a length of cloth. The coin symbolized detachment from "laying up treasure on earth"; the ring, allegiance to the Master; the rock candy, the rejection of the ability to derive sweetness from anything but Allah; the nutmeg — which stood for one's *head* — the sacrifice of self-will, of the *headstrong* ego; and the cloth — which represented one's funeral shroud — the renunciation of attachment to life itself through the willingness to embrace *fana,'* annihilation in God. I took this step because I knew I had had enough of flitting from flower to flower in the spiritual life; now I wanted the Hive. So I said to myself: "Stop, choose one path, stay with it, and sink or swim." So I sat in the Nimatullahi circle for twenty years, rarely saying more than a few words, and concentrating on two themes: *Remember God and forget yourself*, and *put God's Will above your own will — even your will to see Him and be united with Him.* By this method I allowed Him to slowly recollect my scattered psyche, disordered by years of alcohol and drug use, psychic experimentation and unguided spiritual aspiration. ("Forget yourself" does not mean "ignore the actions and agendas of your *nafs*, your lower self"; it means "stop working to build and maintain your identity, give up your fear of losing it, and stop making claims.") During that time, Ron Harris said two things that have everything to do with the question of *identity*. The first was: "We are not here to become 'Sufis'"; and the second: "The only 'Master' is God."

Jenny, however, almost balked before she took this final step. Her misgivings were primarily due to her meeting with one Mr Niktab—old, thin and white-bearded, Dr Nurbakhsh's main representative—the *Shaykh al-Mashaykh*. He was the one who ultimately conducted our initiation, which consisted of whispering to us the words of the *dhikr* we were to use and writing the Name of Allah with his finger on our hearts. When Mr Niktab first met us, he said to me: "We search the world over to find sincere seekers such as yourself"—pretty obviously in order to see if he could inflate my spiritual pride only to puncture it further on, as on the later occasion when he told me, apropos of nothing, "you—you're nothing much." I don't remember being either inflated by his flattery (which only made me vaguely suspicious of him) or deflated by his insult, since I saw both as parts of a "Sufi teaching technique" that was undoubtedly effective with certain people under certain circumstances, but which was clearly not designed for universal application. Then he asked me: "What is your conception of Sufism?," to which I replied "There is only God" (as if that represented my actual station at the time, which it certainly did not). Next he turned to Jenny, and rather insolently challenged her: "And *you??*" "I, I don't know what to say" she replied, flustered.

This is what is known as "getting off on the wrong foot"; it was an encounter that definitely foreshadowed Jenny's future problems with the Nimatullahi Order, which led her to drop out after two or three years, leaving me to fend for myself. Because it was clear that some of the dervishes had no intention of accepting her as a sister-in-good-standing. When she made an observation on one occasion about the reality of higher worlds, one of the male dervishes snapped: "That's just thought!" Another dervish told me, in a "helpful and friendly manner," that he saw Jenny as "mentally challenged," after which I had to call him on his affront and ask him to apologize to her, which he gladly did; by that worthy action he changed an unconscious vice into a conscious virtue. One of Dr Nurbakhsh's most useful teachings was: *If you are still capable of taking offense, you haven't yet reached the stage of the soul-at-peace.* I am pretty good at ignoring insults directed at myself, but not so good at standing by and letting the people I love be disrespected; that's where my "spiritual detachment" comes to an end. Some might say: "You can't stand to see your wife be insulted because she is an extension of your ego"—something that might conceivably be true, if only there were no such thing as love on earth...For my part I was unwilling to accept an insult offered to my wife behind her back as somehow acceptable because it was "an understanding between us guys" that the little woman didn't need know about, realizing that a Devil's-bargain like that is precisely a curse designed to come between husband and wife—this, according to the Qurʻan, being the main goal of the evil magic that was taught to mankind by the angels Harut and Marut in Babylon [Q. 2:102]. Like many of the American dervishes, the man who had dissed Jenny worked for Microsoft, so he was undoubtedly tempted by the more toxic aspects of his milieu to see anyone who was not part of the culture of hip computer nerds as a hopeless Deplorable from the hinterlands—especially if she happened to have a Kentucky accent! (That's California for you.) Nonetheless, the Nimatullahis strongly emphasized *adab*, etiquette, sometimes quoting the saying that "Sufism is all *adab*." Leave it to those who preach against over-indulgence to be gluttons, against sexual sin to be libertines, and against discourtesy to be oafs—oafs, at least, according to the better standards of Western civilization. But who is still civilized enough in the West to teach these proprieties to clueless immigrants from the Middle East—or, for that matter, to contemporary deculturated Americans? "The tribe without a history is not redeemed from time" said T.S. Eliot... Furthermore, after Jenny had been out of the *khaniqa* for some time, the dervishes invented the story (with zero evidence) that we had divorced, after which one of the attractive Iranian girl-dervishes cocked her eye in my direction, setting her sights on me as available, vulnerable and likely to be caught on the rebound. Luckily for us, by that time we had become friends with Huston Smith; when I told him about the sort of treatment Jenny had endured at the hands of the Nimatullahis, he was quite surprised, observing that "her sincerity is transparent." *That*, however, might have been the very problem; there is no worse affront to the cunning than sincerity. Or had Mr Niktab initiated all this cold-shouldering by putting an invisible mark of some kind on Jenny that affected the group psyche? The more likely cause was simply Jenny's difficulty with certain groups—especially emotionally immature groups like the San Francisco poets—that her abusive family-life and the sibling-rivalry her mother had set up with her younger sister had made her vulnerable to. And few groups have ever been more "poetic," more prone to confuse aesthetics with spirituality, than the Persian dervishes! All the best and some of the worst of that orientation can clearly be seen in the exquisite poetry of Hafiz. Wine, wine and more wine, invisible wine, spiritual wine, under the influence of which nothing could be more spiritually *unhip* than *sobriety* (al-Hallaj as the wild and crazy hipster, al-Junaid as the straight, Philistine old fogey)—and who could be more sober and stoic, in her deepest essence, than Jenny Donne? Beyond that, were the Nimatullahis able to so swiftly break my addiction to alcohol simply because they offered me a better wine, the wine of the fountains of Paradise, which the Qurʻan tells us produces neither madness nor headache, neither sloppiness nor hangover? Did the Order somehow function as my spiritual halfway house, with their own highly effective methadone program?

Only God knows for sure. But whatever their method was, it worked. I sat in that *khaniqa* in San Francisco twice a week for 20 years, concentrating on my *dhikr*, hardly saying a word, while slowly and laboriously recollecting the dissipated psyche that, over the previous 20 years, I had blown to the four winds—with grass, with booze, with psychedelics, with poetry, with unguided kundalini-yoga, with Leftist politics, with the "lyric sorcery" of Carlos Castaneda, and with every conceivable brand of New Age psychic experimentation—slowly, slowly picking up the pieces that fit while discarding the foreign fragments that didn't, working on the spiritual station that the Christians call "recollection" and the Sufis *jam*,' "gathering."

And did I ever need it. But for Jenny's part, the fact is—and I have seen this many times—she often has a very strange effect on people. One group (let's call them "the sheep") accept her as the wise, sincere and loving person she obviously is, while the opposite group (the "goats") unexpectedly repress her, slight her, demean her—possibly (I have been forced to speculate) due to a deep unconscious *fear* of something that she represents. I believe that Jenny somehow participates, by God's decree, in a kind of imposed obscurity—an invisible *hijab* if you will—as if He somehow wanted to keep her all for Himself; consequently she often functions (in line with her Libran nature) as a *hidden snare of justice* capable of exposing the obsessive and unconscious discourtesy of those in whom a particular kind of worldliness has become second nature; she acts as a stumbling-block that's invisible to them until they trip over it and fall on their face. On the other side of the same coin, there are some people who, when encountering a profoundly arcane dimension of the Divinity, have the immediate impulse to hide it, to declare it *haram*, a word that denotes not just "forbidden because corrupt" but also, as with the *Masjid al-Haram*, the precincts of the Kaaba in Mecca, "forbidden because sacred"—an impulse that is essentially based on fear. They fear that the vision of that mystery will destroy their whole picture of reality, along with their own meticulously-crafted self-identity—an apprehension which in turn invokes, on a deeply unconscious level, their fear of the end of the world. And it may be that both of these factors have played a part in the way Jenny has been treated over the years, at least by a certain class of people. Yet there is still a secret in her, as indeed there is in all of us, that all this "well-informed speculation" can never fully elucidate; therefore I must pray to God that He will keep the deepest secret of her nature safely hidden from any eyes but His.

The central teachings and practices of the Nimatullahis were those of classic Islamic *tasawwuf*. Unfortunately, however, the dervishes tended to identify "Islam" with the exoteric aspect of the religion and "Sufism" with the esoteric aspect, but in such a way that Sufism's intrinsic relationship to

Islam, its identity as Islam's inner spiritual core, remained uncertain. The Iranian Revolution had been traumatic for the Sufis of Iran, particularly those who had accepted a degree of patronage from the Shah—as Dr Nurbakhsh might well have done, at least according to certain indications. The Sufi orders have suffered persecution under the Iranian Revolutionary government; the fact that the Nimatullahis maintain *khaniqas* in the Western nations has undoubtedly placed them under a certain amount of suspicion. And it is true that the Islamic character of the Order slowly faded during the years I was connected with them; for one thing, the Muslim daily prayer (*salat* in Arabic, *namaz* in Persian) was gradually discontinued, though it remained "optional" for the dervishes (Sufis) in their own homes. I have no doubt that Dr Nurbakhsh had attained a high spiritual station—but as the connection of the Nimatullahi Order with Islam and its Prophet continued to weaken, I had the impression that it was becoming less and less possible for the dervishes to derive real benefit from the Master's spiritual presence. It felt to me as if we were attempting to draw light from his individual person rather than his transcendent function. And since it is impossible to really participate in the spiritual destiny of another, this left me with a kind of "so near yet so far" feeling, though I have no way of knowing whether anyone else felt that way. People came, stayed, left, but their reasons for moving on were never shared and never discussed.

When I first began to practice the Nimatullahi *zekr* (*dhikr*), I had an interesting experience: it was as if I were not silently pronouncing it, but as if the Master were pronouncing it for me, and in me. And since the Master was the authorized representative of Allah, I began to come into the field of the principle that "only God is the Doer." We do not have the power on our own to walk the spiritual Path; only Allah possesses that power. Our sole contribution is to express our willingness to walk it, by virtue of our *niyat*, our intent—the intent to embrace *taslim*, the total submission of our will to God's Will. Though Allah may have led us to the Ark and pointed it out to us, we board the Ark by our own volition—and it is also up to us to resist the temptation to jump ship at every port where we drop anchor. But the Ark alone carries us—that, and the Wind of God that moves it, across the face of His Ocean.

According to Nimatullahi dogma, the Master of the Path must be perfect—because if he is not perfect you will worship him, and worshipping the Master is the same thing as worshipping yourself. And it is certainly true that all idolatry is, in a way, self-idolatry. This, to my mind, is a very subtle and interesting proposition, since it implies that if you do end up worshipping the Master—as plenty of us did, at least on and off—this only proves that he is not worthy of that worship. But why construct such a maddening paradox? A perfect being apparently deserves worship, or something like it—yet that very worship goes to proves that the being in question is *not* perfect; what kind of a Gordian Knot is that? In any case, the relationship between the murid and the Pir was apparently constructed (theoretically at least) so as to induce the dervish to project the *imago dei*, or (in Jungian terms) the Self archetype, onto the Master — and then to gradually realize, in the face of many endlessly disappointing instances of self-worship/Master-worship, that only Allah deserves our worship and is really capable of receiving it — a pretty dicey maneuver, in my opinion. And in view of the fact that Dr Nurbakhsh was a practicing psychiatrist who received his degree from the Sorbonne, one can easily see the similarity between this method and the famous *transference* phenomenon that Freud defined as the "best tool" available to the psychoanalyst. But did it actually work in a Sufi context? I am far from convinced that it did, except perhaps as a preliminary way of dealing with psychologically disordered people who were not yet capable of fully understanding spiritual principles and acting on them — a description that might well have applied to me at that time of my life. Nonetheless, Nurbakhsh maintained that "Psychiatry has everything to learn from Sufism; Sufism has nothing to learn from psychiatry." [NOTE: Anyone who wants to get some idea of the stunning scope and comprehensiveness of Sufi writing should investigate the books of Javad Nurbakhsh, which are 90% composed of selections from the classical Sufi writers of both the east and the west, arranged according to theme — particularly his 15-volume encyclopedia entitled *Sufi Symbolism — Farhang e-Nurbakhsh* in Farsi — which proves beyond the shadow of a doubt that even though the Sufi way possesses an intrinsic unity because it is based on the Unity of Allah, *tasawwuf* can never be reduced to a standard methodology or a closed philosophical system. Nurbakhsh's books were directly influential on Part Two of my own book, *Day and Night on the Sufi Path.*]

Be that as it may, I met some very interesting people in the Nimatullahi circle. Russ, the *Pir-e dalil*, was the adviser dervish, the *upa-guru* in Hindu terminology (the one who trains) to Ron Harris' *satguru* (the one who embodies the essence of the teaching). He was a Chinese from Taiwan who, before becoming a Sufi, had spent many years under the tutelage of one of the last of the traditional Taoist masters, who reportedly lived to be truly ancient. Others were Jamshipur, a traveling dervish with a tricksterish personality whose role seemed to be to push everybody's buttons; Hamid, a congenial Black man from Jamaica whose ancestral polytheism, after slowly creeping up on him, finally took him elsewhere; Niku, an endearing and suffering soul who had been born a princess to a tribe of nomads in Iran, after which she became for a while a Parisian *bohème* in some way connected with Simone de Beauvoir; one of Shah Pahlevi's generals, whose name I don't recall, but whose face shared certain racial characteristics with that of Aristotle Onassis, lending credence to the idea that the army of Alexander the Great contributed bloodlines to the upper castes of Iranian society; Sherko, a rude and rebellious Kurd who drew pictures of the Jinn but nonetheless had a true streak of religious fervor in him; and Leonard Lewisohn, an accomplished academic scholar of Sufism, especially of some of the more-or-less antinomian types centered in Iran, who sometimes visited us from England. Another fellow-dervish was Natasha, who had been the consort of the neo-Shaman Richard Dobson that Jenny and I met and briefly studied with in the lead-up to Harmonic Convergence. Richard had once visited the San Francisco *khaniqa* with some members of the Native American Church, all under the influence of peyote—but since drugs and Sufism don't mix, he ultimately went his own way. And apparently Sufism and psychic surgery don't mix either. Once, after I had just been worked on by some of the Surgeons who were visiting the Bay Area, I had a dream: Out of East Asia, possibly northern China, came flying a huge black cube, like the sinister ship of the Borg from *Star Trek: The Next Generation*—a cube which, like an inverted, Satanic Kaaba, was none other than the Antichrist. When I told this dream to Ron, revealing that I'd had it right after visiting the Psychic Surgeons, he said to me: "Do you think you might be willing to stop seeing these people?" As it turned out, I was willing; though they still traveled to California from time to time, I never saw them again. My evaluation of this incident was that the time of the Surgeons was coming to a close, that the collective psychic plane was becoming too dark for spiritual seekers to involve themselves with them any more without courting serious dangers. The good Jinn may have the power to open your body and heal it, but the evil Jinn—particularly in times like these—will not be far behind, ready to take advantage of whatever psychophysical weaknesses the actions of the good Jinn may have exposed.

We saw Leonard Lewisohn and his wife Jane in a different context when we traveled to England to visit Dr Nurbakhsh at his headquarters at that time, the London *khaniqa*. Lenny introduced us to the well-known English poetess Kathleen Raine, with whom we enjoyed a perfect latter-day version of a Victorian tea-hour. Lenny built me up to her as "an important poet who had a dream in which Blake spoke to him," Ms Raine being both a major William Blake scholar and a woman who still believed, a-la Percy Bysshe Shelley, in the "divine" status of the young male poet. She was suitably impressed but of course totally ignored Jenny, this being the standard *adab* for both the Nimatullahis and the world of *puer aeternus* poets, and their sponsoring matrons, in the late 20th Century—though Jenny, who now has a greater appreciation for Kathleen Raine after viewing some of her YouTube videos, suspects that this breach in courtesy was more the fault of Prof. Lewisohn than of the distinguished English poetess herself. We also met the poetess's son (I forget his name) who—not surprisingly—radiated an intense aura of refinement, hyper-sensitivity and shame. Also on our spiritual-tourist itinerary was Westminster Abbey, whose celestial radiance not even 500 years of Anglicanism had been able to entirely snuff out. I saw the Stone of Destiny in the Coronation Chair, open and unguarded, before it was returned to Scotland; would that I had kissed it! My other main impressions of England—this was my first visit there—were that workmen still worked with shovels and pick-axes and milkmen still made deliveries, an amenity that had disappeared from the States some time in the early 1960s.

Lenny's big project, when I was with the Nimatullahis, was to hook the poet Robert Bly into the Order—Bly, whose works sometimes appeared in the *Temenos Academy Journal* along with those of Kathleen Raine, one of the Academy's founders, Wendell Berry and many others. (Temenos, which has flourished under the patronage of the Prince of Wales, now King Charles III, is a sort of quasi-Traditionalist world of highly aesthetic spirituality and/or highly spiritualized aesthetics.) And since Lenny identified as a poet as well as a scholar, of course Bly would be just the kind of big fish whose initiation would totally validate his worldview; ultimately, the Professor did succeed in reeling him in. My difficulty with this development was that Bly's book *Iron John*, which was to become a central pillar of the "Mythopoetic Men's Movement," started to become something like an unofficial addition to the teaching-literature of the Nimatullahis. This was quite unfortunate to my mind, since Bly (a bit like D. H. Lawrence in *The Plumed Serpent*) tended to exalt the bloody authenticity of Pagan violence in the name of re-kindling the chthonic masculinity of the wimpy late 20th-Century *puer aeternus*, as well as adopting a generally Jungian-polytheistic attitude to Divinity, a worldview in which Zeus, Jesus, Allah and the Great Mother all live together in a big hotel called the Collective Unconscious. His Jungianism at that point was most directly influenced by the Neo-Jungian James Hillman, whose psychic polytheism led him to claim that Multiple Personality Disorder (now known as Dissociative Identity Disorder) was the "natural" state of the human psyche, as well as leading him ever closer to the denial of individuation and the Self archetype. Psychic balance was to be maintained by overcoming the ego's imperialistic attempt to introduce a false unity into the psychic contents, which were essentially multiple and should be allowed to remain so. He was right in his analysis of the spurious unification proposed by the ego and the multiplicity of the undeveloped psyche, but wrong as wrong could be in his denial that a true, integrated unity-of-psyche was possible, and essential to the traversing of the spiritual Path, as a reflection within the psychic substance of the realized Unity of God.

All of this was diametrically opposed to the stated teachings of the Nimatullahi Order, as well as those of Islam and Sufism in general—and this was not something that I could allow to be preached in my presence; I'd come too far to get to Sufism to let the rug be pulled out from under my feet. So I wrote and published a book called *Hammering Hot Iron: A Spiritual*

Critique of Bly's Iron John. What Bly never understood about my book—if he ever read it—was that I had expressed great admiration for his intent in writing *Iron John* and for many of his insights, while pulling no punches in critiquing those aspects of it which I saw as contradicting either the Sufism he now professed or the doctrines of the Perennialists that I was then in the process of fully understanding and adopting—doctrines that were drawn from all the world's great revealed religions and wisdom traditions. The pressure I put myself under in writing that book while sitting twice a week in a Nimatullahi *khaniqa* as my central spiritual practice—one of the main principles of the Order being cordial *adab* with one's fellow dervishes—can perhaps be imagined by those of an empathic nature, though not easily described by me. On one occasion I actually met not only with Bly but with James Hillman, in San Francisco—this was just before *Hammering Hot Iron* was published—on which occasion I let Hillman know that I would be attacking him in my next book. I cannot imagine a clearer demonstration of how dedication to principle can sometimes make you pretty ruthless. Be that as it may, *Hammering Hot Iron* has an almost audible *break* in it, where the center of my worldview visibly moves from the psychological/mythopoetic level where C. G. Jung, Marie-Louise Von Franz and Joseph Campbell were the psychopomps, to the properly metaphysical level where Schuon, Guénon, Coomaraswamy, Nasr, Nurbakhsh and Huston Smith, as well as the scriptures, saints and sages of the world's major religions, were the voices of authority.

But Lenny did tell us a particular Sufi story that I thought was very enlightening. On one occasion he was visiting another *tariqah* that indulged in *karamat*, miraculous and paranormal actions—one of which was to cut themselves with knives and swords and emerge uninjured. Lenny was attending a *majlis* (group gathering) of this *tariqah* when he saw one of the dervishes lean onto a razor-sharp sword, which cut deeply into his belly. Shocked, he ran over to the seemingly wounded man, asking if he needed help. The dervish proceeded to remove the blade from his belly, revealing that he had not bled in the slightest and had received no wound. "Are you unfamiliar with such happenings in your *tariqah*?" he asked in a haughty manner. "With us they are commonplace." I always saw this as an indication that it actually takes greater spiritual power to remain humble and courteous to one's brothers and sisters than to perform miraculous feats. Which would be a more beautiful world—one in which everyone could perform miracles or one in which everyone treated his or her fellow human beings with sensitivity and respect?

During my stay with the Nimatullahis, which largely ended in 2004 when Jenny and I moved to Kentucky, and ended for good in 2006 when Dr Nurbakhsh passed away, my intellectual standpoint—largely under Jenny's influence—was becoming more and more firmly grounded in the Traditionalist/Perennialist worldview. But since I detected, even then, a tendency in the Traditionalist world to grant Love a more-or-less secondary status vis-à-vis Gnosis or Knowledge I clung to the Nimatullahis as representing a more Love-oriented or *bhaktic* Path—which was what they at least claimed to be doing—but a Path that was still open to the Gnosis that the Traditionalists continually emphasized. In other words, I was both *self-divided* and *at war with the thought of my fathers and my kin*—just as Yeats, in *A Vision*, had predicted for my particular phase of the Moon: Please Eleven, the phase of the Consumer, the Pyre-builder.

I experienced the Nimatullahi Tariqah, in the San Francisco of the 1980s, as if I were living in the rich and fading afterglow of an immensely high tradition, breathing in the final perfume of an ancient stream of spiritual power and wisdom that was on its last legs. The traditional apparatus of the Persian Sufism was all there: the *Shaykh*, the *Pir-e dalil*, the *Doudeh-dar* (tea-master), the *wirds* (litanies), the *zekr* (*dhikr* or invocation of a Name of Allah), the *majles* (the gathering), the "low Mass" communal meal (the *sofreh*), and the "high Mass" communal meal (the *deeg-jush*), this last sponsored by a particular dervish who feels the time has come to offer himself to the Master and to God as a supreme sacrifice, and who therefore provides a meal of lamb ground to a paste and mixed with chick-peas, along with other items of high Persian cuisine—this meal representing, precisely, himself. In other words, in the *deeg-jush* the dervish in question sacrificially offers himself, in sacramental form, to his Sufi brothers and sisters, exactly as Christ offered himself to his apostles at the Last Supper. Is this a quasi-Christian influence appearing within a nominally Shi'a form of *tasawwuf*, seeing that Frithjof Schuon characterized Shi'ism as the manifestation of the Christian archetype within Islam? Or are the Last Supper, the Passover Feast and the *deeg-jush* all cultural/religious variations on a common theme more ancient than any of them?

And the music! Classical Persian music is without doubt one of the greatest artistic traditions of the human race, incomparable in its ability to render the dance of longing and loss, of concealment and revelation, between God and the human soul. This music usually came to us in recorded form but sometimes live, depending on the visits of traveling musicians, who were capable of drawing from a simple ensemble of *setar* (percussive "lute"), *daf* (hand-held drum) and *ney* (that breathy Persian flute) a truly celestial expression.

All this I assimilated on a deep layer of my soul, somehow intuiting that I was privileged to have been invited to a unique farewell performance. Persia is old, inconceivably old; over its long history it has been host to a slow, regal, magnificent sunset, a nostalgia of possibly longer duration than any other in civilized history, and one well suited to transmit that other and deeper color of yearning—namely, the nostalgia for Paradise.

But I do mean *nominally* Shi'a. Though the Nimatullahis under Dr Nurbakhsh were one of the few Sufi *tariqahs* that operated in Shi'a Iran, they were as contemptuous of the Shi'a authorities as of the Sunnis, particularly after the Iranian Revolution that had installed the Ayatollah Khomeini and driven both Javad Nurbakhsh and Seyyed Hossein Nasr out of their homeland forever—an exile that only worked to emphasize the prideful and rebellious defiance of the traditional Persian dervishes against the more secular authorities and their exoteric mullahs that had marked the long, though intermittent, history of Sufi-killing pogroms in Iran—an attitude that unapologetically declared: "We are the Kings of Love! That's why so many of us take the name of *Shah*. What are you the kings of, O murderers, but the dungheap of This World?" And the shock of that revolution, and of the anti-Sufi persecutions that followed it, slowly but surely acted to drive the very *Islam* out of the Nimatullahi Order in the West. All the published books of the Order continued to emphasize that no one could be a Sufi without first being a Muslim and following the *shari'ah*—but that's not how things were on the inside. When we were in London, I was incautious enough to mention a piece I had written about the relationship between *shari'ah* and *tariqah* in the presence of Alireza Nurbakhsh, the Master's son who now heads the Order. He went ballistic, cursing the *shari'ah* as freely and openly as any American Islamophobe. In response I chose to believe, on naked will-power alone, that the necessity for *shari'ah* presented in the Dr Nurbakhsh's books represented his true position, taking it as an undeniable axiom that "the Master wouldn't lie!," thereby planting myself firmly, as the American saying goes, on the banks of a river in Egypt. But then, slowly but surely, first intermittently and then permanently, the *namaz* disappeared from the San Francisco *khaniqa*. The Qur'an was never quoted, the name of Muhammad never mentioned. I once asked Ron Harris why we couldn't call down blessings on the Prophet, to which he answered: "My heart isn't in it." On one occasion I was even expressly forbidden to pray the *namaz* in the *khaniqa*—a spiritual shock that nearly tore the heart out of my chest. A dervish from England who was close to the Master told us that Nurbakhsh had said, "We're really Zoroastrians"—yet we never performed any Zoroastrian rites or kept any of the Zoroastrian feasts. As was common with many Iranians who had newly immigrated to the west around the time of the Revolution, the Iranian Nimatullahis began to fall back on their ethnic identity, as well as resurrecting the ancient Persian grudge against the Arab conquerors, identifying it—consciously or unconsciously—with the newly-imposed and oppressive regime of the Shi'a restoration. That's exactly how the cruelty, and the *irony*, of This World, the *dunya* of the latter days, works to crush the Spirit of God out of us, even to the brink of tempting us to reject the Trust itself, thereby abandoning the human form. "And because of the tribulation of those days, the love of many will wax cold" [Matthew 24:12].

JENNY JUMPS SHIP

In any case, after two or three years with the Nimatullahis, Jenny had had enough, so she abandoned the Order—partly because she either saw before I did, or admitted before I was willing to, that the Nimatullahis were in the process of abandoning Islam. So she left me to fend for myself. Worshipping/remembering without her was difficult but not impossible, though the knowledge that she had in some sense been ejected from the Order by group consensus made it harder for me to sit with them than it otherwise would have been. Nonetheless I persisted.

Yet for Jenny, her departure from the Nimatullahis opened up new possibilities. At one of the symposia of the Ibn 'Arabi Society she mentioned her interest in the Traditionalist writers to Prof. William Chittick of the State University of New York (SUNY) at Stony Brook, who suggested that she write to Prof. Seyyed Hossein Nasr at the George Washington University in Washington D.C. Since she had been so deeply influenced by the Traditionalists, I urged her to contact him—which, after overcoming her initial shyness and fear of rejection, she did. She also wrote to Martin Lings in England, and received an encouraging response. It was Dr Nasr, however, who suggested that she contact Huston Smith, and provided us with an introduction to him.

GETTING CLOSER TO HUSTON

After meeting Huston Smith at CCC and the Ibn 'Arabi Society, we finally had an interview with him at his home in Berkeley. I remember asking, on that occasion, a rather poorly-formed question that had been swimming around in my mind: "Who are the Christian Sufis?"—a question that, insofar as it meant anything at all, was answered a few years later when Huston introduced us to Prof. James Cutsinger. This time, however, Huston pointed us toward one Alan Godlas, whom he described as an "esoteric Muslim" who was somehow associated with the Traditionalists. Following this lead we visited Godlas and his wife Sylvia in the East Bay, though little was gleaned from this meeting outside a general "clandestine" feeling, as if we were in the presence of a secret that had not yet been divulged. (We later found out that Godlas had been the local shaykh of the San Francisco Nimatullahi *khaniqa* at one point, though he apparently left under a cloud; as Ron Harris, his successor, described the situation, "he left the door wide open"—whatever that might have meant.) In any case, as Jenny's exploration of the Traditionalist world proceeded, it slowly emerged that there was such a thing as a "Maryamiyya Tariqah"—originally known as the Maryamiyya-Shadhili Tariqah—an "unofficial" Sufi order headed by Frithjof Schuon. Apparently Nasr was one of Schuon's representatives or *muqaddams* in this organization. Consequently, as part of one of our almost-yearly visits to Jenny's family in Kentucky, we traveled on from her parents' home to

D.C. where Jenny was initiated by Dr Nasr as a Maryamiyya *faqirat* (the feminine form of *faqir*, that being a common synonym for "Sufi"). For a number of years after that, she attended (but only once a year) Nasr's *majlis* in Alexandria, Virginia. And it was during one of these meetings that Nasr mentioned to Jenny a fellow Maryamiyya *faqir*, Scott Whittaker, who lived in Berkeley and acted as a kind of unofficial secretary to Huston Smith. Later on we found out that Scott, Huston, Alan Godlas, Graeme Vanderstoel and a few others had held a Maryamiyya *majlis* at Scott's apartment in Berkeley, though these meetings had been discontinued before Jenny's initiation, after which Alan Godlas moved east to take up a professorship at the University of Georgia. In any case, we ended up becoming close friends with both Scott and Huston Smith, often meeting with Huston at his Berkeley home for Chinese take-out and fascinating metaphysical discussions—true Platonic *symposia*. We often drove Huston to his various lectures in the Bay Area, where I would man the book table.

Huston characterized our little gatherings as a "rag-tag *tariqah*," an even more "unofficial" group than Schuon's Maryamiyya, but congenial to all of us and without the inconvenience of any visible chain-of-command outside of our sincere admiration for Prof. Smith, both as a senior spiritual intellectual and a gracious and generous host. Huston had grown up in China as the son of Methodist missionaries, so he came by his appreciation for Schuon's Transcendent Unity of Religions more experientially than intellectually, seeing that China before the Maoist revolution had room for Confucian, Taoist, Buddhist and even Christian influences, all of which (Christianity possibly excepted) were organically integrated into Chinese society. As Huston explained, the Confucians were the "civic religion," the Taoists (unless I'm mistaken) generally officiated at the marriages, and the Buddhists took care of the funerals. And Huston himself retained at least one delightful habit derived from traditional Chinese etiquette: the practice of escorting departing guests to the property-line—in his case, the street below his house—to see them off.

Huston himself was what I've called a "serial monotheist." Though raised as a Methodist Christian, after he and his family immigrated to the States following the Chinese Revolution he became deeply involved with the Vedanta Society. Later, during his Tibetan Buddhist phase, he was instrumental in "discovering" Tibetan polyphonic chant and introducing it to the West; when we knew him he was still involved in Tibetan refugee re-settlement, having rented a small downstairs apartment in his home to some Tibetans. He was also a supporter of the Native American Church, providing testimony about the salutary effects of peyote on Indian culture in support of the legal case for the official recognition of the Church under the First Amendment, which the NAC eventually won. (His wider involvement in "psychedelic spirituality" has already been mentioned.)

During most of the time we knew him, Huston was a practicing Muslim and *faqir* of the Maryamiyya Tariqah; this, however, was about to change, as you will soon see.

We were associated with Huston during the period when he supported the Intelligent Design movement, which included an introduction, along with Dr Nasr, of a talk by William Dembski (author of the ground-breaking book *Intelligent Design*) at the Graduate Theological Union in Berkeley; around the same time he also threw his support behind the attempt of the Department of Education of the state of Kansas to teach other possible explanations for the origin and development of life outside of Darwinian evolution. It was in the context of another of his many interests, however, that he and I ended up on different sides of an important question, though this was merely a small bump in our common road and led to no residual bad blood.

The story is as follows: At one point Jenny and I had become acquainted with one Lee Penn, whose important book, *False Dawn: The United Religions Initiative, Globalism and the Quest for a One-World Religion* I was privileged to edit for Sophia Perennis Publications. This book meticulously details (among other things) the heavy involvement of national governments, prominent foundations and globalist think-tanks in the Interfaith Movement of the western nations. Lee had been a member of a large Episcopalian congregation in San Francisco, which, with mounting dismay, he watched change from a more-or-less traditional, High Church Anglican orientation to one of extreme Liberal ecumenism. This happened largely under the influence of Bishop William E. Swing of the Episcopal Church of California (now retired), Founder and President of the United Religions Initiative, which at one point was probably the most extreme, Liberal and ambitious of all interfaith organizations, a movement whose initial goal (later moderated) was to unite all the major world religions under an umbrella organization that resembled, and might at one point even have become officially connected with, the United Nations—a move that Lee certainly did not support, since it represented the subordination of the religions to the authority of secular powers. On reading the literature of the URI I ran across a number of statements by prominent officers of the Initiative that seemed to indicate an intent to *prohibit religious proselytization*, which was presented as something roughly equivalent to imperialism and/or the violation of national borders, though in the religious rather than the military sphere. But since the right to proselytize is integral to any religious freedom worth the name, I composed a short declaration supporting this right which Jenny and I signed, and then presented to Huston, who also signed. This, however, resulted in a tense phone call from Bishop Swing to Huston, after which he asked us to expunge his signature from the declaration, which we did—and so that was that.

Huston Smith was from another era; it might not be too much to say that at one point he *was* that era — or at least what was left of it; I believe this was one of the reasons he didn't naturally warm to my little challenge to the URI. When Huston began investigating the world's religions, he did so on the basis of a Liberalism that still had some true liberality to it. He was like an anthropologist who traveled to live with the primitive tribes he studied, gained their confidence, participated in their rituals, let his worldview be fundamentally influenced by their beliefs, but then always eventually returned to "civilization" to regale his listeners with tales of his fabulous discoveries and exploits, thereby helping the still-dominant culture of the west to expand its intellectual horizons and deepen its appreciation and empathy for various more exotic, more "marginalized" cultures — a general tendency that undoubtedly peaked in the "spiritual revolution" of the '60s and '70s, and since then has mostly evaporated, along with the unchallenged dominance of the West. But since I was younger, and was generally of a lower social class than Huston, I had already had to deal with plenty of the damage and the contradictions the counterculture brought with it, and with the negative effects of that culture on U.S. society as a whole — things that Huston was blessedly shielded from, and which he could still partly shield us from while we knew him. For example, as Jenny and I were beginning to move in the direction of the kind of "paranoid conspiracy theory" mindset that has become dominant in the 21st Century, Huston still held to the original light-hearted hippie dismissal of the CIA origins of the mass use of LSD, the theory that "we were a CIA experiment that got out of control" and had therefore grown beyond the ability of that organization to mess with us. And when I tried to remind him of the damage that LSD had done to many psyches, and to introduce the idea that mounting "raids on the mysteries" through powerful artificial means might have a sacrilegious aspect to it, as in the parable of the man who attended the Wedding Feast without a wedding garment in Matthew 22:1–14, he replied that since the *Atman*, the Transcendent/Immanent Self or *imago dei* is common to all human beings, the temporary removal of the veil concealing that Self, by any effective means, was a legitimate approach toward Liberation and Enlightenment. Nonetheless he did caution against an over-reliance on psychedelics, since the goal of the spiritual life was to produce "altered traits, not altered states." But his outlook still diverged rather profoundly from the stated principles of the Traditionalist School he was identified with toward the end of his life, which was strictly opposed to the idea of "drug-induced mysticism" — Schuon had apparently commissioned Whitall Perry to criticize this approach, which he accomplished in an article entitled "Drug-induced Mysticism: the Mescalin Hypothesis" — and emphasized religious orthodoxy above all (in its theory if not always in its practice, as we shall see). Based on this divergence, Rama Coomaraswamy once told us that if he were running the Maryamiyya

Tariqah he would never have accepted Huston as a member. Nonetheless I remember a glowing review of Huston's book on psychedelics, *Cleansing the Doors of Perception* that was published by one of Dr Nasr's close associates in the Maryamiyya in his journal *Sophia*, which was in radical opposition to something Nasr had said to us during one of our yearly meetings, namely that Richard Alpert was "a terrible man" because he advocated the use of drugs for "spiritual" purposes. So currying favor with the more prominent members of the Maryamiyya "club" apparently superseded a loyalty to spiritual principles, at least on certain occasions.

Nonetheless it did seem as if Huston had left his psychedelic phase entirely behind—until, that is, he was approached by one Bob Jessie, director of something called the Council on Spiritual Practices, who presented him with a collection of his old articles on psychedelics from the '60s and said to him: "Look, Huston—you have a new book, and we'd like to publish it." Huston's response, according to his predominantly accommodating and generous character, was to write a little more text and provide an introduction, thus producing the book that was ultimately released as *Cleansing the Doors of Perception* (his worst book in my opinion), with the result that most of the people who now questioned him after his lectures only wanted him to talk about psychedelics—or, as they were then starting to be called, "entheogens"—for several years afterwards. I met Bob Jessie once at one of Huston's events. He immediately struck me, at least typologically speaking, as an intelligence agency spook who was preparing the way for the kind of re-legitimization of psychedelics in academia and the psychotherapy world that we see happening today, now that the "entheogens" are much more firmly under the control of the Powers That Be than they even were in the hippie era. On that occasion I asked him a question based on something I'd just heard him say, and he immediately denied ever having said it.

During this late phase of Huston's career we participated in a rather hilarious event at a motel in San Francisco's Fishermen's Warf, to which we drove him as we often did in those days. It turned out to be a recording session for a *TV ad for peyote*, sponsored by a group called Dreamcatchers, which was made up of two or three Anglos and a Hollywood-style Native American in a Hawaiian shirt, Bermuda shorts and dark glasses—not a style of dress likely to be worn by a typically traditional American Indian, most of whom would dress in long pants and long-sleeved shirts. The motel room was set up as a studio where they videoed Huston making a glowing testimonial for the effects of peyote, more or less on the order of "I unreservedly recommend this wonderful cactus; it made me the man I am today." (Peyote, Breakfast of Champions.)

Nor was that the only rather anomalous event that Huston's accommodating character put him in the way of. At one point he received an invitation from J. Z. Knight, channeler of the well-known spirit-entity

Ramtha, who had an "ashram" in the Spokane area, situated at an abandoned racetrack, where she ran something on the order of a Gurdjieff boot camp by putting her followers through various extreme physical exertions. Ms. Knight wanted to pick up a recommendation from Huston to help her group secure a seat on the Spokane Interfaith Council. Huston's wife Kendra cautioned him against getting involved with them, since it was clear to her that they only wanted to use him. Huston dismissed her concerns, however, because no one "used" Huston Smith. He gave of himself freely, not to mention the fact that (as one newspaper article later observed) "he never met a religion he didn't like." I'm only grateful that the practitioners of Voodoo, Santería or Satanism never came to him asking for endorsements!

Huston's tale of his encounter with Ramtha and the entity's "hostess," that he later recounted to us at a café table, was highly entertaining but also rather disturbing. Apparently, even though J. Z. Knight was known to be a teetotaler, Ramtha himself was a serious alcoholic—with the result that, during a channeling session, the Entity in question—while employing the helpless body of Ms. Knight—*vomited all over Huston Smith*. Even after this mishap, however, Huston gave Ramtha a "qualified endorsement." He should probably have taken this event as one of those *signs on the horizons* that the Qur'an talks about—except for the fact that, unless you are aware of the signs *in your own soul* that those outer events are the reflections of, even the most obvious and clear-cut omens from the outer world will remain opaque to you. And guess whose name ended up on one of the newspaper accounts of Huston's excursion into the world of channeling? That of Hunter George—possibly the same one-time redneck guru who had been part of our Santa Venetia Presbyterian Church some years before. In his article he expressed his misgivings about Huston's position vis-à-vis J.Z. Knight, which were pretty much shared by Jenny and myself.

But Huston's life was not all intelligent sunlight and/or happy oblivion while we knew him. When his daughter Karen died of cancer, he delivered a tearful and moving tribute to her at a bookstore in Berkeley, where he confided to the group that this sad event had finally convinced him that the *personal* human consciousness survives bodily death. And some years later his granddaughter (from a different child), Serena Karlan, also met a sad end when, along with her boyfriend, NBA basketball star Bison Dele, she was murdered by Dele's brother on a catamaran in the South Pacific in what might have been a drug deal gone wrong. Yet Huston's spirit stayed buoyant to the end. Not long before his death at 97 he was visited in the nursing home by one of his friends, Prof. Philip Novak of Dominican University (formerly Dominican College) in San Rafael. By that time Huston was deaf, mostly blind, and bedridden—yet he still had enough spark left in him to wryly comment on his condition by singing to Novak a few bars of the Duke Ellington song (lyrics by Bob Russell),

"Don't Get Around Much Anymore." Happiness (as we usually understand it) may be fleeting, but bliss is eternal.

SAINT JOHN MAXIMOVITCH AND EASTERN ORTHODOX CHRISTIANITY

During this time of exploring and connecting with the Traditionalist world, I was drawn (mostly through Jenny's influence) into the outer circles of Russian Orthodox Spirituality in the Bay Area, though I was careful to maintain my Sufi Muslim practices and connections. One of the major ports-of-entry for us into the world of Eastern Orthodoxy had to do with an episode that occurred while I was working with the homeless service agency Project MOVE. During that time Jenny developed a worrisome gynecological health condition. It turned out to be nothing, but on the day Sarah Howard took her to a doctor to be checked out, I went hiking in the hills above our house in Bayside Acres, on the road to Black Mountain, worried about her and praying for her. And it was during those prayers that I somehow became aware of the existence of one Saint John Maximovitch of Shanghai and San Francisco. I can't recall whether I saw a vision of him, or heard his name in my mind, or thought of the cathedral where (as I later found out) his relics lie in repose—the Cathedral of the Blessed Virgin Joy of All who Sorrow on Geary St in the City—but in any case, as soon as I got home, I began the research that quickly led to a conscious knowledge of him and his history. Not only that, but *on that very same day*, Jenny had found a book about him in (I believe) the San Rafael Public Library! So St John Maximovitch, Vladika John as he was affectionately known, unexpectedly walked into our lives in a way that couldn't be denied. We discovered that he was a theologian, a hierarch and a "fool for Christ"—roughly equivalent to the *malamatiyya* in the Sufi world, who engage in "unorthodox" behavior so as to mortify their social vanity and that of their followers—an extremely rare combination of functions for an Orthodox saint. But he was, above all, a great wonder-worker, known for his many miracles of healing, clairvoyance, etc., both during his life and through his intercession from the next world after his death. Furthermore, as we later found out, St John had been a kind of mentor or *staretz* (Russian Orthodox elder) to Fr Seraphim Rose, whom you will soon meet. This half-otherworldly encounter led Jenny, with me in tow, to explore the greater Eastern Orthodox world of the Bay Area.

The Geary Street cathedral was part of ROCOR, the Russian Orthodox Church Outside Russia, which was the most conservative and traditional of the Russian Orthodox jurisdictions, having been founded by the old White Russian immigrants fleeing the Bolshevik Revolution. ROCOR firmly rejected any allegiance to the KGB-controlled Patriarch of Moscow until the fall of the Soviet Union, after which part of the jurisdiction re-united with Moscow, except for a contingent of hold-outs who wanted nothing to do with any state-controlled church. A few of those who had immigrated from Russia as children were still alive in San Francisco in the early 1990s; it was these pilgrims and their descendants who formed the ethnic core of fervent, traditional Russian Orthodox piety for the Bay Area. (In contrast, we found the Greeks to be relatively lukewarm and worldly. At the Greek Orthodox cathedral of the Ascension in Oakland I once heard a priest, who sounded like a tour guide for some archaeological site, talk about angels in the past tense, as if they were figures from ancient mythology and folklore that people used to believe in many centuries ago. "But what happened to them?" I queried, "did they all die off?" Nor will I ever forget the time when the Orthodox writer Christos Yannaras, whom we once heard speak in Berkeley, answered the question from a member of the audience, "what writers should pious Orthodox Christians read?" by suggesting that they read Sartre and Nietzsche! He also claimed that Nihilism as an intellectual movement could be traced back to Thomas Aquinas and Scholastic Philosophy, in line with what often seems to be the central tenet of modern Orthodox theology, namely that "whatever we may believe, first and foremost we reject the beliefs of the Catholics!" The Scholastic nominalism of William of Occam might indeed be one of the roots of Nihilism, but certainly not the philosophical realism of Aquinas!)

St John Maximovitch of Shanghai and San Francisco was the ROCOR bishop for the See of San Francisco from 1962 till his death in 1966. Besides his role as a hierarch and theologian, he was also (as I've already said) recognized as a wonderworker—one might even describe him as a kind of Orthodox Padre Pio. He was known to levitate during Divine Liturgy, and the miraculous healings attributed to him, both during his life and after his death, are numerous and well-attested. Certain stories about him also suggest the miracle of bilocation, though I don't believe that this ability was ever attributed to him explicitly. For example, someone would be near death in the hospital late at night with no way to contact him, but then he would suddenly walk into the room, bless the sick person and quickly leave again, after which that person would start to get better. As for his being numbered among the Fools for Christ—those who affect mental imbalance so as to deflect social vanity—he often went barefoot, even while dressed in his episcopal robes and carrying the staff of his office. The story is told of one occasion when a self-important Russian matron invited him to dine with her and her friends, this being quite a social coup for her—and of course she paid great attention to her dress and her makeup for the important occasion. When the Archbishop arrived and everyone sat down to dinner, they were served the common Russian dish of borscht and sour cream—but when the bowl was placed before Vladika John, he dipped his fingers into it and began to smear the mixture on his face as if it were makeup, while miming all the motions of a woman powdering her face and applying rouge before a mirror. In other words, he ruthlessly *satirized* his hostess in a way that must have been intensely embarrassing for her—so watch out for those Fools for Christ! Only someone who can truly read souls could have practiced such psychological surgery without violating the virtue of charity and doing real damage. (The antics of the ego in the presence of the Sacred are hard to account for in any case, and not always what one would expect. Once, while browsing the Cathedral bookstore, I watched as a man entered, strode defiantly up to the clerk, and held his finger under the clerk's nose. "Smell that! That's *real* spirituality, not the fake holiness of some of the people around here!" After he'd left I asked the clerk what all that had been about, and was told the following story: "That man had a obsession with one of our holy icons that exudes miraculous oil"—a substance commonly known as *myrrh*, though to me it actually smells more like roses—"so finally our pastor simply gave it to him. He's still obsessed with it, but now he uses it as a way to put the rest of us down. He thinks he *owns* holiness." So the man with the miracle-working icon had become a kind of walking parable, which every reader is free to interpret for him- or herself.)

The Cathedral of the Holy Virgin Joy of All who Sorrow, at least according to some (not all of them Orthodox Christians), is the holiest site in North America; it radiates an indescribable aura of Heaven-on-earth.

The first time we ourselves visited there it was to venerate the relics of Blessed John Maximovitch, which were then situated in a glass coffin in the crypt below the sanctuary; later on, after St John's "glorification"—the equivalent of the Roman Catholic "canonization"—the coffin was moved up into the sanctuary itself. The relics were described as incorrupt, though they in no way resembled the relics of a saint like Bernadette Soubirous, whose body still looks as if she were alive but only sleeping. His body is naturally (or supernaturally) mummified, dried and blackened (one of his hands was visible) but not decayed. As for the Cathedral itself, it was like a continuously-operating spiritual powerhouse designed to generate Grace, where a service of one kind or another was always going on, accompanied by the sonorous intoning of the priests in Old Church Slavonic and punctuated by bursts of the celestial Byzantine chant from the hidden choir loft. Where Gregorian chant transmits the sense of penance and exile, the Byzantine version unapologetically renders the immediate presence of the Glory of God. But amid all this beauty and solemnity, the Cathedral still had a quality of informality about it, almost like a community center. People would come and go, arrive to pray and venerate the relics of St John then move on to their next errand—not to mention the fact that the children, of whatever age, were uniformly respectful and knew exactly what to do, how to kneel and cross themselves, now to venerate the saint; nonetheless, for all the glory of it, it was still so unaffected and natural—"supernaturally natural" as Frithjof Schuon might have said... And when I myself venerated the relics of St John Maximovitch, it was as if all the darkness were being pulled out of my soul by some celestial vacuum cleaner and carried far away. His coffin was like a door to Paradise.

Nonetheless, through all of this, I maintained my connection with the Nimatullahi *khaniqa*, the *namaz* (the five daily Muslim prayers) and the *zekr*, because that was where I was getting my work done. Yet the burdens of that work—especially in an environment where a degree of dishonesty about who the Nimatullahis really were and their real relationship to Islam was unavoidable—made it necessary to have some "back-channel" source of Grace, without which I couldn't have maintained my commitment to the Sufi way; that's how divided my soul and my practice were in those days.

Before John Maximovitch came into my life, that compensatory support was provided by the "divine light" channeled by the Johrei Fellowship. When my aunt Barbara died I flew to Los Angeles, acting as a kind of emissary for my mother, to pray at her grave and pick up some of her belongings. While there I visited the Los Angeles Johrei center, the U.S. headquarters of the Fellowship, where the energy was about three times as powerful as it was at the San Francisco center; while receiving it I prayed for Barbara and imagined her being reunited with her late husband Charles. Then I visited and spent the night at the Los Angeles-area Nimatullahi *khaniqa*. While sitting across the table from the local shaykh, I saw that I was having a strange effect on him; he seemed very disturbed. "*It couldn't be*, could it?" he said, "that you're following the wrong Pir? That just *couldn't be*..." Apparently he *felt my dividedness*. This was the last thing I ever expected to hear from an officer of the Nimatullahi Order—yet his question was far from irrelevant. I couldn't answer it then, nor am I entirely sure of the answer even now. Dr Nurbakhsh was definitely a step I needed to take during one phase of my life; nonetheless my relationships with priests, shaykhs and gurus has always been an extremely rocky one; all of them seemed like substitutes for Something indefinable, Something infinitely greater. Nonetheless, as soon as St John appeared, I abandoned Johrei for good; the sparrow-hawk had been chased out of the sky by the Eagle. But my relationship with the Nimatullahis still continued, surviving our move to Kentucky in 2004. It only ended with Dr Nurbakhsh's death in 2006.

MY MOTHER'S LAST YEARS

When my aunt Barbara died my mother inherited what was left in a trust that someone, possibly my grandfather, had set up in both their names. While it was not a vast amount, it relieved my mother of her immediate economic worries, seeing that our own trust had become pretty depleted, and she was also freed by that death from the influence of a sister who had oppressed her throughout her life. She had a surge of renewed energy and began to make plans for the future... but then, soon after Barbara passed, she was diagnosed with macular degeneration: her eyesight began to fail. Not long afterwards she moved to a well-run Catholic assisted-living community in San Rafael, Nazareth House, where she was fortunate enough to be in the company of several people she'd known in earlier years, not to mention some elderly priests—even a bishop—who provided her with valid sacraments, since they were old enough to have been ordained by legitimately consecrated bishops and still used the traditional sacramental forms that had largely been discontinued after Vatican II. And she donated to Nazareth House her beloved piano that she'd kept in her San Anselmo apartment, even though she was too old to play it—the one I remembered from my childhood.

My mother's failing eyesight gave me the opportunity to pay a small portion of my debt to her by taking care of her, running errands etc., both while she was still in her apartment and after her move. At one point, during the difficult years when my relationship with Jenny had put a lot of stress on my relationship with her—not through any vindictiveness or manipulation on Jenny's part, but purely because my mother refused to let me go—when on one occasion I had told her that I wanted to become more economically independent so I could begin to repay her generosity to me, she retorted: "I want *nothing* from you!" (Under the regime of the *Princeps Huius Mundi*, all generosity is oppression and all gratitude is shame.) But now I was able to shop for her, to help her balance her checkbook, to drive her to doctors' appointments, to be with her through a mastectomy she underwent at an advanced age, etc. etc.

She was in Nazareth House for maybe five years, until her health began to seriously fail. Soon afterwards the day came when she was moved to the Nazareth House infirmary, clearly dying. She was having problems getting enough air and had obvious edema, so we knew that her heart was failing. Remembering how hard she had been on Jenny, I suggested that she give Jenny her diamond engagement ring, which she graciously agreed to do from her death-bed, thus making sure that she wouldn't die without doing what she could to rescind her unconscious curse against my wife and my marriage. Then, a day or so later, one of the nuns asked my permission to give her a shot of morphine, obviously (as I now see) in order to ease and possibly hasten her death. I agreed. Did I realize at that time that I might have been participating in a mercy killing, signing my own mother's death-warrant? I'm still not sure; given the state of shock I was in, and seeing that the whole thing had been presented to me as "this is just how we do things," I didn't have the presence of mind to fully realize what was happening—though I recently read an article that claimed (rightly or wrongly) that administering morphine to the dying should not be identified with euthanasia. Be that as it may, I returned to our home for a short rest, and by the time I drove back to Nazareth House she was dead. Then, after we began breaking down her apartment there, we discovered a nearly-full jar of her digoxin pills. Having come to the conclusion that she had already lived too long—something that she had shared with us on more than one occasion—she had simply stopped taking her heart medicine.

The "requiem mass" that was said for her at the new, smaller Dominican Convent that had replaced the old Mother House after the fire, was the only Novus Ordo mass I had ever attended, nor have I gone to one since. It featured some kind of lugubrious, faithless, repetitive English song or chant, and was completely devoid of any sense of piety or Grace or care for the soul of the departed. Not only that, but in my mind's eye I saw a clear image of the *Princeps Huius Mundi* mentioned above. The funeral of my mother was (for me) also the final funeral of the Catholic Church.

THE COURTHOUSE GANG

After my mother's death I went to the Bank of Marin where the accounts related to my mother's trust were held, of which Jenny and I were the beneficiaries. I had my picture ID, my mother's death certificate, and a copy of both the trust document and her will, to prove who I was, that she had passed on, and that the trust was now in my name. But when I asked to see an accounting of the assets the teller refused to reveal them, claiming that the only person with the authority to do that was Maggie Carlin*, my mother's money-manager. "FRAUD!" I yelled at the top of my lungs. That cry resulted in a hurried call to Maggie, who opted to grant me the rights that she was in no way free to either grant or withhold. This led to a "rough patch" between me and the people at Custodian Properties* where Maggie was CEO. She worked with a lawyer named Mick Mead*, a member of what is aptly termed "the Courthouse Gang." They seemed pretty eager to get ahold of what had been my grandmother's house and now belonged to me, probably due to its highly desirable location; some years earlier they had suggested that we sell it (undoubtedly to a buyer they would put forth, most likely a proxy for themselves) and move into a condo, which in the long run would have been a disastrous move for us. My guardian angel, however, put me in touch with one of his local human representatives, a legal aid lawyer, who after a nominal fee gave me just the advice I needed, free of additional charge, in a couple of phone calls—that I should not get into a conflict with the Gang, but just compose an amendment to the trust that would neatly dissolve it and transfer the assets to my Wells Fargo bank account, then quietly fade away—which I did. Later, in Kentucky, while nostalgically surfing the web to see how Old Marin County was getting along, I ran across a story by a woman who had been ripped off by Mick Mead and Custodian Properties for every penny she had. I phoned her up and we had a highly illuminating conversation. "How did you ever get your money *away* from those people!?" she asked, incredulously. My answer, as of today, is that they saw me as what, to them, was a recognizable type: an over-protected Marin County trust urchin of the Baby Boom who had no worldly wisdom whatsoever and so would believe anything they said—which was *almost* true (almost, but not quite). I came to this conclusion based on one clear memory: While I was at the Custodian Properties offices on one occasion, Maggie got a call from one of her clients from the Silver Peso Bar in Larkspur, undoubtedly requesting another emergency dip into the piggy bank to pay the bar tab. Soon the long-haired tattooed client and his hippie girlfriend arrived to pick up their CARE package; they had exactly the same nervous and overawed expressions on their faces that I later saw on the faces of the Marin County homeless people I worked with, when they were required to interact with legitimate solid citizens who actually worked indoors and lived in real houses. Undoubtedly—after gossiping with my mother about what a disappointment I had been—Maggie thought I was one of those. That Maggie and Mick might have been ripping her off all along never crossed my mother's mind, of course; because she was the Marin County Widow of a Prominent Huband, all of her friends and associates were necessarily beyond reproach. Nor did Maggie remember that, back when the trust was being drawn up, I was the one who suggested that it be made a *revocable* trust rather than an irrevocable one, so all the Gang could do on that occasion was include a clause to the effect that "it is your mother's express wish that, after her demise, you keep Maggie Carlin, Mick Mead and Bob Ladroni* (another Gang member) as your financial advisers and consultants, since they have her unqualified and undying trust" etc. etc.—a touching sentiment, but without the force of law. (On a later occasion, during a stock market crash—my mother had already passed on—I had directed Ladroni to sell all my assets and convert them into cash. "Oh Charles!" he had remonstrated, "how greedy of you!" Without that "greed," however—greed for my own money—Jenny and I would have been wiped out, and Carlin Mead and Ladroni would have had less of a juicy apple pie to divide up. So I was actually being *generous* to them at that point, though such saintly generosity was not destined to last much longer.)

ORTHODOX CALIFORNIA

On the other hand, in the other part of my life, our meeting with St John Maximovitch turned out to be the herald of a wider connection with the world of Eastern Orthodox Christianity, which started to arrive (as new phases of life often will) through many doors at once. One of these doors was a book that Huston Smith shared with Jenny called *Not of This World* by Damascene Christiansen, a monk (now abbot) at the St Herman of Alaska Monastery in Platina, California, in the northern Coast Range. It was the biography of Fr Seraphim Rose, an American Eastern Orthodox priest who had founded, along with a certain Fr Herman Podmoshensky, something called the St Herman of Alaska Brotherhood, of which the Platina monastery was a part. The Brotherhood continues to publish Seraphim Rose's books. My favorite is *The Soul After Death*, in which he makes a clear distinction between such things as "near-death experiences" and the "thanatology" of writers like Elizabeth Kübler-Ross on the one hand, and traditional Orthodox teachings on the nature and significance of death on the other. According to Fr Seraphim, the pop thanatology of the New Age may have some insight into the initial separation of soul and body, but it is completely ignorant of, and consequently often tends to deny, the next and most crucial stage of the death process: the judgment of the soul before God. Huston, as a Perennialist, had problems with Seraphim Rose's religious exclusivism, yet he was fascinated with his life story. Fr Seraphim had been secretary to Alan Watts at one time and had studied with the traditional Taoist sage Ji Ming Shen at what was later to become the California Institute of Integral Studies; he had also been influenced, particularly in his spiritually-based social criticism, by the writings of René Guénon. And just as Samuel Lewis had been a kind of bridge between the hippie spirituality of the '60s and the world of traditional *tasawwuf*, Seraphim Rose had acted as a similar bridge between the pre-hippie intellectual Bohemia of the Bay Area and the world of Eastern Orthodox Christianity, a function that the Brotherhood he founded continued to fulfill in the later post-hippie Punk world, particularly through their bookstores in San Francisco, Berkeley, Santa Rosa and elsewhere. One of their more audacious and risky tactics was to appeal directly to the dark and gloomy worldview of the Punks and the Goths through cheaply-printed pamphlets with titles like *Death to the World*, featuring photos of monks in black costumes covered with mysterious "occult" signs — the *megaloschema* habit of the advanced Orthodox monastic — along with piles of human skulls such as were to be seen in some traditional Orthodox monasteries on Mt. Athos and elsewhere. These were the skulls of earlier monks who had prayed, fasted and died at the same monastery, on display to remind the living that death must come to all. The Brotherhood was saying, in effect: "Punks and Goths! If the world looks dark to you, so it has always looked to us; we have chosen to die to it in this life because in essence it is nothing but the realm of death. 'If the world hates you,' said Christ, 'that's because it hated me first: but don't worry, be happy, because I have overcome the world.'" Sometimes the Brotherhood would even admit Bay Area street people directly to their monasteries as novices, knowing that they could never afford the expense of a seminary education, so it shouldn't be surprising that the St Herman of Alaska people were often distrusted by the more conventional Orthodox priests and believers in the established seminaries and parishes. And this distrust was only inflamed by the fact that a New Age monastic order for both men and women known as the Holy Order of MANS had converted *en masse* to Eastern Orthodox Christianity in 1988, under the leadership of one Vincent Rossi (whom Jenny and I later became acquainted with), thereby transforming itself into the Christ the Savior Brotherhood, which became closely associated—though exactly how I haven't been able to determine—with the St Herman of Alaska monks. (In its original New Age incarnation the Holy Order of MANS had operated Raphael House, a well-respected homeless shelter in San Francisco. I visited them there once, hoping to "interview" someone, if I remember correctly, on the subject of spiritually-based social action—though the monk assigned to talk with me, a Jewish-looking young man dressed in a dark navy-blue suit with a priest's white collar, did nothing but stare at me significantly with a faint smile playing about his lips, just as if he were some ex-Scientologist who felt that he had passed on to higher things. Luckily Vincent Rossi turned out to be much more human and engaging.) Jenny also attended some lectures by Fr Herman, both at St Paisius Abbey in Forestville (which she'd first heard about through *Gnosis Magazine*) and at one of the bookstores run by the Brotherhood in Santa Rosa. (St Paisius Abbey later moved to Stafford, Arizona). We also visited the St Herman of Alaska Monastery in Platina, California, in the company of one Mark Fitzgerald*—a rather extreme individual you'll hear more about soon—where we prayed at the grave of Seraphim Rose. The monastery possessed a great trove of saints' relics, though I got the distinct impression, for some reason, that Fr Seraphim's grave was filled with strife and conflict. (I had exactly the same feeling about the supposed burial place of King Arthur and Queen Gwinevere near the ruins of the Abbey of Glastonbury in England.) Later we visited quite a list of Orthodox sites in the Bay Area: several of the St Herman of Alaska bookstores, St Eugene's Hermitage in Inverness (which later, as the Monastery of St John Maximovitch, moved to Manton, California), the Ascension Greek Orthodox Cathedral in Oakland, St Seraphim's Orthodox Church in Santa Rosa, All Saints Antiochian Orthodox Church in Rohnert Park, Holy Assumption Monastery in Calistoga, St John the Baptist Orthodox Church in Berkeley, The Nativity of Christ Greek Orthodox Church in Novato, St Nicholas Orthodox Church in San Anselmo, Old Holy Virgin Cathedral on Fulton St in SF, Holy Trinity Greek Orthodox Cathedral on Green St, and Saint Tikhon of Zadonsk Russian Orthodox Church on 15th Ave. Nonetheless, the Cathedral of the Holy Virgin Joy of All Who Sorrow on Geary St remained the spiritual center of all these excursions.

Another base we touched in the Orthodox world of California was Fort Ross, a restored Russian fort on the northern coast in Sonoma County that represented the southernmost limit of Russian expansion in North America, a territory that was initially opened up by the Russian fur traders who hunted the sea otters; it included a traditional Orthodox chapel. At one event at Fort Ross we heard some Russian tourists talking about how beautiful the site was and wishing it was still theirs; as one woman said to Jenny, "You should hear them talk about Alaska."

We also visited the beautiful little Holy Assumption Monastery in Calistoga, on the banks of the Napa River where it's only a tiny creek; the chapel of the monastery was a replica of the one at Fort Ross. It had only one monk in it, Father Sergious Gerken, who had been for some years at Mt. Athos. An enthusiastic gardener, he was doing his best to turn his narrow strip of land into an image of Paradise, with traditional beehives made of jute, a cedar of Lebanon and even some papyrus from the banks of the Nile. Then there was the day at All Saints Antiochian Orthodox Church in Rohnert Park when a priest Jenny didn't know singled her out after Divine Liturgy and started telling her, for no obvious reason, about an Orthodox female saint who had helped prevent the arrival of the Antichrist, a function known in Greek as the *katechon*—which was strange, because that was when I was in the middle of writing my book *The System of Antichrist: Truth and Falsehood in Postmodernism and the New Age*. Nor will I ever forget our visit to Saint Tikhon of Zadonsk Russian Orthodox Church on 15th Ave. in San Francisco—which, before it became a church, had been the residence of St John Maximovitch. The faithful had preserved the saint's cell exactly as it had been while he was alive; I was allowed to visit it, even to sit in his big semi-reclining chair. He spent his nights in that chair because he basically never slept; there was no bed in his cell. I saw his staff with its heavy metal head, his icons, a life-sized portrait of him, and various objects that I recognized as gifts from the local Catholics: a set of rosary beads (the Orthodox use the prayer rope or *lestovka* ["ladder"] rather than the rosary, with knots instead of beads, when they recite the Jesus Prayer), and a bottle for holy water identical to the one I had had as a Catholic child. Sitting in that chair I went into a state of what I would call "infused recollection"; all the scattered fragments of my soul swiftly returned to their center in the Spiritual Heart, like bees to the hive. The effect was temporary yet unforgettable, since it showed exactly what was required of me if I was to heal from my earlier dissipations in the psychedelic counterculture and the New Age.

And then there was our profound experience of a miraculous icon of the Virgin which had been traveling from church to church in the U.S., and made a stop at the Church of St Seraphim's in Santa Rosa. A woman in Michigan had purchased an icon from somewhere outside the U.S. (Mt. Athos? The Holy Land?) and had been venerating it daily, when it suddenly started to exude miraculous myrrh. When we saw it at the

Santa Rosa church it was mounted above a wooden trough designed to catch the constant trickle of the fragrant oil, which kept materializing from nowhere. We stood in a line to venerate the icon, and after we had done so a deacon dabbed a bit of the oil on our foreheads with a Q-tip, causing us to experience a powerful and instantaneous illumination that totally transformed our consciousness. We had experienced one of the "stock miracles" of Eastern Orthodoxy, which are undoubtedly based on long-established channels of spiritual influence passing through the unseen world and maintained by angelic guardians.

ST NICHOLAS ORTHODOX CHURCH AND THE ORDO MARIANA

Since Jenny (to back-track a bit) had so completely immersed herself in the world of Eastern Orthodoxy, it was obvious that she needed to find a church where she could worship according to that form. She soon settled on St Nicholas Orthodox Church, part of the OCA (the Orthodox Church in America, a Russian jurisdiction) in San Anselmo, a fairly short drive from our home in San Rafael. She was baptized there by full immersion in the year of 1997, clad in a vermillion-print shift that we still have, in a redwood hot tub on the church grounds. It was a true Baptism, not simply a conditional one, since she had never been baptized as a child. Even before she took this step, however, Orthodoxy had already emerged in the world of Frithjof Schuon's Maryamiyya Tariqah when Huston Smith invited us to meet Prof. James Cutsinger of the University of South Carolina, a Christian disciple of Schuon who held the post of one of his "Christian *muqaddams*." He led a Christian version of the Maryamiyya called the "Ordo Mariana"—the very "Christian Sufis" I had spontaneously queried Huston about some years earlier. It was a rather strange meeting, since on the same day it was to take place I began to develop a serious "cellulitis" infection in my foot. Debating whether to meet Cutsinger or go to the ER, I chose Cutsinger, whom we met at Huston's house that evening; he was traveling at that point with his mother. It was through this meeting that we began to learn that the Maryamiyya were not exclusively a Muslim Sufi order but also a kind of portal through which people attracted to Schuon's writings but identifying with other religions than Islam could be connected with the more Traditional and metaphysically-oriented versions of the religion of their choice. Eastern Orthodoxy was more-or-less the preferred form of Christianity for Schuon's followers, partly because the Hesychasm it embraced was very similar in form to normative Sufism, complete with the *Shaykh* in the guise of the Greek *Geron* or Russian *Staretz* (all three words mean "elder"), and the Jesus Prayer—*mnimi Theou* in Greek—that was precisely the Christian form of the Sufi *dhikrullah* or "remembrance of God," which is the literal meaning of *mnimi Theou* as well. Both the Christian and the Muslim forms were precisely in line with the central method of Mariyamiyya spiritual practice, the Invocation of the Name of God. Nonetheless Schuon — who, in the journal *Studies in Comparative Religion*, had said of the Second Vatican Council something like "the Catholic Church is being destroyed before our eyes but no one seems to care," and who, according to something James Cutsinger conveyed to Jenny, had also observed on one occasion that Orthodoxy can sometimes "tyrannize the soul" — also had a Christian *muqaddam* for *sedevacantist* Catholicism, none other than Rama Coomaraswamy. Some of Schuon's people (including Cutsinger) seemed uncomfortable with Rama, but since he was the son of Ananda K. Coomaraswamy, René Guénon's only true colleague who was sometimes described as the co-founder of the Traditionalist School — besides being a board-member of Seyyed Hossein Nasr's Foundation for Traditional Studies, the publishers of his Traditionalist journal *Sophia* — Rama couldn't be ignored.

In any case, after meeting with Cutsinger I went to the ER and found that the infection had blossomed in the past few hours. This led to an incapacitating illness of longer than a month's duration that put me on crutches and was always threatening to take my life by turning into blood poisoning. I was living on penicillin and pain pills, but the wound refused to heal — until I soaked my foot in a bucket of boiled comfrey root, after which it rapidly cleared up. Looking back, it seems as if all the major spiritual transformations in my life have been preceded by serious accidents or illnesses.

Jenny, too, had faced a dilemma, since she definitely wanted to convert to Eastern Orthodox Christianity but wanted to stay in good standing with the Maryamiyya as well, and felt that Dr Nasr might not look kindly on her desire to "convert" to Christianity, which (in exoteric terms at least) meant that she would be seen as "apostasizing" from Islam — though Schuon emphasized that, from the esoteric/Perennialist point-of-view, adopting one revealed religion as a spiritual Way did not necessarily imply rejecting the others. And, as we shall see, Jenny's suspicions about Dr Nasr's attitude turned out to be spot-on. As for his actual relationship to and feelings about Frithjof Schuon, whom he accepted as his Shaykh and whose authority he invoked for his own right to act as a Sufi teacher, the true nature of this would surface later. When Dr Nasr initiated Jenny he had asked her, "Do you want to meet the Shaykh?" (Shaykh Isa, Frithjof Schuon) — to which she replied "I'll leave that up to you"; consequently they never did meet. And to tell the truth I'm just as glad that they didn't, since Jenny's American Indian blood gave her a facial bone-structure very similar to some of the women portrayed in a number of Schuon's nude "shakti" paintings, which made me worry that he might be inclined to snap her up as one of his "intrinsic" or "vertical" wives — but more on that later.

Around this time we were coming closer to another member of Huston's "rag-tag *tariqah*," Scott Whittaker, who ended up becoming one of our dearest friends, until his untimely death a couple of years later. Dr Nasr had mentioned him to Jenny while she was in Washington as someone who worked at Shambhalla, the famous Berkeley spiritual/esoteric bookstore on University Ave. We found him living in an apartment so crammed with books, stacked to the ceiling, that a good-sized earthquake could have buried him under a heap of second-hand knowledge. Besides being a Maryamiyya *faqir* and some-time secretary to Huston Smith, he was a student of Neo-Platonism and a proficient and creative mathematician who was deep into abstruse calculations and researches that he couldn't fully explain to me due to my lack of knowledge of that discipline—though I had the impression that he was doing his best to resurrect a basically Pythagorean worldview by defining the exact points where quantitative mathematics provides the basis for qualitative metaphysical symbolism. When we first met him, ill health combined with a deep intellectual introversion had made it difficult for him to communicate with us on a human level, though over the course of our relationship he gradually emerged from his shell.

Then the day came when one of Scott's friends from Schuon's group in Bloomington, Indiana, Barry McDonald, was visiting the Bay Area, so Scott introduced us. During our get-together at a SF café Jenny mentioned that, based on Nasr's guidance, she had never met Schuon, to which Barry replied: "Since Shaykh Isa (Frithjof Schuon) is your shaykh, at least he should know of your existence. Why don't you write a letter introducing yourself to Sayyida Latifa?"—Schuon's first and only legal wife in terms of Swiss and U.S. law.

So she did. But when she revealed this fact to Dr Nasr, he went ballistic. That's the first time we realized that he considered Jenny to be his disciple, not Schuon's, and that all was not one great harmonious unity in the Maryamiyya world. During one of our yearly visits to Nasr at the George Washington University, I asked him why Schuon's scandal-generating dance events, the "Indian Days" in which he lived out his appreciation of Native American spirituality at some undefined point between fantasy and reality, were any different from the hippies, with their fringed buckskin jackets and headbands (who also had their "traditional" medicine men) "playing Indian in California?" "I really couldn't say" he answered. I also remember an occasion when he lamented the departure of the Nimatullahi Order from Islam as a "disastrous development." [For the "Indian Days scandals," see the articles "Abuse Charges Aired, Denied" by Andrew Welsh-Huggins in the *Herald-Times* and "Sect Leader, 'Wives' Freed on Bond" from the *Vincennes Sun Commercial*, both Bloomington, Indiana newspapers. The articles appeared on October 16, 1991. The indictment in question was later quashed.]

So Jenny was temporarily stymied. How was she to maintain her relationship with the Maryamiyya while pursuing her interest in Orthodox

Christianity? The solution we finally came up with was that she should do an end-run around Nasr and apply directly to Schuon for permission to embrace Orthodoxy—so she wrote to him, and he graciously consented. Nor was Nasr in any position to object. So, from then on, her point of contact with the Traditionalist world changed from Washington D.C. to Columbia, South Carolina where James Cutsinger taught (and his residence in nearby Aiken), and Bloomington, Indiana as well, though we only visited the Maryamiyya in Bloomington after Schuon's death in 1998. (Later, after Jenny's departure from the Ordo Mariana, which disappeared basically because Cutsinger lost interest in it, she made a number of Catholic pilgrimages in Kentucky and Ohio, though I won't list these until *Chapter Twelve*.)

So the years from (roughly) 1990 to 2015 were definitely a time of pilgrimage for us. When God still seems to be "elsewhere," it is natural to want to travel to find Him, or at least to read His signs—but when "heaven and earth cannot contain Me, but the heart of my loving slave can contain Me" is realized, then the outer pilgrimage begins to lose its attraction. As the Sufis put it, when travel *to* God is finished, travel *in* God begins.

Now, however, I need to go back to the year 1997 to tell the story of Jenny's connection with St Nicholas Orthodox Church in San Anselmo, and related events.

The priest at St Nicholas was Fr Stephan Meholick, a native of Pennsylvania whose family hailed from the Carpathians, from the Hutsul people, darkly celebrated in Sergei Parajanov's great motion picture *Shadows of Our Forgotten Ancestors*, a tribe whose often-disputed territory became part of the Ukraine after World War II. The Orthodox Church in America, the jurisdiction that St Nicholas belonged to, is a more-or-less traditional church, though more liberal than ROCOR.

Fr Stephan was an artistic soul who delivered great sermons, though he confided in me once that he would much rather be a hermit somewhere on a lonely hilltop than pastor of a congregation. The church maintained the traditional Divine Liturgy (in English) though it was unfortunately saddled with a more-or-less postmodern "catechist" named John Burnett. He would attend services dressed in a T-shirt printed with skulls, seemed to think that the resurrection of the dead was some kind of uncanny, arbitrary process akin to a vampire rising from his coffin, and considered traditional Orthodox Hesychasm to be a kind of "New Age spirituality." "If you want to do the Jesus Prayer" he once said to me, "go to Spirit Rock"—Jack Kornfield's rural Buddhist retreat center in the San Geronimo Valley.

St Nicholas seemed to prove the validity of Frithjof Schuon's caution that Eastern Orthodox Christianity can sometimes "tyrannize the soul." It was intensely group-oriented and called for a near-total identification and a massive expenditure of life-energy. The beautiful and mystically-profound services were incredibly long and detailed — especially those for Pascha (Easter), an all-night liturgy that, sometime in the wee hours of the morning, morphed into a Russian folk event with the traditional red-dyed Easter eggs, a vast feast with dishes like suckling pig, during which the congregation massively over-indulged themselves to break the Lenten fast, little costumed skits reminding one of medieval western mystery plays, etc. etc. — through all of which ceremonials the grace of the Divine Liturgy was stepped down and distributed throughout the various contemporary and ancestral layers of the collective Orthodox soul. And the women of the congregation were expected to cook and cook and cook, as if cooking were a kind of eighth sacrament.

On one occasion Jenny went to an Orthodox conference that took place at a Catholic retreat venue called The Mercy Center in Burlingame. (Earlier, after the fall of Santa Venetia Presbyterian Church, I had attended a "spiritual director's institute" at the same Center, in a vain attempt to find some trace of an "esoteric Christianity." The main thing I learned there, after we had all taken the neo-Jungian Meyers-Briggs personality test — from which I discovered that I was an "INTJ," an Introverted, Intuitive, Thinking, Judgement-oriented type — was that Feeling-type women tended to be profoundly judgmental of and threatened by male Thinking types such as myself, seeing us all as if we were the natural allies of their "objective, rational, judgmental" male relatives who likely believed that Feeling is basically women's-work and that Religion is all hogwash.)

One of the presentations Jenny heard at the Orthodox conference she attended had to do with the healthy vs. the dysfunctional group-dynamic in church congregations. According to the theory held by the presenter, every congregation has its "in-group," but in toxic churches the priest is a member of that group while in healthy churches he is not. There was certainly an in-group at St Nicholas, where sanctity (or something like it) was considered to depend on being in the good graces of the priest. Fr Stephan, however, didn't particularly encourage people to get into his good graces; he just wanted (in part of himself at least) to be free of the burden of the congregation he was tasked with shepherding — the result being that no matter how intensively someone dedicated him- or herself to gaining admission to the in-group by kissing up to him, this was never quite achieved in any secure or lasting way, resulting in an increasing sense of frustration. And one got the impression that Fr Stephan himself was continually falling short of full membership in the in-group that he himself represented. As for Jenny, she remained in some ways in the group's outskirts, under the shadow of those more fully dedicated to achieving full *social* membership. And this in-but-not-of status proved profoundly painful to her on the occasion of the death of Scott Whitaker, as we'll see below.

PROF. JAMES CUTSINGER

Jenny's "secret, esoteric *staretz*," James Cutsinger — who, as she discovered to her surprise, had once visited St Paisius' monastery just as she had, and who actually dropped by St Nicholas at one time while she was worshipping there, before she knew him — ultimately provided her with the sense that, no matter how difficult her relations to the congregation might become, she had an additional, outside spiritual identification that she could fall back on when her sense of alienation from her "exoteric" group became too hard to bear. (This idea of Orthodox Christianity as "exoteric" and Schuon's Ordo Mariana for his Christian disciples as "esoteric" finally didn't hold water for us, but for a while it did provide Jenny with a degree of needed psychological support.) But the central gift Jenny received from Prof. Cutsinger was the Invocation of the Divine Name in one of its Christian forms, as taught by Frithjof Schuon; when we further researched it we found that it had actually been used in that form at Mt. Athos, so Schuon didn't just make it up. It might be described as a verbal analogue to the traditional Orthodox icon "The Virgin of the Sign"; Jenny still uses it today. Beyond the inestimable value of that foundational offering, Cutsinger allowed us to witness a brilliant mind that dealt with certain abstruse points of theology and metaphysics in a unique and paradoxical way, yet one that sometimes seemed to lack the compensatory qualities of balance and substance. He had some sort of a background in the aesthetic of High Church Anglicanism, which cast a certain aristocratic or dramatic effect over his religious outlook; on the one occasion when we prayed (Jenny a participant, myself more-or-less an observer) in his private oratory, I asked myself: "Is this prayer or theatre?" Before we knew him, he had been involved with an Episcopal retreat-house in Aiken, South Carolina known as Rose Hill, where religious conferences were held; on looking over the proceedings of some of these events we were struck by the high quality and relevance of many of the dialogues. Later on, however, in partnership with one Owen Jones, who bankrolled the operation, he acquired Rose Hill and attempted to turn it into an exclusive, private, Eastern Orthodox academy run more or less on the Catholic Great Books model, but with an uncomfortable, contradictory, semi-clandestine strand of Schuonian Traditionalism running through it — an institution that lasted (if I remember correctly) two academic years before it folded. This outcome was partly due to the fact that Jones had the money while Cutsinger had the brains, thus invoking the perennial tension between those competent in the ways of this world and those conversant with the ways of the other one. Nonetheless, he organized the greatest interfaith event I ever attended, which providentially took place shortly after 9/11 — a conference called "Paths to the Heart" where Muslim Sufis and Orthodox Christian Hesychasts met to share their perspectives on the meaning of the Spiritual Heart (*Kardia* in Greek, *al-Qalb* in Arabic). Seyyed Hossein Nasr spoke for the Sufis; Bishop Kallistos Ware (perhaps the most accessible and reliable writer on Eastern Orthodoxy in English, at least on the popular level) and Vincent Rossi (one-time leader of the Christ the Savior Brotherhood) spoke for the Hesychasts; and Cutsinger spoke (rather uneasily) for the Schuonian Perennialists. I can imagine no more appropriate and helpful response to the Twin Towers attack than that conference. The only jarring note in the proceedings was Cutsinger's own presentation, which began as a luminous exposition of the ontological hierarchy—the Ladder of Divine Ascent in the phrase of the great Orthodox saint John Climacus ("John of the Ladder")—but whose apex was, however, not the Beatific Vision but the Transcendent Unity of Religions, something that to my mind should have been placed on a much lower rung. And, as he later told me, he also interpolated certain passages from Kallistos Ware's books into his lecture, without attribution, so as to "prove" to the Bishop that he was actually a Schuonian Traditionalist without realizing it. This (not surprisingly) did not go over very well. Nonetheless the published proceedings of the conference represent a rare excursion into "esoteric ecumenism" that will hopefully stay in print because it should never be forgotten. (Interestingly enough, Cutsinger was not the only Orthodox Christian who was interested in Sufism in those days. In Marin County we met one Fr Jonah Paffhausen, a close friend of Fr Stephan, who, when he heard I was a Sufi, became fascinated, and said we should really talk some time, which unfortunately we never did. It was Fr Jonah who informed me of the fact that St Gregory Palamas (1296–1359) had been captured on one occasion and held for ransom by the Ottoman Turks. During his incarceration he had apparently had an opportunity to dialogue with some Sufis, which has led to speculation about whether or not Palamas' famous doctrine of the unknowable Divine Essence and its Uncreated Energies might have been influenced by the equivalent Sufi doctrine of the mysterious Essence of Allah (*al-Dhat*) manifesting as His Attributes, His Names, and His Acts—though he could certainly have gotten a very similar doctrine from Dionysius the Pseudo-Areopagite. Fr Jonah, while he was in the Orthodox Church in America, took over St Eugene's Hermitage in Inverness and turned it into the Monastery of St John, which later moved from Marin to Tehama County. He rose to the rank of Metropolitan in the OCA before jumping ship to ROCOR, after which he was known for his cordial relationship with Patriarch Kirill of Moscow. (Whether his friendship with the Patriarch—or with Fr Stephan—has warmed or cooled since the beginning of the Russia/Ukraine war I have no way of knowing.)

James Cutsinger also introduced us to two Orthodox Christians who ended up having a significant place in our lives: Vincent Rossi (already mentioned above), who once led a beautiful patristics class at our house in San Rafael, and Alvin Moore Jr., Cutsinger's godfather, who at one point had enjoyed a prominent position with the Library of Congress and who, like Cutsinger and Rama Coomaraswamy, was a board member of Seyyed Hossein Nasr's Foundation for Traditional Studies. He acted as Jenny's unofficial Christian *muqaddam* for a while, and was particularly known for his beautiful Christmas cards: reproductions of traditional Orthodox icons, each accompanied by a short, beautifully-written metaphysical meditation on a theme suggested by the image. Though Alvin Moore did quite a bit of translation for the Traditionalist world and published articles in various Traditionalist journals, his best and most essential writing probably appeared in those Christmas cards. He had a rather stiff and chilly demeanor that unsuccessfully hid his great generosity, to both Jenny and myself. He encouraged her to write her two books on Dante (*Dark Way to Paradise: Dante's Inferno in Light of the Spiritual Path*, and *The Ordeal of Mercy, Dante's Purgatorio in Light of the Spiritual Path*) which, instead of relying overmuch on Aquinas, provided a detailed exegesis of the first two books of the *Divine Comedy* based mostly on the Greek Fathers and the writers of the Traditionalist School. And in many ways he inaugurated my own Traditionalist writing career by urging me to produce a book rather than editing a journal as I had planned; that book was *The System of Antichrist: Truth and Falsehood in Postmodernism and the New Age*.

Strangely enough however, as the years went by, James Cutsinger's interest in Orthodox Christianity seemed to cool a bit. At one point he transferred his allegiance to Byzantine Rite Catholicism—Orthodox in form, yet still in communion with the Vatican—since he felt that the Eastern Orthodox were not sufficiently open intellectually; certainly they were not very open to the ideas of Frithjof Schuon! Later on he seemed to lose his original degree of interest even in Schuon, since he began to teach a range of non-traditional doctrines derived from the "esoterism" of the counterculture, drawing on sources like G. I. Gurdjieff and Alan Watts. I remember an evening when Jenny and I were talking with him in a restaurant in Columbia, SC, and his eyes lit up at the thought that I had actually "been there" at the center of the hippie counterculture! He asked me on that occasion how some of Schuon's more off-the-wall practices (not his ideas) were essentially different from those of the Neo-Pagans, but I could provide no coherent answer; he was seemingly being lured away from Traditionalism/Perennialism by the same ideas and cultural milieu that Traditionalism/Perennialism had providentially saved me from. He had even been influenced by a young and attractive witch in one of his religion classes who had burst into tears and called him the equivalent of an "old meanie" because he refused to include the "ancient religion" of Wicca (which had mostly been invented by Gerald Gardner, who died in 1964) in his list of approved traditional faiths. Nonetheless he never officially broke with the Orthodox world. After he passed away in 2020 his body was buried at the St Paisius Monastery in Stafford, Arizona, run by the St Herman of Alaska Brotherhood, a monastery which he had visited (just as we had) in its earlier location at Forestville, California.

As for Alan Watts, a story about his interaction with the outer layers of the Traditionalist School needs to be told. On one occasion he had been invited to dinner by Rama Coomaraswamy's mother, Doña Luisa (who, incidentally, had also corresponded with Thomas Merton at one point). Watts arrived stone drunk, bottle in hand, at which point Doña Luisa relieved him of it, placed it outside the door, and told him that he could pick it up on his way out.

HUSTON SMITH TRIES TO CONVERT TO EASTERN ORTHODOXY

So it was becoming clearer all the time that many signs in the "rag-tag *tariqah*" were pointing toward Eastern Orthodox Christianity. James Cutsinger's influence was becoming more timely and available than that of Schuon or even Nasr, and so when Jenny secured Schuon's permission to convert — she was baptized in the Spring of 1997 — Scott Whitaker soon followed. Some time during the period when Scott was a catechumen, a candidate for baptism — he was only finally baptized when he was at the point of death — Huston gave me the gift of a lovely traditional homespun cotton jellaba, hooded in the North African style, a garment that I prayed in for many years until it became so full of holes that it had made me a candidate, if I had elected to repair it, for the emblematic patched garment of the Sufi. A short time after he had given it to me, however, he asked for it back (temporarily), since Dr Nasr would be in town and Huston needed to present a suitably Muslim appearance for their meeting, and for whatever prayers and *dhikr* they might perform together. Even though the Maryamiyya *majlis* that Huston had conducted was pretty well disbanded by that time, I got the impression that Nasr still considered him to be something on the order of "the Maryamiyya *khalifa* for the west-of-the-Mississippi region."

This episode was an omen of things to come. At one point we drove Huston to venerate the relics of St John Maximovitch at the Cathedral on Geary St, and he was so struck by the spiritual power of the place that as soon as he emerged from the building he turned around and went in a second time. Not long after this he let us know that he was planning to convert to Eastern Orthodox Christianity, which would have been right in line with his life's pattern of deeply immersing himself for a good number of years in one religion after another so as to fully absorb the essential flavor of each. And, given his advanced age, this meant that he was likely to die in the Orthodox Church. All that was required now was for him to ask for formal permission from his own *khalifa*, Dr Nasr. However, given Jenny's wise decision to ask Schuon, not Nasr, for her own permission to convert, we had definite misgivings about how Nasr would respond, particularly since Schuon had just recently passed away (in 1998), which meant that this particular route to Orthodoxy within the context of the Maryamiyya was no longer open to Huston as it had been to Jenny. And these misgivings were soon justified when Nasr refused Huston's petition.

But it was the piece of "spiritual direction" that Dr Nasr gave Huston on this occasion that was to have far-reaching and less-than-fortunate consequences. The story as Huston told it was that Nasr had essentially said: "Huston, you have a rare configuration of soul that allows you to profitably practice two religions at once. Therefore you should continue as a Methodist Christian as your *exoteric* practice, while maintaining your Maryamiyya *wirds* and *dhikr* as your *esoteric* practice." This, of course, directly contradicted the standard Maryamiyya/Traditionalist rule against syncretism and the mixing of religious forms. Nasr's proposal was right in line with his "neo-Traditionalist" tendency to interpret the Transcendent Unity of Religions as giving Islam precedence over all the other faiths, since the Qur'an, though it explicitly accepts the validity of former Divine Revelations, nonetheless defines itself as the Criterion according to which the degree of departure of the followers of those faiths from the original purity of their own Revelations must be judged.

This way of "balancing" things did not go over well with Huston. "Dr Nasr just wants to hold on to Big Huston Smith, and is willing to flatter me while betraying one of his core principles to do it," he told us. The upshot was that Huston Smith ended his life as neither a practicing Christian nor a practicing Muslim — since his Methodism had been no more than a flimsy external identification and a piece of old family history for many years — but rather as a person without any formal religious affiliation in the full Traditional sense. This was an outcome that Traditionalist doctrine considered to be extremely unfortunate — so why didn't the Traditionalists prevent it rather than helping to create it?

THE DEATH OF SCOTT WHITAKER, AND WHAT I LEARNED FROM IT

For as long as my wife and I knew him, our friend Scott Whitaker's health was quite poor, due to a serious autoimmune disease known as pyoderma. Eventually he turned up with metastasized colon cancer, passing away in November of 1998. In him we lost a true spiritual friend.

Scott was actually baptized in the hospital, Alta Bates Medical Center in Berkeley. And though I am a Muslim and was at that time a dervish of the Nimatullahi Order, I was allowed to be "acolyte to the acolytes" during both his baptism and his reception of the sacrament of the sick, both administered by Fr Stephan. Jenny and I spent many days visiting him in the hospital, and I was present in his room up to an hour and a half before his death. (Jenny was there the whole time.)

As Scott was dying, I realized that it is possible for someone who is suffering profoundly to burn up other people's karmic impurities in the fires of that suffering. I believe that Scott did this for me, and for several others. This is essentially Charles Williams' notion of vicarious suffering, and I am told that Eastern Orthodoxy has a similar doctrine. What a spiritual Master can sometimes do during his life, some spiritually advanced souls can apparently do at the point of death.

I saw that death, like birth, comes in waves: contractions. I understood this because I in some sense "midwived" Scott's death; at least that's how I experienced it. I felt the contractions. It was as if, as I meditated beside his death bed, I was allowing him to die "through" me, as I spontaneously visualized his soul ascending to Paradise.

My sense of Scott's death on the subtle or animic level was distinct from my experience of the journey and destiny of his immortal soul. On one occasion when he almost died—he temporarily stopped breathing—I felt the "etheric field" in the room around him wobble. And the aura of his body after death—in no way identifiable with his soul, but more on the order of a psycho-physical residue, identified by René Guénon with the Hebrew *ob* and the Roman *lares*—was like a sort of crystalline mist.

During the Eastern Orthodox sacrament of the sick, administered the Wednesday before he died, the last day he was really conscious (he passed at 1:30 next Saturday morning), everyone around his bed felt the heavens open. Father Stephan was as amazed as the rest of us; he said had never experienced anything like it. Heaven came down for Scott, then lifted again. After that point his relationship to his physical form was extremely tenuous. His body was still breathing, but his spirit had already largely departed.

After the exaltation of the time immediately before and after his death, the mammoth job of cleaning out his incredibly cluttered apartment and distributing his vast library of spiritual books began. Scott's step-father, who had traveled with his mother from New Jersey, said "let's just rent a dumpster and throw them all out," seeing them as useless trash and not realizing that they were likely worth many thousands of dollars. A number of Scott's friends, old and new, and several people from St Nicholas Orthodox Church (which he had recently joined), including Father Stephan, made up the work party. I took responsibility for the rescue and distribution of the books, which may have numbered as many as 7000, including those in storage, many if not most of them spiritual classics. The apartment was in a terrible mess, since for several years he had been too depressed and physically ill to take care of it; rats had even begun to eat some of the books. Yet everything in it was a jewel, a treasure. This is why I say that the act of cleaning out his apartment was like Christ harrowing Hell. The books concretely symbolized the souls of the righteous in Hades under the Old Dispensation; Scott's death, like the crucifixion and resurrection, inaugurated the New Dispensation. Consequently the physical work we did was also, by virtue of its inescapable symbolism, a spiritual act. Since his collection was too large to donate to any existing library, either public or institutional, and after Jenny and I took possession of his Traditionalist books and a few spiritual classics from a number of different traditions, we distributed his Christian books to St Nicholas Orthodox Church; his Jewish books to a Bay Area synagogue; other Christian books to the San Francisco Theological Seminary in Ross; his Buddhist and Hindu books to Jack Kornfield's Buddhist retreat center, Spirit Rock, in the San Geronimo Valley of Marin; and his books on Sufism and Islam to the San Francisco Nimatullahi *khaniqa*. Most of his books on Romance and the Courtly Love tradition we gave to San Domenico, a Catholic girls' boarding school in San Anselmo (now co-ed and no longer Catholic).

I learned through this work that the distribution of the personal effects of the deceased both symbolizes and concretely aids in the distribution of that person's psychic legacy—the accidents of his or her personality, including the imprints of lived experience, as well as influences from the dead, the living, and the ancestors: everything which that person had collected during life to weave the psychic garment of his or her immortal soul. The passing on of such a legacy symbolizes, and up to a degree actually accomplishes, what René Guénon called *metempsychosis*. As he made clear, the soul does not literally reincarnate, yet both the living and the unborn can inherit elements of the psychic personality—the memory, the worldly destiny and possibly even the spiritual merit (or at least its psychic reflection)—of the deceased.

The conscious reception and purification by the living of these personality-elements of the deceased, through a spiritually-based grieving process, aids in the journey of the soul after death. I must emphasize that this has nothing whatever to do with the *salvation* of the soul, merely with the ease or rapidity with which a soul that is already essentially saved rises to its eternal destiny.

It is this level of things that's represented by the Eastern Orthodox doctrine of the "tollhouses," so reminiscent of the Egyptian Book of the Dead, as well as by the doctrine of the *bardos* from the Tibetan Book of the Dead, particularly the Second Bardo. The tollhouses, mythically or symbolically conceived of as something on the order of customs sheds, are stages in the soul's progress after death, "borders" which cannot be passed until certain pieces of earthly "baggage" are left behind.—thus they are the rough equivalent of the Roman Catholic Purgatory. They do not, however, possess the force of dogma in Orthodoxy, and many Orthodox theologians deny their equivalence to Purgatory, which they consider to be heresy; others would dispense with the tollhouses entirely, though St John Maximovitch apparently accepted them. And, certainly, to believe that the passage of the soul through the tollhouses has anything to do with its salvation—as if a "failure" at one of the tollhouses could actually result in one's damnation—would be heresy indeed. Their reality is on a lower level than that of salvation or damnation; they are psychic rather than spiritual. Nonetheless, it is important for the living to help the souls of the departed negotiate them, basically through *apatheia* or loving detachment, expressed in terms of a spiritually-grounded process of grieving and letting go.

The three classical stages of the mystical path are Purgation, Illumination and Union. The tollhouses relate to Purgation; the spiritual traveler who "dies before he is made to die" (in the words of the Prophet Muhammad, peace and blessings be upon him) passes through the tollhouses in this life. Purgation does not *cause* Illumination, or Illumination, Union; to believe this would be to believe that the soul can attain union with God entirely through its own efforts. Rather, it would be better to say that virtual Union manifests as Illumination, and virtual Illumination as Purgation, which is the same thing as saying that the perspective of God, or Grace, supersedes and embraces the perspective of man, or works.

According to the *Bardo Thödöl*, the *Tibetan Book of the Dead*, which is based on the paradigm of reincarnation, there are three *bardos* or time-periods in the after-death state (the Fourth Bardo being earthly life). The First Bardo is the moment of death, when all form is transcended and the light of the Void or the Original Mind shines clear; the Second Bardo is the period when the psychic material released from the dissolving subjectivity of the deceased dawns in a series of archetypal forms; the Third Bardo is the period when the soul, if it has failed to achieve immediate liberation in the First Bardo, or proximate liberation (probably to be identified with Paradise) in the Second Bardo, and has not fallen into one of the hells, chooses its next homeland and its next parents in the process of seeking rebirth. To me, as a Muslim who does not believe in literal reincarnation, this can simply mean that those the Qur'an (specifically in the *Surah al-Waqia*) calls "the foremost" attain direct annihilation in God, and subsistence through God, after their deaths; those designated as "on the right" attain Paradise; and those "on the left" fall into the Fire. As for re-birth, it might be admissible to say that those who identify almost completely with their own subjectivity, though they have committed no major sins, may seem to "follow" that subjectivity, that "psychic legacy," after their deaths, as it is inherited by the already-living, the newly-born, or those about to be born. To the living souls who have appropriated elements of the earthly experience of the deceased, it may seem as if they are actually the dead one reincarnated, while in reality the deceased soul is in a kind of ghostly "Limbo"—which Dante, we should remember, situates in the "highest" region of Hell—unable to let go of the accidents of its former personality, and therefore attempting to re-experience earthly life by means of them, as they come to be attached to a new, and unique, human incarnation. (It should go without saying that those among the living who become objects of the attention of ghostly souls in Limbo are themselves likely to be over-attached to their contingent, temporal personalities—wanderers in the wilderness of *sangsara*.)

Scott's death reflected the First Bardo; and his beautiful and elaborate Russian Orthodox funeral at St Nicholas Church (during which I bent over his open coffin to kiss his ice-cold forehead), represented the Second Bardo; the cleaning of his apartment and distribution of his books and the subsequent re-consolidation of our web of relationships after his loss, under changed circumstances, related to the Third Bardo. (The grief process seems to straddle the Second Bardo—the pain of letting go, compensated for in Scott's case by our reception of the radiance of what *he* was letting go of—and the Third Bardo: that different pain, more difficult in many ways, of receiving new earthly life after Scott's passing, a life which we could not fully accept without a deepening realization that, in terms this terrestrial world, he was really no longer with us.) Whenever something or someone dies, something or someone else is born, whether or not we have the insight to discern it and the stamina and detachment to consciously accept it. Nonetheless this new something or someone is not a literal reincarnation of the person or thing that has passed, but rather a new and unique advent, a fresh act of Divine creation, though it may draw upon material released by what has just died in order to form a "body" for itself in this world.

The First and Second Bardos are analogous to the Hindu *Deva-yana*, and the Third Bardo to the *Pitri-yana*. The *Deva-yana* or "Path of the Gods" is the afterlife course which leads, through the waxing half of the Moon's cycle, to final liberation through the Door of the Sun; the *Pitri-yana*, or "Path of the Fathers" (the ancestors) is the course which leads, through the waning half of the Moon's cycle, to existence as an ancestral spirit, and ultimately to rebirth. In Neo-Platonic terminology, the First Bardo is roughly analogous to *pneuma* or Spirit, the Second Bardo to *psyche*, and the Third Bardo to *soma*, the physical body.

After Scott's death, my attention to him was split between the Way of the Ancestors and the Way of the Gods. I saw that if I gave to *Pitri-yana* whatever was accidental and contingent in my relationship to and memory of Scott, through a healthy, purgative nostalgia, I lightened his journey, whereas if I deliberately dredged up those memories, or held on to them, or tried to pull them back, through a pathological, morbid nostalgia, then I blocked his path. (In René Guénon's view, this is what most spiritualist mediums are doing when they attempt to "channel" the departed.) I also saw that, in terms of *Deva-yana*, by which I mean Scott's eternal destiny, if I tried to either hide from or to deliberately contact his spiritual essence,

I veiled him from me. If, on the other hand, I simply "stood in wait," without either extending my consciousness toward him or letting myself forget him—a form of *adab* or "courtesy" that the "sober" Sufis apply to their relationship with Allah—then my relationship with Scott was correct. My care to avoid either pulling back his contingent self or memory on *Pitri-yana*, or reaching for his essence on *Deva-yana*, is part of what made a true contact with that spiritual essence possible. When I visited his grave shortly after his death, at the Mount Tamalpais Cemetery in San Rafael (his grave was right next to that of Ron Silveira, one of my classmates at Marin Catholic High School, whom I didn't know had died) I found it easy to feel his presence, because he hadn't quite left. Later it was more difficult; he seemed to be attending to pressing other-worldly business. But then, it became easy again—possibly because he had begun to experience the "resurrection of the body." I could now spontaneously talk with him from time to time, much as I had done in life. (A heavy, necromantic evocation of his soul, however, would have been just as much an act of discourtesy as an uninvited invasion of his home during his earthly life; it would have been more likely to destroy our relationship than deepen it.)

THE RESURRECTION OF THE BODY

Both Christianity and Islam teach the resurrection of the body as orthodox doctrine. What does this mean? Are all the scattered atoms of the corpse magically brought together again, even if they have become parts of other living things, including living human bodies? I don't believe that is the case. But neither does the departed exist throughout eternity as a formless ghost.

The Vedanta speaks of a subtle body, the *suksma sarira*, which, according to the *Brahma Sutras*, survives until final Liberation. Jesus, after his resurrection, appeared in a palpable though "glorified" body, not a re-animated corpse (though his physical remains were apparently subsumed into that higher body), and both Mulla Sadra and Ibn al-'Arabi, as Muslim esoterists, hold that a body is necessary to the soul at every stage of existence.

From one perspective, a human being can be defined as a polar relationship between the one spiritual Source and his or her formal manifestation, neither of which exists alone, being complementary manifestations of a single Reality. The spiritual pole has precedence over the formal, since Spirit in fact represents this absolute Reality in the mode of polarity with its own manifestation, yet one pole never exists without the other. The dissolution of the material body therefore necessitates a "re-polarization" between Spirit and its manifestation on a different level, thus situating the individual being on a new ontological plane. This re-polarization or posthumous "resurrection of the body" may be delayed by the after-effects of passion and ignorance, making necessary a temporary alienation of the soul from its bodily manifestation in the state of Purgatory, but the re-polarization, or re-union, of soul and body is nonetheless inevitable, resulting either in the eternal subsistence of that person in a glorified body — eternal at least until the dissolution of the present universe — or else the soul's quasi-eternal union with the body of its willful refusal of God in Hell. In the normal course of things no damned soul can be redeemed from Hell, given that damnation is a choice and death takes the soul beyond time, beyond the point where such a choice can be willingly revoked — nonetheless Hell itself is not eternal, since all the hells and all the paradises, all the realms of form, are ultimately reabsorbed into the Absolute on the dissolution of universal manifestation, the *mahapralaya*; this, not the eventual salvation of every individual soul, may be the real meaning of Origen's doctrine of *apocatastasis*. The eternal design of each soul as originally and perfectly conceived in the mind of God remains, but it remains not as a blessing but rather as a condemnation of the soul that has betrayed it. Nonetheless God has the power and the right to redeem any soul from Hell if He so chooses — but if He indeed can liberate any soul He wishes from the infernal regions, that soul's free will cannot be redeemed along with it, seeing that an eternal refusal of God is Hell's name and definition — and an entity without free will does not satisfy the full definition of a human soul. Perhaps all that can be redeemed is that soul's psychic *materia*, which ultimately becomes reintegrated in the Universal Soul from which the material for all individual souls is drawn. Be that as it may, unless the material body remains incorrupt, as in the case of some saints, or else spontaneously dematerializes so as to travel directly to the higher level of being destined for it in unbroken union with its animating principle — as has been very rarely reported for some of the greatest *mahasiddhas* like Milarepa — it dissolves at death, after which the spirit re-manifests a new, integral form for itself on a subtler level — subtler, yet somehow *more concrete* than our present bodies, designed for this terrestrial environment. As Scott said shortly before he died, "What do I have to complain about? I'm simply going to get a new body; that's something I've needed for years and years." As for the ultimate "dissolution" of this synthesis of subtle body and individual soul in union with the Absolute, this does not happen by a *negation* of individual identity but by an eternally-deepening realization of that individual's pre-existing identity with ever wider and deeper universes of Being, culminating in the Vedantic *Tat Twam Asi* — "That (the Absolute Brahman) Art Thou" — the identical realization that Meister Eckhart expressed when he said, "my truest 'I' is God." The soul is not *negated* in God but *fulfilled* in God. What is negated or dissolved is not the soul but the *ego* — which is, precisely, the soul's *resistance* to the realization of its identity with those ever-widening realms of Being, and ultimately with the Absolute itself.

THREE WAVES OF DARKNESS

This concludes the account of the enlightening side of Scott Whitaker's death; yet that death also included an extremely dark side, one that undoubtedly reflected the contradiction between Scott's high spiritual idealism and his distinct lack of what Jung called "Shadow integration." He was in many ways the innocent soul who attracts spiritual darkness, the lamb preyed upon by wolves.

And the first wave of that darkness was truly dark. Myself, Jenny, and Scott's mother, who had traveled to California from New Jersey with his sister to be with him in his last days, along with another woman from the St Nicholas parish, were there in his hospital room as his end drew near. I was not there at the final moment, however, because I suddenly became highly agitated, so the others suggested that I take a break from the ordeal by returning to a house in Albany, just north of Berkeley, that had been offered by an Episcopal priest and his wife as a place for Scott's mother and sister to stay until Scott's *agon* was over. It was while I was resting there that I got a phone call from Jenny, telling me that Scott had passed away.

A few days later, however, back at our house in Bayside Acres, Jenny started to become extremely disturbed — a state that culminated in a truly terrible memory that she had been repressing. She remembered that, not long before Scott's death, a male nurse on the night shift at Alta Bates had come into the room and asked Scott's mother for permission to draw *two liters of blood* from Scott, supposedly in order to "perform tests"; thankfully she refused. In other words, he had asked her to let him drain almost half the blood in Scott's body, an operation that would undoubtedly have killed him. And what "tests" would have meant anything at that point? That he had metastasized cancer was already well known, and he obviously had only hours to live.

As soon as I heard this, I concluded that the night nurse must have been a Satanist, seeking human blood for some infernal ritual, and with the added "hope" that, if he were able to induce Scott's own mother to agree, unknowingly, to his murder, the evil of the crime would be vastly compounded. (Those pawns of the Devil who are specifically trained in how to employ human death for evil purposes undoubtedly know exactly how to exploit the shock and grief of the dying person's loved ones to work their evil will in service to their Master — and what better job for an enslaved and dedicated Satanist than night nurse in a hospital's terminal ward? Perhaps his attention had been attracted by the richness and beauty of the Russian Orthodox sacraments that Scott had received in his hospital room, the deep sonorous chant, the odor of frankincense. What a rare and perfect chance this would have presented to pervert something high and sacred!) The next day I phoned Alta Bates to report, not that they had a Satanist on their staff (which might have strained credulity), but rather that one of their employees was a "mercy killer." Since I knew Scott's room number, and Jenny remembered the date and the time of the event, they now had all the information they needed to identify the individual involved. A few weeks later I got a call from a woman at the hospital who told me that they were taking my complaint "very seriously."

ST NICHOLAS TAKES POSSESSION OF THE CORPSE

The second wave was harder to understand, though one aspect of it can be laid at the familiar doorstep of the group ego. After Scott passed away a strange thing happened to Fr Stephan: he suddenly became terrified of death. He told us that even though he had been present at many deaths, none of the others had affected him like this. The heavens had opened for all of us when he gave Scott the last rites at Alta Bates, but now this uncharacteristic fear had taken hold of him. At the same time, though Jenny was deeply in mourning for the death of her friend, nobody in the congregation could see it — and when she told Fr Stephan of her grief, he heartlessly dismissed it as overblown and self-indulgent. At the same time, undoubtedly based on Fr Stephan's visionary experience while administering the sacrament of the dying, the congregation of St Nicholas almost immediately glorified Scott as a saint and adopted him as an intercessor, though they had hardly even known him or paid any attention to him while he was alive. Jenny had not only been much closer to him than any of the others were, she had even been largely responsible for his entry into Orthodox Christianity — but none of them remembered that. Because of her relatively low status in the congregation, they actually repressed the fact that she had even known him. And it was this, after many months of struggle with the impenetrable emotional blindness of so many people she'd once felt close to, that finally made it impossible for her to continue to worship at St Nicholas Orthodox Church. Instead, she started driving to St Seraphim's Church in Santa Rosa every Sunday, a round-trip of more than 70 miles. It was a good church, probably healthier than St Nicholas had become by then, not to mention the fact that one of its members was Vincent Rossi; the material hardship of worshipping there was negligible when compared to the emotional hardship of St Nicholas after Scott's passing.

MARK FITZGERALD*

The third wave of darkness that followed Scott's death, not as dark as the first one but certainly dark enough, came in the person of one Dr Mark Fitzgerald, a psychiatrist and Maryamiyya *faqir*. It was through this obsessed and haunted individual that we began to see how the Traditionalist world, like every spiritual world we'd ever traveled through, was not without its dark side, as we were to learn with greater clarity from other sources, farther down the road. One of the earmarks of that world, especially within Schuon's circle in Bloomington, was a clash between profound spiritual insight and an insufficient grounding in the sort of traditional, formal safeguards that work to protect such insight from distortion and attack. Guénon himself was apparently susceptible to such attacks; he even said that he was not qualified to act as a formal spiritual guide or *shaykh* because of the spiritual damage he had sustained during his earlier investigations of the occult. In our own case, such attacks were not slow in arriving—and their first target was Jenny.

Soon after the death of Scott Whitaker, Alvin Moore put us in touch with Dr Fitzgerald, who was on his way from the East Coast to California, and was thinking of converting from Islam to Christianity; Mr Moore hoped that we might be able to help him in this transition, as well as introducing him to the spiritual resources available in the Bay Area. When we first met him we got the impression that he was a new friend who was in some sense a compensation for our loss of Scott—quite a dark compensation, as it turned out. If Scott had been in many ways oblivious to evil—he had said to us once, "but how could there really be Satanists? How could people actually worship evil?"—it was as if Mark was host to the very evil that Scott had been unable to see. (Mark also introduced us to Schuon follower Patrick Laude, another Maryamiyya *faqir*, presently a professor of Theology at Georgetown University, who was soon to be author of *Frithjof Schuon: Life and Teachings*, a book that presents aspects of Schuon's theory and practice, particularly its Native American elements, as if they had been a kind of shamanism—a characterization that I don't particularly agree with. At one point I witnessed Mark, a mischievous smile on his face, doing something magical to Dr Laude, some kind of "etheric tickling" apparently, an invisible and inaudible influence that caused the Professor to dissolve in helpless laughter.)

Mark Fitzgerald was without a doubt the most sinister individual, objectively though not *necessarily* in any intentional way, that it has ever been my misfortune to meet, a person who was undeniably affected with a degree of demonic obsession that sometimes suggested full possession. He was even involved in some way with a severe injury that Jenny received—yet for some reason, probably because he himself was so undeniably injured, more deeply than any of the rest of us, I could never get angry at him. He was closer to being transpersonally toxic than personally offensive—though his personality wasn't the easiest force to deal with either; he was pretty insulting to Jenny and even went so far as to bad-mouth her to Alvin Moore. But instead of being angry with him, I was simply afraid of him—though I wasn't afraid soon enough, as it turned out, to do me or Jenny any good.

Mark Fitzgerald was the proverbial "crazy psychiatrist," who was able to secure employment by taking on situations that nobody else would touch. He applied for work at the worst psych wards, where he could undoubtedly make a real contribution partly because he was at least half as crazy, and just as crazy-psychic, as the inmates were. He was seriously bipolar, though like many people affected with that illness he would often stop taking his meds; the manic phase of his cycle was so seductive, and apparently opened him to such profound insights, that he was even willing to pay for it by the worst agonies of depression.

As a child he had suffered unbelievable traumas. On one occasion his drunken father, fooling around with a shotgun, had accidentally shot his younger brother, who later died; his father had attempted suicide in the car on the way to the hospital. In later life he had become involved with a series of dark spiritualities: first witchcraft; then the Gurdjieff work (a bit less dark); then Cheyenne shamanism, which might not have been dark at all if it were not for the damaged soul that Mark brought to it. His next step had been Islam in the form of Schuon's Maryamiyya—when he had gone on the *Hajj*, one of the other *hajjis* had perceptively called him "the King of the Jinn"—and when we knew him he was investigating, with our help, Eastern Orthodox Christianity and Traditional Catholicism, apparently with a view toward entering the priesthood. He had met not only Schuon but both Rama Coomaraswamy and Malachi Martin, and later Alvin Moore. None of them had apparently had enough discernment-of-spirits to grasp his condition (nor did we, until it was too late), though both Rama and Fr Martin had advised him to become a practicing Catholic for at least ten years before seeking Holy Orders—a piece of advice he ignored.

Mark was somehow wedded to destruction. The first time we were scheduled to meet him was at a café in Berkeley, but we couldn't get there because the police had cordoned off the surrounding streets due to a bomb threat. On another occasion, driving from Marin to meet him at his apartment in Alameda, we couldn't complete the trip because the Richmond-San Rafael Bridge was closed due to a refinery fire. On another attempt, Alameda (a military town) was also closed to make room for some urban warfare exercises. And when we finally got together to venerate the relics of St John Maximovitch on Geary St in San Francisco, as we saw him coming down the sidewalk toward the Cathedral a bar-fight exploded onto the street as soon as he passed the doorway; it almost knocked him over. Nonetheless we took him on an extended tour of the natural beauties and spiritual resources of the Bay Area. We introduced him to Huston Smith, to the Eastern Orthodox world of churches and bookstores, to the Nimatullahi *khaniqa*, drove him to the St Herman of Alaska monastery near Platina in the northern Coast Range, and finally took him to meet a Traditional Catholic priest in Daly City. He was ultimately ordained as a Traditional priest himself at Alvin Moore's home in Albuquerque, New Mexico; the last we heard of him he had plans to "minister to the Indians" in Las Vegas, New Mexico. Did he intend to mix the graces of the Traditional Catholic sacraments with some form of shamanism? I never found out for sure. All I can say is, I pity any Indian unlucky enough to run afoul of him. Be that as it may, the gathering signs of spiritual darkness surrounding Mark Fitzgerald made it necessary for us to break with him at one point—something that threatened to lower us in Alvin Moore's estimation, since the evidence for Mark's connection with the demonic kingdom was not available to him—either that or he didn't possess the criteria to correctly evaluate it.

Nonetheless I did learn some true things from Mark, mostly having to do with the nature of emotions. I learned that the fundamental negative emotions, whose energies are related to the basic elements of the ego—the *nafs*—are *fear, hurt, anger,* and *sadness* (Air, Water, Fire and Earth). Hurt and sadness, though they may be hard to tell apart, are not the same: hurt is the sharp sense of being violated due to the disappointment of expectations, while sadness is the desolate feeling of being lost in an empty world. Nonetheless, these four negative emotional tones also have their positive or "redeemed" aspects. Sadness for example, when redeemed, becomes *repose in Being*, the contemplative *apatheia*; likewise hurt, when redeemed, becomes *submission to the Will of God manifesting as total non-resistance to change.* I also learned that emotions are not entirely subjective or psychological; in an equally valid sense they are objective energies, moving through the subtle etheric plane like clouds across a daytime sky.

But we weren't destined to escape unscathed from our encounter with Mark Fitzgerald, which only showed its fangs after he had left the Bay Area. I had a dream one night that Mark was approaching me with a cocky smile on his face; behind him was Jenny, who was being carried on a stretcher. I and some invisible companions quickly drew knives to defend her. Then, a few days later, while I was working at the Marin County Library, she fell in our house and broke her hip. Recalling this event, I am moved to recite the *Surah al-Falaq*:

> *I seek refuge in the Lord of Daybreak*
> *from the evil of that which he created:*
> *From the evil of the darkness when it is intense,*
> *And from the evil of malignant witchcraft,*
> *And from the evil of the envier when he envieth.*

Damage to the physical body is hard, but—as Jenny always emphasizes—it's nowhere near as hard (in most cases) as emotional damage to the soul.

THE SHADOW OF ORTHODOXY (AND CATHOLICISM)

Seen from a distance of years, I can confidently state that the shadow of Orthodox Christianity, outside of its lack of the kind of explicit sacramental theology that characterized pre-Vatican II Catholicism—which lack results in some Orthodox priests preaching things like "Orthodoxy has an infinite number of sacraments" (something that Bishop Kallistos Ware, for one, would certainly not agree with) — seems to be a deeply-unconscious worldliness, coupled with a prideful possessiveness of "the spiritual treasures of the true faith." Those treasures are entirely real, but the possessiveness with which they often become associated is a dangerous delusion. The Roman Catholic Church, ever since the Counter-Reformation, fought an entirely conscious rear-guard action against the secularism and degeneracy of the modern world, a campaign that only came to an end (except for a "faithful remnant") with the Second Vatican Council, where an accommodation to the world known as *aggiornamento* ("bringing up to date") officially replaced the "My Kingdom is not of this world" of Jesus Christ. Orthodoxy on the other hand, like Islam, never had a Renaissance, or a Reformation, or a Counter-Reformation, with the result that, as Rama Coomaraswamy put it to us once, the Orthodox have no idea what Modernism is — the Modernism that Pope St Pius X called "the sum of all heresies." One of the results of this large blind spot is that modern Orthodox theologians, even while declaring their absolute rejection of Catholicism, will sometimes accept, with maddening irony to those in the know, the post-conciliar heresies of the Novus Ordo Catholic Church as "Orthodox" doctrine without the slightest idea of where they came from. For example, Jenny and I heard preached in more than one Orthodox church in California and at least one Orthodox church in Kentucky a doctrine that denies the intrinsic immortality of the human soul, claiming that such an idea was wrong because it was "Greek." Never mind that Orthodox Christianity grew up in the Greek culture-area of the eastern Mediterranean that included Byzantium — thus "Greek Orthodoxy" — or that Platonism made a massive contribution to Orthodox theology, at least in its mode of expression — or that saints universally venerated in the Orthodox world, such as Dionysius the Pseudo-Areopagite, were Christian Platonists or Neo-Platonists. The doctrine in question, known as "conditionalism" or "annihilationism," holds that "the soul is immortal by Grace not by nature," and therefore that those who reject the Atonement of Christ do not go to eternal punishment as the Gospels declare, but are simply annihilated, either immediately upon death or after the general resurrection. This notion, which contradicts both scripture and the preponderance of opinion of the Church Fathers, apparently entered Orthodoxy from Evangelical Protestantism in the 19th Century; some even trace it back as far as the Deist, rationalist and quasi-materialist philosopher Thomas Hobbes of the English Enlightenment. And it is certainly in agreement with the declaration of Cardinal Joseph Ratzinger, who was to become Pope Benedict XVI, in his book *Introduction to Christianity*, that "the notion of an immortal soul is now 'obsolete.'" What this idea fails to consider is that all things are given their natures by God through an act of gratuitous creation, *ex nihilo*, which means that the universe itself, since it is a creature, does not exist "by nature" but only "by Grace," and God certainly has both the right and the power to create a being—humanity—who, though contingent, is nonetheless immortal by participation in His immortality. Neither Jenny nor I could accept any doctrine that denies the immortality of all human souls since it is at odds with "the mind of the Fathers," and inevitably leads to the idea that one could commit all imaginable sins and never have to pay for them; death is not the Moment of Truth and the encounter with Divine Justice according to a conception like that, but simply a dark nihilistic void that cancels all debts—the inevitable consequence of this being that Hell is now and always has been empty of human souls. (As for the *eternity* of Hell, I also have certain difficulties with that doctrine—difficulties that, as already indicated above, I have tentatively resolved by speculating that, while repentance in Hell is impossible, nor can individual souls escape the rigors of Divine justice simply through annihilation, the "day" will come—at what Origen called the *apocatastasis* and the Hindus the *mahapralaya*, the return of universal manifestation to its transcendent Source—when Hell itself, along with all the Paradises of Form, will be reabsorbed into the eternal reality of the Godhead.)

Anyone who wants to understand the definitive Orthodox argument against conditionalism should read *The Immortality of the Soul* by Constantine Cavarnos. Jenny phoned Carvarnos on one occasion to complain about this teaching in contemporary Orthodox churches; he was shocked to hear that such a doctrine was being preached. And so, for all the beauty of the Orthodox churches and the Divine Liturgy, and the valid sacraments celebrated according to the ancient, traditional forms, and the miracle-working icons, when false doctrine is being openly preached, that's the time to say good-bye. The upshot was that Jenny, after we moved to Kentucky and became better acquainted with Rama Coomaraswamy, moved on from Orthodoxy to *sedevacantist* Catholicism, which has the great good fortune of being hated not only by the world but by the apostate Novus Ordo Catholic Church as well, and even by some of the Orthodox—though, as Jenny asks, why should they complain in particular about *sedevacantist* Catholicism when, according to their own doctrines, the entire Western Church has been apostate since 1054? Only, I would say, because they secretly identify with the post-conciliar Catholic Church, mistaking what is merely established for what is truly orthodox. Such contradictions as these, however, will never trouble the easy, comfortable, convinced Orthodox believer of today. Such a person has no difficulties with logical inconsistency since he or she will likely never notice it—possibly because consistency itself is easily dismissed as "the hair-splitting, Jesuitical casuistry of the Latin church." Given that Orthodox sanctity, gnosis and loyalty to revelation far transcend mere philosophical thought, to require acceptance of even the simplest $2 + 2 = 4$ logical proposition is considered to be beneath the dignity of the Orthodox mind—or, as I should rather say, beneath the pride of the Orthodox system-of-sentiments. And I shudder to think (though, from my present vantage-point, I have no way of knowing) what further impetus the Russia/Ukraine war may have added to the Orthodox temptation to become eaten up with worldly identifications. During Jenny's Orthodox period we met a large, bearded Russian iconographer named Alexander, who gave us a keen sense of how the oppression of Orthodox Christianity under Communism might actually have kept the faith honest. Under the Soviet system, "icon-writing" was illegal, so Alexander and his colleagues had to carry on their art in secrecy, which put them in the path of what Dietrich Bonhoeffer called "expensive grace." What will perhaps never be known is whether Russian Orthodoxy was better off (in a strictly spiritual sense) under state persecution than it is now under the "cheap grace" regime of state patronage.

It would be going way too far, however, to imply that Communism never changed or damaged Orthodoxy. Every religion emphasizes group-identity to one degree or another—the Buddhist *sangha*, the Muslim *ummah*, the Christian Mystical Body—but when group-identity takes precedence over individual sanctity or enlightenment, the religion in question has been transformed from a Way into an idol. Group religious identity exists to support individual sanctity, not replace it—and Orthodoxy as we knew it was certainly not immune to this kind of idolatry. The developing dogma claimed that "we are only saved in Community," immediately reminding one of the Marxist doctrine that negates individual human destiny in favor of the destiny of the class, in this case the proletariat. The Desert Fathers of Egypt and Syria however, to whom the life of the anchorite or hermit was central, held the opposite view, even going so far as to warn against excessive Christian "fellowship" as an occasion of sin. Some of the monks would only come out of their caves once a year, on Pascha, and travel to the city to attend Divine Liturgy; on these occasions they were often admonished by their elders to "guard your souls and your consciences, monks—we are going to church!" It is undeniably true, however, that those who have put God first in their hearts form a "supernaturally natural" community, a "communion of the saints." This community, however, is not socially but supernaturally based. True Christian community is not a product of any effort to promote fellowship; rather, the fellowship it manifests is the end result of "the flight of the alone to the Alone." The healthy and spiritually supportive congregation is not born in the world's marketplace but in the monk's cell—with the proviso that the first and last cell is the Spiritual Heart. There is a tendency, however, in both Orthodoxy and Novus Ordo Roman Catholicism, to make religious affiliation paramount, to call for the dissolution of the individual ego not in God but in group identification. How much of this collectivist bias might have entered Orthodoxy from contemporary Catholicism is hard to say, but there is no doubt in my mind that pre-Vatican II Catholicism (like the Traditional Catholicism of today) placed much more of an emphasis on individual spiritual practice, mostly via the rosary. I know this because I was there. Since the Mass was in Latin, the faithful could simply accept the prayers of the priest as establishing the sacred ambience that allowed for, and supported, individual devotion. The priest was doing his thing, talking with God on behalf of the people, at an altar that faced not toward the people but toward the Beyond. But when the altars were de-commissioned, despoiled of their sacred relics, and the "table" turned toward the congregation, priest and people were sealed together into a group-identification that excluded all sense of the Divine Transcendence — an orientation that, in Orthodoxy, is still supported (symbolically at least) by the *iconostasis*. (Those who want get a clear visceral sense of the significance of this loss of Transcendence in the Novus Ordo Catholic Mass should try to find a DVD or streamed version of the TV movie *Catholics* — later re-titled *The Conflict* — starring Martin Sheen, Trevor Howard and Cyril Cusack.)

JEREMY HENZELL-THOMAS AND SACRED ENGLAND

In 2001, a few years before we emigrated from California, I was unexpectedly tapped by Shaykh Kabir Helminski of the Mevlevi Sufi Order, who had published my poetry book *Doorkeeper of the Heart: Versions of Rabi'a*, to contribute to *The Book of Character*, one of a series of volumes published by The Book Foundation, dedicated to revisioning Islam for the 21st Century; some of the things I wrote for that project formed the basis of my own book *Virtues of the Prophet*. The Foundation paid my way to England, where I met with British Muslims Jeremy Henzell-Thomas and his wife Tanya. As the generous hosts they were, they made it possible for me to touch two of the sacred bases — one light, one dark — that meant Britain to me: Glastonbury and Stonehenge.

Stonehenge on the day we visited was nearly deserted, and presented a fairly informal aspect: nothing but some tall, undressed stones standing in a green cow pasture. Yet as I meditated upon them, a powerful impression was transmitted, which I set down in the following poem while waiting at Gatwick Airport for my flight back to the U.S.:

A Visit to the Stone Clock

Sun Moon and Stars work on wires, across an iron sky
Over bloody Stonehenge.

Wizards torture power
Out of known tensions of conjunction and opposition
To lay down on Britain
An iron rule.

> They cry down the Guardians themselves,
>   ground their massive charge—
> Till ancient terror of magic sails along the lines
> From stone to stone:
> No mercy, only titanic power
> In those sentinels.
>
> May we never dare to remember
> What they most certainly knew.

Whether this grim sense of wizardry derived from the original character of the place, or from one of the darker phases in its long history, or only from the neo-Pagan ambience laid down in recent years, is impossible to say; yet I can't forget William Blake's negative take on Druidry, which, in line with the contemporary conception, he connected with Stonehenge, though the temple was actually built much earlier than the advent of Celtic/Druidic England. As S. Foster Damon says in *A Blake Dictionary*:

> Blake accepted the common belief and used Stonehenge as a symbol of the evil Druid religion and its human sacrifices. It was built by the warriors, and is Natural Religion (*Jerusalem* 66:2,8). Here the daughters of Albion torture their victims (*Jerusalem* 66:20); here Brittania murdered Albion with "the knife of the Druid" (*Jerusalem* 94:25).

Glastonbury was infinitely more congenial and uplifting. I found it a hive of New Age activity, with every other shop a Witch Shoppe or an Elf Shoppe or a Pagan Shoppe; the scent of White Sage (imported from California) filled the air. One shop, however was run by Eastern Orthodox monks; that's where I purchased an Orthodox icon of Our Lady of Glastonbury, around whose border appeared a series of portraits of the local Celtic or Saxon saints. The psychic ambience was a cacophony of dissonant vibrations and disembodied voices—but as soon as one stepped into the precincts of the ruined Abbey, dissolved by Henry VIII who also had its abbot executed, a preternatural quiet descended. After passing by a New Age damsel, undulating and with her arms raised to heaven, as if in hopes that the sons of God might look upon her and find her fair, we came to the reputed tomb of King Arthur and Gwenivere, and then to the Chalice Well, in whose waters I performed the *wudu*, the Muslim ablution-before-prayer. I saw and touched the Glastonbury Thorn, or rather a descendant of the original, after which we left the Abbey grounds and climbed the hill on which stood the Glastonbury Tor, *lingam* to the Chalice Well's *yoni*, together recapitulating the Lance and Grail of the Arthurian romances. When I reached the top of the hill where the Tor stands, hollow like a chimney standing open for sanctified souls to ascend like smoke, I immediately asked my companion Jeremy, "Which way is NORTH?" "You must mean 'which way is WEST'" he replied—the track of St Brendan, the quarter of Numinor and Skellig Michael, the

True West. "No, NORTH" I answered, because that's my orientation — or, more accurately, my *boreation*: toward Caer Sidi, "the revolving castle," the name the Welsh gave to the constellations surrounding the North Star, "the still point of the turning world" in Eliot's phrase, the visible point of Eternity in the created order. North is a pretty tough direction, being the direct route to Hyperborea, "the land behind the North Wind," totally avoiding the Western Path, whose gate is simple physical death, mitigated by unconsciousness and the laying down of the body: if you embark on the Northern route instead, you will have to pass, fully alive, through the arctic cold of death-in-life to get to Hyperborea, the land of eternal Spring. As Blake expressed the awe of that passage in *The Book of Thel*,

> The Eternal Gates' terrific porter lifted the northern bar...

Among other things, my visit to the Abbey of Our Lady of Glastonbury, which according to legend was the first Christian site in England, founded by Joseph of Arimathea, gave me insight into the otherwise cryptic meaning of the Prologue to William Blake's *The Marriage of Heaven and Hell*, and resulted in the following exposition:

An Exegesis of the Prologue to William Blake's The Marriage of Heaven and Hell, *Inspired by a Visit to Glastonbury, With an Appendix on the Legend of the Grail*

I am an American poet whose bloodlines flow mostly back to Britain. On a recent visit to Somerset, guided there by my British host and hostess who dearly love the place, my British ancestral mythopoetic unconscious was stirred and opened:

> Rintrah roars and shakes his fires in the burdened air
> Hungry clouds swag on the deep.

Rintrah, according to S. Foster Damon's *A Blake Dictionary*, is the symbol of God's wrath in William Blake's mythology. The clouds are ships of the Royal Navy under full sail, "swaggering" on proud and warlike missions for the Empire; these first two lines are allusions to the atmosphere of the times in which Blake was writing, times of the American Revolution, the British counter-revolution (which led in England to popular protests much like those in America against the Vietnam War), the French Revolution, and, in reaction to it, the suppression of domestic liberties; Blake himself was once tried for sedition.

> Once meek and in a perilous path,
> The just man kept his course along
> The vale of death.
> Roses are planted where thorns grow,
> And on the barren heath
> Sing the honey bees.

The monks at Glastonbury, where the Thorn grew, and who (as I learned from a friend of our hosts, who served us her rose nectar made according to a monkish recipe) cultivated roses (sacred to the Virgin Mary, the patroness of Glastonbury Abbey), kept to the straight path of salvation, the path of self-annihilation, of death-before-death, in the Vale of Avalon, which, as a mask of the Celtic otherworld, is also the vale of death. And monks, like bees, live in cells. I myself saw beekeepers in Glastonbury.

> Then the perilous path was planted,
> And a river and a spring,
> On every cliff and tomb
> And on the bleached bones
> Red clay brought forth.

The monks were martyred and planted in their graves, but planted only to sprout up again in resurrection — and the bloody spring of Glastonbury (the water so *chalybeate*, so infused with iron, that it tastes like blood) is their martyr's blood springing from the ground, reddening (as I saw with my own eyes) with iron rust the little cliff of masonry over which it pours, then flowing into Arthur and Gwenivere's tomb (which is directly down hill from the spring), they who represent all the dead of England, and the Earth too — in aggregate none other than Adam the Primordial Humanity, whose name means "red clay." The vivifying blood of the martyred monks raises Arthur from his tomb (who is Adam, and thus a type of Blake's Albion), clothing his bones and Gwenivere's in living flesh. (There is strife in that tomb; I fear for the day it is opened.)

> Then the villain left the paths of ease
> To walk in perilous paths, and drive
> The just man into barren climes.

If "the perilous path" is the path of religion, then it was King Henry VIII who took the perilous path of declaring himself pope of the English church, and driving the monks, the just men, from their monasteries.

> Now the sneaking serpent walks in mild humility

The priest of the Church of England has now abdicated his spiritual function and become the propagandist for British imperialism, the hypocritical spirit who fills the sails of those "hungry clouds."

> And the just man rages in the wilds where lions roam.

The Holy Spirit, having abandoned King and Church, has gone into the social wilderness to inspire marginalized and wrathful prophets — like Blake himself.

But the resurrection of Arthur is ambiguous, in line with Blake's identification of the Druid religion (Arthur's mentor was Druid Merlin) with vengeance and political oppression, as opposed to the reign of Christ, based on the forgiveness of sins. So if the return of Arthur is the return of Primordial, Adamic Man, it is also the revolt of pagan Druidism and the cult of the warrior-king against the "just men" of Christianity—a revolt personified by King Henry, which has ultimately led in our time to the capitulation of a large sector of the Anglican/Episcopal church to Neo-Paganism, including even (in America at least) witchcraft. (It is really the standard-bearer in this regard. Not only is contemporary England arguably the most secular nation in the history of Western Europe, but the Episcopal Church in the U.S., according to a recent survey, has the largest number of *atheists* of any Christian denomination.)

Well are Blake's books called Prophetic! When Blake wrote, in that lyric from his *Jerusalem*, "And did those feet in ancient time/ Walk upon England's mountains green?" he was alluding to the legend of Joseph of Arimathea, who is said to have been a tin merchant and great uncle of the Virgin Mary, and to have taken the boy Jesus to England on one of his trading journeys, landing near the mines of Somerset, the Vale then being an inlet if the sea. And when he wrote: "I will not cease from mental fight/ Nor shall my sword sleep in my hand/ Till we have built Jerusalem/ In England's green and pleasant land," he was, in a way, declaring himself a one-man non-Roman Catholic esoteric English counter-reformation.

And the Grail

The Chalice Well at Glastonbury, with its water that tastes like blood, is, precisely, the Holy Grail. The site was reputedly the earliest Christian site in Britain, founded by Joseph of Arimathea, who, according to legend, brought the Grail containing Christ's blood to Glastonbury after the crucifixion; the monks would readily have identified that chalybeate water with the blood of the Savior, who is sometimes called a Fountain of Living Water.

The Chalice Well incarnates the lesser, feminine, psychic mysteries, the return to the "Adamic" state, to the human essence as God created it, the realization of the Earthly Paradise. The Tor on the hill directly above, sacred to St Michael, on St Michael's Ley, is the Vertical Path, the *axis mundi*, a ray of the greater, masculine, Spiritual mysteries which lead to the transcendence of the human state, to Union with God. (First Lethe, then Eunoë; first the Earthly Paradise, then the *Paradiso* itself.) St Michael in his icons is most often pictured carrying a lance—and so the mystery of the pairing of the Grail with the ever-bleeding Lance in the Grail romances, that so exercised Jessie Weston, is no mystery: the blood which mingles with the pure water of the Chalice Well ultimately comes from Above; the spear of Longinus piercing the side of the crucified Christ, the lance of St Michael, and the upright beam of the Cross itself (like the Tor, and like Blake's engravings of "Jacob's Ladder" and "The Last Judgement") are renditions of the *axis mundi*, the path that unites the created universe with its invisible Source.

And one more thing: On the border of the Orthodox Christian icon of Our Lady of Glastonbury (who is overshadowed by a smaller figure of St Michael, bearing the lance, and who bears in her right hand the Thorn and in her left the Christ Child, himself carrying a globe of the heavens) are represented many ancient, local Christian saints, one of whom is St Kea. Upon my return to California I consulted Eastern Orthodox lay nun Katherine McCaffrey, a trove of spiritual and historical lore, about who these saints were, and encountered the story, in one of her reference books on Eastern Orthodox saints, that St Kea was King Arthur's chaplain, who packed Gwenivere off to a nunnery after her adultery with Launcelot and the dissolution of the Round Table. He was Arthur's *staretz* (Russian) his *geron* (Greek). So he was undoubtedly the same figure as the Sir Kai of the Round Table, Arthur's *seneschal*, which also means "elder" or "old man." Kea is the Church image, and Kai the knightly or warrior image, of the same man. Sir Kai was a foul-mouthed, vain and curmudgeonly older knight, threatened by the prowess of younger and stronger men; imagine this as the picture keen young warriors would have had of a pious, admonishing, older Christian monk—St Kea—in a time when the Christianization of Britain was far from complete.

I returned to America with a vial of water from the Chalice Well (which was being periodically blessed at that time by Glastonbury's Orthodox monks), half of which I gave to Kitty McCaffrey for her freely-given teachings, while the other half still contributes an increasingly rarefied and therefore ever-more-homeopathically-concentrated fraction to the holy water we still use to purify our home, here in Lexington, Kentucky.

I BECOME A METAPHYSICAL WRITER

Under the influence of the Traditionalists, of Seraphim Rose (to a degree) and of Islamic Sufism, I began to crank out books on traditional metaphysics, comparative religion, comparative eschatology, UFOlogy (one of Fr Seraphim's areas of research), demonology, the metaphysical exegesis of mythopoesis, and spiritual psychology, from 2001 till the present day. I did what I could to update Guénon's critique of false spiritualities, and apply Schuon's doctrines to various areas he neglected, or wasn't particularly interested in, including the genre of traditional folk ballads (though Ananda Coomaraswamy had apparently planned to write a book on that subject) and the western romantic tradition. The Traditionalist/Perennialist world was rich with intellectual stimulation and went a long way toward helping me purify my soul, on the intellectual level at least, from the false notions I had embraced in my years with the hippie counterculture and the New Age. This is not to say, however, that Perennialism didn't have certain problems of its own, as I have already mentioned above. Frithjof Schuon for one, like so many "gurus," Catholic priests and Evangelical Protestants in the late 20th century, was hit with major scandals, though nothing was ever proved against him in court. He was investigated at one point by an Indiana grand jury, but no indictment ultimately emerged.

EVALUATING THE TRADITIONALISTS

Nonetheless, despite the scandals and the negative reports by various disgruntled followers from the Schuon world we encountered over the years, I would certainly recommend that anyone who is serious about the spiritual Path, unless he or she has already embraced an entirely congenial version of that Path, should read the works of the Traditionalists, including the books of Frithjof Schuon, which saved me from so much darkness and gave me the kind of solid intellectual standpoint without which I could never have embarked on a true spiritual Path. At this point, however, I feel that I have absorbed from them all I was destined to absorb, which is why I now consider myself a "graduate" of the Traditionalist School rather than an active member. But though I call myself a graduate, and am now concentrating almost exclusively upon Islam and the Sufi Path, still, I haven't thrown away my diploma. For some spiritual temperaments, the Traditionalists or Perennialists are the best possible introduction to comparative religion and traditional metaphysics, though in the area of spiritual psychology and practical guidance on the Path they have less to offer. Nonetheless, like virtually no-one else in the modern world, they have enunciated certain *necessary* principles relating to religion, its source in God, and its relationship both to the metaphysical order and to human society and history. I believe that a knowledge of these principles is indispensable if we are to correctly orient ourselves to the spiritual quality of our time: a time of enforced religious pluralism, of the weakening, adulteration and perversion of the ancient Divine revelations and wisdom traditions, as well as of the availability of unexpected channels of Grace—the sort of Grace that our apocalyptic times require, and that God has therefore mercifully provided.

In my view, however, One of the ironic blind-spots of the Perennialists is that they sometimes seem to believe that the intellectually elevated treatment of the world's religions and wisdom-traditions, at least within the context of the modern world, began with them, with René Guénon or else with Frithjof Schuon; the notion that they might have had certain useful predecessors or heralds even in the hippie counterculture (Richard Alpert, for example, or Alan Watts, or Huston Smith in his counterculture years) would be a shocking scandal to them—nor am I certain that the generation of Perennialism-identified seekers that followed Schuon is sufficiently aware of the renewed interest in Perennialism among even some Gen-Z-ers; too many of us older folks seem to believe that "revelation" ended with Frithjof Schuon, who was more or less "The Seal of the Perennialists." And Schuon himself seemed generally oblivious to the course of spiritual seeking that some of his students had followed to arrive at his door; he undoubtedly saw the lowlife Bohemian aspects of the counterculture and consequently dismissed it—one of his more prominent followers, Mark Perry, in an email to my wife and myself, referred to the hippies as "human weeds"—but Schuon was largely unaware of its undeniably Traditionalist aspects, chaotic and intermittent though they were, as well as of certain resemblances between his own organization and the hippies he deplored, as witness his attraction to the mystical aspects of many different religions, his interest in Native American spirituality, his appreciation for "sacred nudity" as expressed in his "*shakti* paintings," his difficulties with "organized religion" etc. etc.—though he was clearly operating on a much higher level, both intellectually and aesthetically, than they were. Seen from a Tolkienesque standpoint, and given the obvious drawbacks of caricature as cultural analysis, it's as if the hippies were the Hobbits and the Schuonian Perennialists were the Elves.

Be that as it may, I can confidently state that the works of the Traditionalist writers (with a few notable exceptions) can provide a thorough introduction to Traditional spirituality—on the intellectual level. On the existential level, however, Frithjof Schuon's belief that his high degree of metaphysical understanding authorized him to found a Sufi *tariqah* that departed in several important respects from the tradition of orthodox *tasawwuf*, while still holding on to the "orthodox" and "Traditionalist" labels, ended up imposing a more-or-less heterodox *praxis* on Schuon's almost entirely orthodox *theoria*, a stark though unacknowledged contradiction that has been profoundly confusing and heart-wrenching to many over the years. Rama Coomaraswamy, for one, said to us that "this has never happened before!" Nonetheless, in hindsight, this development can be pretty well classified as one of the drearily predictable manifestations of the Latter Days. Did Schuon's *tariqah* ultimately serve the assimilation of his true teachings, or did it stand in the way of that assimilation? And did the contradictions it generated, like those arising from any war or personal disaster, put certain people through the kind of spiritual transformations and purifications that they would otherwise never have had the courage or the opportunity to face? As we Muslims say when confronted with unanswerable questions like this—at least unanswerable in this world—"and Allah knows best."

MY FRIEND RANDY CARSON, AND MY LOSS OF HIM: THE REACTION AGAINST TRADITIONAL SPIRITUALITY BY THE DARKNESS OF THIS WORLD

When you undergo a major change in your life, a true *metanoia*, sometimes you don't immediately grasp all the implications of it. You know that you've entered into something new, but you may not realize that you will also have to let go of certain things that have *suddenly become old*. You act as if you can simply build your new life on top of your old one, treating it as one more definable acquisition or layer of experience, with no demolition of the earlier structures or any establishing of a new foundation required.

If you operate according to this limited view, however, old patterns that haven't been cleared out yet may imperceptibly creep up to eat into your new edifice like termites—either that, or your old life may suddenly jump you from a dark alley, commit a kidnapping (spiritually speaking) or mount a home invasion. Old ways that you once identified with always hate to be betrayed; if you have the heartless temerity to leave them behind, simply ditch them, in their silent outrage they may plot their revenge, and then assault you when you least expect it. (The same thing often happens after you have experienced a high spiritual state: the lower aspects of your soul will rise up in response, either to drag you back to your former level and negate the effects of the Grace you've received, or else to be purified by that same Grace, after which their toxic residues will be eliminated and their spiritually helpful aspects integrated into your new pattern of life.)

As my identification with the hippie counterculture and the New Age continued to fade, I began to glimpse the evil in them that had been hidden from me by that very identification. It had been staring me in the face all along, but I couldn't see it because I had chosen to fix my eyes on the ideal while ignoring the actual. As I've observed so many times in this book, I was in Søren Kierkegaard's "despair of possibility"; my mantra in those days (from the album "Everything You Know is Wrong" by the Firesign Theatre) was: "Could be, could be!"—forgetting what Bill Trumbly had said when I asked him what he'd learned from LSD, which is definitely worth repeating: "I learned that everything is possible, but nothing is likely." God, however, is what *must* be—and what was required to be in my life at that moment, after I had finally seen the evil of the world I'd been immersed in for so long, was a violent blow up with my best friend Randy Carson, one that ended our relationship of many years at a single stroke.

Randy's spiritual path was *aikido*, the subtlest of the Japanese martial arts. Based on that practice he had developed a powerful and sophisticated method of conflict resolution, which he later put to work to catalyze the startup of several major tech corporations; at one point he even applied his skills as a mediator between the Orthodox Christians and the Muslims on the island of Cyprus. He ultimately became a world class management consultant and social mediator. Yet—at least when I knew him—the quality of "blessed are the poor in spirit, for they shall see God" was not in him. Spirituality, to him, was not a gift to be received with gratitude, but an achievement to be gloried in.

I had first known Randy as an itinerant poet living the life of a nomad in a Ford van with his wife Rachel*. When he arrived in Marin County he asked after the local poets, and was directed to me and Calvin Scott; we ended up reading poetry together in the Poets in the Schools program. Though Randy lived more or less the life of a hippie, he did not really have a hippie character. He was not a habitual dope smoker and was serious about Zen and the art of haiku; his bible was the classic *Zen in English Literature and Oriental Classics* by R. H. Blyth. In those days he was an exemplary character in every way, and a true friend. In some ways he was like an older brother to me, someone who combined the best of the Bohemian lifestyle with a solid and responsible character that was rare in the counterculture—which means that if the Devil gets him, Randy will make quite a trophy. I stayed with him through the birth of his two daughters, and often visited him at his home in Inverness.

However, this life situation was not to last. After a rocky divorce, which was obviously deeply traumatic to him, his connection with the "peaceful" martial art of aikido—in which he became highly proficient, a black belt at least—went to his head. The true spirit of that art is expressed in the book *The Art of Peace* by the founder of aikido, Morihei Ueshiba, known as Ō Sensei (Great Teacher)—yet on one occasion his aikido instructor actually broke his ribs on purpose with a single blow, to "teach" him in the most emphatic terms that he was relying on personal skill and power rather than the immanent Will of God that the Chinese call the Tao—an attitude that was totally opposed to the spirit of aikido. At the same time his move from public sector social service to the exalted echelons of the *private sector itself* lifted him to a level of drunken hubris that reminded me of nothing so much as the performance of Jack Palance as the Roman centurion in the movie *Barabbas*, fighting from a chariot in the Colosseum against Anthony Quinn on foot, who played the title role. I remember how once, after we'd watched Akira Kurosawa's great film *Seven Samurai* together at a cheap local showing in Point Reyes Station, he declared, intoxicated with the image of martial valor: "We're *warriors*, man!"—which was certainly not in the spirit of the last two lines of the film, spoken by two of the survivors, the veterans of many engagements, whose companions-in-arms had been killed in battle: "Again we have survived—" "Again we are defeated."

As for the traumatic aspects of his divorce, one story is highly revealing. His wife Rachel, who had a background as an undercover operative with the Pinkerton Detective Agency, one told him: "The reason I don't want to have sex with you any more is that I'm afraid of getting pregnant—so get a vasectomy." Randy complied, after which she came back with: "Sorry—I guess that wasn't really it." Rachel worked for Planned Parenthood at one point; I first became suspicious of that organization when I heard her describe unborn fetuses as "parasites." Those suspicions were reinforced when allegations later emerged that Planned Parenthood had engaged, legally or otherwise, in the sale of infant body-parts. I hasten to add that, while the attitudes of Randy and Rachel toward abortion emerged in some ways from the counterculture, the original hippies often had an entirely different take on that issue. Ken Kesey once wrote, in the *Whole Earth Catalogue*, that abortion-on-demand was the major fly in the ointment of the whole emerging Liberal-counterculture ethos. And the well-known hippie spiritual leader Steve Gaskin, who used to speak at a venue known as The Family Dog on the Great Highway in San Francisco, and later on led of one of the most successful of the hippie communes—"the Farm" in Lewis County, Tennessee, which is still in operation—was also opposed to abortion. As an alternative, the Farm publicly offered to deliver any baby for free and then find a loving family to raise it—and if the birth mother ever wanted the child back she could have it. Ultimately most women who accepted or considered Gaskin's offer opted to keep their babies. Even Gavin Arthur, the astrologer who had cast Lew Welch's horoscope and known W. B. Yeats—radical sexologist and gay liberation pioneer that he was—recounted his memory of once having been aborted himself (since he believed in reincarnation) which he described as the most horrible experience imaginable. So it might not be going too far to say that the "classical" hippies loved life, while the ultra-Liberals of today generally hate it.

Be that as it may, my relationship with Randy was destined to become the flashpoint that highlighted the depth of the change I'd gone through when I rejected the counterculture and adopted the worldview of the Traditionalists and the Sufi Path. We had been spiritual seekers together in the counterculture years, and also a little later during the time when the general "default religion" was Buddhism—so when we finally went our separate ways, we were not entirely aware of how deeply we had diverged. My years with Santa Venetia Presbyterian Church, even though no church ever smoked more marijuana or was closer to the hippie commune I'd never had in the '60s than Santa Venetia, was still the beginning of that change, while my induction into Traditionalism and Sufism completed it, since this step required me to break with the counterculture consciously. This was due to the fact that the Traditionalist world, for all its problems, was still on a vastly higher spiritual plane than the counterculture, or what the counterculture was then turning into. But Randy had never made that break; he simply grew beyond the earlier hippie phase of the counterculture and embraced its New Age "yuppie" phase, as spearheaded by the kind of people who were generally centered around Esalen Institute. He took with him into the corporate world whatever the yuppies could glean from hippie spirituality, Buddhism, the Sino-Japanese martial arts, neo-shamanism, and the creations of the developing counterculture intelligentsia, packaged as various management-training paradigms, through the frameworks of "Organizational Development" or "Organizational Transformation," on the theory that (or based on the excuse that) we should "work within the system to change the system." I, on the other hand, was cleaning houses along with my wife in rich laid-back Marin County, and later working with a homeless service agency. And since I had become a serious alcoholic at one point, I had to "clean up my act" more radically than he was ever required to. Where he had expanded, developed and advanced, I had only *repented*, and—since there was nowhere else for me to go—I was forced to place myself in God's hands. Randy's way was spiritual achievement, with all the accolades that accompanied it; my way was spiritual poverty, the path of the Sufis, the *fuqara*—a word, the plural of *faqir*, that means "the poor"; the very "poor in spirit (who) shall see God" spoken of in Matthew 5:3. In part of myself, of course, I still wanted to be wealthy and recognized, yet it was decreed for me that my only access to that wealth would be through the patronage of Allah as *Al-Ghani*, "the Rich." All I could do was stand with the other beggars at His back door, and not even try to push to the head of that impoverished, ragged line, seeing that *God is rich (without need), and you are poor (and needy)* [Q. 47:38].

Various signs of the impending crash between myself and Randy began appearing. On one occasion he showed me a book he was very impressed with—a book on "Nazi spirituality." He also had a coffee table book of black and white photos of Japanese samurai executioners, possibly those who played the role of the *kaishakunin*, the "squire" of the man who commits *seppuku*, ritual suicide, whose job it was to behead him after he disembowels himself. He told me (though I haven't been able to confirm that such things actually take place in today's Japan) that these men "practiced" on condemned criminals, something that was certainly not in line with the spirit of *kendo* (the Way of the Sword) as expressed by D.T. Suzuki in his *Zen and the Samurai*. What does beheading unarmed opponents have to do with the honor of a warrior? Be that as it may, the event that actually precipitated the blowup had to do with Randy's daughters, Olive* and Ruby*.

The clash and final parting of our ways happened like this: At one point, with nothing apparently leading up to it, Randy revealed to me that his daughters had volunteered to be sex councilors on a "sex hotline" out of San Francisco; I believe that even Olive, the older daughter, was still under age at the time, and Ruby certainly was. In the course of their "training" they had visited a number of S&M and fetish-oriented sex clubs, something Randy was entirely OK with; he actually seemed proud of his daughters for demonstrating such *maturity*. (At one point, not surprisingly, Olive expressed her desire to train as a surrogate sex therapist.) Then, using the expertise they'd gained, his daughters instructed their father in a new and improved form of masturbation that involved stimulation of the prostate.

It was on that occasion that I discovered one of the ways in which evil *recruits* you; as a journalist covering the Vietnam War once put it,

"I learned that you are as responsible for what you see as for what you do." If I had been oblivious enough or weak enough to let those horrible revelations pass without the appropriate response, if I had repressed them or shrugged them off like I was supposed to, then evil would have hooked me — perhaps permanently; this is how the unexpected disclosure of dark realities can be used to *coerce compliance*. But I didn't shrug them off — thank God. I offered instead the appropriate response, which was to rip into my former friend with all the fury that was in me, accusing him of corrupting his own daughters as no father should ever be allowed to do, and finally ending that perfectly deserved and terminal condemnation with: "AND NOW — GOODBYE!"

That was the moment when my old life that I thought I had left behind rose up to bite me — and I have no doubt that it did so consciously and deliberately, based on the strategic plans of the demons who managed it. The gauntlet had been thrown down; the ball was now in my court. All that those demons required of me was that I *remain silent*; that I make it easy both on myself and on my friend Randy; that I call upon my identity as a counterculture afficionado and a "man of the world" to take those revelations in stride, seeing that to openly express how shocked and appalled I was at what had happened to my friend would have been insufferably *unhip*. "Just put hipness above holiness" the demons whispered, "and everything will be cool." So what if Randy had as much as groomed and trafficked his own daughters? What's wrong with that? After all, he was not trafficking them to lowlife criminal types, but to the successful, upscale, legal world where they would become not *prostitutes* (heaven or hell forbid), but licensed surrogate sex therapists, frequenting sophisticated society and making good money — and even *working without pimps*. My reaction, however, was in no way cool; it was incandescent as the surface of the Sun; it burned like an acetylene torch through the steel chain that had once united us.

But why, exactly, was this violent reaction necessary? Couldn't I just have calmly faded away? I still believe that the answer is "no" — because that revelation was a deliberate assault on me personally and on everything and everyone I loved. If I had *simply accepted* that profoundly poisonous manifestation and tried to play it cool, that world of decadence and degeneracy — to speak as precisely as I can — would have had me by the balls. In moral terms it was nothing less than an attempted abduction, and when the thugs are trying to wrestle you into the back seat of the car you'd better fight tooth and nail, with every weapon at your disposal.

Everybody repeats the words of Jesus, "Judge not lest ye be judged," but few quote the whole passage, which goes on to say "For with what judgment ye judge, ye shall be judged: and with what measure ye mete, it shall be measured to you again" — in other words, "because you will be judged by the identical standards according to which you judge another, you'd best proceed at your own risk." Jesus was not saying "never judge"; if so, he certainly didn't practice what he preached. What else was his characterization of the Pharisees as "whitewashed tombs filled with rotting corpses" but the sternest judgment possible? What he was actually declaring was that the judgment of God is objective and impartial; once it is called for it falls on the entire situation and everyone in it. *Invoking Divine judgment does not make you immune from it.* On that occasion I *was* judged according the criterion I'd used to judge the spiritual state of Randy Carson; I judged precisely so that I *would* be judged, which is why I was purified—or began the long process of becoming purified—of the identical guilt that I'd imputed to him. Whether he was purified of it too I can't tell, because, after I unloaded on him all the secret horror and revulsion that had been building up in me for years—disgust with the "hipness" of the counterculture, revulsion with the "New Age Yuppies" I'd so recently identified with in my pass through the New Age, terminal nausea with the whole *California* thing from beginning to end, with that world of heartless narcissism and deified madness and cold glamour and idealized suicide and hopeless poverty in the midst of riches, with hipness and celebrity as its core values, which was then in the process of being eaten up by the worldliness of the power motive—because after that I never saw him again. I spewed him out of my mouth.

And that was 30 years ago. I can only pray that my words were one of the factors that finally tore that evil out of the soul of Randy Carson *bodily*, by the roots—though whether or not anything like that happened in the intervening years I will never know. In any case, I can thank Randy for making necessary the kind of emotionally violent explosion that I needed—due to my own attachments and blindness—to fundamentally change the course of my life. And though I can hope that he changed too, I can't know for certain that he was even supposed to change. Karma has to be satisfied; every Name of God, whether vast or constricted, has to be manifested; every human being must play his or her assigned and chosen role in the Divine economy. So I can't say whether or not Randy needed to change in the way I imagined for him; all I can be sure of was that *I* needed to change. And I did.

Nor was Randy alone in the kind of corruption he revealed to me that day; certain parts of the aikido world were also apparently vulnerable to it as well, since *hubris* is a common occupational hazard for even the "peaceful" warrior. One of Randy's aikido instructors, Nathan Boone*, had put the moves on Olive while she was still under age. Did Randy alert the authorities? Did he drop Boone as an instructor? Did use his martial arts skills, which went beyond aikido, to deal with Boone in the appropriate manner, and teach him a lesson he would never forget? Not in the slightest. He still accepted Boone as a teacher, and continued his training under him—because Nathan Boone was one of Randy Carson's doorways to *power*. On one occasion Randy had told me: "The most important thing in my life is aikido. Second comes my job. Last of all comes my family." I have no doubt whatsoever that he was telling the truth. "Attachment to power is a great weakness" I remarked to him on one occasion—and saw him jump.

One of the big debates in the counterculture during those years—or in what the counterculture was morphing into—was: should we work within the power-structure or outside it? Should we "drop out" (like Timothy Leary had said) so as to "form a new society within the shell of the old" (like the Wobblies had said), or should we "work inside the system to change the system"? Randy, in his big move to the private sector, had opted to work inside the system, applying the more-or-less counterculture values that were represented (at least for him) by the art of aikido to bring the power of Peace, on a practical and marketable level, into the world of the elites. Anyone who chooses this path, however, will need to confront the question of which is the more likely outcome: that he or she will actually have the power to change the values and attitudes of the power elites, or that those elites, through an all-enveloping environment of covert flattery and intimidation, will end by co-opting the idealistic insurgent and turning him or her into a tool of their own agendas (cf. *The Devil's Advocate* starring Al Pacino)? The main difficulty in answering this question is that the point of co-optation is very hard to see, mostly because it is not actually a point but a process—one that, by the time the insurgent has begun to congratulate him- or herself on having gained access to those elites so the work of values-transformation can finally begin, is already far advanced. And in view of the fact that two of the central elements in the ethos of those elites are the Luciferian union of Sex and Power at the expense of Love—such as came to light with Jefferey Epstein and Ghislaine Maxwell—and the progressive liquidation of the family, I would judge (from my own less-than-omniscient standpoint) that by the time he started virtually pimping out his daughters, Randy Carson had already been thoroughly co-opted by the powers he had so idealistically dedicated himself to transforming.

But there's one more part of the story that remains to be told, one question that still has to be asked: *What was I doing there* that I should have to come to blows, spiritually speaking, with Randy Carson? Were there no earlier indications of the way things were drifting, no warning signs? Had I let many things pass that I should have heeded a lot sooner, and then acted on? *Was there no sexual evil in my own soul?* From my present vantage point I now see that Randall C. Carson *was* the sexual evil in my own soul—projected, externalized, rising monstrously before me, and designed specifically to scare me straight. Or at least that's all he was to me at that moment. Many followers of pop psychology, or pop spirituality, used to believe that if you project your own evil on an external person or object, that person or object could in no way actually deserve such a projection, seeing that there is really no evil in the world; all the evil is inside you. There is even an element of truth in this idea, since the only way I can concretely deal with most of the evil I see in the world is by purifying myself of my own share of it. "Forget trying to change the world, just change yourself" is usually very good advice. But this certainly doesn't mean that the evil we see in the world is all a delusion: that evil is really out there. And if we can't erase or mitigate a particular evil, though it may be our duty under certain circumstances to make the attempt, then it is our absolute duty to separate ourselves from it.

But simply to make Randy Carson the scapegoat for my own sexual evil—no matter how richly he seemed to deserve that role—turned out not to be enough to complete my separation from the darkness he represented for me. A deeper purgation was needed, which appeared in the form of the painful *prostate* infection I've mentioned above, the after-effects of which took maybe two years to finally disappear, and only with the help of several different healers, including a Shen therapist and the Philippine Psychic Surgeons during several of their periodic trips to California. I've finally come to the conclusion, quite late in life, that the narcissism of the poetry scene and the hip spiritual counterculture—among which I must include not only Chögyam Trungpa but finally even Frithjof Schuon (given certain tendencies he shared with the hippies, including his fascination with Native American spirituality, his difficulties with religious authority, his identification of nudity with the "natural" and "primordial" humanity etc.)—could not have been maintained without the help of the delusive glamour of misplaced sexual energy. There's nothing like *maya* of depersonalized sex for casting a spell of false beauty over intolerable actions and situations that otherwise would inspire only loathing and disgust.

This whole episode was one of the first intimations of the death of California in my soul. It made me realize that I was living in a society where things like this were increasingly acceptable, and that was one of the major reasons Jenny and I moved to Kentucky in 2004. Unfortunately, it's becoming harder all the time to get away from California just by leaving California; as always, the Golden State remains the wave of the future. And the real problem, of course, is not California, but This World, which is not the kind of problem that can be solved by finding an alternate Earth somewhere else in the universe where "earthly" problems do not exist. This World in the spiritual sense is not the Earth but the system of the collective ego—and your title to membership in that system is your own individual ego. Sometimes the only way you can locate that ego is to first project it on the outer world, become disillusioned with it in that form, and then withdraw the projection by a process known as "conviction of sin" and "repentance." But you can't repent *for* somebody else or *of* somebody else, only of whatever it was in you that put you in the way of him. And even though leaving the scene of the crime may make it harder for the habitual demons of those circumstances to locate you, you are still fully capable of recruiting or manufacturing all the replacement demons you need to keep your deep-seated attachments well fed and clothed—until, that is, "the axe is laid to the root."

The conflict with the forces of decadence, in the world and in my own soul, that had formally commenced on that day, 30 years ago, is still going on—but at least I have clearly known, ever since that day, the real names of the protagonists. And those protagonists have now surfaced again, in this year of 2023, possibly more clearly than ever before, when the Archons of Hollywood and the Liberal media were unexpectedly forced to show their hand by the motion picture *The Sound of Freedom*, a reality-based film about the fight against the international criminal networks engaged in the sex-trafficking of children, based on the work of ex-homeland security agent Tim Ballard and starring Jim Caviezel, the actor who played Jesus in Mel Gibson's movie *The Passion of the Christ*. How openly outraged the Hollywood and media moguls were—including the editors of *The Rolling Stone* (since we must never forget the role of the '60s counterculture in the development of this monstrosity, as witness Allen Ginsberg's role as a founding member of NAMBLA) by the idea that people would actually care about the well-accepted (in certain elite circles) though not well-publicized practice of child sex-trafficking, and even risk their lives to do something about it! (And, parenthetically, the idea in some people's heads that *The Sound of Freedom* is a MAGA-oriented film, *even though Donald Trump, just like Bill Clinton, hung out with Jeffrey Epstein*, shows exactly how group-identification is so often a case of collective insanity that blinds its victims to the blindingly obvious truth.)

So my willingness to set foot on the territory of Traditional initiatory spirituality ended by invoking some truly shocking consequences, things I could never have foreseen; and, as we will soon see, there was more of the same to come. Like the old spiritual proverb goes, "If you don't have room in your house for an elephant, don't make friends with an elephant-trainer." The biggest elephant of all, of course, is God, of Whom the Holy Qur'an says: *There is no refuge from Allah but in Him*.

In conclusion, since curses are bondage to the thing cursed, I can only end with a blessing: I hope that Randy Carson learned the lesson he was tasked with learning, whatever it was supposed to be; I hope he got through the darkness of those very dark times; I hope he made a decent life.

WOLFGANG AND RAMA

Sometime in the '90s, through some channel or other, we got in touch with a radio personality in Kansas named Bryce Warnick, who was interested in the Traditionalists; he later put us in phone contact with both Wolfgang Smith and Rama Coomaraswamy—Rama a Catholic follower of Frithjof Schuon, Wolfgang another Catholic who was more-or-less intellectually identified with the Schuonian Traditionalists at one point, though he never officially joined them and later had serious difficulties with them. The result was that both of them became close "phone friends." Bryce had set up the famous radio interview between Fr Malachi Martin and Art Bell on the wildly popular talk show Coast-to-Coast AM, devoted (mostly) to conspiracy theories and the paranormal. Later on I was able to get Rama an interview with Art Bell on the same program by presenting him as a Traditional Catholic priest, exorcist and colleague of Fr Martin—and the connections I made at that time also led to my being interviewed twice on C2C myself on the subject of UFOs as a postmodern demonology, not by Art Bell but by George Noory; the last time was in 2021, on the publication of my book *The Alien Disclosure Deception*.

Wolfgang Smith (1930–2024), whom I've never met in person, was probably the central contemporary figure in the push to re-interpret cutting-edge physics, specifically quantum mechanics, according to Traditional metaphysics. He is well-versed in both fields, as few others are, having traveled to India in his earlier years to consult with yogis and gurus, and studied the Vedanta as well as Christian mystics such as Meister Eckhart and Jacob Boehme. As a scientist and mathematician, he developed the equations that allow orbiting space-craft to re-enter the atmosphere without either bouncing off or blowing up. Later on he dialogued with Fr Malachi Martin and met with Frithjof Schuon, but eventually broke with him, due both to the Bloomington scandals and to his own negative re-evaluation of the Transcendent Unity of Religions. He and his wife Thea were *sedevacantist* Catholics for a while, worshipping at Mel Gibson's "private, by-invitation" chapel in Malibu, California, but a personality clash with Mel ultimately arose, so he finally settled as a conservative Novus Ordo Catholic with some interesting ideas of his own, including an application of certain Aristotelian/Thomistic concepts to quantum mechanics. Late in life he was "discovered" by one Rick Delano, who produced a film about Wolfgang's life and teachings entitled *The End of Quantum Reality*, and helped him set up a foundation to propagate his ideas, known as the Philos-Sophia Initiative Foundation. All of this led a number of young people interested in the interface between science and spirituality to gather around him, forming a group who call themselves "the Wolfgangsters"; they presently maintain a blog on Facebook.

But it was Rama Coomaraswamy—he passed away in 2006—who was to become truly decisive in our spiritual lives. Rama was a *sedevaccantist* Catholic and the closest thing to an *informal* spiritual guide that Jenny and I had ever known. Though burdened with ill health and his struggle to preserve what remained of the Catholic Church, and far from what we would think of as a "charismatic" personality, there was a powerful spiritual light coming out of him.

Rama was the son of the prominent Anglo-Indian writer from Sri Lanka on Traditional art and metaphysics, Ananda Kentish Coomaraswamy, who (a you'll remember) is often named as co-founder, along with René Guénon, of the Traditionalist School. Though he was born in the United States, his father took him to India when he came of age to undergo a traditional Brahmin initiation. He later realized, however, that he could not fulfill the *dharma* of his caste while living in the West, so he opted to become a Roman Catholic, since this Path—at least before 1962, and for 2000 years before that—was the most Traditional one available to him in his present circumstances. Nonetheless he returned to India several times, at one point working with Mother Theresa in her ministry to the dying. And since he had trained as a cardiac surgeon, he ended up becoming Mother Theresa's cardiologist.

After the Second Vatican Council arrived, however, Rama was appalled to see the entire structure of the religion he had adopted crumbling before his eyes. This led to an exchange of letters between him and Mother Theresa in which he begged her to appeal to Pope John XXIII not to let this disaster happen—all, of course, to no avail. I still have the half-edited manuscript of their exchange on my computer, Rama's letters long and detailed and argued like theological legal briefs, Mother Theresa's letters short and admonishing, mostly in the vein of: "My dear Ram, You are hurting Jesus, we must obey the Pope." (I was privileged to fully edit another of his books, *The Problems with the Other Sacraments Apart from the New Mass*, which was published by Sophia Perennis; his other three books are *The Problems with the New Mass*, *The Destruction of the Christian Tradition*, his *magnum opus*, and *The Invocation of the Name of Jesus: As Practiced in the Western Church*.) Finding that it had become impossible for him to worship in the "Novus Ordo" Roman Catholic Church, he moved first to the Society of St Pius the Tenth, conservative Catholics who remained in communion with Rome, then to the Society of St Pius the Fifth who are *sedevacantists*, finally becoming an "independent believer" within the *sedevacantist* world. Concurrently, sometime in the '70s, he became connected with Frithjof Schuon's Mariyamiyya Tariqah, ultimately functioning as one of Schuon's "Christian *muqaddams*"; he also became a member of the board of Seyyed Hossein Nasr's Foundation for Traditional Studies, which published the influential

English-language journal *Sophia*. (An even more influential journal was *Studies in Comparative Religion*, while the third main Traditionalist publication in the English-speaking world that lasted for any length of time was *Sacred Web*, edited by the Canadian barrister and Ismaili Muslim, Ali Lakhani, which is now in its second, on-line incarnation.) And it was clear to us by the time we knew him that Rama had definite problems with Schuon as well. He testified before an Indiana grand jury in Schuon's dance-event scandals (the legal issue was based on reports that the dances were sometimes attended by underage girls), though he never told us exactly what he said to them since his testimony had been sealed. However, it was clear to us from the attitudes toward Rama of many in Schuon's group that they felt he was not toeing the party line. To openly eject him from the Traditionalist School, however, would have been to remove one of the pillars of their legitimacy—the name he carried of his illustrious father—so whatever kind or level of break he might have made with the Schuon world never became publicly explicit.

Rama's fate, due to his single-minded pursuit of doctrinal purity, was to become increasingly alone. In later years he developed bone cancer, which kept going into remission and then coming back; during that period he received the last rites of the church either three or four times. After he became too ill to continue as a surgeon he retrained as a psychiatrist, and was ultimately ordained as a Traditional *sedevacantist* Catholic priest, in which capacity—as I've already mentioned—he worked as an exorcist in the New York area for a time, in partnership with Fr Malachi Martin, with whom I corresponded briefly near the end of his life, mostly on the subject of UFOs. I complained to him that most UFOlogists had a limited view of their subject because they didn't understand metaphysics; he agreed that a lack of metaphysical knowledge was what "queered the pitch" when it came to a right understanding of the phenomenon.

Rama separated himself from the Society of St Pius X because he believed they were in a false position, accepting the post-conciliar popes as valid yet electing not to follow certain of their rulings. His own position was that a Catholic *must* follow the rulings of a valid pope, since the pope is infallible when speaking *ex cathedra* on matters of faith and morals, and consequently that if certain doctrines openly taught by the post-conciliar popes are false, this can only mean that those popes have lapsed into heresy, and consequently are no longer popes—thus his *sedevacantism*. So in terms of his chosen tradition, he was more strict on a doctrinal and practical level than many other conservative Catholics. He fully accepted the doctrine of "no salvation outside the church" as far as the Christian world was concerned—and yet, as a Perennialist, he also accepted the validity of other Divine Revelations and the possibility that more than one such Revelation might enjoy Divine sanction at the same time, while rigorously avoiding (unlike "Pope" Francis!) the temptation to mix practices taken from different religions. This was also the fundamental stated position of the Schuonian Traditionalists, who recommend strict Traditionalism when it comes to one's particular chosen or destined faith (a principle Schuon himself did not always follow, however), but do so in the context of a Perennialist universalism that accepts the validity of all the major revealed religions: Hinduism, Zoroastrianism, Judaism, Christianity and Islam, as well as Buddhism (which Guénon saw as a kind of Hindu heresy until Marco Pallis and Ananda Coomaraswamy set him straight), Taoism, insofar as it still exists in its full Traditional form (which is doubtful), and the ancient Revelations that came to the primal peoples of the Earth, in particular certain Native American tribes. And it should surprise no one when I say that walking the tightrope between exclusivist Traditionalism and universalist Perennialism is not an easy course for anyone. It is so difficult, in fact, that I sometimes think that *only Rama*, of all the people I met in the Traditionalist world, really met that mark. Schuon himself, though he extolled orthodoxy in his writings, was certainly far from orthodox in his own practice—whereas Rama, like no one else in the Traditionalist/Perennialist universe (Alvin Moore possibly accepted) truly practiced what he preached. (Those who want to know more about Rama should look up his interview with Art Bell for the Coast-to-Coast AM radio program mentioned above; it is presently available on YouTube. Also important is the film *Hostage to the Devil* about Malachi Martin, produced in Ireland and directed by Martin Stalker, in which Rama briefly appears at an exorcism in his home in Connecticut conducted by Fr Martin; Jenny and I visited him there once. In the scene where four people are seen praying in front of a window, he is undoubtedly the figure on the extreme right, seen from the back; we recognized his voice.)

After getting to know Rama by phone, we finally met him at a conference on Thomas Merton and Sufism at a seminary in Louisville, Kentucky, in 2001 while we were still living in California; the second and last time we met was at his home in Connecticut in 2005, just after our move to the Central Kentucky city of Lexington. Finally, in 2007, while visiting our friend Eric Galati in Long Island, we drove to Connecticut to pray together at Rama's grave. Here is the eulogy for him I wrote shortly afterwards:

Rama Coomaraswamy: A Eulogy

Rama Coomaraswamy was what is called a *mensch*. How is one to pay just tribute to such a man? It is not enough, finally, to speak of his personality, or his writings, or even his great personal kindness. One needs to say something about his character—his principles, that is, since in the case of a fully-realized human being, principles and character are one and the same.

In terms of the *explicit* teaching he gave me, his principles were three:

1) You need to be affiliated with an orthodox spiritual tradition.
2) You need to realize that little can be expected from this world, which is a vale of tears.
3) You need to prepare yourself to be alone.

Rama was a man of great existential capacity. Intellectually he was more fully "informed" than most men ever become, but there was hardly a piece of knowledge in him that was not also a "realization," a part of his very being, his muscle, bone and marrow. No abstract speculation, no hazy impressionism, no lyricism, just solid, working knowledge—the literal meaning of that virtue of "wisdom" which begins with the fear of God. And though we must always remember that only in God are Potency and Act identical, because God is Pure Act, still we can say that Rama Coomaraswamy, late in life, was a man almost without *potential*. He had graduated from the school of his father Ananda, the great expositor of traditional art and metaphysics; from the school of the greater Catholic Church he saw in the process of deconstructing itself root to branch, noting the stages of its dissolution as a physician notes on his chart the steady decline of his patient's vital functions, her shallow, rapid breathing, the slowing and increasingly irregular beat of her heart; from the school of the "traditional" Catholic church that provided him at least (and there is nothing at all "little" about this "least") with the grace of a valid sacramental order; and from the school of Frithjof Schuon, who transmitted many great truths—the last of which was a clear demonstration of the difference between intellectual understanding and existential realization. The great ocean of life finally washed him up on the shore of his own solitude, despite his wide family connections, the many who received the guidance that he gave without stint or any expectation of recompense, and the more fortunate few who could call him friend. He knew, if anyone ever knew it, that each of us must meet God, and death, alone.

And who can match his "professional" achievements, given that nearly all of them were the direct reflection of his spiritual capacity? Surgeon; psychiatrist; Mother Theresa's cardiologist; writer on metaphysics and "church history"; perennialist philosopher who could yet speak to the Catholic world, without dishonesty or contradiction, as a traditional Catholic exclusivist; ordained Catholic priest in one of the several traditional apostolic successions; and, finally, a practicing exorcist, one-time colleague of Fr Malachi Martin. And sufferer, too: in his seemingly endless, years-long battle with bone cancer (now so sorrowfully ended—sorrowfully for us, not for him), he received the last rites of the Catholic Church three times (and during his last illness, undoubtedly a fourth). God brought him to the door of death, sent him back, called him again, sent him back again, over and over, until he was as *harrowed* as a man can ever be—harrowed like the good ground, receptive to the seed of the holy Word who is Christ the Lord. What he was destined to know, he knew; what he was destined to become, he became. He fought the good fight; he finished the race.

Dr Coomaraswamy can truthfully be described as an "intrinsic" exorcist. His power in this regard did not stem only from his knowledge of and his right to perform the traditional Catholic rite of exorcism; he was an exorcist in his very substance: one who knew the mystery of iniquity to its depths, and yet never despaired of the goodness and power of God. To talk with him, even on the telephone (as my wife and I would, from time to time, when the spooks got a little too thick on the ground for comfort), was often a "theurgic" experience; there was light coming out of him.

In his strict, operative adherence to his chosen tradition, in his down-to-earth quality, his *canniness*—who would have thought that a great Bohemian-cosmopolitan, Anglo-Indian *artiste* like Ananda would have turned up a saturnine, dry-witted *Yankee*?—he compensated in a way for his father's self-confessed imbalance of the intellectual vis-à-vis the existential in the spiritual life, his tendency (in the words of the Qur'an surah *The Poets*), to *say* that which he *did not*. The great and undeniable blessings of that father were triumphantly realized in the son, and, God willing, a few shortcomings made good (but God knows best).

In the months before his death I found myself writing a book on the inner spiritual meanings of traditional British and Appalachian folk songs entitled *Folk Metaphysics*, and in the course of it I slowly came to realize that it was as if I were picking up on a stream of lore coming from his father Ananda—not so much through my reading of him, which was not that extensive, but through other channels. Dr Coomaraswamy told me that his father had made a collection of such songs, and had intended to write something on them, a project he never found time to complete. I also had my only two dreams of Rama during that time; in both of them he was radiantly happy. So I suspected something was afoot.

One of the last things Dr Coomaraswamy said to me (in relation to exactly what I can't remember) was: "Don't start writing poetry now—it's the language of the gods." He didn't realize, I guess, that I already had little to lose in that regard, having begun my writing career as poet—a spiritual debt I am still struggling to pay off. So instead of composing an elegiac poem on the passing of that great and saintly man, I will simply quote a few stanzas from the traditional Appalachian ballad "I Am a Poor Wayfaring Stranger":

> I am a poor wayfaring stranger
>   Traveling through this world below
> There is no sickness, toil or danger
>   In that fair land to which I go.

> I know dark clouds will hover o'er me
>   I know my path is rough and steep
> But golden fields lie out before me
>   Where weary eyes no more will weep.
>
> I'll soon be free from every trial
>   This form shall rest beneath the sod
> I'll drop the cross of self-denial
>   And enter in that home with God.

If any soul was ever loosed from the bent bow of this world to find itself, in the space of a single breath, quivering in the bull's-eye of the white rose of Paradise, it was his. Yet we are all in need of the strength and solace of prayer through the rigors of death; so let us pray for that soul, but do so in the knowledge that whatever surplus might remain, over what little may be required of him to pay his toll, will be laid up for us in the vaults of eternity, where neither moth nor rust can corrupt, nor thieves break in and steal.

      o o o o o

Soon after Rama died, Jenny dreamt of him; he was standing on an ocean beach. In the dream he told her, "Now I am dying, and you are two of the people I wanted to touch in with before I left." In our world he was already dead, but in his he was still in the middle of the death-process. Then he turned his back to her and gazed out across the vast ocean — the Ocean of Infinity.

JENNY GRADUATES FROM THE TRADITIONALIST SCHOOL

Not long before our move to Kentucky, Jenny began to feel that her time under the spiritual tutelage of Frithjof Schuon was drawing to a close — so one evening she prayed to the Virgin Mary to "adopt" her, since she no longer wanted to relate to the Virgin through the mediation of Schuon's Maryamiyya Tariqah — which he had named after her — but to do so directly, without intermediary. The next morning, after spending some time in our garden, she came back into the house to report: "I've just seen the most amazing bird in our vacant lot!" After she described it to me I concluded that it could only have been a bald eagle — an eagle with a snake in its mouth! In all my 50 years in Marin County I had never seen an eagle of any kind, either flying or at rest, at least not certainly — except for "Goldie," the handicapped golden eagle who lived permanently at the Marin Wildlife Center in San Rafael — and now a bald eagle had appeared right in our little suburban lot. And it was Jenny who saw it, though shortly afterwards I saw what might have been a juvenile in the mass of ivy growing up the phone pole at the top of our path, smaller than an adult and without the white head, but making the same characteristic yelp of the bald eagle, a lot like the cry of a seagull, though more percussive and penetrating. I immediately saw this as an omen, and connected it in my mind with two things: first, the fact that Frithjof Schuon had been given the name Brave Eagle when the grandson of the great chief Red Cloud adopted him into the Lakota tribe on the Pine Ridge reservation in South Dakota; secondly, that the Eagle is the heraldic bird of St John the Evangelist, who was adopted by the Virgin Mary when Christ on the cross told her, "Woman, behold thy son," after which he turned to John and said, "Behold thy mother" [John 19:26–27]. Based on this striking event, I knew that Jenny's prayer had been answered.

CHAPTER TWELVE

The Planet of Kentucky

SOMETIME IN 2003 OR 2004, THE DAY CAME—
rather suddenly—when we knew we were going to leave California for good. After an emergency eye operation (fairly successful), I saw that we would either have to borrow against our house to pay the medical bills—which we never considered doing—or we would need to sell out and to pull up stakes. And though the transition was rigorous and shocking, in another way its very inevitability made it easy: hard in terms of stress and effort, easy in terms of the energy of certainty. As Frithjof Schuon so rightly said, necessity carries its own graces along with it, since—as Ibn Sina and others of the followers of Aristotle taught—God is Necessary Being. Consequently we decided, or it was decided for us, that we would sell the sweet little house that had belonged to my grandmother, a house that I had known all my life, and move to Kentucky, for the simple reason that—even with all the dark memories it held for Jenny—it was the only other home base we knew, one we had been visiting almost yearly for a quarter of a century. Then, not much later, after Jenny prayed one Sunday at the Nativity of Christ Greek Orthodox Church in Novato that God would send her a buyer for our house, she struck up a conversation with a woman she'd never met before, sitting in the pew behind her, and found that the woman had been simultaneously praying that God would send her a house to buy. Consequently we struck a deal with the first potential buyer we talked with, who offered us $11,000 more than our projected asking price. We didn't even need to list the house or pay a realtor's commission, proving that the mills of God don't *always* grind slowly; like it says in Isaiah 65:24, "Before they ask, I will answer." So we sold the house for a hefty sum, since—though it had only one real bedroom, termites, one half-bathroom, a damaged roof and no garage, it was situated in highly desirable Marin County, one block from the shores of San Francisco Bay, and we were selling near the peak of a housing boom. The angels of that great transition were our *honest* accountant, John Soderblom, who had aided us in our fight with Maggie Carlin over the trust; Johrei channeler Kathy Blackwell, who, as a real estate agent, helped us with the paperwork for a nominal sum and generally navigated us through the whole process; Jenny's mother Lola, who immediately lent us $30,000 to cover closing costs and travel expenses, for which we quickly reimbursed her as soon as we reached Kentucky and deposited the big check; and Xenia of St Petersburg, the Orthodox saint, wonderworker and fool-for-Christ that Jenny venerated, who had lost her husband to drink

and afterwards became a homeless wanderer, and whose strong point as an intercessor seems to be her power to help people find *where* and *with whom* they really belong. That done, we sold our two nearly used-up cars, rented a Penske van, loaded all our worldly possessions into it with the help of some sturdy but pious Mexicans—young men who felt the beauty and the gravity of our move but who, because they didn't speak English, could only transmit their feelings through the soulful expressions on their faces (and possibly their silent prayers)—and hit the road for our next destination, 2000 miles to the east, driving hard against the solar headwind that blew in from the rising dawn ahead, to begin the next chapter of our lives.

The night before we left, walking Fourth Street in San Rafael, we ran into George Lucas himself. It was as if Marin County were feebly trying to dissuade us from leaving it by showing us a truly memorable example of "all the wonderful things we were leaving behind." But the truth is, we never really "had" George Lucas, nor was Marin County any longer a shape that our souls could recognize. Possibility and nostalgia were ending; actualization had begun. In leaving California "behind" for points East, we became early scouts and fur trappers for the great exodus from the once-Golden State that has swelled to a torrent in recent years, while firmly contradicting Lew Welch's suicidal principle that "*This* (Marin County) *is the Last Place/ There is nowhere else to go.*" Sorry, Lew, but it was not the Last Place, thank God: there *was* somewhere else to go.

THE RETURN OF JENNY DONNE

So I drove Jenny and myself cross-country, over two-thirds of the continent, in our yellow Penske van, accompanied by our sober, wise, faithful little cat, Juniper. We'd bought a cage for him to ride in but he protested his incarceration so loudly that we gave him early release, with the result that he simply slept curled up on Jenny's lap the whole way. When we arrived in Lexington we spent that night at Jenny's sister Mary Anne and her husband Craig's house, where I had the following dream:

> I am viewing an object resembling the Ark of the Covenant, except that the two wingéd Cherubim surmounting it, between whom was the place on the actual Ark known as the Mercy Seat where God's Presence manifested, had been replaced by the figures of two Native Americans in a similar posture. Between them, an invisible hand was smudging the "Medicine Ark" with cedar smoke.

This dream indicated to me that we were now in the spiritual territory of Frithjof Schuon, not that far from his followers in Bloomington, Indiana, from James Cutsinger in Aiken and Columbia, South Carolina, and much nearer to Dr Nasr in D.C. than we had been in California. And there are indications that cedar was used as one of the elements in the sacred incense of the Hebrews, as it certainly was, and is, by many Indian tribes.

We finally arrived at Jenny's mother's house in Pike County in August, near the Virginia and West Virginia borders, which we used as a base from which to scout houses to buy in Lexington — and by October, with the further intercession of St Xenia, we found the house that was to be our home (Xenia told us it would be the third we looked at), a two-storey brick place with a grape arbor and a big back yard — twice the room of our house in California, and with a welcoming aura that only basically good people can leave behind. As soon as we moved in I reproduced as best I could the dream of the Native American Ark of the Covenant by smudging our hearth with cedar smoke.

Nonetheless, when I moved from California to Kentucky with Jenny, it was as if I had traveled into the darkness of her past. As for Lexington, a fading island of traditional gentility, it was an atmosphere congenial to us, a small city that still "worked" and had all the products and services that we needed, including alternative healing resources, plus some people who — before they passed on — became good friends. Lexington is set in the middle of the Bluegrass, which has something of the feel of the English countryside and is divided by the same style of traditional stone fence that's found in England and Ireland, with the top course set vertically, built of rough undressed limestone that makes a kind of natural brick. It was easy to drive out into the beautiful horse farms, the wooded hills, the Kentucky River area, and try to get lost — which was impossible, since every road still led back to Lexington. Some of the farms in the surrounding area were owned by fabulously wealthy horse-shaykhs from the Arab Emirates — one of whom was Mohammed bin Rashid Al-Maktoum, the Crown Prince of Dubai — who would fly in and out using the private airstrip reserved for the super-rich just north of town, thereby avoiding customs. Queen Elizabeth also traveled to the Bluegrass from time to time to visit her race horses. The animals of the area were quite a menagerie: horses of all colors, blue-hued bays, spotted appaloosas, plus donkeys, mules, llamas, sheep, pigs, steers, swans, peacocks; and one Spring while driving on a rural road I saw a camel and stopped to feed him some succulent weeds that grew on the wrong side of his fence; he ate heartily but showed little gratitude. His companion in the same paddock was a buffalo. And it was fun to trek back through the history of the place and the surrounding area, discovering charming old churches and taverns. We visited the place on the shore of the Kentucky River where Daniel Boone founded one of his first settlements; the meeting house where the big Cane Ridge Revival took fire from the Holy Spirit in 1801; the Shaker settlement at Pleasant Hill that we drove to one time with a visitor from Japan who wanted to see an "arts and crafts" site that had been mentioned by Traditionalist writer Ananda Coomaraswamy, Rama's father — not to mention the old distilleries, including an abandoned complex, overgrown with brush and vines, that we discovered on some bottom land below the cliffs near the Kentucky River, an imposing brick castle with towers and battlements that used to be part of Old Crow. And then Henry Clay's palatial home in Lexington; the house Lincoln's wife Mary Todd grew up in; the building that used to provide student housing for Transylvania University, which was the academic Mecca of the trans-Alleghany region before the University of Kentucky was founded — a site where Confederate president Jefferson Davis had lived for a time as a young man — and the old Lexington cemetery where several of my Strother forebears still kept lodgings. And then there was the famous Narcotics Farm on Leestown Pike, now a minimum-security Federal prison, the institution mentioned in the writings of William Burroughs, who had "taken the cure" there at one time, and also in the movie *The Man with the Golden Arm* starring Frank Sinatra. The idea of the place, from a time when opioid addiction was not yet a rural thing, was that healthy country living, fresh air, sunlight and pitching hay were just the things that ghetto-bound urban junkies needed to get straight. It didn't work of course, but it did lead to various interesting developments, including some amazing jazz combos made up of master musicians from the big urban areas — not to mention a curriculum of arcane experiments conducted by the CIA as part of their MK-Ultra mind-control program, who made deals with some of the junkies trying to the kick the habit that, if they would agree to let the spook-doctors experimentally dose them with God-knows what weird drugs (not just LSD but a number of others that most people have never heard of), they would be paid for their time, their inconvenience and their physical and emotional damage *in junk* — a practice not entirely in line with the stated purpose of the place, to say the least. (I've always felt that somebody ought to commission a bronze statue of William Burroughs to be placed beside the front entrance, decked out in his gentleman farmer outfit of Sunday suit and dress straw hat, shotgun held vertically at his side in a grim Beat parody of "American Gothic.") We were using the past to slow down present time, until the store of past time available for that purpose was entirely used up: the work of collecting ghosts, those thin, half-conscious memories who tend to get stuck in various cultural backwaters and forgotten territories from the human past... You could still do that in the Commonwealth in the days before Covid, following Mark Twain's observation that "When the world ends I'd like to be in Kentucky, because it's always twenty years behind the times..."

So Lexington was cool. But when it came to Pike County, the coal mining region of rural-industrial America in the heart of Appalachia where Jenny grew up, entering that land I always felt like Orpheus seeking his lost wife Euridice in Hades, armed with nothing but a lyre tuned in Phrygian mode and a fairly good singing voice, to move the stones on the hillsides — and, even heavier than they were, the sealed hearts of some who occupied the houses. As we drove down and down from the ridge on the west side of the Big Sandy watershed, the pressure on the back of my neck always palpably increased.

When Jenny and I first got together we felt almost like brother and sister, as if we had occupied the same womb—which is another way of representing the knowledge that we had known each other before birth, and had left that world with the agreement that we would seek and find each other in this one. When Jenny was a little girl, as you may remember, she had told her mother, "After I grow up I'm going to move to California and marry a poet." I still partly wish I'd been born in Kentucky a few years earlier than I had been in California so I could have been there to defend her during her horrendous childhood—but since I couldn't do that, it was my duty (apparently) to go back with her to Kentucky and suffer along with her, to the extent of my capacity, some of what she had suffered as a child.

Moving back to "the scene of the crime" was a big risk for Jenny, but given our economic situation there were few alternatives. She had escaped "hillbilly/bourgeois" oppression in her 20s by moving from Kentucky to California; now, in her 50s, she was required to escape a growing "Liberal" oppression by moving back to Kentucky from California, in a time when the Golden State, in the eyes of many residents, no longer represented "freedom." It had become the Brazen State or the Leaden State—but still nowhere as leaden as Pike County, Kentucky! For a period of time the turn in the U. S. toward more traditional values, including some of the more interesting aspects of the Alt Right—a phase of things that was mostly buried in its turn by the subhuman ghoulishness of Wokism—represented a real liberation for both Jenny and myself. That liberation reached its apex, and also its doom, in the person of Donald Trump, who swept it all together into one big pile of dry leaves, set it on fire and reduced it to ashes. At least Louisiana's Huey Long was a real populist who came directly out of the people he claimed to support and aspired to lead. Trump, on the other hand, was/is a rich New York sleazeball who had no real affinity or care for the forgotten working class and the ex-Southern Democrat rural whites he appointed himself the leader of; his relationship to them was entirely opportunistic. Of all the many good reasons to deplore Hillary Clinton, who added the term "deplorables" to the lexicon of American English, perhaps the worst of all was that she gave us Donald Trump! Driving from Lexington to Pike County one day, before the 2016 election, we saw written in big letters on the roof of a rural barn: "ANYONE BUT HILLARY!" We also saw an ad for a T-shirt, modeled by a pretty girl, that read: "I was DEPLORABLE before it was hip." But since we moved to Kentucky in 2004, we had more than a decade where we could learn from and feel supported by an intelligent conservatism, while still preserving some of the more positive and realistic values we had learned from the older Left, the Left as it was when "social justice" was a hopeful banner of human liberation instead of what it later became, a hateful slogan of social control. The worldview of that older Left-wing was 180 degrees opposed, in some ways, to today's anti-working class and virtually anti-human "Left," the sinister witch's brew that sprang from cultural Marxism and the virtually total co-optation of the Leftist liberation movements of the '60s by the social engineers, the mind controllers and the CIA—the same people who were able to make the Trotskyites into a major tributary to the Neo-Conservative movement by painstakingly transforming their anti-Stalinism into a blanket anti-Russianism. The "Liberals" of today are not really liberal, nor is the "Left" still properly leftist, any more than the Catholics (most of them) are, in any historical or traditional sense, actually Catholic. But seeing that human beings are in the habit of following names rather than realities, this is a hard thing for many people to grasp.

Nonetheless, what Jenny discovered by moving back to the Commonwealth of her birth was, first, that she was no longer the hopelessly abused child she had been when she left, that she was *strong enough to live here*, and second, that the evil that had tried to smother her when she was young was still alive and well and as evil as ever, since it did its best to kill both of us—which meant that her earlier difficulties had *not been her fault*. They weren't something that could be overcome by maturation and character-development on her part, as her parents had claimed, but a darkness that was really out there in the world she'd come from—though it certainly took plenty of maturation and character-development for her to face that world and not be destroyed by it.

As soon as we'd settled in Lexington I scoured the web to see if there were any Sufis in town. Through this method I found Dr John Parks and Maryam Hand, both of whom were associated with the Shadhili Tariqah. Maryam, who produced a slim volume of spiritually perceptive and personally candid and transparent verse entitled *Piercing the Veil*—published by Finishing Line Press who later did a collection of Jenny's poems, *Black Sun*—and who was a near-homeless divorcee from a prominent doctor husband when we knew her, later moved to a rural farm/commune run by the Shadhilis in Pennsylvania and married a fellow *faqir*. John Parks, also an initiated Shadhili *faqir*, was a retired psychiatrist and at one time a close associate of Roberto Assagioli, the Italian psychiatrist who originated Psychosynthesis; Dr Parks had also been Medical Director of the Blue Grass West Mental Health Center in Frankfort, Kentucky at one time. (See his interesting article "Biopsychosynthesis" at https://synthesiscenter.org/articles/0132.pdf .) He had a background with the Vedanta Society as well as Sufism, and was one of the founders of the Lexington Christian/Muslim Dialogue, which still meets, and which played an important part in my life by hosting my second major foray into peace activism, the debut of the Covenants Initiative (see below).

It was through Dr Parks, at a class he led in Lexington on the ideas of Ken Wilber, that we met Kathleen Cummings, whom he later married. Kathleen was a woman who, since her rather unexpected and clearly devastating divorce, had traveled the world as a pilgrim; when we knew her she was in a state of perpetual oscillation between Catholicism and Buddhism. She had an obsessively pushy and judgmental streak in her character that she recognized but couldn't control — she was better at relating to animals than human beings — yet that in no way jeopardized our friendship. It was through her that we learned of the nearby Korean Buddhist monastery, Furnace Mountain Zen Center, that she had been connected with for a while; it's built in a striking architectural style of Chinese rooves with glazed, perfectly-interlocking, dark blue tiles. Jenny and I went there to meditate once, though we did so according to our own contemplative forms. She also told us of the existence of a community of non-ordained Catholic hermits who had collected around the Trappist Abbey of Gethsemani, about an hour's drive west of Lexington near Bardstown. They were not even an official Cistercian "third order" for householders, but appeared to be more of an informal gathering of natural contemplatives, somewhat like the Beguines and the Beghards — either that or a group of virtually homeless persons who had nowhere else to go, but who were still capable of accepting (as not everyone can) the hospitality of Catholic monks; the Trappists had apparently allowed them to "squat" on their extensive property. It seems as if Kathleen had been connected with them too for a while — and it was through her that we met Matt Haltom, who was very helpful in connecting Jenny with a Traditional *sedevacantist* Catholic group near Lexington.

But when we arrived in Kentucky Jenny was still an Eastern Orthodox Christian, so she scouted out some of the local Orthodox churches, one Greek Orthodox, one Russian (OCA) and one Antiochian, whose founding congregation had been made up of Arab Christians, mostly from Syria and Lebanon. Christian Arabs have a long history in Kentucky. Dawahares, a department store chain that went out of business in 2008, was founded by them, and the governor of the Commonwealth as of this writing, Andy Beshear, as well as Dr Harbie, Jenny's ophthalmologist, are from the same stock. Jenny settled on the Antiochian church, St Andrew's, whose priest, Father Thomas Galloway (an ex-Catholic) was immensely helpful to us in a number of later health crises and other difficulties. Yet the shadow of Orthodox Christianity that I've analyzed above, its tendency to unconsciously adopt decidedly unorthodox doctrines due to its misunderstanding of the modern world, finally meant that Jenny couldn't continue with that form of Christianity. It was at the point of this difficult realization that our connection with Rama Coomaraswamy became so crucial in Jenny's next spiritual re-location.

STRANGER IN A (STRANGELY FAMILIAR) STRANGE LAND

As a California boy who married a woman from Eastern Kentucky, I found myself enrolled in an intensive course in Appalachian family dynamics, both positive and negative, from which I ultimately graduated (hopefully with honors) as the bulk of her extended family slowly died off. Before that, however, I had been required to learn just how prejudiced California could be, especially liberal Bay Area California (Bakersfield might have been a different story), against Oakies, Crackers, Red Necks and Hill Billies — the kind of people known today, courtesy of Hillary Clinton, as "Deplorables."

As I've already indicated, almost my entire social group — the remnant of my adolescent peer group, made up mostly of people I'd gone to high school with or who had attended other Marin County high schools at the same time — rejected me when I got together with Jenny, either because of her or simply because I wasn't "supposed" to get married to anybody. Nor did my mother ever really accept her. She refused to celebrate Christmas with us, preferring to spend it instead with her Lesbian Catholic friends. Obviously, in some fundamental way, she didn't want human life to go on, a sentiment apparently shared by a big chunk of Jenny's family as well, seeing that neither she nor her sister nor either of her two female cousins had children. As for us, we felt that our lives were not stable or ordered enough to bring children into the world, so we produced books instead (many old family lines, like that of Lew Welch, finally terminate in an Artist), which means that both our families, as culturally different as can be imagined, showed signs of the anti-fertility tendency that is now becoming dominant in many parts of the world, resulting in plunging birth rates. That's why we feel so lucky to know Lee and Julia Speray, host and hostess of the little Traditional Catholic house church where Jenny worships, and their four children: Veronica, Bernadette, Cecelia and Raphael. What a privilege it has been, for me personally, to watch those kids grow up.

But that's a number of different stories. The one I want to tell now, about one of the things I learned after visiting Kentucky from California almost yearly for 30 years before finally moving here with Jenny in 2004, demonstrates how large California and Californians loom in the Kentucky mind, both positively and negatively. We now live on a street in Lexington named "Pasadena," near to which is another street called "Sun Seeker Court." Apparently the subdivision we now occupy was originally conceived, around 60 years ago, as a kind of "Southern California of the Bluegrass." (You can also see this mysterious affinity in the cartoon sitcom *The Simpsons*, which seems to come, for some unknown reason, out of the tension between California and Kentucky. The secret Kentucky identity of the all-American town of "Springfield" appears in the character of "Cletus the slack-jawed yokel" and — for those in the know — a guest appearance by former Kentucky governor Martha Layne Collins, not to mention the fact that Springfield, Shelbyville and Simpsonville are all towns in Central Kentucky, and the further fact that "Mr Sparkle," which in one *Simpsons* episode is a cartoon character representing a Japanese dishwashing detergent, is actually the name of a car wash in Lexington. When the residents of "Springfield" want to buy fireworks for the 4th of July, they have to travel to Tennessee, and on one occasion I saw a *legal advice kiosk* in downtown Lexington that was likely the origin of fly-by-night lawyer Lionel Hutz's "I Can't Believe It's a Law Firm." This is the esoteric secret of *The Simpsons*: look for it and see if you agree.)

On the other hand, when we visited the well-known Kentucky writer Wendell Berry back in the '70s — Wendell being a sort of "Gary Snyder East" — in the guise of fellow American poets, at his farm near Port Royal in Henry County (Wendell had been one of Jenny's teachers at the University of Kentucky; Steve Sanfield, another California poet and a friend of Snyder's, was there at the same time), his little daughter piped up and said: "We don't like people from California, do we Daddy?" Instead of reminding her of the manners appropriate to the family of a respected Kentucky writer and gentleman "hobby" farmer when entertaining literary guests from out of state, he just stared dreamily off into the distance as if to say, "... out of the mouths of babes, out of the mouths of babes..." So it wouldn't be wrong to say that we were awash in a sea of prejudice from both California and Kentucky, as well as from both the California and the Kentucky sides of our families — even though if you aspire to "renounce the world," finding yourself a victim of prejudice, despite all its obvious drawbacks, can help point the way. Nonetheless, as a kind of merciful compensation, when Jenny met the aunt of Wendell's wife Tanya in Mill Valley, California — a painter — she revealed to us a dark family secret: that a lot of Wendell Berry's poems of "traditional, agrarian" Kentucky had actually been written in Marin County! This led me to wonder if Wendell ever dropped acid with Ken Kesey like his fellow Kentucky poets Gurney Norman and Ed McClanahan reportedly did; in my mind's eye I see him having a radiant LSD vision of Piers Plowman that determined the whole later course of his career... (And apropos of McClanahan: His daughter Kris, a true mistress of the healing arts, who had grown up as one of the kids attached to Ken Kesey's Merry Pranksters, became my acupuncturist for a while in Lexington. During one of her treatments I told her my memory of visiting Kesey's place in Oregon during my travels as a hippie pilgrim. As I was walking up the gravel road toward his residence, I saw a diminutive figure ahead in the distance, slowly approaching with a limping gait. As we drew closer to one another, I realized that this apparition was in fact — a parrot. When he was a couple of feet away he cocked his head, looked up at me with one eye, and said: "*Hello!*" The official Greeter Parrot. "I remember that parrot," Kris said.

Small world. The second-string greeter I met next was Kesey's lieutenant, Ken Babbs, who went into a well-practiced routine designed to prevent Kesey from being inundated with fans and curiosity-seekers, diverting me to a barn where I was invited to sleep the night. Should I have introduced myself as a respected literary figure who had been published by Lawrence Ferlinghetti's City Lights? The thought never entered my head.)

At that point however, though I was aware of the abuse Jenny had suffered in her earlier years, I still had the generally positive if not romantic view of Kentucky and Appalachia held by the average California hippie, the view of the *Foxfire Books* enthusiast and folk-lore and folk-music afficionado, supported by the memory of the Kennedy-era Liberalism and labor Leftism that saw Appalachia as both a valuable cultural resource and a rural vanguard of the labor movement, rather than as a no-man's land of backward Neo-Nazis that was best quarantined from coastal urban America and left to die on the vine. (That original view has not yet entirely disappeared, but I've had to seriously modify it due to subsequent experiences.) The remnant of the old Appalachian Left, like the people at the community cultural collective, performance venue and radio station known as Appalshop in the town of Whitesburg in Letcher County, still remember the visit of Robert Kennedy to that area in the 1960s as a ray of Liberal hope. For some crazy reason, however, the more modern view of Appalachia as a hinterland of expendable Deplorables and "useless eaters" is also called "Liberalism," immediately putting me in mind of Confucius' saying that one of the essential things we must do to restore civilization to a land sunk in barbarism is to "rectify the names."

JENNY DONNE, LOCAL ARCHETYPE

Jenny's identity in other people's eyes has always been a mystery to her. The California prejudice against Oakies, Crackers and Hillbillies is fairly easy to account for, but who she has often been assumed to be in the Commonwealth of Kentucky is hard to explain and even harder to get a clear picture of. Exactly what archetype from the collective social unconscious has so often been projected on her, and why? Once when we met Wendell Berry after a lecture at the Lexington Theological Seminary—this was the first time we'd seen him after our move to Kentucky from California—he said: "My my, Jenny Donne has come home." (His reaction to me, on the other hand, was a glare of hatred and loathing, as if I were a terrorist or human trafficker who held Jenny as my hostage.) But who, exactly, was this "Jenny Donne"? She certainly got no privileges in the Commonwealth from being whoever that person might be. Jenny always got the feeling, accurately or otherwise, that Wendel hadn't particularly respected her in college either, that he had no qualms, as a Flatlander from tobacco country, against implicitly putting her down for coming from Eastern Kentucky. And another Kentucky poet, Richard Taylor, had much the same "prodigal's return" reaction when we met him at his book store, Poor Richard's, in the state capital of Frankfort; obviously he remembered her as a significant figure from his past. He told her that he would be glad to stock any of her books, but when she showed him a copy of her *Dark Way to Paradise, Dante's Inferno in Light of the Spiritual Path*, he reneged on his offer. "Nobody would want to read a book like *that*," he said. It was from Taylor that we got the impression that poetic Kentucky is a kind of colonialized art ghetto where Arts Council grants are distributed to promote and establish local color, and prizes specifically given for poems about hound dogs, whiskey stills and old grannies rocking on porches—but heaven help the rebel (Wendell Berry officially excepted) who tries his or her hand at elevated themes or shows an appreciation for high culture: no Dantes or Shakespeares will be allowed emerge from the Dark and Bloody Ground, to show their seed-heads above the average height of the local corn. My own speculation is that Jenny, like Thomas Hardy's Tess of the d'Urbervilles, represented—to the dark depths of the Appalachian psyche—some kind of once-aristocratic bloodline, more likely a spiritual rather than a genetic one, that had fallen on hard times at one point and been reduced to peasant status, only to be reborn as "the Fairest Maid of the Valley" so often celebrated in the old ballads. She certainly could have been just such a Maid according to her high school yearbook photo, with her beautiful Japanese or Native American eyes (as an adolescent she had identified for a time with Lady Murasaki, author of *The Tale of Genji*), eyes that became more Anglo some time in her 20s, though her more mature physiognomy was no less beautiful. Her difficult destiny might have stemmed from the fact that she had grown up in a time when the Fair Maid Archetype was no longer in demand, unless the Maid in question was a professional or sexual hustler, angling for marriage to some big local lawyer or politician. That numinous archetype still existed, deeply repressed, in the collective unconscious of the region, though now it appeared either as an atavistic siren working to lure its victims back to their shameful Hillbilly past, or else as a hallowed ancestral ghost pointing a finger of Divine Judgment at the heartless mores of modern life in the name of more wholesome, more traditional, more *human* times. It was as if Jenny, like the figure of Carrie in the Stephen King movie of the same name, represented an outraged cultural innocence now transformed into a sentence of doom against its tormentors, in the same way that the Greek goddess Persephone was seen as incarnating both violated maidenly innocence and infernal witchcraft, the curse of the Furies. (Carrie=*Kore*. Stephen King's obvious intent in *Carrie* was to present a contemporary version of the Persephone myth; "Kore," an epithet of Persephone that means "Maiden," became "Carrie" in the film. Carrie's relationship with her mother mirrors Persephone's with her own mother Demeter, goddess of agriculture and fertility, and just as pigs were sacrificed to Demeter/Kore in the Eleusinian Mysteries, so Carrie in the motion picture is drenched in pigs' blood.) The reader may feel that this archetypal view of Jenny is rather excessive on my part, based on something like an "unresolved anima-projection" (speaking in anti-romantic Jungian terms); all I can do is emphasize again how mysterious some people's prejudicial and negative reactions to Jenny have been to me personally, especially in Marin County. She is essentially sweet-tempered, sober, and self-possessed, friendly but not addicted to imposing herself on others; what do they unconsciously sense in her that calls up such strange responses? It's as if she provokes some sort of fear in them. And those who don't have this reaction generally appreciate her as sincere, sympathetic and spiritually intelligent. It's as if people immersed in the world hate her, while those with a healthy distrust of worldly values see her as she is. Writing this I am reminded of the words of Jesus Christ from the Gospel of John: "If the world hate you, know that it hated me first . . . but be of good cheer, because I have overcome the world."

MYTHIC KENTUCKY

Since Kentucky was an entirely different cultural and psychic environment than the one I'd grown up in, with different plants and animals, different speech-patterns, different smells and different "ancestors" — though my mother's family, the Strothers, had spent several generations in Lexington in the Bluegrass on their way from Virginia, before moving on to Missouri and California — I needed to acclimatize to it on several levels, one of which required the creation of a "mythic Kentucky" to match the mythic California and Marin County of my youth. I accomplished part of this myth-making by writing a book, which began when we heard traditional folk singer Jean Ritchie perform at the Appalshop in Whitesburg, Letcher County. She sang one of her signature selections, "Fair Nottamun Town," a mysterious song with cryptic, paradoxical verses that seemed to hold some hidden meaning. She told us that there was a curse on the song, to the effect that anybody who figured out what it meant would lose all his or her luck. The title of the curse-defying book I wrote based on that encounter was *Folk Metaphysics: Mystical Meanings in Traditional Folk Songs and Spirituals*. And this temporary but necessary mythification of Kentucky was certainly aided by the old wayside taverns and stone churches of the Bluegrass, some of them dating back to the 1700s, as well as by the time when, driving through the countryside just north of Lexington, we spied an exact full-sized replica of an Irish round tower on one of the big horse farms, just like the one at Cashel, the kind that the Irish monks built to protect themselves from Viking raids. We later learned that it had been built by Tony Ryan of Ryanair airlines. Irish immigrants, plenty of whom were stone masons and horse breeders, were an indispensable part of the horse industry in the Commonwealth — many became jockeys — as well as being partly responsible for the traditional stone fences that line so many of the country roads. And on top of that, fox hunting is still legal in Kentucky — so if King Charles is ever deposed or abdicates (both distinct possibilities), and if the U.S. ever breaks up into separate principalities (as some people apparently hope), we might have a job for him here. We even have a large stone castle west of Lexington, though when Queen Elizabeth came to visit her horses in the Bluegrass she called it "a Mickey Mouse castle." (A Mickey Mouse castle for a Mickey Mouse king?)

And Jenny, for her own part, has this to say about one aspect of Ancestral Kentucky:

> The population of Kentucky, like that of the American Colonies in general, hailed mostly from the British Isles of the 17th and 18th centuries. And, because of their isolation, the People of the Mountains kept a spirit from that time, earlier than that of the empires that were later built by Britain and America; you might say that they missed the 19th century entirely.
>
> Also, I believe it is likely that a percentage of the mountain people were descended from the ones we call "indentured servants," some of whom had become indentured willingly while others were taken against their will. According to "revisionist historian" Michael Hoffman in his book *They Were White and They Were Slaves*, not all people who ended up coming to America involuntarily came from Africa. Mostly in the 1600s, British and Irish children were kidnapped and forcibly taken as laborers to the New World; at one point Whites from the British Isles performed most of the forced labor in the Colonies, though some Black slaves had already been imported. Only later was the bulk of this labor taken over by the Blacks. And these White servants, or slaves, suffered the same kind of separation from their loved ones that the Blacks would have to endure later on. A percentage of these indentured workers, after their periods of servitude were complete, would likely have migrated west to Kentucky.
>
> The ballad "Henry Lee," as sung by Ralph Stanley and others, may contain echoes of the indentured servanthood of immigrants. The Lady in the ballad wants Henry Lee to sleep with her, but he refuses because he has a far-away true love in a "merry green land" — so she kills him with her "little pen knife," and the other Ladies of the community help her cover up the murder. Then she calls to a little bird to come and live in her "golden cage," but the bird refuses, saying that if she would kill poor Henry Lee she would just as likely kill a little bird like him. The Ladies and the golden cage, and the fact that the Lady gets away with murder, indicate that she is of a high social degree. When she asks him to "get down, get down" and spend the night with her, this could mean that he was a rider who had arrived from elsewhere, from the

"merry green land" where his true love lived. And in another version the chickens crow late at night at the moment Henry is killed, likely indicating that he was already living on the Lady's land. These things always made me wonder if Henry Lee were not her indentured servant.

These mountain people descended from indentured servants would naturally hold on to the spirit and feeling of the British Isles as they had known them before their forced departure; they were not adventurers looking forward to a new life, but people pining for the home they had lost through oppression, exploitation and violence. Consequently the old ballads of Britain, which were transmitted by oral tradition, formed an important part of these people's historical memory. It is partly due to this that the English dialects of southern and central Appalachia retain certain speech patterns from the 18th century, the Elizabethan age, and even the time of Chaucer, along with other elements of folk memory and belief. I remember as a child hearing about something called "Old Christmas"—which spooked me because, as I was told, that was the night when the animals knelt in the fields. Old Christmas is the date of the Nativity according to the old Julian calendar rather than the newer Gregorian one.

This archaic quality was not something that the people I knew when I was growing up were interested in or particularly wanted to remember—yet the feeling of it still lingered. And both I and Charles believe that certain feudal elements hold sway even now, on a deeply unconscious level, in the folkways and family relations of Eastern Kentucky.

Every land has its curses, though a period of imposed cultural dominance by a later social regime can sometimes hide the toxic effects of those earlier "generational spirits" until the dominant cultural stratum starts to lose its hold and the vengeful ghosts of the massacred and the dispossessed slowly begin, almost imperceptibly at first, to rise from their graves. And beyond the dark legacy of indentured servanthood that Jenny believes had a part in forming the culture she grew up in, moonshining certainly played a big role in making Eastern Kentucky in some ways a land of unquiet ghosts. Jenny's coal mining grandfather Allard Plunkett* was a successful moonshiner, something that was even more true of his own father John who had apparently been the top moonshiner of the whole area, a fact that came to us through oral tradition from Jim Plunkitt* (same name, different spelling), the family genealogist who manages the Plunkett Family Association Facebook account. When we met him in Fremont, California, Jim said that he had seen a written report, letter or memo from the sheriff of Pike County that named John Plunkett as Local Enemy Number One. So Jenny's great-grandfather likely functioned as the boss of an organized criminal enterprise, making him something on the order of a rural Mafia Don. That social position undoubtedly came into being partly due to the Whiskey Rebellion of 1792, through which the U.S. Federal Government asserted its authority over the until-then relatively independent settlements on the western frontier, thereby adding another layer of ancestral oppression to Kentucky's "dark and bloody ground."

Jenny's father's family, the Donnes, seem to have had a bit of criminal background too, but nothing like the Plunketts. There was the Donne Gang, a band of Quaker farmers, Tories during the Revolutionary War, who opposed independence, so their "gang" status was probably mostly in the eyes of the Patriots — though of course the worst mark against the Donnes is their distant relationship to Richard M. Nixon. But what of my own family background? The worst crime of my closest family seems to have been the undrinkable wine my father made during prohibition, a couple of bottles of which we kept in our garage just for nostalgia's sake, and my paternal grandfather's divorce (a scandal at that time) and alcoholism. The guilt for whatever oppression the Widmanns, my aunt Barbara's family, laid upon the peons who worked their coffee finca in Guatemala hopefully didn't pass to me since I was no blood relation, nor (God willing) did whatever curse might have been attached to the 33rd Degree Mason pin I found in my father's bedside table after his death — not his pin (he was an Elk) though possibly my grandfather's, but in any case a badge of obloquy to both my ex-Catholic and my contemporary Conspiracy Theorist sensibilities; its influence was hopefully diverted by my anti-Masonic writings. But the worst stain upon my bloodlines, besides whatever illustrious crimes were committed by various kings and nobles back in England and France, undoubtedly came from the slaveholding Virginia planters of my mother's family — though the Strothers lost their fortune at one point, thereby hopefully "laundering" a certain amount of the karma that passed from them to me. (It's interesting, isn't it, how the crimes of the oppressed are taken as proof of degeneracy, while the crimes of the oppressors are praised as high achievements.) In our own time, ancestral guilt has become a dogma of Woke ideology — but if you subscribe to that theory and go back far enough, then no hands are clean — including those of the Blacks, whose chiefs often sold off their own people to the slave-traders, some of whom were Arab Muslims (Islam being my own religion), who drove them to the coast and sold them in turn to the Europeans and the Americans. But as for myself, I do not subscribe to the ancestral guilt theory. I didn't oppress those peons or whip and sell those slaves, nor did Jenny cook moonshine or commit whatever crimes were necessary to keep a large illegal booze operation running. We will be judged only for our own crimes — and our shortcomings, lies and evasions — because our wills are free. According to the Quran, 35:18, *no bearer of burdens will bear the burden of another.* Likewise "The son shall not bear the iniquity of the father, neither shall the father bear the iniquity of the son: the righteousness of the righteous shall be upon him, and the wickedness of the wicked shall be upon him" [Ezekiel 18:20]. So what does Exodus 20:5 mean when it says "Thou shalt not bow down thyself to them, nor serve them: I the Lord thy God am a jealous God, visiting the iniquity of the fathers upon the children unto the third and fourth generation of them that hate me"? Two things: first, that the guilt referred to is specifically related to the worship of idols, one of the biggest and most traditional of which is *family identity*, and that the psychic toxicity—*not* the intentional guilt—of older generations may pass to younger ones, either psychologically through learned behavior or psychically through what are called "generational spirits," one of whose favorite ploys is to try and convince you that the damage done to you by your parents and grandparents is somehow your own fault, just to make sure that you shift the blame instead of renouncing it by passing on the same damage to your children; that's one way those evil spirits maintain the congenial atmosphere that lets them thrive. Only the love of God has the power to cancel the curse and cut the lines of generational poison. This act of cancellation is not without suffering of course, but the suffering is well worth it in view of the honor and glory to come. As Jenny says of her family darkness that so wounded her as a child, "That's not my heritage; your heritage is what you love," thus paraphrasing Ezra Pound, who wrote, in "Canto LXXXI":

> What thou lov'st well remains, the rest is dross
> What thou lov'st well shall not be reft from thee
> What thou lov'st well is thy true heritage...

Yet the ancestral darkness remains until it is released; it takes fire to separate the dross from the true gold. And a big contribution to that darkness was certainly made not only by the Whites but by the Native Americans, as both victims and perpetrators. My wife's mother's family, whose ancestral home is in Pike County, Kentucky, near the Virginia and West Virginia borders—the land of the famous Hatfield-McCoy feud over timber rights—obviously have a lot of American Indian blood in them. Kentucky was often a refuge for Native Americans fleeing war and forced exile from their lands further east, and it stands to reason that some of the Cherokees, along with other tribes, would have made their way to Eastern Kentucky as refugees from their people's dispossession. So the Hillbilly Kingdom was founded in part on a historic crime: the dispossession of the Cherokees by Andy Jackson, and their exile from their ancient home, to die, or else survive, on the Trail of Tears to Oklahoma—and that after the Cherokees had acted as loyal allies to Jackson in the War of 1812 and the Battle of New Orleans. (The "civilized" Cherokees had their own working homesteads, their own written language and alphabet and newspapers, even their own Black slaves! If the status of *slaveholders* did not ultimately fit them to be called "civilized" in White Virginia and Tennessee, what else could?) The memory of that betrayal is still so fresh among many Indians that you'd better not buy anything from a Native American or pay a debt owed to him or her with a $20 bill, even to this day, since it bears Jackson's image.

A profound impression regarding the Trail of Tears, if not a clairvoyant vision of a darkly buried past, impressed itself on me when I encountered Jenny's family. I haven't been able to fully corroborate it, but I still can't shake it: that when the time came for the Cherokees to be relocated, the women were faced with an excruciating choice: either to go along with the men and lose their homes, and possibly their lives, or else stay behind in hiding so as to more-or-less remain attached to the land as chattels when the "Americans" moved in, on the chance of becoming a consort, married or otherwise, to some unattached White Man, a choice that would have been reinforced by the traditional matrilocal organization of Cherokee culture: "Well tended homestead on cleared land; good soil and drainage; available Indian labor." (And no clan could be more matrilocal, if not matriarchal, than Jenny's mother's family!) Those who stayed put to intermarry with the Whites, whose descendants then later emigrated west to Kentucky as either settlers or refugees, so as to give Jenny's her high cheek bones, shovel-shaped eye teeth concave on the back side, and "Mongolian spot" on the sacrum like the Mayans have, also passed down their ancestral curse: the shame of those women who betrayed their menfolk so as to remain on their land and save their lives. Imagine a degree of oppression under which even survival becomes a source of shame!

In both Oklahoma and Kentucky the Plunkett name appears in the Cherokee Rolls, a fact that Jenny and I discovered when we visited the Harry Caudill Memorial Museum in Whitesburg in Letcher County, Harry Caudill being the author of the well-known classic of local history, *Night Comes to the Cumberlands*. The Rolls were compiled when Cherokees applied for the money awarded in 1905 because of a 1902 lawsuit in which the Eastern Cherokee tribe sued the United States for funds due them under the treaties of 1835, 1836 and 1845, in compensation for the expropriation of their lands. Partly out of this ancestral crime, the American version of the Rape of the Sabine Women from Roman history, came the profound capacity of the hill folk to perpetrate, endure, and deny, long-term multi-generational violence and abuse, not just between families, as in the Hatfield-McCoy feud, but within them. This resulted in a tendency to grim silence and an almost superhuman ability to lie about evil even in the act of perpetrating it, that has passed down through the generations—diminished perhaps, but still unbroken.

So Eastern Kentucky is not a place and a culture where Native American blood is likely to be taken as a source of pride, at least among the middle classes—as such blood still is, for example, to the Baskerville family, Virginia tidewater aristocrats and tributaries to my mother's family, the Strothers.

The Baskervilles were slaveholding planters, proud of their descent from Powhatan, a prominent chief of the eastern seaboard, through his daughter Pocahontas; it's from her (I'm told) that I inherited the "Baskerville nose," thin but with a definite hook to it. Those high planters had no truck with trash Negroes, trash Whites or trash Indians, but marriage with an Indian "princess" of what they considered to be aristocratic blood was something they recognized as a venerable tradition that gave them a legitimate *spiritual* title to the land they tilled. But Jenny's mother's family, though they look Indian enough (and probably are) to claim membership in a surviving tribe and open a bingo parlor, never mentioned their Native American ancestry and probably would have denied it if we had ever broached the subject. (Even the Plunkett background as moonshiners had to be told us on the sly by Jenny's mother's cousin Jeanette, who was from the "no-count" branch of the family; in a holler where the housing selection was cabin/mansion/trailer, cabin/mansion/trailer, Jenny's mother was mansion — more or less — while cousin Jeanette, who lived right next door, was trailer.) Even Jenny's uncle Juble, the family genealogist, didn't dare go into the family's Indian blood, though he was proud to find possible connections between the Plunketts — the anglicized version of the French name Planquet* — and the Bourbon kings of France. (The French, the Irish, the Scots — Europeans of Celtic ancestry — never had much of a problem mating with Indians of any status; it was mostly the Anglos, for some reason, who were squeamish in this regard.) And the saddest thing is, the suppression of the great Indian contribution to the bloodlines of so many American families acts to turn a noble ancestry — though not without its dark ancestral sins, with which every human bloodline is tainted — into a vengeful and haunting ghost.

Yet the people of Kentucky and the greater South certainly do not uniformly reject their Indian ancestry. The fictional Chickasaw chief Ikkemotubbe was an important figure in William Faulkner's mythology of his fictional Yoknapatawpha County, Mississippi, while the influence of the Cherokee musical tradition on the "old time mountain music" of Appalachia is apparent in the songs of the Cherokee musician Walker Calhoun. The high traditions and sacred theurgic practices of the First Nations peoples of North America, as well as their more bloodthirsty habits, are a formidable spiritual influence for both good and evil that lies hidden in the background of the contemporary religious and cultural landscape.

And there are layers even older than that. Kentucky is in many ways a more ancient land than California, older geologically (the Appalachians vs. the Sierras), older in terms of U.S. history, but also possibly older from the standpoint of pre-Columbian culture — though the theory recounted above that at least one Native American site in Marin County, California has been more-or-less continuously occupied for 8000 years works against this easy assumption. The westward expansion that would make the lands lying to the east the "old country" is a European pattern, not a Native American one.

One influence that might have started me musing in the direction of Ancient Kentucky was my meeting, at my mother-in-law's house in Pike County, with Cordell Damron, the "Hillbilly Edison," whose research on laser technology — not in any well-staffed laboratory but in his own home in the Appalachian Mountains — made him of great interest to the engineers who were working on the Star Wars program of orbiting space weapons in the late 20th Century — as well as to the CIA, who kept him under surveillance to make sure his findings didn't find their way into unfriendly hands.

Among the yarns Cordell spun were two that suggested the existence of an almost inconceivably ancient *industrial* civilization of the kind that many "fringe" archaeologists like Graham Hancock, both professional and amateur, now believe in under the name of "the Silurian Hypothesis," based on discoveries of rare and far-flung artifacts, some found embedded in ancient rock strata, that give every impression of having been manufactured by a high technology comparable to our own.

Cordell's story was as follows: On one occasion he was contacted by a strip miner of his acquaintance, who told him: "Cordell, it looks like we've found something inside a vein of coal that you really need to take a look at." The find was a mass of objects imbedded in the vein that gave every appearance of being — pipes. Metal pipes. Given that the Earth's coal deposits were formed approximately 250 million years ago, this — if there had been any way to authenticate it — would have been an extraordinary find to say the least. (I neglected to ask Cordell if he happened to have taken possession of any samples of these "pipes," but if the reader is moved to research the matter he or she may find some clues in the Cordell Damron Archive presently housed at Berea College in Berea, Kentucky.)

Cordell's second yarn was just as striking — the story of another day of strip mining that had apparently turned up a perfectly-proportioned adult human skeleton, no taller (if I remember rightly) than about 18 inches.

Interestingly enough, many Native American tribes had similar names for the land now called Kentucky. The Wyandots called it *Kah-ten-tah-teh*, meaning "Fair Land of Tomorrow" or "Land Where We Will Live Tomorrow." The Shawnee name was *Kain-tuck-ee*; according to John Johnson in *Indian Tribes in Ohio* it means "At The Head Of The River." The Mohawks and the Delawares named it *Kentucke*, "Place of the Meadows." Kentucky's first historian John Filson, however, translated *Kentucke* as "Dark and Bloody Ground" or "The Middle Ground," the first meaning possibly derived from the Cherokee Chief Dragging Canoe, speaking in the Great Council at Sycamore Shoals in March, 1775, who told the Whites that there was a dark cloud hanging over the land they were seeking to acquire.

Why does a similar-sounding word applied by various Indian tribes to the same general area, some of whom lived at a considerable distance from it, possess so many apparently different meanings? It may be that these tribes inherited this place-name from a common source—possibly the mound-builder culture which, according to Indians themselves, pre-dated their own arrival. And though some white archaeologists now claim that the present native population of Kentucky is directly descended from the mound-builders, the fact is that they did not use the old ritual earthworks, even though they sometimes occupied the same sites, which at least demonstrates a great civilizational revolution, even if it was not racially based. It is well-known that place-names will often be retained by tribes and nations who occupy a given area after they supplant, drive into exile or massacre the original inhabitants, even if they have little or no knowledge of the languages of those earlier populations. Many Celtic place-names were retained in Saxon Britain, and over half of the states that make up the U.S. still keep their Native American names. It's as if the newer populations desire, consciously or otherwise, to venerate and/or take possession of the *genius loci*, the "spirit of place" of their new home, so that the land will sustain them.

But if "Kentucky" is the true and ancient word for the land still called by that name, how can we account for the wide variation in the meanings attributed to that name by various tribes? What do "Land Where We Will Live Tomorrow," "At the Head of the River," "Place of the Meadows," "The Dark and Bloody Ground" and "The Middle Ground" have in common? Some of the differences are easily explained: "At the Head of the River" may denote the watershed of the Kentucky River or the Big Sandy, "Place of the Meadows" the Bluegrass, and "The Dark and Bloody Ground" the wars between hunting parties from different tribes over the abundant game to be found in the area. But what, if anything, is the common theme that made this whole land *Kentucky*?

Territories once occupied by ancient races who have emigrated, been slaughtered, or died out are often identified, by later populations, as Otherworlds, Lands of the Dead; the death of 90% of the native population by smallpox during the 1600s would certainly be enough to explain this identification in the case of Kentucky, though there may be other and older reasons for it. They are felt to be "haunted" by their earlier inhabitants; consequently they sometimes become "forbidden" lands, whose *genii loci* are considered to be too dangerous to appropriate, placate or have any dealings with. This may be why some areas of Kentucky were not claimed or settled by Native Americans when the whites arrived in numbers, but were used largely as hunting-grounds—a civilizational regression from earlier, more settled lifestyles that could have resulted from the smallpox pandemic. And if we consider the various apparently incompatible meanings given to the word "Kentucky" according to mythopoetic etymology, we may watch as those meanings apparently converge upon the notion of an Otherworld, a Land of the Dead.

    The idea of a Garden of Paradise, found in the Abrahamic, Near Eastern and Celtic religions, is still with us today. It is considered to be the place of our origin, but also the paradise to which sanctified souls will return when their earthly journey is done. Thus it is both Source and Destiny, both "the Head of the Rivers" and "the Land of Tomorrow." It is also often an area of meadows, a tract of level ground. Since at least the 18th Century we have seen mountains as beautiful and romantic — but our earlier ancestors, who often had to traverse them, had different notions. They were considered dangerous, inconvenient, cumbersome; they were "cumberlands," hard tortuous areas that nobody would naturally think of as paradises or happy hunting-grounds. The spiritual meaning of mountains in many world mythologies has to do with notions such as the inaccessibility of the gods (Olympus), or nearness to Heaven (Sinai), or a difficult ascent (Dante's Mount of Purgatory), more than with any sense of rest or reward for a life well-lived; the Terrestrial Paradise at the summit of Dante's Purgatory was the origin of the human race, but not our eternal resting-place. To the degree that a paradise was seen as the prize won by the just, it was most often pictured as a level area, easy to stroll through, like the Pure Land of Amitabha in Buddhist lore. So it is readily understandable that the Bluegrass — though certainly not the Cumberlands — would contribute some of the quality of an earthly Paradise to the ancient word *Kentucky*. And sacred territories were considered "Middle Grounds" by many archaic peoples; the ancient Persians and the ancient Chinese, who thought of their homelands as sacrosanct, named them "The Center of the Universe" (Persia) and "The Middle Kingdom" (China). [NOTE: Most linguists would consider relating "cumbersome" to "Cumberlands" to be a case of spurious etymology, since they trace "Cumberland" back to "Cymri," a name that means "Welsh" in Welsh. And Dr Thomas Walker, who first explored the Cumberland Gap in 1750, named the river north of the Gap the Cumberland River after the patron of his expedition, the Duke of Cumberland, which is why that mountainous area — cumbersome though it certainly is — is now called the Cumberlands. Be that as it may, word-derivations are not always linear and singular. If the Cumberlands of Britain were indeed difficult to travel through, that fact could easily have spawned the adjective "cumbersome," just as the cumbersomeness of their American version might have influenced Walker to name them after his patron. A word, unlike a man, can have many fathers.]

    But what of the Dark and Bloody Ground? Certainly the narrow hollers of Eastern Kentucky, dark, twisted like sheep's-guts and painful to pass through, which served as hideouts for Native Americans fleeing the wars that troubled the Eastern Seaboard after the coming of the White Man, in many ways deserve that name. And we have also mentioned its possible derivation from the intertribal skirmishes over hunting-rights. But if Kentucky is truly a Land of the Dead, taboo to many Native Americans as a place to settle, it in some ways fits the definition of a *fallen* Paradise. The Garden of Eden in the Book of Genesis became just such a lost or fallen Paradise, made taboo to humankind by Jehovah after Adam sinned; the "angel with a flaming sword which turned every way," posted by God at the gates of Eden to bar humanity's return, stood as a sign of this divine curse. If Kentucky truly is a Dark and Bloody Ground, this may be part of the reason.

My speculations on Ancient Kentucky had their origin in a dream my wife Jenny had, who dreamed of a house of evil in Pike County, Kentucky, whose residents kept a large black-winged bird, like a Condor. As soon as she told me the dream I immediately remembered that the ancient and original name of the Inca sun-god Viracocha, who reigned in the Andes Mountains where the Condor glides, was *Kon-tiki*, and a few minutes on the Web taught me that the Condor was one of Viracocha's royal emblems. The Aztecs, who migrated from a place in North America they called *Aztlán* — immediately reminding us of *Atlantis* — were sun-worshippers practicing human sacrifice, and some sources give the meaning of the syllable "Kon" in Kon-Tiki as "sun." Was the mound-building culture of the Ohio Valley in some ways continuous with similar cultures in Mesoamerica and South America? Did they too worship the sun and sacrifice human victims? We may never know. It is known, however, that a single forest once stretched from the limestone highlands of Appalachia to another region of limestone, the Yucatán in Mexico. Inca legend has it that Kon-Tiki was white, bearded, and blond-haired or red-haired; the same is claimed for the Aztec/Toltec Quetzalcoatl and the Mayan Kukulcán. Several Amerindian informants from North America have held that the mound-builder culture that preceded them was of a different racial stock — and various Kentucky caverns, including Mammoth Cave, Short Cave and Salts Cave, have yielded red-haired mummies (see *Weird Kentucky* by Jeffrey Scott Holland). Similar mummies have been found in the Paracas and Nazca areas of Peru. And it is worth noting that the Native Americans of Appalachia, in common with most North American tribes, have their legends of the Thunderbird, whether it be conceived of as a myth, a cryptid or a paranormal apparition. So if the mound-building Ohioans (or Mississippians), and the pyramid-building Toltecs, Aztecs and Mayans, as well as the Inca (or pre-Inca), were indeed united by a common cult of sun-worship, possibly deriving from an earlier race with fair skin and red or blond hair, then "Kon-Tiki" and "Kentucky" could, just conceivably, be the same word. Those migrating from the east, through the dark and difficult Cumberlands, would have reached a point where they could first see the Bluegrass from the outlying mountains. Emerging from "some dark holler/Where the sun refuse to shine" (as the song goes), they would have gazed down, with relief and wonder, into a vast open area, a sea of grass filled with light: the Land of the Sun. What better seat and homeland for a Pan-American sun god—seeing that, to populations entering America from the north and moving southward, Kentucky at one point would have become the Old Country, the Grandmother Earth? And if a shadow now lies across this land, it may be because the worship of that god died in Kentucky, which is why his loss—and his curse—are still felt here, perhaps by a sudden and inexplicable dark edge to the mellow golden sunlight. The story of that curse is clearly told, for example, in the work of Lexington photographer Ralph Eugene Meatyard (an afficionado of Jazz and Zen Buddhism who knew and collaborated with Guy Davenport, Wendell Berry and Thomas Merton)—though the spirituality of the Shakers with its Native American influences and the spirit healings of Edgar Cayce, another photographer who came from Hopkinsville, might have acted, to a certain degree, as a balm and a mitigation. Human souls can still be saved, one by one, out of this way-station, but as for the land itself and the ancestors it holds, they are not saved—nor will they ever be till the graves are opened and Jesus Christ comes back again, to judge the living and the dead.

But until that happens—and to lighten up the atmosphere a bit while still preserving its mythopoetic aura—I can report that Jenny once discovered, with the help of a story told by "conservative" Kentucky poet Guy Davenport, a connection between Kentucky and *The Lord of the Rings* mythology of J. R. R. Tolkien. Once upon a time, as recounted in his book *The Geography of the Imagination*, Davenport met another Kentuckian, a history teacher, in the town of Shelbyville near Lexington, a man who had been a fellow-student of Tolkien's at Oxford. The man had no idea, until Davenport told him, that his old classmate was now a famous published author whose books were popular among the hippies. He told Guy Davenport that Tolkien had often queried him, during their long walks, about the interesting surnames and Christian names current in his part of the world (names like the "Dingus Pigman" for example, or the "Paris Music," that I found in some old Pike County phonebooks at my mother-in-law's house), and this reminded the poet of something that had caught his attention while reading Tolkien's works. So he consulted a Lexington phonebook and found the names of most of the Hobbits; in a Shelbyville phonebook he found the rest. In other words, "Took" (perchance the same name as Robin Hood's Friar Tuck?), "Baggins," "Belladonna," "Frodo" and "Bilbo" are apparently Central Kentucky names, proving that (at least on one layer of things) Jenny and I presently live in the actual Shire—though this in itself will not protect us, I'm afraid, seeing that the Nazgul are now on the march.

KENTUCKY RELIGION

In common with all areas in North America and most of the world, the spiritual landscape of Kentucky is complex. Some have called Kentucky "the buckle on the Bible Belt," and that was undoubtedly true at one point, and remains partly true today, as witness the Asbury Revival of 2023 at Asbury University in the town of Willmore just west of Lexington, which drew people from all around the world. But I may in fact have lived long enough to see that belt start to become unbuckled.

The traditional Christian piety of Eastern Kentucky was most evident in the older and less "successful" members of Jenny's mother's family: "Aunt Anel" Hampton (Jenny's great aunt by marriage), her son Arnold, and Esta Plunkett, the wife of Jenny's uncle Juble. My attendance at the funerals of these three immersed me in the holy and living spirit of the Old Time Religion, as well represented by title of the traditional fiddle tune "Glory in the Meeting House," and the tune itself.

Aunt Anel was a traditional Christian visionary. An angel once appeared to her, standing on a golden shield, to prophesy the coming of a "great separation," apparently the end of the world; she wrote a poem about it. Her house, on the other side of the creek from Jenny's mother's house, a bit dumpy and sway-backed, overflowed with love and welcome: it was the very self and essence of "down home." I talked with her once after she was old and bed-bound. She'd had another vision more recently of uncanny elves with conical hats sitting in a neighbor's apple tree, which explained — she said — why the tree hadn't borne fruit that year. "We've got a lot of those things in California" I told her, after which she liked to recount to people how "Charles says that California had lots of those very things I saw in my vision." And they've only increased their range since then.

The Old Regular Baptist funerals of Anel, Arnold and Esta showed salt-of-the-earth folk Protestantism at its finest, a religion in which God, to make up for the loss of the sacred Sacramental Order preserved by the Catholic Church for 2000 years — or 1500 years if you take it only to the Protestant Reformation — allowed as how *sola fide*, "faith alone," might open a door through which the Holy Spirit could enter, if He so elected. Like sunlight through a hole in the roof, like rain soaking through parched, dry earth, the Mercy of God comes to the human heart through whatever channel is available to it, no matter how narrow, crooked or "unofficial." All that's necessary beyond that is a sound barrel to hold the rainwater and a clean mirror to reflect the light of the Sun. But do we still know how to polish that mirror? And are the coopers still at work?

In the Old Regular Baptist churches the sexes are separated, men on the right, women on the left, as in some of the more traditional Eastern Orthodox churches; this works to set up a "tantric" polarity between the sexes to get the holiness energy flowing, something that takes place in the "nave" of the church where the yet-to-be saved are seated, those who haven't been baptized yet. As for the "saved" or the "elect," the ones who act as ministerial team, these sanctified souls occupy, as their sanctuary, a raised platform at the head of the room. As opposed to the often dry and repetitive sermons of some of the mainline Protestants, composed the night before or drawn from a sheaf of past writings, the Old Regular Baptists will only preach when the Spirit moves them. I remember how, at one of those funerals (I forget which), the preacher stood up to preach and then confessed that the Spirit had not spoken to him on that occasion, so he sat down again.

The elect would literally "get themselves into the Spirit" by walking back and forth across the Sanctuary, opening themselves, making themselves available to Him — they would "walk all over God's heaven," in the words of the old spiritual, right before our eyes: bewildered, intensively questing, then transfigured! And when the Spirit arrived they would preach by immediate, direct inspiration — partly due to the fact that, since they had the Bible nearly memorized, they could provide that Spirit (the *Forma*) with plenty of material (the *Materia*) for Him to assemble and work with. They preached, in other words, by the Bardic method, according to which — whether through Spirit or through Muse — the preacher or poet composes *ex tempore* by drawing from the vault of a fully-stocked memory, bursting with mythopoetic lore. And of course the common ecstatogenic technique of hyperventilation-while-preaching was also in evidence. But the thing that really struck me was the fact that, though the Baptists officially deny the reality of Purgatory and therefore say no prayers for the dead, on one occasion the Spirit, speaking through an Old Regular Baptist preacher, actually called for such prayers — as if that Spirit were really a secret Catholic who was forced to hide this identity while moving among Protestants. As they preached, they opened the door to Heaven: you could just barely glimpse the radiant, illuminated crack through which their Spirit-inspired words kept pouring in.

I feel deeply privileged to have witnessed such openings — particularly since most of the congregations were getting on in years; the young, no longer content to follow in their elders' footsteps, were mostly headed elsewhere. Our first indication of this was when we met a young waitress in the Courthouse Café in Whitesburg who was taking a correspondence course in shamanism; around the same time, while browsing in a bookstore off Highway 23 near Pikeville, we found some "how to" books on witchcraft. Both of these things would have been no surprise in California, but in Kentucky they were a new development. Slowly we began to get the sense that, for the younger generations at least, Christianity was being replaced by a fascination with the paranormal. More cryptid stories were emerging. A popular internet program devoted to paranormal subjects called the Pennyroyal Podcast, based in the Pennyroyal Plateau region of

Eastern Kentucky, was attracting a large audience; one of their claims was that a local cult, which included some prominent businessmen and lawyers, worshipped a figure called the Green Man, who occupied a cave somewhere in the hills. Our friend Dr John Parks, the retired psychiatrist (you'll meet him soon), told us that, to his certain knowledge, there were four different Satanist groups operating in the Bluegrass. And the last time we visited Long Fork to prepare Jenny's mother's house for sale after her death, we saw — in a small field attached to the trailers next door where Lola's cousin Jeanette and her husband J. E. once lived (they had both passed by that time), on a slice of land now occupied by one Rick Chaney who had married their daughter-in-law after her first husband died — a life-sized (or death-sized) skeleton scarecrow; whether it was a real skeleton or a plastic one we never discovered. But whatever it was, it was a sign for us of the profound spiritual change that had come over that part of the world. Eastern Kentucky had always been host to various magical beliefs inherited from the peasant cultures of the British Isles, and possibly from the Cherokees as well, though after the '60s it was almost impossible to tell what was actual folk belief and what had been imported later from western occultism and/or the New Age. But for many generations Christianity had been dominant; this, however, was now beginning to change before our eyes. The "Pagan Belt" culture so perfectly pictured in the TV series "Northern Exposure" that ran on CBS from 1990 to 1995 was now invading the Bible Belt. (The equivalent cultural transformation for Great Britain is accurately portrayed in the detective series "Midsomer Murders.") And Jenny's uncle Dale's funeral, as you will see below, was the perfect example of a post-Christian Christianity, exactly as predicted by Flannery O'Connor in her novel *Wise Blood*, with its "Holy Church of Christ without Christ."

Jenny and I had a personal brush with that world when we attended a book-signing at Joseph Beth Bookstore in Lexington featuring one Tracy Damron, an attractive blonde supermodel-type from Pike County and a kind of New Age witch (vaguely reminding me, now that I think of it, of Jeannette Pomeroy); she'd written a book on various spiritual subjects. She had been the wife of Steve Nunn, an unsuccessful gubernatorial candidate and son of former Kentucky governor Louie Nunn; Steve went on to murder a later girlfriend and is now in state prison. She told us the story of the time when a young lover of hers, apparently taking it into his head to meditate under water, was found sitting naked in the lotus posture at the bottom of a swimming pool, dead. As she continued with her interesting revelations she handed each of us a feather which she said would establish a psychic connection between us and her. Simultaneously I developed an attack of ventricular tachycardia and had to drive home early so I could take some medication for it; I was undoubtedly terrified.

As for the feather, I immediately threw it away and prayed to God for protection, as well as reciting the Surah al-Falaq of the Qur'an, in which the reciter takes refuge in the *Lord of Daybreak* from *malignant witchcraft* (literally, "women who blow upon knots").

Every part of the world harbors tendencies like this, which are traditionally kept in check when Christianity or some other God-revealed religion is culturally strong in a particular area. But when the High Religion begins to weaken and fade, all the low religions come out of the closet. As for how this might have affected Jenny's mother's family, one possible vector of ancestral darkness could have been Jenny's great grandmother Annie Plunkett, who she never met, the wife of John Plunkett, the big moonshiner of the area. Jenny's mother described her as a very weird individual, and the stories Annie told used to scare Jenny's aunt Irene. When I first heard of Annie I wrote a poem (which I never kept) in which I said she was a witch. In the poem — as originally in my mind's eye — I asked her what she saw, and she replied: "I see war, and hate, and horror, and a horrible love!" And since Jenny has recently been wrestling with the feeling, now that most of her family has passed on, that a "generational spirit" looking for a new home might be obsessing her, I began to wonder if Annie Plunkett could be the source of this influence, since for a man powerful in the outer world to marry a woman who claims to be powerful in the inner one (as in the case of Steve Nunn and Tracy Damron) — whether or not we call such a woman a witch — seems to be a common practice in Kentucky, and elsewhere. Then, just the other night, I dreamt that we had buried Annie Plunkett's body somewhere in the garden of my childhood home in California; in the process of digging it up again I unearthed one of her shoulder-blades, which was small enough to be the shoulder-blade of a bird. The next day I consulted my favorite dream-interpretation machine, Google, and discovered, while searching under "magic/shoulder-blade," that *scapulimancy* — divination using a shoulder-blade (scapula), a practice called *slinneanachd* in Scots Gaelic — goes back as least as far as the Druids, and used to be common in many parts of the world. This, of course, proves nothing — yet at this point it wouldn't hurt to say *audhu billahi min ash-Shaytan al-rajim*, "I take refuge in Allah from Satan the rejected." (Which puts a better feeling in your heart, dear reader — the old time Christian religion or the weird world of the witches? As I see it, the coveted gift of "discernment of spirits" is sometimes nothing but spiritual good taste.)

To back-track a bit, and tie up some of the threads of spiritual influence that ultimately converged on Kentucky, it was during one of the years we were visiting in Long Fork from California, before we moved to Kentucky permanently, that we drove to Washington D.C. to visit Dr Javad Nurbakhsh at the Washington Nimatullahi *khaniqa* on MacArthur Boulevard.

We'd stayed the night before at a motel in Lexington, Virginia, home to the Virginia Military Institute where Stonewall Jackson had taught. We'd had a short yelling-match that night, detoxing from the oppressive vibes we'd absorbed at Long Fork; we arrived in D.C. the next day. When we came into Dr Nurbakhsh's presence—he was half-reclining on a pad or mattress on the floor, as was his habit—and greeted him, we saw him shrivel up into an intense state of physical contraction for a moment, then relax. So it was clear to me that he had immediately absorbed my load of psychic poison, "taken on my karma" in the terminology of the time, then released it (or most of it) to Allah. Since then I've wondered whether his long-term poor health (he was a diabetic, Type One I believe) had partly to do with his work of taking on the suffering and spiritual darkness of his *murids*. Later I did my best to release my problems directly to God so they wouldn't burden him, though I'm not sure I really had the power to divert them in that direction, since he was, at that point, the proper established channel for that operation. And I was also able to witness his meeting with Dr Seyyed Hossein Nasr, at that time a *muqaddam* (representative) of Frithjof Schuon in Schuon's Maryamiyya-Shadhili Tariqah; he was teaching then (as now) at the George Washington University, and had known Nurbakhsh in Iran. They were like the Sun and Moon, Nurbakhsh golden like the Sun (his name means "Light-giver"), and Dr Nasr, who showed great deference to him, silvery like the Moon.

Later, on another trip from California to Kentucky, after Jenny had left the Nimatullahis and been initiated by Hossein Nasr into the Maryamiyya Tariqah, we made *three* consecutive trips during the same summer from Long Fork to D.C., this time so Jenny could visit Dr Nasr and attend *majlis* at his own *zawiya* near Mount Vernon. (On the cornerstone of George Washington's mansion I saw carved the Masonic symbol of the crossed axes, with a dot below their intersection, which immediately reminded me of the insignia of the Nimatullahi Tariqah, featuring two crossed battle-axes, in which the dot was replaced with a *kashkul*, a begging-bowl made out of the shell of the sea cocoanut, the largest seed in the world. Did the Nimatullahis get that symbol from the Masons, or did the Masons get it from some ancient source from which it also passed to the Nimatullahis?) The act of traveling three times in a row, forth and back, from the spiritually destitute environment of Pike County to the immensely more elevated and light-filled circle of Dr Nasr, precipitated some obscure inner alchemical transformation in Jenny's relationship with her family and her past life with them—one that, augmented by our several later trips to the remnant of Schuon's circle in Bloomington Indiana after his death, might have been signaled by the mysterious appearance, on Long Fork Creek, right in the middle of that hillbilly holler, of a Native American tipi, painted in the exact heraldic colors of the Maryamiyya—ochre, orange, maroon etc.—along with a real estate sign advertising the services of Abodes, a company owned by one of Schuon's major followers, Michael Pollock. We never found out exactly who lived in the tipi—he was just described as "some Indian"—but we both felt that this strange occurrence represented the appearance of a short-lived beam of the Schuonian *maya* that had somehow found its way into Jenny's old neck-of-the-woods.

Beyond that, two further incidents of the hidden workings of the Spirit in Eastern Kentucky, of the Light that shines in the darkness though the darkness can't comprehend it, are worth mentioning. On one occasion, when I was waiting in a hospital with Jenny's family while Arnold Plunkett*, Jenny's mother's third and last husband, was being tested for prostate cancer (negative at that point, positive later), I struck up a conversation with an Evangelical minister in the waiting room. It turned out, amazingly enough, that he had also encountered the Psychic Surgeons in the Philippines just as I had, in his capacity as a missionary, and had even worked with them! He, the Surgeons, and some Muslim *hakims* (Sufis perhaps?) had come together from their radically different points of departure, on those distant islands, to bring God's healing to the sick. What an amazing "coincidence" that I should run into him!

And then there was the mysterious, near-miraculous event that occurred during a time when Lola was gravely ill in the hospital—so ill that the doctor had showed up in the waiting-room to tell her family, "It looks like we've lost her—I'm so sorry." Then, unexpectedly, a minister appeared that nobody knew, a Black man, and asked to see Lola Plunkett. After being admitted to her room he prayed for her, then left the hospital, apparently without introducing himself. From that moment on her condition began to improve; she was released from the hospital a short time after. Jenny and I later wondered if he had actually been an angel, until the family found out who he was and visited him at his church. Either on that occasion, or earlier when he might have talked with Lola in the hospital—though it's hard for me to imagine that she was in a position to talk with anyone at that time—he revealed that her husband had summoned him, though Arnold claimed that he'd never contacted him and didn't know him. Had the doctors actually called him in, as they might have done in the past with good results for seemingly hopeless cases? Had he been informed in prayer of Lola's need, possibly by an angel of healing? Or possibly, as Jenny speculates, by the soul of her father, Fred Donne, Lola's first husband, who had died some years earlier? No one knows. But after this incident Lola claimed that she'd completely lost her fear of death—though whether it would have been better for her to have kept a little of that salutary fear is a question I can't begin to answer. She had apparently gone through something like a near-death experience, but she never elaborated further.

CATHOLIC KENTUCKY

Farther west from Lexington, mostly west of the Bluegrass, lies old Catholic Kentucky which, along with Louisiana, makes up the original Catholic missionary territory of the United States, settled not by the later Catholic immigrants, the Irish, the Poles and the Italians, but by the French. The center of that world is Bardstown, and the center of that center is the Abbey of Gethsemani, founded by French Cistercians of the Strict Observance—better known as Trappists—where the most famous Catholic monk of the 20th Century, Thomas Merton, was cloistered (rather restlessly so, as it turned out). Bardstown is the site of the Proto-Cathedral, the first Catholic cathedral west of the Alleghanies, and the surrounding area is filled with many beautiful, old, historic Catholic churches. This Catholic zone stretches north to Louisville, the Ohio river, and then across it into the Greater Cincinnati area, which presently functions as the heartland of traditional *sedevacantist* Catholicism in North America. (For those unfamiliar with this term, the *sedevacantists*, the best known of whom is undoubtedly the actor Mel Gibson—though some might wish to include Steve Bannon as a potential candidate—believe that "the Seat is vacant," that the Roman Catholic Church has been without a valid Pope since Pius XII—that is, ever since the Second Vatican Council. So what's their problem, you ask? It's enough to remind the reader once again that Pope Francis said, in an interview with Vatican radio, "God does not exist"—proving that the Almighty has held back the major part of His lightning until the Last Day—and to point out as I did above that his predecessor Benedict XVI, when he was Cardinal Ratzinger, declared in his book *Introduction to Christianity* that "the notion of an immortal soul is obsolete.") As for our sole contact with Francis' "Novus Ordo" church (as the *sedevacantists* call it) in Kentucky—outside, that is, of the Abbey of Gethsemani—on one occasion we did visit a convent of the Missionary Sisters of Charity, Mother Theresa's order, with its gazebo housing a shrine to the Virgin, in the town of Jenkins not far from Virgie—Jenkins being possibly the worst and most depressed-and-depressing town in that area outside of (maybe) Robinson Creek. It was home to a group of nuns who represented the tiny, flickering, last gasp of the Catholic Church in a decidedly non-Catholic area. Only the living death of Jenny's mother's house, where time hung heavy, like water slowly dripping from a limestone stalactite, growing an eighth of a millimeter per year over the centuries, could make that isolated Novus Ordo outpost seem like a tiny patch of light.

THE ABBEY OF GETHSEMANI

One of the spiritually helpful practices Jenny received through her Maryamiyya initiation was a short, 2-hour long monthly "retreat," allowing for the intensive practice of *dhikr* in one of its approved Christian forms, a practice that is known to most people as "the Jesus Prayer." This led to our habit, for some years, of driving around 60 miles west to Bardstown, then another 12 miles to the Abbey of Gethsemani. Once we got there, all we had to do is walk into the church, with its bare gray interior walls perfectly suggesting spiritual poverty, climb the stairs to the choir loft, and pray. We needed no reservations, and nobody disturbed us.

Gethsemani as we knew it was a fading spiritual powerhouse. It seemed to cast a radiance of subtle grace over the whole surrounding territory; nonetheless this influence, over the years we went there, appeared to be slowly receding. The remaining monks were a skeleton crew of old men; from our choir loft we watched them in the nave below where they would file in several times a day to pray the Hours. A young novice would sometimes appear, only to be gone the next time we visited. As they prayed and sang their hymns (in English), one got the impression that they were singing their own requiem, especially when rendering one mournful song whose chorus concluded with the words, "at The End of the Age."

Catholic monasticism, and the Roman Catholic Church as a whole, was experiencing a renaissance in North America when Merton came to Gethsemani, part of it due to Merton himself and his best-selling spiritual autobiography *The Seven Storey Mountain* (the title a reference to Dante's *Purgatorio*). As the '60s unfolded, however, Merton became — partly under the influence of the Second Vatican Council — more and more of an "interfaith" figure, as well as a recognized voice in the anti-Vietnam War peace movement. A book of reminiscences about Merton that was published after his death (whose title I don't recall, nor can I locate a copy of it since I lent mine to someone and never got it back) included chapters by Lawrence Ferlinghetti and Joan Baez. The broadening of Merton's interests and contacts beyond the Catholic world is demonstrated in a series of books published by Gray Henry through her press Fons Vitae (Gray remains closely associated with the Traditionalist School) which include *Merton and Buddhism, Merton and Sufism, Merton and Hesychasm, Merton and Judaism, Merton and the Protestant Tradition, Merton and the Tao, Merton and Confucianism,* and *Merton and Indigenous Wisdom*. He had connections with a Qadiri Sufi Shaykh, corresponded with a number of the Traditionalists, and met not only with several Tibetan lamas but also with the Dalai Lama, as we learn from the story of his final journey that appears in *The Asian Journals of Thomas Merton*. Merton had been getting antsy in Gethsemani for some years, so when a more liberal abbot appeared who was willing to temporarily relax his "vow of enclosure," he hit the sky for Asia, where he had been invited to speak at an interfaith conference for monastics in Bangkok. He felt on the eve of his trip that his long spiritual pilgrimage was finally beginning to flower, and that might well have been true — though not in this world. Immediately following his speech at the Bangkok conference, which concluded with the words "so I will disappear from view," he died by electrocution in his bathtub after returning to his room, when an electric fan accidentally fell into the water. (Some, of course, speculated that he had been assassinated, but nothing was ever proved.) It is noteworthy, however, that the title of his last speech, as I've already commented on above, was "Marxism and Monastic Perspectives." It was certainly not a paean to Marxism, yet his willingness to dialogue with the Marxists in a "friendly" manner, as equals, after what they had done to both the Catholics and the Eastern Orthodox in Russia, China and Eastern Europe—not to mention their invasion and destruction of Tibet—might in itself have crossed some red line in the Unseen World. And another strange thing was that Thomas Merton's end was an almost exact parallel to the fate of the main character in Herman Hesse's novel *Das Glasperlenspiel* (*The Glass Bead Game*). The Grand Master of a mysterious monastic order that governs a principality (somewhat on the Tibetan model) is inducted as a child into the Order by traveling monks who discover him, much as the Dalai Lama or other Vajrayana *tulkus* (incarnations) are discovered as children. The entire *raison d'être* of the Order is to carry on an endless metaphysical tourney known as the Glass Bead Game. Over the years the protagonist rises through the initiatory grades, till he ultimately becomes the Grand Master—then he abruptly decides to abandon the Game and quit the monastery. He goes out into the world with a new-found sense of expansiveness and freedom, decides to take a swim in a cold mountain lake, and immediately dies by drowning. I wrote a poem once (I no longer have a copy of it) about Merton's death in which I intimated that he had somehow been killed by the Tibetans, unintentionally yet inevitably, through a clash of archetypal spiritual identities; in that poem I called him "the last Catholic."

"If only," I sometimes say to myself, "Thomas Merton had concentrated on Hesychasm, crafted a specifically Catholic form of the practice of the Jesus Prayer designed for householders, and then presented it to those young Catholics of the '60s who were vainly seeking a formal mystical Path within the Roman Catholic Church—a Path they later found, or thought they had found, in this or that Eastern religion. If only he had given them a form of contemplative prayer that might have taken the place of the Liberation Theology and 'promiscuous Liberal ecumenism' offered by the Second Vatican Council, things might have been very different in the Catholic world." As perhaps the greatest writer on Catholic contemplative spirituality of the 20th Century, judging from such books as *New Seeds of Contemplation* and *The Sign of Jonas*, he might have been able to pull it off. As it was, the only one to do anything like that was Rama Coomaraswamy in his book *The Invocation of the Name of Jesus:*

As Practiced in the Western Church—a book written by a less prominent author and one that appeared much too late to appeal to the kind of mass audience that Merton could have commanded.

And as Merton went, so went Gethsemani. At one point the monks were able keep the institution afloat through their two cottage industries—cheese and coffins—but by the time we were going there the Abbey had begun to morph into a kind of interfaith retreat house, hosting events led by Tibetan Buddhists and others. And as Gethsemani went, so went the "Novus Ordo" Catholic Church.

Yet it was still a wonderful place to meditate. Once while doing my Nimatullahi *zekr* in the choir loft, I unexpectedly *returned to consciousness*, and realized by that return that I had been essentially non-existent for an extended period of time; I concluded that I had most likely "experienced" (or rather *not* experienced) what the Sufis call "Absence," and the Hindu yogis, *nirvikalpa samadhi*.

TRAVELING AGAIN

So after our move to Kentucky, our life of travel resumed and expanded. From Lexington we branched out, taking frequent trips not only to Gethsemani but to Pike County, over the high ridge to the east and down into the valley of the Big Sandy, to visit the Old Folks, half a state away, as well as to Morehead to see Jenny's uncle Dale, his wife Eileen and their daughter Angie. We took a trip to a spot near Bowling Green in the west of the state to view the total solar eclipse, and to the town of Augusta north of Lexington on the Ohio River where Rosemary Clooney had lived and her son George Clooney had been born, imagining the big day in the century before last when the showboat would arrive and all the restless, cooped-up girls started to dream of being stylishly abducted by a burly riverboat sailor or some slick professional gambler, representing the Great Outside World. Also near the Ohio we visited Gray Henry—the Maryamiyya *faqirat* Sayyida Aisha, director of Fons Vitae, successor press to the Islamic Texts Society, one of the greatest of the Traditionalist publishing houses, concentrating mostly on the writings of classical *tasawwuf* and including the writings of my own present Sufis, the Shadhili/Darqawi/'Alawi *silsila*—just so we could drink tea with her in her famous Mongolian *yurt*. We took a tour boat ride on the Kentucky River, flanked by high vertical cliffs, and drove several times to the well-restored Shaker Village of Pleasant Hill nearby, built by that strange, celibate, female-led colony of Protestant nuns and monks. It had a characteristic fey aura of suspended animation and preternatural quiet, the same feeling I got in Inverness Farms at Bloomington, Indiana after Frithjof Schuon passed on, that being another point of interest and pilgrimage we visited several times, thanks to the hospitality of Barry and Rebecca McDonald. Schuon's group also frowned on reproduction, though they were by no means celibate! During one of those visits I placed a branch of cedar that I'd broken from a tree at Pleasant Hill on Schuon's grave. Our connection with the Bloomington of the latter days was congenial, all-in-all—until, after the death of Javad Nurbakhsh, I began investigating whether the Maryamiyya Tariqah might be the next stop on my inner pilgrimage. Not long before Schuon had "retired" due to the well-known scandals, though he still presided over the Bloomington circle, he delegated his function to two (at least) of his *muqaddams*, Seyyed Hossein Nasr and Martin Lings. So I decided to investigate Lings's branch of the organization while Lings was still alive, since a representative of that branch (whose name I don't recall) lived in Bloomington. On that visit Jenny and I were sitting with Barry in his enclosed porch across from a grove of tall trees, filled with beautiful multicolored birds, listening to him tell with a haunted expression of a recent trip to India where he had visited the temple of "a Goddess worse than Kali," when the representative of the Lings branch arrived. One thing he said, with a supercilious smile, really stuck with me: "But why should people suffer?"—as if human suffering were something that one could simply opt to undergo if he or she were addicted to "voluntaristic, passional mysticism" (in Schuon's terminology), or else opt out of if one were a true *gnostic*, someone whose metaphysical discernment lifted him, or her, above all that messiness. "These people obviously don't know the score" I said to myself, and dropped the idea of joining the Maryamiyya then and there—though my decision was also influenced by the nightmares I'd had at the motel where we spent our first night in Bloomington. On top of that, when we got home to Lexington I found that I'd lost my wallet in Indiana, though someone found it and mailed it back to me (*alhamdulillah!*).

Our visits both to South Carolina to see James Cutsinger and to the remnant of the Schuon circle in Bloomington—one of which included a meeting between Jenny and Schuon's first and only legal wife, Catherine Schuon (Sayyida Latifa)—began before we left California and continued for some time after our move. By the 1990s, travel, for both of us, had been transformed into pilgrimage; we hardly took a trip of any length except for a spiritual purpose. We visited Nurbakhsh, and later Hossein Kashani, shaykh of the Washington D.C. Nimatullahi *khaniqa* after Nurbakhsh had moved on to England, and touched base with the *khaniqas* in New York and Chicago. While in Chicago we also visited the All Saints Antiochian Orthodox Church, whose pastor, Fr Patrick Henry Reardon, was editor of the interesting and somewhat traditionally-oriented Christian journal, *Touchstone*. We traveled to Holy Cross Orthodox Monastery in West Virginia and also to the Orthodox Monastery of the Holy Cross in Setauket, Long Island, whose Abbot, Maximos, was a "graduate" of the

Schuon world; he had studied under Prof. Cutsinger. We were able to share with him some of our developing misgivings about the less "Traditional" aspects of Schuon's manifestation, and to receive from him two wonderful gifts: a beautiful Coptic icon of the last supper painted on papyrus, and a set of Muslim prayer-beads—known as a *tasbih*—that he had picked up in Jerusalem. And on one occasion (at Cutsinger's invitation) we also venerated a traveling miraculous icon at the Holy Trinity Cathedral in Columbia, SC, in which town we also visited the Orthodox bookstore of a man who called himself Pilgrim John, where we purchased a copy of the amazing book *Prayers by the Lake* by Nikolai Velimirovich, whom I like to call "the Orthodox Rumi," as well as touching in with the St Elizabeth the New Martyr Russian Orthodox Church (ROCOR), whose priest, Fr Mark Mancuso, was another graduate of Schuonian Traditionalism.

But for all this patronizing of orthodox traditions, my life was not yet purified of unorthodox, quasi-spiritual manifestations. For example, about a year after our move to Kentucky, the day came when we learned that a female white buffalo calf had been born in Shelbyville, Kentucky, at Buffalo Crossing, a buffalo ranch and tourist destination. She was named Cante Pejute (Medicine Heart). So I bought some sweet grass at a Lexington head shop and—thinking of course of Schuon's "vertical" (unofficial) wife Sharlyn Romaine, Sayidda Badriyya, the latter day incarnation of the White Buffalo Cow Woman of the Lakota according to Schuonian mythology—I drove with Jenny to the ranch and left the sweetgrass for the calf, though I didn't get to see her... It was one more spiritual half-step that never got completed. I was still addicted to ghost religions, still in the habit of making subtle connections between the signs to transmit whatever unread psychic messages the ether might unexpectedly come up with, but doing so outside any living spiritual center or commitment, just to prevent the world's encroaching materialism from petrifying my worldview—like those people who hope that the Sasquatch, the UFO or the Loch Ness Monster will finally appear to save them, or at least give them some momentary room to breathe, the kind of people who take ghost-hunting tours of old Kentucky hotels, hoping to encounter a patch of frigid air or see the magnetometer needle twitch significantly, letting them be redeemed once again—at least temporarily—by one more anomalous sign, omen or magical synchronicity...

And my memories of Bloomington, Indiana began to feel just as ghostly to me. What had once seemed like the high plazas and colonnades of Deva-loka gradually began to look more like a row of abandoned warehouses, or a de-commissioned gothic cathedral in a dying city. Rama Coomaraswamy once told us he believed that demonic activity was taking place in Bloomington, and one of my present 'Alawi *fuqara*, Paul Yachnes (Sidi Safwan)—a refugee from Schuon's circle—recounts a significant incident that seems to corroborate this. After leaving the Maryamiyya Tariqah, and while spending the night in a house-*zawiya* of a Maryamiyya *faqir* in another town, he heard a clear voice from the empty air declaring that "I am Mahound!," which he attributed to a Jinn. *Mahound*, for those who don't know, is a derogatory term for the Prophet used by medieval Christians, who believed that Muhammad was a pagan false god worshipped by the Muslims. Was some Jinn ironically satirizing Schuon's tendency to see his own professed religion of Islam as in some ways inferior to the Vedanta, to Kashmiri Shaivism and to his own "plenary esoterism"? When he was told that a new mosque had opened in Bloomington, he was reported to have said: "It's not *my* fault!" (and I tend to agree).

Since I lack the authority to judge anyone else's spiritual Path—which does *not* mean that I always lack the discernment to avoid what I see as spiritually dangerous to myself—I must allow that the Maryamiyya may still be spiritually alive for some people. But for all its transformative influence on my intellectual outlook, which saved me from so much darkness and illusion, it was never quite alive for me. The residual *maya* of Schuon's powerful but ultimately ephemeral manifestation outlived him for quite a few years, undoubtedly because the luminous doctrines he expressed and the astounding consortium of colleagues he brought together worked as a real step for so many... but then came the day when that spiritual battery finally lost its charge, and the light went out—at least for me. After that, it became necessary for me to begin separating the wheat from the chaff in Schuon's manifestation. The only thing I can say for certain at this point is that—at least when taken alone—Schuon's Transcendent Unity of Religions, though it can provide a useful orientation for certain people under certain circumstances, is in no sense a spiritual Path.

But since Frithjof Schuon and the Traditionalist School had been our main identification for almost twenty years, when the Schuon world began to falter and fade, identity-crisis and the bewilderment that goes with it threatened to dominate our lives. But as it turned out, God had a new phase in store us, a stretch of years which were ruled by four factors, three of which I've already recounted. The first was a 20-year-plus burst of creativity, stretching from 2001 till the present day, during which time I wrote and published some 20 books—not to mention the YouTube videos and internet interviews that went with them—as well as editing a book by Rama, one by Lee Penn, one by the Lithuanian Maryamiyya *faqir* Algis Uzdavinys—a profound scholar of Mesopotamian, Egyptian, Greek and Muslim esoterism and mythopoesis—two books on Dante by Jenny and one book of her poetry; the second was our friendship with Rama Coomaraswamy, which gave Jenny her entré into the world of *sedevacantist* Catholicism; the third, my initiation into the 'Alawiyya Sufi Tariqah; and the fourth and (so far) the last, the Covenants of the

Prophet Muhammad with the Christians of the World, which I consider to be a direct overflow of the 'Alawi *baraka* (grace, spiritual influence) into the outer world of society and history.

PILGRIMAGE; DEATH; INJURY; PURIFICATION

And finally our habit of pilgrimage and spiritual seeking came to fruition. In 2005 we visited Rama Coomaraswamy at his home in Wilton, CT; the next year he died. That year of 2006 was quite a rigorous year for us. In February Jenny fell and broke her other hip, then developed a serious post-operative infection which required a new operation, after which she had to receive weeks of infusions of powerful antibiotics at a walk-in clinic. During this ordeal she actually offered up her suffering to God as a prayer that I would somehow find the insight and courage to break with the Nimatullahi Order—a prayer that was in fact answered. In September of that same year we attended a large Traditionalist conference in Edmonton, Alberta, Canada at the University of Alberta, sponsored by the journal *Sacred Web*, which is where we began to get the sense that the sun of the Traditionalist world was slowly but surely beginning to set. The next year we traveled to the New York area again to meet with our friend Eric Galati; the three of us went to pray at Rama's grave in Connecticut, then drove past his earlier home in Greenwich. On that trip Jenny and I also met with Dr Faiz Khan, a Long Island physician, who had recommended that I investigate a particular Sufi *tariqah*, a lesser-known *silsila* (teaching lineage) of the 'Alawiyya (not to be confused with the Tariqah 'Alawiyya based in Yemen) which was part of the greater Shadhili stream of *tasawwuf*, springing specifically from the great Sufi shaykh Ahmed al-'Alawi of Mostaganem in Algeria, the subject of Martin Lings's book *A Sufi Saint of the Twentieth Century*. Frithjof Schuon himself had taken *bay'at* (initiation) with Shaykh al-'Alawi at one point. Faiz was gracious enough to drive us from New York to Alexandria, Virginia to meet a representative of that order, Paul Yachnes, who introduced me to its teachings and practices, and showed me photos of their present Shaykh, Sidi Rachid; Mr Yachnes and some of his colleagues turned out to be past members of Schuon's circle who, since they were unwilling to follow Shaykh Isa any longer in some of his less Traditional manifestations, had sought and apparently found the source of the light they had seen imperfectly reflected in him. Faiz had been associated with Faisal Rauf, known for his association with the famous and ill-fated "Ground Zero Mosque" that ran into so much opposition due to its plans to locate near the area in Manhattan that had been largely destroyed in the Twin Towers attack on 9/11/2004. Faiz's connection with Rauf was through a *silsila* of the Qadiri Tariqah whose American branch—at least as far as Faiz was concerned—had come to a bad end. I always got the sense that he thought of me as a kind of offering to Allah on his part to atone for his decision not to continue observing his connection with *tasawwuf*.

In his initial introduction of the 'Alawiyya to me, Sidi Safwan had mentioned that those who choose to take *bay'at* with the shaykh of their *silsila* would sometimes become ill, either after initiation or while contemplating it—clearly a kind of initial purgation, a "holocaust of karma" such as often happens in the presence of Spiritual Truth and Power, when the *nafs*, the lower self, rebels (as it inevitably will) against the Divine Presence but is ultimately purified by It. This prediction came true in a formidable way when, on December 13, 2008—which just "happened" to be my 60th birthday—Jenny and I were seriously injured in an automobile accident while on our way home from a visit to her uncle Dale and his wife Eileen in Morehead in Rowan County. (Jenny's mother and her husband Arnold were there at the same time.) I'll tell the story of the aftermath of this calamity and the ordeal of our convalescence below, but first I'll need to set the stage by painting a detailed though not unbiased portrait of Jenny's mother, Lola P. Donne, as well as her third and last husband, Arnold Plunkett.

LOLA DEAREST

As a Californian I already had one strike against me in some Kentucky circles, though I can truthfully say that my 19 years in the Commonwealth have been almost entirely congenial to me, and—for all their difficulties and near-tragedies—some of the happiest of my life. They have also been the most productive, since I have been able to write and publish—thanks to the perceptive generosity of my publisher James Wetmore of Sophia Perennis—nearly two dozen books of "metaphysics and social criticism," spiritual psychology, metaphysical exegesis of mythopoesis etc. etc., plus a book of collected poetry built around my Blakean/Gnostic epic, entitled *The Wars of Love and Other Poems*. My wife Jenny also produced the two books of Dante exegesis I've already mentioned, entitled *Dark Way to Paradise: Dante's Inferno in Light of the Spiritual Path*, and *The Ordeal of Mercy: Dante's Purgatorio in Light of the Spiritual Path*—the first of which Jenny's mother lived to see, only to react with silent, jealous outrage, an outrage based on the fact that, according to her, it was unalterable divine law that Jenny was to achieve nothing, do nothing, and be nothing. She was also considered no less than a traitor to her bloodlines for moving to California, even though she had to do it to save her life. I've imagined that Lola's unspoken reaction to that move might have been something on the order of, "If you were going to betray your Kentucky roots, at least you should have moved to *southern* California instead of hippie San Francisco and come back as a movie star or something." In any case, Lola Plunkett, as well as Jenny's father, Fred Donne, and her last husband, Arnold, will be the main subjects of the following account.

Writing about the almost inconceivable pettiness and blindness of Jenny's parents, despite their material generosity, in some ways feels petty in itself. Do people really want to hear one more "Mommie Dearest" story of an abusive childhood? Because the truth is, you can't fight deadness; taking a militant attitude toward an incurable lack is a serious misstep, as in the proverbial notion of "beating a dead horse" or the fable of the Tar Baby from the Uncle Remus tales. Childhoods like that are as common as dirt, and in any case my readers have plenty of problems of their own. Yet how someone could survive such beginnings without the help of any friends or protectors or even any explicit religious faith, and not descend into drug addiction, homelessness, serious mental illness or suicide, is a profound mystery, since to have your reality totally denied by the people you're closest to, the only people you know, is nothing short of attempted murder—an attempt that too often succeeds. To survive that kind of long-term assault conclusively demonstrates, in my opinion, how we are not entirely the products of our social environment or our genetics, but bring something essential with us from another world when we come into this one; it also clearly suggests the reality of such things as guardian angels. And I believe that the formidable yet largely invisible strength that Jenny developed during the time of her upbringing—which might better be termed her "downhammering"—partly explains the power she had to save me from the near-fatal deceptions and dissipations I was immersed in when she found me. She could do that because she *wanted to live* more than I did, and I was strongly attracted to precisely that brand of fierce certainty. Suffice it to say that it is not really possible to tell the true story of Jenny Donne, of what I consider to be her unique spiritual achievements, without recounting the history of her family darkness. Some would say, and part of me would also say, that it might be best to seal these accounts until all can be settled by the true Judge and Healer in the next world, seeing that the human race—especially in its present state—can in no way provide the necessary discernment and absolution. And some aspects of this case have in fact remained sealed. Yet truth, even the hardest truth, has its own rights and justification. Beyond that, to tell the true story of a cruel oppression also opens the door to an understanding of what motivated the oppressors, what woundings, what depths of loss. When Truth unseals the evidence, Mercy (God willing) may soon follow it.

Jenny's mother was immensely generous on the material level, though we tried our best not to depend on her financially but simply to cling to the slim perch that God and my family had provided for us, making sure at the same time that my own mother had enough to live on; thank God she never had to suffer material deprivation on account of us. But on the psychological and interpersonal level, it was a different story. In that quarter of things, Lola was a narcissistic mommie-dragon of the first order, a woman who most likely suffered from some other form of personality disorder as well, possibly borderline autism; in the classic narcissistic family structure so deftly portrayed on YouTube by Dr Ramani Suryakantham Durvasula, Jenny was the designated scapegoat. Yet her mother had actually saved her life on more than one occasion, possibly to compensate for her role in a dark family conspiracy that had viciously abused Jenny for many years, if not actually tried to kill her. It was as if Lola secretly *had* more compassion for her daughter than she ever *showed*—if that makes any sense. And it was not an easy thing for Jenny, traumatized as she was, to accept such substantive material help from her mother, since it made it that much harder for her to stand up against the woman who had so often abused her in the emotional sphere and continued to do so. Yet stand up she did.

Judging from Lola's photographs from her high school yearbook and later, I am convinced that something truly terrible must've happened to her in childhood and/or young adulthood. In high school she exhibited a fierce, almost megalomaniacal pride and self-confidence, but in later photos she is hardly recognizable as the same person, her round, wide-cheekboned face long and narrow; obviously she was in a state of deep depression. As for the cause of her condition, my best theory is that she was in a lifetime state of depression and anger and self-hatred because she had rejected the man she loved, a carpenter, in order to marry the man her parents had proposed, or imposed: Fred Donne, a high school principal and basketball coach, ten years older than her, for whom she apparently had few positive feelings on the personal level but who could help her get ahead in her professional life. Her father had been a coal miner—and one of the few avenues for a Kentucky coal miner's daughter out of the blue collar and into the professional class in those days was the "schoolteacher" identity, a career in education. Lola went far in that world, becoming a full professor at Eastern Kentucky University and head of the Department of Counseling and Educational Psychology which she herself developed. But though her home library was full of books on psychology, she had less insight into other people's feelings and motivations than anyone I've ever met. It was as if she had devoted a lifetime of study to trying to get some understanding of what most people learn simply by growing up, and had still failed to master her subject. It is a grave indictment of the U.S. academic system that someone could have been so successful in an academic career based on a subject which, according to every objective criterion, she had gotten an F in. This is because drive and ambition are routinely mistaken for competence and intelligence in this society; according to the "fake it till you make it" theory, immortalized by Elizabeth Holmes of Theranos fame, making it means that you will never have to stop faking it.

Among other modes of abuse, she enabled Jenny's father to beat her for the first 16 years of her life, an ordeal that only ended, as I recounted above, when Jenny appeared at school with an injured eye and her blouse covered with blood. (Her father, a prominent man in the community, was "cautioned" by the local sheriff on a visit to the family home, although no further legal action was taken.) Lola maintained that she had always protected Jenny from her father's attacks, but the truth is that she had protected Jenny's sister while letting her husband Fred take out his violent urges on Jenny, possibly to avoid against becoming a target herself. But since she was a mistress of cold, silent rages, adept at getting other people to act out her feelings while she always "kept her cool," one must ask how much of Fred's violence was born in the soul of Lola.

Jenny's mother was totally dedicated to lying. To her, denying reality and then enforcing her delusional version of reality on other people was a sign of self-actualization and character-strength—which is to say that she had the sort of personality disorder that produced in her a toxic amalgam of pride and stupidity, which so often go together, since pridefully denying reality inevitably undermines one's sense of it. On one occasion, for example, she accused Jenny (to me) of being genetically defective, not realizing that this necessarily reflected rather poorly on herself as well. She was affected, in my opinion—the opinion of an amateur psychologist who had to learn "street psychology" just to save his life—by a type of character-neurosis probably best described as "the power of positive thinking." I had always suspected that Norman Vincent Peale's brand of entrepreneurial Christianity was little more than an exhaustively researched-and-developed and theologically justified form of lying—a theory that has been richly corroborated by the inter-presidential political strategy of Donald Trump, who actually attended Dr Peale's church in his youth.

Among her delusions was the notion that she had Parkinson's disease, which was (of course) never diagnosed. On one occasion, in the presence of Jenny's uncle Juble (who really did have Parkinson's, or a similar organic tremor), she said: "Yes I do have Parkinson's disease; the reason I show no signs of it, however, is that I have a high degree of self-control." (Imagine the level of dedication-to-repression that could define a Parkinson's tremor as a case of undisciplined "acting out"!)

Disease meant a great deal to Lola; she looked upon it as a mark of distinction. Once she traveled by car with family members to a clinic in Georgia to be screened for heart disease because, according to her, this condition could only be detected by that particular institution. When she was given a clean bill of health and told that she had no sign of any form of heart disease, she cried all the way home to Kentucky; apparently the news that her heart was physically sound had literally broken her heart. This episode indicates that she must have essentially thought of herself as a *body* rather than a complete human being, body, soul and spirit. If her heart ached, the condition could only have an organic cause—and this from a university teacher of psychology! Clearly she was quite a bit ahead of her time in this regard. The idea that she might actually be deeply depressed was unacceptable to her; depression, in her estimation, was purely a disease of the losers, the *declassé*.

Nonetheless, since she saw herself largely as a body (plus persona), Lola treated her daughter too as a body (minus persona)—a body that she was dedicated to feeding and nurturing, but which she would severely punish if it ever showed any telltale signs of developing a soul. She maintained Jenny in 1970s San Francisco on an allowance of $200 a month, which allowed her to rent a bare room on Fillmore Street for around $80—a room that would probably cost $1200 today—and still have enough to eat, clothe herself from the Goodwill or the Salvation Army, and attend various poetry readings and other cheap-to-free cultural events. Jenny wonders if her mother really did this out of the fear that, if her daughter became too desperate in California, she might decide to end her exile and *return home*, precipitating God-knows what upheavals. Lola also helped us out financially several times, after we were married, in a more substantial way—for which, all negative feelings apart, I am profoundly grateful. And so, though we worked as house-cleaners for quite a while and I made a few chunks of money through writing projects, without the help (and finally the inheritance) from both sides of the family, we would have been totally lost. The greatest gift we were given by our circumstances—in line with which I have often described myself as "independently poor"—was *time*, and I vowed to use that time not in frivolous self-indulgence (though I did not entirely succeed in this) but rather to create something of value to humanity that could never have seen the light in any other way. It was through this kind of work that I hoped, in Gurdjieff's words, to "pay the debt of my existence"; consequently a dedication to artistic, intellectual, socio-political and spiritual achievement, partly so as the negate the gnawing guilt of economic dependency, has in many ways been the keynote of my life. And the only way I could achieve this, in the last analysis, was to recognize my total dependence upon God; since there was no way I could see myself as a "self-made man," I was required to recognize Him as my sole Creator and Sustainer, to seek employment only through Him, to do and create what He wanted me to do and create, and to dedicate the fruits of my actions to Him alone.

But for all her substantial help, Lola was still a fury to us in many ways. It was as if she was in so much pain, in pain so deeply denied, that if she ever realized the depth of it, it would crush her like a bug. And the only way she had found to escape that pain, outside of prescription opioid use, was to torment her daughter, to dump the full weight of her own self-wounding, and self-hatred, and grief, and despair, on Jenny. For a full quarter of a century, in her phone calls from Kentucky, she would reduce Jenny to tears at least once a month. Once, when Jenny was feeling relatively strong and confident, she said to her something like: "Oh, Mother, why do you always have to be on my back?"—and her mother immediately burst into tears, as if to say: "How cruel and ungrateful a daughter you are, Jenny, not to let *even your own mother* drive you to despair!" Jenny was the one true scapegoat Lola had been able to cultivate over the course of her life; if she lost this last protective barrier against the darkness of her feelings, what would become of her? How could she go on?

And perhaps her cruelest attacks against Jenny were based on her delusions, the most thoroughly worked-out of which was as follows: "My daughter was diagnosed with autism, therefore I made the hard sacrifice of studying psychology so as to dedicate my life to finding a cure for my poor autistic daughter." Not a single word of the above statement, outside of the fact that she did indeed study psychology, is true. Nonetheless this profoundly delusional woman was able to found and head the Department of Counseling and Educational Psychology at Eastern Kentucky University, giving credence to the common cliché that psychiatrists and psychologists are often crazier than their patients. Psychological insight she had not, but there was no denying her drive and ambition, and the raw nerve that it took for her to assert them. And if she had lacked those impulses, no matter how imbalanced and obsessive she might have been in expressing them, her daughter Jenny might never have come into my life.

On one occasion, after we had moved to Kentucky and long after her father's death, Jenny expressed the desire to go to the Wyatt Family Reunion, the Wyatts being a branch of her father's family. She was interested, as a poet, because of the possibility that the family was descended from the famous Elizabethan poet Sir Thomas Wyatt, who wrote the luminous lines: "They flee from me that sometime did me seek/ With naked foot, stalking in my chamber..." Lola discouraged this, telling her that she didn't plan to attend herself and that nobody there would be interested in seeing Jenny without her. Then she actually did attend the Wyatt reunion, even though she was no blood relation to them, and afterwards crowed to Jenny about what a wonderful time she'd had. (Games like that were very common.) This incident reinforced Jenny's conviction that her flight to California had not been a caprice, as her mother always maintained, but an enforced exile; a scapegoat can't really fulfill its assigned function unless it is driven into the wilderness.

Jenny believes that her difficulties with her parents came from her having been born with an essentially loving nature, which went against the basic value-structure of her family, who—for all their nominal

Christianity—appeared to identify love with the weakness and the Christian sentimentality of earlier, more "backward" generations: warmth is weakness, coldness is power. Her uncle Juble and his wife Esta were the most loving and generous members of the family, and Juble was capable of having real interests that weren't immediately translatable into social or professional cash-value; he knew how to love things for themselves alone, and consequently he was at the bottom of the family pecking-order in terms of his generation. And this identification of love with weakness was certainly not limited to Jenny's immediate family, but was and is a fundamental part of the culture she grew up in, a kind of rural ghetto culture where two of the dominant ways of relating to other people were first to find out whose ass to kiss, and next to determine who you could shame and terrorize with impunity, a culture where the only avenue of escape on many people's radar-screen was, and is, a cold-blooded dedication to success. (Come to think of it, that rural ghetto culture filled with child abusers and opioid addicts, which is also host to pockets of positive traditional values, spiritual beauty and genuine humanity, isn't all that different from the larger American culture as a whole...) A distant cousin of Jenny's, a 10-year-old girl, once informed her parents (both lawyers, since divorced) that she had told a boy she knew that he was not invited to her party because it was only for girls. This made the little boy cry, but instead of being reprimanded for this embryonic act of cruelty, she was praised for it by her adult relatives; the story of her childish exploit was recounted proudly at family gatherings. And this attitude, as we all know, is now spread throughout the entire world, except for isolated areas of resistance; this is the worm at the root of the human enterprise. And so when I asked Jenny, "What did you get out of this lifelong experience of family darkness for your spiritual life, your *real* life?," her answer was: "I learned to love human dignity, and always to seek it." As Jeffrey Epstein and Ghislaine Maxwell taught us, or should have taught us, the worship of power—*whether by the powerful or the powerless*—is inseparable from human degradation. People so often seek power as a way to escape degradation, but if that quest is pursued over the dead body of love, it is defeated before it begins: "There is no Might nor Power except in Allah."

Jenny also tells the story of the day in her childhood when she and Lola were window-shopping at a nearby town; she was ten years old at the time. In the window of a furniture shop she saw a doll dressed as a bride, and told her mother: "I want that to be my last doll." They entered the store and Jenny began talking to the salesman, expressing her interest in the doll—but at the same time Lola was silently pinching her arm; she told the man "we'll be back for the doll later." Out on the street she said to Jenny, "Couldn't you tell that I was pinching your arm? That doll was much too expensive" (it was $9.00). Later, however, at another store in Jenny's home town, Lola bought her another doll that Jenny wasn't interested in at all, one dressed in a ball gown; it cost $15.00. Besides Lola's rejection of her own socially-enforced marriage, Jenny sees this as indicating that her mother didn't like or accept who her daughter actually was and was working as hard as she could to impose a false identity on her. The bride doll had what Jenny now understands as a sacred quality for her. Matrimony is a sacrament to the Catholics, and little Catholic girls used to be dressed as brides for their first communion. As Jenny sees it, the bride doll symbolized the sacred dimension while the "debutante" doll represented the marketplace of this world. Meditating on this incident, she came to realize that she had not simply been at odds with her family, but at odds with the whole world she was born into; for most of her life she has been like an immigrant trying to find her place in a foreign nation—or, as perhaps we need to say at this late date, a foreign planet.

Near the end of her life, Lola married a lowlife thug and/or local solid citizen named Arnold Plunkett, a member of the same extended Kentucky clan, though his degree of relatedness to her has been hard to determine; due to this marriage her original married name of Lola Plunkett Donne became transformed into Lola Donne Plunkett (or possibly Lola Plunkett Donne Plunkett). She apparently believed that her higher social position would allow her to control Arnold who, as a retired grammar school principal, was lower in the social scale than she was (though he probably had a higher income)—but that's not how it turned out. In reality he was extremely abusive to her, not through a hot temper that might have gotten the sheriff involved but in a more cold and calculating way. The state of her health required that she have constant care, and her preferred way of securing this (she told us once) was to get married again. But since Arnold knew this, he could easily terrorize her by threatening to move back to his house up the creek (part of a compound of other small houses belonging to him and his sons), then actually doing so—and then moving back, and later moving out again, over and over—a course of slow torture that nearly resulted in her death. So her initial idea that she would be able to dominate him based on her higher status as a retired college professor and her ownership of the biggest and most pretentious house in the valley proved to be a serious miscalculation.

Arnold Plunkett was a man I might have liked, if only he had not harbored a criminal intent targeting me and my family; he possessed talents and character-traits I could've appreciated—stylistically if not morally—if only they had been pointed in a different direction. He had a real intellectual curiosity that enabled him, unlike Jenny's mother, to show an interest in things for their own sakes. And he really cared for his children. But somehow (as we shall see) he could also plan acts of fraud and virtual grand theft while still seeing himself as a salt-of-the-earth respectable community member who was only asserting his rights as a locally-born son of the hills as against myself, a carpetbagger from California, and equally against the rest of the family (virtually all of them as locally-born as he was) by virtue of his marriage to Lola—a ceremony which, in his eyes, gave him natural title to the house and land she represented, even though she had willed them to her daughters. As her husband he began to see himself as the kind of indigenous squire and landowner who might even aspire to run for State Legislature, in view of which he cultivated relationships with local petty power-brokers like Clayton Little. Sadly, these plans came to naught, though he did serve a term as president of the Plunkett Family Association; when collecting available items to expand the scope of your identity in the quest to become "somebody," you must take what you can get.

Once, while we still lived in California, Lola had summoned us to come back to help her deal with a difficulty that had developed with Arnold—she described him at that time as "the best thing and the worst thing that ever happened to me"—a difficulty that she characterized as "giving him some time off from taking care of me so he won't burn out," likely indicating that his game of repeatedly threatening to leave her, then leaving her, then coming back again had begun to manifest, though we couldn't see that at the time. So we agreed to visit and help where we could. I was just recovering from a bout of uveitis in one of my eyes which was probably the cause of the cataract which then began to appear, but I decided to take the trip anyway because Lola seemed to be in real need. Earlier she had told us that she'd married Arnold specifically because she knew she needed care and wanted to avoid assisted living and/or a nursing home, and so during this trip I naively expressed my admiration to him for his willingness to be party to such an arrangement—after which I got the distinct impression that this was the first time he'd heard of it. Did my sincere compliment only inflame an already smoldering situation? Over the years I've found that some scenes are so toxic that any attempt to improve them only makes them worse; what such psychic vampire-situations need is not an infusion of positive energy, but simply to be given as little energy as possible, of any kind. As Lew Welch said in his "CHICAGO POEM":

> You can't fix it. You can't make it go away.
>   I don't know what you're going to do about it,
> But I know what I'm going to do about it. I'm just
>   going to walk away from it. Maybe
> A small part of it will die if I'm not around
>   feeding it anymore.

Unfortunately, however — or maybe fortunately — we couldn't simply walk away from it at that point; we still had a part to play in Jenny's family drama that nobody else (apparently) was either willing or able to assume.

For Lola's part, she used Arnold as a kind of weapon against the rest of her family. He fought with her sister Irene's husband, Chester, and with Jenny's sister Mary Anne's husband, Craig, and with Jenny's cousin Marquetta's husband, Oliver, and also with me. Irene, for one, was terrified of him. And Lola felt she had to take Arnold's side in these conflicts, at least passively, since to admit the humiliating position she'd put herself in by marrying him was too much for her to face, and she still needed him as a caretaker. On top of that, Arnold — with Lola's acquiescence — attempted in some ways (short of physical violence) to continue the abuse that Jenny had suffered from her own father, an abuse that had abruptly stopped many years earlier thanks to that visit from the sheriff, and had ended for good with no chance of a repeat performance when her father died.

Jenny's father's funeral is well worth mentioning at this point. One of the "mourners" at the gathering was a woman who had baby-sat for Jenny when she was a child. As soon as she saw Jenny she approached us, cackling like a witch, and began "reminiscing" with her about how "Didn't I *whup* you when you was a little girl!" as if this were a fond memory that Jenny would appreciate because it took her back to the good old days. And a similar thing happened, much later, at her uncle Forrest Dale's funeral, who was the last of that generation. No prayers were offered, the name of Jesus passed no-one's lips; instead the centerpiece of the event was a "eulogy" (or possibly "kakalogy" would be a better term) delivered by the pastor, who had been a student at the grammar school where Dale was principal. It was all about how Dale had "whupped him good" and so set him on the straight and narrow — so Dale's claim to fame, for which he should be fondly remembered by all, was something that might have sent him to jail in our own times, where he could conceivably have occupied a cell right next to the ghost of Jenny's father. Recently a statistic came out that child abuse actually decreased in Kentucky during the Covid pandemic; the likely reason given for this was that *many of the schools were closed!* Was bullying being counted as child abuse, or was the abuse actually coming from the teachers? Being "whupped" is undoubtedly to some people's tastes in Eastern Kentucky (and elsewhere) — possibly because getting whupped earns you the right to whup in turn, so as to "pay it forward" — but Jenny's tastes, being more literary and spiritual, definitely ran in other channels: *human* channels, as I would describe them.

After Arnold's intent to abuse her became evident, Jenny let her mother know that she intended never to be in the presence of this man again, largely because his daughter Judy had threatened to sue her (see below), a decision that Lola deliberately misinterpreted as "vowing never to see your mother again." (When I told Arnold about Jenny's early beatings, in a misguided attempt to "clear the air" in a family where clearing the air was not only impossible but illegal, his response was: "She probably deserved it.") Then, when Christmas came, Lola called her up and told her how she and Arnold and *everybody else* in the family had had such a *wonderful* time at Marquetta's house—all except Jenny, of course, who unfortunately hadn't been there due to her unreasonable and disrespectful decision to no longer endure Arnold's presence. The only problem with her story was that Jenny had actually been at the event in question, though Lola and Arnold were nowhere to be seen. (Jenny decided not to confront her with the lie; what was to be gained?) So apparently her lying-power had finally begun to break down due to the feebleness of old age and the ever-closer approach of the Moment of Truth.

Lola's anger and aggression against the rest of her family—and herself—was not always apparent, but from time to time it broke out. It sometimes became visible when she was driving a car. On one occasion when she was driving me, Jenny and several other family members furiously down a narrow two-lane road, she pulled up behind a coal truck and then abruptly swerved left to pass, with zero visibility. If another car had been in the oncoming lane this could have been the end of all our lives, including hers. I had to order her to take care and slow down—something I doubt that anyone else in her family (Jenny excepted) had ever dared to do.

As I've already recounted, Lola had an extensive library with many interesting volumes on psychology and other subjects, but as soon as you talked with her about anything substantive you realized that ideas meant nothing to her. She was not even slightly interested in ideas, insights, perceptions, art, religion, psychology or politics outside of their bearing on her professional life; the fact is that she wasn't interested in much of anything. She had no hobbies, no pets, no films or books or television programs that she particularly liked—not even soap operas, mostly because she couldn't follow the plots or understand the basic motivations of the characters—and no real interests outside of social position, which is why she joined so many clubs and organizations, becoming the president of most of them. It was obvious that she had advanced her career by memorizing what she was supposed to know and say and playing the role required of her—and so when she abruptly took early retirement (something that is apparently common in people with Narcissistic Personality Disorder who are beginning to run out of the energy necessary to keep up "the Act"), she returned from her college apartment in Richmond to her home in eastern Kentucky, to sit in her reclining chair for the rest of her life, watching television and trying her best to understand it. During this time she also became addicted to opioids, which the doctors continued to prescribe to treat various conditions of chronic pain, both real and imagined. As she once expressed it to me, "I just sit here all day thinking beautiful thoughts."

Lola the Respected Professional and Lola the queen bee of a clan of partly middle-class hillbillies were clearly two different people. I remember one car trip with her, Jenny, Jenny's sister Mary Anne and Jenny's father Fred from her apartment at Eastern Kentucky University in Richmond back to her home in Pike Country. In Richmond she spoke in elevated, measured tones, with the studied elocution she'd likely picked up at the University of Mississippi (Ole Miss), but by the time we'd gotten to Pike County she was talking in the hushed, rapid, spooky voice of a superstitious hillbilly woman who believed in ghosts, curses and the evil eye. Nonetheless she was still able to play the role of a Respected Retired Professional to the Pike County community and the more unsophisticated elements of her own family—until she married Arnold, that is, a retired elementary school principal with a bad reputation, after which she lost face and became seriously *declassé*.

A character like Lola's does not, of course, develop in isolation. To begin with, the Commonwealth of Kentucky has (intermittently) the worst child abuse rate of any of the 50 states, and eastern Kentucky is likely the epicenter of the pandemic. This may partially have to do with the unconscious survival of an essentially pre-modern construction of family authority in that area, according to which the paterfamilias holds the rights of life and death over his wife and children, though not literally of course... Certainly Arnold ran his family like a gang-boss; as long as he was the Sire, the True Father, his three sons—married or not, fathers of their own children or not—could never be real adults; they could only be "the boys." Likewise, when he tried to assert his authority over me, he began by doing everything he could, all reality to the contrary, to define me as his son! And what else but an implicit allegiance to Father Rights could explain Jenny's father's avoidance of jail time for assault and battery?

So the region, the clan and the family were fertile ground for the development of a character like Lola's; when Jenny's uncle Juble, the genealogist, asked Jenny's grandmother for some family stories, her response was: "If you start poking around in the past you might find out some things you'd rather not know!" Suffice it to say that whoever has read the comic/ironic tragedies of Flannery O'Connor, based on an uncompromising analysis of a collective cultural disorder where unquestioning obedience to the dominant social stereotypes is as mandatory as is a complete ignorance of their real nature—something that can only be called a "disorder" because the people affected by it are culturally oppressed, seeing that unconscious obedience to collective norms is common in all social groups—will know exactly what I'm talking about. Lola's family was happy to accept her (pre-Arnold that is) as a Professional Wise Woman and an admirable success story in a culture and generation where almost the only routes of upward mobility out of the coal mines were either emigration to Ohio or Detroit or Indiana or Chicago, mostly for factory work, or else the school system. Lola well knew that only a culture as unsophisticated as that of Appalachia would be certain to see her as a Well-Respected Retired Professional Educator, but that while interacting with her supposed peers at the university, she was always in danger (or felt herself to be in danger) of suddenly being recognized as an impostor, a no-count hillbilly who was only impersonating a real professional woman, someone who had absolutely no ideas or even opinions of her own nor any interest in developing them — so she most likely decided to quit while she was ahead, abandon her studied role and head for the hills before her acting ability broke down entirely.

The family under Lola's rule also implicitly accepted (at least for a while) the idea of the "arrogant, irresponsible Californians" (us), a myth that was undoubtedly reinforced by Jenny's irresponsible notion of "running off to California" to save her life. This myth rose up and bit us on the occasion of the funeral of Chester, the husband of Jenny's aunt Irene. After the funeral service, while sitting in our car in the church parking lot, the dumb-ass constable who was directing traffic came over and told us, "Wait here, I'll let you know when it's time to leave for the interment." But he never did come back, so by the time we realized that everybody else had left, and had burned rubber out of the parking lot to catch up with them, it was already too late. The graveyard where the interment was to take place was in Inez, a town quite a ways to the north. We broke the speed limit trying to get there until a state trooper pulled us over — though when we told him we were late for a funeral, he waved us on. (Forget the law: in Appalachia the Funeral always has precedence.) But when we got to Inez no graveyard was immediately apparent, so after roaming around aimlessly for a while we drove back to Irene's house in Pike County. We expected that the family would say, "Where were you? We were all worried," after which we could tell the story of the dumb-ass constable and the ensuing chase. *But no.* While we were away they had apparently invented the story (or been told by "someone") that, as flighty irresponsible Californians, we had simply decided to bug out on the interment on a momentary whim, since people from California (and this is not entirely untrue) have no sense of "family values." This brand-new idea had so rapidly become a fixed and unchanging article of faith that when we told Irene what had actually happened that had made us late, her response was: "I don't believe you." Even the undeniable fact that we had actually returned to the funeral party seemed to have no significance for them. Such a degree of prejudice and delusional group-think can only grow out of a depth of narrow-mindedness that is extremely hard to wrap your mind around. One example of this mental tininess is the time when a professor friend of Jenny's I've already told you about, James Cutsinger, phoned her at Lola's house from South Carolina, to which Jenny's mother responded with shock and disbelief: "*Jenny* (of all people) got a call from a *Real Professor* from *the University South Carolina!!*" This was nearly enough to produce a stroke, a heart-attack, or at least a dead faint. A similar shock awaited her when, on a visit with us to Mission Dolores in San Francisco, she suddenly realized, with a look of panic on her face, that the walled churchyard with the old tombstones was *not* the familiar family graveyard of Appalachian Kentucky that any *normal* person could understand, but a *foreign* graveyard with *Mexicans* in it — Mexicans who might even be *Catholics!!* These reactions paled in comparison, however, with another one she recounted from her past. According to that story, she had been sitting at a counter somewhere next to a man she knew, had accidentally taken a sip of coffee from the man's cup — and had then realized, to her horror and chagrin, that the coffee had *sugar* in it! "I *never* take sugar in *my* coffee!" she confided to us in hushed tones, her face pale enough to suggest an approaching metaphysical crisis affecting her whole sense of reality. I believe we can see here the true origin of the mindset described by Bob Dylan, in his song "It's Alright Ma (I'm Only Bleeding)," as "pettiness which plays so rough." Its origin is *fear* — in this case a collective regional fear which in earlier years was fear of the coal company gun thugs, the sheriff, the revenuers and the rival moonshiners, plus the ravages of crop failure, malnutrition and feud violence, but which was now being misapplied — as fear so often is — to anything outside the tiny circle of familiar daily concerns.

Lola's total lack of the slightest interest in ideas or art of any sort, coupled with a firm belief that she actually did have such interests, meant that her daughter's intellectual pursuits — she published poetry and in later life wrote two books on Dante's *Divine Comedy* — made Jenny a living reproach to her. "*I should have been the writer in the family!*" she maintained. (Then why did you never write anything, Lola? Because to do that you would need to have had a real interest in things.) When Jenny showed her the cover-image of her first Dante book — *Dark Way to Paradise: Dante's Inferno in Light of the Spiritual Path* (Lola never showed the slightest interest in what was inside) — she entered into one of her formidable, jealous, silent rages; congratulations of any kind were of course out of the question. She had, however, at least *planned* to write one book, on the subject of the Lost Jonathan (or John) Swift Silver Mine, an Eastern Kentucky legend. Lola had somehow taken it into her head that the Jonathan Swift in question was really Jonathan Swift the famous Anglo-Irish satirist, author of *Gulliver's Travels* and *A Modest Proposal* — though how he was able to find and lose a silver mine in Appalachia while pursuing his career as a writer and courtier in England was never fully explained. If she had ever written and published her book, it would certainly have been an interesting excursion into revisionist history.

But undoubtedly the darkest episode in Jenny's mother's life as we knew it was her passive participation in the death of her husband Fred, Jenny's father. Fred had a serious health condition which caused his kidneys to totally kick out from time to time, though he was never on dialysis. Once during a visit by Jenny's parents to our home in California I succeeded in cutting one of his attacks short—they usually sent him to the hospital—through the use of a ginger compress and bear-berry (uva-ursi) tea. His Appalachian heritage undoubtedly made him amenable to being treated with herbal medicines and home remedies; he himself had showed me how to recognize and harvest some of the local herbs and barks. I also saw that he had a serious chiropractic subluxation on his spine near the kidneys; I pointed this out and recommended that he get it taken care of, but he never did, and so the problem persisted. Then, when he and Lola were at their vacation home in Florida, he had his last attack. The local physicians, unfamiliar with his case, conjectured that his pain might have to do with a gall bladder condition. On the phone with Lola I loudly implored her to tell the doctors about his kidney condition, since he was apparently exhibiting all the symptoms of his habitual attacks, and get his physicians in Kentucky to fax his medical records to the doctors in Florida. Her response was, "I'm sure the doctors here know what they're doing; I see no reason to bother them." So they performed exploratory surgery looking for a gall bladder condition, and Fred died. After his death Lola felt liberated; she had a moment of exaltation thinking about all the things she wanted to do now that she was no longer saddled with a husband she hadn't loved. Then, not long afterwards, she began to decline rapidly, both physically and mentally, as if her negligence of Jenny's father on the occasion of his last illness, though it was probably mostly due to the kind of high regard for the medical profession that has since largely evaporated in that part of the world since the advent of "gender affirmation surgery" and the Covid vaccine, had been the last straw when it came to her own state and condition. This led us, I believe, to a deeper understanding of what, in her life of lying, had been the first big lie. As a young woman, as I've already mentioned, she had been in love with a carpenter, but her father—a coal miner, a prominent moonshiner, and a man of high standing in his rural community—had apparently forbidden the match, and ruled instead that she was to marry Fred, a man with much better prospects, a high school principal and basketball coach. This last role naturally gave him real social position in the Commonwealth of Kentucky where basketball is king; he was an example of the old Kentucky stock of very tall white men, like Lincoln was, who made up the core of Kentucky basketball before the Blacks took over. I can only imagine that the origin of the deep depression she exhibited in some of her old photographs must have been the deeply-denied shame of having betrayed herself and the man she loved for the booby prize (at least in emotional and spiritual terms) of social status and professional advancement—though without that hard-bought achievement, where would Jenny and I have been in later years? This might partly explain why she never moved to Lexington or Richmond after her retirement, like so many of her professional class would gladly have done if they'd had the chance, but remained on her mother's land instead, a narrow strip of bottom-land in a Pike County holler; it's as if (as she once actually told us), since her adult life had been essentially loveless, she had opted to spend the rest of her days living in memory of her parents, so as to stay close to the only love she'd known in her life. That's where she built her two-storey "prefabricated southern mansion" with the hollow sheet-metal columns, a house I like to call a "spite house"—something on the order of a spite fence, since she also built it in that location to outshine her sister Irene, whose smaller house was next door, and for which Lola had torn down her parents' home. In the group photograph of her father's family, Irene is the unattractive dumpy sister, while Lola is the comely young maiden, the local princess, gazing up worshipfully at her father—coal miner, moonshiner and squire of the holler, all the privilege and status of the ancestral landlord still weakly evident under the reality of poverty, oppression and exploitation. And that worship destroyed her life. Instead of marrying the man she loved, or at least moving out of Appalachia to the Bluegrass, she elected to pitch her tent on her father's grave and remain there for the rest of her life, faithful to the end. She also did her best to so demoralize Jenny that she too would never get away—but Jenny broke the curse, fled to California, and married me; consequently she had a life.

So I believe that the First Lie that began Lola's career as enemy of the truth was that she had really wanted to choose Fred and social advancement over a life with her beloved. How often do we opt to misrepresent to ourselves a hard stroke of fate, or else an abdication of personal responsibility, as an act of sovereign free will? I've seen the same thing in the homeless population I used to work with in California. "There's no way I was *kicked* out on the street" they would claim; "I'm an unbridled Gypsy spirit like Johnny Appleseed or Emperor Norton, here of my own free choice." If they were ever to admit the real truth, they couldn't go on. And once the first Big Lie is told, lie after lie must be issued and defended to keep the original sin alive. Yet for all her manifest curses directed against Jenny, she also gave a secret blessing to her and to our marriage when, through Irene, she passed on to Jenny the engagement ring, with its tiny chip of poor-man's diamond, that had been given to her by her one true love. So somewhere, somehow, even though she lacked the courage to stand by her blessing, part of her wished Jenny well. Nonetheless, her abusiveness was the still dominant factor. To take only one example out of many, when Jenny was in the hospital undergoing an ablation procedure (an electrical cauterization of the heart) for her atrial fibrillation, we had to instruct the nurses not to put through any more calls to her from Lola due to their abusive nature.

As for her husband Arnold's influence on her social standing, it was nothing short of disastrous, not to mention his effect on her personal life. Most likely — as you will soon see — he ended up stealing her will, probably on two separate occasions, in hopes that if she died intestate, the house, which she had willed to her two daughters, would pass to him instead. Through Arnold we witnessed what showed every sign of being Lola's karmic retribution for her abuse of Jenny (retribution, not redemption), and learned in the process how revenge is far from sweet. On one occasion when we were visiting Kentucky from California, she kindly lent us her car so we could visit James Cutsinger in South Carolina — for all her abuse she had always been generous to Jenny on a material level — but this made Arnold angry. He hated that she let us stay in one of her perpetually unused upstairs bedrooms when we came for a visit — "What is this, the *Hotel California?*" he snarked — but he also hated that we had the gall to plan other stops on our journey than just the Hotel. When Lola had first married him he had attempted to explain to me, in an obscure and circuitous manner, that "now things were going to be different around here"; apparently his theory was that, since he had been born in that holler, and had married Lola as I had married her daughter, he now had certain aspects of a father's authority over me as head of the house and lord of the estate. In any case, while we were away in South Carolina on a three-day trip, he deserted her again. "I don't have to take this, I can do my own housework," she said to herself — and as she attempted to vacuum the floor while suffering from serious osteoporosis, she broke her back. When we returned we found her in bed in serious pain, so we drove her to the hospital. "Shall we contact Arnold?" we asked. "No!" she said. We finally did contact him, however, and when he arrived he tried to blame us for her injury. "I *knew* this would happen if you went to South Carolina!" "You were her caretaker, not us," I answered; "we were 300 miles away when the injury happened; you were 3 miles away. We left on a trip to see friends; you deserted her."

Then, while we were visiting her at her hospital room, Arnold and his gang of a family trooped in and presented her with a paper to sign. "According to this paper" said Arnold, "you grant us the right to stay at your house for 10 days after you die." Sweet! She never did sign it, however, for the following reason: Some time earlier that day, Arnold's daughter

Judy (a "big physical therapist" according to Lola), who had been wiggling and squirming around the hospital in evil glee, had let the cat out of the bag: "You're going to find out there's something wrong about the will!" she foolishly divulged. As soon as I heard that I immediately drove back to Lola's house, went to the safe (which was providentially unlocked) and found Lola's will—apparently the original—*unsigned*. I immediately drove back to the hospital, and so when Arnold brought out his "after you die" document, I whipped out the will, and showed Lola that it had never been signed. "Why thank you, Charles" she said, "I was so sure that I had already signed it." So she signed it in the hospital in the presence of witnesses, as well as of Arnold and his family; needless to say this did not endear me to him. (I speculate that he had given her a copy of the will rather than the original to sign, and then destroyed the copy, leaving only the unsigned original, making it appear that no will had ever been signed.) Next I took the signed will down to another floor where there was a copy machine to make copies for us, Jenny's sister and Lola's lawyer—and while I was there, the security guards showed up. Earlier in the hospital room Jenny had screamed some choice epithets at Judy, who was kissing up to Jenny's mother while cutting Jenny out (the family believed that, due to this, Judy had the right to "sue Jenny for everything she's got," which she had actually threatened to do, and would certainly win the case), so I had steered Jenny out of the room and escorted her to the chapel to pray and calm down. I thought the guards had something to do with Jenny's outburst—*but no:* a complaint had been lodged against *me!* Apparently Arnold had hoped against hope that when the guards accosted me I would run or struggle, end up either in jail or shot, and somehow the whole nightmare, in which his best-laid plans to steal Jenny's and her sister's inheritance had shamefully come to nothing, would all go away. But when I showed calmness, restraint and lack of fear, the guards apparently figured that it was all a tempest in a teapot and took no action; therefore I was able to leave a signed copy of the will with Lola's lawyer and return the original to the safe. Interestingly enough, however, after Lola's death the signed original was not in the safe—and since Lola could no longer climb to the upstairs bedroom where the safe was located, no-one else had access to that safe but Arnold Plunkett. Nonetheless the signed copies proved to be legally binding. Two of the many things that are most conducive to human degradation are wealth and poverty, since both can result in worship of This World.

Arnold had his chance to exact his revenge on us, however, when Jenny and I were injured in the serious car-crash I've already mentioned, ending up with busted legs, plus one wrist and one ankle each; though Jenny was hurt more seriously, we were injured in exactly the same places. And the only place where we could recover with any degree of care was at Lola's house, which she generously made available to us. This ordeal, which as you'll see went far beyond physical pain and damage, showed every sign of being the Sufi purification prior to initiation that Sidi Safwan had predicted—and perhaps it was also designed to prepare Jenny's soul for her entry into Traditional Catholicism, which was to happen a few years later.

During our 11-week stay, Arnold refused to mail any of our letters, including those with checks to pay the agency that was providing our in-home medical help; he threatened to beat me while I was still in a wheelchair, but retreated hastily up the stairs when I wheeled myself toward him in a threatening manner. He went so far as to turn our in-home help against us, explaining how disrespectful we were to Lola and issuing orders to them (which they obeyed), even though we were the ones paying their wages. And he raised the issue of the will once again, though not in any intelligible way since for us to have a frank discussion of our differences would have required him to admit to criminal wrongdoing. Significantly, our help had no sense that Arnold was actually Lola's husband since he showed no signs of it; at that point he was spending most nights at his own smaller place up the holler. They called him "the man who runs the house."

Then there was the dark and stormy night when, lying awake after midnight as I often did, since it was hard to sleep under those conditions—though I was firmly under the influence of the artificial peace provided by pain pills—I heard Arnold leave the house by the front door. Earlier that day he had been walking around the house, thinking out loud: "Let's see now, we've got to *scare* Irene some way" (Irene lived alone just next door) "so she will want to move in here with Lola and care for her so I can take a break and move back to my own house for a while..." Then, when morning came, we learned that somebody had apparently put a shot possum on Irene's doorstep in the middle of the night. "Must've been kids that did it as a prank, teenagers," was Arnold's explanation. How strange it was, at least to me as a fairly rational individual, that Arnold's daughter Judy would actually tell us about the irregularities with the will that Arnold had so meticulously engineered, and that Arnold himself would declare his intention to frighten Irene into moving out of her house within close hearing-range of *me*, the last person in the world you'd imagine he would want to know about it. My only explanation, though it is a speculative one, is that Eastern Kentucky culture is so devoted to the repression of unpleasant realities and the general habit of blocking out unwanted perceptions that both Arnold and his daughter were confident that neither I nor Jenny would ever *admit to ourselves* what we'd actually heard or seen. This would also explain how Jenny could be sent to school at the age of 16 with an injured eye and covered with blood—because her parents totally repressed the significance of such a spectacle, and relied on everybody else in the community to repress it too: a conspiracy of blindness.

During the 11-week ordeal of our convalescence, Arnold's near-hypnotic ability to convince other people of the truth of various slanders directed against his adversaries resulted in the dumbest of our home health aides coming to believe that she knew the entire history and interpersonal dynamic of a family she had first encountered only days earlier, the main element in this dynamic being "Charles and Jenny have been very mean to poor Lola." Based on this principle, the gullible girl became extremely abusive to Jenny, who was in pain and couldn't walk—and when Jenny burst into tears, her response was: "Yer acting like a TWO-year-old! The people here are ILL; YOU'RE only INJURED!" On top of that, when our friend Eric phoned us from New York, she felt compelled to make it clear to him just what bad people we were, so we handed the phone to her so she could fully inform him of how "your friends are *terrible people!*" Nonetheless she must have finally scared herself straight, awakened herself to the fact that she'd truly blown it as a home health aide and might even be liable to legal action, since she abruptly left the agency she'd been working for, and soon afterwards left the state. It was during these conflicts with Arnold and our "help" that I felt the power of "resist not evil" and began to understand that your anger against your enemy is actually the triumph of your enemy's anger against you. The main lesson to be learned was about the power of self-control and "suppression of rage"; unless that's already in place, *loving* your enemies—the post-graduate course—will be no better than a dishonest and powerless fantasy.

But perhaps the most macabre happening during our convalescence was the night Lola burst into the living room of her house where our hospital beds were set up and said "I caught you! I heard you fighting." When we only gazed at her with a calm yet profound look of shock and puzzlement, she said "Oh. It must have been the TV." But the TV wasn't on, and had not been on. When Lola realized this, her response was: "Hmm. It was probably just my dentures again." Apparently she was under the belief that her dentures sometimes acted like a crystal radio (such incidents have actually been reported) and were picking up some of the local programming. But when we later recounted this incident to a psychologist we were consulting about the possibility that Lola had Alzheimer's, her response was: "It sounds more like schizophrenia to me" (schizophrenia—or *maybe...*).

This incident opens the door of memory to other happenings that were so strange they verged on the paranormal. When Jenny and I returned to Lola's house from our trip to South Carolina we got in late, so we retired to our room without waking Lola; it was only the next morning that we discovered her lying in her bed with a broken back. The night before, however, in our darkened room, we had *both* seen bright red blotches of color in the air above our bed, and heard her voice as if talking in her sleep—but there is no way we could normally have heard any such thing from that part of the house. It may be that the majority of married American men are led to ask themselves, at one time or another, whether their mothers-in-law might be possessed by demons; in any case, that question definitely presented itself to me on more than one occasion. Things vaguely suggestive of demonic activity included the time when, slumped in her reclining chair either asleep or heavily sedated on opioids, a deep, guttural masculine voice issued from her mouth for a moment, uttering a string of unintelligible words. On another occasion, the day after Jenny and I had done something we almost never do, which is to listen to an acoustic music group at a local café, she phoned us and, in the lowest, twistiest, most insinuating voice imaginable, asked: "Been going to the *clubs??*" as if clairvoyantly catching us in some act of unforgivable degeneracy. Then there was the time when, as soon as she stepped into Jenny's sister's house in one of her silent rages, all of the wiring blew out: obviously a *coincidence*, but, at least to my mind, a very significant one.

None of this, of course, proves anything. But by far the strangest occurrence was the time when I looked out the sliding glass doors at the back of her house and saw Lola—who had great difficulty walking due to a broken osteoporotic ankle that had never properly healed, to the point where she nearly needed a walker—absolutely *sprinting* up the steep grassy hill behind the house like an Olympic athlete toward her then-husband Robert Damron (whom she had briefly married between Fred and Arnold, before she had their marriage annulled because it had never been consummated), as if to do him seriously bodily harm. There is no way I could have run up that steep an incline myself in my late 50s, and she was already in her 70s. Later that day Robert took me aside and asked, with a spooked look on his face, "Charles, can you tell me what's going on in this madhouse?" As it happens I did have an idea of what might be going on, but since I didn't feel comfortable saying something like, "Well, we suspect Lola of being demonically possessed of course—preternatural strength being one of the surest signs of such possession—but that's not so rare these days so I wouldn't pay it any mind," I just put him off with some evasive excuse. "Magical realism" is not just a literary form invented by Gabriel García Márquez; it's the way things actually are. As for growing up in a madhouse—though this was a different one, not in Virgie but in another Pike County town, Belfry—here's the poem Jenny wrote about that, and about the excruciating spiritual alchemy she conceived of to deal with it:

The Blood

> The room around the wall is peopled and deranged.
> I must get away from the wall and go toward the
> tree that never has leaves. My body wrapped
> around it will be its leaves. My blood comes up
> within me, like heat and I am becoming the
> flower of the tree. I am sinking into my blood.
> As I die my blood remains in the invisible parts of
> the tree. I can feel my blood forming and appearing
> within a time and space I can never know.

Be that as it may, after we survived our Pike County convalescence, returned to our own house in Lexington and were on the mend (a couple of weeks early, since we had to get out of Long Fork to save our lives), I decided to contact a lawyer, since I was not entirely sure that Arnold's campaign to cut us out was entirely over. The lawyer was only someone connected with an internet legal service that provided free advice in hopes of landing clients, but when I showed his report to Lola—it had recommended that I file a police report and consider pressing both civil and criminal charges, including kidnapping (which was admittedly pretty far-fetched)—she passed it on to Arnold, after which he showed it to a lawyer of his own. I never heard what transpired between them, but my conjecture is that the lawyer must have said something like, "Well, Arnold, they really don't seem to have much of a case, but if I were you I'd cool it just to stay on the safe side." We had no intention of taking any legal action—getting out alive and saving the will was victory enough—but of course Arnold didn't know that.

And it was during our convalescence that two other highly interesting events took place. The first was a letter I received from none other than Charles Windsor, Prince of Wales, the present King Charles III of England. It was written by his secretary, thanking me on behalf of His Highness for the gift of my book *Who Is the Earth? How to See God in the Natural World*. The second was a telephone conference-call organized by Maryam Hand, inviting me to participate in a group Sufi *dhikr* whose participants would chant a Name of Allah—*Al-Ghani*, the Rich—specifically to petition for the relief of economic distress. (Maryam was at that point a murid of Sidi Muhammad Sa'id al-Jamal ar-Rifa'i ash-Shadhili [1935–2015], one-time custodian of al-Aqsa Masjid on Jerusalem's Temple Mount.) As we were chanting that Name, Arnold Plunkett scampered in, as if impelled by an invisible force, to inform us that Lola, since she was planning to buy a new car, had decided to give us her old one to replace the car we'd lost in the crash. What do you do, how do you react, when someone's emotional cruelty is matched only by their material generosity? What else can you do but refer all bounty and all chastisement back to Allah, showing forbearance in the face of human persecution and expressing gratitude for human munificence? Furthermore, given our state of virtual incarceration during our convalescence, there was little else we could do. We were being put through a course of intensive spiritual training under strict discipline, where necessity is the mother of virtue.

As for the end of Lola's story, her approaching death didn't seem to change her character much or induce her to make any embarrassing admissions; like so many of us (and like essentially all materialists) in part of herself she apparently believed—for all her strictly nominal Christianity—that death is the final refuge from justice. Very few people attended her funeral, the funeral of (as she would have it) a loved and respected pillar of the community and a true Appalachian success story. And given that Arnold had threatened, at one point, to "post a deputy at Lola's funeral" (he was always looking forward hopefully to the day of her death) in case Jenny or I decided to "act out," we were pretty close to missing the event ourselves. On top of that, the preacher Arnold hired to perform the service, after bad-mouthing the flowers we'd bought for being too large and spoiling the view of the coffin, proceeded to bad-mouth Lola's children (undoubtedly as coached by Arnold as he had coached our in-home medical help, and possibly also the dumb-ass constable at Chester's funeral) under a thin veneer of rather suspect Biblical commentary, to the effect that "Jesus always said 'love your Mom'—and that He did, yes sir, Jesus loved his Mom"—no matter that what Jesus really said was "I am come to set a man at variance against his father, and the daughter against her mother, and the daughter-in-law against her mother-in-law" [Matthew 10:35]. As I've learned over the years, some of these Appalachian "full gospel" Old Regular Baptists and members of similar sects don't actually *read* the Bible in any thorough way. Since their theology is largely limited to the principle of "whoever says unto me 'Lord, Lord' shall enter the Kingdom of Heaven," if they actually cracked the book it might result in some uncomfortable surprises.

Lola's funeral ended with the equivalent of "OK, boys, let's load 'er up," followed by the hollow clunk of a coffin on the bed of a hearse. Pack 'er up and be done with it, was the general attitude. By contrast, her sister Irene's funeral was a real outpouring of community love and grief. As the sub-dominant sister, Irene had been required by contract in common law to do her sister's bidding—as when Lola had rousted Irene and her husband Chester out of their house and ordered them to drive with her into town right before we were due to arrive on a car-trip from California, just so we would be welcomed by two locked and empty houses, no explanatory note, and the sighing of the wind in the trees. But when Irene died it became clear that she, the local school teacher as opposed to the big college professor, was the beloved sister of the community; hers was the biggest of the maybe eight funerals of Jenny's kin that I've attended. (Funerals are big events in that part of the world, much bigger than weddings — so much so that they almost suggest an indigenous American ancestor-worship, whose major feast is Memorial Day. When the Hall & Jones Funeral Home moved to Virgie, Jenny's father expressed his relief that "now Lola will finally have a social life.") In stark contrast to the community's thin representation at Lola's funeral, everybody and their cousin turned out when we sold off the contents of her home, as if their secret dreams of looting the Big House had finally come to fruition.

I will begin to draw this account to a close with two poems. The first was written by Jenny many years ago, after her escape to the West:

My Birth Dress

As soon as I was born, my birth dress was put around me
like an incubator. When I quit my kicking, voices accumulated
within the room.

These were the voices of the women who had made the dress cloth
with insect shadows over it. There was snow inside of
the arms and legs of these women, but when they looked into
mirrors they could only see insects.

One of the women had no neck, so the other hung my birth
dress over her arms and said it was a necklace that sinks
into the ground during the daylight hours. This woman always
kept her arms and legs covered in the daytime.

This woman is my mother. When I look into the hollow
that exists between the nighttime and morning I see only her.

And because I was born backward she can never see
me. She remembers that, as the sun went away she went to her
mirror and combed her hair while it was becoming wet.
She heard my feet as they started to come out, and then
her memory of me ends.

Sometimes if you can just tell something like it really is, you've begun to free yourself from it; this is one of the many implications of Jesus Christ's promise that "the Truth shall make you free."

The second poem is by me. It was written on the occasion of Lola's death in 2012, which was the only death I ever fully witnessed:

A Death

Standing at my wife's mother's bedside at the moment of her death,
We watched as it passed over her face: first, terror at the grim horsemen,
Then total astonishment: eyes blind to this world but wide open to the next,
Her attention expanded, dispersed, into the clear light of Death
Like a towering cloud mass breaking up on the surface of a
Vast, empty sky.

Her body left behind, deflated,
Breath of the spirit now departed,
A flattened bag of flesh,
Like a tawny desert as the sandstorm that's just buffeted us
Begins to move away, shrinking towards a horizon
That both beckons us
And stops us cold
With the gesture of "Halt! *Not yet*" —

Returning us to the usual concerns,
The turning wheel of our days, their familiar rhythms,
Now shrunken and puppet-like in the face of that

    Magnificent

        waiting

SKY

As Lola was dying, the only thing remotely resembling Extreme Unction was provided by Jenny, who dabbed some oil from the perpetually-burning lamp at the glass coffin of St John Maximovitch on her forehead, to the puzzlement of the attending relatives. As for me, after she died I had only one dream about her — not as rolling in hellfire nor being purged of her sins by being beaten with blackboard pointers and heavy textbooks. The scene was a road on a hillside just above the high school in my California home town of San Rafael. From there I could look down a bank to a new building rising from the high school grounds. On the lowest storey of the building was a window, and behind that window, alone in a room, sat Lola with a mournful expression on her face; next to her was a vase holding a single flower. So the judgment, the *post mortem*, did not show incorrigible evil intent, but simply — ignorance. She had been sent back to school and was beginning on the lowest level of the school building, the kindergarten level (since the street in the dream was the one on which my father had driven me daily to Catholic kindergarten); though in life she just hadn't *gotten* it, in the next world she was being given a fresh chance to learn her ABC's. If I've ever been shown a vision and emblem of God's Mercy, His reluctance to despair even of the hardest cases of human cruelty — when based, that is, on simple human ignorance — this is it. And that dream agrees substantially with Jenny's assessment of Lola Dearest as of this year of 2023: "My mother wanted to do the right thing, but she didn't have the slightest idea of how to go about it."

So that was all I was given to see. If real, rigorous purgation has been part of her destiny, maybe I am simply being protected from being damaged by such horrible sights. The desire to watch our adversaries fry in fire and brimstone is inseparable from our low opinion of Divine Justice, as if God's retribution would somehow be incomplete without our own puny, self-interested revenge thrown in on top of it. And the same goes for His Mercy, which is absolute in its own terms without needing to ask for any help from our own weakly sentimental and self-deceptive attempts to feel love for those we can never sincerely love without God's help—a fact that led William Blake to observe that "Pity divides the soul." So whatever Lola's eternal destiny may be, all we can really do, besides remembering her acts of substantive help to Jenny and myself that her cruelty seemed deliberately designed to hide, is leave her to God and be done with it—though prayers for the dead, if offered in that same spirit of *apatheia* and detachment, are never useless. We can never know what secret good may lie in the souls of those who have hurt us, nor what secret depths of the Divine Mercy may be hidden under the cloak of His Wrath and His Majesty. And even if the intended recipient of our prayers is sealed off from their influence, God can still use them elsewhere for His own mysterious purposes.

The only way out of bitterness, desire for revenge and participation in the evil we condemn is the mysterious activity known as *forgiveness*. You and I do not possess the power to forgive; only God can do that. All we can do with our own limited strength, without God's help, is intend not to retaliate. Only God has the power to change our feelings of anger and hatred into those of love and compassion. Nonetheless we do have the power *to pray that He will do this*; when faced with violence and enmity, let us not forget to exercise that power. As for Jesus' promise in the Sermon on the Mount that those who hunger and thirst for justice will be satisfied, its inseparable companion is: "Vengeance is Mine sayeth the Lord"—because sometimes our anger, especially when it expands beyond all boundaries and becomes bigger than we are, comes from our misappropriation of the Wrath of God, to which we have no right and which is none of our business. And if we are arrogant and foolish enough to place ourselves between that Wrath and its destined target, hoping to throw our own little stone onto the heap of Divine retribution, that Divine Wrath will roll over us like a tank. Our own feeble wrath is based on nothing but conceit and arrogance, while God's Wrath springs, precisely, from *Love*. It is Love itself that makes that Wrath so devastating; as Jesus said, "Love your enemies, do good to them that harm you, and you will heap coals of fire on their heads"—because the ego's resistance to Love is the essence of hellfire. That fire would turn into cool refreshing rain if those bound to the ego could only recognize it as the power of Love ... but in truth we have no power to influence the choices of others. All we can do is intend not to resist the formidable power of Love ourselves, then step aside and let it do its work.

[NOTE TO THE READER: This detour through Jenny's and my memories of her mother may seem out of place to some in a memoir like this, as if it were based on a childish attachment to something that could not have had any serious consequences. I've learned the hard way that it's nearly impossible for even the most sympathetic and perceptive people to get a clear picture of someone else's *social* oppression—especially if the one laboring under that oppression is not part of a race or class or gender that has been officially designated as "oppressed"—nor can they easily realize that such oppression, even if it is enforced only by pettiness and small-mindedness, can sometimes be, quite literally, a case not only of attempted murder but of murder complete, though the final outcome is often long-delayed. My experience over 37 years of my wife's oppression at the hands of her mother, during which time I had to dedicate a large chunk of my life energy to compensate for that influence, has had a major effect on my character, for both good and ill. Though it was certainly an unrelenting burden, it was also something, given my attraction to poetic idealism and metaphysical elevation, that undoubtedly helped me avoid the worst forms of the "grandiose ascension" and titanic fall of the Jungian *puer aeternus* that the poet Robert Bly talked about in his book *Iron John*, and which my childhood and young adulthood in Marin County, California had set me up for. Therefore, to the advice of "let it go, it's not worth remembering" I answer: "It's impossible to let go of something while you're still repressing it. Letting go has to be a conscious act; to let go of an attachment you must remember it completely, along with the entire load of emotion that goes with it." And if the reader is tempted to accuse Jenny and myself of the sin of *co-dependency* for sharing our burdens and our struggles, my response is: "If this be co-dependency, make the most of it."]

DESTINATION

Jenny's mother, as you may remember, died in 2012, but for the main line of my own spiritual Path I'll have to backtrack to 2010, when I was sufficiently mended after our car-crash to drive myself and Jenny to Alexandria, Virginia, so I could join the 'Alawiyya Tariqah by taking *bay'at*—through Sidi Safwan—with the shaykh of our *tariqah* at that time, Sidi Rachid. Shortly before the trip I had a dream that Javad Nurbakhsh had been hospitalized, though I hadn't heard news of him in years—and as soon as we returned home to Lexington after that pivotal journey, I discovered that Dr Nurbakhsh had passed away on the very day I had accepted initiation into the 'Alawiyya.

HOW I WRITE (A SECOND DIGRESSION)

The only thing I really know how to do, in a completely reliable way, is write. Writer's block? Never heard of it. In the case of "Muse-inspired" lyric poetry, when a poem comes in from wherever they come from, it's all there in the first instant. You may not have recorded one word of it, yet you know that it's already complete in some other world—as unmistakable as a smell. The work is not to compose or construct it, but simply to bring it through. And when I graduated from an exclusive concentration on lyric poetry to composing metaphysical essays, and later to the kind of narrative that makes up much of this book, I used the same method: the insight, the story, was somehow already fully there, complete in the world of memory or some other world. So writing by this method is analogous to a pregnancy: suddenly *somebody else* is undeniably on the scene; you know this because you've caught their unique scent. You may not yet know the first thing about what they will be like, yet certainty that they are exactly who they are is already in place. Once that unique soul, that *form*, has magnetized to itself all the *matter* it needs to construct a body for itself, you will see its living face. But in order for it to do this, sufficient material—and sufficiently varied material—must be made available to it to choose from. The soul striving to be born into this world needs food, water, air, shelter, as well as (on the subtle level) the correct feeling-tones and psychic impressions; if one necessary element is missing, the pregnancy will fail. So part of the work of writing, at least according to the way I do it, is to get into the habit of constantly translating all available insights and experiences into verbal structures, as soon as they appear. You don't have to remember these structures or write them down, nor does this process of composing and collecting linguistic material need to be fully conscious; recorded or not, remembered or not, those structures will nonetheless be stored away somewhere, ready to be called upon and put to use as soon as a living but not-yet-incarnate form makes its appearance, demanding to be born. But here we can see—on the more negative side—how writing and contemplation are polar opposites. Writing, like every form of expression, is expenditure—expenditure of what contemplation has earned; if expression outweighs contemplation in your life, then you are in a state of dissipation and debt. Contemplation, since it is inseparable from *listening*, may inspire writing, and writing has the ability to translate what is learned in contemplation into concepts and imaginative forms that the lower levels of the mind can understand. Yet it is still true that the material writing draws upon is collected through talking to yourself, while the essence of contemplation is to learn how to *stop* talking to yourself, so that you can listen to the higher Voice that emerges from, and is inseparable from, the Great Silence. The First Speaker, whose speech is Silence, is God, God as the *logos*; this is why, in terms of the human being as the servant of God, listening comes first and speech follows after. The poet is, first, a *trouvère*, a "finder"; only later is he or she a *poietes*, a "maker."

In *The Marriage of Heaven and Hell* William Blake wrote: "The Prolific would cease to be prolific unless the Devourer, as a sea, received the excess of his delights." In view of this I must *eternally* thank James Wetmore of Sophia Perennis Publications for publishing virtually everything I've written for the past 20 years. I can see him loading them into a truck, driving them to market, and displaying them attractively in racks or on tables, so that the Devourers can nibble at and/or stuff themselves with the excess of my delights, relieve me of the burden of them and make room for more. And though I began my latter-day writer's life with *Doorkeeper of the Heart: Versions of Rabi'a* in 1988, which was published by Kabir Helminski of Threshold Books, and *Hammering Hot Iron: A Spiritual Critique of Bly's Iron John* in 1992, published by Quest Books, the real "debriefing" began with *The System of Antichrist: Truth and Falsehood in Postmodernism and the New Age* in 2001—which I wrote and published while I was still living in California—and continued in all the books that followed as soon as we'd moved to Lexington, Kentucky, books in the genres of metaphysics, metaphysics and social criticism, metaphysical exegesis of mythopoesis, Islam, Sufism, UFO demonology and spiritual psychology, all of which were published either by James Wetmore as director of Sophia Perennis or by him in tandem with John Riess as co-partners of Angelico Press. Many of these books came out of my attempt to apply Traditionalist/Perennialist ideas to areas that were mostly neglected, if not deliberately avoided, by the major writers of the Traditionalist School clustered around Frithjof Schuon, including folklore, mythology, comparative eschatology (though Martin Lings's *The Eleventh Hour* is a classic in this genre), demonology and political science—areas that René Guénon, for one, was much more open to. As for my most characteristic genre, "metaphysics and social criticism," I did my best to bring the elevated metaphysics of René Guénon and Frithjof Schuon together with the unavoidable "conspiracy theory" mindset of the 21st Century—with some interesting results.

JENNY AND THE TRADITIONAL CATHOLICS

Jenny's thorough, relentless and one-pointed quest for the true Catholic Church, which took place mostly but not entirely after I had established my connection with the 'Alawiyya Tariqah, was in some ways unexpected, but always felt exactly right. Somehow the Western Church spoke directly to her soul—but why? Her family had been weakly-observant Baptists; the Traditionalists mostly emphasized Eastern Orthodoxy, which Jenny accepted as a valid church with valid sacraments; and her most intense experience of Christian community had been with a mainline Protestant church following the social gospel. Why Roman Catholicism? Was she in some ways re-living my past in connecting with the Church as I remembered it from my childhood, just as I had entered her past by encountering, and surviving, the darkness of her family? That might have been true up to a point, but there had to be more to her attraction to Rome—which was certainly foreshadowed by her attraction to Dante—than the influence of my past. Certainly no one would expect Jenny's experience of my Catholic high school friends, or of my mother and her Catholic nun friends, to put Catholicism in a positive light for her. Her own explanation is that she was born, somehow, with an essentially medieval soul, which only Roman Catholicism truly resonated with. Her love of traditional Western Civilization, including the whole ethos of Romance and Courtly Love, made Traditional Catholicism—though in a profoundly secret way—her inevitable spiritual destination.

The world of Traditional *sedevacantist* Catholicism is filled with believers dedicated to informing themselves as deeply and comprehensively as possible about the 2000 years of Catholic tradition, theology and spiritual guidance, as well as to defining and maintaining the grace and efficacy of the Traditional sacraments. Yet the lack of any central authority governing Traditional Catholicism as a whole, coupled with the reduction of the function of the bishop from administrator of an organized diocese to little more than an ordainer of priests, necessarily results in the problem that Rama Coomaraswamy characterized as "every priest his own Pope." This state of affairs inevitably meant that Jenny's road through the Traditional Catholic world would be filled with many bumps and detours and chuckholes. Nonetheless, by the grace of Providence, she ultimately found what she was looking for.

Outside of the tendency in contemporary Eastern Orthodox Christianity to deny the universal immortality of the soul, Jenny found that the Russian Orthodox Church in Kentucky had much more of a Protestant feel to it than did the churches of the Bay Area, built as they were on the solid foundation of a deep traditional Russian piety, thanks to St John Maximovitch and the old White Russian believers who were just then breathing their last. Like the Novus Ordo Catholics, the Orthodox Christians of Kentucky (and Indiana) were beginning to replace the deep contemplative inwardness that had once blossomed as the sacred Hesychasm of Mt. Athos with a shallow, glad-handing "Hi, Neighbor!" fellowship, mostly derived from "mainstream" Protestantism. Quite a few Protestants were converting to Eastern Orthodoxy at that time, and they tended to bring their mainstream Protestant sensibilities and character-formation with them, as well as their inherent anti-Catholicism, which tended to blend confusingly with the much older Orthodox Christian denial of the authority of Rome that dated back nearly a thousand years to the time of the Great Schism. The fact that both the Protestants and the Orthodox rejected the Pope let them see much that they had in common, but hid from them their great and inherent differences. Furthermore, the Protestant rejection of the Catholic doctrine of Purgatory undoubtedly worked to reinforce the similar Orthodox tendency, though the Eastern Orthodox didn't so much deny the reality of after-death purgation as the notion of Purgatory as a separate "place," tending rather to explain posthumous purgation in terms of a temporary sojourn in Hell. And I am reasonably confident that once the Protestant rejection of Purgatory was imported into Orthodoxy it did much to reinforce the "conditionalist" or "annihilationist" heresy that I've analyzed above.

Be that as it may, the day came when Matt Haltom, a Traditional Catholic whom Jenny had met through Kathleen Cummings, told her about a Traditional Mass that was taking place at the home of Jean and Kirby Bischel, in Georgetown just north of Lexington — and even though Jenny still identified and worshiped as Orthodox, she decided to attend. There she met four people, outside of the Bischels, who were to become very important to her. The first was Bishop McGuire, the celebrant, who had come down from St Gertrude's Catholic Church in the Cincinnati area to say Mass for the Traditional Catholics of the Bluegrass. Number two was Christian Plunkett, undoubtedly a distant relative of hers through her mother's family, who proved to her that there were actually such things as *good* Plunketts! (Christian later made contact with Arnold Plunkett through the Plunkett Family Association, though I was able to give him what he needed to protect himself from that contact by recounting the history of our near-fatal run-in with Arnold after our auto accident.) The third was Lee Speray, at whose house-church near Lawrenceburg, west of Lexington, Jenny now worships. The fourth was one Vili Lehtoranta, a native of Finland, who was studying for the priesthood at Bishop Donald Sanborn's Traditional Catholic seminary in Florida. Later, after he was ordained, he became a priest at St Gertrude's — and during the time I was in the ICU due to the serious episode of diverticular bleeding that developed when I had sacrificed virtually everything, including a big chunk of my life-energy, to bring news to the world of Dr John Andrew Morrow's re-discovery of the Covenants of the Prophet Muhammad with the Christians of his time (see below), he drove down all the way from Cincinnati, Ohio to Lexington, Kentucky, in response to an appeal from Jenny, just to pray for me in the hospital. (I had unwittingly laid my life on the line by vehemently laboring to convince John Riess and James Wetmore of Angelico Press that Dr Morrow's *The Covenants of the Prophet Muhammad with the Christians of the World* HAD to be published; I'll tell that story next.)

After this service at the Bischels' home I began driving Jenny to St Gertrude's in West Chester near Cincinnati; soon afterwards she placed herself under the posthumous intercessorship of Rama Coomaraswamy by officially becoming a Traditional, *sedevacantist* Roman Catholic as part of the St Gertrude's congregation. St Gertrude's was and is one of the few "established" *sedevacantist* church compounds in North American, with its own full-sized buildings and elaborate furnishings, providing an entirely appropriate setting for the solemnity of the true Catholic sacraments. Later on Jenny began catching weekly rides to St Gertrude's from the Bischels. St Gertrude's had been founded by some of the priests, including Fr Anthony

Cekada and Bishop Daniel Dolan, who had taken the *sedevacantist* position—largely through Rama Coomaraswamy's influence—and later followed him out of the Society of St Pius X to found the Society of St Pius V.

It was through Lee Speray that Jenny met one Bishop Webster from Knoxville, Tennessee, who was saying Mass at a little dilapidated once-Protestant country chapel just outside of Louisville, known in its Catholic incarnation as the Church of St John the Baptist, whose congregation had been founded by a priest (by then deceased) who had known Rama. It was placed in a beautiful county setting of low wooded hills, right next to a little farm with such an array of beautiful and varied livestock that it reminded one of the Garden of Eden: cows, sheep, goats, llamas, geese, ducks, chickens, peacocks...a lovely place to worship. Bishop Webster himself used to drive us to Mass there. On one occasion, when I told him of our experiences with Arnold Plunkett, the Bishop said: "he sounds like a Freemason"—which was very interesting given that Arnold has actually joined the Freemasons a few years before. (I was becoming a little too Catholic for my own good at that time—for a professing Muslim—since I was in the period when the Nimatullahis were beginning to disappear from my life and the 'Alawis had not yet arrived.) Later that church was taken over by one Father Leonardo, a chubby, "charismatic" little cleric, still living with his parents, who later turned out to be a sterling example of the "every priest his own pope" syndrome that Rama had warned us against. It was at St John the Baptist that we attended the wedding of Lee and Julia Speray. Julia, who hailed from Pennsylvania, was a woman who would've looked perfect in a 19th Century frock and bonnet. She took to motherhood like a spaniel to water and later turned out (with Lee's help of course) four perfect Catholic children. Christian Plunkett had been corresponding with Julia's father on *sedevacantist* subjects, who had lamented that his daughter, as a Traditional Catholic, had few ways of meeting eligible young men—but then Christian remembered Lee, who was in a similar predicament, so he proceeded to introduce them. Also at that church we met one Sister Dymphna, who dressed in a traditional nun's habit—but since she seemed to be without a functioning contemplative order at that time (though I could be wrong there), she wore the Maltese Cross, the emblem of the Knights of Malta, who have a historical connection with the Knights Templar. Since viable and well-organized dioceses and contemplative orders are hard to come by in the *sedevacantist* world, sometimes Traditional priests and nuns, in need of a higher authority to help them practice the virtue of obedience, will attach themselves to various Catholic chivalric orders, who still have their own buildings, officers and sources of funding. Jenny remembers that the priest who had founded St John the Baptist, and had known Rama, had been one of Dymphna's high school teachers.

It was around the time that Jenny began attending mass at St John the Baptist that a schism occurred at St Gertrude's. Part of the congregation split off, led by one Fr Ramola, and formed a new church, St Theresa's, in Lebanon, Ohio. Jenny ended up visiting and worshipping at both churches. During the same period she would sometimes attend Mass at Lee and Julia's apartment in Frankfort, first as celebrated by Bishop Webster, next by a priest from Ireland, Father McGilloway, and finally by one Fr Michael Oswalt from Alabama, who had been a seminary-educated Novus Ordo priest before he became a *sedevaccantist*. At the same time she continued to attend Fr Leonardo's Mass at St John the Baptist.

Later Fr Leonardo somehow prevailed upon a wealthy Black member of his congregation, Judge Gary Payne (retired) to buy him a huge old abandoned Lutheran church in urban Louisville, more or less on the "buy it and they will come" theory, which told him that once he had a big, legitimate "real" church to offer, Traditional (or else disaffected Novus Ordo) Catholics would materialize out of nowhere and fill the place to overflowing. Fr Leonardo's idea was perhaps traceable back, at least in my mind and according to my own brand of satirical humor, to the "build it and they will come" notion from the 1989 Kevin Costner film *Field of Dreams*—something that worked quite well in the movie, but not so well in real life: they bought it, but nobody came. The place needed extensive repairs that the congregation couldn't afford and cost an arm and a leg to heat in the winter, so it eventually had to be re-sold at a loss. Later Fr Leonardo alienated the Sperays and others of his original congregation through his cranky ideas and controlling ways. He would refuse communion to people he wasn't getting along with, claimed at one point that smoking cigarettes and eating non-organic food were mortal sins, and finally fell in with some mentally-challenged food-freaks who taught that consuming raw pork was the way to perfect health . . . all of which led Lee Speray, after his Leonardo phase was over, to apply to him the Latin phrase that is used whenever the white smoke rises from the Vatican chimney signaling that a new pope has been elected: "*habemus papam*." On one occasion Jenny and I were invited by a member of Leonardo's circle to his home in Frankfort to attend the baptism of his and his wife's new child; he had asked Jenny to act as Godmother, a role she gladly accepted. But when Fr Leonardo handed the child to his parents and his godfather (Christian Plunkett) after the baptism, he deliberately left Jenny out, passing the child to *me* instead, who, besides not having any appointed role in the baptism, was not even a Christian! Later I phoned Fr Leonardo and asked him if Jared, the father, had informed him that he had wanted Jenny to act as Godmother, since it is my habit never to a let a slight offered to my wife in my presence go unanswered. Leonardo hemmed and hawed for a moment, and then told me that, no, he hadn't. Next I phoned Jared and, expressing surprise that

Fr Leonardo had left Jenny out of the baptismal ritual, asked him if he had remembered to tell Leonardo that Jenny was to be the Godmother. He told me that he had definitely informed him. "That's strange" I replied, "because I just talked with Fr Leonardo and he told me that you hadn't... it must just have been a case of poor communication."

After Jenny stopped going to Fr Leonardo's Mass, and before she limited herself to worshipping at St Gertrude's exclusively, she attended a Traditional Mass several times at a rented space in Frankfort; it was celebrated by one Father Bernard Hall, who came down from his home base at a house church called the Infant of Prague Chapel in the Cincinnati area to serve the Traditional Catholics of Central Kentucky. (Based on the number of traditional Mass groups in and surrounding it, Cincinnati can probably be described as the center of *sedevacantist* Catholicism in North America.) Father Hall was a Traditional Catholic from England, who grew up in the town in Yorkshire that the Brontë sisters came from, either Thornton where they were born or Haworth where they later relocated, I forget which. He received a scholarship to study at the same university in Scotland, St Andrew's, that Prince William had attended. He was also well-acquainted with Rama Coomaraswamy; during a period when he was having difficulty legally immigrating to the United State, Rama even considered adopting him as a son. Fr Hall was instinct and overflowing with the traditional English culture that Jenny loved; in his sermons he was just as likely to quote from Shakespeare or Chaucer as the Bible or the Church Fathers.

Then the day came when Jean and Kirby Bischel moved to the Cincinnati area, which meant that Jenny lost her ride to St Gertrude's. Soon after this she began attending Mass at the house church of Lee and Julia Speray near Willisburg west of Lawrenceburg, which was a lot shorter trip from Lexington than the long drive to Cincinnati. This church was destined to become the most stable and also the most accessible Mass that Jenny has yet been able to find in Ohio and Kentucky — but a number of complicated hurdles still had to be jumped before that Mass could be solidly established.

The main problem was finding an appropriate priest. Fr Leonardo had already revealed his shortcomings, and Lee Speray and his older brother Steven had theological differences with Bishop Webster, who turned out to be a "Feeneyite"—a follower of Fr Leonard Feeney, who held that only Baptism by Water is valid and capable of bringing salvation, not Baptism of Desire or Baptism of Blood. This essentially means that someone who has already been fully catechized and is looking forward to the day or his or her Baptism, but who happens to die the night before, will go to Hell, as will someone who was willingly martyred for Christ but hadn't yet received the formal sacrament. In other words, the Feeneyites deny the mercy of God, picturing Him as a punctilious and heartless tyrant, and also essentially denying His omnipotence by binding Him to rules and regulations that, though authored by Him, properly apply only to human beings. The next pastoral candidate was Fr Hall, who Jenny was rooting for, but Steve Speray, the *de facto* congregational theologian, author of several self-published books on Catholic doctrine and host of the website "Catholic Top Gun," tested him and found him wanting in his strict adherence to Catholic Tradition as the *sedevacantists* understand it. At that point we were afraid that Steve might turn out to be one of the types that was all-too-common in the *sedevacantist* world, that of the influential member of a given congregation (usually wealthy, though this limitation did not apply to Steve) who, because the authority of a bishop was lacking, arrogated to himself the properly episcopal right to hire and fire the priest, and took pride in assuming that role. This, however, turned out to be the furthest thing from the truth.

JOHN AND KATHLEEN PASS ON

Among our closest friends in Lexington were the retired psychiatrist and initiate of the Shadhili Tariqah John Parks and his wife Kathleen *née* Cummings, whom you've already met. Kathleen had been central in introducing Jenny to the Traditional Catholics of the Lexington area though she was not really one of them herself, and my relationship to John helped compensate for my not having a Sufi *tariqah* in town to practice with. We were not destined to have them as friends for as long as we might have wished, however. Since John was getting on in years, Jenny and I ended up visiting him in the hospital on more than one occasion — once after he'd needed to have a heart valve replaced, for which operation his heart needed to be lifted out of his chest, and once for a bleeding kidney, which turned out to be nothing serious. Soon after this episode, however, Kathleen turned up with advanced brain cancer. She survived the necessary operation, but was not given long to live; ultimately she was sent home to die, which happened a few weeks later. And only a short time after that, John followed her on the same road.

John and Kathleen had been living on a farm near Waco, Kentucky, in the beautiful foothills of the Appalachians, with its own fishing lake and a striking view of a nearby mountain that was known for its Native American graveyard. The place had two notable distinctions. The first was that it was said to be one of the places where Daniel Boone had hunted and fished; the second was its reputation as a good place for UFO-watching. People would drive up to a little elevated flat area on that land in the evenings and watch as our "alien" visitors put on their usual aerial performances. In view of this it's an interesting fact that the piece of land in question abutted the Bluegrass Army Depot, which some have characterized as "Kentucky's Area 51."

As Kathleen drew near to death the *Tibetan Book of the Dead* was recited over her, since Buddhism was one of her two religious identifications. Then Matt Haltom asked her if she wanted to receive the Traditional Catholic sacrament of extreme unction. Her answer was "yes," so Matt contacted Fr Oswalt in Alabama, who drove all the way up to Kentucky just to administer that sacrament, after dark, to one lapsed Catholic on the point of death.

Jenny and I were there for the occasion. As Fr Oswalt recited the Latin words of the rite, I noticed two things: first, that one of Kathleen's caged birds (Jenny heard this too) seemed to be reciting the words along with him, in bird-fashion only of course; and second, that John Parks couldn't stand to be in the same room where the rite was being performed, but went downstairs to the lower room until it was over. This was a bit strange, since, even though he was a Muslim, he'd apparently had no problem with the recitation of the *Tibetan Book of the Dead* — he may even have recited it himself — and also in view of an episode that had happened in Kathleen's hospital room as she was recovering from her operation. One of her visitors had been a Jewish woman, a Buddhist, who had said, loud enough for everyone to hear: "I hate people who pray" — including, in her category of hated people, Jenny (a Christian), myself, and John Parks (the two of us Muslims who prayed five times a day). On that occasion John stayed in the room. In other words, he could abide the presence of a Buddhist woman who hated people who prayed to God just as he did, but not that of a Catholic priest who also prayed to God. Here we can see how "This World" has unwritten rules that appear in no book, but which are all too often obeyed without question.

After the rite was over I asked Fr Oswalt (it was quite late at night), if he'd like to have a cup of coffee with us at a local all-night café so we could get to know each other. He declined however, saying that he needed to be on the road since he had to say Mass next morning, down in Alabama.

That's dedication for you. And that's the priest that Steve Speray finally accepted as worthy to be the pastor of Jenny's little house church near Willisburg, which goes by the name of the St Vincent Ferrer Mission. Fr Oswalt came through a Traditional Catholic group called the Congregation of Mary Immaculate Queen (CMRI), one of the more stable and reliable of the *sedevacantist* organizations. Both while he was based in Alabama and after he moved to Illinois, he drove, and still drives (I believe), to five states every month, to say Mass for small Traditional Catholic congregations. Fr Oswalt is the salt of the earth. His sermons are essential Catholic doctrine and morality and nothing else. He is an ascetic and a zealot, though not the kind of zealot who becomes filled with animus against sinners and unbelievers; he has no time for that. Nor is he the kind of priest who is cut out to be the pastor a large and complacent congregation, becoming fat and comfortable and having tea and light conversation with the church matrons on a Sunday afternoon. (That he was expected to fill this kind of role was apparently one of his problems with his church in Alabama.) His relationship to Jenny's congregation is in no way social, but entirely sacerdotal. As soon as Mass is over he's already in his car with his dogs, on his way to the next assignment: a true circuit-rider, like a number of my Methodist ancestors on the 19th-Century American frontier. Under Fr Oswalt, Jenny finally found her true spiritual home. As for Steve Speray, as soon as Fr Michael Oswalt was in place, he ceased being a theological attack dog and became simply one more sheep in Fr Oswalt's flock, proving that his loyalty was entirely to the true Catholic Tradition, not to his own potential role as the power-broker behind the priestly throne. Perhaps only someone like myself, who has been from one end to the other of the religious landscape in North America, would be capable of realizing just how rare a thing that is.

THE DAWN OF THE COVENANTS

From the year 1988 when my "tour of duty" in the New Age came to an end until the year 2013, I remained entirely outside the world of activism. I had already seen how almost every major political effort in today's world, whether for peace or social justice or environmental protection, had been largely co-opted by the powers that be. With lightning speed I discerned—or believed I had—the essential contradictions in all the social movements that I surveyed, ran them ahead in my mind's eye to their ultimate conclusions, and found them barren. The only kind of choice I saw in any sort of idealistic effort to "save the world" was that between Gog or Magog, so I was content to sit things out till I found myself in an entirely different world, one where earthly hopes and agendas have no meaning.

Then—unexpectedly, providentially—an opportunity presented itself for me to return without prejudice or the need to rely on any degree of willful blindness to my earlier activist identity. In 2013 my publisher James Wetmore showed me a proposal from one Dr John Andrew Morrow for a book entitled *The Covenants of the Prophet Muhammad with the Christians of the World*, asking me what I thought of it. (He would sometimes do that with submissions he received from various quarters, since he respected my opinion.) I took one look at that proposal and told Mr Wetmore to jump on it quick, since Dr Morrow's book was the most crucially relevant document that I could possibly imagine, both in terms of its ground-breaking research in religious history and of its relevance to that precise historical moment—the moment of the rise of ISIS. When first I talked by phone with Dr Morrow—a Metís (person of mixed

Native American and European ancestry) from Quebec whose Muslim name is Imam Ilyas 'Abd al-'Alim Islam—I said: "Our press doesn't have a large marketing budget for your book—but I think we can make a movement out of it"—and I was right. So *The Covenants of the Prophet Muhammad with the Christians of the World*—I did some editing on it and contributed a foreword—was published in October of 2013. Between that time and now, Dr Morrow's book has indeed become the basis of an international Muslim/interfaith peace movement—the Covenants Initiative—in the United States, Europe and the Muslim world. I should add at this point that my connection with this movement has in no way been dictated by my Sufi *tariqah*, nor am I at all inclined to preach it to them; I have acted strictly as an individual. Yet insofar as the Sufis practice the most radical form of submission to God imaginable—submission to the point of self-annihilation—then, if involvement with this movement is indeed God's will for me, it must be considered as one of the fruits of Sufism in my life. One indication of this is that during my work with the Covenants I wrote and published a book on Sufism entitled *Day and Night on the Sufi Path* (Angelico/Sophia Perennis, 2015), which includes the following poem I wrote about the advent of the Covenants in my life:

> I was sleeping safe in my scabbard—
> Then God drew me like a sword.
> I awoke to war: to victory and defeat.
> The clean design woven in air by this
>   flashing of blades
> Was drawn from the lettering
> Of the Mother of the Book,
> Written down before first breath
>   was drawn on earth,
> Or the earthen floor laid to receive
> The prints of beasts and men.
> The pounding of feet in battle
> Writes the pre-eternal script of the stars
> On the Guarded Tablet,
> And all these forms of bodies
> Transfigured in their moment of struggle
> Have long since gone to their rest
> In Garden or Fire.
> *It was not you who threw when you threw,*
> *But God threw*;
> And the outcome, and the *agon*,
> And all the exquisite uncertainty—
> To human eyes—of the hour of contest—
> *He* enacted, and *He* knew.

The Covenants Initiative made its official debut in 2013 at the Bilal Mosque in Lexington, Kentucky, at an event sponsored by the Lexington

Christian/Muslim Dialogue, one of whose founders (as you'll remember) was John Parks. Dr Morrow drove down from Indiana to help inaugurate it. During my presentation I expressed my belief that the globalist elites, in their massive campaign to control and/or deconstruct all the major world religions, have been playing a double game of sponsoring the interfaith movement (or elements of it) in the "developed" nations, hoping to weaken the doctrinal frameworks of the faiths by influencing them to soft-pedal any "divisive" doctrines, while at the same time inciting interfaith conflict in the "developing" world in hopes that the religions might eventually destroy each other, or at least justify by their violent excesses a firmer secular hold on them by the globalist powers, which the infiltration of the interfaith movement by those same powers had already laid the groundwork for. In order to reach these tentative yet fairly well-informed conclusions, I drew upon my wide personal experience of the vast spectrum of American religious beliefs and practices in the late 20th century and the first years of the 21st, as well as my half-century of (intermittent) social activism in the U.S. peace movement. When the time came for question-and-answer at the Lexington mosque, a Muslim whose accent identified him as being from the Indian subcontinent made a very interesting revelation: "I can confirm from my personal experience that there really is an agenda to foment interreligious violence. In the village where I grew up, on certain nights, unknown *agent provocateurs* would throw slaughtered pigs into mosques and slaughtered cows into Hindu temples, predictably resulting in Hindu/Muslim riots the next day." And, as I later realized, since both pigs and cows were used, the perpetrators were likely neither Muslims nor Hindus, but after the provocations had been issued and emotions inflamed, nobody had the presence of mind to draw that rather obvious conclusion.

That event was the beginning of a 7-year effort, one that only went into suspended animation when Covid came. During those years my writing shifted from the articulation of ideas in the relatively abstract vacuum of the inner mental world, to the writing and composition of actual events, events that would later take place in the outer world of society and history, though everything I wrote I wrote by dictation from some unseen source: as William Blake put it, "the authors are in Eternity." Such synchronicities may seem like magic to those foolish enough to identify with them, but what they actually are is the operation, via what Wolfgang Smith calls "vertical causality," of the Will of God operating both *on the horizons* and *in their souls*—in both inner and outer worlds—simultaneously. Here's a short history I wrote of our movement, covering the years from 2013 to 2019, which details most of the salient points:

A HISTORY OF THE COVENANTS INITIATIVE

The Covenants Initiative began in 2013 with the publication of the ground-breaking book *The Covenants of the Prophet Muhammad with the Christians of the World* by Dr John Andrew Morrow. The covenants or treaties of the Prophet with various Christian communities, which Prof. Morrow re-discovered in obscure libraries and collections, as well as in a number of ancient monasteries in the Middle East which he contacted in search of these vital documents — also providing exhaustive historical research and textual analysis to establish their validity — uniformly command Muslims not to kill, rob or in any way oppress peaceful Christians, or stop churches from being repaired, or tear down churches to build mosques, or even prevent their Christian wives from going to church and taking spiritual direction from Christian priests and elders. On the contrary, the Prophet commands all Muslims to actively defend these communities "until the coming of the Hour."

Here is the English translation of the text of the first Covenant, granted by Muhammad to the ancient Monastery of St Catherine at Mt. Sinai:

> *In the Name of Allah, the Most Compassionate, the Most Merciful.*
>
> This covenant was written by Muhammad, the son of 'Abd Allah, the proclaimer and warner, trusted to protect Allah's creations, in order that people may raise no claim against Allah after [the advent of] His Messengers, for Allah is Almighty, Wise.
>
> He has written it for the members of his religion and to all those who profess the Christian religion in East and West, near or far, Arabs or non-Arabs, known or unknown, as a covenant of protection.
>
> If anyone breaks the covenant herein proclaimed, or contravenes or transgresses its commands, he has broken the Covenant of Allah, breaks his bond, makes a mockery of his religion, deserves the curse [of Allah], whether he is a sultan or another among the believing Muslims.
>
> If a monk or pilgrim seeks protection, in mountain or valley, in a cave or in tilled fields, in the plain, in the desert, or in a church, I am behind them, defending them from every enemy; I, my helpers, all the members of my religion, and all my followers, for they [the monks and the pilgrims] are my protégés and my subjects.
>
> I protect them from interference with their supplies and from the payment of taxes save what they willingly renounce. There shall be no compulsion or constraint against them in any of these matters.
>
> A bishop shall not be removed from his bishopric, nor a monk from his monastery, nor a hermit from his tower, nor shall a pilgrim be hindered from his pilgrimage. Moreover, no building from among their churches shall be destroyed, nor shall the money from their churches be used for the building of mosques or houses for the Muslims. Whoever does such a thing violates Allah's covenant and dissents from the Messenger of Allah.

Neither poll-tax nor fees shall be laid on monks, bishops, or worshippers for I protect them, wherever they may be, on land or sea, in East and West, in North and South. They are under my protection, within my covenant, and under my security, against all harm.

Those who also isolate themselves in the mountains or in sacred sites shall be free from the poll-tax, land tribute and from tithe or duty on whatever they grow for their own use, and they shall be assisted in raising a crop by a free allowance of one *qadah* [unit of dry measure] in every *ardabb* [=6 *waiba*=24 *rub'a*] for their personal use.

They shall not be obliged to serve in war, or to pay the poll-tax; even those for whom an obligation to pay land tribute exists, or who possess resources in land or from commercial activity, shall not have to pay more than twelve *dirhams* a head per year.

On no one shall an unjust tax be imposed, and with the People of the Book there is to be no strife, unless it be over what is for the good [Q. 29:46]. We wish to take them under the wing of our mercy, and the penalty of vexation shall be kept at a distance from them, wherever they are and wherever they may settle.

If a Christian woman enters a Muslim household, she shall be received with kindness, and she shall be given opportunity to pray in her church; there shall be no dispute between her and a man who loves her religion. Whoever contravenes the covenant of Allah and acts to the contrary is a rebel against his covenant and his Messenger.

These people shall be assisted in the maintenance of their religious buildings and their dwellings; thus they will be aided in their faith and kept true to their allegiance.

None of them shall be compelled to bear arms, but the Muslims shall defend them; and they shall never contravene this promise of protection until the hour comes and the world ends.

As witness to this covenant, which was written by Muhammad, son of 'Abdullah, the Messenger of Allah, may the peace and blessings of Allah be upon him, to all the Christians.

As sureties for the fulfillment of all that is prescribed herein, the following persons set their hands...

The signatures of the witnesses to this Covenant include those of four future caliphs — Abu Bakr, Umar, Uthman and 'Ali — along with those of many of the Prophet's companions. Muhammad issued similar Covenants to many Christian communities in Arabia, Iraq, Syria and Armenia, as well as making Covenants with the Jews, the Zoroastrians and the Sabaeans. All these documents have similar provisions, along with special features relevant to specific communities. Before the fall of the Ottomans at the end of World War I, the Prophetic Covenants were known to most literate Muslims and virtually all scholars in the Muslim world, as well as many Western scholars. They were attested to by Muslim historians and in many cases renewed annually or every few years by Caliphs and Sultans. They formed the basis for official Ottoman policy toward religious minorities.

Emir 'Abd al-Qadir al-Djazairi [1808–1883], the great freedom-fighter against French colonialism in Algeria, when he defended the Christians of Damascus from massacre at the hands of the Druzes, was following the Prophet's Covenants to the letter. When the Ottoman Empire fell, however, the Covenants began their descent into obscurity, since they were now seen as little more than the irrelevant documents of a defunct bureaucracy.

As soon as *The Covenants of the Prophet Muhammad with the Christians of the World* appeared it was widely recognized as of central relevance to our post 9/11 world, where religion as a pretext for conflict has in many ways replaced the secular ideological struggles of the 20th century. Since 2013 the Covenants Initiative, which that book inaugurated, has become an international peace movement within Islam; as of several years ago, over 700 articles on the Prophetic Covenants have been published, and Dr Morrow has granted many interviews and given multiple speeches in the United States, Canada, Europe and the Middle East. The Initiative invites Muslims to subscribe to the theory that the Covenants of the Prophet are legally binding upon them today, and to sign the following Declaration to that effect:

> *We the undersigned hold ourselves bound by the spirit and the letter of the covenants of the Prophet Muhammad (peace and blessings be upon him) with the Christians of the world, in the understanding that these covenants, if accepted as genuine, have the force of law in the shari'ah today and that nothing in the shari'ah, as traditionally and correctly interpreted, has ever contradicted them. As fellow victims of the terror and godlessness, the spirit of militant secularism and false religiosity now abroad in the world, we understand your suffering as Christians through our suffering as Muslims, and gain greater insight into our own suffering through the contemplation of your suffering. May the Most Merciful of the Merciful regard the sufferings of the righteous and the innocent; may He strengthen us, in full submission to His will, to follow the spirit and the letter of the covenants of the Prophet Muhammad with the Christians of the world in all our dealings with them. In the name of Allah, Most Gracious, Most Merciful. Praise be to Allah, the Cherisher and Sustainer of the worlds.*

This Declaration, which appears in the book itself, has allowed many Muslims from all walks of life, including prominent scholars and religious leaders, to lend their support to our efforts, both scholarly and political.

The central thrust of our scholarly effort, as carried on by Dr Morrow and other researchers influenced by his work, has been to subject these documents to a rigorous western-style textual and historical analysis, thereby establishing a documentary paper-trail stretching back from the earliest extant copies of the Covenants to their original authorship by the Prophet Muhammad himself, peace and blessings be upon him, with many of his better-known companions acting as scribes and witnesses. The effect of this achievement has been to provide, almost for the first time, an historically-verifiable record of the *sunnah* of the Prophet in his dealings with the People of the Book that is *not dependent upon the hadith literature*, thus going a long way toward establishing the political documents of the Prophet—the Covenants and the Constitution of Medina—as a third foundational source for the Islamic tradition outside of *hadith* and Qur'an.

The potential applications of this perspective are twofold. To begin with, those Qur'anic *ayat* relating to how Muslims are to interact with the other Peoples of the Book that had once seemed obscure or ambiguous can now be better understood in light of Muhammad's actual known practice as revealed in the Covenants—and as soon as the real intent of the Qur'an is seen in the light of this prophetic *sunnah*, a new criterion is established that allows us to distinguish true from spurious *hadith* with greater confidence, according to whether or not they are in line with the intent of the Qur'an as clarified by the Covenants. In other words, to the degree that the Covenants illuminate the Qur'an, the Qur'an can winnow the *hadith*.

Secondly, a renewed appreciation for the pivotal significance of the Prophetic Covenants, as well as the Constitution of Medina, has given Muslims something that they've desperately needed in these times: a way to oppose terrorism and establish human rights and social justice in an entirely traditional and Islamic way, without imitating western models of progressivism and modernity, of "equality" and "the rights of Man." This is an important consideration in view of the fact that most of these ideologies ultimately derive from the French Revolution, which was a revolution not only against power and privilege, but also against religion, against God. According to the Prophetic Covenants, Allah, not humanity, is the Guarantor of human rights and the Delegator of human responsibilities.

In the course of our scholarly researches we developed ongoing and cordial relationships with St Catherine's Monastery in the Sinai and the Simonopetra Monastery on Mt. Athos. A copy of *Covenants of the Prophet Muhammad with the Christians of the World* was presented to Pope Francis through the agency of Shaykh Yahya Pallavicini, President of the Comunità Religiosa Islamica Italiana (COREIS) in Italy. In February of 2019, the Vatican co-hosted a seminar in Rome along with the Caux Round Table on the Covenants of the Prophet; in October of the same year, a conference on the Covenants took place in Istanbul co-sponsored by the Vatican and including the Caux Round Table, a representative of the Armenian Orthodox Church, the Syrian Orthodox metropolitan vicar of Mardin in southeastern Turkey, and one of our academic colleagues from the Hamad Bin Khalifa University in Qatar, Ahmed El-Wakil. It was centered around *The Covenants of the Prophet Muhammad with the Christians of the World*.

As for the political wing of the Covenants Initiative, in 2014 Dr Morrow embarked on a European tour, co-sponsored by the Canadian government and Radical Middle Way, speaking to French ministers in Paris, EU officials in Brussels and the Hague, and in the UK at Oxford, Cambridge and the House of Lords; the same year he spoke at a televised meeting in Abu Dhabi before ambassadors and foreign ministers of several Muslim nations. Early on, our work garnered expressions of support from Bartholomew, Ecumenical Patriarch of the Eastern Orthodox Church, from Theophilos III, Greek Orthodox Patriarch of Jerusalem, from Dr Mohamed Gameaha of Al-Azhar University in Egypt, from a number of Catholic prelates, and from Ayatullah Khamenei, Supreme Leader of Iran. In 2016, Dr Morrow served as an advisor to the Organization of Islamic Cooperation.

Also in 2016 the Covenants Initiative was contacted by Bishop Francis Kalabat, leader-in-exile of the Chaldean Catholics of Iraq, now living in the United States. Bishop Kalabat asked the Initiative to issue a call for the actions of ISIS to be declared genocide. This became the Genocide Initiative, which we posted as a petition on the Change.org website. In March of that year, the Fortenberry Amendment, defining the actions of ISIS as war crimes and genocide, was passed unanimously by the U.S. House of Representatives, followed shortly by a statement to the same effect by Secretary of State John Kerry. The work of the Covenants Initiative was hailed in an article in the premier U.S. armed forces publication *Stars and Stripes* as one of the factors that led to the passage of the Fortenberry Amendment. Also in 2016, Dr Morrow was part of a delegation of Muslim leaders to the Obama White House. In the same year he received an Interfaith Leadership Award from the Islamic Society of North America. In 2017 he was awarded a Certificate of Special Congressional Recognition by the U.S. House of Representatives, addressed President Rouhani of Iran at the United Nations, and was invited to participate in the Arba'een Pilgrimage in Iraq by the New Horizon Conference along with a group of intellectuals, professors, scholars, diplomats, political advisors, analysts, journalists, and artists. In 2018 he advised the Kingdom of Bahrein on the subject of the Covenants; in the same year, along with myself and my wife, as well as Craig Considine and Abdul Malik Mujahid, he spoke on the subject of the Prophetic Covenants at the Parliament of the World's Religions in Toronto. In 2019 he lectured on the Covenants before political leaders, Shi'a Ayatullahs and religious leaders of many faiths in Iraq. In the same year, in partnership with the International Museum of Muslim Cultures of Jacksonville, Mississippi, USA, he was instrumental in developing a traveling exhibition dedicated to the Prophetic Covenants entitled "Muslims with Christians and Jews: Covenants & Coexistence." Also in 2019, the Covenants of the Prophet Foundation [501 (c) (3)] was established in order to continue the work of the Covenants Initiative.

When ISIS burned St Mary's Cathedral in the Philippines in 2017, the governor of the Autonomous Region of Muslim Mindanao immediately invoked the Covenants of the Prophet to prove that such actions were "un-Islamic"; there is every reason to believe that this response was largely due to the efforts of the Initiative. And in November of 2018, when the Supreme Court of Pakistan acquitted the Christian woman Aasia Bibi on charges of blasphemy, the justices extensively quoted from *Covenants of the Prophet Muhammad with the Christians of the World* in their written decision; since then, the (now past) Pakistani prime minister, Imran Khan, referenced the Covenants in a number of his speeches. In view of these successes, we can now confidently assert that the Covenants Initiative has been among the major ideological counterforces within Islam to ISIS, al-Qaeda and other Jihadist movements.

In the course of his quest for the Prophetic Covenants, which began even before 2013, Dr Morrow has brought many little-known and some heretofore unknown documents to light. He also issued an appeal to all monastic and other institutions possessing authentic copies of the Covenants to provide texts and photos of them which could be archived in the West for safekeeping—in some cases just ahead of ISIS, who were also searching for them, but only to destroy them. As for the six Covenants that appear in *The Covenants of the Prophet Muhammad with the Christians of the World*, he arranged for them to be printed in a separate booklet, *Six Covenants of the Prophet Muhammad with the Christians of His Time*, which has been translated into 14 languages. Subsequently, Dr Morrow convened a consortium of scholars, both Muslim and non-Muslim; together with them he wrote and published a three-volume anthology of "Covenants studies" entitled *Islam and the People of the Book*. This work includes studies of the Covenants concluded by Muhammad with Jews and Parsees as well as Christians, clearly demonstrating that it was the Prophet's intent to found a defensive confederacy of all the religions who believe in the One God. He also published a popularized version of his research as a book entitled *Messenger of Mercy*, complete with some highly significant new material, including the unexpected fact that the Covenants used to be required reading in the U.S. State Department as training for those diplomats assigned to work with the Ottoman Empire, and the possibility that, based on the contents of Thomas Jefferson's extensive library, they might conceivably have had an influence on the drafting of the U.S. Constitution. Be that as it may, given the great pressure being exerted upon the traditional religions in today's world, the numerous attacks against churches, synagogues and mosques, the religious genocides and the ongoing political co-optation of many of the ancient faiths, we believe that Muhammad's interfaith alliance, as exemplified both by his Covenants and by the Constitution of Medina, can act as a model and an inspiration for new and desperately needed efforts toward interfaith mutual aid and protection in the 21st Century. (For a more complete treatment of the Prophetic Covenants and chronicle of the Covenants Initiative, I refer the interested reader to *The Islamic Interfaith Initiative: No Fear Shall Be Upon Them* by Dr John Andrew Morrow, Cambridge Scholars, 2021.)

THE COVENANTS IN A LARGER CONTEXT

No Muslim should ever forget the following two *hadith* of the Prophet:

Someone who unjustly kills a *dhimmi* [member of a protected religious minority within Islam, including Christians and Jews] cannot get a whiff of Heaven. [Sahih Bukhari, *Jizya*, 5]

Whoever oppresses a *dhimmi* or loads a work that is over his strength or takes something away from him by force, I am his foe on the Day of Judgment. [Abu Dawud, *Kharaj*, 31–33]

The Covenants of the Prophet, which have left a clear historical and textual trail that traces back to their original composition by the Prophet himself, are precisely in line with *hadiths* like these. As soon as Dr Morrow began to make these documents known to the Muslim world—which had begun to forget their existence, or at least their continuing significance—Muslims from all walks of life, including many prominent scholars, began to join our movement and make it their own. As I've pointed out above, less than a year after the publication of *The Covenants of the Prophet Muhammad with the Christians of the World*, Dr Morrow was denouncing ISIS before the House of Lords in London. And, from one point of view at least, our movement (or at least the first cycle of it) culminated in 2016 in the Marrakesh Declaration, issued by the leaders of many Muslim nations after a convention in Marrakesh, Morocco, which renewed the traditional protections granted to non-Muslim religious minorities within Muslim nations, based on the Prophet's Constitution of Medina. We were told by officials of the Islamic Society of North America that our work with the Covenants Initiative was one of the inspirations for that Declaration.

It is my belief that the success of the Covenants Initiative—which, outside of the labor of the publisher, editors and printers, and various informal alliances that we have made with journalists and other activists, has basically been the work of two individuals and the exhaustive scholarship of only one—can only be explained by the fact that God willed it. It is a part of the virtue of faith to remain open to this possibility, while remembering that God's Will can be expressed in innumerable different ways in our lives, that no human being is exempt from that Will, and consequently that to receive a command from Him is in no way a badge of status, spiritual or otherwise, but rather a serious duty that must not be ignored.

And the Covenants also turned out to have an unexpected connection with the doctrines of the Traditionalist School, though nothing could be further from the stance and practices of Frithjof Schuon than the kind of activism that brought the Covenants to light. In *The System of Antichrist* [Sophia Perennis, 2001] I had called for a "united front ecumenism" of the world religions against three things: non-traditional religious fanaticism, false psychic religion, and militant secularism. I presented this form of interfaith action as the proper outer or exoteric expression of the Transcendent Unity of Religions, as opposed to "promiscuous Liberal ecumenism," whose ultimate goal seems to be the dissolution of all the traditional faiths via the attempt to create some sort of One World Religion. United front ecumenism exerts no pressure on the religions to syncretize their doctrines with a view toward worldly unification. Instead, it posits their *transcendent* unity by showing how the forces of religious fanaticism, psychic pseudo-religion and militant secularism have declared war on all the world religions, thereby demonstrating that these religions represent a common threat in the eyes of those forces, and consequently that all the true religions must spring from a single common Source that those forces oppose. This is not to say that there can't be a legitimate form of "esoteric ecumenism" (Schuon's term) which discerns the metaphysical First Principles that all revealed religions and wisdom traditions hold in common, only that the *necessary plurality* of these revelations and traditions is itself one of those First Principles. I never believed that I would live to see anything resembling a true united front ecumenism, so I just described what I thought it might look like and left it at that. Then, twelve years later, the perfect incarnation of united front ecumenism, the Covenants Initiative, simply fell into my lap, and then went on to become an international movement. As William Butler Yeats put it, "In dreams begin responsibilities."

Looking back over the route by which the Prophetic Covenants came into my life, I now see that my earlier pass through the Eastern Orthodox world, following Jenny, finally bore fruit when it came to spreading the word of the rediscovery of the Covenants, since the first Christians I thought of reaching out to were Orthodox hierarchs, the Ecumenical Hierarch Bartholomew and the Greek Patriarch of Jerusalem Theophilos III, both of whom replied with letters of support. Not only that, but the first time I had heard of the famous *ashtiname*, the original Covenant granted by Muhammad to the Monastery of St Catherine in the Sinai, was on the website of a Nimatullahi dervish from the New York *khaniqa*, Irving Karchmar, author of the quasi-Nimatullahi novel *Master of the Jinn*; so at least my years of immersion in Orthodoxy and Nimatullahi Sufism had recognizable effects in the *zahir*, the outer world, even if they were not entirely fulfilled for me in the *batin*, the inner one.

SACRED ACTIVISM IN A TIME OF RELIGIOUS DEGENERATION

While true spiritually-based social action, even militant action, can certainly be carried on within a Christian framework, it will always be secondary to the interior life and the grace of the sacraments. After all, as Jesus Christ (peace and blessings be upon him) said, "My kingdom is not of this world." Unlike Christ, however, Muhammad (peace and blessings be upon him) was sent not only as a mystical sage and a moral teacher, but also as a husband, a father, a business man, a diplomat, a judge, an administrator and a military leader, not to mention a *rasul*, a law-giving prophet. Consequently "sacred activism" within a Muslim context is less subject to internal contradictions than a hybrid spiritual/political theory like Liberation Theology is within a Christian context. On the other hand, the integration into the religion of Islam of the perennial human necessity for militant action becomes a great danger when the essential spirituality of the religion, including the "organized mysticism" of the Sufi orders, becomes weakened. The vast damage done by an "Islamicist" militancy when it cuts itself loose from the "just war" doctrine and rules of warfare to be found in the traditional *shari'ah*—not the latter-day perversions of the *shari'ah* promulgated by the Wahhabi/Salafis—should be obvious to all. The evidence of intermittent support for certain Islamicist elements by the United States and other outside powers must also be taken into consideration, in light of which it should be painfully clear that it is next to impossible for Islam to wage any kind of just war against western neo-colonialism when terrorist armies, fighting in the name of Islam but not according to its principles, are willing to accept funds and arms from the West. By the same token, the "turn the other cheek" doctrine of Christianity, which represents the height of spiritual heroism when the faith is strong, is in danger of becoming a culpable form of cowardice in the face of political, moral and spiritual evil when the faith loses force. It's as if Christianity, in its decadence, is vulnerable to infection by the Dark Feminine principle—something that is certainly visible, for example, in the Catholic pedophilia scandal—whereas when Islam degenerates it tends to manifest the Dark Masculine principle in the form of terroristic brutality. The corrupt Muslim soul is desiccated; the corrupt Christian soul is putrescent. And just as Christianity continues to abandon its virility in the face of internal decay, militant secularism and the Islamicist threat—though we must remember here that more Muslims than Christians have died at the hands of terrorist groups such as the so-called Islamic State—so the compromised manhood of Islam, which has also been weakened by both external attack and internal decay, may become even more vicious and perverted under the influence of Christian weakness and apostasy—a weakness that tempts militant Islam, or rather *something that is no longer true Islam* as soon as it succumbs to this temptation, to every kind of excess. Thus effeteness and barbarism create each other. Regarding the passivity of degenerate Christianity, it should be remembered at this point that, according to traditional Catholic moral theology, to become "an occasion of sin" for other people is sinful in itself. Cowards are a standing temptation to bullies, therefore anyone who will not defend him- or herself from invasion or unjust oppression bears part of the guilt of the oppressor, not to mention the fact that those who won't defend themselves will certainly not be willing or able to defend anybody else! If, on the other hand, Islam and Christianity can find the power to sincerely and discerningly contemplate each other's virtues, to the point where they gain the ability to see the same virtues within their own traditions, no matter how deeply hidden these treasures might have become, the interfaith movement could turn into an occasion for mutual strength and support in the cause of God rather than one of mutual compliance and capitulation to the power of the global elites.

Nor would such an alliance always need to be led by scholarship and activism alone. As ISIS was rearing its ugly head and the Covenants Initiative was spreading, a spontaneous movement grew up among Muslims in many parts of the world, through people who had likely never heard of the Prophetic Covenants, to protect Christians from attacks by the Islamic State. Some who volunteered for this heroic work even died as martyrs, not in defense of their fellow Muslims but of their Christian brothers and sisters. The story of these events has almost been buried in the contemporary suppression and re-writing of history, but you can find it if you look. [See https://charles-upton.com/2020/07/10/muslims-defending-christians-around-the-world/]

SOME FURTHER HISTORY

In 2015, Jenny and I traveled to New York to see our friends Eric and Irena Galati, during which time Dr Morrow and I spoke on the Prophetic Covenants at the Islamic Society of Long Island, as well as at the Nur Ashki-Jerrahi Sufi Lodge in Manhattan, based at the Dergah al-Farah, where I was also unexpectedly asked to read from my epic poem "The Wars of Love" by a *faqir* who knew and appreciated it. And as the Covenants Initiative grew, Dr Morrow, as if by miraculous providence, continued to discover new Covenants or new versions or copies of older ones, often in the archives of ancient monasteries in the Near East, with which some of our allies or emissaries made contact. To all intents and purposes, as mentioned above, this work presented itself as a race against ISIS, who were also seeking the Covenants of the Prophet—not to enshrine them, however, but to destroy them, along with the monasteries that held them and the monks who guarded them, since those documents explicitly declare groups like theirs to be under the curse of Allah and His Prophet. Beyond this race against time, our other major concern was not to let ourselves be co-opted either by the Sunni Muslims who were beholden to Saudi Arabia or the Shi'a Muslims of Iran. Both were bidding for us, hoping to reduce the Prophetic Covenants to fodder for their respective propaganda machines and/or geopolitical ambitions. It took some doing to play one party off against the other, though all Dr Morrow usually had to do was simply say "no" to invitations coming from either camp.

All this mostly happened during the first Trump years, and it probably couldn't have happened without him. This is *not* to say that he in any way supported our movement—far from it. He simply rattled the system of business-as-usual hard enough to let various unpredictable cracks in the carapace open up. Nonetheless he did achieve some truly great things in his first term, including his lightning-fast deconstruction of the whole Devil's-pact of the U.S. military and the CIA that had grown up under the Obama administration with the Jihadist groups that ultimately resulted in ISIS, who were a band of mercenaries organized and recruited for the purpose of countering Russia in Syria and Iran. (As evidence for the existence of such a pact, in 2016 a colleague of ours was part of a delegation of Muslim leaders who met with the National Security Adviser at the Obama White House. The Muslim leaders were told: "ISIS is losing ground in Syria and Iraq, and so ISIS fighters will now be *returning to the United States*. Therefore, *we want your help in re-integrating these returning fighters into U.S. society*, for which Federal grants are available"—not in identifying them so they could be arrested and sent to Guantanamo, but in putting them on comfortable ice until their next assignment. When our colleague heard this he said to himself: "Doesn't this woman know that ISIS has a hit list of U.S. Muslim leaders, and that some of those leaders are in this room right now?") And though I certainly don't deny that Trump has been unconscionably hounded by his enemies in the political establishment and the media since his first presidential campaign, I basically see him as a narcissistic and nihilistic bully who worships only himself, someone who became the "populist" leader of the White working class that the Democrats had abandoned (or the remnant of that class) only because no more worthy leader made his or her appearance, plus the fact that he had enough pure *chutzpah* to assume a vastly incongruous position: that of a New York billionaire in a red baseball cap who delights his base by his willingness to satirize, ridicule and threaten the people they hate, thereby successfully diverting their attention from the fact that he had done little if anything substantive to improve their condition or advance their interests. Yet what if he were to move us farther away from the threat of World War III by compromising with Russia and China, allowing each its pre-eminence within its own sphere-of-influence, instead continuing to back the U.S. push to dominate the whole world, while simultaneously taking greater pains to defend the independence of our nation against the inroads of these two superpowers? What if he were to become a heroic leader simply because he was driven to it against his will? Here we can see, again, how people are far from simple. The Black Knight wears a tiny gold locket around his neck, beneath his mantle; the White Knight carries a vial of poison hidden somewhere on his person. Only Allah possesses the true Scales that can judge between good and evil. (And, parenthetically, let no one assume that my criticisms of Trump indicate that I have any degree of support or sympathy for Joe Biden, whose policies and those of his handlers have moved the world—with a certain amount of help from Vladimir Putin—ever closer to World War III.)

Be that as it may, there might actually have been a more direct relationship between Donald Trump and the Covenants Initiative that appeared on the surface, though there is no way I can prove its existence. This possibility can be traced back, surprisingly enough, to Seyyed Hossein Nasr, who had been so helpful to Jenny and me in the past. Sometime in the 20-teens I received a phone call from one Sam Hirbod, an Iranian-American billionaire; he told me that Dr Nasr had been following my "career" with interest, and had suggested that he look me up. He told us that he was about to meet with some people in the newly-elected Trump administration, if not with The Donald himself, through the offices of a Jewish billionaire of his acquaintance. Sam appeared to be the *simpatico* and super-rich angel that every social movement dreams of. In response, I quickly produced (with Dr Morrow's help) a document entitled "War on Five Fronts: A Comprehensive Plan to Defeat ISIS," since I figured that handing Trump a document like that, one *produced by Muslims*, represented our best chance to prevent the launching of any anti-Muslim pogroms sponsored by the new administration. I was definitely helped in this effort by my background with the Sanctuary Movement for Salvadoran refugees and Santa Venetia Presbyterian Church, since this experience helped me understand that ISIS was really just another death squad, though on a much larger scale than the Salvadoran variety, one initially organized and armed by the U.S. and a consortium of western nations, plus Saudi Arabia, Turkey and Israel. Sam apparently did meet with members of the Trump administration in 2017, though I never got up the courage to ask him if he had actually passed that document on to any of them.

Then, in 2018, Jenny and I flew to Toronto to meet Dr Morrow and speak (all three of us plus two other speakers, Craig Considine and one more who shall remain nameless) at the Parliament of the World's Religions, where we made a formal presentation of the Covenants to Jenny as representing the Christians of the World. She was without a doubt the appropriate recipient of this gesture, since one of my major motivations for throwing myself into the effort to publish and disseminate the Prophetic

Covenants was to do what I could to save Islam's reputation (and my own) from the formidable danger of Jenny's negative judgement in the face of the crimes of ISIS against Christian communities in the Middle East. My denunciation of that Satanic organization as an open enemy of Islam was well received by our rather small audience, which included a number of turbaned Muslims from overseas, though it didn't go over well with our nameless speaker, who demanded that my speech be cut out of the video of the proceedings, which it was. Later on in the same year, Sam Hirbod invited me to speak at his newly-opened Hub Foundation in the East Bay, for which Jenny and I made our one and only return-trip to California (so far) after our move to Kentucky in 2004. We met our last two California friends, Ellen Frank and Marty Glass (author of the unique volume *Yuga: An Anatomy of Our Fate*, published by Sophia Perennis, who is now no longer with us) in Berkeley, and aimed to touch two further bases in San Francisco: the Russian Orthodox Cathedral of the Holy Virgin Joy of All Who Sorrow on Geary St, which had become such an important spiritual resource for us when we lived in the Bay Area, and City Lights Book Store on Columbus Avenue in North Beach. We got to the Cathedral to venerate the relics of St John Maximovitch, but our ride to City Lights fell through, thereby precisely defining the present shapes and affinities of our souls. Nonetheless, through our meeting with Sam I got wind of another possibility for our movement: the connection of one of Sam's associates with the respected Muslim/American poet and documentary filmmaker Michael Wolfe, a sometime resident of the Beat/Hippie town of Bolinas, editor of Joanne Kyger (Gary Snyder's first wife) and Bobbie Louise Hawkins (wife to Robert Creeley), author of the books *The Hadj* and *One Thousand Roads to Mecca*, and producer of the award-winning film *The Sultan and the Saint* about the actual meeting, during the Crusades, between the Sultan of Egypt and St Francis of Assisi. I later met with Michael Wolfe in Lexington to discuss a possible documentary on the Covenants.

So it was all "naturally" falling into place: A successful Muslim filmmaker with a background as a Marin County poet (as I had been) who knew the Beats (as I had) would make a documentary on the Prophetic Covenants and the role of our Initiative in resurrecting them, the project to be funded by an Iranian/American billionaire who had come to us through my Traditionalist School connections. All appeared neat and sweet—except that it was not to be. Sam's fortune was mostly invested in the hospitality industry—he had just bought the San Jose Fairmont Hotel—so when Covid-19 arrived, he lost big time. On top of that, Donald Trump, even after Sam's "overture," did little that was likely to make a rich Iranian/American feel optimistic about the future, what with Trump's son-in-law Jared Kushner cozying up to Israel and Trump's declaration that, as far as the United States was concerned, Jerusalem not Tel Aviv was the capital of the Jewish state. Nonetheless I'll have to admit, in hindsight, that the disappearance of this possibility was not all negative, since we noticed that the idea of telling the story of the Covenants Initiative in cinematic terms was beginning to eat into our will to actually carry the movement forward, film or no. If Dr Morrow and I became famous, if we "went down in history," what more needed to be accomplished? Wasn't that what we'd been after all along?

Actually, no. But it should continually amaze us all how the mere *story* of something, the *identity* associated with it, will insidiously take the place of the thing itself, as if that thing's only "cash value" were its publicity or ego value — a delusion that's profoundly intensified by the present culture of social media, "selfie" photographs and celebrity worship. The keynote of our time is the exaltation of shadow over substance, as if nothing has any meaning in itself outside of the question of whether or not other people, as well as ourselves, opt to identify with it — this being the degenerate shadow of *democracy* itself. This delusion has now gone so far that laws are actually being passed to punish people who deny the validity of other people's arbitrarily adopted identities, even if these identities have no basis in reality whatsoever. Because what, after all, is "reality"? Maybe there's no such thing — and *if* there's no such thing, then any fantasy dreamt up by anyone at all will inexorably begin to assume the status of an absolute reality and a human right, the denial of which will necessarily constitute a punishable heresy, or blasphemy, or violation of civil or criminal law. Obviously this can't go on. As William Burroughs so ominously remarked long ago, as part of his analysis of *image* as a kind of addictive junk, junk likewise being defined (in his terminology) as "cooked-down image":

WILL HOLLYWOOD NEVER LEARN?

In any case, the Covenants Initiative was saved from the hell of notoriety and unreality by the evaporation of its publicity-shadow, leaving behind the substance of its achievements. Whether any major new manifestations of social action are destined to arise from Dr Morrow's rediscovery of the Prophetic Covenants is anybody's guess. However, speaking only for myself, I can say that the Covenants Initiative has already fulfilled the *socio-political dharma* which that Buddhist dharmic astrologer attributed to me so long ago. That part's done. As for the contemplative element of my life, my direct relationship to God *beyond all terms of relatedness*, that part remains to be deepened and perfected — eternally so, since in God, Who is the final End to everything, there is no end.

ARCHBISHOP VIGANÒ AND THE RELIC OF ST CHARBEL

But one fascinating sub-plot to the Covenants Initiative story still remains to be told. Since our initial impulse was to reach out to major

Christian authorities world-wide, of course we wanted to approach the Vatican. Pursuant to this I contacted the Apostolic Nuncio (Vatican ambassador) to the United States, Archbishop Carlo Maria Viganò, who graciously agreed to forward a message from us to Pope Francis. This may or may not have been the origin of an initiative of the Caux Round Table, with Vatican backing, to reach out to Ayatullah al-Sistani of Iraq, perhaps the most respected leader of Shi'a Islam and a man not beholden to Iran. But then I saw, on the Vatican website, that Vatican Radio interview with Pope Francis I keep harping on, where he openly declared that "God does not exist"—which was OK, apparently, because the Three Persons of the Trinity do exist, and the more the merrier. However, since this idea denies the Unity of God as defined in the *Credo in Unum Deum* of the Nicene Creed, and essentially degrades the Trinity to a trio of pagan gods, I became concerned that this unprecedented papal announcement might provide ISIS and similar groups with an excuse to kill more Christians (as if they needed one). So I contacted the Archbishop again, asking him if there was any *delicate* way for him to relay my concerns to the Holy Father. This time I heard nothing back from him.

Then a Kentucky connection surprisingly appeared. Kim Davis, the county clerk of Rowan County where Jenny's uncle Dale and his family lived, made the national news by refusing to sign marriage licenses for gay couples; this resulted in such couples descending on Kentucky from all over the country, demanding to be married in Rowan County. And soon afterwards, not surprisingly, Kim Davis failed in her re-election bid. (When Jenny asked Dale's wife Eileen, supposedly a conservative Christian, what she thought of Ms. Davis, she described as her a "troublemaker," which can be explained by the fact that Eileen was from a generation where Conventionality and Tradition could legitimately be identified—which is certainly not the case today.) Then, however, when Pope Francis visited the U.S. in 2015, Archbishop Viganò arranged for Kim Davis to be in the receiving line to meet the Holy Father—but when Francis realized who she was, the Pope (at least silently) went ballistic. And it was soon after this that Archbishop Carlo Maria Viganò lost his position as Apostolic Nuncio. The offending heresy, as it turned out, remained on the website for years—until Viganò came out as a major public critic of Francis, after which he had to go into hiding to protect himself from Vatican agents. It was only then that the "God does not exist" blasphemy was scrubbed from the Vatican website. So the Covenants Initiative ended up having a distant through real connection with the major public spokesman for conservative, anti-Francis Catholicism; it was as if Rama Coomaraswamy were overshadowing our movement from beyond the grave. Viganò, like so many conservative Catholics, was until recently a *sedevacantist* in all things but the admission that a Pope who openly teaches heresy is no Pope, though now (as of 2024) he has finally crossed that line. The name for the rather self-contradictory theological position once held by the Archbishop, and the Society of St Pius X as well, is *sedeprivationism*—which simply means that, while a true Pope does in fact exist, nobody has to obey him or believe anything he says because he is fundamentally damaged goods. (If so, then why hold on to him?)

And it may be that Rama had another, more arcane influence on our movement. Shortly before his death in 2006 he gave us an amazing gift: a first-class relic (part of the body or blood of a saint) of St Charbel Makhlouf, a Lebanese Catholic monk, hermit and wonderworker, who never showed his face outside his cowl, keeping his eyes always on the ground, so that no-one knew what he looked like until the day he was found dead in his cell. He was venerated by both Christians and Muslims, and innumerable miracles have been attributed to him both during his life and after his death. From time to time Jenny and I pray with that relic, asking the saint to carry our prayers to Allah (the name for God used by both Muslims and Arab Christians); the relic appears to function as a talisman that puts one in touch with the Angelic Hierarchies. (I must emphasize that I never attempt to directly invoke the angels as if I had power over them, since to do this would be to begin to transform them into familiar spirits and myself into a magician, and this is one of the first steps toward pagan polytheism—but if God elects to send them on missions in response to my prayers, I always welcome them. And if He moves me to pray with their help, I always pray to Him first.) Then the day came when I was suddenly seized by the impulse to ask God to roll back the mad dogs of ISIS, so I prayed that prayer with the relic of St Charbel—during which I saw, in my mind's eye, angelic armies pouring in to attack and conquer the Satanic troops of Daʻesh—and maybe two days later, Russian troops entered Syria to finally bring them down. I must hasten to emphasize that *I did not create this effect*. The power of petitionary prayer is based on the reality that Dr Wolfgang Smith has named "vertical causality," which manifests in our world in terms of what Jung called "synchronicities." God's Will is born in Eternity and enters time, not through causal tendencies arriving from the past but strictly through the gate of Now—or, as the Sufis explain it, God only answers the prayers that He Himself has commanded us to pray. Apparently He had already determined that ISIS had gone too far and needed to be stopped—and so, through His Mercy and election, I was allowed to be present for that Divine act, as part of the occasion for a prayer that operated first through His Grace, secondly through the intercession of St Charbel, and only as a terminal echo through my own receptivity to that Grace and that intercession. The magician foolishly thinks that he is the doer; the witness to miracles knows, with unbreakable certainty, that the only Doer is God.

THIS WORLD — AGAIN?

So as it turned out, the whole development known as the Covenants Initiative was quite an unexpected change for me, one that brought to fruition a 50-year effort on my part to construct a working synthesis between spiritual aspiration and social action. In the 1960s my Social Activist Self was simply part of the hippie crowd, making the antiwar scenes that were already there to be made. In the 1980s I really had to choose sides, though there was little question as to which side I would choose — that of opposition to U.S. intervention in Central America — seeing that I was backed up by a strong religious peer group and could conveniently hide behind the skirts of a charismatic female leader (as I did again, soon after, with Project MOVE). But in the 20-teens, with the Covenants Initiative, I followed a male leader for the first time (unless you could call Lew Welch a "leader," though this is not really an accurate characterization since he was not an activist except by sentiment) and was directly instrumental during those years in founding the very movement that defined my role. For a quarter-century I had thought that activism of any kind was a thing of the past for me, since it was my firm conviction that we were in a "damned if you do and damned if you don't" situation where the contradictions inherent in *any* of the available ideological positions were so radical that it was impossible, in good conscience, to support any of them. It was as if the Devil had drawn the sides, seasoning each shining constellation of idealistic good will with a liberal dose of mortal evil, so that damage would be done and darkness spread no matter which side you took. But then, with no warning whatsoever, as if in a blinding flash of light, the Covenants of the Prophet appeared: beholden to neither the Occidental Left nor the Occidental Right, based on a sound doctrine of human rights that owed nothing whatsoever to the French or Russian or Chinese revolutions, representing an *almost inconceivable* synthesis between theocracy and democracy, and — given that the Prophet Muhammad, peace and blessings be upon him, had declared that the Covenants, with their plan for a Federation of the Peoples of the Book against two oppressive world empires (Byzantium and Persia), were directly inspired by Allah — representing a social manifestation with Divine sanction behind it, one that was astonishingly and inexplicably appropriate to the needs and quality of the time. I *saw* all that and so said an unqualified "yes" to it, with the result that I was able, for the first time in a half-century of incomplete and frustrated efforts, to participate in an action that might actually have left an enduring mark on the world — if, that is, the world itself endures. And to top it off, I was able to dedicate my work with the Covenants to my dear wife Jenny, a committed Christian, as proof that I in no way denigrated her religion, even though I had moved on in my own spiritual journey from Christianity to Islam. Without the Covenants

Initiative, the pressure of maintaining a religiously-mixed marriage in the age of ISIS might have been too much for us to bear; but as it was, the Covenants actually helped save our relationship, just as they had helped free Aasia Bibi from a Pakistani prison. God's actions, whether tremendously dramatic or quietly nourishing and guiding, always have infinitely more to them than meets the eye.

EPILOGUE: THE BIRDS OF KENTUCKY

Since I still live in Kentucky, how can I conclude the story of it, tie it all up in a sack, like I did for my time in California? One way, as appropriate or arbitrary as any other, would be to ask: "What is the most significant event of your sojourn in Kentucky so far? What work are you most proud of?"

There are several possible answers to this question, but this one (though it is limited by a certain cuteness) is perhaps my favorite: I taught a dove to fly. For three Springs in a row the mourning doves had built their nest on a ledge above our back door. The third Spring there were two fledglings occupying it — "squabs" as the young doves are called. The stronger one had flown off with its mother, who seemed disinclined (I thought) to return to the nest; the weaker was left behind. Would it fail to risk the air and lose its life? Unwilling to see that happen, I stood before the squab and raised my arms straight up on both sides of my head. Imitating me, the squab too raised its wings; then, undoubtedly catching sight of those thin, silvery *lines of the air* along which all birds fly — as I discerned one time while reviving a bird who had knocked itself out against our window in California — it jumped from its nest, and flew.

CLOSING
The Planet of Remembrance

SO NOW THIS BOOK IS GETTING NEAR ITS END. What do you do when your autobiography ends and you yourself are still walking around, breathing up everybody else's air, leaving your big carbon footprints all over the landscape, just like you owned the place? We must finally admit that all conclusions are arbitrary. You only cease when you've had enough, enough of digging up other people's bones, and your own—enough of stirring the pot of "me."

Looking over what I have written under the title of *Giving Myself Away*, I see that my life has been filled with more conflict and spiritual darkness than I'd earlier been willing to admit; undoubtedly I was posed these challenges because I needed to learn how to stand my ground without holding grudges or becoming bitter or losing hope, and how to work against the dissipation that's inseparable from the life of a writer by making emotional sobriety and psychic recollection the center of my spiritual work, though the perfection of these virtues still eludes me by a wide margin.

While composing this book, as I recalled each major episode of my life I would go through a real catharsis. Waves of toxic psychic residues, each one different, each with its own specific color, flavor and frequency, would up rise through me and disperse into the ether. Sometimes I would even be sick for a day or two. It's been a holocaust of the idols, a process of deconstructing the residual subpersonalities that are always left behind by any powerful experience after that experience has become a memory—a real "bonfire of the vanities." Why leave Purgatory for the next world? There's no crucible for expediting and deepening the soul's purification like a living human body.

To the narcissist, personal history is supremely fascinating; to the person seeking self-transcendence and annihilation in God, the obsession with personal history becomes actively nauseating at one point—not just the more degenerate aspects of it, but all of it. Repentance from any sin has three stages: first comes the repentance of the intellect, which is the understanding that a particular act is something that compromises your human integrity; next comes the repentance of the will, which entails the intentional renunciation of that act; and finally comes the repentance of the emotions. The will may have fully renounced a particular vice, yet repentance is still not perfect if that vice still has its attractions. Only when the sinner goes beyond a willful "no" to his sin and actually becomes disgusted by it—when he says to himself, "how could I ever have been attracted to *that?"* — is his repentance complete. And while the sin of the ordinary believer is his involvement with this or that recognizable vice, the sin of the Sufi (as the Sufis say) is his attachment to his sense of separate existence. When a young man boasted to the Sufi woman saint Rabi'a al-Adawiyya that he had never committed a sin, her reply was: "Alas, my son, thine existence is a sin wherewith no other sin may be compared." Disgust is unpleasant, but at one stage of the spiritual Path it is a very good sign: because disgust is "infused repentance." All that's required after that, as the Sufis also say, is for you to "repent of repentance." Alcoholics Anonymous may liberate you from drink, but after that you'll need to liberate yourself from Alcoholics Anonymous, otherwise you'll be a repentant alcoholic for the rest of your life — and there's so much more to life than that.

When almost the last wave of the catharsis produced by writing this book rose and passed away, I had a dream:

> A Jewish man was complaining about some Jew in the 1600s who had single-handedly blocked the progress of Judaism, even up to this day. Then Jesus Christ appeared and cried: "It wasn't him who blocked Judaism, it was me!" [I fully agree with Jesus here, by the way.] Next he looked with great severity at someone with a shallow, frivolous attitude, doing his best to frighten him with the anger in his eyes. The main problem with this version of Jesus, however, was not his vindictiveness; the main problem was — that he was me! In this dream, *I* was Jesus Christ!

Upon awakening I realized that the Jew of the 1600s must have been Shabbetai Zevi, the false Messiah who electrified international Jewry — and then, shockingly, converted to Islam, thus putting a wet blanket on Jewish messianism for the next several centuries. But what was this dream really about? What was it trying to tell me about my own condition?

When you are attacked and wounded by dark spiritual forces, by the unexpected yet inevitable "stroke of Fate," you are immediately confronted with three possible responses. The first, unless you are a saint, is virtually impossible to choose, at least until you have gone through a long course of spiritual effort and struggle: it is to accept the wound as an act of God, in the unbreakable understanding that everything God does is for the greater good, whether or not you can even begin to imagine how that could be. The second is simply to despair and allow yourself to be destroyed. The third — is to fight back. But how can you fight back against dark spiritual powers without some spiritual power of your own? To combat the infernal entities — who are ultimately the unwilling servants of the Majesty of God, even though there is no way you can accept this now — you need to have God on your side. But to accept help from God, God as you hope Him to be as against that other face of God you can't accept yet for Who and What it is since it is much too formidable to deal with, you will need to identify with the Power of Light, at least as a servant of it, but also sometimes—perhaps unconsciously—as an *instance* of it. In other words, after having made the third choice, you may be secretly tempted to see yourself, not God, as the source of that Power.

In this fallen universe, we have to act; even deliberate inaction is an unavoidable action in a world like this. And every act in which we identify ourselves as the actors involves *sin*; this is what the law of *karma* (which simply means "action") is all about. "All have sinned and come short of the glory of God" [Romans 3:23] means: all *must* sin. Every action is a sin because all actions are necessarily partial. We choose to do this but not that, to avoid this but not that, and by so doing we shatter to pieces the primordial Unity of Being. Only pure contemplation of What Is, contemplation in which action and non-action are one, avoids "missing the mark" (the literal meaning of "sin") and so hits the Target. The source and essence of sin is not choosing the wrong action (though this is certainly sin's result), but acting in the belief that *you* are the doer, whereas in reality the only Doer is God. So the root of all sin is *self-will*, and—since, in reality, only God is the Doer—self-will always involves an unconscious identification with God. As my dream teaches, you *become Jesus* as it were, and so turn Him into a vindictive partisan of good against evil, instead of what He really is, and what you also really are: the Human Form as the mirror, in this world, of the total Reality of God as the Sovereign Good, not just the relative good that opposes evil—the locus-of-manifestation for all His Attributes, all His Acts, all His Names. And for a human being to identify with Jesus Christ as I did in my dream—Christ whom the Christians call Divine—is certainly to participate in the spirit of Antichrist. So *the primal sin is identification*. Once you have become "this or that," God is ejected from His proper place in the human spiritual Heart and becomes—depending upon who you think *you* are—merely This or That definable Thing in some abstract, spiritual sky. Obviously you can't will to overcome self-will simply by "being good," since this vice manifests as both self-willed transgression and self-willed obedience. But as soon as identification ends, self-will ends along with it. You are no longer the doer because you are no longer anything; you are nothing but one more unique instance of God's Self-knowledge. And once this dissolution of identification is established, then God, Who is the only Doer, acts not only *upon* you but *through* you, thereby leaving the Satanic powers of self-will no territory in which to operate; these powers are finally conquered not by opposing them, but rather by eliminating their total field of action.

In Sufi terminology, the mass of self-created identities we need to be purified of is called the *nafs* (the soul, the self). The *nafs* leads us into the whole world of obsessions, distractions and addictions precisely because she is in pain—and, in the most fundamental sense, the pain of the *nafs* is based on her memory of her pre-eternal union with God, which she has now lost through coming into this world (or, as the Christians say, through "original sin"), and on her habit of attempting to rely upon this former union, upon *identification* with God, now that the time for primal union has passed. This is the origin of the self-will that is her essence. Created beings have departed from their original home in the Unity of God, where they were perfectly identified with Him by virtue of their non-existence, and have entered this kingdom of dimensional existence we call "the universe"—the realm where they can no longer identify with Him, but are now required to obey Him.

The *nafs*, however, will not accept this demotion in rank; she wants to retain all the rights of God she knew in her original condition of Union with Him, even as she experiences the primal pain of separation from Him—a pain that would be annihilated in a flash if only she were willing to submit to God instead of identifying herself with God. She continually asserts these illegitimate rights in all her dealings with us; she does this only to hide from herself the pain of separation—in other words, to hide it from you—and to attempt to conceal it from God as well by putting up barriers to His ability to contemplate her through the Eye of the Heart.

But nothing can be concealed from God. He is *Al-'Alim*, the Omniscient and *Al-Shahid*, the Universal Witness; His Eye breaks through every cloud, His Vision penetrates every veil. Consequently anyone who attains the Knowledge of God will be empowered to witness the *nafs* with the Eye of God, which has now become the Eye of the Heart; this is the point where Knowledge of Allah begins to be transformed into a higher realization, into what some Sufis have called the Knowledge of the *Nafs*. As the Heart's Eye opens she is stripped of all her masks, all the passions she covered her face with to hide from her primal pain of existence as apparently separate from God. And when the pain of the *nafs* is completely revealed, then she can no longer hide herself as prideful tyranny and self-will, but will appear exactly as she is: as *desperate need*. You have experienced her power, her seduction and her deceit; now you must experience her pain, and come to the realization that all her seductions and manipulations are based not on the free exercise of her power, as she would like to believe and to make you believe, but only on her desperation, and her attempts to flee and deny and hide from that desperation. All things are in need of Allah—absolute need. Whatever denies this need by asserting its own self-sufficiency earns His wrath; whatever admits this need and turns to Him in supplication invokes His Mercy. No degree of triumph, no degree of distraction, no degree of flight, can cure the pain of the *nafs*; only the Love of God can cure it—at least that's what the Sufis say.

But am I really *giving myself away* in this book? Am I really deconstructing the *nafs*? Or am I only building another secondary self that I will now have to worship and obey, live down or live up to, or risk becoming "nobody"? "I read your autobiography, but now that I've met you I see that you're not like yourself at all! *Liar!*" Only true prayer, either shirked or consummated, can answer this question. By myself, in dialogue only with myself, I can't even know if I'm really being sincere; only He can know that. Who I think I am is all delusion; who He knows me to be is reliability and certainty.

THE ROOT OF IDENTIFICATION IS SELF-WILL

So the central task of the spiritual Path is to overcome identification, the deeply-ingrained tendency to say "I am this or that." The problem is that identifications are endless, virtually infinite; if we were to try to remember every one of them, and then detach from and release them one-by-one, there would not be enough years in any lifetime to finish the job. What is needed is to find the *one root* of all those identifications, and then sever it. What is that root? It is none other than *self-will*. God knows exactly who we are, and precisely what actions we must perform and avoid to remain true to who we are. But to identify with anything whatsoever is to say: "I don't want to be who God knows me to be, I want to be something else; I don't want to do what God knows I must do, I want to do something else"—which means that every identification, every intention to be "this or that," no matter how seemingly positive, no matter how apparently unconscious or unintentional, is an act of disobedience—and the only way to sever the root of *all* identification is to submit to the Will of God in this moment. If the essence of every type and degree of vice or ignorance is identification, the essence of every true act of faith and repentance is *islam*, a word that means "complete and willing surrender, whose outcome is peace." Submission to God's Will goes far beyond obedience to moral rules and the fulfillment of ritual obligations—though these are the necessary starting-points—until it ultimately begins to express itself as discernment and acceptance of the true nature of the present moment (in terms of the intellect), without denial, distraction or editing, as well as immediate response to the demands of that moment (in terms of the will), without resistance, delay or argument. To know the true nature of the moment is to participate in God's Knowledge; to respond to the precise demands of the moment is to be strengthened by God's Action. When identification dissolves, when self-will is broken, then nothing exists any more in the realm of knowing but God's Knowing, nor does anything remain in the realm of action but God's Doing. What God knows is always so; what God does is already accomplished.

It may seem strange to the reader however — it even feels a little strange to me — that I should end the story of my life as it has been so far with a "teaching," with something on the order of "the moral of the story." That, however, is how I actually see things. "Raw" experience that we haven't assimilated through reflection and insight becomes what we colloquially call "baggage," something we have to lug around with us wherever we go; it only slows us down. But experience we've learned to see in its "metaphysical transparency" becomes one with our essence; it is no longer some extra, added factor.

A CONVENIENT PLACE TO END

So when the age of the Covenants Initiative had properly ended, then the time of Covid-19 came — which, in Gurdjieff's terminology, I like to call "the stop exercise" — and locked everything down. Even if you weren't in lockdown officially, some degree of lockdown was (and is) inevitable — lockdown of both the body and the soul. But the Heart — if it's got the Key — knows how to escape that lockdown. Due to the isolation imposed by Covid, it was as if experience had stopped flowing in from the world, through the outer man, and so the inner man was activated. The archives were opened. Vast truckloads of Memory were taken out of storage and set on their trek toward the archives of Eternity — not just my own personal memories, but the memories of the entire earthly and human past. This book is the contents of only one file box among many millions now taking that final journey.

(And, speaking of Covid, I have one more little story to tell — parenthetically — the story of one of my two real "Edgar Cayce experiences." Soon after the pandemic arrived I had a dream: nothing but the words "Covid island cure." Immediately upon awakening I entered those words into Google, my favorite dream interpretation search engine, and found that the president of the island of Madagascar had recommended that his people use the herb *artemisia annua* — sweet wormwood — as a Covid preventative; so I started using it myself. Then, a couple of years later, I found an article about a National Institutes of Health study which determined that sweet wormwood was effective against Covid-19, and against cancer as well.)

So this time, you might say, is the time of the resurrection of the dead, the return of the Ancestors — and the only way those Ancestors can rise from their graves is to rise *through us*. In days like these, whether deliberately or only by default, in full waking consciousness or in the depths of mortal distraction and sleep, we offer our bodies to be the purgatories of souls we will never know. In my epic poem "The Wars of Love," which (as you'll remember) took me thirty-three years to write, this is what they wanted me to say:

"We are those
Who lie slandered under the name of death.
We have incontrovertible reason,
Proof to silence laughter.
From palaces of torture,
From twenty terms in the grey, damp, infinite dusk
We raise our voices and salute you,
Who still sit laboring in your dream —
You living men and women, clothed as we were
In the sweetness and the dignity
Of human flesh. We are the strength of your arms and your loins,
The voice of your living memory.
Speak us, man! Tell our story.
We've been muttering too long in our ruined halls, those narrow beds,
The groves still barren of our voices;
We've lain too long in the seed-houses, the uneasy archives,
   the crucibles of sleep.
Beware! The dead are hungry for those who will not live;
The ones who die into a coward's dream we consume;
We eat, and are not satisfied.
But as you remember Him, He will also remember us in our chambers
   of darkness
Till the river of our endless dying flows East again,
Toward the rising sun."

Once, while she was living in San Francisco, Jenny dreamt of a stunningly beautiful blonde woman in a long red dress, standing next to a globe of the Earth. The woman said: "Holes will now start to appear in the world, and whatever we put into those holes will become absolutely real." This was a kind of companion-dream to her dream of Marilyn Monroe (recounted above) where Marilyn, in giving all her clothes away, began to fear that as soon as she discarded the last garment she would cease to exist. This is the time, long awaited, when our "consensus reality" has finally broken down under shock after shock — the time when those holes have begun to appear not just for the sensitives, the visionaries, but for everyone. First the official acknowledgement of the UFO phenomenon; then Covid, climate change, transgenderism, China and Taiwan, Russia and the Ukraine, economic instability, the deconstruction of our political system, the disintegration of our social fabric even up to the point of possible civil war — the universal availability of Artificial Intelligence, appearing *as* us and speaking *for* us, as if to totally obliterate the human voice and face — and now the Hamas/Israeli/Houthi/Hezbollah/Iran war which threatens to spill over every seawall and cross every boundary. When our collective image of reality starts to fall apart, when self-image-plus-world-image breaks down (self-image as represented, in Jenny's dream universe, by Marilyn Monroe, and world-image by the beautiful woman with the globe) — then, through the cracks and rifts and bullet-holes in what's left of our habitual taken-for-granted reality might come *anything at all*. What actually will come, for each of us—apart from the ordeals destined to be suffered by the whole human race—depends entirely on the direction and quality of our attention. Are we oriented toward beauty or toward ugliness? Are we centered in lies or in truth? In refinement or in lowlife? In compassion or in vindictiveness? In self-respect or in degeneracy? In courage or in cowardice? In integrity or in self-betrayal? Or is the goal of our aspiration something that lies completely beyond these pairs-of-opposites? Like the song says, "what you see is what you get." Now is the time when "what you have spoken in darkness shall be heard in the light, and what you have whispered in sealed rooms shall be cried from the rooftops" [Luke 12:3], when all of us will be forced by the apocalyptic energies of the times to live out the entire consequences of whatever deep-seated attachments we have failed to let go of, whatever views of self-and-world have become fixed and petrified in us, whatever secret idols we still worship—to fully express them for all to see, and for *us* to see: this is the true significance of *apocalypse*, a word that means "revelation." Therefore, as the facades of world-identity crumble and the masks of self-identity fall, be prepared, dear reader—as soon as the specific Glitch in the Matrix that has your name on it opens, directly in front of you—to release your concentrated spiritual attention like an arrow to the center of the Target, to the Reality that lies behind the performance. If the seed you release comes from God, it will posit Paradise; if it comes from the *nafs*, the ego, it will posit the Fire—and the best thing of all that you can posit is not the thing that *you* most want but the thing that God wants, even if you can't even begin to know what that thing is. As the Sufi Bayazid Bistami teaches us in his short prayer, "O God, You know what I want," what God wants is what you *really* want, whether you know it or not. So all I can say—in terms of unsolicited advice, which can certainly be irritating, and which anyone is free to reject—is: "maintain vigilance, keep a steady hand and a cool eye, and shoot straight."

But at least I had found the spiritual Path that had been clearly presented in my Lifetime Dream, dreamt at the age of six or seven—*or had I?* Because, with amazing decisiveness, just before Covid put the world in quarantine, the whole thing suddenly and unexpectedly fell apart, at least according to the traditional definition of what constitutes a viable Sufi *tariqah*. Our shaykh was hit by a sexual scandal that made the feeble attempts at self-sabotage launched by Chögyam Trungpa and Frithjof Schuon look like the work of rank amateurs. Not only that, but his offending actions were secretly videoed by his wife and then sent (by someone else) to *all* his followers in every part of the world! What was done in secret was cried from the rooftops beyond any shadow of a doubt in that situation, consequently the whole thing, mercifully, was over (comparatively speaking) in the twinkling of an eye. But why, after a lifetime of seeking spiritual guidance, and after apparently finding exactly what I was looking for according to the pattern I had been shown as a child in the Dream of My Life, was it suddenly and definitively withdrawn? Had I committed some secret sin that made me unfit to be guided? Had God finally abandoned me? Or had the darkness of the late Kali-yuga and the incipient rise of Antichrist finally closed all the doors of Grace, leaving the human race to wither on the vine? I saw that if I were to subscribe to such beliefs, then they would effectively be true, at least for me; what you see is what you get. However, another interpretation soon presented itself, which I expressed in the following verses:

> The Shaykh was the only channel for
>   God's guidance,
> Since if Truth does not assume a human form
> It cannot touch our humanity.
>
> But then the Shaykh was gone;
> This is the darkness at the end of my
>   lifetime dream.
> So now there is only the need and the
>   Presence,
> Only He Who Is, and *I who am not* —
>   except by the free and undeserved
>   generosity
> Of He Who Is.
> All that once placed us face to Face,
> All that worked so hard to unite us
> Now no longer stands between us.
>
> But if I remain facing need alone, need
>   that veils the Presence,
> I will lose the awareness of that need,
>   in my dark self-involvement —
> And so that terminal darkness at the
>   end of my Lifetime Dream will be
>   despair indeed.
>
> So *turn around now, watcher* — no more
>   story of "me"
> Out there dancing on the horizon;
> No more parade of beginnings and endings,
>   of shifting identifications.
> It is in the Presence of God that our need is
>   most clearly seen;
> It is in the face of that need that the
>   Presence is known exactly as It is,
> And so can never be lost — while need is
>   still acknowledged —

> Until the rising of the final Sun,
> When the Presence overwhelms it,
>   annihilates it, fills it to overflowing,
> So that no helpless, starving beggar remains,
> Hanging on the doorsill of the King.
> "Blessed are the poor in spirit"
> (The dervishes, the *fuqara*)
> For they shall see God."
>
> Why did the Shaykh have to leave?
> Only so that the Comforter could come,
> So that *experience* would no longer
>   be necessary.
> You are no longer traveling *to* God
>   (now that you have given yourself away)
>   but *in* God—
> So the time has come to leave the raft on the
>   shore of the Ocean
> And press on deeper into the Interior.

Once, while sitting in the circle of the Nimatullahi dervishes at the San Francisco *khaniqah*, I had a vision of the Prophets: Adam, Noah, Abraham, Moses, Jesus, Muhammad and—interestingly enough—Zoroaster. I saw images of each, felt the quality of each. And when I asked, "which one do I have the greatest affinity with?" the answer came: "Abraham." He too found himself ejected from the spiritual universes of his time—specifically, from the vast, zodiac-driven megamachine of the Mesopotamian ritual system—precisely so he could meet the Great Mystery alone in the wilderness, one-on-One, which is how he earned the title of *khalil-Allah*, "the friend of God." And though I am neither a prophet nor a saint, I can still identify with that particular brand of exile. We have no right to reject the great revelations that God has sent us—but what if they (seemingly) reject us? Religion is the best of pursuits but the worst of idols, which is why God sometimes commands us: "Meet Me naked beyond the range of human eyes; then put your clothes back on—your chosen religious, ritual and theological forms—and return to your destined people." (From the perspective of the present day I am beginning to see that Frithjof Schuon, while he followed the first of these directives, failed to realize the necessity of the second.) So I still follow the Sufi path, even after our great disaster; I haven't lost it. And though I am richly blessed, perhaps for the first time in my life, with true spiritual brothers and sisters, what I have lost is the function of a living human *mediator* between myself and God: He and I are now face to Face and breast to Breast—except for those times when my wavering faith plunges me into impenetrable darkness, or when my temporary Absence indicates that the Presence we once shared is now entirely Him.

To forget God is to forget everything; to remember Him is to be present to everything in the same moment, a moment *outside time*, and find your destined place in the eternal order. But since such a "conclusion" can't be located on the timeline of the passing days, it might be best to end this book (arbitrarily, as all endings must be) by repeating, one more time, the concise words of Lew Welch from his "HIKING POEM/HIGH SIERRA," words perfectly designed to wipe the slate clean:

> Trails go nowhere.
> They end exactly
> where you stop.

INDEX OF NAMES
[*An asterisk following a name indicates an alias*]

Aasia Bibi, 557, 569
Abba, 332, 334
Abbot Maximos (Holy Cross Monastery), 509
Abd al-Qadir al-Djazairi, 554
Abraham (prophet), 31, 579
Abu Bakr (caliph), 553
Abu Dawud, 558
Achilles, 195
Adam, 140, 145, 188–89, 454, 497
Adams, John, 379
Adams, John Quincey, 379
Adi Da (Da Free John), 346, 375
Adler, Mark, 278
Alabama (band), 202
Al-'Alawi, Shaykh Ahmed, 1, 52, 130, 133
Al-Buzaidi, Shaykh, 130
Alegría, Fernando, 332–33
Alfred the Great, King, 72
Al-Ghazali, 294–95
Al-Hallaj, Mansur, 402
'Ali ibn Abi Talib, 553
Al-Junaid, 402
Allen, Don, 106, 109, 194
Allen, Steve, 74
Allende, Salvador, 330, 332–33
Allison, Mose, 223
Allman Brothers, The, 202
Al-Maktoum, Mohammed bin Rashid, Crown Prince, 478
Alpert, Richard (Ram Dass), 114, 158, 167, 197, 340, 396, 415, 457
Amin, Idi, 283
Amos (prophet), 192
Anacreon, 87
Anactoria, 247
Anderson, Dame Judith, 391
Anderson, Walter, 36, 289
Andrew, Prince, 241
Antoninus, Brother (William Everson), 98
Appleseed, Johnny, 528
Aquinas, St Thomas, 2, 418, 434
Arberry, A.J., 150
Argüelles, José, 44, 50, 359–60, 364–66
Aristophanes, 80
Aristotle, 122, 206, 344, 476

Armstrong, Neil, 105
Arthur, Chester A., 104
Arthur, Gavin, 104, 461
Arthur, King, 425, 452, 454–56
Asimov, Isaac, 162
Assagioli, Roberto, 481
Augustine, St, 4, 43, 83, 322,
Autsen, Pete, 13, 281

Babbs, Ken, 485
Bacall, Lauren, 388
Baer, Max, 388
Baez, Joan, 80, 94, 148, 157, 379, 506
Baez, Pauline, 80
Bailey, Alice A., 367
Baker, Dick, Roshi, 115
Ballard, Tim, 467
Band, The, 163, 202
Bannon, Steve, 505
Barks, Coleman, 397
Bartholomew, Ecumenical Patriarch, 556, 559
Basie, Count, 388
Baskerville (family), 15, 72, 492–93
Bassanio, 315
Baudelaire, Charles, 158
Bayazid Bistami, 344, 577
Beardsley, Aubrey, 57
Beatles, The, 78, 90, 142, 148, 163, 182, 226, 315
Beatrice Portinari, 11, 57, 273
Beckett, Samuel, 157
Bedoya, Alfonso, 289
Behan, Brendan, 157
Bell, Art, 468, 471
Bell, Richie, 267
Belushi, Jim, 332
Belushi, John, 209, 330–31
Benedict XVI, Pope (Joseph Cardinal Ratzinger), 448, 505
Bergier, Jacques, 162
Bernadette Soubirous, St, 99, 419
Berry, Chuck, 388
Berry, Tanya, 484
Berry, Wendell, 32, 407, 484–86
Beshear, Andy, 494

Bethards, Betty, 260, 265, 362
Bettis, Mike, 113, 389
Bhagavan Das, 114
Biden, Joe, 563
Big John (radio personality), 302
Bilbo Baggins, 498
Bin Laden, Osama, 99
Bird, Christopher, 170
Bischel, Jean, 543, 546
Bischel, Kirby, 543, 546
Bishop, Elvin, 388
Black Elk, 159, 174, 370
Blackburn, Marquetta, 522–23
Blackburn, Oliver, 522
Blackman, Marsha, 341
Blackwell, Katherine, 288, 341, 392, 476
Blake, William, vii, 4, 7, 15–16, 23, 54, 72–73, 76, 83, 89–90, 94, 99, 103, 110, 112, 114, 120–21, 145–46, 174, 182, 200, 212, 260, 295–96, 309, 312, 322–24, 376, 406, 452–56, 513, 538, 540, 551
Blaser, Robin, 229
Bly, Robert, 18, 97, 100, 168, 228, 277, 325–26, 397, 407–8, 539, 541
Blyth, R.H., 460
Boehme, Jacob, 468
Boff, Leonardo, 320, 329
Bogart, Humphrey, 388
Bolen, Jean Shinoda, 271, 365
Bonaparte, Napoleon, 8, 230
Bonhoeffer, Dietrich, 118, 287, 450
Bonnie Prince Charlie, 282
Boone, Daniel, 547, 478
Boone, Nathan*, 464–65
Borkowsky, Eugenia, 108
Borkowsky, Miriam, 107–8
Bowery Boys, The, 234
Boyce, Jack, 89, 193, 195, 314
Boz Scaggs, 388
Bradbury, Ray, 162
Brand, Stewart, 158
Brautigan, Richard, 106
Brecht, Berthold, 352
Bridget, St, 104, 365
Brodie, James, 127
Broughton, James, 98
Brown, Claude, 158
Brown, Edmund G. "Pat," 392
Brown, Jerry, 78, 391
Brown, Norman O., 157
Brown, Vinson, 159

Bruce, Lenny, 97, 157
Buck, Beryl, 390
Bucke, R.M., 158
Buckley, William F., 217, 230, 249,
Bukhari, 558
Bukowski, Charles, 109
Bullock, Kenneth George, 41, 89, 271–72, 277, 279
Bunting, Basil, 107–8
Burbank, Luther, 170
Burckhardt, Titus, 375, 395
Burdick, Brad (Antler), 114
Burke, John, 392–93
Burnett, John, 430
Burns, Robert, 19
Burr, Raymond, 210, 249
Burroughs, William, 46, 89–90, 101, 103, 157, 159, 226, 231, 235, 266, 291, 479, 565
Butler, Mrs (neighbor), 289–99
Byron, Lord, 112

Caddy, Eileen, 170
Caddy, Peter, 169–70
Cain, Fr, 66
Calhoun, Walker, 493
Camara, Dom Helder, 320, 329
Campbell, Joseph, 160, 184, 319, 329
Camus, Albert, 158
Captain Beefheart, 388
Cardenal, Ernesto, 148, 320, 328
Carlin, George, 157
Carlin, Maggie*, 422–23, 476
Carnegie, Dale, 356
Carrie (character in film), 486–87
Carson, Olive*, 462–64
Carson, Rachel*, 459–60
Carson, Randy*, 183, 185–86, 231, 265, 342–43, 357, 379, 459–67
Carson, Ruby*, 462
Caryn (adolescent friend), 85–86, 165–66, 179, 279
Cassady, Neal, 104–5, 111
Castellani, Rocky, 388
Castro, Fidel, 330
Caudill, Harry, 492
Caux Round Table, 555–66
Cavangnolo, Rich, 346
Cavarnos, Constantine, 499
Caviezel, Jim, 467
Cayce, Edgar, 259, 354, 498
Ce Acatl Quetzalcoatl, 44

Index of Names

Cekada, Fr Anthony, 544
Céline, Louis-Ferdinand, 158
Chaitanya, Sri, 233
Chaney, Rick, 501
Charbel Mahklouf, St, 567
Chardin, Teilhard de, 77, 196, 352, 359
Charlemagne, 282
Charles III, King, 407, 488, 534
Charles of Anjou, 238
Charles, Prince of Wales, 407, 534
Chatterton, Thomas, 84
Cherkovski, Neeli, 114
Cherokees, 491–92
Chesterton, G.K., 161
Child, Francis James, 121
Chishti Tariqah, 126, 374
Chittick, William, 411
Christiansen, Fr Damascene, 423
Christopher, Brother, 98
Chrysostom, St John, 137
City Lights Publishers, 100–1, 107, 110, 236, 278, 332, 485, 564
Clapton, Eric, 143
Claremont de Castillejo, Irene, 271
Clark, Arthur C., 162
Clark, Tom, 291
Clavijero, Francisco Javier, 44
Clay, Henry, 479
Cleaver, Eldridge, 158
Clinton, Hillary, 480, 483
Clooney, George, 508
Clooney, Rosemary, 508
Clover, 388
Clow, Barbara Hand, 355
Cockell, Don, 388
Cocteau, Jean, 28, 159
Cohen, Leonard, 100, 219
Cole, Charles Octavius, 65
College of Marin, 87–88, 114, 129, 176, 375, 380
Collins, Al "Jazzbo," 289
Collins, Martha Layne, 483
Commander Cody, 388
Communist Party, 108, 214, 327, 346, 351, 355, 371, 379
Community Congregational Church of Belvedere-Tiburon (CCC), 398, 411
Como, Perry, 178
Connery, Sean, 219
Conroy, "Bondo Bob," 383–84
Considine, Craig, 556, 563

Coomaraswamy, Ananda K., 158, 375, 394, 398, 408, 428, 469, 478
Coomaraswamy, Doña Luisa, 435
Coomaraswamy, Rama P., 81, 350, 375, 380, 394–95, 398, 414, 428, 434–35, 446, 448–49, 458, 468–474, 478, 482, 507–8, 510–12, 542–44, 546, 566
Cooper, James Fennimore, 16
Coppola, Francis Ford, 106, 164, 214, 325–26, 393
Corso, Gergory, 87, 98–99, 107, 158,
Cosa Nostra, 113
Costner, Kevin, 545
Cox, Harvey, 82
Coyote, Peter, 148, 327, 391
Crane, Hart, 56, 210, 286
Cream, 143
Creedence Clearwater Revival, The, 202
Creeley, Robert, 106, 194, 289, 564
Cregg, Hugh Anthony Jr., 102
Cregg, Magda, 17, 77, 87, 89, 101–4, 125, 130, 139, 169, 192–96, 202, 222, 228–29, 279, 314–15
Creighton, Hannah, 327
Crème, Benjamin, 369
Crosby, Stills, and Nash, 142, 153, 225,
Crosby, Stills, Nash and Young, 213
Crowley, Aleister, 134, 161, 201, 256
Crumb, Robert, 126, 150
Cuddy, Terry, 107, 210
Cumberland, Duke of, 496
Cumby, Constance, 355
Cummings, Robert, 105, 482, 543, 547–48
Curtis, Tony, 384
Cusack, Cyril, 451
Cutsinger, James, 394–95, 398, 411, 427–28, 430, 432–35, 477, 509–10, 526, 529

Da Free John (Adi Da), 346, 375
Dalai Lama, 99, 135, 266, 303, 506, 507
Daley, Jeff, 363–64
Dalton, Roque, 330
Damon, S. Foster, 172, 452–53
Damron, Cordell, 494
Damron, Robert, 533
Damron, Tracy, 501–2
Danny, Wakoff, 327
Dante Alighieri, 11, 23, 99, 112, 133, 145, 148, 162, 273, 303, 434, 439, 486, 496, 506, 511, 513, 526, 541
Darwin, Charles, 77, 369, 413

Davenport, Guy, 498
Davis, Jefferson, 479
Davis, Kim, 566
Davis, Reverend Gary, 222
Davis, William Heath, 28
Dawahare (family), 482
Dawson, Augusta, 35
Dawson, Bill, 35
de Beauvoir, Simone, 405
De Mille, Cecil B., 128
De Mille, Richard, 128
De Quincey, Thomas, 159
Dede, Sulieman, 169
Delano, Rick, 468
Dele, Bison, 416
DeMarco, Paddy, 388
Dembski, William, 413
Democratic Party, 78, 327, 392
Dempster, Milen, 327
Denny, Sandy, 131
Depp, Johnny, 113
Devlin, Sharon, 134
Dewey Dell (Faulkner character), 154
Diaz del Castillo, Bernal, 28
Dick, Philip K., 162
Dickens, Charles, 21, 69, 247
Dickinson, Emily, 99, 120
Diego, Brother, 328
Dietrich, Barbara, 89
Dietrich, Frank, 89, 108, 271, 274, 286
Diggers, The, 148, 391
Dingman, Tony, 106, 316, 325
Dion, 153
Dionysius the Pseudo-Areopagite, 448
DiPrima, Diane, 98
Disney, Walt, 35, 256
Dobson, Richard, 128, 294, 373–74
Dōgen, 90
Dolan, Bishop Daniel, 544
Dominican College, 52, 63, 384–85
Dominican Convent, 63, 367, 385, 422
Dominicans, 30, 32, 63–64
Don Genaro, 128, 285
Don Juan Matus, 127–29, 236, 257, 285
Donleavy, J.P., 157
Donne* (family), 490
Donne*, Fred, 269, 504, 513, 515–16, 525, 528, 533, 567
Donne*, Jenny, 1, 6, 11, 15, 17, 26, 31–32, 40, 47, 49, 60, 62, 71–72, 81, 84, 89, 92, 101, 106–7, 115, 167, 171, 175, 186, 194, 225, 256, 258–59, 261, 268–86, 288, 290, 294, 298, 300, 316–17, 320–24, 326–27, 329–31, 335–36, 339–41, 343, 345, 351, 402, 477–82, 485–89, 514–20, 522–39, 541–49, 559, 561, 563–64, 566–67, 576
Donne, John, 117, 194
Donne, Lola (Lola Plunkett*), 269, 402, 476, 501, 504, 513–39
Donnelly, Ignatius, 44
Donovan, 157
Dorn, Ed, 107
Doyle, John, 25, 113, 153–55, 158, 213, 215–16, 277, 279, 283–84, 297–98
Doyle, Kirby, 92
Dragging Canoe, Chief, 494
Drath, Phil, 327
Dreamcatchers, 415
Dubbs, Charles and Eileen, 338
Dullea, Fr John, 66, 76, 78, 83–84
Duncan, Isadora, 211
Duncan, Robert, 98, 106, 162, 307
Durante, Jimmy, 13
Duvall, Robert, 106
Dylan, Bob, 70, 80, 83, 107, 148, 157, 163, 165, 202, 205, 212, 222, 328, 526

Eason, Gianna, 327
Eastwood, Clint, 228
Eaton, Charles le Gai, 375, 395
Eber, 174
Eber Scot, 174
Eckhart, Meister, 161, 442, 468
Eleanor of Aquitaine, 15, 32
Eliade, Mircea, 88, 108, 160
Eliopanzo Peter Deal (hitchhiker), 214
Eliot, T.S., 2, 77, 112, 235, 402, 453
Elizabeth II, Queen, 478, 488
Ellett, Betty, 312
Ellington, Duke, 388
Elliot (hitchhiker), 207–10
Ellison, Ralph, 158
El-Wakil, Ahmed, 555
Emerson, Ralph Waldo, 81, 147, 150, 160
Engles, Friederic, 327, 351
Epstein, Jefferey, 241, 465, 467, 519
Esalen Institute, 113, 360, 363, 369, 461
Escher, M.C., 150, 183
Essenes, 192
Estes, Clarissa Pinkola, 271
Evans-Wentz, W.Y., 160, 237, 256
Everson, William (Brother Antoninus), 98
Evola, Baron Julius, 395

Fagin, 247
Fältskog, Angetha, 334
Fanon, Franz, 157
Farabundo (*see* Martí, Farabundo)
Farabundo Martí National Liberation Front (FMLN), 330, 348
Fariña, Mimi, 142, 379
Fariña, Richard, 142, 157
Faulkner, William, 12, 154
Feeney, Fr Leonard, 546
Ferguson, Marilyn, 355
Ferlinghetti, Lawrence, 1, 77, 87, 90, 97, 107, 109–10, 114–15, 126, 148, 236, 323
Fibber McGee and Molly (radio characters), 35
Fifth Dimension, The, 145
Filson, John, 494
Firesign Theatre, The, 157, 290, 459
Fitzgerald, Edward, 160
Fitzgerald, F. Scott, 381
Fitzgerald, Mark*, 425, 444–47
Forché, Carolyn, 331
Foster, Graeme, 236
Fowler, Gene, 183–84
Fox, Deki, 367
Fox, Jon, 367
Frances (friend in Canada), 219
Francis of Assisi, St, 564
Francis, Pope, 471, 505, 566
Frank the Sorcerer, 244–46
Frankie, Aunty, 16
Fraser, Kathleen, 273
Frazer, Sir James, 95, 105, 160, 184
Freemasons, 23, 83, 260–61, 354–55, 358, 544
Freire, Paulo, 328
Fremont, John C., 59
Frodo Baggins, 73, 328, 489
Fromer, Irving, 327
Frost, Robert, 97, 119, 163
Frye, Northrup, 76
Furnace Mountain Zen Center, 482

Gable, Clark, 113
Galati, Eric, 471, 512, 561
Galati, Irena, 561
Galloway, Fr Thomas, 482
Gameaha, Mohamed, 556
Gandhi, Mohandas K., 150, 252, 318
Garden School, The, 52, 65–66
Gardín, Carlo, 74

Gardner, Gerald, 434
Garfinkel, Harold, 128
Garfunkel, Art, 214, 217, 222, 332
Gargery, Joe, 15
Garibaldi, Giuseppe, 34
Garrison, Jim, 212
Gaskin, Steve, 461
Gate of Horn, 371
Gates, Bill, 357
Gawain, Shakti, 358
Geller, Uri, 290, 373
Genaro, Don, 128, 285
Genet, Jean, 158
George I of Greece, King, 238
George, Hunter, 430
Gerken, Fr Sergious, 426
Gethsemani, Abbey of, 482, 505–8
Giacomini, Gary, 379, 390
Gibran, Kahlil, 211
Gibson, Mel, 47, 398, 467–68, 505
Gide, André, 158
Gilbert, Jack, 89, 261, 271–73, 279
Gillespie, Dizzy, 112
Ginsberg, Allen, 1, 87, 90–92, 97–98, 100, 105, 110–11, 115, 120, 145, 148, 150–51, 158–59, 164, 172, 187, 205, 213–14, 266, 289–96, 319, 323, 350, 361, 397
Glass, Marty, 564
Global Family, 363–64, 371
Goble, Chester, 522, 525, 535
Goble, Irene, 503, 522, 525, 528, 531, 535
Godlas, Alan, 411–12
Godlas, Sylvia, 411
Goethe, Johann Wolfgang von, 143, 150, 160, 323
Gogarty, Oliver St John, 157
Gonne, Maud, 104
Goober, 312
Goodman, Paul, 157
Gorbachev, Mikail, 363, 371
Gorcey, Leo, 234
Gore, Leslie, 25
Graham, Bill, 392–93
Graham, Billy, 99
Graham, Leanna*, 335–37
Graham, Martha, 211
Grateful Dead, The, 61, 107, 129, 176, 388, 391, 393
Graves, Robert, 95, 130, 160, 184, 314, 375, 394
Graziano, Rocky, 210

Green Gulch Zen Center, 115
Gregory Palamas, St, 433
Griffith, Andy, 312
Grimm, Jacob, 141, 207
Grimm, Wilhelm, 141, 207
Guénon, René, 1, 22, 41, 43–44, 54, 77, 158, 174–75, 197, 224, 261, 325, 375, 394–96, 398, 408, 424, 428, 437–38, 440, 445, 456–57, 469, 471, 541
Gurdjieff, George Ivanovitch, 138, 160, 169, 245, 371, 416, 434, 446, 517, 575
Guthrie, Woody, 205
Gutierrez, Gustavo, 320
Gwinevere, Queen, 425
Gyalwa Karmapa, 16th, 169, 171–75

Hadhazy, Dean, 384–85
Hafiz, 8, 150, 402
Hall, Fr Bernard, 546
Hall, Huntz, 234
Haltom, Matt, 482, 543, 548
Hamid (dervish), 405
Hampton, Anel, 499
Hampton, Arnold, 499
Hampton, Jeanette, 493, 501
Hampton, Lionel, 388
Hamsun, Knut, 387
Hancock, Graham, 494
Hand, Maryam, 481, 534
Harbie, Dr, 482
Harding, Esther, 271
Hardy, Thomas, 486
Harpo, Marx, 107
Harrer, Heinrich, 303
Harris, Ron, 76, 399, 401, 405, 410–11
Harrison, George, 148
Harvey, Andrew, 100
Hatfield (family), 491–92
Hawken, Paul, 170
Hawkins, Bobbie Louise, 106, 194, 564
Hawthorne, Nathaniel, 56
Hearst, Patty, 123
Hegel, Georg Wilhelm Friedrich, 77, 191, 352
Heinlein, Robert, 162
Hell's Angels, The, 112–13, 206, 389
Helm, Levon, 202
Helminski, Kabir, 451, 541
Hemingway, Ernest, 381
Hemple, Drew, 359
Hendrix, Jimi, 143, 152, 168, 274, 328

Henley, William Earnest, 7
Henry VIII, King, 452, 454
Henry, Gray (Sayyida A'isha), 506, 508
Henry, O., 28
Henzell-Thomas, Jeremy, 451
Henzell-Thomas, Tanya, 451
Heraclitus, 73, 93–94, 196
Herbert, Frank, 162
Hermetic Order of the Golden Dawn, 134, 354
Hernon, Charles, 334–35, 340
Heron, Gil Scott, 213
Hesse, Herman, 158, 207, 507
Hilarion (entity), 376
Hilarion the Great, St, 367
Hillman, James, 407–8
Hirbod, Sam, 563–64
Hirschman, Jack, 108, 148, 217, 230, 277, 323
Hitchcock, Alfred, 210
Hitchcock, William Mellon, 200–1
Hitler, Adolf, 8, 118, 147, 301–3, 305, 351
Hoffman, Abbie, 148, 202, 213
Hoffman, Dustin, 253
Hoffman, Michael, 488
Holland, Jeffrey Scott, 497
Holmes, Elizabeth, 515
Holmes, Sherlock, 106
Holy Virgin Cathedral Joy of All Who Sorrow, 417, 419–20, 425, 435, 564
Hopis, 172–73, 202
Horiuchi, Bruce, 153
Horn, Erica, 127
Hot Tuna, 388
Houdini, 211
Howard, Ken, 375
Howard, Sarah, 177, 188, 298, 378–93, 417
Howard, Trevor, 451
Hubbard, Barbara Marx, 358, 360, 363, 366, 376
Hudson, Walter, 15
Huerta, Rebecca, 389–90
Huerta, Tim, 389–90
Huneke, Rev. Doug, 62, 330
Huxley, Aldous, 83, 157–59
Hyemeyohsts Storm, 159
Hypatia, 260–61

Ibn Abbad of Ronda, 22, 149
Ibn al-'Arabi, 204, 375, 441,
Ibn al-Qabturnuh, 73, 119

Ibn 'Arabi Society, 398, 411
Ibn Sina (Avicenna), 476
Ikkemotubbe (Faulkner character), 493
Illuminati, 83
Inayat Khan, Hazrat, 160
Innocent III, Pope, 80
Inti Illimani, 328, 332
Irons, Jeremy, 379
Ishi, 60

J. E. (relative to Jenny Donne* by marriage), 501
Jackson, Andrew, 491–92
Jackson, Stonewall, 503
Jagger, Bianca, 328–29
Jagger, Mick, 206, 339
James, William, 20, 109, 144, 158, 330
Jeffers, Robinson, 98
Jefferson, Thomas, 557
Jerrahi Tariqah, 561
Jessie, Bob, 415
Jesuits, 77, 150, 449
Jesus Christ, 12, 30, 54, 57, 60, 62–63, 70, 81, 83, 94, 98, 100, 148, 178, 192, 233, 283, 295, 350, 356, 407, 426–27, 441, 448, 455, 463–64, 467, 469, 487, 498, 506–7, 522, 535–36, 538, 560, 571–72, 579
Ji Ming Shen, 424
Jiménez, Juan Ramón, 326
Jobs, Steve, 494
John XXIII, Pope, 469
John the Baptist, St, 192, 326
John Chrysostom, St, 137
John of the Cross, St, 151, 161
John Maximovitch, St, 417–20, 423, 425–26, 435, 438, 446, 537, 542, 564
Johnson, John, 494
Johrei Fellowship, 280–88, 343, 362, 392, 420, 476
Joktan, 174
Jones, Jim, 99, 162, 361
Jones, Owen, 432
Joplin, Janice, 146, 152, 202, 253
Jordan, Michael, 105
Joseph of Arimathea, 453, 455
Josephina (psychic surgeon), 264–65
Joy of Cooking, 338
Joyce, James, 86, 155–57, 166, 186
Judas, 295
Jung, Carl, 76, 79, 92, 136, 142, 151, 156, 160, 188, 195, 198, 271, 278, 280, 292, 306, 319, 325, 339, 365, 370, 375, 394, 405, 407–8, 431, 443, 487, 539, 567
Juniper (cat), 477
Justinian (Byzantine Emperor), 261

Kalabat, Bishop Francis, 340, 556
Kandel, Lenore, 87, 112
Kane, Kathy, 26
Karchmar, Irving, 559
Kardec, Alan, 262
Karlan, Serena, 416
Kashani, Hossein, 509
Kaufman, Bob, 107
Kaufman, Parker, 107
Kea, St, 456
Keats, John, 330
Kemp, Lysander, 73
Kennedy (family), 227, 485
Kennedy, John Fitzgerald, 152, 212
Kennedy, Monsignor Thomas I., 367
Kennedy, Robert, 159, 485
Kerouac, Jack, 89–91, 95, 97–98, 101–3, 105, 158, 205, 221–28, 287
Kerr, Jerry, 19, 21
Kerry, John, 556
Kesey, Ken, 112, 158–59, 200, 209, 286, 461, 484–85
Khamenei, Ayatullah, 556
Khan, Faiz, 512
Khan, Hazrat Inayat, 160
Khan, Imran, 557
Khayyam, Omar, 147, 160
Khrushchev, Nikita, 53
Kierkegaard, Søren, 269, 271, 278, 310, 367, 382, 459
King, Bob, 385
King, Martin Luther, 111, 311, 318, 320
King, Stephen, 486
Kinney, Jay, 358
Kipling, Rudyard, 16
Kirill, Patriarch (of Moscow), 433
Kirpal Singh, 170, 176
Kleps, Art, 201, 340
Kniebus, Rebus, 290
Knievel, Evel, 290
Knight, J. Z., 415–16
Knox, Helena Margarita, 183–84
Kohles, Fr Donald Michael, 81–82
Kornfield, Caroline, 161
Kornfield, Jack, 160–61, 312, 391

Körte, Sister Mary Norbert, 87, 114–15, 129
Krassner, Paul, 78, 144, 202
Krippner, Stanley, 363, 372
Krishnamurti, Jiddu, 169–70
Kroeber, Alfred, 60
Kubler-Ross, Elizabeth, 355, 424
Kundera, Milan, 360
Kurosawa, Akira, 460
Kushner, Jared, 564
Kyger, Joanne, 564

Lacey, Fr Francis, 76, 306
Ladroni*, Bob, 423
Lakhani, Ali, 470, 486
Lamantia, Philip, 98
Langford, Mrs, 39
Lao Tzu, 50, 90, 105
Last Poets, The, 213
Laughlin, James, 331
LaVey, Anton, 162
Lavin, Cappy, 379
Lawrence, D.H., 407
Layla, 11
Leadbeater, C.W., 367
Leary, Timothy, 112, 148, 158, 167, 179, 190, 200–1, 237, 340, 465
LeBerge, Stephen, 256, 369
Led Zepplin, 202
Lee, Annabelle (Poe character), 57
Lehmann, Benjamin Harrison Jr., 391
Lehtoranta, Fr Vili, 543
Lemmon, Jack, 332
Lencioni, Ed, 69–71, 83
Lennon, John, 142, 148
Lenore (Poe character), 57
Leonard, George, 157
Leonardo, Fr, 455–57, 544–46
Levenda, Peter, 159, 200, 373
Levertov Denise, 98, 120
Lévi, Éliphas, 395
Lewis, C.S., 161, 242, 338
Lewis, Huey, 87, 102–3, 341
Lewis, Samuel (Sufi Sam), 125–26, 136, 160, 175, 363, 374, 424
Lewisohn, Leonard, 119, 406
Lindbom, Tage, 395
Lings, Martin, 130, 155, 375, 395, 399, 411, 418, 428, 509, 512, 515, 541
Litchfield, "Whitey," 388–89
Little, Clayton, 521
Livingstone, David, 159

Lohr-Bailey, Helga, 327
Long (family), 36
Long, Butch, 36, 39
Long, Earl, 17
Long, Floyd, 36
Long, Joe, 36
Long, Judy, 36, 39
Long, Lori, 36, 39
Longinus, 455
Looking Horse, Arvol, 170, 176–77
Loras, Jelaleddin, 169, 176
Lorca, Federico García, 106, 118–19, 158, 194, 216, 326, 330
Louis XIV, King, 17
Lowell, Amy, 211
Lucas, George, 271, 477
Luke, Helen, 271
Lundberg, Ferdinand, 157
Luria, Isaac, 101–2
Luster, Betty, 289
Luster, Helen, 93, 289–90
Lyons, Mike, 337–38

Machado, Antonio, 326
Magi, 192
Maharishi Mahesh Yogi, 148
Mailer, Norman, 223
Majnun, 11
Makow, Henry, 200
Malcolm X, 99, 158
Malraux, André, 158
Mamas & The Papas, The, 210
Mancuso, Fr Mark, 510
Mandaeans, 192
Mandell, Arnold, 128
Manriquez, Rafael, 332
Manson, Charles, 99, 142, 148, 162, 206, 361
Mao Tse Tung, 13, 187, 351, 412
Marciano, Rocky, 388
Marcos, Ferdinand, 262
Marcuse, Herbert, 157
Maria-Rosa (Salvadoran activist), 339
Mariah, Paul, 289
Marie-Louise von Franz, 79, 271, 339, 375, 394, 408
Marin Catholic High School, 66, 74–79, 82, 90, 98, 272, 328, 378, 441
Marin Committee for Central America, 49, 327–30
Maritain, Jacques, 395
Marlene (poet and stripper), 274

Marpa, 303–4
Márquez, Gabriel García, 12, 533
Martí, Farabundo, 348
Martin, Fr Malachi, 398, 446, 468, 470–72
Marx, Harpo (see Harpo Marx)
Marx, Karl, 49, 77, 94, 107, 109, 150, 153, 214, 318–20, 338, 342, 347–48, 351, 358, 369
Mary, Virgin, 284, 297, 454–55, 474–75
Maryamiyya Tariqah, 411–15, 427–30, 435–36, 444–46, 474, 503, 505, 508–11
Mattison, Avon, 360, 362, 367
Maugham, Somerset, 160
Maxim, Joey, 388
Maximos, Abbott (Holy Cross Monastery), 509–10
Maxwell, Ghislaine, 465, 519
May, Elaine, 157
Mayakovsky, Vladimir, 100
McAlister, Fr Daniel, 66
McBride, John, 74, 76–78
McCaffrey, Katherine, 456
McCarthy, Joan, 329–30
McCaull, P. H., 78
McClanahan, Ed, 484
McClanahan, Kris, 484
McClure, Michael, 112, 115, 277
McCoy (family), 491–92
McDonald, Barry, 429, 508
McDonald, Country Joe (and the Fish), 97, 193, 253, 277, 388
McDonald, Rebecca, 508
McDougal, Mrs (teacher), 68
McDowell, Mississippi Fred, 258
McGowan, David, 159, 200
McGucken, Archbishop Thomas, 67
McGuinness, Mary, 80, 90
McKenna, Terrence, 159, 197
McKenzie, Scott, 229
McLuhan, Marshall, 77, 157, 229
McNamara, Robert, 360
McNear (family), 11–13, 68
McNear, Erskine, 13
McNear, Lawrence, 13
McPherson, Aimee Semple, 335
Mead, Mick*, 422–23
Meatyard, Ralph Eugene, 498
Medrano, Tony, 328
Meholick, Fr Stephan, 430–31, 433, 436–37, 444
Meisner, Jim, 80
Meltzer, David, 319

Melville, Herman, 164
Merry Pranksters, The, 484
Merton, Thomas, 31, 99–100, 135, 161, 331, 347, 435, 471, 498, 505–8
Mertz, Fred and Ethyl, 338
Merwin, W. S., 291
Metzner, Ralph, 158, 167, 430,
Mevlevi Tariqah, 126, 169, 176, 451
Michael, St, 455–56
Micheline, Jack, 323
Michell, John, 173
Milani, Judy, 215, 252
Milarepa, 92, 267, 286, 304, 306
Milé, King, 174
Millay, Edna St Vincent, 211
Miller, Steve, 388
Mills, C. Wright, 157
Milton, John, 99, 322–23
Mississippians, 497
Mitchum, Robert, 388
Miwoks, 61, 285
Molly (Mormon girl), 213
Monroe, Marilyn, 17, 355, 370, 576
Monroe, Robert, 355, 370
Moody, Raymond, 355
Mooney, Michael, 40
Moore, Alvin Jr., 395, 433–34, 445–47, 471
Morrison, Jim, 117
Morrison, Van, 153, 388
Morrow, John Andrew (Ilyas Abd al-'Alim Islam), 117, 318, 349, 352, 543, 549–65
Moses, 579
Mother Theresa, 389, 398, 469, 472, 505
Mound Builders, 495, 497
MS-13, 348
Muhammad, 1, 70, 99, 299, 305, 318, 345, 349–50, 352, 378–79, 410, 439, 511–12, 543, 549–68, 579
Muhammad Sa'id al-Jamal ar-Rifa'i ash-Shadhili, 534
Muir, John, 228
Mujahid, Abdul Malik, 556
Mulla Sadra, 441
Mulligan, Buck, 156
Mumtaz Mahal, 261
Murao, Shig, 101
Murasaki, Lady, 486
Murgatroyd, Mrs, 39
Murphy, Michael, 369
Musashi, Miyamoto, 357
Music, Paris, 489

Naone, Dana, 291
Naqshbandi Tariqah, 160
Naropa, 267, 291, 303
Naropa Institute (now University), 114, 289–91, 293–94
Nasr, Seyyed Hossein, 1, 375, 394–95, 398–99, 408, 410–13, 415, 428–30, 432, 434–36, 469–70, 477, 503, 509, 563
Natasha (dervish), 406
Nation, Carrie, 350
Nava, Gregory, 332
Nazirites, 192
Needleman, Jacob, 169–71
Neem Karoli Baba, 167
Neihardt, John G., 159, 370
Nelson, Willie, 202
Neruda, Pablo, 98, 319, 326, 332–33
Neumann, Cornell, 237
Neumann, Erich, 271
Newhart, Bob, 157
Newman, Paul, 17
Nichols and May, 157
Nichols, Mike, 157
Nicholson, Jack, 89
Nicholson, R.A., 150
Nietzsche, Friederich, 50, 418
Niktab, Mr (Sufi shaykh), 401–2
Niku (dervish), 405
Nimatullahi Tariqah, 23, 76, 175, 374, 399–411, 420, 429, 436, 438, 446, 502–3, 508–9, 512, 544, 559, 579
Nimrod, 184
Nin, Anaïs, 270
Nityananda, 169
Noah, 64, 579
Noory, George, 468
Norman, Gurney, 158, 484
North, Colonel Oliver, 348
Northbourne, Lord, 395
Norton, Emperor, 528
Novak, Philip, 416
Núñez de la Vega, Francisco, 44
Nunn, Louie, 501
Nunn, Steve, 501
Nurbakhsh, Alireza, 410
Nurbakhsh, Dr Javad, 23, 25, 399, 404–6, 408, 410

O'Connor, Flannery, 501, 524
O'Meara, Fr George, 66
Ō Sensei (Morihei Ueshiba), 460

Obama, Barack, 556, 562
Ochs, Phil, 148
Ohioans, 497
Old Man of the Mountain, 192
Oldmeadow, Harry, 395
Olson, Bobo, 388
Olson, Craig, 477, 522
Olson, Mary Anne, 477, 522, 524
Onassis, Aristotle, 122, 206, 405, 476
Opaso, Christina, 327, 330,
Opaso, Cristián, 327–28
Oppen, George, 108
Orage, A.R., 371
Orbito brothers (psychic surgeons), 265
Ordo Mariana, 427, 430
Orlovsky, Peter, 98, 323
Orwell, George, 157, 237
Ostrander, Shiela, 355
Oswalt, Fr Michael, 84, 268, 548–49
Ottenstein, Eddie, 153

Pacal Votan, 44
Pacino, Al, 465
Packard, David, 384–85
Packer, Duane, 355
Padre Pio, 418
Paffhausen, Fr Jonah, 433
Paganini (family), 61
Pahlavi, Mohammad Reza, 161
Palance, Jack, 460
Pallis, Marco, 375, 395, 471
Paracelsus, 109, 134, 179
Parajanov, 73, 430
Parker, Charlie, 107
Parks, John, 481–82
Pascal, Blaise, 81
Pathways to Peace, 360–62
Paul, St, 6, 81, 299
Pauwels, Louis, 162
Payne, Judge Gary, 545
Peal, Norman Vincent, 316, 356–57
Pedroli, Andy, 53
Péguy, Charles, 317–18
Peleg, 174
Penn, Lee, 413, 511
Perkoff, Stuart, 93
Perry, Mark, 457
Perry, Whitall, 375, 395, 414
Peterson, Jordan, 97
Pettengill, Fr David M., 76
Pharisees, 350, 464

Philip of Macedon, 238
Pia (Marin County mulatta), 379
Pierce, Angela, 11–12, 70, 284
Pigman, Dingus, 498
Pilgrim John, 510
Pilson*, Gene, 324
Pink Floyd, 388
Pinochet, Augusto, 332
Pitt, Brad, 303
Pittle, Dave, 335
Pius V, Pope St, Society of, 544
Pius X, Pope St, 448
Pius X, Pope St, Society of, 544
Plato, 27, 51, 94, 127, 224, 371, 412, 448
Plimpton, George, 217, 239
Plotinus, 151
Plume, Rev., 260
Plunkett* (family), 490, 493, 543
Plunkett*, Arnold,* 504, 513, 520–25, 529–35, 543–44
Plunkett*, Angela, 508
Plunkett*, Annie, 502
Plunkett*, Christian, 543–45
Plunkett*, Eileen, 513, 566
Plunkett*, Esta, 499, 519
Plunkett*, Forrest Dale, 501, 508, 513, 522, 566
Plunkett*, John, 489, 502
Plunkett*, Juble, 493, 499, 516, 519, 524
Plunkett*, Lola, 269, 476, 501, 504, 513–39
Pocahontas, 15, 493
Podmoshensky, Fr Herman, 424
Poe, Edgar Allen, 10, 57, 128
Polish, Michael, 89
Pollack, Jackson, 216
Pollock, Michael, 504
Polony, Csaba, 49
Pomeroy, Jeanette, 253–54, 501
Pope Francis, 80, 99, 505
Portia, 315
Post*, Doreen, 324
Potter, Harry, 141–42
Pound, Ezra, 100, 108, 112, 118, 150, 212, 278, 322, 491
Powers, Jeannie, 13
Powhatan, 15, 493
Presbyterian Church (USA), 362
Presbytery of the Redwoods, 320, 347, 362
Presley, Elvis, 249
Pringle (family), 33, 42
Pringle, Alison, 42

Pringle, Bob, 42, 44, 48
Pringle, Brooks, 42–43
Pringle, Catherine, 42–43
Pryor, Richard, 157
Psychic Surgeons, 130, 251–66, 283, 406, 466, 504
Putin, Vladimir, 563

Qadiri Tariqah, 506, 512
Quaid, Dennis, 89
Quan (family), 11
Quicksilver Messenger Service, 100, 388
Quinn, Anthony, 460

Rabi'a al-Adawiyya, 451, 541, 571
Raine, Kathleen, 406–7
Rakosi, Carl, 108
Ram Dass (Richard Alpert), 114, 142, 148, 159–60, 167, 178, 197–98, 236, 396
Ramakrishna, Sri, 160, 167, 206, 233
Ramana Maharshi, Sri, 111, 160, 167
Ramani Suryakantham Durvasula, Dr, 515
Ramola, Fr, 545
Ramsay, Jay, 100
Ramtha (entity), 414–16
Ransom, Elwin, 338
Ratzinger, Joseph Cardinal (Pope Benedict XVI), 448, 505
Rauf, Faisal, 502
Reagan, Ronald, 21, 343, 348, 356
Reardon, Patrick Henry, 509
Red Cloud, 475
Reich, Charles A., 151
Reich, Wilhelm, 354
Reiser, Oliver L., 359
Reps, Paul, 160
Reverdy, Pierre, 311
Rexroth, Kenneth, 77, 108, 150,
Rexroth, Mariana, 77, 108
Reznikov, Charles, 108
Riess, John, 541, 543
Riley, Rev. Lou, 327, 333
Rilke, Rainer Maria, 69, 114, 143, 386
Rimbaud, Arthur, 154, 158
Ringrose, James, 35
Ritchie, Jean, 222, 327, 487
Rivera, Diego, 48
Roberts, Adelaide, 24
Roberts, Jane, 256, 354, 358, 369–70, 396
Roberts, Megan, 24–26
Roberts, Oral, 99

Robinson, Sugar Ray, 388
Robles, Daniel Alomia, 332
Roddenberry, Gene, 107
Rolling Stones, The, 148, 332, 163
Rolling Thunder, 169–70
Romaine, Sharlyn (Sayyida Badriyya), 510
Roman, Sanaya, 355
Romanoff, Peter Andreievich, 391
Romero, Archbishop Oscar, 321
Ronstadt, Linda, 388
Roosevelt, Theodore, 147, 220, 228
Rose, Fr Seraphim, 161, 355, 417, 424–25
Rossi, Vincent, 425, 443–44
Rossman, Jared, 164
Rossman, Michael, 164
Rouhani, Hassan (President of Iran), 566
Rousseau, Jean Jacques, 140
Rubin, Jerry, 111, 148, 202, 213
Rue, Ray, 13
Ruggles, Gene, 283–84, 324
Rumi, Jalaluddin, 22, 99, 150, 178, 181, 397, 510
Russ (Sufi adviser), 405
Russell, Bob, 416
Russell, Leon, 388
Russell, Peter, 355
Ryan, Tony, 488

Sahl, Mort, 107, 109, 159
Sales, Grover, 107
Salome, 17
Samson, 192, 222
San Francisco Theological Seminary, 126, 135, 171, 376, 438, 485
San Francisco Zen Center, 115
Sanborn, Bishop Donald, 543
Sand, Nicholas, 201
Sandburg, Carl, 97, 163, 211
Sanders, Ed, 291, 293
Sandinistas, 148, 320, 330–31, 352
Sandino, Augusto C., 50
Sanfield, Steve, 484
Sant Darshan Singh, 176
Santa Venetia Presbyterian Church, 167, 171, 186, 292, 300, 310, 312, 317, 320–21, 330, 333–47, 351–54
Sappho, 247
Sarah (wife of Abraham), 31
Sartre, Jean-Paul, 103, 142, 158, 418
Savate, Nino, 290
Saybrook Institute, 372

Schaya, Leo, 175, 187
Schelkun, Greg, 283, 362
Scholem, Gershom, 234
Schroeder, Lynn, 355
Schucman, Helen, 354
Schuon, Catherine (Sayyida Latifa), 429, 509
Schuon, Frithjof, 1, 122, 142, 158, 176, 183, 187, 233, 352, 375, 394–99
Schwab, Paul, 83
Schwartz, Jack, 235
Scott, Calvin, 459, 379, 385
Sedevaccantist Catholics, 81, 84, 268, 398, 428, 449, 468–74, 482, 505, 511, 541–49, 566
Seeger, Pete, 148
Segundo, Juan Luis, 320
Serra, Fr Junipero, 59
Serrano, Nina, 330
Seth (entity), 354, 358, 369, 396
Shabbetai Zevi, 571
Shadhili Tariqah, 130, 411, 481, 503, 508, 512, 534, 547
Shah, Idries, 160, 374, 394
Shah Jahan, 261
Shakers, 478, 498, 508
Shakespeare, William, 25, 57, 99, 178, 222, 315, 379, 486, 546
Shams Tabrizi, 178
Sheen, Bishop Fulton J., 66
Sheen, Martin, 451
Shelley, Percy Bysshe, 112, 406
Shor, Barbara, 372–73
Shore, Dinah, 205
Sidi Rachid, 512, 539
Silveira, Ron, 441
Simon, John Oliver, 319
Simon, Paul, 214, 222, 332,
Sinatra, Frank, 117, 217, 321, 479
Sir Kai, 456
Sister Dymphna, 544
Sister Joan, 30
Sister Mary Ellen, 64
Sister Pat, 30
Skerl, Jim, 231, 234
Skinner, B.F., 157
Sly and the Family Stone, 388
Smith, Huston, 1, 375, 395, 398, 402, 411–17, 423–24, 427–29, 435–36, 446, 457
Smith, Karen, 416
Smith, Kendra, 416

Index of Names

Smith, Wolfgang, 461, 551, 567
Smoley, Richard, 358
Smothers Brothers, 157
Snow, Paula, 183
Snyder, Gary, 1, 87, 91, 100, 107, 112, 115, 120, 140, 150, 152, 158, 251–52, 285, 315–16, 380, 484, 564, 567
Son of Sam, 361
Sons of Champlin, The, 388
Spacek, Cissy, 332
Spangler, David, 355
Sparky (radio character), 302–3
Spatola, Adriano, 108
Spence, Lewis, 44
Speray, Bernadette, 483
Speray, Cecelia, 483
Speray, Julia, 483, 544–46
Speray, Lee, 543–46
Speray, Raphael, 483
Speray, Steven, 41, 547–49
Speray, Veronica, 483
Spicer, Jack, 16, 81, 87, 98, 100, 107, 148, 162, 218, 228–29
Squire, Charles, 174
St Andrew's Orthodox Church, 482
St Cyr, Lili, 388
St Gertrude the Great Catholic Church, 543, 545–46
St Marie, Buffy, 100, 253
St Nicholas Orthodox Church, 336, 425, 427, 430–32
St Raphael's Church, 9, 62, 66
St Raphael's School, 66, 68–74
St Vincent Ferrer Mission, 548
Stalin, Josef, 108, 351, 481
Stamper brothers (Kesey characters), 286
Starhawk, 358
Starr, Blaze, 17
Steadman, Frances, 327
Steely Dan, 230, 236
Stein, Gertrude, 28, 90
Steinbeck, John, 30
Stevenson, Robert Lewis, 28
Stewart, Jimmy, 210
Stone, Oliver, 332
Strong, Maurice, 360
Strother (family), 15, 72, 110, 487, 490, 492
Strother, Catherine, 249
Strother, Walter, 15–16
Studer, Carolyn, 186, 320, 333–35, 347
Sufi Ruhaniat International, 363

Sun Tzu, 357
Sun Yat Sen, 11
Surubi, Fr, 81
Suzuki, D.T., 462
Suzuki, Sunryu, 124, 160
Swami Mukhtananda, 169, 346
Swami Satchidananda Saraswati, 167, 177
Swami Shivananda Saraswati, 167
Swami Vivekananda, 160
Swift, John, 526
Swift, Jonathan, 157, 526
Swift Deer, Harley, 294
Swing, Bishop William E., 413
Synge, John Millington, 157
Syrian Orthodox Metropolitan Vicar of Mardin, 555

Tam (dog), 39–40
Tarnas, Richard, 150
Taylor, Richard, 486
Tess of the d'Urbervilles, 486
Theodora, Empress, 261
Theodosia (entity), 260–61
Theophilos III (Greek Orthodox Patriarch of Jerusalem), 556, 559
Theophrastus Bombastus von Hohenheim (Paracelsus), 109
Theosophical Society, 161, 169, 235, 355, 358–59, 369
Theresa of Avila, St, 161
Theresa of Lisieux, St, 98
Thich Nhat Hahn, 160–61
Thomas Aquinas, St, 2, 418, 434,
Thomas, Dylan, 17, 117, 119, 158
Thompkins, Peter, 170
Thompson, Hunter S., 112
Thoreau, Henry David, 157
Tierney, Fr, 67
Tili, 260, 303
Tilopa, 267, 303
Tiny Tim, 211
Tobener (family), 13, 29
Tobener, Chuck, 13
Todd, Mary (Lincoln), 479
Toffler, Alvin, 355
Tolkien, J.R.R., 73, 131, 161, 179, 244, 458, 498
Tomlyn, Lilly, 157
Took, Belladonna, 498
Tower of Power, 388
Trotskyites, 481

Trudeau, Gary, 202
Trumbly (family), 30, 80, 83, 153–58, 190, 257, 278–79, 290
Trumbly, Bill, 69, 80, 87, 141, 153–54, 156, 158, 215, 252, 283, 289
Trumbly, Bob, 74, 153–56, 207–8, 210–12
Trumbly, Dan, 153
Trumbly, Doug, 126, 153–56, 226, 251, 277, 283, 289, 297
Trumbly, Jenny, 215, 252, 283, 289
Trump, Donald, 467, 480, 516, 562–64
Trungpa, Chögyam, 111, 114, 135, 160, 169, 172, 266–68, 289, 290–96, 303–4, 361, 397, 466, 577
Tuck, Friar, 94, 498
Tugboat Annie, 9
Turini, Janice, 80
Twain, Mark, 16, 56, 210, 479

Ueshiba, Morihei, 460
Umar (caliph), 553
Underhill, Evelyn, 158
Upton, Bonnie, 9, 11–12, 15, 25, 29–34, 42, 52, 54–58, 65, 248–49, 253–55, 257–59, 266, 272, 275, 278, 281–84, 296, 298, 302–3, 367, 420–23, 541
Upton, Charles Hemenway, 16–18, 281, 490
Upton, Lilian, 15–16, 21, 53, 64, 258, 286, 297–98, 312–13, 422, 476
Upton, William Freeman, 9–10, 13–22, 24–33, 35, 38, 40–42, 52, 60, 71, 78, 81, 85, 96, 152, 164, 184, 186, 190, 207, 227–28, 238, 243, 247–48, 253–58, 262, 266, 268, 275, 283, 285, 288–89, 297, 302, 382
U.S.–Soviet Dream Bridge, 371–72
Usher, Roderick (Poe character), 57
Uthman (caliph), 553
Uzdavinys, Algis, 511

Vajrayana Buddhism, 111, 171–75, 266–68, 290–96, 507
Vallee, Jacques, 290, 373
Vallejo, Cesar, 49, 98, 319, 326, 330
Van Buskirk, Alden, 330
Vanderstoel, Graeme, 412
Vangelisti, Paul, 108–9
Vargas, Roberto, 148, 321
Vaughan, Reuben Vance, 172, 238
Vedanta Society, 355, 412, 481

Velimirovich, Nikolai, 510
Viganò, Archbishop Carlo Maria, 565–67
Villon, Francois, 94, 98–99
Virgins, Vestal, 104, 365
Von France, Marie-Louise, 79, 371, 339, 375, 395, 408
Vonnegut, Kurt, 162
Voznesensky, Andrei, 100, 236–37

Wagner, Ma, 9, 13
Wain, David, 89
Wakoff, Danny, 327
Walker, Thomas, 496
Wallace, Amy, 127, 136
Wallace, Irving, 127
Wallace, Yusuf (Sufi), 216
Ware, Bishop Kallistos, 433, 447
Warhol, Andy, 210
Warnick, Bryce, 468
Wasserman, Paula, 71, 168, 183, 186, 217–31, 297, 232, 236, 297
Waters, Frank, 159
Watts, Alan, 157, 160, 328, 424, 434
Waugh, Evelyn, 30
Wavy Gravy (Hugh Nanton Romney Jr.), 78, 226
Wayne, John, 388
Weber, Max, 357
Webster, Bishop, 544–46
Welch, Lew, 1, 16, 17, 28–29, 32–33, 49, 53, 77, 87–98, 102–4, 106, 109–10, 112, 115, 116–29, 131, 136, 137–40, 148, 152, 154, 159, 164, 184, 189–94, 205–6, 210, 228, 232, 243, 251–52, 268, 271–72, 274, 283, 285, 287, 299, 305, 307–9, 312–17, 319, 322, 325, 363, 374, 391, 461, 477, 483, 521, 568, 580
West, Nathaniel, 158
Weston, Jessie, 455
Wetmore, James, 513, 540–41, 543, 549
Whalen, Philip, 87, 91, 107, 115
Whaley, Arthur, 108, 150
Whitaker, Scott, 431, 435–45
White Buffalo Cow Woman, 170, 176, 188, 510
Whitman, Walt, 90, 99, 112, 120, 164, 208, 211
Who, The, 163, 166,
Widmann (family), 490
Widmann, Barbara, 33, 490
Widmann, Charles, 33–34

Index of Names

Widmann, Rudi, 33–34
Wilber, Ken, 162, 482
Wilde, Oscar, 211, 272
Wilhelm, Richard, 141, 150
William of Occam, 418
Williams, Charles, 203, 437
Williams, Robin, 235, 291
Williams, William Carlos, 28, 90, 108, 123, 211
Willoya, William, 159
Wilson, Mike, 147
Wilson, Woodrow, 15
Winchell, Walter, 15
Wolfe, Michael, 564
Wolfe, Thomas, 210
Wolfe, Tom, 157
Wolfgangsters (Facebook group), 469
Woodman, Marian, 271
Woods, James, 332
Wordsworth, William, 33
Wozniak, Steve, 357
Wright, Frank Lloyd, 312
Wyatt (family), 518
Wyatt, Sir Thomas, 518

Xenia of St Petersburg, St, 476, 478

Yahya Pallavicini, Shaykh, 555
Yannaras, Christos, 418
Yeats, William Butler, 5, 25, 89, 104, 112, 117, 119, 121, 134, 148, 158, 229, 241, 272, 275, 306, 314–15, 409, 461, 559
Yevtushenko, Evgeny, 100
Yogananda, Paramahansa, 160, 260
Yogi Bhajan, 167–68, 177, 260, 297
York, Barbara, 334
Youngbloods, 388

Zappa, Frank, 240, 388
Zealots, 350
Zen, 90, 115, 120, 124, 126, 138–39, 148, 160–62, 221, 282, 337–38
Zevi, Shabbetai, 571
Zimmer, Heinrich, 177, 375
Zodiac Killer, 361
Zoroaster, 361
Zukovsky, Louis, 108
Zuur, Cheryl, 327

www.ingramcontent.com/pod-product-compliance
Lightning Source LLC
Chambersburg PA
CBHW021756220426
43662CB00006B/72